Pathways of Memory and Power

Pathways of Memory and Power

ETHNOGRAPHY AND HISTORY

AMONG AN ANDEAN PEOPLE

Thomas A. Abercrombie

THE UNIVERSITY OF WISCONSIN PRESS

The University of Wisconsin Press
2537 Daniels Street
Madison, Wisconsin 53718

3 Henrietta Street
London WC2E 8LU, England

Library of Congress Cataloging-in-Publication Data
Abercrombie, Thomas Alan, 1951–
    Pathways of memory and power : ethnography and history among an
Andean people / Thomas A. Abercrombie.
        632 pp.   cm.
    Includes bibliographical references and index.
    ISBN 0-299-15310-X (cloth: alk. paper).
    ISBN 0-299-15314-2 (pbk.: alk. paper).
    1. Aymara Indians—History.   2. Aymara Indians—Religion.
    3. Aymara Indians—Rites and ceremonies.   4. Festivals—Bolivia—K'ulta.
    5. Ethnohistory—Bolivia—K'ulta.   6. K'ulta (Bolivia)—History.
    7. K'ulta (Bolivia)—Politics and government.
    8. K'ulta F2230.2.A9A24   1998
984'.12—dc21   96-38814

For my parents,
N. Thomas and Margaret Elizabeth Abercrombie,
and for Chloe

Contents

Illustrations

Photographs

Preface

GENEALOGY OF A PROJECT IN RESEARCH AND WRITING

Like peoples and the writings we call histories, scholarly projects also have a past. The research that gave rise to this book, for example, did not start out as a study that could have produced the information and arguments I now advance. A brief survey of the transmutations that led from graduate school to this book (and from a Ph.D. in anthropology to a job in history) may help to account for (if not excuse) its lapses and inadequacies.

In January of 1979, a few days after surviving a massive snowstorm as well as my proposal hearing in Chicago, I set out for Bolivia with my wife and fellow fieldworker, Mary Dillon, who accompanied me in Bolivia while carrying out her own research on Aymara language and culture. I carried with me a faculty-vetted research plan that I thought to be relatively straightforward. Having read most of the ethnographic works then available on the mixed civil and religious authority hierarchies of the Andes, and naturally having found this literature wanting, I set out to overturn the prevailing functionalist-materialist interpretations of Andean fiesta-cargo systems and to replace them with a subtle, context-sensitive analysis of the cultural meanings inherent in the ritual duties of fiesta sponsors and the exercise of political office.

Following leads provided by fiesta-cargo research in Mesoamerica (ably reviewed in Chance and Taylor 1985), those anthropologists of the Andes who concern themselves with authority structures and saints' festivals have tended to focus primarily on the costs incurred by festival sponsors in a potlatch-style outlay of resources, the way that such sponsors rise by virtue of their festival careers toward local political office (see, for example, Buechler and Buechler, 1971; Carter 1964; Stein 1961). In the prevailing jargon of such studies, the career "ladders" climbed by fiesta sponsors and holders of yearly political office constitute a "prestige hierarchy," in which the increasing expense of each successive step up the ladder correlates directly with its occupant's degree of local prestige and thus political power. Most such studies also subscribe to one side or the other in the reigning structural-functionalist debate of the 1950s to the mid-1970s, over not if but *how* these fiesta-cargo systems and prestige hierarchies promote social solidarity and help to close corporate communities. If an increase in spending correlates with a rise in prestige in such a social system, then the question is whether that system serves to legitimize asymmetries of wealth by granting the rich a form of ritual mystification of privilege, or whether it serves to level potential asymmetries of wealth through a redistribution in which the "haves" are granted temporary power and prestige in exchange for their material surpluses.

While they attend to the inequalities of sponsor wealth and festival expenditure, such approaches, I felt, have neglected to analyze (and in some cases, even to describe) other important details: the exact nature of the rituals involved, the role of the saints and other sacred beings in the everyday lives of community members, and the local significance of the authority roles to which sponsorship of fiestas lead. Without such information, it is impossible to apprehend the culturally constituted values that might motivate participation in such a system, other than attributing to them our own culture's "commonsense" interpretation of the goal of much symbolic activity, namely, the maximization of individual economic advantage.

Not all such studies invoke such terms, but most bring functional premises in through the back door by calling attention to how fiesta-cargo systems create "prestige hierarchies," a term usually used as a euphemism for "hierarchies of wealth." In a way that starkly contrasts with the care these authors take to seek out native terms and interpretations of other matters, the accrual of "prestige" is applied as a self-evident (functional and utilitarian) explanation of ritual expenditures, the value that inspires participation in fiesta-cargo systems. Inspired by the pioneering work of Isbell ([1978] 1985), I proposed to discover the values that motivate people to engage in fiesta-cargo careers and the meanings inherent in their activities.

As if that in itself were not enough for a year-long period of research that was to begin with study of the Aymara language, I planned to do much more. During the late 1970s anthropological practice began to shift. Under attack was the discipline's customary concern with supposedly isolated and self-contained traditional societies, an artifact of social anthropology's origin as a handmaiden to colonialism, and also a product of the presuppositions entailed in functionalist as well as structuralist theories. Such concerns led me to qualify my research proposal in complementary ways. On the one hand, I sought to understand the transformations suffered by ritual authority systems as a result of the interface between local orders and more global processes: So I proposed to study ritual-authority systems in the Lake Titicaca area, where a rapid process of conversion to evangelical Protestantism and political fission seemed to go hand in glove with relatively high levels of participation in the mostly urban national culture of nearby La Paz. I therefore sought to highlight the interplay between the definition of the social unit and the meanings encoded in festival and political practice, which I felt would be clearest in a context where both the boundaries of social groups and the legitimacy of the fiesta-cargo doxa were being questioned. Thus I aimed to understand what meanings festival participation and civil authority posts have for their participants by focusing on a moment of meaning change.

While I believe that I have been fair in my characterization of the fiesta-cargo literature, it might appear to those familiar with Andean ethnography as more a caricature. That is because so little of the ethnography published in the 1970s and 1980s has dealt with fiesta-cargo systems (see, however, Rasnake 1988a, whose research-in-progress was influential when I began to do my own research).

Those decades saw the publication of a considerable amount of ethnography on the Andes, but ethnography influenced by other research paradigms, largely ethnohistorical and ecological. In effect, much of Andeanist ethnography aims to reconcile the pre-Columbian past with the postcolonial present. At the same time, many of these works have also sought to reconcile the three most influential approaches to the Andean past: the predominantly materialist project of John V. Murra to describe an Andes-specific type of political economy, the historicist project of John H. Rowe to mine chronicles and archives for material to construct a chronological history of pre-Columbian Incas and their colonial heirs, and the structuralist efforts of R. Tom Zuidema to comprehend complex Andean social structures through the lens of Inca cosmology.

Seeing as how the reconciliation of such apparently contradictory approaches has been the aim of much frenetic theorizing in the post-structuralisms and postmodernisms of the last few decades, it came as no surprise that some seminal works (like those of Tristan Platt, Deborah

Poole, Joanne Rappaport, Roger Rasnake, María Rostworowski, Frank Salomon, Irene Silverblatt, Michael Taussig, Gary Urton, and Nathan Wachtel, to mention but a few)[1] have enlivened Andean ethnography while crossing the frontiers of materialism and structuralism, semiotics and history. Using various theoretical frameworks, they have leapt beyond the functionalist concerns that characterized 1950s and 1960s "community studies," landing in the deeper waters of cultural signification. Most have also heeded Murra's and Zuidema's admonitions that the pre-Columbian past and ethnographic present can each help to inform the other. On the other side of the aisle, seminal works by historians Sabine MacCormack, Karen Spalding, and Steve J. Stern, among others, have also engaged such matters, drawing on the resources of social history to blend materialist and culturalist approaches, and, breaking with an older tradition of treating "indians"* as passive players in stories about conquering Spaniards, have adopted the anthropologists' "bottom-up" perspective to seek out indigenous points of view.

We now have many beautifully detailed analyses of not only Andean forms of political economy, vertical ecology, everyday reciprocity, and systems of kinship and marriage, but also Andean symbolic practice,

---

*Throughout this work I have adopted the terms of reference used in sources and in everyday discourse. Thus "indian," referring in colonial and modern sources to Native South Americans, amerinds, indigenous peoples, and in some contexts *campesinos* or "peasants," is not my analytic category, but a category of ascribed and/or asserted collective identity that requires analysis. It may have been more correct, but also awkward, to have left this term in the original Spanish *"indio,"* along with the other group categories such as *"español"* (Spaniard) and *"negro"* (African or black), and other terms for mixtures of these fundamental categories (such as *"mestizo," "mulato," "sambo," "pardo," "castizo," "criollo,"* and a host of others). I will argue that in the earlier colony, "indio," "español," and "negro" were categories of *nación* (nation, in an old regime sense), being transformed into categories of presumed race only in the late eighteenth century, when "español criollo" was displaced by the color term *"blanco"* (white), and "indio criollo" by the insult term *"cholo,"* applied to an upwardly mobile indio who had failed to conceal his true identity (see Abercrombie 1996 for a fuller treatment of this issue).

I have chosen to use common English translations of these terms, but also to violate conventional capitalization rules. "Indian" is capitalized in English because it corresponds to the geographic entity India; "Creole" is treated as a proper noun because it signifies (in the Caribbean) a kind of language or cuisine, which are not among the usages I examine here. I thus choose to use these terms in the lower case, retaining capitalization only for more proper geographic designations such as "Spanish" and "Spaniard," "Andes" and "Andean." Although "Spaniard," "indian," "mestizo," and like terms henceforth generally appear without quotation marks, I use them always in a qualified sense, as cultural constructs of difference rather than labels for some prior racial or ethnic realities.

cosmologies, ritual cycles, and a host of particular rituals in particular places. The anthropological euphoria over the discovery of many surviving and beautifully complex cultural forms within Andean communities has had a salutary effect on the scholarly literature and, ultimately, on the evolution of new political stances among Andean nation makers toward "indigenous" cultural forms in rural "peasant" communities.

Yet the appeal or discovering effective cultural resistance, of revealing the Spanish overlay as merely a thin veneer covering a clandestine but ongoing survival of a coherent and purely Andean cosmology, has at times led ethnographers to overshoot the mark. Joseph Bastien's (1978) otherwise admirable and sensitive account of an aesthetically appealing Kallawaya hydraulic mountain cosmology, for example, reaches so far beyond the Christian "overlay" that Kallawaya sponsorship of Christian saints' festivals, and the political structures that emerge from such sponsorship, nearly disappear from the monograph. A fine and heartfelt ethnography by Catherine Allen (1988) captivatingly engages the reader in the ethnographer's experience, especially in the difficult-to-convey forms of everyday Andean sociality that operate through the chewing of coca and the drinking of alcohol. Yet in foregrounding the uniquely Andean features of consuming, exchanging, and offering coca and alcohol, the apparently Spanish and Christian features of this experience rhetorically fade into insignificance. Both ethnographies also avoid much engagement with the relationship of their communities with nearby towns that link them, as isolated places, with the road network, markets, and antithetical identity projects of city people and the elite of the national state. The elided towns in both ethnographies, not coincidentally, served or serve as ritual and political centers of fiesta-cargo systems into which the "isolated" communities were integrated.

Such studies demonstrate the degree to which Andean cultural formations have resisted the predatory encroachments of both colonial- and republican-period "civilizational" projects. They offer useful tools in the development of *indigenista* and *indianista* identity projects and their goals of ethnic solidarity and nationalism, which highlight the heroic qualities of successful colonial resistance and seek to turn this resistance against systematic discrimination and imperialism. It is relatively easy to foreground cultural continuities and hence write a cultural-resistance success story solely by privileging terms that carry "indigenous" inflections: *ayllu* rather than *cantón*, *jilaqata* instead of *cacique*, rituals directed towards mountains rather than towards saints. Yet in such efforts to foreground "an Andean order of things," as suggested by the title of another recent work (Arnold, Jiménez, and Yapita 1992), ethnographers sometimes repeat, albeit with different intent, the "idols behind altars" or "baptized but not evangelized" rhetoric of colonial administrators and extirpators of idolatry.

Colonial officials created a rhetoric that could portray the failure of previous civilization and conversion projects so that their own oppressive projects might gain official approval; to preserve the colony, the process of civilization and conversion had to remain incomplete. Curiously, the staunchest critics of the colonial project forward similar arguments to prove the inefficacy of colonial indoctrination and the resistive capacities of the colonized. What can we make of the fact that indianista "ethnic nationalist" authors and anthropologists romancing fully "other" others share rhetorical strategies with colonial administrators? At the very least, we can conclude that such rhetorics are deployed to forward what are essentially *historical* hypotheses: The most fundamental claim underlying theses of cultural resistance or continualism is that indigenous cultures have been (heroically) impervious to the contingent stream of colonial events. From there it is only a short step to the conclusion that indigenous culture is, as ritual was once thought to be, extra- or even antihistorical. Whether we conclude with the extirpators that indians remain idolatrous because of their ignorant and malevolent obstinacy, or conclude with the indigenous nationalists and romantic anthropologists that pre-Columbian culture remains intact because of the indians' resistance to homogenizing imperialist forces, we forward theses about the outcome of long-term social processes. Such historical theses stipulate that indians resist transformation because they are impervious to history, living in a structural closure that, like the shields of the Federation Starship Enterprise, can withstand the impact of all alien events.

I claim no exemption from such sins. By the time I set out for "the field" after six months of studying the Aymara language in La Paz, I had decided not to pursue my original, comparative project, because I would have had insufficient time for more than one community study. At the same time, I had concluded that to study the transformation of a cultural order, one must first establish the nature of the status quo ante; I chose, that is, to jettison the social transformation project in order to focus on the dynamics of ritual and political life in a single, relatively "traditional" community. Thus I opted out of history, back to the already anachronistic "closed corporate community."

My shift towards what I held to be an apparently historically "cold" fieldsite was a reasoned one, grounded in theoretical concerns. A subtle semiotic account of an Andean town's fiesta-cargo system might transcend the limitations of functionalist and economistic approaches, and account in culturally salient terms for the values that motivated participation in saints' festivals and town council politics. Such a study could then serve as a baseline for a future study of social change.

There were other motives for my shift in fieldsite as well. Further readings on Andean history while in La Paz (under the tutelage of Tristan Platt, who took me on an extended tour of his library) led me to believe that by studying a community where the saints were still revered, where the town council members emerged from festival sponsorship, and where social units like ayllus and moieties still clearly persisted, I might succeed in tracing contemporary social forms back into the documented past, hence discerning the competing influences of Spanish colonialism versus pre-Columbian heritage. Ironically, I too chose to work in a "traditional" community so as to approach history retrospectively.

I stayed long enough in that small town, a place called Santa Bárbara de Culta (capital of a territory and people who call themselves Cultas, rendered "K'ultas" in modern Aymara orthography),[2] to witness the arrival of Protestantism, to see the people of part of the territory submit a petition for peasant union incorporation, to note the massive outmigration of K'ulta people into coca-production zones, and to witness a rapidly escalating process of community fissioning. But these were not what I had set out to study.

By tuning out the "invasive" influences from the city and national culture that were readily apparent in the truckstop town nearest to the "isolated" community I had come to investigate, I was able to convince myself that my fieldsite was an extraordinarily "traditional" one, where pre-Columbian forms still persisted to a degree I could not have predicted, even by drawing on the most romantic of the resistance literature. Had I not, for very contingent reasons, spent much time in the truckstop town of Cruce and also taken the historical turn, I might have tried to write a resistance narrative as my dissertation (although it would have been sorely tested by my teachers' own historical turns and the general displacement of domination-resistance models by hegemony-counterhegemony ones). At any rate, when I prepared for fieldwork in 1978, I had had no inclination to accept the admonitions of Chicago anthropologist R. T. Smith that, in conditions like those of the Bolivian "Aymara,"[3] where a classlike asymmetry of power infused all relations between "indigenous people" and "nonindians," both rural and urban and indian and nonindian cultural systems interpenetrated one another. Had I taken his advice (or given heed to the work of Jean Barstow

[1979], who was completing her dissertation as I prepared to leave for Bolivia), I might sooner have shifted away from domination-resistance paradigms towards a more historically grounded and less romanticizing approach. As it was, that shift was more fortuitous than reasoned.

By the time I left K'ulta territory in July of 1980, my Aymara had improved enough for me to appreciate how much I still did not know about the fiestas and politics I had come to study. I had learned that while K'ultas are adamant Christians, whose saints' festivals are arenas in which fiesta sponsors gain the respect of their peers, enabling them subsequently to exercise legitimate authority during turns as members of the council of Santa Bárbara de Culta, the ritual duties of saints' feast sponsors and council authorities also include more clandestine performances, above all frequent animal sacrifices. Offering their most valued animals, male llamas, to Christ (whom they also hold to be the sun) and to the Virgin (who is at the same time the moon), K'ultas give their celestial deities animal substitutes for themselves, and by doing so seem to take on attributes of herd leader and shepherd, by which in various speech forms they characterize control over the animal world typical of their pastoral life-ways, but also typify the pastoral language by which a biblical deity exercises sovereignty over people.

However, such new avenues for approaching the meanings enacted in Andean fiesta-cargo systems began to open up only at the end of my fieldwork period. At the very end of my stay, I also discovered that festival sacrifices are marked out by complex libation performances, which, like the myths I heard, seem a rich source for understanding the meaning of sacrifice, fiesta, and also K'ulta ways of thinking about the past.[4] Although I had only the barest glimpse of such things after a year's work, I had heard many local narratives, left my mark on town council documents, and poured a great many libations for beings from the past who still live on in the mountains and plains of K'ulta.

Once I realized that a year's work in K'ulta territory was not enough to enable me to flesh out these understandings, I began to seek funding for a second year of field research, but this proved impossible. Instead, several shorter return trips proved invaluable, and eventually I completed a dissertation exploring these themes, "The Politics of Sacrifice: An Aymara Cosmology in Action" (University of Chicago, 1986). In the end, however, I devoted about a third of the dissertation to what I called an ethnohistory of K'ulta. A serendipitous eligibility requirement for one of the application forms I had sent for—Fulbright IIE—led me to write a proposal for "ethnohistorical" research in Buenos Aires, where I had heard that colonial documents on Bolivia are to be found.

In late August of 1980, I launched myself into the laborious grind of archival research. Seeking to historicize my account of accommodated cultural resistance, I found that writing a history of the colonized requires a good deal of creativity. The formerly "standard" sorts of sources turned out to be quite insufficient; the "vision of the vanquished" resided in between the lines, in small nuggets of information lodged within litigation records, census materials, and the humdrum documents of notarial books and parish registers. Such techniques had already been explored for the writing of Andean history by pathbreaking luminaries such as John V. Murra, Franklin Pease, and María Rostworowski as part of an endeavor called ethnohistory, and were also very much in vogue among practitioners of analogous efforts that are elsewhere called history from below.

The end product of this almost accidental combination of ethnographic and historical research was a dissertation, in which a history of the K'ulta region drawn from written sources uneasily coexists with a relatively standard sort of ethnography. Neither part of the endeavor benefited from any particular effort to query the relationship between my own historical and ethnographic project (as investigation, power-laden fieldwork, or writing effort) and those of the people past and present about whom I wrote. A full decade has passed in the transformation of dissertation to book, during which academic fashions have changed and I have completed additional research. During that decade, I also became a historian, successively enamored by new and more culturally sensitive approaches to popular history, ethnographic history, and microhistory. Not surprisingly, what I offer here is something essentially new.

As I began to rework my dissertation for publication, I became increasingly dissatisfied with both its historical and its ethnographic parts. The former, it seemed to me, may have offered an "ethnohistory," a "history from below" of a non-Western people, but it did so within Euro-American historical canons. I had created a written past for a people who had not written their own, but I now found that the past I provided them was not one they would recognize. Sweeping them up into the narrative project of colonial and imperial history, my ethnohistory in fact colonized the K'ulta people's past, as well as that of their ancestors, about whom I wrote without much attention to how *they* would have understood their pasts. In my ethnographic fieldwork, I had realized that the people of K'ulta indeed make their own history, understanding through mostly unwritten forms of social memory their relationship to the past. So too, after I had read Spanish colonial writings more closely, it began to appear that the colonial project itself had in many ways aimed to erase Andean ways of understanding the past, in order to colonize Andean forms of historical consciousness. At least some Spaniards even seemed to have understood the nature of their project, although they conceived it as the substitution of the universal truth for indian errors and superstitions.

I do not pretend to offer here an objective account of the past and present of a historically subordinated people. Instead, I present three interrelated and multivocal stories: an account of my ethnographic fieldwork (part 1), an account of past conflicts in historical consciousness between rural communities and colonizing states (part 2),[5] and a detailed study of some persisting K'ulta ways of understanding the relevance of the past to the present (part 3). All three parts aim to expose the power-laden discourses that produced the evidence presented here, whether that of my ethnographic encounters, colonial encounters of the past, or the internalized "intercultural" self-consciousness of K'ulta people who theorize in their practices about their relationship to powerful forces not only of the animated landscape in which they live but also of the national state and international capital.

Juxtaposing in this way a reflexive ethnography and reflexive history, I aim to unmask the politics of ethnography and of history, but not to call ethnographic and historical practice into question. Instead, I hope to demonstrate that, in the study of the people and relationships of colonial situations, our motives, goals, and discursive strategies are enmeshed in the very kinds of struggles about which we write. As we strive to hear an indigenous voice in documents produced for the state's archives, we find those very documents to be a discursive frontier, a barrier of miscommunication erected between colonizer and colonized. And as we carry out ethnographic fieldwork to find indigenous meaning worlds, we discover them to be concealed in clandestine spaces.

Once, such frustrating experiences were destined to be relegated to diaries and working notes, or they were humorous anecdotes to be discarded when we had overcome the obstacles between us and the indians. Here I choose to focus on that discursive frontier, in the belief that it is fundamentally constitutive of the relationship between colonizers and colonized, states and subordinated peoples, and therefore also constitutive of the forms of self-understanding of each. By foregrounding the resistances, silences, lies, and other barriers that we, as ethnographers or historians, encounter in our efforts to "get into" the lives of persons in living societies or documented pasts, we may uncover keys to the intercultural situation that we set out to study. That is my goal here.

*   *   *

The writing of a book is perhaps never the product of a single hand. This book has risen from several years of research nurtured by numerous teachers, colleagues, and students, and developed in many conferences, conversations, correspondences, and friendships, making the effort to recall all the debts I have incurred nearly overwhelming.

To Mary F. Dillon, who accompanied me in much of the field research and many an archival foray, and offered countless hours of conversation and collaboration on Andean themes over several years, I am deeply indebted.

When I was an undergraduate at the University of Michigan, the unique convergence in my life of two extraordinary Australians, John Earls and Michael Taussig, drew me towards Andean anthropology and history. Without their encouragement and the continuing inspiration of their work, this book would not be in the reader's hands. Fellow anthropology undergraduates Joseph Gaughan and David Stoll have over the years helped to sustain me through the slings and arrows of academic and personal life.

Between hammer and anvil at the University of Chicago's forge of aspiring anthropologists, many persons contributed valuable comments and criticisms on various chapters of the dissertation that eventuated in this book. Above all, my friend and mentor Terence S. Turner has lent his critical acumen and support at several crucial junctures in the production of this book. For their advice and commentary, I am indebted to John Coatsworth, Jean Comaroff, John Comaroff, Nancy Munn, Don Rice, Marshall Sahlins, Michael Silverstein, S. J. Tambiah, Valerio Valeri, and the late Sol Tax, among other present and past University of Chicago faculty members. The cross-disciplinary courage and humane scholarly example of Bernard Cohn and George Stocking have also been important. I like to think that at one time or another the late Chicago luminaries Mircea Eliade, A. K. Ramanujan, and Victor Turner also left their stamp upon my work. Early drafts of various chapters benefited enormously from the input of fellow graduate students Fernando Coronil, Mark Francillon, Paul Goldstien, Carol Hendrickson, Bruce Mannheim, Rafael Sanchez, Julie Skurski, and Charles Stanish.

For completion of the dissertation from which portions of this book have been drawn, ethnographic research in Bolivia and archival research in Bolivia, Argentina, and Spain was supported by Fulbright-Hays (1979–80); Fulbright IIE (1980–81); the University of Chicago Center for Latin American Studies Mellon Fund, the Whatcomb Museum, and

Sigma Xi (1982). Additional research for this book, ranging from archival work to brief visits to K'ulta, was completed in the margins of other postdoctoral projects funded by the Council for the International Exchange of Scholars, U.S.–Spain Bi-national Commission (1987); Fulbright and SSRC (1988); the Wenner-Gren Foundation for Anthropological Research (1990); Fulbright-CIES (1993); and by University of Miami Max Orovitz Awards and General Research Awards in 1991, 1992, and 1994.

Numerous other institutions also provided essential support. Part 1 was drafted during breaks from another project while a Fulbright fellow in Seville, where José Hernández Palomo and the Escuela de Estudios Hispanoamericanos helped provide critical working space. A preliminary draft of the Introduction was worked out in context of a February 1994 conference organized in Paris by Thérèse Bouysse in memory of Theirry Saignes. Parts of chapter 8 were completed for a 1993 conference on Andean kinship in St. Andrews, Scotland, organized by Denise Arnold and Tristan Platt. Chapter 5 and 6 were given impetus by preparation of lectures for a postgraduate seminar presented at the Universidad Nacional de Jujuy, Argentina, during August of 1994. Thanks for the opportunity go to Marta Ruíz, Alejandro Isla, and a challenging group of scholars in Jujuy. Chapter 7 was first redrafted from a dissertation chapter for *Borrachera y memoria,* edited by my late friend Theirry Saignes and published by HISBOL, La Paz, 1993. I thank HISBOL for permission to republish portions of that article, and Siglo XXI Editores for permission to reprint drawings of Felipe Guaman Poma de Ayala (from *El primer nueva corónica y buen gobierno,* Rolena Adorno and John V. Murra, eds., 1980), which illustrate the text.

The directors and staffs of numerous archives have provided repeated help. In particular I must thank those of the Archivo General de Indias (Seville), the Archivo de la Real Academia de Historia (Madrid), the Biblioteca Nacional (Madrid), the Archivo General de la Nación de Argentina (Buenos Aires), the Archivo Judicial de Oruro (Bolivia), the Archivo del Tribunal de Poopó (Bolivia), the Archivo de Derechos Reales (Oruro, Bolivia), the Archivo Histórico de Potosí (Casa de la Moneda, Potosí, Bolivia), and above all, the late Gunnar Mendoza, past director Josép Barnadas, current director René Arze, and the excellent staff of the Archivo Nacional de Bolivia (Sucre). At the Escuela de Estudios Hispanoamericanos, where chapters 2–4 were drafted during 1993, special thanks go to José Hernández Palomo for his help in facilitating work space in the world's most enchanting city.

At various junctures, ideas and issues developed herein have benefited from discussions with or comments by Xavier Albó, Arjun Appadurai, Denise Arnold, Monica Barnes, Rossana Barragán, James Boon, Christina Bubba, Thérèse Bouysse-Cassagne, Marisol de la Cadena, Fernando Cajías, Verónica Cereceda, David Cook, Alexandra Parma Cook, Jean-Jacques Decoster, John H. Elliott, Jane Fajans, Nancy Farriss, Antoinette Fioravanti-Molinié, Ed Franquemont, Christine Franquemont, Teresa Gisbert, Martha Hardmann, Inge Harmann, Olivia Harris, Billie-Jean Isbell, Javier Izco, Catherine Julien, Michael LaRosa, Brooke Larson, Edward LiPuma, Sabine MacCormack, Gabriel Martínez, Enrique Mayer, Walter Mignolo, John V. Murra, Scarlet O'Phelan, Benjamin Orlove, Sherry Ortner, Tristan Platt, Karen Powers, Susan Ramírez, Roger Rasnake, Mercedes del Río, Silvia Rivera, Guido Ruggiero, Frank Salomon, Stephen Sangren, Linda Seligmann, Raymond T. Smith, Geoffrey Spurling, Steve J. Stern, Burkhardt Swartz, David Tuchschneider, Henrique Urbano, Rafael Varón, Nathan Wachtel, Mary Weismantel, Norman Whitten, Juan de Dios Yapita, Elaine Zorn, and Tom Zuidema. Along with their scholarly input, the friendship and support of the late Thierry Saignes and Lucy Therina Briggs were also of great significance.

Students in courses taught at the Departments of Anthropology of Cornell University, Stanford University, the Universidad Técnica de Oruro, and the University of Chicago have offered insightful challenges and insights. Graduate students at the University of Miami also provided comments on draft chapters. Special thanks go to Sarah Elizabeth Penry and Douglas Trefzger, who commented on the manuscript as a whole and offered many suggestions for improvements in argument and style.

Anonymous readers for the University of Wisconsin Press as well as Duke University Press provided important criticism and suggestions for revision, some of which I have heeded. Paul Gelles, Florencia Mallon, and Gary Urton each provided detailed and critically important comments on the draft manuscript as a whole, and they have saved me from many a false turn in argument and indelicacy of style. I am also indebted to editor Rosalie Robertson of the University of Wisconsin Press, whose efficient support shepherded this work through the entire publication process in the most humane manner imaginable. Argument and style have also benefited enormously from the meticulous efforts of copy editor Robin Whitaker.

No doubt I have forgotten key names in my litany of gratitude; my apologies to those I have inadvertently slighted. My thanks also to all those who have wittingly or unwittingly helped me capture the evanescent idea or elusive connection; it is not possible to repay the debt or damage for so many ideas borrowed, begged, and stolen from others, theirs no matter how much I have bent them to my own purposes. My apologies in advance to the reader of this book, who must suffer the consequences of my inability to have heeded correctly the sage advice of so many fine teachers and fellow students.

Pathways of Memory and Power

Chapter One

Introduction
From Ritual to History and Back Again, Trajectories in Research and Theory

> Men make their own history, but they do not make it just as they
> please; they do not make it under circumstances chosen by
> themselves, but under circumstances directly encountered, given
> and transmitted from the past. The tradition of all the dead
> generations weighs like a nightmare on the brain of the living.
> And just when they seem engaged in revolutionizing themselves
> and things, in creating something that has never yet existed,
> precisely in such periods of revolutionary crisis they anxiously
> conjure up the spirits of the past to their service and borrow from
> them names, battle cries and costumes in order to present the new
> scene of world history in this time-honoured disguise and this
> borrowed language.
> —Karl Marx, *The Eighteenth Brumaire of Louis Bonaparte*

Around the year 1520 (a year in which the commoners of Castile's towns
rose up against Charles V and burdensome aristocrats and, in the
Caribbean, Cortés pursued his conquest of Mexico), the following story
unfolded: An Aymara *mallku* named Inca Colque, hereditary lord of the
diarchies Killaka, Asanaqi, Awllaka-Urukilla, and Siwaruyu-Arakapi,
dispatches a group of young married men on the great Inca highway to
Cusco. After formally requesting their services and entreating them with
a banquet and copious libations of corn beer, he tells them that it is their
turn, their *mit'a*, to undertake personal service to the Inca emperor. An
imposing figure dressed in lavish Inca shirts laced with gold and silver
threads, Inca Colque rides in a litter on the shoulders of fifty Uru
retainers when he inspects his territory and people, having earned the
shirts, the right to ride the litter, and the title Inca precisely for his
services to the Inca empire in peace and war. Raised to the status of *unu
mallku*, "lord of ten thousand households," Inca Colque may well

have received these honors during the Inca ruler's personal inspection tour of Qullasuyu, if not in the periodic sacrificial pilgrimage-ceremony of *capac hucha,* the imperial ritual of the "opulent prestation."[1] Having entered on good terms into a personal relationship with the Inca Huayna Capac and become a stand-in for the Inca administration as well as their "natural lord," he has become a fearful figure to his assembled people. But he is also generous, adept at transforming patrimonial gifts into an asymmetrical obligation. To the assembled group he commits his young grandson Guarache, who is to learn the imperial language, Quechua, and take up one of the duties (such as feather-worker) appropriate to noble youth in the Inca capital, joining them in the carefully orchestrated stages of their initiation as privileged future rulers.

The group takes to the Inca highway, the *qapaq ñan* ("great road" or "opulent way") that leads from the farthest corners of the realm directly to Cusco. Fed and clothed from Inca storehouses along the way and housed in Inca rest houses and supply depots at regular intervals along the road, the group wends its way on the well-made road through the territories of once-hostile neighboring groups.

The group stops at the Inca administrative center of Jatun Qulla, where the memory of a great pre-Inca warrior-mallku lives on, notwithstanding his transformation after defeat by the Inca into the leather of a ritual drum on which the meter of Inca epics is now banged out. Greeted with welcome food and drink and shown to their night's quarters, the group moves directly to the great hall facing the town's large plaza. Great numbers of corn beer storage jars draw their attention, before Inca priests begin to serve them large cups of the refreshing but intoxicating beverage. When each one is handed a ceramic beaker, painted with scenes from the mythic past, he is told to which *wak'a* he should dedicate the drink. After many commensal toasts, each one has recalled a genealogy of the gods that interweaves their own, local past with that of the ruling Inca.

In the morning, they will continue on the way to Cusco, the Inca "world navel," where they will participate in more religious rites at the very center of the Inca empire. Through them, they will learn the imperial ritual calendar enacted in lyric song-dances and sacrifices at wak'a shrines along *ceque* lines. Dancing along ritual paths that radiate through the Cusco valley from the Qurikancha (one of which reaches deep into Qullasuyu, corresponding to the "line of travel" of creator deities that emerged from Lake Titicaca), they will become adept in the religiously grounded political organization of the empire, and they will understand the festive and sacramental value of work they may, seven years later, undertake in Inca fields producing corn for the vast quantities of beer that this complex interweaving of Inca and "ethnic" gods and genealogies requires.

Unlike the others, young Guarache, unmarried son of their paramount mallku, Inca Colque, will remain in Cusco to be raised within the age-graded ritual "schools" in which Incas inculcate the privileged elites of conquered peoples in cosmopolitan values.[2]

Over a period of several weeks in late 1575, don Juan Colque Guarache, hereditary lord of a people called Killaka (and son of the Guarache raised in Cusco), assembles Spanish and native witnesses to answer a set of questions about his genealogy and his family's services to the Inca state and to Spanish colonial authorities. With the intervention of Spanish courtroom officials, a scribe, interpreter, and numerous witnesses, he constructs a *probanza de servicios y méritos,* a "proof of services and merit," chronologically recounting an event sequence reaching from Inca times to his own present. Like the thousands of other legally sworn "curriculum vitae" that crowd the shelves of Spanish and Latin American archives, Colque Guarache's probanza construes an account of the past—a historical narrative—that places him at the subjective center of events in the most favorable possible light. With special emphasis on support and supply in journeys of Inca and Spanish conquest, on the provisioning of troops and supplies for the Inca conquest of Chichas, the posting of spies on the roads to aid the Crown's war on rebellious conquistadors, and the levying of laborers for the mines of Potosí, Colque Guarache's services appear as a series of vectors reaching out from his home territory of Killaka to the farthest corners of Perú. Directed to Philip II of Spain and to imperial archives via postroad and dispatch ship, the probanza includes an appeal for specific boons (assessed in coin and in Spanish-style aristocratic privileges) that his services warrant.[3]

One day during 1549, Pedro Cieza de León, in the midst of a journey from Cusco to Potosí down the qapaq ñan, the Inca road that is now trunk route of Spanish colonial journeys, stops on the shores of Lake Titicaca to question local native leaders. Eager to understand how the Andean past can be reconciled with the universal history of a Bible that mentions neither the Indies nor indians, and to satisfy his curiosity about how the impressive ruins of Tiwanaku could have been built by predecessors of the barbaric people he has encountered here, Cieza probes with pointed questions about the distant past, and records—in his travel narrative account about the Incas—the fragments of native fables that contribute to his own historical theses. The stories his interlocutors tell him describe the superhuman acts of their culture heroes, performed during foundational journeys that created the landscape through which the events are remembered. Anticipating much later historical theorizing, Cieza fixes on apparent commonalities between such stories and biblical narrative, especially the theme of a universal flood, in an effort to draw the Andean past into universal history. He records one myth fragment that suggests, to him, that Tiwanaku must have been built by "people like ourselves," referring to Europeans, who were subsequently annihilated by less civilized Aymara invaders. In a few suggestive paragraphs, Cieza lays the groundwork for many other theorists (from seventeenth-century Spanish chroniclers to Thor Heyerdahl and Erich von Däniken) for whom determined forms of social memory have left no space for an autonomous American history or an independent Amerindian form of historical consciousness (see Cieza de León 1986).

It is midmorning on September 7, 1982, in the hamlet of Vila Sirka, not far from the highland Bolivian town of Santa Bárbara de Culta. A group of Aymara-speaking men, mostly brothers and cousins bearing the patronym Mamani, are seated on stones around a small stone altar within the llama corral, atop a deep cushion of dried llama dung. Acting as *awarint wasu wariri*, the "alcohol cup server," don Bartolomé Mamani offers a small shot of diluted cane liquor, served in an unusual silver cup (a miniature pair of yoked silver bulls stand in the center, belly-deep in alcohol). He hands the cup to his cousin Manuel, who pours a few drops at each corner of the altar, intoning the words *jira t'all misa taki,* "for the dung-plain altar." After gulping down the remainder of the serving, he hands the cup back to don Bartolomé, who refills the cup and urges each man present to imitate don Manuel. Fifty shots later, thoroughly inebriated, don Bartolomé and the other elders in the corral complete their ritual, which they call *amt'añ t'aki,* a "memory path." By then they (and their wives, seated on the ground a few meters away, engaged in a gender-parallel performance)[4] have recalled and intoned the names of many ascendant ancestors and a litany of ever more distant mountains, plains, and other sacred places, mapping out in their minds a centripetal journey across the living landscape that embodies their past.[5]

One morning in January of 1988 as I walk through the marketplace in Oruro, Bolivia, a sidewalk vender calls out my name when I step over her small array of brushes. At first sight I see only another of the ubiquitous bowler derby- and *pollera*-clad "cholitas" whose wares dominate urban street markets, but after a closer look and a brief conversation, I recognize doña María, a woman I had first met in 1979 not long after beginning ethnographic work in the countryside. Back then, she had gone about in the homespun outfit of the rural indigenous population, as had her husband, Julián Mamani, nephew of the libation specialist Bartolomé Mamani. When I ask about him, doña María explains that he is locked up in Oruro's prison. Not long afterward, spurred by long-standing mutual obligations, through which personal relations are transacted in the countryside, I wind up serving as a combination expert witness and character reference for Julián.

Having rejected what he felt to be a custom-bound and backward lifestyle, Julián had sought to escape the past by selling pieces of it. He had already pleaded guilty to several counts of theft, having taken colonial paintings and silverwork from a series of rural churches in his home district, after, he argued, he had been duped by a wily antiquities dealer in La Paz. Caught in the crossroads town of Cruce with his cash (and unsold loot) in hand, he had nearly been lynched by his own kinsmen, among whom he had become persona non grata. Julián had taken the easy road to capitalist success (and an urban lifestyle) by converting the sacred objects of his people's heritage into a more transcultural form of capital, but he had in fact robbed himself of his own past. Having now been schooled in the regimes of time and work discipline behind the steel gate of San Pedro prison, he would not be returning to a rural llama-herding lifestyle, as he had promised the judge; he would spend his future eking out a living making brushes and brooms as his jailers had taught him, as a newly minted member of the urban proletariate.

Finally the day arrives for my testimony on his behalf. Julián Mamani is escorted from jail to a hearing room of the Superior Court of Oruro, where I wait just outside the door. When he arrives, he reaches out to shake my hand and stealthily presses into my palm a many-times-folded piece of paper. Worried that I might say the wrong thing, he has concocted my testimony for me. Having learned to read and write during three years in prison, my friend has been able to instruct me secretly in my testimony through the silent medium of writing. The note contains a first-person statement that he hopes I will memorize and repeat in court, establishing his generally good character.

On the paper I read the following words: "I have known the peasant Julián Mamani for many years. He is a simple farmer and herder. An illiterate, ignorant, and naive indian, he is incapable of understanding the value of the goods he stole or of planning such thefts without help." Uneasily, I conclude that, under the circumstances and in the social context in which I find myself, the statement is the truest thing I might say. So after being sworn in and granted special credibility on account of my status as ethnographer of Julián's home town, I say more or less what is on the paper.

Ironically, a now literate Julián had written out a statement for me to memorize so that I could affirm his *il*literacy and his humble desire to return to the innocent peasant life that he in fact hated and from which he was in any event now cut off. Julián's story is now permanently inscribed in an *expediente,* a trial record, filed in the archive of the Superior Court of Oruro. So too is my own expert witness testimony, where in future decades or centuries aspiring historians may marvel at the demeaning stereotype of rural indigenous people offered up by a late-twentieth-century anthropologist. Or will they instead see in the record an innocent member of a pristine, "oral," indigenous culture, caught up in the evil machinations of a neocolonial world of state power and capitalist culture?[6]

Sitting in a courtyard in the crossroads town of Cruce late one afternoon in October of 1979, a septuagenarian, don Pablo Choquecallata, responds to my ethnographic questions with a heroic history of his hometown, with himself and his personal life-story at the center. Beginning with his role in building the stretch of the Pan American Highway where he founded Cruce in the late 1930s, don Pablo names and dates the standard milestones of progress from first house to first store to first school. In other conversations, don Pablo reaches deeper into the past, recalling his childhood in a nearby hamlet and his 1930s military service in the Chaco War, ending with internment in a Paraguayan concentration camp. He remembers the 1940s president Gualberto Villarroel's National Indigenous Congress, which he attended as a delegate, and its denouement, when the president was hanged from a lamp post in La Paz's Plaza Murillo. Don Pablo then narrates a series of journeys undertaken while serving as one of the yearly rotating authorities of his community, to the archives of Poopó, Oruro, and Sucre, in search of his people's colonial land titles.[7]

Many months later, don Pablo takes down a cigar box from a high shelf in his bedroom and presents me with a typescript document that he has not mentioned before. At his request, I read it to him and an audience of local authorities. It records their fathers' and grandfathers' travels to Bolivian archives to obtain this copy of a late-nineteenth-century document. At the same time, it records eloquent petitions drawn up by the ancestors of my audience for presentation to the Bolivian president, some of which contain precise references to articles of the Bolivian constitution and to what are described as "the principles of Political Economy." Assembled authorities, however, grow bored with this part of the document, being very familiar with the kind of legal petitions they themselves draw up from time to time, when someone who can read and write can be found to help. Instead, they want to hear the oldest parts of the document.

When I come to the copies of colonial writings imbedded in this sheaf of papers that Pablo Choquecallata himself once carried to the president in La Paz, I find that they are indeed land titles, dating as far back as 1593. My audience's interest rises when I come to the iterations by land judges of boundary markers along a circuit delimiting the territory to which they and their predecessors have for the past four hundred years laid claim.

The document not only lists boundary markers, called (in colonial Perú as in sixteenth-century Castile) *mojones,* but also describes the ritual circumambulation of the border by land judges and the hereditary native lords of Asanaqi, who stake their legal claim to territory through this act and subsequently take legal "possession" by yanking up plants and throwing stones and clods of earth. All such acts are duly recorded by the notary who accompanies the entourage, describing performative acts as well as the particular characteristics of each mojón. The land title resulting from this recorded ritual is meant for the archive, creating an "archival memory" by which a rote, word-for-word and act-for-act recollection of the territory and its possession can be later reconstituted. Such mojones and possession ceremonies derive from Castilian society, where, before the ready availability of paper and the rise of archival culture, these ritual acts were once a Castilian technique for engraving these legal transactions in the unwritten archive of social memory.

At each boundary marker, the judge reads out a copy of the sequence thus far constituted in the presence of cross-border neighbors, who might be expected to protest. When they do not, general consent to the mojón's position is recorded on the copy. In an extraordinary act which both inscribes the ritual circuit and makes inscription into commemorative monument, the judge then inserts this copy of the title into a bull's horn and places this point upwards into the deepest recesses of the pile

of stones that makes up the mojón. As necessary supplements to one
another, writing, ritual, and the landscape itself together constitute a
memory in words, acts, and places by which to moor the quotidian
experiences of future generations in a tangible past.

At least one stretch of the mojón list in the document is very familiar
to several members of my audience during this reading. As local
authorities of a polity derived from one corner of Asanaqi territory, my
audience finds the document's sequence of boundary markers not only
familiar but also meaningful, notwithstanding their inability to read. For
apart from their roles in adjudicating local disputes, collecting taxes, and
otherwise mediating between the Bolivian state and their local community, it is their duty to memorize lists of mojones and walk the border
they define in a yearly commemorative ritual akin both to colonial land
judges' demarcation and possession ceremonies and to Inca wak'a rites
along ceque lines.[8]

HISTORY AND MEMORY, NARRATIVE AND LANDSCAPE

Each of these vignettes describes what might be termed a frontier
situation, a moment in the intersection of distinct yet interdependent
cultural realms. As a journeyman of the frontier practice of ethnography,
the act of entering into the space of another culture in order to write
about it for people like myself, I entered into contexts that were already
frontiers, in which many generations have engaged in delicate communicative negotiations between local society and more global state forces.
Whether Asanaqi to Inca, indian to Spaniard, or rural community or
individual to the Bolivian government, all have found themselves engaged not only in political struggle but also in a struggle to mark out
relatively autonomous spheres in which to gain control over the meanings of their lives. Crucial to this endeavor are efforts to gain and retain
control over the definition, transmission, and interpretation of the past.
As ethnographer, historian, and author of this book, I have not only
thrown my hat into this same arena of discursive contest, but have also
become part of it, if only in transitory ways. In this book, which itself
repeatedly violates the disciplinary frontier between ethnography and
history, I seek to recognize and question the reciprocal impact of my
projects and those of the people whose stories I here relate, by taking a
reflexive turn in history as well as ethnography.

Each of my vignettes also recounts a moment in the realization of
social memory, the many permutations of which are the main subject of

this book. Following a trail blazed by Connerton's *How Societies Remember* (1989), which drew heavily on *annaliste* sociologist Maurice Halbwachs' pioneering interwar work on commemoration and collective memory, I seek to explore past and present forms of social memory in a single region of the Andean highlands.[9] Examination of the foregoing examples will help to forward a preliminary definition of what I mean by social memory and to foreground the shapes it has taken in pre-Columbian to postcolonial contexts.

In each of the above vignettes, specific individuals address, within distinct and well-defined contexts, the defining relationship between persons, social groups, and their pasts, whether through commemorative enactment, active inscription, testimony in court, or engaged investigation. They strive to place themselves in a historical context, tapping into diverse kinds of memory sources in a self-defining act. Existing at a wide range of historical moments, all share a concern with time and the implications of its passing. All seek to ground present individual and collective concerns in temporally distant origin moments tied to them through duration, generation, and transitive relations to ancestral figures and places of shared significance. All share a manifest concern with the intersection of personhood, time, and movement through the landscape that we call travel.

Although I extract some of these exemplary vignettes from historical investigation of documentary texts (one account, that of the Asanaqi mit'a journey to Cusco, being an imagined text) and others from ethnographic annotations of fieldwork experiences, this distinction in method and source does not satisfactorily classify the activities described in the examples. The activities of Asanaqi visitors to the Inca administrative center of Jatun Qulla share much in common with the ethnographic example of the Mamanis' llama corral libations. So also do Cieza's efforts as chronicler have much in common with the probanza production of don Juan Colque Guarache and the archival investigations of don Pablo Choquecallata, who would surely draw on the written documents he guards to write his own history, if only he knew how to read and write.

On the basis of these external similarities and differences, one might divide my examples into two categories: In some, the written word mediates past experience, while in others, "traditionally transmitted" myth and ritual mediate it. Such a distinction, as clear to sixteenth-century Spaniards (who invariably commented on pre-Columbian Andeans' lack of writing and the consequent uncertainty of their history) as it is to modern observers, suggests that a great chasm divides written from oral cultures and, perhaps, the disciplinary domain of anthropologists from that of historians. Since the present work seeks to bridge the gap and cross disciplinary divides, as the example of simultaneously written and enacted journeys along sequences of boundary markers suggests, we must explore such distinctions.

Rather than resort to the unexamined prejudices of easier targets, let us see how an especially insightful historiographer, Jacques Le Goff, treats the issue. In a brief sketch of an entity he calls "ethnic memory," which he distinguishes from the explicitly historical memory made possible by the emergence of writing, Le Goff proposes that "the principal domain in which the collective memory of peoples without writing crystallizes is that which provides an apparently historical foundation for the existence of ethnic groups or families, that is, myths of origin" (1992: 55). Le Goff carefully avoids explicit insistence on a clear distinction between peoples with historical consciousness (through writing) and those (without writing) who must make do with mythical consciousness, but he implies the distinction, nonetheless, in his subsequent analysis. Although collective memory in nonwriting societies organizes collective identity through myths of origin, genealogies of its leading families, and the technical knowledge transmitted by practical formulas imbued with magic, "writing permits collective memory to make a double advance with the rise of two forms of memory": commemoration by inscribed monument, and the written document, which stores information and communicates it across time and space (ibid., p. 58–59).

Without writing, the Andean past suffered distinct disadvantages from the Spaniards' point of view and according to traditional canons of historiography. Apparently responding to this stigma, some (mostly literary) postmodernist scholars have suggested redefinitions of writing which level the playing field, bringing pre-Columbian Andeans into the literate world. In essays that make subtle distinctions between the writing and reading of linguistic texts and the Andean "representational" form most akin to them, the system of knotted strings called the *quipu* (sometimes spelled *khipu*), Tom Cummins and Walter D. Mignolo nonetheless suggest the potential equivalence of such systems, a suggestion underscored in the title of the volume in which their essays appear, *Writing Without Words: Alternative Literacies in Mesoamerica and the Andes* (Boone and Mignolo 1994). Other scholars privately suggest that the quipu was more than just akin to writing as a mnemonic device, that it actually conveyed a phonological system for the representation of speech. As I will later argue, it seems more likely that the quipu functioned as a mnemonic device for narrative purposes by its structure as an iconic model of transit lines in space, a manipulable model of the ceque systems that connected significant topographic points, recalling the ritual movements that helped to shape the boundaries of the social by linking social groups to narratively coded pasts associated with the landscape.

Without granting writing to preconquest Andeans, other scholars have shifted the locus of attention in the study of colonial and postcolonial relationships to discourse, privileging linguistic communication (if only by treating all communication as languagelike) above other kinds of conception and expression. Studies in the growing field of "postcolonial discourse" (for example: Seed 1991, 1992; Barker, Hulme, and Iversen 1994) have come under attack for rhetorically downplaying the violence and coercive use of power attendant to colonial and republican state relations with indians (see the thoughtful review in Mallon 1994). From the perspective of our topics, however, the most serious problem in analyzing colonial relations as discourses, and of suggesting that pre-Columbian social memory resided in forms of "writing without words," is that it marginalizes and obfuscates precisely the kinds of nonlinguistic modes of conception and communication—the embodied and enacted forms of social memory—that were (and are) centrally important in the Andes. It follows, then, that one cannot undo colonial projects by granting writing to preconquest Andeans or by restoring the Andean voice to accounts of colonial discourses. Instead, we must first focus on the process whereby nonwritten and unvoiced forms of social memory were erased from Spanish accounts of the Andean past.

The advantages of writing and the disadvantages associated with the lack thereof in the pre-Columbian Andes became especially clear to both Andeans and Spaniards when they attempted to write Andean histories (see chapter 5). Like Le Goff, chroniclers of the preconquest Andes, lacking the apparently context-free transmissions from the past called writing, surveyed the forms of still-persisting social memory available to them as sources and chose to privilege oral narrative, especially myths of origin. Also like Le Goff, many chroniclers marveled at the mnemotechnical possibilities of the knotted-string device called the quipu (for Le Goff a "rare exception" to the absence among nonliterate societies of serious interest in word-for-word memorization or exact acts of memory [1992: 57]). Among the chroniclers of early postconquest Peru, only a few ethnographically inclined colonial authors, such as Juan Polo Ondegardo, recognized the power of the memory work carried out in singing and dancing (performances of a balladlike genre of music and dance called *taquies*) between holy sites along the transit lines that Andeans called ceques, and which we might term topographs. Most sixteenth-century observers saw only oral narrative as a reasonable facsimile of and source for the written event chronicle.

By privileging the kind of nonwritten memory that seemingly approximated written records of event sequences—that is, the origin narratives that sixteenth-century Spaniards called *fábulas, burlerías,* or *ironías,* and that we call myths—historians and ethnographers of the past four and a half centuries generated an unfortunate legacy. By grouping together mythic narrative and the event sequences of eyewitness testimony (recorded in the act by the ethnographer or read out of old writings) as the "stuff of history," Andeanist historians found important keys to writing histories of the Andes but obscured Andeans' *own* histories, the culturally specific social memory forms through which pre-Columbian to twentieth-century Andeans have engaged their pasts.

In this book, a work in the disciplinary borderlands where ethnography and history meet, I set myself to a double task. On the one hand, I carry out a familiar sort of "objective history," subjecting ethnographic observations and documentary sources alike to the techniques of source criticism, weighing the reliability of each source, the potential distortions or lies imparted to them by the special interests or the coercive effects of the colonial power imbalance of scribe and witness. On the other hand, I aim to represent or reveal some of the ways by which Andeans of the past and present have understood their pasts through other sorts of registers, including oral narrative and ritual action. Since evidence of the latter comes either from historical documents or from ethnographic writings, which both often sought to portray Andean social consciousness as timeless and ahistorical, the two projects necessarily coincide.

Seeking the soundest evidence, I build up a narrative image of the Andean past, from preconquest times, through successive colonial and republican transformations, to the present. In this effort, applied to ethnographic sources in parts 1 and 3 and to documentary sources in part 2, I trace the impact of what I take for the most significant moments of social transformation, but always with special attention to the changes undergone by Andean ways of recounting and accounting for the past.

Everyone engaged in the project of understanding the meaning of pre-Columbian Andean ceques, wak'as, or taquies knows that serious obstacles litter the scholarly path. Sometimes the cultural prejudices of colonial authors, which dictated what kinds of things were penworthy (such as myths of origin and other oral narratives), led to silences about certain Andean memory practices. Conversely, at times Andean cultural practices were so alien that they remained nearly imperceptible to Spanish eyes. Likewise, insistent Counter-Reformation condemnations of the idolatrous, heretical, and diabolical quickly subjected much Andean practice to "extirpation," exiling it for both Andean and Spaniard to the clandestine realm of the unspeakable. As a result, in evaluating documentary sources on the Andean past, we must exercise a dual kind of source criticism, attending not only to the kinds of events, practices, and memory forms that colonial chroniclers describe (or to what twentieth-century Andeans volunteer about their practices) but also to the structure of their silences.

Thus in part 1, I attend to ethnographic silences—the gaps in the ethnographic record as well as the structured diffidence on the politics of the ethnographic encounters that produced them. In part 2, I turn to documentary lapses, seeking to reconstruct the kinds of social memory— such as taquies, ceque transits, and capac hucha pilgrimages, as well as their even less understood colonial derivatives—that were so poorly inscribed in colonial writings. In part 3, I turn to a different sort of historical enterprise, suspending the historian's rules of source criticism and purported empirical objectivity in order to describe ways of understanding the past that violate such rules. Only after I have exposed the politics of my ethnographic fieldwork, in part 1, and provided the most "other culture"–sensitive historical background of which I am capable, in part 2, will the full power as forms of historical consciousness of the myth narratives, libation topographies, and other K'ulta pilgrimages in space-time (as described in part 3) perhaps become apparent.

The structure of the book, sandwiching a more traditional form of historical inquiry between large chunks of ethnographic writing, may in some ways constitute a liability for my project of breaking down old distinctions between "mythic" and "historical" peoples, and of demonstrating the analogous ways that, with or without writing, social memory is constructed, contested, and revised. Dividing the material according to whether the source is documentary or ethnographic risks reemphasizing the very frontier I seek to blur.[10]

I accept this risk for two interrelated reasons. On the one hand, in spite (or because) of the fact that my own career has led me to cross the disciplinary battle front, I recognize that, while the methods, ethics, and consequences of historical and ethnographic work share more than their practitioners might like to admit, there is at least some justification for disciplinary specialization in the different problematics of querying and writing about dead versus live people. On the other hand, I choose to divide ethnographic from historical sections of the book so as to avoid suggesting that, by twining the two kinds of sources together into a single narrative thread, the resulting story would be more complete. The social memory that K'ultas construct through myth and ritual practice sharply contradicts the general line of social memory construed by historians and nationalist ideologues. Rather than trying to reconcile such contradictions, I hope to illustrate through contrast their distinctly constituted politics of memory and forgetting. Colonialism produces not only a contention of societies and cultures but also a conflict of histories.

Yet even as I acknowledge gaps between the predominantly written (and Spanish-dominated) record of the colonial past and the mainly nonwritten modes of historical consciousness in contemporary K'ulta, I also seek to highlight the continuities and similarities between such techniques. Only by doing so can my account of K'ulta social memory hope to challenge those who might disparage the K'ultas as a "people without history" because for the most part they do not write.

According to a much-worn historians' touchstone, highlighted in yellow in every western civilization textbook, ancient post-Socratic Greeks initiated the discipline of history by marking the distance between historical and mythical consciousness (and subsequently between the historian's territory and the anthropologist's). Historians, the argument goes, being aware that objective social conditions emerged from the activities of men like themselves rather than from the activities of gods, radically undermined the comfortable certainties of mythical consciousness with their pens, banishing myth to the realm of uncivilized and superstitious "ethnics." Yet as Le Goff notes (citing Momigliano), Herodotus, Thucydides, and other "great" historians of Greco-Roman antiquity chose to write exclusively or preferentially about the recent past, according primacy to eyewitness testimony (Le Goff 1992: 186 [Momigliano 1977: 161–163]). By default they left the most distant past, the time of origins, unexplained, susceptible to rationalization by nonhuman first causes. As generations and centuries of historical texts have piled up one upon the other, the "recent" past (documented by now-dead eyewitnesses) has grown very deep and wide. The writing system perfected by men like "Simonides of Ceos, the son of Leoprepe, the inventor of the system of mnemonic aids, [who] won the choral singing prize at Athens" (264 B.C. inscription on a marble slab in reference to an event of 477 B.C. [Le Goff 1992: 66]), has left us mountains of text fragments purporting to be eyewitness testimony about the impact of human agency on events. But founding moments remain beyond the reach of documented human agency, relegated to the poetic memory techniques such as that of Simonides' choral singing.

As Le Goff notes, along with many other authors, the arrival of writing did not automatically displace all other forms of collective memory. In the case of sixteenth-century Spain (and the rest of Europe), the Bible actually served as a charter and touchstone for an immense range of commemorative activities, providing the rhythmic or habitual substance of everyday life. The calendar and its eschatology were reduced to experiential miniature, projected iconically onto yearly, weekly, even daily routines, thus chaining the supposedly sequential experience of duration to cyclic reenactments and repeatedly erasing contingency and the cumulative transformation of life in favor of an endless recurrence of the biblical narrative of covenant, sin, confession, penance, absolution, and redemption. Regardless of the fact that their "charter" was a written document rather than an oral narrative, the "civilized and Christian" life-ways Spaniards sought to impose on Andeans could well be judged a form of "mythical consciousness." For Le Goff, such examples illustrate how the European legacy of prewriting techniques of collective memory continued from antiquity into the Middle Ages, leaving a residue in modern times that was still strong in the Renaissance period, when so many books on the "arts of memory" emerged, along with so many chronicles.[11]

Daily, weekly, monthly, and yearly routines marked out by the ringing of church bells and regular confession and participation in the Eucharist accompanied, in Spanish towns as well as Peruvian ones, periodically enacted obligatory collective rituals such as the processions of Corpus Christi, an array of saints' festivals, celebration of the monarch's (and Christ's) life-crisis rites, tribute-collection rituals, rites and pilgrimages of personal service to the Crown, and regular administrative inspection and census tours known as visitas. All these events share qualities ascribed to visitas in a recent landmark reanalysis of such events: "[They] were understood to *enact* as visible reality a programmed politico-social order (*policía* was a common term for it) as opposed to the ragtag product of history. Visiting was a theater of ideology, giving that bundle of imagined patterns called social structure a temporary primacy over practice. In this respect it had a strict Incaic precedent: the *capac hucha*. . . . As much as the *capac hucha,* a Spanish *visita* created the social order it pretended to discover" (Guevara-Gil and Salomon 1994: 4–5; emphasis in original).

We might add that such rites, regarded as hegemonic devices of the state, simultaneously commemorated and brought into being the specific relationship among space-time, subordinated social groups and rulers, and subjectivities (in the ontological as well as political sense). In this regard, Spaniards' efforts to distinguish themselves from indians on the basis of a unique European relationship to the past enabled by writing seem forced or overwrought.

Perhaps we can conclude that the urgency of their efforts to end the practices they identified as idolatry, and to erase the Andean techniques of enacted social memory that recalled it, derived not from the great contrast between barbarous and idolatrous enacted memory and the civilized and Christian sort inscribed in Spanish ritual calendars, but to the unnerving similarity between them. Recognition of such formal parallelism between Spanish Christian ways and the "almost Christian" and "almost civilized" collective practices of Andeans raised the potential for relativist social theory. It threatened to make patent the constructed and therefore conventional or arbitrary nature of *civitas* and Christianity. Unlike the human authors and authorities missing from the Andean past for its lack of writing, the *author*ity of Spaniards' ritually enacted civitas and Christianity was God himself, whose deeds themselves structured space and time (in calendars and their architectural-topographic icons of heavenly agency) when mortals recalled and commemorated them. A recognizably analogous and alternative form of social memory could be nothing other than satanic mimicry, designed by the devil to conceal Truth from Andeans.[12] Thus Andean forms of social memory became errors and superstitions, the very memory of which it became the Spanish duty to erase.

Similar suspicions are raised by the fact that, ever since the sixteenth-century arrival of writing in the Andes, written and oral forms of communication have coexisted with one another, sometimes leading to reciprocal influences. Perhaps, then, making distinctions between Spaniards and Andeans along the axis of letters is not as useful as we might think in characterizing the cultures of either colonizers or colonized. Even while centuries of experience with the legal effectiveness of textual memory has led Andeans to venerate pen and ink as well as document bundles, reverence for writing has not erased their equally deep respect for the nonwritten arts of memory.

The example of don Pablo Choquecallata—for whom respect for and engagement with the documented past can coexist with a tradition of mythic narrative and the recalling through libations of the social past "written" on the landscape—might suggest to some readers that the Spanish civilizational project failed. I think it hasty, however, to conclude that Andeans adopted Spanish reverence for writing but preserved their own alternative forms of historical practice, clandestinely remembering their pre-Columbian ways. For Spanish colonialism was an exploitative relationship grounded in a civilizational mission, a project to transform Andean social life. And in this regard, the colonial confrontation of histories resulting from the Spanish colonization of Andean pasts did not take place mainly in or through the written text, or even primarily in the realm of verbal narrative.

Those Spaniards who concerned themselves with the conscience-assuaging civilizational project that accompanied colonial raids on Andean silver sought to impose on Andeans the calendars and ritual commemorative forms of Spanish Christianity. To the degree that they succeeded, they did so by forcibly transforming preexisting social groups by abolishing the techniques and locations of preexisting Andean social memory and by reinscribing Andean social life within new forms of space and time. The study of long-term shifts in the Andean manner of engaging the past, therefore, necessarily involves studying changing institutions, settlement patterns, architectural forms, economies, political organization, and modes of travel, of ways of perceiving space and time inflected with deep implications of power and kinds of social hierarchy.

I might, then, conclude that this is a book about long-term transformations of rural Andean "cosmologies" under the unfavorable conditions of subordination to colonial Spanish and creole-dominated republican state regimes. And so, indeed, it is. It is also, however, about the forms of counterhegemony that Andeans have been able to deploy through complex interplays of public and clandestine practice that invoke ancestral beings in sacred landscapes that are also inhabited by the saints. Andean culture as a self-contained order of signifiers has not resisted four and a half centuries of state domination by colonial and republican forces, because such cultural logics are virtual realities, imagined by anthropologists. Cultural meanings are always deployed in social action, in lived contexts, by real people who must experience and account for unpleasantness like asymmetries of power. Not Andean culture, but *Andeans,* like don Pablo Choquecallata, have resisted the forces of social domination by drawing on a collectively construed social memory to *understand* the hegemonies to which they are subject, so as to redeploy them creatively in the form of counterhegemonies. Theses on cultural resistance that locate only a precolonial Andean past in the clandestine practices of living rural Andeans, it would seem, fail to recognize Andeans' intellectual capabilities.

Is it only anthropologists and historians who are to be granted the ability to recognize, understand, and counter the nefarious impact of historical experience in the Andes? Or must we also account for Andeans' own ways of undoing the sorcery of history with its memory? Those who grant exclusive rights to historical and ethnographic method, and then go on to suggest that their project is to give a history (or a metacultural analysis) to a group of people otherwise lacking it, must answer for themselves as well as for their "science." They must explain how it is that scholarly debates carried out in luxury hotel boardrooms, or in books published by academic presses, can serve people living in difficult conditions elsewhere. They must also come to grips with the degree to which intellectual projects like theirs help to reproduce their own privileged position, not only vis-à-vis some distant "ethnic other" but also with respect to the workers in those hotel laundry rooms or to the homeless people who beg for change just down the street.

Although I do not claim such authority, the same admonition goes for me when I suggest the possibility of representing in this book some alternative (and "other") forms of social memory. As I strive to show in part 1, ethnographic and historical projects cannot be extricated from power-laden contexts and projects of colonial, imperial, and national states, nor can ethnographers or historians rise above the fray. This is so, first of all, because it is through our links to power—indexed by letters of introduction, affiliations with embassies and research institutes, signed and sealed authorizations by state or peasant union authorities, and more generally our relative wealth and status evinced by the ways we speak and dress and the goods we possess—that we gain access to archives or rural towns. Whether we treat them as such or not, these diverse emblems of our powerful connections serve as potent instruments of coercive persuasion and also as comforting safety nets by which we can quickly escape messy or dangerous situations. I traveled to K'ulta and to foreign archives with a thick packet of letters signed by consuls, government ministers, and department and province authorities, all of which were duly inspected by local authorities in K'ulta.

But when K'ultas invert my trajectory and travel from the country to the city to trade, file petitions, or seek access to archives, they do not do so from such a position of power. Likewise, they are not for the most part in a position to contest what I write about them. No matter what strategies of writing I employ here, it is my voice, not theirs, that speaks through these pages.

At the same time, this work is enmeshed in the rise and fall of intellectual paradigms and theoretical fashions that are not those of K'ulta. In an effort to redress such problems in part, I peg my presentation and arguments not only to debates over authority, objectivity, and truth, but also to discourses of ethics in work among "ethnics."

ETHNOGRAPHY AND HISTORY IN A POSTCOLONIAL INTERCULTURE

This is, then, a book that draws on a combination of participant-observation ethnography and archival investigation to explore in the Andean context the relationship between memory and history, and to juxtapose ethnographic, historical, and "social memory" records, recollections, reconstructions, and commemorations of the past. Its most fundamental argument is that historians, and in some cases anthropologists, have been guilty of extraordinary hubris in their accounts of ancient or non-European forms of historical memory and in the portrayals of non-European pasts that they have presumed to reconstruct for "peoples without history."

I privilege the term "social memory" (of which writing and the writing of histories constitute a special case) as an attractive alternative to some uses of the term "culture," because the latter, in noun phrases such as "Aymara culture" or "the culture of K'ulta," seems always to convey the existence of a static "system of symbols and meanings" existing in some virtual "structure," floating in intersubjective mind space. I use the term "social memory" to convey the embodied ways by which people constitute themselves and their social formations in communicative actions and interactions, making themselves by making rather than inheriting their pasts. Recollecting and commemorating the past always takes place in contingent contexts where power is at play. As a result, alternative forms of social memory and alternative possibilities for construing the social are always in contention.[13]

Substantiating this pronouncement requires more than further theoretical argument. It demands substantive exemplification. I seek to do just this through the primarily ethnographic cases developed in part 1 and part 3, and the predominantly historical ones developed in part 2. In my final chapters, I draw on the revaluation of ritual that has ensued in part from anthropology's historical turn (for a concise account, see Kelly and Kaplan 1990). Rather than the antithesis of the historical event, as ritual was once understood, it may be the case that all ritual (including, of course, explicitly "historical" commemorations, but also saints' festivals and sacrifices) may be regarded as an instrumentality of history, a veritable historical engine.[14] At the very least, I will show how the people of K'ulta construct their own identities, their historical identities, by ritually formulating and transforming their relationship to the past.

By accentuating the ways in which Andeans have actively engaged Spanish and Bolivian creole ethnocidal policies and adapted imposed forms to their own ends, I aim to minimize the risk of falling prey to anthropological nostalgia for a time when we could pretend to study beautifully hermetic "other cultural" worlds, untarnished by contact with the rapacious and polluting "Western culture" or capitalism. The insistent note of lamentation heard in works by the French practitioners of anthropological history Nathan Wachtel (1977) and Serge Gruzinski (1993: esp. 260–281), whose concepts of "destructuration" name a progressive and conclusive displacement of indigenous forms by colonially imposed ones, has too often led other anthropologies to answer them with claims about successful cultural resistance. Whether asserting that native culture has been destroyed or that it persists behind a thin veneer of feigned Christianity and adherence to colonizers' codes of values, such arguments rest on semiotic theories of virtual cultural closure. They err in suggesting that native society before colonialism, or any society, was ever a static and closed structure.

However, another view of "culture" produces different conclusions. I do not mean to suggest that colonialism did not "violate" native societies, only that they were not pure and closed semiotic orders before the conquest, just as sixteenth-century Spanish society was in no sense closed and unchanging. Both Andean social forms and Spanish ones were in the midst of rapid transformation at the time they were thrown together, and both were also transformed as a result of their confluence. The meaning orders we call culture are not hothouse flowers, but rather products and producers of lived experience in all its messiness. From that point of view, the historian's question ought not to be "How and when were native cultures destroyed by invading ones?" but "How at various points in time have indigenous people (and for good measure, colonial Spaniards as well) taken account of the colonial experience in the poetically structured narratives and practices that we call myth and ritual?"

Moving onto a historical frontier pioneered by Stern (1982; 1993) and by Spalding (1984), I contend that the institutional matrix and cultural meanings of "ethnic" cultural survival in the Andes have been shaped by native peoples' active and collective engagement with, rather than flight from, the power-infused cultural programs of state elites. In response to Counter-Reformation insistence on orthodoxy, which constrained natives' room to maneuver in their efforts to synthesize "original" and "imposed" institutions and belief systems, the native synthesis took the form of an active interplay between relatively orthodox public practice and clandestine supplements, where native intellectuals and ritual specialists ran less risk of persecution as "idolatrous dogmatizers" or heretical proselytizers. Over time, the tense relationship between orthodox Hispano-Christian practice and heterodox and "pagan" Amerindian practice not only defined the space of conflict between Spaniards and indians, but also was internalized within Spanish-creole and indigenous cultures. Having been defined through their conjunction, neither was fully imaginable without the other. And so the mutually constituting work of both hegemony and counterhegemony (also memory and countermemory) came into play, in Michael Taussig's memorable phrase, "in the sweaty warm space between the arse of him who rides and the back of him who carries. Even there—perhaps especially there on account of its closeness—one glimpses how the poetics of control operates with imagery and feeling located in the subconscious realm of fantasy" (Taussig 1987: 288; Guevara-Gil and Salomon 1994: 27–28 n. 7). How much of that subconscious realm is collectively displaced into the nonpresent, the past and the future, which can be newly shaped by grasping hold of its memory? Not surprisingly, the social memories of groups at both ends of the colonial relationship summon up pasts that can account for that relationship, whether to justify or to undermine. And so social memory, which might in technical jargon be described as conventional sequences of narrative and action tied to meaningful coordinates in space and time, or in more pedestrian language be described as the myths and rituals of cosmology, has come to model the colonial situation itself. And this is as true for the social memory of colonizers as for that of the colonized.

As I suggested, this anthropological romance itself rests on a thesis about social memory, one that holds that Andeans' pasts are immutable, locked up in a closed and virtual purity. As a historical thesis, it echoes those of colonial priests and republican liberals, who also portrayed the indian as immutable, albeit for his barbarous ignorance rather than for his heroic resistance. None of the above, however, represents merely fabricated images of indigenous ways. Indeed, each may grasp, in its

own way, an essential feature of the colonial dynamic: Given the degree
to which colonialism was not just coercive exploitation met by "everyday forms of resistance" (Scott 1985) but also a contest of histories, one
might suggest that both Spaniard and indian forwarded in their respective social memories philosophies of history that *temporalized* their
opposing poles in the colonial asymmetry of power.

Above all, this temporalization in the production of the colonial
cultural dynamic is our object of inquiry here. So too must we attend to
how historians and anthropologists have (often without explicitly theorizing about other cultures' historicity) located indigenous cultures in
time (see Fabian 1983). In the chapters that follow, I provide an account
of when and under what circumstances such temporalization of the
colonial intercultural relationship between indians and Spaniards became an essential feature of Andean societies and of Andean studies. At
the same time, I offer a revisionary approach to the study of colonial
formations, suggesting that much error has resulted from misreading
temporalized intercultural syntheses as separable and independent "earlier and original" and "later and imposed" parts.

I also seek here to query the curiously analogous ways by which
colonial peoples and modern anthropologists and historians have theo-
rized about the relationship between specific (other) cultural forms and
history, and about how certain notions of cultural logics (and also
colonial projects) have tended to obfuscate the ways other cultures might
generate other histories (see Thomas 1989).

The colonial project, and the republican project since independence,
has never had solely political or economic ends, but historical ones as
well: Not only have respective Spanish- and creole-dominant sectors
(which is to say, the forces of the state) sought to define their relationship
with subordinated indians as a historically grounded relationship, rooted
in founding past events, but they have also sought to figure their
Spanish-indian and creole-indian relationship as opposed poles on a
time-line on which Spaniards and creoles, striding onto the high-ground
and into the light can make out indians only by an over-the-shoulder
backwards glance, towards the dark and murky past.[15] The projects of
history are deeply implicated in political-economic programs, allied to
interest and power.

It is to be lamented that the nostalgia-driven anthropological romance
has so often played into such schemata, pining (along with nineteenth-
century romantics, 1930s German folklorists, 1940s indigenistas) for the
lost innocence of their own before-the-fall pasts (preindustrial, preimpe-

rial, and prenationalist), perhaps recoverable in the living fossils that colonizers, empires, and nation-states have made of their colonized, subordinated, and marginalized "subnational" alters.

This book has been shaped by such concerns, as well as by the tension between the poetic forms of historical understanding that I glimpsed in K'ulta (which I have attempted to translate into a language and prose form that is alien to it) and the conventions and conclusions of my own historical investigations. So too has it been shaped by the realization that the historian's conundrum with regard to interpretation of documentary evidence, which has invariably been a product of past interest and power-charged discourses, just as the historian's interpretations are always in some manner interested and power-infused, differs little from the readerly concerns that fuel debates over the nature of ethnographic representation. The "source critical" maneuvers to which historians subject their sources are just what readers of ethnography hope to do with reflexive, confessional, or "discourse centered" ethnographic writing.

It is my hope that my efforts here to displace or supplement the ethnography and history of the "idols behind altars" resistance paradigm does not appear to undercut all the politically salient identity projects (from indigenous nationalism to nationalist *indigenismo*) that now draw on them so heavily. To portray indigenous societies as transformed by colonialism may offend those for whom unchanging continuity is a source of imperialism-resistant national "originality" or of legal bases for claiming land. Foregrounding the constructed nature of social identities and the pasts on which they rest, even when one insists that all such identities and pasts are constructed, is not always politically expedient.

I respond by highlighting the degree to which Andean cultural forms in all their multiplicity are the products of an active intellectual engagement with encompassing political economies, cultural hegemonies, and globalized sociocultural fields. To K'ulta intellectuals present and future, and to indigenista and indianista activists more generally, I do not offer predigested rhetorical ammunition intentionally suited to the discourses of nationalism, but a respectful intervention, accompanied by all the evidence necessary for its disqualification as adequate representation.

Part One

An Ethnographic Pastorale:
Introduction to K'ulta and
the Local Sources of History

Chapter Two

Journeys to Cultural Frontiers

In June of 1979, some six months after arriving in Bolivia, I set off from La Paz with my wife and fieldwork companion, Mary Dillon, on a journey to a small rural town. My destination in that journey from La Paz was Santa Bárbara de Culta, a small and out-of-the-way town, to which I often travel in memory on a well-worn imaginary path. Santa Bárbara de Culta, a town of adobe and thatch houses that is a permanent home for a few families and a political-ritual pilgrimage center for about six thousand people spread across the treeless but hauntingly beautiful mountainscape of its hinterlands, has been a repeated destination in research trips or simply to visit old friends. But much more often, as I have sat before a keyboard while writing and revising this book or stood before a classroom full of students in courses on Latin American ethnography or history, I have conjured images of that town into being, assembling and reassembling the traces it has left in my memory.

Representations of such places have a tendency to take on the features of an exotic travel destination. So after "setting the scene" with accounts devised to establish our presence in such a place, thereby establishing our eyewitness authority for what follows, we ethnographers have tended to disappear from our ethnographies shortly after arrival. In what was once the norm in ethnographic writing, succeeding chapters then backed away from the first-person account, describing rituals and kinship systems and political economies in a distanced and authoritative third person of the omniscient narrator. We have done so because, although travel is the

29

essence of ethnographic experience, ethnographers who travel by plane, bus, or camel to "Third World" destinations are always subject to the fear of being little more than an overblown tourist, seeking the most exotic places and experiences so as to outdo others' accounts of vacationland exploits. Depersonalized "normative distancing" and displacement of fieldnote chronographies by a logical succession of chapters on various domains of life helped not only to conceal the author's (and discipline's) narrative artifice and to obscure the power-laden interpersonal dynamics of "data collection," but also to distance the traveling science-minded ethnographer from the dilettante tourist and his or her self-centered anecdotes.

Yet the travel account has the merit of foregrounding its narrative line and, hero or humbug, placing the narrator at the scene of the drama. I beg the reader's indulgence, then, in bearing with me on a package tour, a travelogue with commentary, that begins, as I did, in Chicago and reaches K'ulta only after a series of transit stops. I justify this apparently subjective writing strategy on aesthetic but also unusually scientific grounds: It will highlight, rather than conceal, the power relations of fieldwork, and will thus enable critics to unravel and doubt the evidence I place into context. I also make the strange case that an account of K'ulta in tourism terms may be more appropriate than any other kind. And I refer here not only to the fact that the people of K'ulta are themselves inveterate travelers. More to the point is the fact that their ways of life, their genealogies, marriages, politics, and very pasts, are remembered as itineraries of travel.

On a trip from the United States to rural Bolivia, arriving at the international airport of La Paz and encountering the city center may be full of exotic new experiences, but the whole scene is also relatively comfortable and familiar. Taxis carry arriving passengers to the downtown hotels of a modern capital city. The traveler discovers upon closer inspection, not far away from the city center, the city's large population of Aymara-speaking people, who live around the urban periphery but dominate its street markets.

For me, of course, La Paz was initially to be only a brief stopover on a continuing journey, one that would lead to a small rural Aymara-speaking community where I would complete the fieldwork requisite for a Ph.D. in anthropology. My journey to K'ulta began as a graduate student of anthropology at the University of Chicago. Yet in spite of wide-ranging readings in Andeanist ethnography and history, I had not yet heard of that place. Indeed, apart from the immediate vicinity of

Lake Titicaca, most of the territory occupied by Aymara speakers went at that time undescribed in the ethnological literature.[1]

Most of the llama herders of the Altiplano are speakers of the Aymara language, which was even more widespread at the time of the Spanish invasion.[2] Today La Paz is the only major city in which Aymara still predominates. The trip up the slope from the La Paz city center to the Altiplano provides the substance for what might be called a vertical sociology, a study in the correlation of differences in ethnicity and wealth to those of altitude. Glass and steel (or at least glass and concrete) skyscrapers at the lower financial-commercial-political core of the city gradually give way upslope to the old colonial center and, yet farther up hill, to one-room adobe homes; a predominantly Spanish-speaking nadir fades into a mostly Aymara-speaking zenith, mediated by the monuments and institutions of the colonial and republican past.

Like the administrative-elite cores of all Bolivia's major cities and provincial capitals, the city center of La Paz is a bastion of the Spanish language, which since colonial times has been the language of state and of the country's ruling elite. In the days of the colony, of course, ruling elites were Spaniards. From the local seat of royal power, the appeals court of the Audiencia de Charcas in the city that is now Sucre, the distant Spanish Crown ruled the territory that is now Bolivia and presided over the extraction of surpluses from indigenous labor through the collection of tribute and through forced indian service in mines and Spanish towns. Such pressures and Spanish projects to acculturate indians forcibly to Castilian culture and the Catholic faith notwithstanding, indigenous societies managed to perpetuate themselves, transformed, throughout the colonial period. They were aided in this both by the colonial preference for indirect rule (indian authorities collected tributes and levied labor for Spanish overlords) and by a succession of laws and discriminatory practices that strove to keep Spaniards separate from indians. The latter also made use of colonial institutions—in particular, the limited autonomies granted to them as members of rural town councils and urban parish communities—and access to forms of legal redress due them as properly constituted subjects of Spanish kings and, later, of Bolivian governments.

If La Paz has a Spanish core, it has an Aymara periphery. For well-to-do Paceños, a kind of architectural model of that periphery is very close at hand, in the kitchen, laundry room, patio, and maid's quarters, where a pollera- and bowler-clad, Aymara-speaking maid is a *de rigueur* sign of respectability.[3] Other laboring people, like the maids whose employers do not provide quarters, live mostly in the Aymara-speaking neighborhoods that developed from colonial indian parishes founded on the outskirts of the Spanish city center. Indigenous neighborhoods rise up steep hillsides towards the very rim of the basin in which La Paz is located. In the 1780s, it was around this rim, from a base in indian neighborhoods, that the armies of Tupac Catari attacked colonial Spaniards and laid waste to the city center during a long siege. Not long after that great rebellion was quashed, creole Spaniards in 1825 took the reins of state from Spain after their own revolution, leading to the liberal program of privatization and ethnocide. Such predations did not, however, go unresisted. Indian rebels were again on the move in 1900 and again in the 1920s, met always by swift reprisals and exemplary punishments.[4]

In 1952 they again laid siege to the city after the Movimiento Nacionalista Revolucionario (the Revolutionary Nationalist Movement) gained power, forcing a reluctant government to enact an agrarian reform law at the point of their picks and hoes.[5] In the 1980s and 1990s, rural people have engaged in mass political action to achieve other ends. Blocking roads to prevent the movement of troops and to keep provisions from reaching the cities, they have protested rises in fuel prices (which increase transport costs and erode the marginal benefit of producing for the urban marketplace) and, in 1980 and 1982, helped to bring down military dictatorships and return the country to democratic rule.[6] In 1992, to mark their own celebration of the Columbian Quincentenary, a pan-indian political movement, with leadership from the La Paz–based indianist parties named after the 1781 rebel Tupac Catari, chose to reenact Catari's siege of the city rather than to commemorate the Spanish conquest of their peoples.

Whatever their politics or the details of their local forms of ethnic-class identification, rural people have been migrating citywards at an increasing pace. The former indian parishes on the slopes above central La Paz have been population saturated. Near El Alto airport on the Altiplano above La Paz, what was once a small migrant community has swelled into a city in its own right, with a population nearing one million. Most migrants to El Alto and to the peripheral parishes of La Paz itself were once full-time farmers and herders in the indigenous communities of the Altiplano. Upon arrival, many join friends, relatives, and associates from their home communities in forming residents' associations, complete with social halls and urban versions of the patron saint festivals of the countryside town (see Albó et al. 1983). This does not mean, however, that one can thus easily identify in the city the large variety of distinct rural "ethnicities" that can be discerned by dress and hat styles in the rural highlands. Migrants usually strive to erase from their persons all external marks of "indio" or "campesino" origins. They do so by adopting the relatively uniform dress code of the urban "popular class," a dress code that itself has a long history in Bolivia's cities.

This cultural frontier, if it can be said to have an existence in geographic space, is located in La Paz at the junction of the Spanish city center and its indian neighborhoods, partway uphill in zones that are marked on tourist maps as the "black market" and "witches market." It is, of course, to this frontier that tourists and ethnographers are attracted when they reach La Paz, whether by exotic fantasies or by having read ethnographies and travel guides. Entering this part of the city, one first passes by rows of tourist shops laden with reproductions of colonial paintings, antique coins, and traditional (read "indian") arts and crafts. Here and there the larger shops face competition from young men in jeans, running shoes, and sweaters selling indigenous textiles from a stack placed on the sidewalk. Other ambulating vendors may pass by with small packets of spices. A bit higher uphill, one comes to the magic stalls of the witches market, followed by the black market, full of polyester pants, blankets, wholesale fruits and vegetables, and a host of other commodities. Higher still, one will find a large and bustling street market, called Miamicito (Little Miami), full of the commodities that best satisfy the modernist fancy: stereos, televisions, stoves, refrigerators, personal computers, and Game Boys. Even if one cannot afford the tour to Disneyworld and Miami malls, their goods are readily available here.

The witches market begins just above the colonial church of San Francisco, along Sagarnaga and Linares streets. Here storefront businesses owned by *cholita*-clad vendors offer magical wares: ready-made incense bundles for a variety of ritual purposes and the elements for such bundles, a variety of herbs, colored seeds, bits of silver and gold foil, pressed sugar cakes with relief images of saints or cosmic powers, and dried animal fetuses. There are also soapstone amulets that serve for love magic and wealth increase, and ingredients for divination rites, sorcery, and curing arrays.

Ask what these things are for and you will get sparse explanations, but will surely be told about the *pachamama*, the "earth mother" goddess to whom practically all Paceños will pour a libation in the presence of a bottle of beer. You may also hear about the power of the mountain gods, especially, in La Paz, the great Illimani, the snow-covered peak that towers above the city. These earth deities, believed to be sacred to indians, hold powers that can be unleashed by tapping into indian magical traditions, available here on the cultural frontier of the witches market.

Although they are the most visible and closest to the city center, these formal magic shops face stiff competition from other dealers in magic who sell their wares nearby on the sidewalk. Here and there you may see a man carrying saddle bags. This will be a Kallawaya sorcerer, a shamanic specialist from a region north of La Paz to whom many city folks of all classes and ethnicities give credence (Photographs 2.1a and 2.1b). From such a man you may obtain insight into the future or find out why life may be treating you poorly. By appointment, Kallawaya *curanderos* will come to your home or business to preside over libations and the burning of incense bundles to effect a change in fortune. Farther along up the street, the poorer relations of magic-store vendors hawk the ingredients of magic bundles from sidewalk displays.[7]

Photograph 2.1a. K'ulta women sell herbal remedies and magic bundles in the Tarabuco market. A K'ulta herbalist (in the white hat) explains her wares to Mary Dillon and Chloe Abercrombie. K'ulta women selling herbs and magic-bundle ingredients had accompanied their husbands on llama-caravan trading trips to maize valley areas, where they are considered expert in herbal healing. Tarabuco, department of Chuquisaca, July 1988. (Photograph by author)

Photograph 2.1b. A Kallawaya curandero with a medicine bag. In the background, up the street, traveling textile vendors hawk their wares, a common pursuit among young K'ulta men. Sagarnaga Street, La Paz, 1994. (Photograph by author)

35

Figure 2.1. Ekeko, the magical mestizo trader. Cult to this Tunupa-turned-traveling salesman aids in the acquisition of material wealth. The figurine should be purchased at the La Paz Alasitas fair, and should be blessed in the mass of Our Lady of La Paz and by one of the Kallawaya curanderos who wait outside with their incense braziers. During weekly or monthly cult, usually on Fridays (day of the *supay*, when Christ is dead in the weekly recension of the passion), Ekeko receives libations and likes to smoke a cigarette. (Author's sketch of six-inch-tall plaster statuette)

In the January fair of Alasitas, linked to the celebration of Our Lady of La Paz, one can buy miniatures in street stalls that, when treated with the proper rituals, may bring one full-scale versions of the items they depict. A perennial favorite is a plaster doll of a standing male figure some four to six inches tall, known as Ekeko (see Fig. 2.1), who is himself a sort of patron of this festival. Portrayed as a mestizo in his poncho and knit cap with ear flaps, Ekeko is the very image of the successful traveling vendor: Only the head, hands, and feet protrude from beneath a cornucopic profusion of consumer goods bundled in his carrying cloth and draped round his neck and waist: miniature sacks of sugar and flour, coca leaves, soap, tinned cane alcohol, boxes of noodles, feather dusters, cocoa, and candies. God of plenty, Ekeko helps to assure prosperity when he is properly attended to. Like all Alasitas goods, he must first be doubly blessed in the La Paz cathedral by a priest at a special mass in honor of Our Lady of Peace, and outside, on the church steps, by one of the curanderos who wait with ready charcoal braziers, ritual arrays, and libations to enliven Ekeko's latent powers. His mouth gapes open in what looks like a maniacal smile or hearty shout, ready to receive a cigarette to accompany his libations on the first Friday of every month.

Ekeko may seem a comic and folkloric figure, but his name betrays profound associations with the past: It is that of a god of ancient highland myths, a trickster who brought forth the peoples of the Bolivian high plains in his travels southwards from Tiwanaku, wellsprings of the world. In spite of these deep ancestral connections, many of the Paceños attending the Alasitas fair opt instead for an array of papier-mâché, plaster, or plastic models of goods-laden trucks, market stalls, and luxury homes. There is also a brisk market in miniature paper certificates, such as marriage licenses, divorce papers, college degrees, and titles to property. Perhaps most ubiquitous in Alasitas stalls are wads of miniature thousand-dollar bills, **passports,** visas to enter the United States, and, yes, airline tickets to Miami.[8] Just so can one appeal to the Virgin and to the ancient powers of mountain and plain, to be transformed into a modern-day Ekeko, returning from a shopping binge in Orlando and Miami dressed in furs and Mickey Mouse ears, laden with new clothes, housewares, and high-tech electronic equipment.

JOURNEY TO A CROSSROADS

Laden with trunks and duffle bags full of just such kinds of treasures, pockets bulging with airline tickets to Miami, traveler's checks in dollars, and letters of recommendation from powerful government officials, my

first trip to my chosen field-site of Santa Bárbara de Culta followed the
old road running from La Paz to Potosí, now the Pan American Highway
but once, along most of its route, a stone-paved road linking the Inca
capital of Cusco with the Inca empire's southern province of Qullasuyu.
This was the path followed by Inca Colque and his mit'a conscripts on
their way to Cusco. Transformed by colonial Spaniards into a trunk
route between colonial cities and silver mining centers, the same road
carried Spanish census takers, indian forced-labor contingents, and
generations of native lords engaged in long-distance commerce or
pilgrimages to state archives.

The La Paz–Oruro leg of my first journey into the countryside began,
as have many since, deep in the natural bowl in which La Paz nestles.
The road circles up and over the rim and emerges onto the Altiplano
(Map 2.1). Even while still engulfed in the ever-growing expanse of El
Alto, one gets a clear view of the imposing snow-covered peaks of the
Cordillera Real, marching off past Lake Titicaca to the northwest and
into Perú. To reach Oruro, however, the bus turns southwards. After
emerging finally from the drab sprawl of new settlements on the edge of
El Alto, one passes by numerous dry-farmed fields. As one moves farther
south, towards Oruro, cultivated fields become fewer, hugging the skirts
of the foothills. In noncultivated areas, a relatively dense cover of spikey
grasses and low shrubs becomes increasingly sparse. The bus races
through some small towns of adobe houses, a few with imposing
colonial churches; on certain days one or more of these towns host a
market, and the roadside is crowded with trucks and rural people
carrying loads on their backs in brightly colored carrying cloths. (Some
of these towns have been service or rest areas—*ventas* or *tambos*—since
the Spanish invasion and before, when this road carried colonial mule
trains and llama caravans.) Near the city of Oruro, the countryside
becomes more arid, and ever larger patches of white crystalline salts
begin to dot the landscape, as do, now and then, herds of llamas and
alpacas, cared for by sling-wielding children.

As the geographer Carl Troll (1968) explained, the Andes are a
tropical mountain chain: A rise or fall of just a few hundred feet can
make a great deal of difference in climate. The Altiplano from Lake
Titicaca to the salt flats of Uyuni is for the most part a treeless expanse
of grass and scrub, interspersed with barren-looking rocky hills. Incessant winds, a long dry winter, and cold nights have favored bunch-
grasses and low shrubs that huddle close to the ground. In the cold
months from May to October, the landscape is dominated by shades of

yellow and brown, replaced by a light sprinkling of green during the rainy warmer months of November to April.

Much of this territory is too dry and cold for any flora other than the grasses and shrubs that provide pasture for the land's sheep and llamas. But here and there on hillsides and in river valleys, Altiplano peoples risk their labor and sow the native crops capable of withstanding the rigors of altitude. Much of the territory can support only the native *quinua* (or quinoa) and bitter potatoes, and a variety of Spanish-introduced barley that is grown, though not to maturity, for animal fodder. In some more-sheltered and well-watered spots, varieties of potato more familiar to North American and European palates can be grown, along with other root crops like onions, carrots, and the native *oca, ulluco,* and broad bean. Visit the marketplaces of La Paz or Oruro, however, and you will find a large variety of not only root crops and grains but also fruits and vegetables, as well as spices, chili peppers, and coca leaves. Most of these cannot be grown on the Altiplano; they are available to Altiplano peoples by bringing them from warmer lands to the east and west of the Altiplano's mountain borders, from the valleys of the sparse rivers that cut deep transverse valleys into an otherwise barren Pacific coastal desert, and from the meanders of large rivers that wander towards the wet tropical lowlands of the Amazon Basin and the Río de la Plata drainage.

After a change of buses in the old mining town of Oruro (now a city of nearly 200,000, and the capital of the Department of Oruro), the traveler can continue the journey (see Map 2.1). By night, it is a bumpy, dusty, and cold trip, interrupted only when a tire or engine part needs repair or when the driver stops for refreshment at a roadside restaurant. In incongruously named places like Hotel Londres or Hotel Paris, one can shake the dust off and, by the light of a kerosene lantern, sometimes get a good meal or at least a tin mug of coffee with bread and the much-appreciated local sheep's cheese of Paria and Challapata. In spite of the clouds of dust and yellowing hillsides of the winter months, a daylight ride enables one to appreciate more fully the changing scenery.

From Oruro south to the provincial capital town of Challapata, the road runs along the foothills of the Cordillera de Asanaque on one side and the basin of the vast Lake Poopó on the other. In a dry time, the lakeshore may be several kilometers away from the road, a shimmering mirage floating over a dusty landscape wandered by whirling dust devils. But, as happened in 1979, when a series of wet years brought sufficient water from its feeder streams, including the Río Desaguadero, which

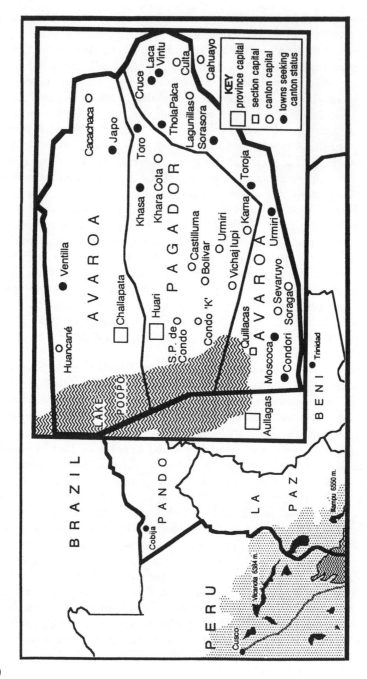

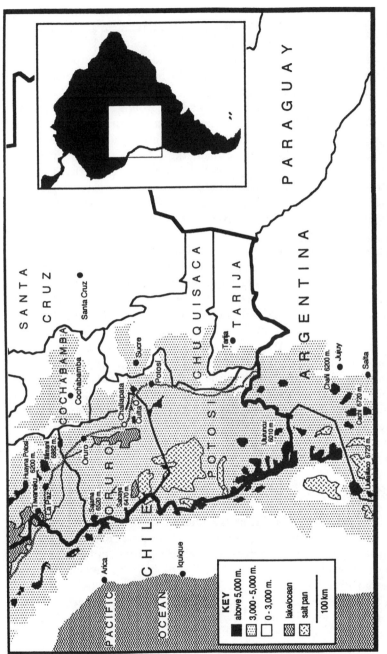

Map 2.1. Bolivia: its topography and political divisions. The inset depicts the cantons and southeastern provinces of the department of Oruro. (Author's renderings, based on *Atlas universal y de Bolivia Bruño*, "Bolivia, mapa orográfico," p. 77, and "Oruro, mapa político," p. 107 [La Paz: Editorial Bruño, 1995]; and *Rand McNally Atlas of the World*, Masterpiece Edition, "Northern South America," p. 242 [1993])

41

snakes south from Lake Titicaca, the lake expanded until its shore reached the road itself. Its shallow, cold, and brackish water hosts abundant plankton and, therefore, also fish and waterfowl. Around Lake Poopó a wide variety of ducks, geese, and wading birds abound, including vast flocks of flamingos, which, when disturbed, burst into a thrashing blaze of red and black.

At several points these same hillsides host groups of squarish adobe ruins of *chullpas,* the tombs of the pre-Columbian ancestors of today's rural people. One such site is built on the slopes of the great mountain called Tata Asanaqi. Just below them the ruins of the old town of Challapata cover a flat area on a hilltop (*pata*) where, perhaps, ritual libations (*ch'allas*) were once poured. "New" Challapata, capital of Abaroa Province, lies nearby on the Altiplano itself, at a fork in the road at the entrance to a narrow river valley where the Pan American Highway turns east and begins the climb towards Potosí.

As one approaches Cruce, the road switchbacks up a steep defile and emerges onto an open plain between high peaks. Fed by mountain runoff, several small streams begin near here in artesian springs. In fact it is here, in the midst of high-altitude Cantón Culta, that the highway passes and then becomes a kind of triple continental divide: Up until this point on the journey, streams have flowed westwards, draining into the evaporation pan of the Altiplano. From here on, many of the streams on the north side of the road are tributaries of the distant Amazon, while waters on the south side flow into the Pilcomayo and pass Buenos Aires before reaching the Atlantic via the Río de la Plata. Just past this junction of drainage basins, the bus rounds a bend and emerges suddenly onto a high, windy, and rocky pampa, where a small number of unpromising adobe-walled stores and restaurants line the road at a different kind of junction.

CRUCE: A SOCIAL FRONTIER

Cruce (Sp. "crossroads") lies at the intersection of the Pan American Highway and a smaller road that veers off to the north towards the town of Macha, in the northern extension of the Department of Potosí. Near the town of Macha (on which see Platt 1978a, 1987b), this smaller road intersects with a less traveled, east-west road linking Oruro and Sucre. Along these roads trucks carry highland products, salt, and urban goods to the northern and eastern valleys and the lowlands that drop towards the warm and moist foothills of the Amazon basin. They return laden with the potatoes, wheat, maize, and fruits that form not only much of the urban diet but also that of the highland rural household. Some rural households of K'ulta, and other towns farther west, choose instead to carry their salt, freeze-dried meat and potatoes, and highland herbs on the backs of llamas to those distant valleys; from May through August, many caravans, some consisting of a hundred or more llamas, cross over the pass on which Cruce sits.

Cruce Culta, as its residents call it, consists of a few dozen buildings fronting these roads (see Photographs 2.2a and 2.2b). One of the many new towns promoted by progress-minded rural people eager for access to what the highway might bring, it was founded in the late 1930s, when the highway was first habilitated for motorized traffic, by the local man who had been chosen to lead the work gangs that improved this section

Photograph 2.2a. A view of Cruce on a market day in 1988. An early customer inspects bulk foodstuffs. In the background, don Pablo Choquecallata's herd of llamas and alpacas emerges from the corral behind his house, on the way to pasture. Cruce Culta, July 1988. (Photograph by author)

Photograph 2.2b. Main Street, Cruce, on a market day in 1988. A truck rumbles along this unpaved section of the Pan American Highway through "downtown" Cruce. In the background is the Hotel Copacabana, actually a restaurant. Vendors in "cholita" costume, wearing full pollera skirt, apron, and bowler derby, sell to predominantly "campesina" customers, in black *bayeta* dress, *aksu,* and white hat. Some vendors, however, are local campesinas, who have switched to the more culturally appropriate costume for a seller on market day. Cruce Culta, July 1988. (Photograph by author)

of road. In the 1960s, after the Bolivian revolution and agrarian reform made universal education a state goal, it was Cruce, rather than the more isolated Santa Bárbara de Culta, that became the seat of a rural school district. Here the cantón's children can complete their primary education. For a variety of reasons, including the lack of transport and long distances resulting from the geographic size of the district, few children progress beyond the first three grades, which are offered in one-room schools scattered in widely separated hamlets, some more than four hours' walk away. Secondary school, available only in the provincial capital of Challapata, is beyond the reach even of most children who complete primary school in Cruce. In fact no one I questioned could remember a single child from Cantón Culta who had been to high school. I should take note, however, that local memory does not always include out-migrants whose local ties have been severed, and over generations many individuals and families have abandoned their homeland for urban life. Later on I will introduce a few of them.

Just as emigration has long been a fact of life in rural territories like this one, so has immigration left its mark. In Cruce it was an early product of the schools. From the first generation of teachers came the first restaurant and sparsely stocked general store, operated by don Antonio. The offspring of a union between a mestizo miner and an indigenous woman in the mining center of Pulacayo, don Antonio had opted to remain in Cruce after retiring from schoolteaching in the mid-1960s and marrying a migrant from the town of Pocoata. Since then Cruce, along with the localist ambitions of its native founder, has continued to grow, at the expense of a dwindling Culta some thirteen kilometers away. Much of that growth has resulted from retiring teachers and in-migrating outsiders like don Antonio and his wife, who upon arrival become known as *vecinos*, "neighbors."

Cruce is home to a variable number of temporary or seasonal residents. A crew of road workers is sometimes lodged here along with their machinery, and when school is in session the town hosts the schoolteachers who staff the cantón's *nucleo*, a regional school into which the children of the cantón's many one-room, three-year schools can in theory (but rarely in practice) continue on to grades 4 through 6. The town's permanently resident vecinos numbered about twelve adults in 1979 (there were perhaps twenty by 1992) and came from almost as many places. A few, like the town's founder (in his seventies in 1979, and still politically active in 1988) are progress-oriented local folk; others, like the first teacher-settler, come from Quechua-speaking mining camps; several, who retain ties to their hometown of Huari, were farmer-herders themselves once, and began their association with the place and their storefront businesses as itinerant peddlers and produce bulkers. Dependent on the money economy as well as on patronal ties to the farming and herding natives of the place,[9] vecinos uniformly know Spanish and, in addition, are more likely to speak to their local clients in Quechua than in Aymara. Most of them, in fact, distinguish themselves culturally from the local population, whom they call campesinos (peasants) in respectful moments but in moments of anger will also tar as backwards and ignorant indios. Cruce is a young town, and so far the handful of local rural folk who have moved there from one or another of the cantón's hamlets, even those few who have opened businesses of their own, retain the ties to local social units that vecinos generally lack.

Some outside-born vecinos resent this incursion of campesinos into the territory of social privilege, and insult these social-climbers with the label "cholo." In moments of outrage the latter, as well as hamlet-dwelling locals, may likewise insult a vecino, or virtually any representative of urban national culture, as a q'ara, meaning (culturally) "peeled," or "naked."[10] The term "mestizo," heard frequently in the cities to refer to culturally or "racially" mixed individuals, is not much used in Cantón Culta.[11] In fact, all these terms of reference and address have been stigmatized to some degree by their use to put individuals and groups in their place in an undesirable stratum of one of Bolivia's systems of social inequality. The term "vecino," which for sixteenth-century Spaniards referred to a select number of fully vested (and, of course, Spanish) town citizens with the greatest degree of privilege, is not free from stigma nowadays. Some vecinos, aware of the rusticity of their status from the perspective of high-status city dwellers, would prefer to think of themselves as criollos, a term with its own history, which since the independence period has referred to the highest stratum in the social hierarchy, at greatest remove from "indio." Even "criollo," however, can be and is stigmatized when pronounced with sarcasm or irony by a social critic from "below."[12]

It is certainly true that rural-dwelling, farming and herding speakers of Aymara and/or Quechua, those whom city people and vecinos call indios or campesinos, are the least privileged, most maligned and disfavored sector of Bolivian society, suffering a degree of stigmatization greater than that of the recent migrant from countryside to city. This helps to account for the fact that, in most of the countryside, there is for such people no unstigmatized term of reference or address (as we shall see, most campesinos in Cantón Culta prefer to call themselves commerciantes on their national identity cards, and few have subscribed to the indianista parties' suggestion that they wear the label indio with pride). And when an individual from the cantón travels to the city, he or she most often changes from the homespun and handmade clothing of the hamlet into store-bought machine-made clothes, purchased in order to blend in more easily with the urban "popular masses."[13]

As a new-town way station between the life-ways of rural subsistence farming and herding on the one hand and the wage-labor and capitalist relations of Bolivia's cities and mining centers on the other, Cruce is an increasingly common sort of place in Bolivia. To us, an ugly roadside strip of unappealing buildings with tin roofs, it is for many campesinos a place where dreams are made, and broken. The mutual confrontation and romance of vecinos and campesinos that takes place there, however, is not a new phenomenon. During much of the nineteenth and twentieth centuries, up until the revolutionary moment of 1952, the old town of Santa Bárbara de Culta, like most other rural "indigenous" towns, was also the site of such struggles. Before the revolution, however, the exploitative power of vecinos was much more entrenched, and the battle lines more sharply drawn. That is because the status of vecino in rural towns originated in efforts by a long succession of late-nineteenth- and early-twentieth-century governments to ally themselves with those who, in the countryside, appeared to be forces of progress and modernity. Thus positions of power went to those who identified with national culture, acted as economic and political intermediaries between indigenous societies and the city, preferred private ownership of land to collective title, patron-client ties to kinship-based reciprocities, and so on (see Platt 1982a, 1984, 1987a). For the most part such privilege evaporated in the revolution of 1952, but the impulses did not. Today in Cruce (and in a few cases, in Santa Bárbara), vecinos might best be defined negatively as residents of a rural town who lack membership in its local ayllus, and hence lack access to collective lands and the herding and farming life that go with them. The status can be defined positively as well, referring to those who can profit by occupying an advantageous place in the intersection of two worlds.

Although they often develop ties of compadrazgo, "co-godparenthood," with the campesinos who work and lay claim to the land, such ties imply asymmetrical reciprocities rather than the more balanced forms of mutual obligation that often link campesino with campesino. It is in fact the vecinos' refusal to adhere to local rules of the game that gives them the freedom to profit and to amass capital; it is that same refusal that makes them so hated. Successful vecinos are outsiders for a good reason. The pressures that are mounted against local campesinos when they begin to act as vecinos, failing to share their wealth, become simply too much to bear.

This does not mean, of course, that K'ulta campesinos do not engage in rather wily forms of capitalist exchange. Indeed, when I first arrived in Cruce, I was often approached by campesinos proffering business transactions. Gringos are rare visitors to K'ulta territory, and on first sight several K'ultas mistook me for the hippy-capitalist textile traders with whom they had dealt before. Several times after campesinos

approached me with warm greetings I was forced to explain that I was
not "Arturo" or "Billy," and that I was not in the market for the textiles
that were then offered to me for sale. One such encounter illustrated the
difficulties inherent in the process that in Bolivia has been called
cholification, that is, an individual's self-transformation from campesino
into vecino.

In 1980 I shared drinks in a Cruce truck-stop bar with a campesino in
his mid-twenties who had mistaken me for such a trader in ethnic
capital. The experience was a strange one, foregrounding for me the
degree to which, as an anthropologist, I had come to collect something
here (ethnographic "data," rather than the hippy capitalists' indigenous
textiles or the tourists' authentic "otherworldly" experiences) redeem-
able for values in my own cultural context. The ironies of the encounter
were heightened by the reason for the young man's interest in speaking
with me, which was to reveal his personal conundrum to someone from
the sort of background that might allow comprehension of his plight.

For years he had plied traditional long-distance trades, but recently
had had unusual success. He had amassed a large number of valuable
textiles from the valley regions where other K'ultas trade mostly for
corn, and he had made contact in La Paz with an enterprising but
unscrupulous American "hippy capitalist." Once he understood the
relative value of certain textiles, he had sought out heirloom pieces that
some of his community members kept in their storehouses, and had also
"found" some possibly pre-Columbian textiles in shaft tombs scattered
about K'ulta territory. Some of these items can bring in thousands of
dollars on the international market, and although my drinking companion had received only a fraction of their worth from his American
business partner, he had amassed quite a fortune.[14]

After numerous drinks, he showed me a thick wad of hundred-dollar
bills and lamented that he could not return to his home hamlet with this
money without sharing it out among his family members, who would
waste it away. Instead, he said, he would invest the money by purchasing
a truck. But that, he felt, would provoke envy among his less-fortunate
kinsmen. His plan, then, was to buy the truck and promptly move to
another town on the highway. My drinking companion was in fact
contemplating a radical shift in status, one that would take him
permanently out of the category of campesino, away from agriculture
and herding and into the role of vecino in some other campesinos'
territory. Not long afterwards, he did just that.

When this young man drove away from Cruce in a new, Brazilian-
made ten-wheel truck to take up residence in another growing roadside

town, he did precisely what another of Cruce's vecinos had done some ten years earlier. Don Cayetano, who owned Cruce's only two-story house, had moved here with his truck from a hamlet in the Macha area. The truck no longer runs, and don Cayetano's dream of trading up to big-time transport and becoming a prosperous member of the Mejillones truckers' union did not pan out. He now ekes out a living for his growing family by running a store specializing in school supplies (as well as a large assortment of other locally useful commodities, including gasoline and diesel fuel, now delivered to him in fifty-five-gallon drums).

Cruce is thus a point of tension within the territory of Cantón Culta, an active frontier that is home to all the contradictions inherent in Bolivia's peculiar tangle of ethnicity, class, and culture. It is also a convenient place to disembark a bus or truck or to wait for one: Many hamlet-dwelling rural people maintain a storeroom here from which to market produce and animals. As such a way station, it is also a good place to find lodgings and to begin the hike into the old town of Santa Bárbara, still the official capital of the cantón.

Don Antonio, the retired schoolteacher turned restauranteur-hosteler and senior vecino in Cruce, kindly consented to rent us a room behind his restaurant, where a road crew and their dumptruck and grader were also housed. Home as well to a pack of dogs, numerous pigs, chickens, and a very loud rooster, don Antonio's patio, onto which our room opened, became a kind of halfway house sanctuary for several reasons. There, it was sometimes possible to obtain bottled gas to fuel a heater to ward off the cold. Given the cultural-frontier facet of Cruce, it was also a space in which our own identity as outsiders was not so much at issue. More important for the present work, the interclass and/or interethnic conflicts that were near the surface there provided insights into phenomena that too easily faded into the background in the hamlets of the countryside. Cruce also served as an important frontier of another sort, making possible interviews that would have been less likely anywhere else in the territory. For as the most vibrant conjunction of local life and the forces of national culture and the Bolivian state, Cruce is a kind of neutral territory in which people from the fractious social groups of the cantón intermingle. This is not true elsewhere, even in the old town of Santa Bárbara that used to provide a similar atmosphere.

There are many new towns like Cruce in Bolivia, and there would be more if the progress-minded movers and shakers in rural communities were to have their way. As an outpost of the national state erected by rural people themselves to help bridge the gap they experienced between their "traditional" life-ways and the city's twentieth-century modernity,

Cruce is one of very many places along a spongey cultural border, not only between vecinos and campesinos, but also between ascribed and achieved kinds of identity—that which others would have one remain and that which one would become. It is simultaneously a battleground, where the most stinging insults are sometimes hurled, and a neutral territory, where individuals may more easily contemplate a change in identity.

When we first settled there, however, I was unable to appreciate fully Cruce's advantages, which paled in comparison with the town's lacks, as seen vis-à-vis my project. I had come to study the intersection of ritual and politics in the fiesta-cargo system, but at that time Cruce had no church, and therefore none of the major saints' festivals of the cantón took place there.[15] Likewise, the cantón's authorities carried out their weekly meetings elsewhere. Along with the church, the office of the cantón's corregidor, where the town council did meet, was located on the plaza of the colonially founded town of Santa Bárbara de Culta, down the road a piece and some distance removed from the Pan American Highway. A few days after arriving in Cruce, therefore, I set out on foot for the more "isolated and traditional" town of Santa Bárbara.

As I reflect on that journey, I am struck by an irony: My method as ethnographer was to leave behind the cosmopolitan and urban world of global capital and rampant and homogenizing consumerism, attempting to shed the implicit knowledge of my own milieu and the privilege and access to power that comes with it, so as to gain access to another, more locally anchored and precapitalist world. In this romantic invasion, I had established a beachhead in a crossroads town, and sought by degrees, leaving behind electricity, conveniences, motorized travel, monetized forms of social interaction, and the privacy that results from such anonymous kinds of sociality, to enter the world of llama caravans, foot plows, and kinship-based reciprocity. My residence there was temporary, but my goals and itinerary were in fact precisely the inverse of those K'ulta people who were building new houses on Cruce's highway, aiming to transform themselves (through immigration to the city) and their homeland (through intensified integration with markets, commerce, and national life). But the relationships between "traditional" values and those associated with what even in K'ulta is called progress is anything but straightforward. It is laden with contradictions. I may have hoped to become an invisible amanuensis through which traditional K'ulta life-ways would inscribe themselves, but very few among the people of K'ulta were willing to regard me as such. For some, I was instead a dangerous interloper, practitioner of the dark sorceries of urban life, to be avoided or driven away. Others, on the contrary, considered me a conduit through which they might gain access to urban values, government development funds, and perhaps cash and manufactured goods. For the rural people of Santa Bárbara, I embodied the potential benefits and dangers of the city and the crossroads town. In La Paz, Oruro, or Cruce, where everyone is an outsider, rural people might have expected to run into unknown entities like me, but not in the countryside. I may have hoped to leave Cruce behind when I walked out of town across the plains towards vecino-free hamlets, but that turned out to be impossible. I was a walking frontier, carrying Cruce and everything it represented on my back, a kind of Ekeko come to life. This was the predicament I put myself in as I sought to carry out the frontier practice called ethnographic research, a predicament that shaped my relations with rural people and led sometimes to frustration, sometimes to insight, and to consequences sometimes felicitous, sometimes unfortunate.

Chapter Three

The Dialogical Politics of Ethnographic Fieldwork

AN ETHNOGRAPHER IN SANTA BÁRBARA DE CULTA

Where the highway winds east from Cruce, it drops a bit and almost immediately enters a broad pampa. One can see several hamlets nestled in sheltered spots in the foothills around the plain. The settlement that I reached on my way to Santa Bárbara was a hamlet on the road, consisting of a one-room school, with a sign identifying the place as Palca, and a half-dozen other buildings, only two of which seemed to be occupied. Yet these were laid out around a sizable plaza, interspersed among the foundations and tumbled-down walls of at least a dozen other constructions. Hoping to try out my still-rudimentary Aymara and to confirm that it was indeed spoken here, I approached one of these houses where an older woman, wearing the black dress and white felt hat characteristic of this area, was peeling potatoes in a doorway. I was only able to get within fifty feet of the house and to utter a well-practiced greeting when she put down her potatoes and began to hurl shrieks and stones in my direction. Chastened, I returned to the road.

Other experiences on that walk increased my apprehensions about fieldwork. As the road crossed the pampa it led me past two or three flocks of llamas, alpacas, and sheep. When I came near, sling-wielding young shepherdesses ducked down behind rocks and turned their backs. Their dogs, however, were not so reticent, charging at me with fangs bared. I soon learned to keep my pockets bulging with stones, nearly absent in some areas, with which to keep the dogs at bay. Farther on, I

52

crossed paths with two young men, dressed in white homespun trousers, homemade vest and jacket, and the apparently universal white felt hats, leading a pair of heavily loaded donkeys towards Cruce. They addressed me first, in Quechua, asking me where I was going. When I replied in Aymara, they switched to it, but my language training had not prepared me to understand their rapid-fire speech and unfamiliar forms of expression. Switching to a rudimentary Spanish, one of the young men suggested that it was not such a good idea to cross this pampa or go to Santa Bárbara, since strangers had been found hereabouts dead, naked, and lacking some of their body parts. With a good deal of giggling, the two young men and their donkeys continued on their way, as I did.

Now two hours' walk from Cruce, I was running low on optimism as well as energy. The day, at least, was brilliantly sunny. The previous night a wintry chill had frozen the pools of water that here and there dotted the plain, and the small streams that flowed over the graveled road surface had been reduced to streaks of ice. But the intense radiation of the midday sun that strikes this fourteen thousand-feet-high plain now melted the ice and raised the ambient temperature to somewhere near 65° Fahrenheit. Herds of llamas, alpacas, and sheep grazed on the short-cropped green plant growth that covered the pampa's lowest and wettest spots, while the yellows and browns of winter-dry bunch grasses faded at the horizon into the reds and purples of the mountains that rose in the distance on all sides. The warmth and the stark beauty of my surroundings helped to put my experiences into perspective.

Certainly, I reasoned, indigenous peoples' historical experience with city people and outsiders justified their wariness and accounted for the apparent hostility that I had experienced. Just the year before, in 1978, the government had once again sent a commission into the region to carry out a survey of individual property holdings (a *catastro*), as a step towards imposing a new kind of tax. The people of K'ulta, who continue to prefer payment of a nominal head tax over a system that would require formal distribution of individual land titles, dispatched the commission with a hail of stones, just as they had taken care of many previous state functionaries over the past century. So, too, only determined resistance had prevented outsiders during the nineteenth and early twentieth centuries from converting ayllu lands into haciendas (even though, too cold to produce readily marketable crops, K'ulta remained relatively insulated from such efforts). Finally, I recalled the rural Andean belief, described in many ethnographies, in the secret identity attributed to some outsiders as evil and magical *pishtacos*, *ñaqaqs*, or *k"arisiris,* who extract the blood and body fat of unwary indigenous victims. Given this array of dangers represented in outsiders, it stood to reason that K'ulta people should shy away from me.

Finally I reached the eastern edge of the plain and came to a narrow track that turned southwards off the main highway, barely passable by jeep or truck. This was the road to Santa Bárbara, and I took it. I found myself walking along two barely maintained and infrequently traveled wheel ruts, which descended gently into a broad ravine cut by a now-dry stream. On both sides of this ever-broadening ravine, small fenced fields alternated with expanses of pasture and rocky outcrops. Here and there, I noticed a *viscacha,* the Andes' bushy-tailed, rabbitlike rodent. Black and white raptors called *alqamaris,* birds something like eagles, circled overhead. As this track curved and looped down the ravine, I noticed that it was crossed at several points by a much straighter path, deeply worn into the ground and even etched into the exposed rock like a series of closely spaced bicycle tracks. Too steep for motorized vehicles, this was in fact a major llama-caravan trail that grazed the town of Santa Bárbara as it carried trade between the salt flats of Uyuni and the maize valleys to the northeast. Indeed, the turnoff for Santa Bárbara lay at a crossroads much older than that of Cruce: Here an ancient artery of subsistence trade destined for household larders and communal storage bins was overlain at right angles by the more recent Spanish silver highway (now the Pan American Highway), a vein that drained these same larders on the way to marketplace, mine, and European bank. Just as K'ulta territory was a watershed dividing both the Altiplano drainage basin from the rivers leading towards the Atlantic and the Amazon waters from those of the Río de la Plata, it was another sort of intersection as well, land that had witnessed the passage of untold thousands of llama caravans on the north-south route, and as many Potosí-bound forced laborers and galleon-bound silver bars.[1]

About a kilometer from this junction, I crested a small rise and Santa Bárbara came into view, a small and quiet town nestled in the folds of a curving hill just above the point where the stream bed I had been following joined a larger river valley. Along this crest where the town came into view I could see other foot trails converging towards Santa Bárbara. One of them, coming from the northwest, was flanked on either side by tall stone pillars forming a sort of gateway just at the point where walkers would first (or last) see the town; I would later find that all the trails converging on the town from distant hamlets were marked in this way. Off to one side of the road, where a footpath angled over a hill towards a hamlet some distance away, I noticed what appeared to be a stone seat, made of large squarish blocks of smooth stone. This was a good place to stop and rest.[2]

From this distance I could make out most of the structure of the town, laid out along the grid-plan lines followed by most Spanish-founded rural towns (see Photograph 3.1). Most visible were the gleaming tin roofs of a large adobe church and its accompanying bell tower, situated on a large town plaza, and a smaller but still impressive school, standing just outside the main cluster of town buildings. Sheltered against the hillsides, the rest of the town consisted of about 120 rectangular, thatch-roofed houses, arranged around small courtyards in groups of three or four. Interspersed among these houses were nearly as many

Photograph 3.1. Santa Bárbara de Culta before the fiesta and the rains. A Vila Sirka Mamani herd passes through town on the way to pasture. The tin-roofed church and bell tower face the plaza (concealed by housetops). In the background is the cemetery, past which runs the access road leading to the Pan American Highway. September 1979. (Photograph by author)

roofless, crumbling house ruins. Clearly, the town had seen better days. Nearly all the houses were built of earthen adobe blocks. Most were windowless, and only a few buildings (the school, the church tower, and a few houses) were whitewashed.

As I approached the town, I noticed very little activity. From a distance I noticed a few women sitting in a courtyard somewhat above the main square, weaving cloth on horizontal looms staked to the ground. A handful of small children played in the otherwise empty streets. Fifty meters from the main square, the road took me past artesian springs enclosed within a large stone corral, feeding a verdant patch of grass. Inside the corral, a pair of donkeys grazed. Entering a large stone-paved plaza by one of the four entranceways at its corners, I came to the center of a very quiet, nearly abandoned, Santa Bárbara de Culta.

After my initial experience approaching houses, I thought it prudent to sit down in the plaza and wait. Looking around, I saw that the church and the other one-story adobe buildings around the plaza were padlocked; some, lacking wooden doors, were closed with large stones piled in the door frames. A few hours later, an old man approached me, again asking me questions in Quechua. I responded with Aymara stock phrases, offered him some coca, which I had carried in a small bag tucked under my belt, and we had a conversation of sorts. I had difficulty understanding his Aymara; again, it was unlike what I had learned. He spoke no Spanish, and so with a great deal of fumbling on my part and patience on his, we made slow progress towards understanding while we both studiedly chose coca leaves and put them into our mouths. I managed to convey that I wanted to meet with the town authorities, that I was interested in fiestas, and that I would like to stay in the town. I learned that the town authorities were, perhaps, to meet on the following day. Soon the old man left me, thanking me for the coca I had given him. I sat alone for a while in the plaza before returning to Cruce.

When I returned the next day at an earlier hour, the town was somewhat livelier, though no authorities arrived in the town hall, or *corregimiento*, which remained padlocked on one side of the plaza. There were a few more of the wary but respectful conversations like that of the previous day, and I was able to learn the name of the *corregidor*, as well as the relative location of his home hamlet. Someone explained to me that he was the town's highest authority, and that he usually met with other authorities called caciques, *alcaldes*, and *alguaciles*, whose absence on this Sunday remained unaccounted for. Perhaps they would meet Wednesday, someone else suggested. Several more such trips and a preemptive visit to the corregidor in his home hamlet were necessary before I finally did meet with the town authorities, accompanied by Mary Dillon and bearing gifts and official papers.

We arrived in Santa Bárbara on the last Sunday of June to meet with the collective leadership of the place, carrying a quantity of gifts, including newspapers and books in Aymara, packets of chalk, notebooks, and pencils for the schools, and a map of the area purchased from the Instituto Geográfico Militar. While we waited our turn before the authorities—others had gotten there before us with a variety of business—we practiced our Aymara with the women and children seated on the ground outside the corregimiento and observed the goings on.

Apparently only men were allowed inside, except for occasional female petitioners. The few women who entered the office did so very discreetly, sitting on the floor near the door, which offered the only source of light for the windowless one-room building. Inside, the corregidor was seated behind a large adobe desk, covered by a locally produced cloth. On his desk there were some papers, a book titled *Código Civil,* a stamp pad, the seal of the cantón, a Coca-Cola bottle filled with a clear liquid, and a small cloth holding a pile of coca leaves. From my vantage outside the door I could clearly make out, above and behind the desk and corregidor, two pieces of cloth affixed to the wall, each with other objects attached. High up, near the base of the thatched roof, there was a Bolivian flag. Three posters were tacked over it: in the center, a reproduction of the Bolivian state seal, and to each side, reproductions of paintings of the Liberator, Simón Bolívar, and first president, José Antonio de Sucre. Just below these national icons a large striped poncho was also affixed to the wall. Hanging from nails at the center of the poncho were symbols of authority, a bundle of *varas* (silver-tipped staffs of office), a braided leather whip, and a silver-trimmed *pututu,* a trumpet made from a bull's horn.

Below and in front of these symbolic arrays, the corregidor sat behind his desk on an adobe bench that followed the wall all around the inside of the room. Near him, seven or eight other authorities listened to petitioners and occasionally interjected their opinions. All the men inside wore the traditional dress of the area: homespun and home-sewn pants of white or black, held up by a brightly colored woven belt and a red and black striped sash, the ends of which hung down at one side. The pants were complemented by a checkered wool vest and jacket, also locally

produced, worn over a store-bought shirt or sweater. Over these some of
the men wore ponchos nearly identical to the one tacked to the wall,
woven from black wool with bands of brightly colored vertical stripes. A
few men carried their ponchos folded and draped over one shoulder. On
their feet, they wore sandals made from rubber tires (*ujutas*) and their
heads were covered by *ch'ullus,* knitted woolen caps with earflaps. Each
man held his white felt hat in his lap, and each also held a small woven
pouch, a *ch'uspa,* containing coca leaves and the alkaline clay that is
chewed along with them.

A few hours passed while we waited for our turn, and I was able to
observe the standard etiquette of each new petitioner. All began their
petitions by greeting the corregidor and then each of the assembled
authorities with a handshake, embrace, and second handshake. Most
then produced a quantity of coca leaves, which were received in both
hands by the corregidor and then added to the pile. My coca was at the
ready, but I was somewhat alarmed to see that most also presented a
bottle. The corregidor then passed his own bottle to the petitioner, who
poured a few drops at each corner of the altar, mumbling a few words
(which I could not make out) before taking a swig of what I soon learned
was an 80-proof mixture of water and cane alcohol. Periodically, the
corregidor distributed small handfuls of coca leaves to everyone in the
room, always received with thanks in two open hands. Now and then,
two men or two women would exchange their coca pouches, touching
them to the earthen floor with a few mumbled words, before placing a
few more carefully chosen leaves into the growing wad that made a
bulge in one cheek.

The atmosphere in the room seemed to alternate between quiet speech
making and loud discussions in which all seemed to speak at once,
punctuated by libations, chews of coca, and occasional joking and bursts
of laughter. I learned from some teen-aged boys outside that most of the
petitioners had come to seek resolution of land disputes. The meeting,
then, combined the attributes of a town council session and a sitting of
a law court of first resort. All the same, the desk seemed to be taking on
the characteristics of a ritual altar, with the corregidor appearing
increasingly to be the officiant of an elaborate offering ceremony. I later
learned that this apparent conjunction of politics, law, and ritual goes
very much deeper, while the kind of libating and coca dedicating I was
seeing here is more akin to the small reciprocities of everyday sociality.
By attending many of these meetings and the rituals through which the
authority of these men is made legitimate, I learned that the power

exercised by them here was vested in them not only by the state, through their nominal appointment by the subprefect in Challapata, but also by the gods, through the highly complex system of ceremony and sacrifice that helps define and bind together the social groups that occupy the cantón's territory. And that, along with the trajectories of mythical consciousness and historical consciousness that intersect in these same contexts, is the primary subject of this book.

At the time, however, I had only the faintest intimations of all that; my immediate concern was to act as appropriately as possible and to avoid being sent packing. The day wore on, and when finally we were called into the town hall, it was to hear that the session had ended and that we should return the following week. Apparently, the assembled authorities hoped that the delay might encourage us to disappear from their lives in the least confrontational way.

When we returned a few days later for the next meeting, however (this time armed with a bottle of alcohol in addition to coca and gifts), our wait was shorter. Only one, urgent case was heard before we were allowed to make our petition.[3] I began by presenting the corregidor with alcohol and coca, after which the already described rituals of libation and coca chewing began. I then read out a prepared self-introduction in Aymara and presented my gifts. After consultations among the authorities, the corregidor asked to see our documents. We produced passports and numerous letters of introduction, including one written by the prefect of Oruro. In Spanish, the corregidor repeatedly queried our purposes, and I responded that I planned to write a book about the history of the town and in particular about its fiestas. At this point, we were asked to sit; the authorities to the corregidor's left made room for me on the bench while a space on the floor was allotted to Mary Dillon.

Deliberations in rapid-fire Aymara then began in earnest. After the first twenty minutes or so, it became clear that the group was divided. At this level of discourse the Aymara was beyond our understanding, but from gestures alone we could plainly see that one authority in particular was disposed against us, while another seemed to take our part. At one point, the corregidor stopped the discussion and noted that there was no hotel here. We could not stay unless someone had room for us. Once again, the room burst into debate, and the corregidor asked us to leave the building. From outside the door, where we sat with other petitioners and interested parties, we listened to impassioned speechifying without comprehension. Finally, after nearly an hour of discussion, we were called back in. The corregidor informed us that it had been decided.

Since we had papers ordering them to allow us to do research (which we did not have), they would do what they must. While some faces from the other side of the room glared disapprovingly in our direction, a man in his midtwenties volunteered to put us up. At this, however, there was more debate. One of the higher-ranking authorities insisted that we should stay with him instead. The two men briefly argued until the corregidor intervened to decide the matter. We would stay with the authority (who, it turned out, was the corregidor's sister's husband) and later, if we wished, visit the young man's household. It was a propitious decision.

Not only was our host, don Manuel Mamani, alcalde of his ayllu for the year, but he also belonged to the ayllu, or social group, within whose territory the town of Santa Bárbara was situated. And unlike most of those present, who hailed from far-flung hamlets, he lived in a hamlet very near to the town itself. In addition to being alcalde and because of his facility with both spoken and written Spanish, he was also the town's (and cantón's) notary and *registro civil*. Putting pen to paper, he made out a formal document giving us permission to reside in the cantón for the purpose of writing a book on customs. Signed by the corregidor, it was then embossed with the seal of the cantón. After making arrangements with our new host, we formally thanked everyone present with the local double-barreled handshake-embrace and returned to Cruce to prepare our move.

On the following day we moved into temporary lodgings, an empty house on the plaza belonging to our host's in-laws. Not long afterwards, our host moved us once again, this time to his nearby home hamlet of Vila Sirka. We were moved into a building on the courtyard of our host's own house complex, a thatch-roofed, one-room adobe house (built initially to serve as a storeroom). Although it was very small—inside dimensions of about six by nine feet, with an adobe platform on one end that served as a bed, and an adobe bench against the back wall—it opened onto a spacious courtyard, in which we often sat to warm ourselves in the sun, while slowly becoming familiar with the daily round and working to improve our Aymara.

GETTING TO KNOW THE MAMANIS: HAMLET AND TOWN, VILA SIRKA AND
SANTA BÁRBARA

Vila Sirka lies almost adjacent to the town of Santa Bárbara, and it was thus possible to experience both the everyday life of a residential hamlet and the collective sphere of the town. But apart from one day each week when the authorities met in the corregidor's office on the town plaza, Santa Bárbara de Culta was extraordinarily quiet during most of that July of 1979. So too was Vila Sirka. The relative absence of life gave rise to doubts about the wisdom of settling in a tiny hamlet near an apparently abandoned town. But don Manuel told us that this degree of quiet was seasonal, resulting from the absence of those on trading expeditions in the warm valleys seeking the foodstuffs to sustain them for the rest of the year. I learned, however, that in spite of the hamlet's thirteen standing houses, only five houses (six, counting ours) were occupied on a permanent basis. And despite Santa Bárbara's 120 standing houses—the great majority of which remained closed and locked—the town lacked permanent inhabitants altogether.

Within Vila Sirka, only four households were regularly occupied (see Fig. 3.1). There was the house in which don Manuel lived (when not in Santa Bárbara performing his duties as notary), along with his wife and their four children. Each of the hamlet's three other households, don Manuel informed us, was headed by one of his male cousins. Most of the land around Vila Sirka (and indeed, around Santa Bárbara) is claimed collectively by the patronymic group to which don Manuel belongs. A kind of patri-stem, this group of four patronym-sharing households belonged to a larger configuration, a patriline, claiming descent from a single, original, male ancestor. In addition to their claim in and around the town, more distantly related Mamanis also occupied two other small hamlets within a half-hour's walk. In the center of these settlements, they defended a large stretch of common pastureland from the territorial ambitions of other patrilines.

Initially through the exchange of gifts of foodstuffs and visits, we very gradually came to know don Manuel's immediate family along with those of his three cousins, and eventually were able to participate in diverse aspects of their lives. In the early weeks, however, contacts were infrequent. I busied myself with a survey of Vila Sirka and nearby Santa Bárbara, of which I made two watercolor maps, one of which may still adorn the wall of the town council office (see Fig. 3.2).

Apart from don Manuel's house in Santa Bárbara, the town also held other, nonpermanent residents. On one side of town, there was a one-room school, and next to it, sometimes, lived a schoolteacher sent by the national rural school system. In 1979 and 1980, the teacher was a trilingual Spanish-Aymara-Quechua speaker from the outskirts of the city of Oruro. Near the plaza was a house that seasonally became a small general store when a family from the Altiplano town of Huari arrived to carry on what for them was a profitable trade. Another house was

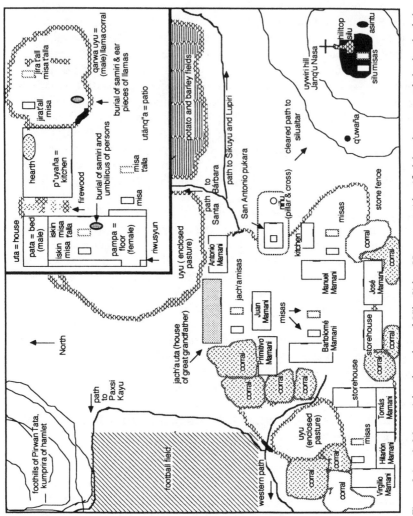

Figure 3.1. A Mamani hamlet: plan of Vila Sirka. Houses are identified by the name of the head of the household (the patriline jiliri). The inset contains details of a patio and house. (Author's rendering)

The inset labels:

uta = house
pata = bed (male)
iskin misa t'alla
iskin misa t'alla
hearth
firewood
p'uyaña = kitchen
pampa = floor (female)
niwusyun
burial of samiri and umbilicus of persons
misa
misa t'alla
jira t'all misa t'alla
jira t'all misa
burial of samiri & ear pieces of llamas
qarwa uyu = (male) llama corral
utánq"a = patio

Main map labels:

North
foothills of Pirwan Tata, kumprira of hamlet
path to Paxsi Kayu
football field
western path
jach'a uta (house of great grandfather)
uyu (enclosed pasture)
potato and barley fields
path to Santa Bárbara
path to Sikuyu and Lupiri
San Antonio pukara
cleared path to siluatar
Antonio Mamani
niru (pillar & cross)
kitchen
misas
Manuel Mamani
José Mamani
jach'amisas
Juan Mamani
misas
Primitivo Mamani
corral
Bartolomé Mamani
storehouse
storehouse
corral
stone fence
corral
corral
uyu (enclosed pasture)
corral
corral
corral
corral
Tomás Mamani
Hilarión Mamani
misas
Virgilio Mamani
corral
corral
uywiri hill Janq'u Nasa
hilltop silu
asiru
silu misas
q'uwaña

62

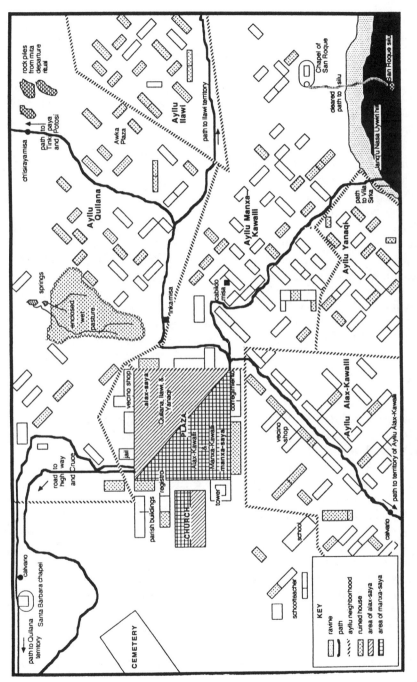

Figure 3.2. Plan of Santa Bárbara de Culta (Author's rendering)

63

occupied about six months of the year by a different itinerant trader from Huari, don Eugenio, a man whose mestizo father had been a powerful vecino and occasional state-appointed corregidor in the 1930s and 1940s and had married an indigenous woman from this town. Then in his late sixties, don Eugenio plied his trade in ambulatory fashion, carrying a bundle of goods on his back from hamlet to hamlet. Both shops sold essentials of rural life: candles, kerosene (for lamps made from tin cans), dyes, coca, candy, cane alcohol from large tin cans, canned sardines, Alka-Seltzer, and dynamite. Apart from money, the trade for these goods involved food and also sheep, the meat and pelts of which they could later sell in the city.

During that cold July, however, the stores remained vacant. A few times a day, people from surrounding hamlets arrived in hopes of buying or trading. The proximity of Vila Sirka and Santa Bárbara led them quickly to learn of our presence. Most assumed that we, being outsiders, would, like good vecinos, have opened a shop. Almost daily, individuals came to our door asking what we had, and opened their bundles to offer small quantities of potatoes, toasted corn, eggs, and sometimes meat, in exchange for what they hoped we would offer. Since we were chronically short of such foodstuffs, we eventually learned to keep an extra stock of sugar, oranges, rice, and coca (we did not go in for alcohol and dynamite). By offering our guests a cup of heavily sugared tea we obtained not only a bit of food for ourselves but also conversation and friendship. Even when the storekeepers returned, such exchanges continued. We were poor businessmen, however, and would often provide tea, candy, safety pins, barrettes, or store-bought bread to our guests at no charge. We also provided food and drink to everyone who stopped by. Eventually, many of our guests reciprocated, especially members of the resident Mamani families, who would send a child with a gift of eggs or potatoes or the fresh-baked bread from local ovens.

Generosity in feeding guests was one way of conforming to local custom, which requires everyone to feed uninvited guests, especially strangers. Exceptions can be made in the case of proven enemies and those who are not true human beings. *Kuntinarus,* the ghosts of the area, and *k"arik"aris,* a kind of magical vampire, as well as certain deities in malignant human form can be turned away if one can identify them in advance.

Since all but known enemies may disguise themselves as friendly strangers, they are difficult to recognize, though many stories of these beings provide clues for their identification. K"arik"aris, who present themselves most often in the forms of cityfolk, priests, and foreigners, sometimes carry backpacks like the one I had worn on my first trip to Santa Bárbara. I learned to carry my possessions in the local way, in a textile bundle tied around my shoulders, and that first experience of a hail of stones was never repeated (though the accusation, in a much more serious form, was). Kuntinarus are incapable of digesting food. Thus when we stopped in a hamlet on a walk through the territory and were offered large quantities of food, we made an effort to clean our plates. Aside from the issue of avoiding suspicion, failing to accept and to finish food is the height of disrespect and impoliteness. One result of all this is that visits must be carefully timed. Going from one house directly to another forces the guest to choose between insulting host or stomach.

For a variety of reasons, our most frequent conversations during our early months in Cruce and in Vila Sirka–Santa Bárbara, other than those with don Manuel and the vecinos of Cruce, were with young, unmarried men. Many of the married men, including don Manuel's three cousins in Vila Sirka, were off on trading trips during much of the dry and cold winter months, seeking the abundant harvests of the valleys or attempting to market in the cities (for cash) some of what they had obtained. The women and old men who remained, and who spent much of the day in the hills and pampas herding their animals, were more reticent, sometimes seeming to avoid us. In addition, because of the relatively recent arrival of rural schools and the more active travel and marketing role of men, few of the women or aged men spoke Spanish. And given their relative reticence, our efforts to converse with them in Aymara were too brief to be productive. Young, unmarried men under twenty-five or so years of age were both the most fluent in Spanish and the most eager to speak with us. They were also the least burdened by time-consuming work. Many seemed to spend much of their time wandering the hills with an eye out for fetching shepherdesses, engaging in courtship rather than in commerce. Dressed to the nines in their homespun clothes, many young men passed through Santa Bárbara in their wanderings, sometimes looking for a small mirror or safety pin that they might purchase as a gift to a girlfriend. Sometimes they would also while away their time in conversation with us.

When they did, their curiosity vied with ours, in the oblique style of information gathering that results from the local etiquette that considers a direct personal question very impolite. After finding we had little to trade for, questions often concerned the asking price of what possessions they could see or what we might have elsewhere, perhaps in our home country. From here, it was a short step to wonder whether we also came from a land with farmers and herders. The market prices of agricultural products and animals back in the United States were of special interest. The people of Cantón Culta travel a good deal—it is not for nothing that they label themselves commerciantes—and the distance and airfare between the United States and Bolivia were often of interest to them. One young man, juggling the relative cost of airfare and the selling price of lamb per kilo, seriously considered the idea of marketing his sheep in Miami.

One of the most oft-asked questions was the price of my hiking boots. Undaunted by the quoted price, many proceeded to suggest a trade involving sheep or llamas. When I would politely decline to sell them, numerous men queried the possibility of ordering a pair through me. While I found that wearing a good pair of boots helped my feet to resist the rough terrain and the extreme cold that descended nightly, I later discovered that reinforced shoes and heavy boots, which some men indeed owned, were especially desirable for use in ritual battles and warfare, serving to protect the feet against sling-thrown stones and for effective kicking in close combat.

There will be much more to say about fighting when we explore the relationship between feuds and festivals, ritual battles and land wars, k″arik″aris and the proper way of dealing with them. Understanding the significance of these relationships requires, however, much more famil-iarity with the meaning of blood, semen, and the fat that adheres to internal organs, which is to say the circulating substances involved in the maintenance and reproduction of human life and human agency in the forms they take in Cantón Culta. Here I will note only that some fighting takes a playful form.

Towards the end of July, a young Mamani woman came to our house in search of what might be called beauty aids—the mirrors, barrettes, and large-sized safety pins that unmarried but marriageable women wear in quantity. She also, however, was bleeding from a cut on the top of her head, and we helped her wash and disinfect the wound. When we looked more closely, we noticed that she also sported a large bump, and she related that a certain young man who had been courting her had scored a direct hit with a small sling-thrown stone. Laughing about it, she reported that she thought she had landed a few shots on him, too. One of the wandering minstrels had failed to get close enough to sing his love song.

COUNTERETHNOGRAPHY: THE ROLES AND PERSONA OF THE ETHNOGRAPHER

The preceding incident was just one of the moments when ethnographic inquiry was conjoined with another role, this time as first-aid providers. Others also asked for medical advice and treatment, sometimes far beyond our competence, which was limited mainly to antiseptic and Alka-Seltzer. When such cases came along, such as the woman brought to us in an apparently advanced stage of tuberculosis and the man in convulsions suffering from a fractured skull, we were able only to advise our friends to seek aid from a doctor in Challapata or Oruro. This was also our approach with the especially touchy subject of birth control. The issue was invariably raised when we were asked why we had no children. In spite of our evasive answers, many people guessed that we might know something about contraception, and one or two men, and many more women, quietly and singly came to our house seeking detailed explanations. Now, the chimerical story of Peace Corps sterilization schemes (made all too vivid in the Sanjines film *Blood of the Condor*) was then widely known in Bolivia; one of the indianist parties based in La Paz had made opposition to such genocidal, imperialist family-planning programs into a principal plank in its platform. Our response to such questions, therefore, was to affirm that birth control was possible and available from a doctor or pharmacist in the city.

Mary, whose research on the Aymara language kept her often close to the house, where she served innumerable cups of coffee and plates of food to visiting men and especially women, learned to spin during hours of polite conversation. To her credit, she was not as insistent about attending secret rituals and completing libation sessions as I was, and was therefore also able to minister to me and others when we needed to be dragged home in a drunken state. This, it turned out, was a characteristic woman's role in festival contexts, where their level-headedness served to save them as well as their menfolk from embarrassment.

Apart from being a pseudostorekeeper and adhesive-bandage provider, I was to take on many other roles as well. I carried a camera to record the place and its goings on, and soon discovered that photographing people is a highly sensitive business, which my subjects sometimes sought out and sometimes avoided. Photography was not unknown, but the people of K'ulta had experience only with Polaroid portraitists of regional fairs and the box-camera photographers of urban plazas, who develop their images on the spot. There was much consternation and suspicion when I could not deliver instant images after snapping a photo. But once I had been able to have some pictures developed and had delivered them to the people they portrayed (to the surprise of many, at no charge), I was frequently sought out for portraits, to a degree that severely strained my research budget. I also found that formal poses were vastly preferred over casual snapshots and that many people greatly objected to close-ups that "cut" part of their bodies. One of the resident vecinos was convinced that I had intended him bodily harm; a lengthy explanation of my aesthetic reasons for preferring close-ups helped to alleviate his fear and anger, which was completely placated once I reshot his family's photographs in the stiff, unsmiling, frontal, full-body style (wearing urban clothing and displaying an array of "national culture" possessions such as radio and bicycle) that nearly all K'ultas preferred as a more dignified form of self-presentation.

There were other roles as well. In early August, just before Bolivian independence day, my comparatively large size and, I suppose, my boots led the Mamani bunch to invite me onto their soccer team, engaged in a round-robin competition with many other teams in the cantón. But I am not much good at soccer or at running for long periods at high altitude (the heavy boots did not help). I was rapidly moved to the goalie position, where size counts for something, but after just two games was politely though permanently sent to the bench, replaced by sixty-year-old don Eugenio. Besides storekeeper, nurse, photographer, and failed goalie, I also became at various times a member of work gangs, undertaker, coroner, peasant union typist, and election judge.

Being the notary as well as alcalde for the year, our host don Manuel kept a small office on the main plaza in Santa Bárbara. It contained little more than two chairs and a desk, on which sat his register books, notary materials, and typewriter. In the office, he recorded births and deaths and performed civil weddings. I was present during numerous such events, all of which were accompanied by the same ritual of coca chewing and libations at the corners of the desk that I had seen in the corregimiento. In one marriage ceremony, I participated in libations dedicated to typewriter, register book, stamp pad, and seal. For each of these services, don Manuel, the first local man to have passed the examination to obtain this post, received a small fee.

Don Manuel often complained that the wealth his clients assumed that he had amassed made him the object of their envy, which in the Andes, can cause illness. Although he seemed perfectly healthy, he *was* in some respects wealthier than most others. His house in Santa Bárbara was the largest and best appointed one in town, consisting of two rooms rather than one and sporting a window. Yet, along with his wife and children, don Manuel preferred to spend most of the time in a much smaller, windowless house in Vila Sirka. He explained that to live in the large house in Santa Bárbara provoked too much envy among his ayllu-mates.

Because of his notarial duties, which included the provision of death certificates, he also kept a pick and shovel for the digging of graves. Now, a measles epidemic swept across the cantón during those cold months, hitting a large percentage of children under ten or eleven years of age. In the temporary absence of our host, who had himself gone to the valleys to trade, distraught men came to our door in search of our host and his implements. Several times I helped to find don Manuel's wife to unlock his town house, and helped as well to dig a grave for a dead child in the cemetery, located several hundred meters outside of town, where it has been since the late eighteenth century.[4] So when grieving men asked me to pray over a child's grave, I did my best to oblige. Most seemed satisfied with what I was capable of, which was the Lord's Prayer in English. That was the extent, however, of my priestly activities.

Later on, when through similar circumstance I was enlisted to help with the burial of a young man, I was asked to play the part of a coroner and to identify the cause of death. I tried to beg off, but the corpse was nonetheless unwrapped for my benefit before I was able to excuse myself on the basis of incompetence. By then I was fluent enough in Aymara to understand that the heightened emotional state of the pallbearer undertakers, which I had interpreted as grief, in fact included a large dose of raw fear. Corpses are not buried by members of the immediate family, but by affines. Burial of his wife's brother or mother's brother is one of the unpleasant tasks incumbent upon a man, who is to them a perpetually subordinated and indebted outsider, a thief of sister or daughter. There is a serious possibility of contagion in the cemetery, not from disease, but from a kind of possession of which uneasy souls, those which have not yet gone west, are capable. Certain souls are especially likely to cause problems, including those who have committed incest and those who have died while drunk, like the young man I was helping to bury. These became kuntinarus (Sp. *condenados*), ghosts who cannot reach the distant land of the dead, and are thus destined to wander endlessly across the places they knew when alive. Stories abounded of strange meetings with a kuntinaru, some of whom may show up on one's doorstep looking as they did when alive, in search of the solace and food that their true forms prevent them from obtaining. I had also learned that to pronounce a cause of death, even an apparently innocent one (given the circumstances of his death, this youth had most likely died of alcohol poisoning), can lead to recriminations and even violent acts of revenge that may set off, or continue, a long-lived and bitter feud.

In yet another capacity, I became recording secretary in a meeting of authorities of one section of the cantón. The meeting was held to petition the government for emergency aid after the harvests of 1979 proved disastrous. My role was to take dictation, typing—in triplicate—requests for state aid. Among the requests was an appeal for the stocking and staffing of a posta sanitaria, an emergency nursing station, stocked with vaccines and medicines, which should have been the prerogative of the cantón. (As mentioned in a previous note, one was eventually built and staffed, in the mid-1980s, but in Cruce rather than in Santa Bárbara.) The same document included incorporation of part of the cantón as a peasant union, or *sindicato,* which the authorities believed that state agencies would require. Many communities have been reformed as sindicatos, but the syndication efforts I witnessed proved to have been made to convey an expedient appearance rather than to transform social life effectively.

I was asked to compile the sindicato roster by copying names, professions, and numbers from stacks of national identity cards handed to me by the authorities. These had been recently delivered in preparation for their distribution after mandatory voting in the presidential elections.[5] We will later plumb the significance of the fact that the peasant union founded in the document corresponded only to the social group, or ayllu, to which my host belonged and the territory in which the town of Santa Bárbara was located, a fraction of the people and territory of the cantón.

To round out this survey of the roles that an aspiring ethnographer may be asked to play in the countryside, I will admit to having served, in the presidential elections of 1980, as election judge, voting booth guard, and one of three vote counters. Rural people have had the vote since the 1950s revolution, and my experience confirmed that they use it fully. In part, they do so because voting is mandatory; one cannot get one's national identity card validated without the evidence of the ink-dipped blue thumb that election judges give voters after they deposit their ballot in the box. The authorities of the town urged me to cast my own ballot, but I refrained from doing so.[6]

A BALANCE SHEET OF CULTURAL POSITIONING

Just as I struggled throughout the fieldwork period to grasp the manner by which K'ultas understand events and define themselves, they sought to place me within the field of possible roles into which gringo (outsider) vecinos normally fit. Clearly, I proved inadequate as hippy capitalist, vecino shopkeeper, nurse, coroner, soccer player, and state official. I suppose that seeing me flounder on the soccer field, botch up the peeling of potatoes, pass out after drinking too much at a festival, or act as uncomfortably as they did in the presence of a corpse, helped to dispel some of my K'ulta friends' fears about me and to establish a sense of common humanity. That and the fact that we, unlike schoolteachers, priests, and other outsiders, had not disparaged their beliefs or practices, or attempted to enlighten them with rational and scientific wisdom, made the sharing of more private events more imaginable. It also, however, opened the way to their more intensive (but always politely indirect) questioning, to which it was sometimes difficult to respond without preemptively contradicting the answers I hoped for from them. It was thus somewhat ironic that we were so often sought out as resident experts not only on our own culture but also on the questions of the ages, such as what happens to us when we die, what the stars are made of, if it is true that the earth revolves around the sun or that men have walked on the moon. Often, of course, such moments resulted from my own inquisitiveness being turned back on me. Still, because the people of Cantón Culta were just as curious about us as we were about them, I had no choice but to answer them. I found that I often learned as much by their questions and their uptake of my responses as by attempting to ask my own.

Standing one night under the moon and stars, for instance, I asked one K'ulta man, a *yatiri* ("one who knows") widely renowned for his cosmological knowledge, about the stars and the constellations that people in the Andes see in dark spaces in the Milky Way. "You," I was told, "know more about that than I do." Then the questions about moon, stars, and souls came back at me. How does one take a teacher's role to explain the heavens to an expert in cosmology, whose knowledge schoolteachers disparage, and still hope for *his* explanation? Fortunately, the Aymara language is especially suited for imparting information without implying that one believes in it. Rather, it requires one, grammatically, to state the source of any imparted information, whether direct personal knowledge (as in eyewitness evidence), reported speech (what someone has told one), or more distant received wisdom, what *they say* (referring especially to information passed down verbally from generation to generation, often in the form of narrative). Now, personal knowledge information is regarded as much more reliable than that contained in reported speech, unless the integrity of the witness is questionable. Received wisdom from the distant past is generally held to be unquestionably true, or at least the best that one can hope for where personal knowledge is impossible. Received wisdom, however, sometimes fails to provide clear answers to today's questions, and also sometimes comes in variant versions that leave room for alternative forms of explanation or clarification. To the yatiri, therefore, I provided a thumbnail sketch of distant balls of fire, earth's orbit of the sun, and NASA moon walks, carefully circumscribing it as information read in books and newspapers, heard from teachers, and witnessed on television—all these being, to my yatiri friend, eminently fallible sources. About the destination of souls and the afterlife, I had only to respond that we would all find out, someday. That, it turned out, was also the standard reply in K'ulta territory.

The next morning when I walked out of our house into the courtyard, the yatiri and his cousin, our host don Manuel, asked for a reprise of the solar system explanation, which don Manuel had also read in his one-volume encyclopedia. Don Manuel produced his soccer ball and an orange for a demonstration, after which I quickly excused myself. A bit later, I ran into don Manuel juggling these two spheres for another man, a stranger to me, who had come to town on business. Left alone with the stranger, I went through the usual explanations of my presence (writing a book on fiestas, preserving a written record of local customs, etc.). Once again, my guest asked details about where I came from and what it was like there. He especially wanted to know if my country had farms and herds, if the weather was the same there as here, if it hailed there too, and if I also saw the sun and moon there. I began by noting that our country was very far away, many months' journey by land, and that we had come by airplane. About the weather, I noted that it was summer there when winter here, and vice versa. He had been plotting the trajectory of this journey with a stick in the sand, eyeing me with increasing wariness. At the reversal of seasons, however, he stopped me, took a few steps back, and stated that I must come from another *muntu* (from Sp. *mundo*, "world"). I had not mentioned other suns or planets, and I tried to assure him that there was only one world and that I was of it, but my ignorance of his culture had led me down the garden path. It also led him hastily away. I do not believe that I ever saw that man again, but our conversation, reported to don Manuel, was a source of great mirth and also of new information. "Muntu," it turned out, is a word for "the other world," which is to say, the place the sun goes at night, where much of what we experience here on *aka pacha* ("this earth," "this plane of space-time") is there inverted. Muntu is also the abode of the dead.

Through use of the personal-knowledge grammatical frame and by assuming too much in the way of shared terminology, I had unwittingly made myself out as a ghost.

Throughout our stay, our relations with members of the community wavered uneasily between the kinship-based reciprocity that requires hosts to feed their guests and kinsmen to palliate relatives' want, on the one hand, and the asymmetrical relationship of vecino to campesino, on the other, based not only on tit-for-tat barter transactions but also on patron-client ties. Kinlike ties were strongest, of course, with our host's family and finally with all the Mamani patriline. Since marriage hereabouts is patronymically exogamous, we also developed good relations with the hamlets and patronymic groups with which the Mamanis have numerous and strong affinal links. For others, however, our status was permanently that of potential vecino storekeepers, or worse. This was true, of course, for the passing strangers who, during these winter months, regularly graze the town with their llama caravans, going to and coming from the warm valleys accessible via a trail that leads past the town. It was also true for the individuals and small groups of people who periodically show up in Santa Bárbara to pay cult to the patron saint's image.

Much later, when I returned to the town alone in February of 1981, a new batch of authorities (all the yearly posts rotate at the new year) urged me to bring my wife and settle permanently, offering to help build a larger house on the very plaza where we could set up shop. But whether the offer resulted from friendship, progressive civil spirit, or awareness of our client-advantageous business practices, I cannot be sure. Yet another man, seeking to obtain some of our goods before our departure (such as our much-coveted small propane range and kerosene lantern), seriously proposed that we trade them for alpacas, which could become, he suggested, the start of a herd, which his wife would keep for us until our return. This was a more attractive, even flattering, proposition. Since shopkeeping vecinos born outside the territory can no longer lay claim to land, the offer seemed to imply that we might claim rights to pasturage, something that by then I knew to derive only from kinship ties. Indeed, when I again returned alone for a few months' stay in 1982, one of the Mamani men went so far as to offer his daughter to me in marriage, suggesting that, because he had no sons, I might settle in to claim land through her. Since he knew my wife, I thanked him for his offer but expressed some shock at it, and said that I knew they did not take bigamy lightly hereabouts. This he shrugged off with the explanation that, because my wife and I looked to him very much alike and because we had no children, he had come to believe that we were siblings in reality. Yet even if he had been correct and I had been attracted to the idea of thus "going native," by then I knew that the land claims of in-marrying sons-in-law are extremely tenuous, expiring at the same time as the father-in-law. I recalled the words of another Mamani man about a brother-in-law living on the family's lands and what would happen upon the father-in-law's death: Roughly translated, he had said, "We shall bid him farewell with stones."

Towards the end of my 1981 stay in K'ulta territory, while seated at a ritual altar with the Mamani men and pretending to be unconscious so as to avoid becoming so, I overheard don Bartolomé Mamani describing me to his distant cousin, who had just arrived in town with his llama herd from the far-off valley in which he lives, and was hesitant to allow me to participate in a sacrifice he was sponsoring. Don Bartolomé, who was the officiant of the sacrifice, told him not to worry and that, although we had seemed strange at first, the families of Vila Sirka had grown accustomed to us. I was, he said, like a grandfather, always pestering them about the proper performance of customary rites. Now, I was somewhat taken aback by being classified as a grandfather by a fifty-five-year-old man. I might have preferred to have been called brother or even son (though not brother- or son-in-law). At the time I thought the classification might have something to do with my beard's having gone from dark brown to white over the course of fieldwork. On reflection, however, I see my friend's point about my peskiness. The same man once bristled when I asked him, during a small-scale hamlet fiesta, when the "*uywa ispira*" libations would take place. According to my calculations, I should have then just walked in on them. In fact, the family was apparently trying to forgo this phase of libations on that occasion, but once I had spoken the words, the all-night ritual had to be hastily prepared and then performed. My eager interest in ritual practice had made me the nagging voice of customary conscience. On another occasion, when I had asked him to describe a sequence of libation dedications, don Bartolomé told me that such words cannot be uttered without in fact performing the libations. When the gods hear their names (and apparently the names of rituals as well), they get thirsty and must be given drink. To awaken their thirst only to disappoint them is to invite their wrath. Therefore to avoid that wrath while acceding to my requests that he, a specialist in libation language, utter the gods' names, my friend had on several occasions consumed and sprinkled on the ground quantities of alcohol. Even if it is the right thing to do, properly fulfilling ritual obligations can be costly to the pocketbook as well as the body.

This should serve to point up the fact that the ethnographer's presence can have a notable impact on the development of the events he or she observes and participates in. Some events, in fact, would not take place at all in the ethnographer's absence. On the whole, I think, we need not worry excessively about the potential distortions of "data" that might result. The hastily gotten-up ritual provoked when I caused the mountain gods to salivate was in essence the duplicate of many other such rites that I did not provoke but managed to see. In retrospect, being a pesky "grandfather" is as unobtrusive as any other role an ethnographer might play, except perhaps that of an actual, invisible, ghost.

Such concerns arose only after our improved Aymara, better manners, and avoidance of the treachery usually expected of outsiders and city folk had convinced a few people that we had the capacity, at least, for becoming fully fledged human beings, though perhaps only those of the lowest order. At the beginning, however, I was admitted to only the most public and innocuous of events, while other life contexts were carefully hidden from view. Yet even the most casual of interviews opened up paths of inquiry, sometimes through my own misunderstanding. And the most formal or public of arenas, such as authority meetings, soccer games, or collective labor, exposed tacit understandings and forms of everyday sociality, which led to significant insight.

Formal interviews, which I employed on just four occasions towards the end of my first period of research, were helpful in filling in gaps in my knowledge and in pointing to further areas of investigation.[7] These, however, were difficult to arrange. Few of the inhabitants of Cantón Culta would consent to lengthy grillings while I scribbled in my notebook, and no one wanted to be seen so engaged. Besides, such sessions do not form part of normal K'ulta experience, in which probing questions are considered rude and information is generally imparted after a slow circling around subject matter that is somehow related to the context of discussion. It was therefore through participation in significant local events, sharing experience about which more could be learned in later casual conversation, that I was able to gather the most useful bits of information on the way of life (and death) of people of Cantón Culta. For example, to the degree to which I have achieved understanding of ideas about the dead or about the mountain gods' thirst, this understanding is a product of collating many distinct experiences over the course of my research. I was not to appreciate the significance of the gods until I had participated in dozens of sacrifices and libation sequences. To understand the role of the dead required observation of many rites in the three-year funerary cycle; local beliefs in ghosts became intelligible only by hearing many ghost stories, including one narrated before a meeting of authorities in a suit over wrongful death. I learned then that I was wise to have refused to pronounce the cause of death of the young man I had helped bury, since most deaths, apart from truck accidents and those of infants and the aged, are suspected of having been the result of unnatural causes.

Yet collating bits and pieces of information from a single area of experience, such as death and burial, proves insufficient to achieve a truly adequate understanding. Interpretation is most rewarding only from the vantage of a much wider frame of reference. In Cantón Culta it is often fruitless to ask for detailed explanations of the meaning of things, since there is no exegetical tradition per se. A well-timed question in the context, say, of an unfortunate death may evoke stories of kuntinarus, but understanding the significance of these stories requires a good deal of presupposed knowledge that one must pick up, as the people of K'ulta have, from other contexts. To achieve a more embracing vision of the K'ulta understanding of humanity's place in the cosmos at large requires participation in the widest possible range of life events.

For better or worse, during the early months of our stay in Cruce and Vila Sirka-Santa Bárbara, I was not only excluded from what most people thought of as the most significant of events, but was often not even aware that they were taking place. This was because so much of ritual life, including critical parts of otherwise very public saints' festivals, takes place quietly, inside the houses, courtyards, and corrals of the closely woven family groups to which we did not belong. Some such events were deemed so "secret" that I was never able to participate. But as we gained the confidence of our host's kinsmen, we were little by little admitted into the fabric of their lives. It was in this way, and only by seeing the relationships among meaning contexts as diverse as llama herding, agricultural practices, funerals, saints' festivals, town council meetings, and sacrificial rites, that I eventually began to appreciate the ritually regulated circulation of the male and female life substances, which move through time as well as space.

Apart from the coca exchanges and pouring of libations in town council meetings, I saw very little of the ritual practice I had come to study during my first months in K'ulta territory. I had learned, however, that the festival season was nearly upon us, and hoped that, by insinuating myself into the activities to come, vistas both broader and more intimate would find their way into my notebooks. The festival year, and indeed the yearly round itself from a local point of view, would soon begin with the secret rites of the first few days of August. Although the published literature makes it clear that this is a special time of year, when the earth is held to be "open" and receptive to offerings, my questions got me nowhere, and I knew of nothing but soccer games. I later learned that some families within virtually every hamlet had carried out extremely important sacrifices and offerings during the first few days (or rather, nights) of August, while I slept soundly.

The rites which I did not see were family-oriented, prepared within the household and performed at private sites on nearby hillsides in the predawn darkness. These activities also served to open the agricultural year and, in consequence, marked the beginning of the return of the cantón's people from their long-distance trading trips. For throughout the month of July, individuals and small groups of mainly men arrived in trucks at the roadside or appeared with their llama caravans over the northern and eastern hillcrests, laden with sacks of foodstuffs that would fill their stomachs for the months to come. Two of don Manuel's cousins reappeared during July, and although both made their entrance into the Mamani hamlet accompanied by a caravan of llamas carrying dried corn, wheat, fruit, and potatoes, both had in fact traveled by truck up to the roadhead, where the animals were brought to meet them for their final entrance. Others from nearby hamlets had left home back in May or June with llamas loaded with salt, and had traveled great distances to amass foodstuffs before returning to Ayllu K'ulta in time for the August rites that open a new agricultural and festival year.

As the days and especially the nights began to warm up, groups of men gathered to break the ground for new fields, build and repair fences, and prepare to sow their crops. They were also preparing for the saints' days of that month, made festive not only for the return of so many prodigal sons but also for plentiful holiday feasting.[8]

During this quiet first month in K'ulta then, I began to piece together the nature of the local fiesta-cargo system and to appreciate the rhythms of a pastoral life style. But slow days of pastoral reverie and occasional conversation were suddenly interrupted in late July by an event precipitated by an unexpected wavering in the council's confidence in me. One afternoon the corregidor again asked to see my papers and, on verifying that they did not include research permission from the subprefect in Challapata (the corregidor's immediate superior), insisted that I seek it.

My trip to Challapata did in fact help to boost local confidence in me, especially among the Mamani clan, for whom Vila Sirka is a patronymic hamlet, but not because of the papers I obtained.

EMPATHY, TRUST, AND MURDER

I was not especially eager to comply with the corregidor's request, since I had already once been arrested in Challapata by a member of the local military police.[9] I had then seen that the subprefect's office is also the entrance to a very unpleasant-looking jail, which I had so far managed to avoid. There being no alternative, I set off for Challapata.

Since I had a letter of permission from the departmental prefect of Oruro, I was not too surprised when the subprefect immediately handed over a signed and sealed letter granting us permission to reside in Cantón Culta, one of several cantóns in his jurisdiction. On leaving the office, however, I stopped to read a wanted poster tacked to the outside of the door. Without offering a reward, it called for all good citizens to aid in the arrest of a group of murderers who had in September of 1978—the year before our arrival—beaten and kicked a man to death on a country trail near the town of Santa Bárbara de Culta. I was chilled to find that the wanted men were all named Mamani. A closer reading revealed that the list of about a dozen names included two of don Manuel's cousins and one of his nephews, our neighbors in Vila Sirka.

None of the Mamani men had struck me as especially murderous (indeed, it was with them that we were forming the closest ties), and I was not inclined to perform a citizen's arrest of our host's kinsmen. At the same time, the dead man's patronym, Carata, struck a bell. He was a paternal kinsman of the man who had vehemently argued against us at our initial meeting with the authorities, when the Mamani family had been our principal support. I am still not clear on all the dynamics of that initial meeting, but the Carata man had not in fact held a position of authority at the time, whereas the corregidor was one of don Manuel's affinal kinsmen, factors that surely had worked to our advantage. In any case, our very presence in Vila Sirka and nearby Santa Bárbara de Culta, and within the Mamani household, seemed to have involved us in a feud between patronymic groups.

A few days later, back in the town, I casually mentioned to don Manuel the arrest order for his cousins. He explained that there indeed had been a fight during the 1978 festival of the Exaltation of the Cross. Afterwards, said don Manuel, the drunken Carata man, on his way back to his hamlet of Paxsi Kayu, must have fallen and hit his head on a rock. Don Manuel's cousin Juan, however, had in fact fallen into the hands of the subprefect and had been in jail, rather than on a trading trip, for the month or so before and at the time of the fight. Furthermore, that particular fight between Mamani and Carata men had not been the first: Mamani men had been injured in the past, and the two groups had a long-running disagreement over the use of a fertile plot of agricultural land. Don Manuel believed that the Caratas had been remiss in taking their case before the subprefect, rather than resolving it locally in the corregimiento.

Over the next few days, don Juan's two sons came to me separately in search of a loan. They needed five thousand pesos in order to replace some llamas that they owed to some unspecified person. By now my feeless photography and lack of business acumen in barter transactions had become legendary in Ayllu K'ulta and had also become a serious budgetary burden, so I did not immediately cough up any cash. Other Mamani men, however, were contributing to the pot, and I eventually did too. The amount, it turned out, was precisely what was needed to bail don Juan out of the *juzgado,* and he was soon back in the local picture. Not exactly bail, the money was the established fine for having broken a pledge, an *acta de buena conducta,* by which Mamanis and Caratas, previous to the untimely festival death, had solemnly sworn not to engage in any further provocations.[10] Because a death was involved, the matter was not settled with the fine (kept by the subprefect). The llamas mentioned by don Juan's sons still had to be gathered as a payment to the aggrieved Caratas. In the context of another wrongful death case, I learned that the standard blood payment consists of ten llamas, the number that are needed for sacrifice in the three-year sequence of funerary rights. The cantón's authorities often require participants in a feud to sign an "act of good conduct," as well as to deliver blood payments, regardless of whether or not guilt is established. Since both accusers and accused are treated equally in such procedures, it is possible for accused parties to make restitution without requiring an admission of guilt and for accusers to settle without withdrawing their accusation.

The four Mamani families of Vila Sirka increasingly opened their doors to us after these events, events that seemed to confirm my status as a reliable Mamani ally. With increasing frequency Mary Dillon and I were welcome in the contexts of everyday life. We could now sit with Mamanis peeling potatoes in the kitchen, work with them in the fields, and walk to the pastures with young shepherds and their flocks. I was able to spend long hours with Mamani men as they wove bolt cloth on treadle looms, which they often set up during the day in llama corrals while their children herded in far-off pastures; Mary was able to join groups of women as they sat upon the ground to weave their amazingly complex warp-patterned textiles. Contexts like these proved invaluable for improving language skills and for opportunities to gain essential understandings. Issues and concerns that to our interlocutors were quotidian, were to us marvelous.

Still, on some issues, the Mamanis remained wary. They managed to keep us in the dark, for example, about certain private ritual practices that were carried out in the first few days of August. Questions about land tenure were also quite clearly still unwelcome. On the other hand, on some matters earlier reticence seemed to fall away quickly. It was not long before an extended weaving session in a quiet corral, a rest break in agricultural labor, or the evening hush around the cooking fire became the context for the telling of stories about the distant past, about mountains that walked, wild animals that could take the form of humans, ghosts that came back to haunt the living, and about the earliest times when the sun first rose in the sky. Other conversations focused on the annual round, trading trips by llama caravan, and the proper technique for freeze-drying potatoes. We spoke too about the nature of marriage and relations with affines, and heard fragments of the genealogies by which Mamanis trace their links with one another and with the patrilines with whom they have intermarried. On each such topic there were sensitive areas, moments of embarrassment when a question opened a problematic issue. Learning to master the elements of a K'ulta etiquette entailed, however, much more than becoming adept at polite conversation. I would later discover that some things, such as the names of deceased ancestors or mountain deities, are spoken easily only in certain ritual contexts (contexts to which I had not yet been admitted), and that the rules of etiquette I was learning are given order by principles of cosmology that are also the lineaments of history.

Surprisingly, the easiest topic of conversation was the saints' festivals I had come to study. In many ways, having announced my purpose as that of writing a book on fiestas seemed to have been the best possible research strategy. Mamanis seemed pleased to discuss the details and timing of the collective festivals that they so much looked forward to. While some individuals lamented the silence that had overtaken the town since Cruce had emerged as a new entrepôt, they were quick to tell us how Santa Bárbara came to life during its fiestas, and especially during the major town fiestas of Guadalupe (September 8), Exaltación (September 14), San Andres (November 30), the moveable feast of Corpus Christi, and above all during the patron saint feast of Santa Bárbara (December 4).

From the fragments of many conversations, I was able to piece together what I thought to be a decent sketch of the three forms of festival sponsorship that were said to be part of all these major fiestas. At the same time, discussions with authorities about the nature of their jobs also promised rapid insight. It quickly became apparent that year-long religious roles of fiesta sponsors are alternated with the likewise annual authority posts—"cargos," in local parlance—in the ranked sequences that throughout Spanish America have been described as prestige hierarchies. The major forms of sponsorship (*mayordomo, fuera,* and *alférez*) and the most significant of town council offices (alguacil, alcalde, and jilaqata) provide the ranks in this civil-religious hierarchy. A careful reading of the literature on such social forms in the Andes, however, had not prepared me for the true complexity of its workings in Cantón Culta. First of all, there are additional roles in both festival and town council. Second, I had to account for the post of corregidor, which is not part of a civil-ritual career. Most important, I had to take account of the fact that the elaborate system of sponsorship and cargo rotation, about which I was learning, does not include all the cantón's constituent social groups. Nor, it turned out, do the town council meetings.

The edifice of understanding that I had built by the end of September (by which time I had witnessed two festivals and assembled a complex model of both social organization and the concatenated systems of festival sponsorships and authority positions) began to crumble by the end of October. The career sequences and schedules of rotation that I had worked out were not incorrect, but new insight proved such models to be superficial. Yet they are a good starting point for a more detailed consideration of the social organization of Cantón Culta.

Chapter Four

Structures and Histories
K'ulta between Gods and State

ETHNOGRAPHIC BORDER CROSSINGS

It is today almost a commonplace in ethnographies such as this to dwell on the imbalance of power in the ethnographic situation. With research permissions, ties to the Bolivian government (in permissions and affiliations), U.S. passport, money, and valuable goods, I was in a relative position of power, reinforced by the fact that it was I who asked the questions and Andeans who answered them. At the time, however, I experienced just the reverse sort of power imbalance. I wanted to stay in the ethnographic game in Ayllu K'ulta and "get information"; K'ultas seemed to hold all the cards.

We may associate the phrase "Let me see your papers, please" with narratives of international intrigue and border crossings, but it is also today an insistent preliminary to fieldwork in the smallest and most "isolated" Andean villages. Without a sheaf of papers to serve as passport into a place like K'ulta, the researcher (foreign or Bolivian) will simply be sent packing.[1] Locally constituted authorities assert their right to police the borders of their jurisdiction, and the outsider who wishes to stay more than a few days or has no apparent legitimate business in the countryside (such as trade) must gain, not only the personal trust of those authorities, but also a favorable vote of the town council. So too did the council decide where and with whom we would stay—with Manuel Mamani, member of the council.

In contrast with our usual border crossings when traveling, say, between the United States and Bolivia, when passport control is but one edgy moment dividing stretches of private life, we seemed in Cruce and Santa Bárbara de Culta to have been let in only as far as the transit lounge. More aptly put, the border was wherever we were.

I had wanted to work my way quickly into K'ulta private life, but instead found myself engaged with K'ulta authorities and eminently public life. After I had learned that the very visible saints' fiestas and authority roles are deeply bound up with a more hidden world of llama sacrifices and shamanic sessions, and both apparently are tied to meanings generated in the quotidian practices of the kitchen and corral, I actively began to seek access to these relatively private and closed arenas. But instead, I found myself most welcome in the plaza, church, and town council office. As outsiders living on the patio of a public official, where K'ulta people came to do business, our presence was unusual but more acceptable than elsewhere. In such a place, visiting K'ultas from other hamlets arrived prepared for public business, and seemed intrigued and honored when we invited them into our house. At the same time, when I walked unexpectedly into the center of another hamlet, a silent alarm seemed to have sounded. I would generally be treated as an honored and powerful guest, seated on a folded poncho in a patio and presented with huge amounts of food. What passes for common decency and polite sociality in K'ulta often struck me as a form of diplomacy; in order to avoid accidental insult, communication is highly structured, and the flow of information is controlled. In such situations, the silent pauses in pleasant conversation are heavily saturated by the unsaid.

From the perspective of a U.S. citizen and viewed on the context of ordinary travel, these experiences may seem unusual. When we cross national borders or enter another city, we do not expect to be put up next to Parliament or city hall and escorted into government meetings, especially when we are not citizens. We expect, rather, to merge into the everyday life of the private citizen. But if one reflects on the matter a moment, the private life we expect to enter when we travel is the alienated world of human relations as mediated by money and bureaucracy: hotels, restaurants, stores, businesses, museums, golf courses, and universities. We are welcome in truly private life, in people's kitchens and living rooms and backyards, only by becoming friends or relatives.

In K'ulta, the space of public social interaction is extremely limited, and it belongs to council authorities and sponsors of religious festivals. It takes place especially at well-marked places and during particular moments and seasons, in the saints' festivals and accompanying markets, which are attended by many outsiders. Even so, during festivals outsiders tend to stick to the most public places in town—the church, plaza, and streets. Stone-fenced patios of festival sponsors remain off limits until the loud crack of an exploding stick of dynamite announces that the patio is open to all who wish to partake of the banquet feast that certain festival sponsors offer.

In K'ulta, such sponsors, who are council authorities-in-training and the authorities themselves, mediate between the hamlet life of patrilines and the collective society of the cantón, which is an officially recognized unit of the Bolivian state.[2] Indeed, through their activities they represent the community to the state and the state to the community. Their acts give "indigenous communities" a territorial and social shape. Yet even though the current shape of K'ulta, as a collective social group, is a product of its authorities' negotiations with the state, it would be misleading to conclude that peoples like the K'ultas are an epiphenomenon of the national state. For the Bolivian state and all the intermediate governmental units between nation and cantón are also a product of the continued insistence of authorities in places like Ayllu K'ulta on defending their existence and rights as a collectivity.

It is also misleading to suggest that K'ulta is an ancient entity, a "naturally" constituted people who have successfully resisted all efforts to colonize and transform them. Having come into existence in something like its present form during the seventeenth and eighteenth centuries, K'ulta as a social group has no continuous past reaching back to pre-Columbian days. Nonetheless, I had already caught glimpses of certain private or secret practices, carried out before the dynamite blast and after the festival outsiders went home, that did seem like continuities with a deeper past: llama sacrifices and myths of origin involving foxes and condors and the sun, divination with coca leaves and shamanic seances addressed to mountain gods, all of which K'ulta authorities seemed intent on keeping out of view. I seemed destined to be admitted only to sessions where authorities transacted official state business and festivals in honor of saints that harkened to Spanish Catholicism.

Such experiences have led many ethnographers, myself included, to believe that their calling is to discover and understand this clandestine world of meaningful practice. The very existence of the clear boundary maintained by authorities between a clandestine realm and a much less indigenous-looking public sphere has suggested to us ethnographers that the hidden practices are the site of a more authentic and original culture, while the public practices correspond to the "modern and foreign" impositions of the colonial and national states and the Catholic church. The temptation on reaching such (false) conclusions is to flee from the authorities and saints' festivals, in the written ethnography if one cannot do it in fieldwork practice, just as I and many others have fled from truck-stop "progressive" towns like Cruce into supposedly more "traditional" places like Santa Bárbara de Culta. That was the impulse that led me—after heeding the dynamite blast invitation to festival banquets, accompanying processions with saint images around the plaza, and sitting through many council meetings—progressively to seek the trust of the Mamanis and to invite myself into their most private ceremonies.

What I found by my end run around the authorities' border defenses, however, is that secret practices are permeated by Christian and Spanish themes. Moreover, sacrifices to mountain gods seem often to be the duty of council authorities or, rather, the means by which such authorities are trained and designated. K'ulta culture, that is, is not to be found on one or the other side of the frontier between clandestine and public practice; it is to be found at the frontier itself. The scale and kinds of social groups and types of authorities that have confronted and mediated state power from the Spanish conquest to the present have undergone many transformations; so too, then, has "indigenous culture," shaped for centuries through the collective interfaces between households or hamlets and powerful states.

At the same time, we shall see, the authorities put forward by peoples like the K'ultas are also the principal repositors of social memory. The ritual techniques they must master on their way to becoming authorities are those by which K'ultas construe their past. Many of those techniques, indeed, derive from pre-Columbian practices, but the memories they transmit are very much shaped by present concerns, as are all the revisionist accounts of the past we call histories. Authorities use their memory techniques to remember the past in a determined way, for specific ends, but their duties are not solely to recall the past. They are also charged with the business of meeting with outsiders and going out to meet the world, visiting government offices, learning how to file petitions, and paying taxes, giving out as little information as they can while playing the part of the community's intelligence officers. Guardians of tradition, authorities are also agents of change.

I had come to Santa Bárbara de Culta to question its people about their customary practices and about their past, but I discovered that it was a two-way street. I was also subject to interrogation, for the useful knowledge I might possess about prices and travel and goings on in the city, for insights into urban and cosmopolitan culture and also into the past as I understood it. To remain there, I had to submit myself to K'ultas' ethnographic and historical queries. If my purpose was to carry out the frontier practice of ethnographic research, the frontier space of the authorities was, not the worst, but the best place to do so. It was not a barrier, but the dynamic and creative edge of cultural invention and social memory. The systematic discrepancy that I had noted between the number of council officers that should have been at a meeting of the cantón council and the number who actually attended (a result of internal factionalism within the cantón) was one sign of local dynamism. Another was that I was intensively scrutinized by some K'ultas, such as Julián Mamani, not so they might use whatever knowledge they gained for local purposes, but so they might find a way out of K'ulta altogether. The frontier on which I worked was a contested space, full of contradictory projects and laced with dissension. For those who stay in K'ulta, most such dissent and contest is played out in the context of council meetings. I would later discover that "missing" members of the council had not simply withdrawn from collective projects, but had formed themselves into new councils, in search of recognition as independent cantóns. Sparse attendance at meetings in Santa Bárbara, then, was an index not of council weakness but of the strength of the institution. Let us see, then, just what kinds of powers K'ulta authorities embody and how they come to hold their several kinds of offices. I begin not with an insider's perspective, but from the outside looking in, as all visitors to K'ulta do.

COUNCIL AND CORREGIDOR, AYLLU AND CANTÓN, FIESTAS AND CARGOS: SOME FORMAL INSTITUTIONS OF K'ULTA LIFE

Cantonal offices are in theory occupied by elected officials; members of the cantonal council, according to laws dating back to the early colonial period, are chosen by popular vote and installed for a yearly term of office beginning on New Year's Day. These elected officials then choose three candidates from among the "most apt" for the office of corregidor, the highest-level authority of the cantón, who acts as the state's representative in the cantón and mediates cantonal affairs to the subprefect. (As we shall see, the term "corregidor" was used for a quite different kind of state authority in the colonial period, occupied by royal appointees to oversee justice and tax collection in colonial-era provinces.) The subprefect in turn reports to the prefect of the Department of

Oruro. Both are presidential appointees, reflecting the party patrimonialism of this democratic-authoritarian state structure.[3]

A new set of yearly chosen cantonal council members *do* travel each year to Challapata to be sworn in before the subprefect, and with them they bring three candidates from whom the subprefect chooses the corregidor. But although popular elections are indeed held within the cantón for the election of Bolivia's president, there is no voting involved in the selection of cantonal authorities. Still, one can say that local government at the level of the cantón (like the elected municipal offices in provincial and departmental capitals) is more representative and democratic than state authority at the provincial or departmental level. Who then, are the authorities of the cantón, and how do they accede to office?

Like all the cantóns of the region, Cantón Culta/Ayllu K'ulta is internally subdivided.[4] Many local authorities told me that Cantón Culta is composed of five ayllus, which are both territorial units and units of social organization, membership in which is determined by birth (Map 4.1). In theory, each ayllu sends three authorities to the weekly meetings of the cantonal council in the town of Santa Bárbara. The highest ranking of these is called jilaqata or cacique, charged with resolving disputes within the ayllu and representing ayllu members in disputes with individuals from other ayllus. Next in rank comes the post of alcalde, whose job it is to collect the head tax that each head of household owes to the national government, payable in the office of the prefect. Alcaldes also act as police officials, intervening with a whip to break up fights. Finally, there are alguaciles, who act as the deputies of the jilaqatas, empowered to keep vigil over the jail and to round up the principals in disputes brought before the council.

In fact, the bulk of the cantonal council's work consists not of the administration of public works, of which there are very few,[5] or of collecting taxes, which requires little time, but of the administration of justice. Meeting as a collective body, the council constitutes a court of first resort. Having sat through a great many such meetings, I can attest that the council's business is largely taken up in mediating and adjudicating disputes over land. But I also witnessed a variety of other legal cases, including trials for murder, bigamy, calumny, reneged debt payment, bride theft, wife beating, and witchcraft, as well as an investigation into a case of visitation by a ghost and another to resolve an accusation of blood-sucking and body-fat-removing vampirism. In all such trials, the council acted as judge, jury, and executioner, but also as

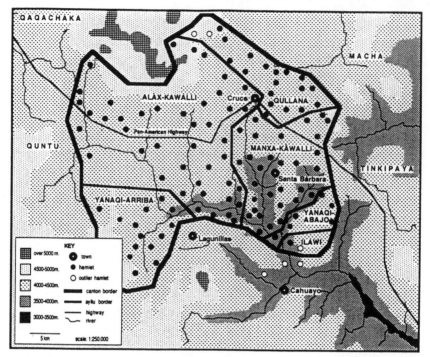

Map 4.1. Ayllus and hamlets of Cantón Culta/Ayllu K'ulta. Patriline-hamlets are also separated from one another by well-known borders. Neither interpatriline nor inter-ayllu boundaries are absolute; patriline territorial claims often overlap with those of other patrilines, and the same is true of ayllu territories. Some pasturelands are shared between patrilines, and others between ayllus. All ayllus hold small patches of land, sometimes settled by a small hamlet, in ecologically complementary zones outside their main contiguous territory, in the midst of another ayllu's territory. (Author's rendering, based on author's fieldnotes and 1:250,000 Carta Nacional, Instituto Geográfico Militar: Sheet SE 19-16 [Río Mulato])

prosecutor, defense attorney, and mediator, with particular roles falling out according to individual authorities' relationships to accused and accuser. In no case did I witness a meeting in which the council failed to reach an accord or final decision. When circumstances prohibited harmonious resolution of a case, it was referred to the higher authority of the subprefect, an event I witnessed twice. Most cases, however, are resolved with the imposition of a fine, formal signing of an act of good conduct, and ceremonies of reciprocal pardon, in which disputants agree to a council-decreed compromise and promise to avoid further provocations.[6]

Figure 4.1.   Jach'a p"ista t"aki: "great fiesta paths," or fiesta-cargo careers, illustrated as sequences of offices and festivals

As I have said, these year-long posts are held by appointment, not by election, but the appointments are neither renewable nor repeatable. Instead, these roles fall to individuals at predetermined points in one of four fixed-sequence fiesta-cargo careers, called *jach'a p"ista t"akis,* "great fiesta paths."

Like the civil posts which they include, these four careers are ranked (see Fig. 4.1). The two shorter careers lead to the midranked post of alcalde. They are named for their focus on one of two male saints. Together they are called *awksa t"akis,* "our father paths," of which San

Andres awksa t"aki, the Saint Andrew path, is the higher ranked. The alcalde who results from this career is therefore of greater stature than the alcalde who is produced by following Exaltación awksa t"aki, the path of the Exaltation of the Cross. The other two careers, which lead to the post of alguacil on the way to jilaqata, are the *tayksa t"akis,* "our mother paths," of which the longest and highest-ranking career is Santa Bárbara tayksa t"aki, leading to the post of "greater" jilaqata.

Formally, the fiesta sponsorship roles that are alternated with "civil" roles to make up a career are also year-long posts, and a new mayor-domo takes over from the old one during the very fiesta of the saint in question. On average, an individual who has embarked on such a career performs one of these year-long civil or religious roles every three or four years. Years of each career role are specified long in advance, as are the "rest" years in between. Every role demands a considerable outlay of resources, sometimes involving the purchase of twenty liters of cane alcohol, several pounds of coca, the manufacture of large quantities of corn beer, and the provision of many sacks of potatoes, corn, flour, and up to ten or twelve llamas to feed festival throngs. Clearly, the two- or three-year gaps between roles are necessary for the recuperation of resources in order to continue the career. Rest years are not, however, devoid of duties: There are ritual responsibilities during every year of a career.

Since the shortest career consists of four roles, and the longest and highest-ranked, of eight, careers are a minimum of twelve years and a maximum of twenty-five years in duration. What is more, the first step on a great fiesta path is not usually taken until after sponsorship of hamlet-level fiestas in the *jiska p"ista t"akis,* "small fiesta paths." And once the "great path" is completed, a man becomes a *pasado* (from Sp., "passed") but is not, therefore, considered "retired." Regarded with respect, pasados also have the privilege of attending council meetings, and they play prominent roles as honored guests in the ritual proceedings presided over by current festival sponsors and authorities.

My discussion of fiestas and cargos has not included the office of corregidor, the putative head of the cantón and chairman of the council meetings attended by jilaqatas, alcaldes, alguaciles, and pasados. This is because the corregidor is not required, or expected, to sponsor any festivals. From the midnineteenth century until the revolution of 1952, this post was the prerogative of resident vecinos (like don Eugenio's father), one of whom was periodically appointed by the subprefect. Since then, the post has been controlled by the town council itself, and the once-powerful corregidor has become little more than a figurehead who formally executes the decisions of the council as a whole.[7]

CITIZENSHIP IN AYLLU AND NATION

He may not have a great deal of power or influence (owing to the fact that, unlike other council members, he has no roles in saints' festivals), but there is one collective ritual over which the corregidor does preside. It was also the first large public ceremony I was to see. I refer to the only civic ceremony celebrated in the countryside, Bolivia's independence day, on August 6. Although it is held without large-scale participation during a time when many people are still away on their trading journeys, it is not lacking in significance. There is organized participation by teachers and schoolchildren. And the cantón's authorities, who must in any case forgo long-distance trade during their term in office, attend this requisite part of their duties in force.

The event is programed by the national government, and in 1979, when I witnessed the ceremony, the corregidor held a copy of the year's guide to festivities as the plaza was made ready. In essence, the backdrop for the speech he delivered was half the size of the symbolic display that hung above his desk in the council office: a Bolivian flag adorned with the national crest and reproductions of the founding fathers' portraits. There was a prepackaged speech, which the corregidor haltingly read out before the assembled authorities, schoolchildren, and a few dozen onlookers. A special feature in 1979 related to the fact that that year was the centenary of Bolivia's defeat by Chile in the War of the Pacific, in which the former lost its coastal department and its ports. There were allusions to the sacrifices of the country's soldiers and to hopes for a recuperation of its seacoast.[8] In tune with the centennial, schoolchildren were required to march to the plaza dressed in the red uniforms of the martyred Batallón Colorado, and most managed reasonable facsimiles made of cloth, painted cardboard, and paper (Photograph 4.1).

The ceremony had begun when these walking icons of national sacrifice (and of citizenship) raised the Bolivian flag over the schoolhouse. Then the aforementioned speech was brought to a close with a series of *"vivas."* "Viva Bolivia!" the corregidor shouted, and the crowd responded, "Viva!" Ditto for Simón Bolívar, Mariscál Andrés de Santa Cruz, and José Antonio de Sucre. Then, in honor of the Department of Oruro's hero, also a martyr of that war, there were "vivas" to Eduardo Abaroa, who had charged to his death rather than surrender, shouting, "Que se rinde su abuela!"[9] More "vivas" went up to the Department of Oruro, to the Provincia Abaroa, and to Cantón Culta. After this, the corregidor enlivened the proceedings with a series of preprogramed contests. Young men ran a foot race stripped to their underwear,

Photograph 4.1. A Mamani boy dressed as a soldier of Batallón Colorado. Manuel Mamani sewed this red-and-white, nineteenth-century uniform for his son's school pageant. The boy poses before patriotic icons arrayed on a wall of the corregimiento: portraits of independence heroes frame Bolivia's seal, above a flag bunting, all arranged over a K'ulta poncho nailed to the town hall facing onto the plaza. Prepared by cantonal authorities including Manuel Mamani at the direction of the cantonal corregidor, the array will serve as the backdrop for a civic ceremony honoring Bolivian independence. Normally, essentially the same array adorns an inside wall of the corregimiento, behind the corregidor's desk-altar. Santa Bárbara de Culta, August 6, 1979. (Photograph by author)

although some, chastened by the taunts and laughter of the crowd, did not run back to the finish line in the plaza. A group of older men competed at potato peeling, while women vied for the title of fastest eater of stale bread. Finally, the corregidor threw handfuls of hard candy into the air, and adults and children alike scrambled to claim it. These contests were some government official's idea of good, clean, and perhaps civilizing fun.

With this the teacher called the children back to the school, where each was served a cup of hot milk and a piece of bread. The food was provided by the lowest-level cargo-holder, the *escolar,* whose regular duty it is to provide bread and milk (prepared from foreign aid packages). The teacher then added his own idea of cosmopolitan panache to the proceedings. He had made costumes for the children, this time of plastic, so that they could perform an urban dance for their elders.[10]

Although it was not much of a day for secret religious rituals, and it lacked the big turnout and intensity that I would later see in saints' festivals, it was clear that people took their membership in the idea called Bolivia seriously. It was also a good day for photography, and was to be my first experience with the chameleonlike identity transformations that most of the cantón's inhabitants can carry out in very short order. Some people sought portraits of their children in their historical military uniforms (also worn by the presidential guard in La Paz). Practically all the younger members of the Mamani crew, as well as some of the authorities, including the corregidor himself, primped for portraits before and after the ceremonies (Photographs 4.2a and 4.2b). They did not, however, want to pose in their everyday homespun outfits, even in the colorful and festive versions that are kept for special occasions. Instead, all and sundry sought mementos of themselves standing stiffly before the flag and founding fathers while dressed in the outfits characteristic of the relatively well-heeled vecinos. Generally speaking, this shift in clothing went from homemade to store bought, and from wool to acrylic. For men, homespun white or black pants were put aside for acrylic trousers, and homemade vest and jacket were replaced by sweater and (in a few cases) sport coat. All those who owned a pair of shoes put them on in place of their rubber-tire sandals. The stocking cap ch'ullu and broad-brimmed, local, white felt hat were put aside in favor of a hatless but well-combed head. Women, on the other hand, rushed to change out of their black homemade dresses and white felt hats and into the cholita outfits kept for travel to cities.

In contrast with the change in clothing undertaken for travel (when K'ultas strive to obtain maximally beneficial positioning vis-à-vis urban

Photograph 4.2a. Julián Mamani and María Colque in everyday wear. The couple stands for a portrait in the Mamani llama corral during qarwa k"ari. In the background, Mary Dillon and wives of Mamani men continue their ch'allas seated around women's misa (a cloth laid on the ground). In the distance is the caretaker hill (uywiri) known as White Nose. In the foreground are sacrificed llamas. Vila Sirka, carnaval 1980. (Photograph by author)

94

Photograph 4.2b. Julián Mamani and María Colque in their traveling clothes (standing third and fourth from the right). This group portrait includes the Mamani youths, taken at their request, after changing into carefully stored city clothes owned by all except the young woman at the far right. Julián's brother and his wife (at the far left) were later killed in La Paz in 1982, in a truck accident while they sat on a witches' market street selling herbs and medicines. In the foreground are four unmarried Mamani women of courting age. All here changed back into "homespun" after posing for the photograph. Plaza of Santa Bárbara de Culta, carnaval 1980. (Photograph by author)

business contacts, to avoid the exploitation and insult that a clothing-identified indian/campesino might there experience), my K'ulta friends carried out this August 6 change of clothes for themselves, to obtain for posterity an image of an alternative identity associated with national culture. The cultural value of this identity is indicated by the term used to describe the change from homespun to store-bought clothes: "*civilizarse.*" While it may derive from experience in the military, where uniforms are contrasted with *ropas civiles* (civvies), the term "civilizarse" is also parsed as "to become civilized," in opposition to the insult of being "uncivilized," which rural people may avoid by wearing these store-bought clothes. We shall see that the textiles worn as part of homespun outfits bear a heavy load of meaning in the context of sacrifice and other rituals that lie towards the "private and secret" pole of a continuum of meaning contexts, in which the store-bought clothes, marking "urban national citizenship," lie at the opposite pole. K'ulta selves must have room for both sorts of identities (and others as well).

Indeed, in reflecting on the moments of embarrassment or reticence that I had run into, it began to seem as if silence on certain issues is regular and structured, corresponding to something like a separation between overt and covert, published and secret information. One might characterize this disjunction in subject matter as a distinction between a public, collective sphere and the business of private life. But I think it is more complex than that. Surely many of the personal stories and myths that I heard and activities that I witnessed in kitchen and corral correspond to a "private" domain rather than a "public" one. In fact, it became increasingly clear that the "secrecy" of some information is a result, not of a conspiracy of silence, but of cultural understandings of contextual appropriateness: Names of dead ancestors are to be mentioned only in the context of funerary rites and certain libation sequences (performed on Mondays); mountain gods will become "hungry" when their names are uttered and will take vengeance unless libations and offerings are immediately forthcoming. Such ritual contexts are circumscribed not only by schedules of proper time and place of performance, but also by hierarchies of inclusion as to who must and who may appropriately perform and attend. At the same time, the separation of beings and practices into topics of relatively "open" and relatively "closed" forms of discourse does not obey some abstract opposition between public and private domains (and as we shall see, there are closed and secret aspects of large-scale public events just as there are open and unrestricted features of private, intrahousehold life), but follows a set of cosmological principles that are also *historical* ones: The most circumscribed subjects are actions directed towards ancestors and mountain gods and unorthodox sacrifices to Christian beings. All such powerful agents from the past are invoked and made present to effect changes in the current state of affairs. So even the most secret of magical rites are at the same time *of* history and *for* history.

In examples like these, a relatively straightforward opposition emerges from what is actually a more complex continuum of contexts from maximally private to maximally public. The contrast between the roles, the means of election, and the kind of legitimacy achieved by the corregidor as opposed to the fiesta-cargo participants is one such set of opposed poles, but so too can we see the contrast in the very activities within the conjoint council (composed of corregidor and rotative authorities). In the Mamani-Carata murder case, for example, a legal action inscribed on paper (and involving the provincial subprefect) assessed a five thousand peso fine; a verbal agreement reached within the council chambers established the blood payment of ten llamas, by which rites unknown to the state might provide both sanction and resolution of the conflict. While I attended the saints' festivals of September, I began to take note of another example of such bifurcation, between loudly trumpeted collective acts performed for all to see, hear, and participate in and other acts carried out in hushed tones and closed circles of invited guests, in sponsors' home hamlets before and after public events in the town. The anthropological romance made those private and secret events into magnets. Unfortunately, they were charged to repel rather than to attract the outsider's gaze.

HOUSEHOLD AND COLLECTIVE RITUALS

During the month of September I was able to attend two major saints' festivals in Santa Bárbara, the September 8 festival for the Virgin of Guadalupe, and the festival of the Exaltation of the Cross on September 14. During these festivals, the town of Santa Bárbara burst to life. Each festival is presided over by three kinds of ritual sponsors, the mayor-domo, fuera, and alférez. In preparation for festival duties, each sponsor kills a large number of llamas and brings the meat, along with vast amounts of foodstuffs, to Santa Bárbara from his home hamlet by means of llama caravan. And with the foodstuffs, the sponsor brings his relatives, especially the people of his patriline. The younger men among the entourage form a music and dance group, dressed in special clothing (with matching jackets) and playing musical instruments (in September, the panpipes known as *sikus*). Thus on the day before the feast of Guadalupe large groups of people descend upon the town from various directions. Upon arrival, each group repairs to a specific patio in the town and to the house kept there by each hamlet and patriline.

On the basis of the ideal model of social forms that I had put together, I imagined that sponsors from K'ulta's five ayllus would descend upon the town and that I would see some pattern of alternation among ayllus and between the two moieties (the upper moiety consisting of Ayllus Qullana, Yanaqi, and Ilawi, and the lower moiety, of Alax-Kawalli and Manxa-Kawalli). Apart from the vibrance and color of the event as it began to unfold, my first surprise was that all the sponsors and all the entourages of llama caravan, dancing musicians, and festival followers came exclusively from the two ayllus of the lower moiety. Qullana, Yanaqi, and Ilawi did not participate. I soon learned that their failure to arrive was one product of a long-running factional battle underway within Cantón Culta and Ayllu K'ulta. This realization began to account for the shortage of authorities in the council meetings I had attended, in which the two Kawalli ayllus had been well-represented; Yanaqi and Ilawi, sporadically present; and Qullana, missing altogether. But I will save description of the fascinating background of K'ulta's factional disputes and analysis of their implication for ritual and political life in the cantón for a later moment. Partial as they may have been, the saints' festivals of Guadalupe and Exaltación were already complex beyond measure, and the meanings enacted in them, beyond my grasp (Photograph 4.3).

The three sponsors that preside over each festival—mayordomo, fuera, and alférez—were accompanied by their wives. Now, each sponsorship role involved a different set of activities, but all performances shared some features. When each entourage arrived in town on the day before the saint's day itself, provisions were unloaded from llamas and four posts were set up at the corners of each patio's stone *misa* (an altar-table). The posts held a canopy, which provided shade and shelter for the long sessions that then unfolded around the misa. Each misa was immediately covered with a textile, and the low benches around it were occupied by the sponsor and his male coterie. Nearby, the sponsor's wife and her female guests arranged themselves around a square textile laid upon the ground. Cans of alcohol and large jars of corn beer were then brought out, and a session of libations began. In each patio, a pair of llamas was rather quickly killed and butchered, and not long afterwards, the entourages began a series of visits among themselves. Later, these groups also processed through the town, visiting the church, the council and corregidor office, the *tiendas* of the resident vecinos, and a few other patios in which certain misas received special attention. At specified moments, the mayordomo's group moved to a misa near the church in a precinct formerly constituting the parish house, the fuera carried a bundle containing a miniature saint's image to the church, and the alférez group retrieved a banner from the church with which he (as always, accompanied by his wife) would lead a procession on the saint's day itself.

Manuel Mamani had told me there would be three sponsors. Yet, as the day before the saint's day (called Vespers) wore on, the number of active patios in town grew to six, with each sponsor's replacement for

Photograph 4.3. Ch'allas at turri mallku ("male condor tower") and the *arku* of Santa Bárbara. Bartolomé Mamani, *wasu wariri,* is at the left in the foreground. Santa Bárbara de Culta, December 1979. (Photograph by author)

99

the following year arriving to take office. At dawn the next morning, the day of the saint, the bands played near the church tower, after which there was another series of visits, now more complex and involving the incoming as well as the outgoing groups. Such visits culminated in banqueting at each outgoing sponsor's altar-table, at which the incoming sponsors were honored guests. After the food was eaten and prodigious amounts of drink consumed, dance groups gathered in the plaza, now incorporating dancer-musicians from incoming sponsors' entourages. Initially, six separate dance groups formed small circles in the plaza, each playing its own repetitive melody. The effect was cacophony to my ears. As the dancer-musician groups jostled against one another, they began to merge, forming two large circles according to ayllu affiliation, for each outgoing sponsor from Ayllu Alax-Kawalli was in the process of being replaced by an incoming sponsor from Manxa-Kawalli (and vice versa). Alax-Kawallis and Manxa-Kawallis now challenged each other in a duel of melody and volume, the circles moving in opposite directions to one another, opposed dancers bumping and challenging one another. Finally, fighting began to break out, first in pairs and then en masse, in the ritual battle known in Quechua as the *tinku* (and in local Aymara as *ñuwasi*, "knuckler"). The traveling vendors who had set up their wares around the plaza's perimeter gathered up their goods and scuttled into open doorways as darkness fell and blood flowed, and so ended the principal day of the saint's festival. On the following day, grudges apparently forgotten, each outgoing sponsor turned over sponsorship to his incoming counterpart. Before midday, all entourages had set out on the return walk to their home hamlets, again accompanied by a caravan of pack llamas carrying banquet leftovers.

Apart from the identities of the sponsors and the saints as well as some other accidents of difference, the festivals of Guadalupe and Exaltación, which occurred with hardly an interval between them, seemed to follow essentially the same script. At the same time, they were alike in relative participation: only two of K'ulta's five ayllus had been involved. Alax-Kawalli and Manxa-Kawalli had been present, but Qullana, Yanaqi, and Ilawi had not been. Over the next few weeks I pondered what I had seen and recovered from the exhaustion induced by nonstop festival activities. In spite of my exclusion from most of the libation sessions, I was nonetheless hung over from the intake of large amounts of alcohol and corn beer. Perhaps only two of K'ulta's five ayllus had participated in the festivals, but the dual organization for which the Andes are famous was still fully present. Also fascinating were the manipulations of saint images, the distribution of body parts of the butchered llamas, and a host of other festival features. Overall, these festivals had been full of new opportunities for observation and understanding, but the experience remained something of a disappointment, largely because, apart from a few isolated occasions, I had not been welcome within the closed circles around ritual altars, where libations had been poured and meaningful utterances pronounced. Exceptions to this exclusion took place at moments when the council authorities were invited to sponsors' altar-tables to be honored and during sponsors' visits to the council office.

On one visit to a sponsor's altar, I had been told to pour a bit of my cup of corn beer in honor of Guadalupe and other cups for Tata Awatir Awksa, "Our Father Shepherd," and Tayksa Mamala, "Our Mother," and it was explained to me that these were the title for Christ and one of the titles for the Virgin Mary. But I saw dozens of such libations, and was sure that I had heard other dedications (especially to *uywiri* and mallku). And when I asked others to explain these dedications to me, I was told by several entourage members that the men around the altar (as well as the women around theirs) were "engaged in superstition," "libating some supays" (demons).[11] Even these meager insights into clandestine practice (and techniques for keeping it so) were rare. For the most part, I stood at the periphery of ritual events with Santa Bárbara's two vecino shopkeepers and the low-status unmarried men, served at the feast but not allowed at the table.

Apparently, my standing with Mamanis and authorities was sufficient to give me a place among them, but I will admit that I was not then certain that this was a good thing. In fact, it seemed that these authorities, specially constituted to mediate between their ayllus and the outside world, had served very well as insulation between me and the semiclosed ritual practices I had wanted to understand. Further questioning convinced me that even more "secret" events, including what sounded like elaborate llama sacrifices, of which the relatively public llama killing I had seen was a pale imitation, took place in the privacy of the sponsors' hamlets before and after the collective and public events of Santa Bárbara. I began to despair that an invitation to the ritual altar would have to wait until Mamanis themselves served as sponsors, and it was possible to follow the whole sequence of saint fiesta ritual from beginning to end, from the household altar to the church altar and back again.

There were other significant events and conversations between late September and mid-November, but the attention of most K'ultas turned to pursuits other than festivals in Santa Bárbara. The town was once again quiet while K'ultas sowed their crops. Out in the hamlets, however, there was much ado, as small-scale hamlet saints' festivals were celebrated, honoring miniature images kept in hamlet chapels.

At the same time most K'ultas spent long hours sowing potatoes and other high-altitude crops in their own fields and those of others. Breaking the soil, planting the crops, and building fences to keep the herds off fields are accomplished through collective forms of labor. Work gangs are brought together through a variety of mechanisms, including the conscription of one's ritually subordinate wife takers, and through the use of various sorts of payment for service. But collective work is above all a patriline affair, during which patriline mates exchange days of labor through the reciprocal arrangement known as *ayni*. It is also a patrilineal affair because it is the patriline that claims title to agricultural land and the patriline that becomes a solidary unit to defend lands when disputes arise. And, of course, when ground is broken for new fields or fences built in previously unfenced areas, disputes do arise, and patriline work gangs are sometimes rapidly transformed into battle units.

Thus the September festival emergence of patronymic dance-fighting "platoons" coincides with their engagement in cooperative labor and in skirmishes over land.[12] Like the well-known tinku battles of the Macha or Laymi versus Jukumani just north of K'ulta, K'ulta's festival ñuwasis are ritualized fights between the dancer-musician groups of opposed moieties, but they may also escalate into more serious fighting when there are active interayllu land disputes. Indeed, several K'ultas told me that it had been the escalation of festival ñuwasis into full-scale battle, a land war called *ch'axwa,* that had driven the deep rift between K'ulta's moieties and led Qullana, Yanaqi, and Ilawi to abandon the festivals of Guadalupe and Exaltación.[13]

This period of collective labor and festival performance is a time of patriline solidarity, ayllu cohesiveness, and rapidly shifting "fission and fusion" of alliances over land disputes, but it is also a time for other sorts of collective labor. Quite apart from agricultural work, fence building (often a source of intergroup friction) and the like, this is also the period during which ayllu labor is most easily mobilized for projects that benefit the community as a whole, such as construction and upkeep of the town's access road and communal buildings. Such collective labor built the access road in the first place, as well as the Pan American Highway and its earlier incarnations (dating back to the Inca and pre-Inca roads that cross the region), the church, town council building, jail, parish house, and schools.

CULTURE AND THE CLANDESTINE

It was to ask the jilaqatas, alcaldes, and alguaciles to send their people for a collective work project that the corregidor called an extraordinary meeting of authorities in mid-October. Now, a crumbling church wall had been repaired through collective labor during the months before our arrival. Normally, a priest resident in the parish seat of Huari visited this vice-parish but once a year, during the feast of its patron, Santa Bárbara. This year, however, he had returned in early June to check the repairs in the church wall and had found the work wanting. In addition to some cosmetic repairs to the new interior plaster, he had demanded that the church's earthen floor be paved with stones. He had also asked for improvements in the parish house. From its appearance—a three-room thatched-roof, adobe structure with shuttered windows, terra-cotta floors, and fading murals—the parish house had been in existence since at least the late nineteenth century. Located on a courtyard adjacent to the church, it was the largest residential structure in town. It sported its own stone-lined canal to bring water from local springs, but also featured the Spartan adobe bed and benches of local dwellings. Now in a sad state, lacking windows for its stone-linteled frames, it was the home of a resident priest until 1938. From 1779 until that date, Santa Bárbara had been a parish seat, with two vice-parishes of its own. The house's only regular occupants nowadays were the hummingbirds that nested under its roof beams. During our stay in the town, the priest spent only one night there, his yearly average. He had not been present during the festivals of Guadalupe and Exaltación.

Apparently, to inspect the work he had ordered, he had promised to return on a date that was rapidly approaching. There was a good deal of discussion, some authorities arguing that recruitment efforts were hampered by the fact that so many men were still away on trading trips in the valleys and cities. The corregidor reminded the other authorities, however, that the priest had also threatened them that, should they fail to properly make Santa Bárbara's church ready, he would have a new church built, in Cruce. Finally, the council agreed to begin work on the church the next week, forgoing repairs to the parish house, apart from adding some thatch to its roof.

To speed up work that had been too long delayed, the corregidor set out for Challapata to request a platoon of soldiers for additional hands.[14] To my surprise, four young rangers showed up a few days later. Sleeping in the school, now in recess, they stayed only long enough to help amass a pile of paving stones near the church door. All spoke

Aymara, which is not surprising, given that many rural youths volunteer to perform the military service required of all male citizens. (Other, less willing, soldiers are caught up in periodic sweeps of market towns and city streets in "recruitment drives.") Some local youths as well as adults admired the soldiers' uniforms, and several locals stood at attention for photographs dressed in the soldiers' uniforms, while the soldiers donned local homespun and posed in fierce stances, topped by the local cowhide and tin *monteros,* hats modeled long ago on conquistadors' helmets and worn in festival dances, ritual battles, and land wars.

When the soldiers left, the corregidor issued a final call for laborers, but very few heeded the call. In fact, some of the authorities themselves were missing. Those from Qullana, of course, were absent as usual, but so too were two of the three authorities of Ayllu Alax-Kawalli. Had they failed to show, hoping that the work would not satisfy the priest, thereby leading to a church in Cruce, within their territory? I do not know.

Apart from this partial roster of authorities, I recognized two of the mayordomos who had served as banquet hosts during the fiestas of Guadalupe and Exaltación. Before beginning work in the church, they joined three other mayordomos in pouring libations at a misa in a small room adjacent to the church, within the parish residential compound. In addition to their service as banquet hosts, these men were also responsible for the upkeep and security of the church and its images. They also each took two five-week turns residing in the town of Santa Bárbara, during which each had possession of the keys to the church. Periodically, individuals and small groups of pilgrims came to town to pay homage to one of the saints—usually the town's patron, Santa Bárbara—and the resident mayordomo would open the church and supervise the proceedings. I had knelt with two such groups in the previous months and watched as they lit candles, burned incense with llama fat in charcoal braziers, and poured libations. Most such devotees, I later learned, were yatiris, a kind of shaman specializing in spirit-mediumship, for whom Santa Bárbara serves as intercessor or *awukatu* (from Sp. *abogado,* "attorney").

Normally each mayordomo ceremoniously ended his turn as key bearer with the arrival of his replacement. The two men together poured libations of alcohol and sweetened tea, and the new mayordomo accepted the keys only after checking off the church valuables against a tattered list. (It was during one of these changing of the guards that I had seen the contents of the locked chest kept under the altar; once saints' clothing and crowns, priestly vestments, and other ornaments had been removed, mayordomos accounted for a series of leather-bound parish register books, which I eventually convinced one mayordomo to let me see.) In preparation for work in the church, however, the assembled mayordomos now moved from their chapel to the bell tower, where they poured (and drank) more libations at its base. This time I heard a few of the libation dedications, including those to *turri mallku* ("male condor tower"), *turri mallku sap"i* (the tower's "root"), Tata Asanaqi (a mountain peak near Challapata), and Churi Asanaqi (a high hill not far from the church). Then they removed the images and valuables (except for the massive gilded colonial retable that rose against the back wall behind the adobe altar) for safekeeping in the corregidor's office.

Joined by these mayordomos, the authorities were now ready to begin their labors. Seeing such a miserable turnout, I decided to lend a hand myself and joined a group of about twenty men in laying the new stone flooring. The work lasted only a few days, during which the authorities' wives baked bread in an earth oven and provided meals of corn mush with potatoes and chili peppers.

We finished our labors around noon on the third day. The mayordomos replaced the images and valuables while I joined the authorities in pouring and drinking more libations at the base of the church tower. It was then that I witnessed an astonishing turn of events. The jilaqatas, with whom I had just been drinking, led two rams into the plaza. Directly in front of the church door, they threw the rams to the ground and cut their throats, collecting the blood in bowls and intoning mumbled words while flicking some blood towards the east. Couple by couple, the authorities and mayordomos, accompanied by their wives, knelt in pairs near the rams, facing the church door. Each person was then presented with a small board with a pair of clay braziers on it, containing burning charcoal onto which pungent herbs, incense, tablets of sugar, and pinches of other substances were placed. Since the man and woman in each couple raised a pair of braziers, a total of four sets of incense offerings were raised in the air while the couple quietly intoned some words. After most of the authorities had finished, Mary and I were urged to kneel and take up the braziers. Don Bartolomé, the ex-authority who seemed to be officiating, approached us and explained that the right-hand brazier on each board was for "Dios," and the left-hand brazier for "La Virgen." Once the fragrance of the incense was rising well, he told us to say the words "Tata Awatir Awksa taki," and "Paxsi Mamala taki." I was able to parse these Aymara phrases as "for Our Father Shepherd," and "for the Moon Lady," and I later learned that these are indeed the honorary titles applied to Christ and the Virgin and, at the same time, to the sun and the moon.

While I pondered this candid performance, by those whom I had thought most culturally constrained, of what seemed a quite un-Catholic ritual, a young boy on the hill behind the plaza spotted the priest's jeep approaching and shouted out an alarm. The incense, the rams, the bowls of blood, all were quickly dragged out of sight into a nearby house while another authority spread fresh sand on the blood-stained ground. I was left alone in the plaza while everyone else scrambled to wash their faces, hands, and feet, and to send out messengers that the priest was in town.

The priest stepped out of his jeep and gave the church a quick inspection, spoke to a mayordomo, and got back into his jeep. With some difficulty, the authorities finally convinced the priest to stay long enough to say mass. Meanwhile, a small crowd began to assemble in the plaza. A chair and table were set up in the center of the plaza, and the priest got out a cash box and receipt book and began collecting fees: Some individuals paid for funeral masses; others, for baptisms. Five or six couples paid the fee for a church wedding, and a number of the sponsors of recent saints' festivals paid for masses in honor of their saints.

Fees collected, the priest then went about the task of reconsecrating the church, sprinkling salted holy water about the walls and floor. By the time he began the mass, some two hours after his arrival, there were perhaps sixty people in the church. All seemed in dead earnest in their devotions during the ceremony, first quietly suffering through a sermon that was more like a litany of abuse. The priest began with reference to the new floor, which he judged the product of poor workmanship and a lack of proper Christian zeal. Speaking in a rarified Chilean Castilian (marked by the *vosotros* verbal declinations) that was, fortunately, largely unintelligible to most of this flock, he admonished all present to take the gringos among them as their guides, to wash themselves more frequently, dress in livelier colors, eat at table with knife and fork, and rebuild their homes to make separate bedrooms for parents and children.

The priest pointedly addressed these chidings to the assembled authorities, to whom he repeatedly referred as his *hijitos* ("little children"). All in all, the sermon struck me as profoundly insulting and deeply ethnocentric, in which the priest painted himself (and the ethnographer) in the well-known, patronizing pose of civilizing missionaries.[15] Yet no one seemed to take offense. In fact, when he emphasized each point by asking his "hijitos" if they understood him, the authorities humbly chimed, "Sí, Padre." Shortly afterwards, when the wine and wafer were eucharistically transformed and consumed by the priest (confirmation and thus direct participation in communion being rare in the countryside), all present seemed deeply moved, as they were, too, by the images of Christ and the saints, to which many lighted candles and fervently prayed.

After he had finished his complex yet relatively rapid combination mass (baptisms, weddings, and funerals included), and while newlyweds and new godparents celebrated in the plaza, the priest headed quickly to his jeep and prepared to depart. I approached the jeep along with a group of authorities. While he sat in his seat with the door standing open, the priest noticed blood seeping through the sand where he had just walked. Pointing towards the blood-stained earth, he called out to us, "What happened here, did you kill a cat?"

The authorities turned towards me, seeming to wait for my response, so I shrugged and played ignorant. After a few difficult moments, the highest-ranking jilaqata finally replied that, no, someone had only been butchering a sheep, for meat. With that, the priest closed the door with a smile, saying, "Next time, give me some of it." And he drove off.

It is only remotely possible that the priest did not know, after more than ten years of visiting churches like these in his far-flung parish, at least something about what had actually taken place. Most likely, he had simply learned to live with the knowledge that a clandestine form of religiosity took place in parallel with that which he controlled. In a later interview with this priest, he argued that these campesinos were good Christians, devoted to God in their own way. Neither fully taking the part of indigenous religiosity, as I have heard some Bolivian priests do, nor despairing the futility of priestly dedication among such unevangelized pagans, as others have done, this priest towed a middle path, turning a blind eye to their heterodox practice while condemning their cultural backwardness.

This kind of laissez-faire missionizing has been characteristic of the Church's role in the rural highlands since the midseventeenth century, when the last of the idol-smashing and orthodoxy-imposing "extirpation of idolatry" campaigns fizzled out. Combining cultural blandishments with a routinized priestly functioning lacking in curiosity has at one and the same time served to underscore the colonial nature of the missionary's presence and made room for, and even cultivated, parallel and presupposed forms of heterodox religiosity such as that which I had witnessed.

Although I had not joined the authorities of Santa Bárbara de Culta in the worship of a golden calf, I had nonetheless become part of the congregation in the performance of an animal sacrifice. Its performers (as well as the priest) clearly preferred that such practices remain clandestine, and I had not betrayed their trust. Earlier, I had earned the trust of my host's patronymic group by my response to the murder case, and doors had opened. Now I seemed to have crossed another threshold, this one opening onto the semihidden aspects of K'ulta's religious universe.

All doors did not, however, open overnight. In fact, by the time I reached the plaza the next morning, blood had been splashed above the lintel of the church door, and I was not then to learn whether it was from the previous day's rams or another sacrifice altogether. It was months before I learned just what the sacrifice was for. At the time, I missed much of the symbolic import of this ritual and, in fact, did not see significant parts of the rite. Some of the libations had been performed in private as the work in the church reached completion; others, around the church tower and in the corregimiento, were simply outside my hearing or beyond my comprehension of Aymara at the time. Since the dead rams had been hustled out of sight, I was not able to note the distribution of the meat or the libations that accompany it, and I apparently slept through the moment when blood was splashed upon the door lintel.

In retrospect, I know that the rite was complex, combining aspects of two relatively common kinds of sacrifice. On the one hand, the blood over the door lintel relates this rite to the *wilara*, a sacrifice performed upon the inauguration of any new (and, apparently, repaired) building, before its owners take up occupancy. The term "wilara" is also applied to sacrifices performed at regular intervals by authorities in honor of their staffs of office. Wilaras are also performed by nonauthorities at moments of special danger. The term might best be glossed as "blood offering"; in fact it is the simplest sort of sacrifice in the K'ulta sacrificial repertoire.

K'ultas distinguish many kinds of sacrifices, above all by the nature of libation dedications and by just how the animals' meat and body parts are distributed among gods and men. This particular sacrifice, however, was more than just an ordinary building dedication. The church, first of all, is not just any building, but a dangerous one, containing the powerful saint images in whose honor great festivals are regularly performed. During their removal from the church and subsequent replacement, the saints had been disturbed, and the special rite known as *lurya misa* had therefore been performed. Lurya misas, which include the doubled and redoubled incense offerings as well as the special libation dedications that I had witnessed, are always accompanied by sacrifices; this one included special blood aspersions required by the physical alterations to the building.

RETHINKING "SYNCRETISM": COORDINATES IN SPACE
AND TIME OF A COLONIAL INTERCULTURE

At first sight, the incense offered to Paxsi Mamala and Tata Awatir Awksa, the references to Turri Mallku and Tata Asanaqi, and sacrifice of rams in the plaza seemed to add up to a rather profound degree of cultural resistance, an entire cultural order preserved under the very nose of Church authority, performed by those local people who had seemed most implicated in the local administration of state authority. What could be less Catholic than animal sacrifice dedicated to mountains, to the sun, and to the moon? The temptation was very strong to adopt the interpretive stance of the "Christianity as a thin veneer," the "idols behind altars," the "baptized but not evangelized" variety of cultural continualism, by which all that I had seen might be analyzed and understood as uniquely Andean, intelligible according to pre-Columbian cultural logics. If K'ultas hear "sun" when the priest says "Christ" and "moon" when he says "Virgin Mary," and if, instead of exemplary Christian lives, they see in each saint the transformative and communicating power of lightning to intermediate for men between the sun and moon in the heavens and the underworld's masculine mountain gods and the feminine plains, then their apparent humility while attending mass and their efforts to pronounce Catholic prayers correctly (in both Spanish and Aymara) must be an elaborate hoax, a centuries'-rehearsed mask behind which their original, pre-Christian belief and ritual system lives on. From this interpretive vantage, one might find the pure, unadulterated Aymara signal by simply filtering out from fieldwork communications the foreign, Spanish-Catholic noise.

Yet when I saw the blood upon the lintel, I did not think only of pre-Columbian Inca sacrifices; I was also put in mind of the sacrifice that Yahweh asked of the Hebrews in Egypt, that of the original Passover from whence derives the symbolism of the Last Supper, and the identification of Christ as the Pascal Lamb, the Lamb of God. Animal sacrifice is central to Old Testament worship, and even if Andeans have seldom been exposed to Leviticus, the Christianity they have for centuries been taught is itself shot through with sacrificial metaphor, not least of which is the Eucharist. Might we then not understand this K'ulta sacrifice, and the sacrificial sequences by which all K'ulta saints' festivals are structured, as a K'ulta reworking of the Christian Eucharist? As we shall see, this is indeed a potent interpretive frame for understanding not only K'ulta sacrifices and saints' festivals but K'ulta authority as well. We shall see that the festival sponsors who become authorities undergo a transformation very like that of the eucharistic Christ, being equated with the victim of an animal sacrifice to symbolically appease a vengeful God and redeem their flocks. But they also quite transparently strive to become more directly like Christ, to achieve a leadership role and legitimate their positions of power by internalizing some of Christ's qualities.

So too did the devotion to the saints, which as far as I could see was entirely heartfelt, betokening something other than a "thin veneer" of Christianity. And the lurya misa itself was certainly in some ways the counterpart of the priest's water-sprinkling reconsecration of the church, an act that can be interpreted as sacralizing space or as a form of desacralization that makes it safe for one to enter.

As I learned more about the "private and secret" aspects of saints' festivals and sacrifices, I was even further disabused of the idea that I ought to separate analytically the Christian-Spanish from the Andean in this K'ulta cultural synthesis. It *is* possible to distinguish relatively "more Christian" and relatively "more Andean" cosmic spheres in the contrast between *alax-pacha* (heaven) and *manxa-pacha* (underworld), a contrast that also seems to correspond roughly to ritual practices in "more public" as opposed to "more private" performance contexts. But the qualities and characteristics of "Christian" and "Andean" deities seem to have interpenetrated one another so thoroughly that the contrast seems in some ways vacuous. Try as I might to seek out the secret and private rites, to plumb local sorceries and sacrifices, I seemed always to find the saints, Christ, and the Virgin at the heart of "native" ceremonies. By the same token, I also found shamans and mountain spirits in the church at High Mass. So too did the K'ultas' Christ and Virgin partake of some decidedly non-Catholic qualities, and underworld gods sometimes displayed quite biblical features.

Indeed, all the gods and saints, rituals and myths, of K'ulta share both Spanish-Catholic and Andean characteristics. The K'ultas' Christ, for example, is in many ways unlike the Christ of the priests. For K'ultas, Christ is a man whose death, at the hands of Supay-Chullpas, led directly to his apotheosis, a rebirth into the heavens as the sun. Yet surely as enemy and tamer of the native Supay-Chullpa "demons," whose exemplary death must (through self-sacrifice) be recalled and repeated over and over again, this Solar-Christ shares common ground with the priests' Jesus, whose iconography in colonial times was unabashedly solar. Likewise for K'ultas, as for missionary priests, the relationship between these two sorts of beings and powers is essential to the order of things, part of the human condition. The difference is that K'ultas juxtapose such powers so as to make themselves kinds of persons *distinct* from city people, vecinos, and priests.

From an analytical perspective, K'ultas' relatively orthodox, public-sphere Christian practice and their relatively heterodox clandestine practices are alike in addressing deities of both heavens and underworld which partake of qualities deriving from mixed Christian and pre-Columbian sources. But we cannot explain K'ulta religiosity simply by asserting that it is a syncretic blend of two traditions. For K'ultas themselves make a distinction between relatively "more Christian" and relatively "more Andean" deities and activities, which the logic of their practice divides between opposing spheres—open and public versus clandestine and private—knowing that, from the priest's and outsider's point of view, libations and sacrifices to mountain gods appear to be a diabolic kind of antireligion. Indeed, that is why they hide some of their practices. K'ultas may believe that some of their clandestine practices are just as Christian as their public ones, but they also know that others will not see it that way.

To understand the apparent paradox of hiding *Christian* practices from priests requires an alternative approach to the old problem of so-called cultural syncretism. In part 3 of this book, I lay out in greater detail some of the features that this alternative approach must have to enable us to extricate ourselves from old ethnological dilemmas, such as the assumption of closure in structuralist and semiotic (as well as functionalist) analysis that has long turned attention away from the active cultural frontier of societies in contact. Here I will only suggest that the dynamics of what might be called an interculture are profoundly historicized in the consciousness of all Bolivians, whether from the city or the countryside and whether self-identified as campesinos, mestizos, or criollos. Both urban-national and rural-"indigenous" cultural formations have come to presuppose one another's presence, producing in each kind of class- and ethnicity-marked position on the Bolivian scene a means of positive identity through contrast with culturally distinct others. In both La Paz and K'ulta, such presuppositions acknowledge the existence of asymmetries of power within the country as a whole;

indeed, the structured system of inequality that was colonialism, subsisting still in ethnically marked "class" distinctions, is directly addressed at the heart of the creole and indian meaning worlds. As we shall see, inequality is perceived as a result of a primordial form of cultural opposition involving conquest of a cultural alter. Achieving effective social agency in K'ulta, like the creation of adequate national citizens, leads rural indians and urban creoles to locate the origin of inequality in a foundational "first time," and in some way to invert or symbolically transcend such inequality through ritual manipulations of historical consciousness. In short, both urban nationalists and K'ulta festival sponsors predicate their personal and collective projects on the existence of the other, and such otherness is an indelible and inevitable part of the world of experience. The division of practice between public and clandestine spheres, then, has been structured by the power asymmetry of intercultural discourse under colonial and postcolonial conditions; it also exists to enable K'ultas to come to grips directly with such asymmetries of power.

Generally speaking, the church of Santa Bárbara and the hamlet altar-table, the heavens and the underworld, *may* be regarded as relatively "Catholic" as opposed to "Andean" spheres, but the ritual activities I saw in both sorts of contexts, related to both sorts of deities, seemed always to strive to bring the two spheres into contact with one another. Without letting the priest catch them doing it, they sought to bring about such controlled contact through the intercession of the saints. Indeed, I learned that most of the pilgrims who I had seen arriving at Santa Bárbara's church were engaged in one part of a lurya misa of their own. Santa Bárbara, I learned, is especially charged with lurya (it is not for nothing that she is the patron saint of electricians), and is often the intercessor, or awukatu, of yatiris, who seek knowledge from the hidden "other worlds" of above and below.

Soon after the priest's visit interrupted the council's sacrifice, I learned that there were yatiris among my neighbors and hosts. Don Juan (who had been released from jail) was a specialist in the reading of coca leaves, and people from nearby hamlets periodically sought him out to discover, by throwing coca leaves upon a cloth, whether tomorrow would be a good day for travel or whether they should sell some sheep to a traveling butcher now or later. Both don Bartolomé and his wife were highly respected curers, capable of determining the cause of illness and removing it from the sufferer's body for disposal elsewhere. I had already noticed that don Bartolomé and doña Basilia were often chosen to pass around the chicha bowl or alcohol cup during libation sessions. They were, in fact, wasu wariri (Sp. *vaso*, "cup," and Aymara *wariri*, "one who bears"), which is to say specialists in libation dedications. Although I did not grasp much of what was involved in libations until months later, don Manuel assured me that his "brother" don Bartolomé was nearly always chosen to officiate at Mamani festivals and sacrifices.

As libation specialists, don Bartolomé and doña Basilia well knew the complex and poetically organized sequences of drink dedications known as amt'añ t"akis, the "memory paths" by which human beings recall and address the gods, both the Christianity associated beings of heaven and the spirits of the underworld, which more than one K'ulta commentator likened to demons.[16] Eventually I would hear their names called out to come for their portions of alcoholic drinks, and I would understand that the yatiris' special task, and by extension that of festival sponsors and authorities, is not so much to keep incompatible "Andean" and "Western" orders apart as to bring two kinds of powers within a *single* cosmic order into controlled contact with one another. Gods of the heavens and gods of the underworld each bear their own kinds of dangers, dangers deriving from their generative and transformative powers, from their roles in foundational "first time" events, and from their association with (or opposition to) the kinds of power wielded by the urban-national-priestly sector. The yatiri, sponsor, and authority share the task of manipulating such godly powers to the benefit of the local community. This task involves engagement not only with generative forces of the earth and sky but also with the powers of church and state and "world system"; through ritual means, such K'ulta ritual-political specialists also become kinds of historians, capable of recasting their position in the present by manipulating and reformulating the past.

Yatiris are therefore kinds of specialists in history, masters of the arts of social memory, and their libation-sequence "paths of memory" are keys to the genealogies of gods and men, social structures, and the meaning of events. Yatiris tend also to specialize in storytelling and are especially fluent in accounts of foundational moments that took place in the distant past. Many such stories are linked directly to specific places on the K'ulta landscape, places that are themselves gods that require drink in libation sequences.

Libation-sequence memory paths serve as one form of K'ulta chronotope, a conventional understanding of the relationship between time (*cronos*), space (*topos*), and agency (of the person whose life-journey charts a path in time and space), such as those that Bakhtin describes for certain forms of the novel (for instance, the Spanish picaresque). Through performance of memorized sequences of libations, the K'ulta memory path becomes a form of historical consciousness with remarkable properties. By mentally moving along the trajectory of deity-places named in a libation sequence, K'ultas move from the here and now backwards in time and outwards in space and, paradoxically, also towards the future. Like a trip along the inside-outside of a Möbius strip, these mental journeys abolish temporal distance and bring the visible past into the present while projecting it towards the invisible future.

Remarkable as they are, however, such journeys along K'ulta memory paths do not abolish the Spanish invasion and the long history of colonialism. Indeed, the relationship of indian and Spaniard, of the Chullpa underworld and the Christian sky, is as deeply implicated in K'ulta historical consciousness as it is in local institutions like the town council and saints' festivals. K'ulta memory paths, the sacrificial saints' festivals in which they take place, and the verbal narratives about the past told in the form of myth can best be seen as efforts to come to grips with colonial and postcolonial situations, to internalize the logics implicated in the systems of inequality in which K'ulta and K'ultas must exist, and to construe themselves as effective social agents in and of that world. To be adequate, an analysis of K'ulta's cultural forms must take account of these imbalances of power and, like the people of K'ulta, understand the impact of those imbalances on the constituted social world. At the same time, such an analysis, like that carried out by K'ultas in their own media, must achieve historical understanding. It would not do to privilege one or another strand of the complex intercultural weave that colonialism produced, to subordinate K'ulta chronotopes to the chronologic of the West, or, the opposite, to claim that K'ulta history is superior to the historian's book. Instead, one must acknowledge their differences and similarities while building up a comparative understanding. Thus I prefer to develop two different sorts of accounts, each internally multiple and laced with dissent and contradiction, rather than producing a single interwoven narrative.

As, by describing in this text forms of social memory that are culturally K'ulta, I seek to build up an intercultural understanding, I also, then, seek to understand the "interculture" in which K'ultas participate. Like an "intertext," this interculture must be found in the convergences and intercommentaries produced over time by K'ultas and their interlocutors on the temporal relationship between colonized indigenous and colonizing Christian or Spanish presumptive ancestors.[17]

The interculture to which I refer was produced through centuries'-long interactions along a cultural frontier that has been the site of a great deal of violence, exploitation, resistance, and accommodation. Its relative indian and Spanish poles have been invented as contrasts of race, ethnicity, class, and estate. Such contrasts were required by colonialism and reinforced by Spaniards' need to prevent indians from becoming Spaniards and indians' simultaneous efforts to resist Spanish civilizing and Christianizing strategies. Spanish colonials sought to impose Christianity and civilization on Andeans and to enforce orthodoxy in belief and practice, importing to the Andes not only Catholicism but also the Counter-Reformation. Under such circumstances, discourse between asymmetrically empowered cultural "others" entrenched a relationship between clandestine and public, between "pagan" and "Christian" activities and powers, making this relationship into a reflex of cosmological principles that were first established when the colonial cosmos was brought into being.

Thus town councils, saints as intercessors, and a sacrificial Eucharist performed for the Solar-Christ have become means of harnessing the magical power of history for the transformation of the present and assurance of the future. Over the centuries a relatively Hispanic, state- and church-linked sphere has become just as necessary in indian constructions of their own identities as a magic-inflected indian sphere tied to earth deities has become for the nationalist ideologues of the creole state.

This is not the place to explore in depth how this interculture works within the meaning contexts of the city and the national political scene; I reserve such an endeavor for another book.[18] Yet as I have elsewhere argued, one can see in urban nationalist pageantry as in K'ulta sacrificial rite, how memories of founding days are "hegemonic fictions read into the past as an outcome of the ideological struggles of the present—an invented tradition, fictions held by both Christianized Indians, such as those of [the Andes], and the Church, as well as by the colonists as a group" (Taussig 1987: 377). Yet if "history has put memory at the service of colonization," certain kinds of intercultural shamanism may yet be able to rework or undo "the history of sorcery with its memory" (ibid., 391–392). In part 3, I will discuss at length how K'ulta ritual forms seek to do just that.

Fortunately we are seeing less and less of an anthropological sorcery that strives to do the same, by rescuing the purely "indian/Andean" through magically making the Spanish and the Christian disappear. It would not have been difficult here to have stripped away references to saints' festivals and town councils, cantóns and corregidors, in favor of a language of ayllu and jilaqata, sacrifices and generative substances, sun, moon, and mountain gods. True, I might thereby have construed yet another example of successful Andean cultural resistance, but I would also have engaged once again in an anthropological romance that seeks out the maximally "other" other, a satisfying proof of the fallibility of cultural imperialism and the shallow emptiness of Western culture. Instead, I became convinced that a K'ulta cosmology and philosophy of history rest on understanding the relationship between underworld and heavens, between more-Christian and less-Christian beings and powers, and between domestic and collective spheres. And all these mediations are accomplished by understanding and manipulating the relationship between the present and the past, by engaging the services of social memory.

FROM HISTORICAL CONSCIOUSNESS TO A HISTORY OF K'ULTA

Unlike a former anthropological romance, the historical consciousness in K'ulta eucharistic sacrifices and libation journeys through space in time actively remembers events of conquest and colonialism and construes Christ, fiesta-cargo systems, and cantóns as critical features of K'ultas' lives, as important as mountain gods and ayllus. Their constructions of their past do not lead back to the glories of an Inca empire or Aymara kingdoms. A long colonial and republican history has intervened between the pre-Columbian past as it is known by Western historical canons and the past as it is construed by K'ultas, and the latter can best be understood as a product of the long-running intercultural discourse in which it is still engaged.[19]

In K'ulta the past lives on in a variety of modes, it is present in the gods of mountains and plains from the distant past, who surge into the present in the landscape itself, in the relatively anecdotal recounting of events from individual experience, in the ancestral wisdom of myth, and in the genealogies of persons as well as in those of the gods. The people of K'ulta also call upon personal and collective stores of written documents, often held as guarantors of rights as well as of memory. As among ourselves, long-past events, those which no living person has witnessed, are recalled to help inform the present, whether to bolster the conviction that things are rightly so the way they are or to explain why some situations must be avoided. Also as among ourselves, certain specialists are considered particularly authoritative in the historian's craft, which in K'ulta consists especially in the arts of memory.

Memories, however, are best kept when well-ordered, and best ordered when they are carefully selected. The arts of memory, that is, require not only remembering but also what might be called structured forgetting. This was made abundantly clear to me when I asked questions in a vein that might have led my interlocutors in K'ulta to dredge up stories of how things might have been before the Spaniards came. By reading works of ethnohistory, I knew that the ancestors of the people of K'ulta must once have belonged to one of the large, dual-organized federations of "kingdoms" that were incorporated into the Inca empire not long before the Spanish invasion of the Andes. I knew as well that the populations of such polities were resettled from far-flung hamlets into towns like Santa Bárbara de Culta by Spanish colonists, where colonial officials came to collect tribute, to levy labor for mines, and to indoctrinate indians into the Catholic faith. For at least two hundred years after the Spanish conquest, these now-colonized peoples were ruled indirectly by descendants of the hereditary authorities, who Spaniards called caciques. Without knowing any of the details of the particular case of K'ulta, I was certain of those basic historical facts.

I found, however, that the people of K'ulta would have none of it. When I asked about the history of the town itself, I was told a story about a miracle in which the image of Santa Bárbara had appeared to a shepherd, and then refused to be moved from the spot where her church was eventually built.[20] When I asked about the Incas, I found that the only ones most people had heard of were stones, the ones that were especially good as ammunition for slings during fights.[21] Only one man had heard of the Incas as a people, conquered by Spaniards long ago. He expressed some sympathy for those unfortunate folk he had learned about from the schoolteacher, and then related a story of another conquered people he knew about. He thought of neither group as ancestral to his own people. Queries about hereditary caciques elicited only unknowing shrugs. The word "mallku," the Aymara title for such lords recorded by early Spanish writers, struck a familiar note, but in reference to condors and mountain gods, not humans. When I asked about the distant ancestors of modern K'ultas, the ones who lived here before the Spaniards and before Christianity had arrived, my interlocutors became indignant.

As far as the people of K'ulta are concerned, they are surely Christians, and so, too, were all their ancestors. To suggest otherwise is taken as an insult, an imputation against local honor. It is just the sort of thing that visiting priests and urban elites say about and to them. Several individuals told me that, of course, they had heard about the non-Christian people who lived before the coming of Christ. I then heard the story of Christ's coming, in the form of the sun, and his conquest of the Chullpa people. Although the Chullpas were not Christians, they were most assuredly not the ancestors of anyone in K'ulta. I was told that the only descendants of those early people were certain fishermen on Lake Poopó who are deprecated for their primitive ways at the same time that they are feared for their ties to primordial powers, powers that also give them a privileged place among shamanic sorcerers. Unlike the Chullpas and Urus, the people of K'ulta, I was repeatedly told, came *after* Father Christ, as Spaniards did.

Frustrated in such efforts to square even the roughest "ethnohistorical" chronology with local historical consciousness, I eventually learned to listen patiently, in the proper contexts, rather than to pursue unwelcome lines of questioning. Thus, I eventually did hear some clues that would be useful to me in my efforts to reconstruct K'ulta's past, by pointing me in the right directions while I did archival research. I also, however, learned that K'ulta ways of reckoning the past are for them as valid as and more satisfying than the "factually" trustworthy chronology of events that I worked towards for my own purposes. In retrospect, it's clear that my purposes, as a historian, are rather more like those of the chroniclers among the Spanish conquerors than those of the indians they conquered. The story of the fall of a great pre-Columbian empire to a small band of European adventurers, and the subsequently directed acculturation of the former by the latter, is one that Spaniards (and creoles) may like to hear but is not so edifying to the conquered. The people of K'ulta have other ways of conceiving the past and its relationship to the present that suit them much better. And it is not, as one might suppose, simply to deny an ancestral defeat, but to learn from it, turning their past to their own purposes, as we do ours.

Historical consciousness is not limited in K'ulta to myth, genealogy, and libation sequence, but also draws upon the documentary record and "personal knowledge" oral history of relatively recent events. I heard stories about land wars, such as the one that had driven a wedge between K'ulta's moieties, about grandmothers struck by lightning, young men whose musical instruments had been charmed by sirens, and hauntings by local ghosts. Often, stories of local feuds opened towards the miraculous: One attempt by Ayllu Alax-Kawalli to secede from the remaining festival system in Santa Bárbara was foiled by the Virgin of Guadalupe, whose image brought such unrelenting bad weather to the Alax-Kawalli hamlet to which she had been "kidnapped" that her "thieves" voluntarily returned her to the Santa Bárbara church.

However, oral accounts of events involving named persons and actual ancestors reach back no further than four or five generations; they are far removed from forgotten people (and sometimes, forgotten social forms) whose stories are told in the documents of archives. In K'ulta I found no one versed in both mythic narrative and the history of documents who, like Paez described by Rappaport (1994) or Arnold's Qaqachaka "titleholder" (Arnold, Jiménez, and Yapita 1992), attempted systematically to harmonize written and oral accounts of the past. I did, however, find documents in the hands of K'ultas and a profound respect for the written word, especially for the kinds of documents that might detail and guarantee K'ulta rights to the lands on which they live. Apart from Cruce's Pablo Choquecallata, several other K'ulta authorities had journeyed to Sucre, La Paz, and even to Lima to scour the archives for "original" copies of colonial land titles that might be used to defend local boundaries. While I searched out the structures and meanings of a K'ulta historical consciousness, accounts such as these also served as sources for my own historical endeavors, bits of "data" abstracted from the meaning contexts in which I heard of them, and as clues in a quest for a history of K'ulta according to Western canons.

By following a K'ulta ritual pilgrimage to Condo and the mountain called Asanaqi and by reading the parish registers kept in the Condo church, I was able to envision a research path that, like the memory paths of K'ulta libation sequences, led at the same time away from K'ulta and into a still-visible past. For K'ultas, of course, the sacred "resting places" along their ritual pathways are physical and topographic, objects that in their invisible interiors still pulse with breath and life from signally important past events, veritable repositories of historical process. On my journey, following the pathway of colonial messengers and documents as well as K'ulta authorities in their quests for legally valid land titles, the resting places were the sacred sites of historians, the archives of colonial church, province, judicial capital, and of the Spanish metropole itself. In those places, the dusty breath of the past speaks out in a cacophony of voices, mostly Spanish ones, and is terribly cluttered with legalistic stock phrases and bureaucratic niceties. Only occasionally does a native voice (almost always interpreted, translated, and shaped for a Spanish audience) rise momentarily above the noise.

As I learned about K'ulta ways of thinking about the past and also of certain customary activities in the present, I was not always stymied in the search for clues for my own historical endeavors. True, the people of K'ulta did not recall a glorious Inca past or accept that they descended directly from pre-Christian peoples. But exposure to some of the means by which K'ultas regard the past led to less-distant connections that oriented me in archival research. Let us see, then, some of the ways that another people's cultural heritage, the contents of their social memory, can be mined as building blocks for our own constructs in cultural history.

One of the duties of authorities in K'ulta is the preservation of document bundles, which few can read but all revere. Thought to contain the community's titles to land, such bundles hold varying sorts of documents, sometimes contained within one another as parts of law suits and legal petitions. One document that I was able to read and study—the Choque-callata document described in a chapter 1 vignette—was thought to contain land titles granted by the king of Spain. It did. Composed of imbedded documents from the sixteenth to the twentieth century, it also recorded the efforts of many generations of authorities to safeguard their peoples' land claims. But the maximal authorities of the document were hereditary lords, mallkus, of an entity called Asanaqi, its capital in Condo. This was a surprise to my audience.

San Pedro de Condo, as well as Asanaqi, came up in other contexts as well. Tata Asanaqi, "Father Asanaqi," was invariably at the head of a list of hierarchically named mountains libated in the ritual sequences the people of K'ulta call memory paths. As a potent mountain deity, he is also addressed as mallku, once the title applied to hereditary lords of Aymara diarchies, now a kind of god (and the form that the mountain god sometimes takes, that of the male condor, also called mallku). Then too there was the customary ritual practice of the jilaqatas that required them to travel in a group each year to attend mass in the church of Condo during the fiesta of San Pedro. In fact, they had gone there without my knowledge while I waited to meet with the town council during my first month of fieldwork. I later learned that they had walked the fifty kilometers to San Pedro de Condo, so that their varas, or staffs of office, could hear the mass. I inquired further, of course, as to what Condo, Saint Peter, and Tata Asanaqi had to do with the jilaqatas and their varas. Indeed, in 1988 I had an opportunity to discuss such matters with two of K'ulta's jilaqatas while they awaited the arrival of the priest for the fiesta of San Pedro in Condo itself (see Photograph 4.4). I learned

Photograph 4.4.   K'ulta jilaqatas pour libations in the churchyard during the fiesta of San Pedro in Condo. After walking to Condo with their varas and carrying whips, jilaqatas of K'ulta drink puro from a bottle in honor of the cross in Condo's arcaded colonial churchyard. They await the mass, during which their varas (now resting inside at the feet of the patron saint) will hear the mass in honor of San Pedro, whom they address with the name of the mountain that looms above Condo, Tata Asanaqi. San Pedro de Condo, June 29, 1988. (Photograph by author)

only that the journey was required because the varas *need* to hear this mass and must pay respects both to the great mallku, Father Asanaqi, and to the holder of the key to heaven, Saint Peter, to whom that festival mass is dedicated.

In K'ulta as well as in Quntu (Condo), Tata Asanaqi is considered to be the most powerful mallku in the region. We shall see that this shared homage bespeaks a common past that guides and empowers the present. For it is through acts such as this sacred pilgrimage that the varas, called *tata reyes* in the ritual language of libations, are transformed into something more than mere emblems of office, and the authorities into something more than just tax-collecting officials.[22]

We have seen that authorities like jilaqatas are "elected" to office through a long-term ritual apprenticeship involving the performance of saints' fiestas. Among other ritual duties, the jilaqata-to-be performs a great number of llama sacrifices, mostly during calendric rites. Such sacrifices always include dedications of alcohol and chicha libations (ch'allas). Some libations are poured to the saints and the gods of above, most especially to Jesus Christ and the Virgin Mary. Interwoven with them, however, are many libations to gods of manxa-pacha, the underworld. Always such libations are performed in an orderly series of hierarchies, naming first the local gods of men, the altar, guardian hill, and mallku mountains of the performers, followed by dedications to similar hierarchies of place deities pertaining to the herd animals, foodstuffs, and the performer's male and female ancestral lines. In the context of the place deities of libators, the top of the hierarchy is almost invariably the mallku Tata Asanaqi. Just behind Tata Asanaqi in status comes the most powerful *local* mallku, a mountain very close to the town of Santa Bárbara de Culta called Pirwan Tata, "Father Storehouse." In the ritual language of libations, this mallku is called Churi Asanaqi. Now, "churi" is a Quechua, not an Aymara, term, meaning "son."[23] As we shall see, this way of expressing a hierarchic relationship between Quntu and K'ulta reflects historical circumstances, for both authorities and gods of K'ulta were once validated in San Pedro de Condo.

Two of K'ulta's jilaqatas told me that they were not the only ones to make the pilgrimage to the town of Condo. Jilaqatas from the nearby towns of Cacachaca, Challapata, Cahuayo, and Lagunillas had also traditionally carried their varas to Condo's church, although the attendance of some had been irregular in recent years.[24] Queries about nearby towns, those within the territory described in the colonial land title, the same ones that sent jilaqatas to Condo, produced yet further clues. I had already learned that among the ayllus of Condo were some that shared the same names as those of K'ulta. My K'ulta friends assured me that these like-named ayllus were in no sense "the same," but at the same time they acknowledged a distant connection between the two places. Seeking explanations beyond shrugs in regard to the coincidence of ayllu names or the self-evident power of a great mountain and a powerful saint celebrated at the fiesta in Condo, I chose to follow the social organizational evidence of the land title, which I felt might account for both ayllu names and mountain hierarchy.

About eight months into my fieldwork, I was able to leaf through the parish registers kept in a chest of valuables in Culta's church, jealously guarded by K'ulta's mayordomos. They were interesting but recent. "Book one" of priests' records of baptisms, marriages, and funerals dated only to the last quarter of the eighteenth century, when Culta was erected as an autonomous ecclesiastic unit, a *doctrina* or rural parish. My curiosity next took me to Condo, where under the watchful gaze of four mayordomos I was able to scan a few parish registers, beginning with that town's "book one," dating to 1571.[25] Although all of K'ulta's ayllus were listed there, along with ayllus not present in K'ulta but found in other towns of the area, there was no mention of the town of Santa Bárbara de Culta. Later baptismal registers of the seventeenth and eighteenth centuries, however, did contain references to a series of vice-parishes visited periodically by the priest of Condo. Alongside the vice-parishes of Cacachaca, Cahuayo, and Lagunillas, Culta first appears as Santa Bárbara de Aguas Calientes. Apparently, its current icy artesian springs were once hot.[26] It also appeared that Cantón Culta/Ayllu K'ulta was a late arrival on the territorial scene, very probably a historical descendant of the larger entity called Asanaqi, produced through some process of political subdivision. Only in the pilgrimage with varas and the libation to mountain gods can we see a memory of a former regionwide political entity called Asanaqi, recalled from a time before historical contingencies—and, in particular, activist town councils—rent it into pieces.[27]

By the end of December, I had made significant progress towards understanding festivals and sacrifices, saints and underworld gods, herders and foxes. As to history, I had amassed leads that pointed in two very different research directions. One set of facts—the jilaqatas' ritual duties in Condo, the homonymous ayllu names in K'ulta/Culta, Quntu/Condo, Qakachaka/Cacachaca, and Challapata, the reverence displayed in K'ulta for the mountain called Tata Asanaqi, and the knowledge that K'ulta/Culta had once "pertained" to Quntu/Condo—led towards a need for archival research to uncover the historical basis for such connections. But other data led in a different direction. With few exceptions, K'ultas have little interest in documentary investigation of K'ulta's origins in pre-Columbian polities, largely, it seems, because they already possess valued and trusted techniques and media for the structuring and preservation of historical knowledge: The story of the origin of modern humanity after the defeat of Chullpa people by the Solar-Christ, tales of the exploits of wild animals that seem linked to ideas about contemporary kinship and affinal relations in a way that historically valorizes them, the profound interest in genealogy, the "roots" of sacred places, and the arts of memory in libation sequences, all suggest that an authentic "ethnohistory" of K'ulta already exists: their own.

These techniques and media do not, however, tell a single story, but many interlaced though divergent ones, linked to individual, patriline, ayllu, and cantonal pasts. Factional disputes have multiplied these divergences and have created yet more separate pasts to underwrite the separatist futures of annexes and ayllus seeking an autonomous existence. Sometimes, stories about interayllu fights recall more than just a structured ritual opposition; they trace moments of definitive rupture. At the same time, a generational divide cuts across these other kinds of historical heterogeneity, with increasing numbers of disaffected youths, schooled and ambitious, questioning the efficacy of the old techniques. Some are tempted to convert to one or another form of evangelic Protestantism, as Manuel Mamani did between the time I left K'ulta in 1982 and my return in 1988. Others, especially those young traders seeking to make and keep a large profit from the textile business, search for new kinds of libations and new kinds of sacrifices, such as those performed by miners and the urban "popular classes," that might help them to achieve goals and ambitions of which their fathers never dreamed.

Sometimes, indeed, the new rituals developed by such dissenters appear to their elders as kinds of diabolical antirituals. Many young traders now keep a skull, taken from the cemetery, in their storehouse, where it serves as a macabre sort of bank. Placing their dollars between their skull's closed jaws, they pour libations and burn incense to it on the Tuesdays and Fridays when evil forces are most active, in order to cause the money to come back to them and grow. Many older K'ultas are aghast at such behavior, which inverts their values. For them, Tuesdays and Fridays are days of evil sorcery. And to remove skulls from the cemetery is not only a sacrilege against the ancestors but also a positive danger, since exposing them to the sky can cause the rains to fail.

The techniques and contents of social memory that I describe in this book are active and changing tools, not inert traditions. The forms that I describe here, and thereby freeze in time, belong to one brief moment in a continuing process of creative collective transformation. As such, they *have* histories, as well as make them.

In subsequent visits to K'ulta and to archives in Bolivia and Spain, I set myself, then, to a double purpose. On the one hand, I began a sometimes dry and tedious investigation, according to the lights of a Western historical canon, of the documentary record produced by Spanish colonial scribes, which, if laid out alongside other advances in archaeology and "ethnohistory" on this Andean region, might tell a

K'ulta story as a congruent supplement to the stories we tell ourselves about the Spanish and Amerindian past. On the other hand, I strove to use the techniques of the ethnographer to appreciate K'ulta brands of history and to plumb not only their multiple conclusions but also their techniques. It is my hope that the gap between these accounts (a gap unavoidably narrowed by the fact that both accounts flow from my pen in the final instance) may serve not to undermine but to supplement each one, and perhaps to cast a critical shadow over the interpretive effects that have ensued from the manner in which indigenous cultural forms have been (mis)placed in time by Spaniards and creoles, historians and ethnographers.

The forms of K'ulta historical consciousness developed in narratives and embedded in rituals, however, may be most intelligible to non-Andeans when we are better disposed to appreciate the conditions in which they have been forged. I offer in part 2 what, to most readers, will be a familiar sort of historical presentation, drawing on documents and interpreting them according to disciplinary canons. Subsequently in part 3, the conclusions of this investigation may then be confronted with my constructions of the less-familiar K'ulta styles of doing history.

Part Two

Historical Paths to K'ulta:
An Andean Social Formation
from Preinvasion Autonomy to
Postrevolution Atomization

Chapter Five

Pathways of Historical Colonization

Stories of an Andean Past from the Archives of Letters and Landscapes

> *Recollection of the past is an active, constructive process, not a simple matter of retrieving information. To remember is to place a part of the past in the service of conceptions and needs of the present.*
> —Barry Schwartz, "The Social Context of Commemoration"

One of my purposes in this chapter is to plumb the Spanish documentary social memory of archives and chronicles for what they might tell us about K'ulta's past.* At the same time, however, I aim to sketch what forms social memory has taken in the Andes. I do so, at least, to the limited degree possible for pre-Columbian and colonial times and, foreshadowing the substance of part 3, the present. I endeavor to juxtapose Spanish colonial and colonized Andean ways of registering the past, not to contrast them as written versus oral, modern versus traditional, or "European" versus "native," but to highlight the convergences of as well as the differences between ways of putting the past to work for the purposes of the present. Above all I seek here to understand the mutual interferences between Spanish and Andean forms of social memory, to help explain how it was (and is) that two "traditions" in contact over a period of centuries can have so largely failed to register one another. Yet, while I may characterize Spanish and Andean techniques of social memory to highlight their similarities and differences, I also strive to foreground one of their most misunderstood patterns of congruence: Neither Spanish nor Andean ways of thinking about the past were (or are) homogeneous. In Spain as in the Andes, doing history has been a contentious affair.

*All the translations of Spanish sources in part 2 are my own unless otherwise noted in the References.

129

Andeans came to value writing, and Spaniards did seek out Andean pasts in indians' oral narratives. But neither came to displace or encompass the other completely. At first sight, it might appear that the people of K'ulta have been deprived of their past. They know Asanaqi and Killaka only as the names of a mountain and a miracle-working saint in a town they think named for him (Santuario de Quillacas, where the image of Tata Quillacas is kept), and they register no memory of mit'a journeys along the qapaq ñan to a fabulous Cusco or of hereditary rulers like Guarache, who ruled over K'ulta territory as a small part of a great pre-Spanish federation. They have instead remembered things differently. By querying K'ultas, it is possible to know the past that they make and what they make of that past.

Drawing on a variety of written sources may make it possible to construct a story about K'ulta's distant past, its prehistory, so to speak, but it may not be possible to understand the pasts of K'ultas' ancestors in the way they do. As I have suggested, most of the forms of social memory in K'ulta are not inscribed on paper, and much of their meaning world is not even construed or construable through oral narrative in the form of stories. Instead, it is to be found in the landscape around them. Through the ways that they walk on it, pour libations to it, name it, and live on it, K'ultas embody in that landscape the lineaments of genealogy and the heritage of their social groups.

Only a few extraordinarily perspicacious Spanish chroniclers began to discover such Andean matters or to write about them. For the most part, Spaniards, who thought of history in terms of books, especially the Book, would have had difficulty in grasping how histories encoded in three-dimensional objects and practices (such as quipus, ceques, queros [wooden chicha vessels], cumbi, and pilgrimage rites at wak'a sites) might be understood. Oral narratives constituted a more familiar genre of historical knowledge, but not in the way Andeans told (sang and danced) them. And of course no Spaniard could put aside the notion that all such practices were connected to that which they called idolatry, superstition, and error.

In any case, not even the most insightful Spanish chronicler actually aimed to understand, as an end in itself, how Andeans recalled their past. When Spaniards made inquiries, they did so in order to achieve pragmatic ends (to collect tributes, to determine which properties might be seized, or to search for buried wak'a loot). Their goal in uncovering the Andean past was usually to destroy it rather than to record it.

Spaniards did engage in methodical rescue of certain kinds of Andean oral narrative, in order to systematize it and discover whether or not it might be squeezed, like a round peg into a square hole, into their own universal history. Often enough, they sought out in Andean narrative providentialist evidence of the Christian God's presence in the Andes before the conquest in order to foreshadow and legitimate their own enterprise there, and perhaps to account for some of the otherwise inexplicable greatness and signs of civilization that they found in the Andes.

Almost all such endeavors, unfortunately, were concentrated on the imperial Incas and their capital of Cusco. The memory work of non-Inca peoples was of very little interest, except as something to be eradicated. Among the texts at our disposal that make reference to preconquest times, there is a great quantity of information on the Incas and very little on the peoples of Qullasuyu, and all of it must be treated with great care. Very little can have escaped transformation in the colonial process of inscription. A host of serious scholars have applied rigorous techniques of inquiry to those sources, tweezing out Spanish influences here, separating truly pre-Columbian information there. My interpretation of the pre-Columbian Andes is based largely on the work of those who specialize in retrieving such information from "contaminated" sources. I then consider the process of contamination itself to plumb the effects of the colonial relationships that produced our documents.

Our efforts to read the documented past of the Aymara-speaking peoples south of Cusco must proceed first to uncover the particularly Spanish meanings and uses of the writings they bequeathed us. We may then ponder what they did and did not learn about Inca life-ways and Inca forms of social memory. That done, we will be in a far better position to plumb the pre- and non-Inca social forms, such as those found in Asanaqi, and subsequently to trace colonial and postcolonial transmutations of sociocultural life. From our vantage (though not from a K'ulta perspective), the pathways in space-time that connect K'ulta's present with its pre-Columbian past intersect not only the Cusco of Huayna Capac but also the Castile of Charles V.

THE CONQUEST MOMENT: A CONFLICT OF HISTORIES

It may appear on first sight that K'ultas suffer from historical amnesia, since they do not recall a glorious past of hereditary native lords, pre-Columbian autonomies, or their ancestors' heroic resistance to Spanish conquest. Yet they tell a "first-time" story that does seem to bear upon the Spanish conquest of Andeans. It is a mythic narrative that tells of ancient times, when the soggy and dark earth was inhabited by a people called Supay-Chullpas. These almost precultural beings—who lacked what K'ultas take to be the essence of their own lives: mortality, animal herds, and an agricultural life regulated by the seasons—were visited by an old stranger named Tatala. The latter is also referred to as Jesucristo, and when the Supay-Chullpas sought to kill him, he did not die but escaped them and, rising into the sky as the sun in the first dawn, destroyed the Chullpas, sending the survivors into the wet and dark underworld, where they still exist.

Very clearly the story has sources both in pre-Columbian oral narrative and in biblical stories imparted by Spanish priests. Told and retold over many generations, it has become an account of the colonial situation itself. Let us begin to sketch our own history of that situation, by turning to the conquest moment of which K'ulta storytellers speak.

Invading Iberians: Feudal Values and Modern Bureaucracy

The unification of Castile and Aragón in the marriage of Ferdinand and Isabel set the stage for the completion, at Granada in 1492, of what had been a slow process of displacement of Moorish control over peoples of the Iberian Peninsula by Castilian, Catalán, and Galician overlords. Although this process is often called the Spanish reconquest, it is in fact a mistake to imagine the existence of a political entity called Spain much in advance of the reconquest's end.

Centuries of reconquest created a "society organized for war," which was also oriented towards religious conversion. To encourage military campaigns in and settlement of the ever-moving southern marches, Christian kings had offered concessions to the military nobility, as well as to the settlers of the towns established on the fortified frontier. We shall later explore the nature of the rights claimed by noblemen to "caretaking" and tax collecting of the inhabitants of the encomiendas and señoríos, the lordly domains granted to them by kings during the reconquest and the competing rights granted to townsmen—and Spaniards were insistently townsmen—by virtue of the fueros, or written constitutions, granted to them by the Crown. Here it is enough to note that the existence of such concessions of power to nobles and towns alike created a serious obstacle to the consolidation of royal prerogative, even after the unification of Castile and Aragón in 1469. It is no accident that the unification of the crowns and the completion of the reconquest (in 1492) coincided with royal efforts to wrest power back from overweening nobles and town councils in order to invest it in a more centralist state apparatus. Under Ferdinand and Isabel, and then their

Habsburg grandson Charles and his son, Philip, nobles were drawn by a combination of threat and enticement away from their castles and into the patrimonial court, while the towns were progressively stripped of their autonomies and made subject to royal administrators called co-regidores.[1]

The election of Charles I of Castile to the crown of the Holy Roman Empire and an attempt to manipulate the voting rights of town representatives in the cortes, the parliament through which royals obtained their subjects' consent in state matters, led to a final outburst of violence in the ill-fated revolution of the communities of 1520 (Haliczer 1981; Maravall 1963), just as Hernán Cortés was venturing into the Aztec realm far to the west. As Charles V, Holy Roman Emperor, the new king presided by virtue of a legitimacy granted by the pope over a Catholic realm with universal pretensions. It was his duty to convert the Indies and to hold fast against Protestantism in the north.

The Crown was enveloped in a vast new bureaucracy; through it, Europe's first centralized absolutist monarchy became more adept at taxation, took direct control over castles, and installed salaried royal representatives to rule the towns. Consubstantial with the centralization of the Crown and the development of the bureaucracy, Castilian monarchs were leaders in the cataloguing, visiting, and representation of their realms. Philip II can be credited with the invention of the questionnaire, created to help take account of his vast territory. The "geographic relations" thereby produced were to be housed in a new palace and symbol of empire, a building called El Escorial.[2] It was adorned with views of Spanish cities (as they might have been seen from a bird's-eye view) and large-scale painted maps of the provinces in the domain that is represented (Kagan 1986), thus becoming a visual and architectural icon of the surveillance and encompassment possible only by focusing the gaze of the state into the private lives of the king's subjects. Such efforts at global summary were an important complement to the daunting bulk of archival documents that crowded the shelves of the Crown archive in the old castle of Simancas (see Kagan 1981; Guevara-Gil and Salomon 1994).[3]

The completion of the reconquest and consolidation of a bureaucratic state, however, did not lead to a significant change in the values by which an aristocratic elite distinguished itself from lowly plebeians (Bennassar 1979). Within Castile, the kingdom from which state structures were extended to the rest of empire, there was no lessening of aristocratic disdain for plebeian manual labor, and possibilities there for the emergence of an entrepreneurial bourgeoisie (which elsewhere led to revolutions both bourgeois and industrial) were slight. Indeed, while the unification of crowns and the squashing of the *comunero* rebels had reduced Castile's need for fortresses and city walls, the new frontier of the Indies provided an alternative outlet for Spain's legion of would-be nobles, a new arena full of infidels to be subdued, where warrior virtues could still lead to ennoblement and, as Sancho Panza hoped for as a Crown reward for helping Quixote in serving the king, insulae to govern. And just as the Crown's intake of American metal wealth underwrote its continued imperial pretensions against Protestant rebels in the north, new indian tributes and increased taxation of Spanish plebeians enabled the Crown to continue to purchase the loyalty of its more ambitious subjects, through grants of rents and honor-filled aristocratic titles.[4]

Spain rose out of fractious multiplicity just as, an ocean away, Tawantinsuyu did. Likewise, the rise and expansion of both empires hinged on the creation of a centralized state bureaucracy. But the Inca and Spanish empires were, of course, radically different, as were the constituent units out of which they were built. In contrast with the Andean case, it is much easier to characterize the kingdoms of Iberia and their unification under imperial rule, largely because the Iberians had inherited a system of writing from an earlier empire, whereas the Andeans had not. The absence of written preconquest sources on the Andes, however, is not our only obstacle. For the written sources we do have *on,* but not *of,* the preconquest Andes were for the most part produced by Spaniards, and in the Castilian language. They were also produced not simply for a Spanish readership but for an official Spanish readership, for the archive. Spanish accounts of things Andean involve the translation of alien concepts into familiar ones, whether intentionally, to establish a familiar ground for readers, or unintentionally, because the writers were blocked by their own ethnocentrism from apprehending an unfamiliar reality in its own terms.

Atahuallpa, whom Andeans called Sapa Inca, became for Spaniards "el Rey Inca"; his empire, Tawantinsuyu, became a *"reino,"* a monarchy. Lesser, regionally powerful hereditary rulers, those whom Andeans called mallkus and kuraqas, became *"señores naturales"* to Spaniards, soon simply called caciques, after a Taino term for chieftain. These were regarded by Spaniards as an Andean analogue of Iberian noblemen, while the social units headed by mallkus and kuraqas were interpreted as "señorios," lordly domains, like those which many conquistadors aspired to govern through an ennobling *merced*, a grant by the king rewarding their loyalty and service to the Crown in the Andean enterprise.

Just as they found in the Andes an analogue to the Iberian aristocratic estate, so too did Spaniards find equivalents for Spain's priests and tribute-paying vassals. Given conquistadors' designs in the Andes, their attitude towards "native lords" was deeply ambivalent. But towards native "priests" and "plebeians," there was much greater clarity. Conquistador religious intolerance, heightened by the religious justifications for conquest in the first place, turned indian priests into devil-inspired pagan dogmatizers and sorcerers, to be eliminated as quickly as possible. Indian tributaries, on the other hand, were a blessing, once the conquistador and Crown could interpose themselves between the "native lord" and his indian "tributaries."

These initial identifications, of native lords, native kings, native vassals, and native tributes, certainly aided both Spaniards and Andeans in making sense of their cultural interlocutors, but they also produced a vast gap in understanding. Such is the effect of cultural pidgins, the communicative vehicles of contact that are created through these hasty equations. Cross-cultural understanding and misunderstanding are simultaneous effects of this kind of communicative situation, which produces a meaning gap. The spark that jumps it can turn the motor of domination as well as the motor of resistance. A few perspicacious Spanish and Andean authors sought to narrow it, but this kind of communication gap is narrowed only by heightening the cultural contrast, bringing difference into sharper relief. Fortunately the paper-happy colonial bureaucracy archived ample clues about just where the equations of cultural translation were least successful; that is where we must look for colonial Andean meaning worlds.

For various reasons (which cannot be fully summarized in the words "colony" and "empire"), the Spanish state did not choose to extend the discovery of coincident institutions to full recognition of Andean equivalents to Spanish social forms. The Crown might have simply granted to native lords the titles and emoluments of Spanish nobility, and transformed mallku into señor, *mallkuña* into señorío. But formidable obstacles lay in the path of such a maneuver. On the one hand, there was the question of native loyalties and the problem of the missionary project that underlay the whole colonial enterprise. It was inconceivable to do without Spanish supervision of the process of civilization and conversion. And a yet more intransigent barrier to an Inca-like indirect form of rule was to be found in the Spaniards themselves, both in those who had migrated to the Indies and those who had invested in the enterprise of colonialism: A multitude of relatively poor and lowly Spaniards hoped to displace the native lords in order to become enriched and ennobled themselves.

In fact, the combined social and scriptural techniques that Spaniards used to achieve their social-climbing goals had already been routinized and legalized in the Caribbean and in New Spain before the Pizarro-Almagro expedition was outfitted for the exploration of the South American Pacific coast. Numerous powerful investors had sunk good money into the project of conquest, and most members of the expedition had nothing else on which to pin their hopes but the future tributes of indian vassals. The die was cast for Inca Tawantinsuyu, determining how it would be shaped by sword and word for Spanish imperial consumption, long before Spaniards made landfall on the coast of what they called Perú.

Although K'ultas do not remember it, some of their ancestors were deeply engaged with the Inca state project. So when Spaniards began their invasion of Tawantinsuyu in 1532, reaching places like Cajamarca and Cusco within a few years, they encountered peoples from Qullasuyu long before they actually conquered Asanaqi and Killaka. Just what happened during those years has been the focus of much historical writing, debate, and revisionism. Because the *relaciones* and *crónicas* that record conquest events were submitted in interested efforts to gain the king's favor, there are perhaps as many versions of the events I am about to describe as there are sources. The same can be said of indigenous sources on the same moments, which were also composed as parts of curriculum vitae. I will, nonetheless, attempt a synthesis, drawing on the work of other historians.

Spanish Incursions on the Inca Opulent Way

Scholars of postinvasion Perú often find themselves searching for explanations for what is commonly supposed to have been an astonishingly swift and easy conquest of a great empire by a small band of European adventurers. Accounts of Francisco Pizarro's conquest of the Incas invariably cite the superiority of Spanish weaponry and armor, a superiority grounded in part on Andeans' unfamiliarity not only with steel, gunpowder, and horses but also with audacious and treacherous Spanish strategies of warfare. Accounts also point to the Spaniards' extraordinary good luck, first in the early offshore capture of indians who later served as interpreters, and then, by virtue of the ensuing communication, of being in position to take advantage of deep divisions and resentments among Tawantinsuyu's varied peoples. Spaniards were also fortunate in arriving during a bitterly divisive succession struggle that pitted two potential heirs of a recently deceased Inca emperor against one another. What is more, this Inca war of succession took place against a backdrop of considerable internal dissatisfaction with Inca rule on the part of recently conquered Inca subjects. Many were all too eager to join with the Spaniards once they had captured the Inca leader, Atahuallpa.[5]

That decisive moment, concluded without the help of disaffected Inca subjects, was perhaps the greatest cause for wonder among all the events of conquest. Indeed, the capture of the great Inca lord, at a time when he was traveling with an army numbering in the tens of thousands, by Pizarro's puny band of Spaniards seems almost miraculous (although accounts of the Cajamarca events do not describe, as do those of the Spanish victory in the later rebel-Inca siege of Cusco, the intervention of saints [see Silverblatt 1988a]).

The event, however, must be taken neither as miracle nor as evidence that indians mistook Spaniards for gods, their horses for all-powerful demons, and their harquebuses for the power of thunder. For Atahuallpa had ensured that Spaniards were carefully watched, and kept an account of all the damage they had done, as well as a detailed list of the supplies they had removed from Inca storehouses. As the Spaniards prepared their trap in the Inca administrative town of Cajamarca, the Inca emperor and his vast retinue stalled for time on an open plain. Atahuallpa had agreed to a parley with the Spanish leader. He planned to enter Cajamarca only after sunset, when the Spaniards would be vulnerable, so he delayed, apparently because his spies had concluded that the horses were ineffective in the darkness (Hemming 1970).

Pizarro's response was to send out a messenger to convince Atahuallpa to enter the trap during daylight hours. The man chosen for the mission was one Hernando de Aldana, a relatively lowly Extremaduran whose linguistic talents made him, it appears, the first Spaniard to have learned the Quechua language.

Precisely what Aldana said to Atahuallpa was not recorded in surviving accounts. Apparently Atahuallpa asked for or attempted to seize Aldana's sword, and Aldana hurried back to the Cajamarca plaza (Lockhart 1972: 213). Following this parley, Atahuallpa mounted his litter and was carried into the plaza while there was still sufficient light for the Spaniards to aim their sword thrusts. Fray Vicente de Valverde, the priest who supposedly presented Atahuallpa with the book that doomed the Inca, remembered Hernando de Aldana as "the first and most important cause of Atahuallpa's capture."[6] Lockhart provides a capsule biography in his study of the Spanish men of Cajamarca:

> At the founding of Cusco in 1534 Aldana settled there and received a good *encomienda*. Within a few years he seemed on his way to becoming one of the principales or leading men of Peru. He performed well during the year-long siege of Cusco by the Indians, and in 1537 was on the city council, closely associated with the Pizarro party, as was normal in view of his Cáceres-Trujillo connections. Yet in the following years he was little heard of, and failed to cooperate with the rebellion of Gonzalo Pizarro in 1544. So alienated did he become that in 1546 a lieutenant of Gonzalo's hanged him for suspicion of plotting against the Pizarro cause. His death, accompanied by prolonged laments, was a pitiful spectacle that turned many against the rebellion once and for all. (Ibid., 213)

It is true that Hernando de Aldana was little heard of in Cusco between 1537 and his death in 1546, but that is a result of the peculiar identity of the encomienda granted to him in 1534, which pulled him away from the Cusco area and into Qullasuyu. For Aldana's prominent action in Cajamarca was rewarded with an encomienda, not in the Cusco area, but in the still-unconquered region to the south, the part of Qullasuyu that four years later came to be called the province of Charcas!

To understand this unlikely turn of events one must accompany Francisco Pizarro and his band of Spaniards (including Aldana) while they collected Atahuallpa's ransom (of which Aldana received a foot soldier's share), executed Atahuallpa, and then marched towards Cusco in triumph.

By the time they garroted Atahuallpa, Spaniards had been joined by vast numbers of indian allies, recently conquered or resentful Inca subjects (such as the Cañaris of the Quito region, the Huancas of the area around Jauja, and the followers of the now-murdered rival Inca Huascar, who had been mercilessly harassed by Atahuallpa's troops), who must have mistakenly regarded Spaniards as a means to achieve their liberty. Once Atahuallpa was dead, Pizarro crowned a replacement, a "puppet Inca" whose leadership might more swiftly bring all Inca Perú under Spanish control. The first appointee, however, died on the journey from Cajamarca to the Inca administrative city of Jauja, where massive stores of food and clothing provisioned Spanish troops. Once Jauja had been refounded as the new Spanish capital city (soon replaced by Lima), Pizarro set out, again with large numbers of indian "auxiliaries," to take Cusco.

Now, among the dispersed and terrified relatives and followers of Huascar, the Cusco-based claimant to the Inca throne, was a surviving son of Huayna Capac named Manco Inca. This Manco had disguised himself as a common indian to escape Cusco and death at the hands of Atahuallpa's armies. Not far outside Cusco in late 1533, Manco and a small retinue threw themselves at the mercy of Pizarro. Among the followers was Guarache, a hereditary lord, a mallku, from Qullasuyu. Guarache's son don Juan Colque Guarache, much favored by the Spaniards, related in his 1570s probanzas how his father Guarache had been a member of Manco's (and Huascar's?) "council of war," and how he delivered himself into Spanish hands at Manco's side.[7] One wonders if it was not Guarache who stepped forward first to negotiate Manco's surrender and, if so, whether the Quechua-speaking Aldana played a part in the event. At any rate, shortly afterwards Pizarro crowned Manco as the new puppet Inca emperor during ceremonies that gave Spaniards their first wide-eyed glimpse of Inca imperial rites.

During a month of banqueting in the great plaza, Manco Inca was accompanied by his mummified predecessors, each of whom received large quantities of the libations that the living offered to them (and drank for them). Miguel de Estete observed the proceedings of 1534:

> ... the deceased Incas, each accompanied by his own retainers, were
> carried into the square in a procession that was headed by Manco
> Inca in his litter with the litter containing Guayna Capac's mummy at
> his side. Having arrived in Haucaypata, the mummies were placed on
> their seats. The feasting, interspersed with sung recitations extolling
> the "conquests made by each one of these lords and his valor and
> accomplishments," began at sunrise and continued until dusk, when
> the mummies were escorted back to their abodes. The entire
> celebration lasted for over a month.[8]

Each mummy would have eaten and drunk with the rest of the celebrants, thus participating in death in the order of sacrifices and libations directed towards wak'as and other deities. In the center of the plaza, stone steps led to a throne of solid gold, on which Manco Inca sat; next to him was the *ushnu,* which was reduplicated in the plaza of every Inca city and administrative center. The ushnu was a kind of well, but rather than providing water, it received the ashes of burned food offerings and large amounts of corn beer. In this way the gods and mummies "ate and drank" their portions of such commensal banquets.

The liquid then flowed away through a system of covered canals that eventually, after passing through the temple of Qurikancha, emptied into the river (MacCormack 1991: 66–71). Like other Spanish witnesses of such rites, Estete was astounded by the power that Inca mummies continued to exert over the living, and by the quantities consumed. For Incas, this was an index of the exhaustiveness of the sacrifices made and libations dedicated. For Estete, however, it was extraordinary excess:

> There were so many people and . . . so much [chicha] in their [wine] skins, because their entire business is drinking without eating, that . . . two covered drainage canals more than half a vara wide that emptied out into the river and which must have been made for cleanliness and to drain off the rains . . . ran all day with the urine of those who urinated into them, and in such abundance as if they were springs that flowed there; certainly, given the amount that they drank, and the number of people who drank it, it is no wonder, although to see such a never before seen thing is cause for wonder. . . . These festivals lasted for more than thirty days running, and so much of that wine of theirs was consumed that, if it had been our wine, according to its cost, all the gold and silver that we took would have been insufficient to have paid for it. (Estete 1987: 141, quoted in Randall 1993: 86)[9]

And so the Andean libation rituals came to be inscribed as forms of excessive drinking, and memory techniques were taken for drunkenness and amnesia, even as the productive capacities that led to such massive consumption were deemed laudable. However, those activities that were associated with ritual drinking, such as taquies, the use of quipus, and all the public gatherings in which mallkus and kuraqas engaged in obligatory fêting of their people, were progressively assimilated specifically to "drunkenness" and generally to the devil-inspired vices such as idolatry that justified the Castilian colonial project. As Randall suggested (1993: 83), given the January-February calendric moment of Manco's coronation, the event coincided with the dates of rituals known as Q"ullaq Ch'away, during which the Inca sent ambassadors to eat and drink with all the kuraqas in great quantity, seeking as well more fields for state production or more production in state fields. Under normal circumstances, that is, in the absence of Spaniards, one would also expect a recently invested Inca ruler to have carried out the capac hucha, the empirewide pilgrimage ritual of the "opulent prestation," through which his personal relationship of mutual obligation with each and every local lord might be reaffirmed or the hierarchic relationship among them changed. If the new Inca had been able to follow in his predecessors' footsteps, he might also have taken to the highways to personally visit, inspect, and set to rights the most distant reaches of Tawantinsuyu. Perhaps he would also have been forced to pacify rebellious subjects.

Very likely he would have engaged as well in new campaigns of imperial expansion, seeking to bring yet more peoples and lands under the broad wings of the Inca state. As Conrad and Demarest (1984) argue, and Polo Ondegardo made very clear, when an Inca died he founded a new lineage; his descendants then cared for his mummy within the palace he had built during life, carrying him to each major sacrificial event, just as Huayna Capac had attended Manco's investiture.[10] The Inca's descendants were charged with providing him (and his gods) with food and drink, which was poured out into jars before the mummies, as Guaman Poma depicts. (See Fig. 5.1.) The dead Inca's food and drink requirements were, however, enormous: Vast quantities were expended daily and in a host of calendric rituals, not only poured out for the mummies, but also consumed by the members of the lineage that he founded in death and consumed in the banqueting of those who continued to work the dead Inca's estates, which remained under production in the name of the dead Inca to provision all the foregoing. If a new Inca did not gain access to the palace, personal subjects, or lands of his predecessor, he was forced to make new arrangements by making new conquests or by redefining relationships that bound conquered lords to Inca lineages. Thus occurred the need for both prolonged personal inspection tours accompanied by armies of conquest, and for the *citua* and capachucha ceremonies that restructured the social hierarchies of empire by realigning the hierarchies of the gods.

Manco, however, was in no position to do such things. Shortly after his investiture, his star began to decline precipitously. Manco found himself a virtual prisoner of the Spaniards, who kept him under a tight rein while they set about a project of systematically looting the empire. Apart from his dignity, the first of Manco's prerogatives to go were his gods: Temples were pillaged, idols were smashed or smelted. The palaces of deceased Incas were taken over by Spaniards, along with the personal servants, the *yanakuna,* who had been charged with caring for the mummies. Spaniards' thirst for gold led to the destruction of many shrines; the mummies and some important gods were spirited away for safekeeping in secret locations. Finally, Manco also lost the one thing without which there was no Inca state: access to the labor of his very subjects. For once Cusco was in his hands, Pizarro began to divvy up the most valuable spoils, the indians themselves. Local lords of the district around Cusco were delivered into the hands of deserving Spaniards in

Figure 5.1. Drinking with the ancestors. The wording at the top translates as "First Chapter. Tomb of the Inca. Inca Illapa Aia [Inca lightning corpse], deceased." The wording at the bottom of the page translates as "burial" (tomb). The Inca and a female companion share a drink of chicha with a pair of mummified ancestors (seated, labeled "Illapa-deceased"), whose drink is poured into the large container. In the background are bones within a chullpa-type tomb, labeled "pucullo." (From Guaman Poma de Ayala 1980: 262)

142

encomienda, which granted the Spanish lord the right to collect tribute from his new subjects and to make use of their labor in productive enterprises like mining and the transport of tribute goods, for the construction of new palaces, and as servants in his house. It was not Manco who would carry out personal visits, new conquests, and capac huchas, but, in their own ways, Spaniards.

Among the native lords given away to Spaniards in Pizarro's early encomienda grants was Guarache, Hernando de Aldana's prize for his services outside Cajamarca. The unu mallku of the Killaka federation, lord of ten thousand vassals, was handed over to Aldana in encomienda fully four years before the battles through which Spaniards conquered the region in which Killaka indians lived. Possibly, Aldana was able to collect some booty through long-distance delivery ordered by Guarache. He must, though, have been chomping at the bit to gain more direct control of Killaka tributes and labors, Killaka treasures, and perhaps Killaka silver mines. But from 1534 to 1538, Spaniards had other preoccupations. The conquest and visitation of the land of Aldana's encomienda had to wait because there were more pressing matters to attend to: civil war between the Almagro and Pizarro factions over possession of the Cusco region, and a full-scale rebellion led by the puppet Manco Inca, including a prolonged siege of Cusco, during which Aldana served well. Even then, a hard-fought Spanish invasion of Qullasuyu was necessary before Aldana was able to take full legal possession of the Killaka indians in September of 1540. When he did so, in the former Inca mining center of Porco, where his indians were already at work, he insisted that the scribe take note of his protest at participating in the ceremony of possession (in which he held the hands of his indians' native lords) "notwithstanding that I have already been in possession of them for seven years" (AGI, Charcas 53, item 1, fol. 11v.)[11]

Although Pizarro may have promised Aldana an encomienda of Guarache's indians, the grant itself could not have taken place until after Pizarro had refounded Cusco as a Spanish town. In Manco's investiture ceremonies of January and February 1534, Spaniards had a chance to gain insight into a world of Inca meanings: Pizarro's act of refoundation in March of that same year ought to have been equally instructive to Andeans. In order to gain the jurisdiction necessary to place indians under the protection of individual conquistadors in the act of encomienda (giving the encomenderos the right to collect tribute on behalf of the Spanish king from his indian vassals), he first had to assert Crown sovereignty over the conquistadors as settlers and citizens of a municipality, the instrumentality through which Spaniards enjoyed rights delegated by the king. Crown sovereignty over citizens of the municipal jurisdiction of Cusco arrived in the same manner that it had earlier come to Jauja, and years before to Cortés' Vera Cruz: Pizarro erected a pillar called a *rollo* (also called a *picota* [see Bernaldo de Quirós 1975]), a part of every Castilian town foundation and still to be seen in Castile as in the Indies, from which criminals would be punished for crimes committed in the municipal territory. It was built in the main square atop preexisting steps, which MacCormack suggests may have been the foundation of the ushnu into which the corn beer was formerly poured and offered to gods and mummies during every Inca rite, including Manco's coronation (Mac-Cormack 1991: 72). After thus closing off the conduit through which offerings had traveled to the unseen world, Pizarro then extended Crown sovereignty to Cusco, and thus to its town council and to himself, by carving marks into the rollo with his dagger (MacCormack, Ibid., citing Betanzos 1987: 52b). After that ritual act, all that was left was the assignment of house plots to the town's new vecinos, those granted the rights of citizenship. Unlike a Castilian town, however, Pizarro excluded a majority of the town's inhabitants from citizenship. For in the Indies, only Spaniards merited the full civil (or more correctly, civic) rights of the status of vecino, and even then such status was limited to those Spaniards who held indians in encomienda. But there was no law against punishing indians on that rollo. Nearly forty years after it was first erected in Cusco's plaza, the site of Manco Inca's coronation and the most sacred rituals of the Inca empire, that place of punishment was to be the scene of the execution of the last of the rebel Inca rulers, Tupac Amaru I.

So it was through his encomienda, by having been granted tributes of Guarache's people, that Hernando de Aldana became a vecino of Cusco, eventually becoming a member of the privileged city council. I will return in chapter 6 to the to the issue of municipal rights and the deep significance of urban life for Spaniards, which, forty years after Pizarro's whittlings on a rollo inaugurated civilized life in Cusco, came to haunt indians in their own home territories. For now, however, I return to the story of how Aldana came to control more effectively Guarache's indians of Killaka. Like the Spanish refoundation of Cusco, that story also leads to blade marks on a symbol of sovereignty and jurisdiction, in the ritual act that founded the City of Silver, La Plata, hometown of the encomenderos of the province of Charcas.

During the years intervening between 1534 and 1538, when Gonzalo Pizarro and his brother Hernando led a force of a few hundred Spaniards and several thousand indian allies into Qullasuyu, Spaniards had faced continuing resistance from Inca armies. When they were not engaged in the gathering of booty, they were sallying forth in armed conflict with indians and with one another.

In July of 1538, six years after Spaniards had captured the Inca Atahuallpa in Cajamarca, a band of about two hundred Spaniards led by Hernando and Gonzalo Pizarro rode south from Cusco accompanied by upwards of five thousand indian auxiliaries under the command of the new puppet ruler named in Manco's stead, Manco's brother Paullo (Barnadas 1973).[12] Their goal was twofold: to crush remaining pockets of indian resistance and bring the southern reaches of the Inca empire firmly under Spanish control, and to gather booty in the form of gold and silver, which Hernando Pizarro might carry with him on a second return trip to Spain. A new haul of precious metals, he must have reasoned, might soften the news of Hernando's murder of Almagro, which in fact did not sit well with the Crown, coming on top of the matter of the regicide of Atahuallpa. Once Qullasuyu and the king were pacified, Francisco Pizarro, as marquis of the conquest and governor of Perú, would be in position to administer the extraction of indian surpluses, which would be accomplished through the institution of encomienda.

Stretching from Cusco southwards as far as the northern highlands of present-day Argentina, Qullasuyu was perhaps the most populous of Tawantinsuyu's four constituent suyu districts, and as time would tell, it was certainly the richest in the precious metals that Spaniards held so dear. Progressing southwards, the invaders no doubt followed the Inca highway along which the inhabitants of the region had traveled when contributing their labor service to the state, or when delivering agricultural products, minerals, and animals produced under Inca administration. On leaving the immediate vicinity of Cusco, the Pizarro brothers and their fellow conquerors would first have passed through the territory of a people called Kanchi, and then through that of the Qana, before arriving at the shores of Lake Titicaca and successively entering the lands of the Qulla people, the Lupaqa, and, at the southern and eastern sides of the lake, the Pakax. It was these peoples, whose territories reached south to the Inca tambo of Caracollo, who were in the most proper sense termed Collas by the Spaniards. Spaniards traveling beyond the tambo of Carcaollo entered into the lands of peoples they dubbed "los aullagas y carangas," "los carangas y charcas," and later, "los carangas, aullagas, quillacas, charcas, y chichas."

Spurred to action by their experiences with Almagro, the native lords of the region around the lake resisted the Spaniards' advance, beginning by removing the bridge of tethered reed boats that provided passage across the Desaguadero River, which flows southwards from Lake Titicaca to Lake Poopó. For their intransigence (or just as likely, for failing to deliver the gold and silver sought by the Pizarros) the native lords of the region paid dearly. Perhaps two hundred of the lords of the Qulla and Pakax were gathered together in a large building in a town called Pucarani, where Hernando Pizarro had them burned alive (Saignes 1985b). Intent on "pacifying" a vast new region so as to swell the numbers of new indian subjects and find new sources of precious metals, the invaders and their indian auxiliaries pushed on to the southeast, along the Inca highway.

The well-constructed Inca road that the expedition must have followed provided not only secure footing for men and horses but also a series of well-supplied rest houses. Some of these, indeed, had numerous storehouses filled with dried corn, freeze-dried potatoes, and quantities of cloth, certainly enough to have supplied both Spanish expeditions, with enough left over for subsequent Spanish needs during the civil wars of the 1540s and 1550s. This system of tambos and the road connecting them were the products of Inca intervention in the domains of several major pre-Columbian polities, uneasily united under the Inca domination that commentators have regarded, in explicit comparison with ancient Rome, as a "Pax Incaica."

However long the societies of Qullasuyu had been beholden to Inca rulers and their pilgrimages diverted to Cusco, it was too brief to have erased local memory of pre-Inca autonomies. Once Cusco had fallen and the central Inca administration had come unglued, the native lords of this high plain, unencumbered by the presence of Inca administrators, were in a position to act in their own interests. Thus, Spanish efforts to gain administrative control of Qullasuyu came just as the large, Inca state-run system of agricultural production in Cochabamba, the Inca silver mines of Porco, and the elaborate systems of transportation, storage, and imperial cult began to break down. To the invaders' great advantage, the vast camelid herds and supply stores formerly under state control remained in place, along with the silver deposits that had been worked under Inca directive. Everything was in place, that is, to provide Spaniards with the motive (mineral wealth and a new supply of vassals) and the means (stored supplies of food and clothing for the short term, and for the long term a self-reproducing labor pool accustomed to the provision of services to extralocal powers) for a profitable colonial enterprise. With the collapse of the Inca state structure, state fields, supply stores, herds, and highways were under the control of the native lords of Qullasuyu. The peoples of the social units led by these lords had every reason to continue supporting their leaders and providing the periodic labor service on community lands by which elite households, as well as the communities' gods, were maintained. All that Spaniards had to do was to bend such lords to Spanish will, to make them deliver tribute and labor service to support Spanish households and social-climbing designs.

Accounts of the 1538 Spanish expedition into southern Qullasuyu are sketchy, and its exact route cannot yet be determined. We know, however, that after defeating a major indigenous offensive, the bulk of the Spanish force laid jurisdictional claim to the territory as a whole in the customary way, by founding a new town and seat of government on the site of the indigenous settlement of Chuquisaca, dubbed La Plata, or the "City of Silver." There are few passable routes between Lake Titicaca and Chuquisaca. Most likely the invading party followed the main Inca highway south along the plains between Lake Titicaca and Lake Poopó, a route that was not only self-evident but also known to those members of the expedition who had traveled it three years before with Diego de Almagro's expedition to Chile. On the east side of Lake Poopó, which then was called Lago de los Aullagas, a major branch road led eastwards, first to the storehouses and tambo (and Inca administrative center) of Paria, and then on to the enormously productive state-run maize fields of Cochabamba (see Map 5.1).

Along the way, Hernando Pizarro decided to return to Cusco, his quota of precious metals apparently fulfilled. He left the expeditionary force under the leadership of his brother Gonzalo. Not long after that, Gonzalo's party met a serious native challenge at a place named "Cotapampa," probably Cochabamba.[13] There, a concerted force of warriors of unknown number (the lords concerned might have mustered many thousands of soldiers) cornered the Spaniards in some Inca buildings. A messenger managed to escape through enemy lines to plea for reinforcements in Cusco, and Hernando Pizarro himself answered the call at the head of a detachment of six hundred Spaniards, enough to break the siege and dishearten native resistance.[14]

Back in Cusco the following year, Franciso Pizarro assigned the tributes and labor power of the new territory's indians to those Spaniards deemed most deserving.[15] Not surprisingly, native lord Cuysara, in

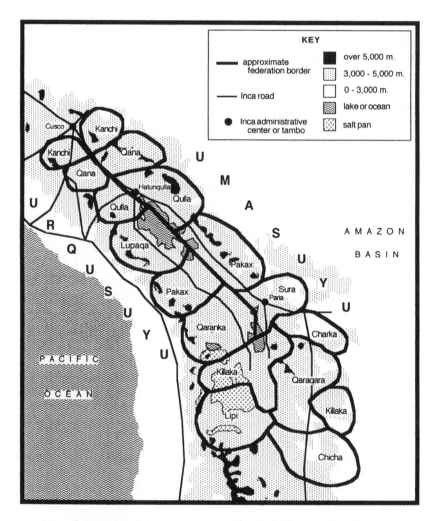

Map 5.1. Federations of diarchies, suyus, and Inca roads of Qullasuyu. Federation boundaries are notional approximations. Inca roads have not been fully mapped in Qullasuyu. (Author's rendering; drawn after information in Bouysse-Cassagne 1987: 211, Fig. 13; Julien 1983: 14, map 2; Hyslop 1984: 258, Fig. 17.1)

whose lands the Inca mines of Porco had already been located by the Pizarro brothers, was handed over to Gonzalo Pizarro.[16] Hernando Pizarro was granted the caciques and indians of "the province of the Chichas," located just to the south of Porco. For himself, Francisco Pizarro set aside the lord and indians of a district he called Puna, consisting of the diarchy of Siwaruyu-Arakapi, one of the four parts of the Killaka federation. Its appeal, no doubt, was its location, sandwiched between the indians of Gonzalo's and Hernando's grants and in easy reach of the Porco mines. Along with their shares of the booty from the distributions of Cajamarca and Cusco and their control through encomienda of many other indian groups between Cajamarca and Qullasuyu, these new grants laid the foundations for a vast Pizarro fortune, much of it converted into land and interest-producing investments in Spain after Hernando Pizarro's return there (see Varón Gabai and Jakobs 1987).

With Franciso Pizarro's seizure of the "Repartimiento de Puna," the Siwaruyu-Arakapi diarchy was separated from Guarache's control as principal mallku of the Killaka federation. A Pizarro associate, General Pedro de Hinojosa, was given the indians of Awllaka-Urukilla, cutting another large slice out of the Killaka pie. We have seen that the remaining two diarchies of the federation, Killaka and Asanaqi, had already been granted to Hernando de Aldana as a result of his role in Atahuallpa's capture and the fortuitous presence of Guarache at Manco Inca's surrender on the outskirts of Cusco in 1533. The surviving encomienda title (presented by Aldana's descendants) dates from late 1539, signed in Cusco by Francisco Pizarro; the ceremony of possession, in which he held his caciques' hands, took place in Porco, the Inca silver mine that caciques had shown to Gonzalo Pizarro, on January 22, 1540.

Like many such early encomienda grants, the documents do not provide much detail about the nature of the Killaka and Asanaqi diarchies. Other than legal niceties and a summary of Aldana's warrior services to the king, which still formed the basis for claims of mercedes and hopes for ennoblement, the title mentions only the names of Guarache and Acho, the two "cacique governors" of the Aldana grant, and a list of further names, some being towns or hamlets, others corresponding to the names of Killaka and Asanaqi ayllus still in existence, and yet more being the names of subordinate caciques and principales under the authority of Guarache and Acho, and after each one the number of indian tributaries who would henceforth deliver goods and labor to Aldana.[17]

It seems unlikely that Aldana even knew where all these places were, much less that he was able to confirm the numbers or fathom the social structural logic that tied these people and places together. Part of the logic, after all, was a vast network of *paqarinas* (the openings in the earth from which pre-Columbian ancestors sprang) and ritual pathways, linked to narratives of origin and sacrificial calendars that were at that time quite unknown to Spaniards. Certainly the forms by which these social groups were tied to land was poorly understood. Many of the places listed in the grant are distant outliers in ecologically distinct zones; others were held under Inca arrangements which, concealed from Spanish administrators, could be converted into "community lands" held under tutelage of Guarache and Acho.

The new encomenderos no doubt immediately put their new subjects to work, under the relatively free-wheeling conditions that prevailed. In theory, encomienda did not provide title to land, but only a right to collect reasonable tributes from a group of indians through the auspices of their "natural lords." According to the political theory of the day, such grants could be made only to further the cause that justified the Spanish conquests, the evangelization of idolatrous indians. But not much evangelization seems to have taken place during the 1540s and 1550s. Tributes were collected, and indians were sent to work in silver mines and gold beds, yes. Spaniards, however, were busy founding cities, building lavish houses, and investing the easy proceeds of their conquest in Spanish and Peruvian land and bonds. They were also busy fighting with one another in the extended civil wars that began with the Pizarro-Almagro controversy and became more generalized when the Crown and the Council of the Indies moved to curtail conquistador pretensions. The fame of Peruvian silver spread quickly among Spanish adventurers, who were now crowding Caribbean and Mexican haunts. Others began to pour into Perú from Spain. Polo Ondegardo, for example, came to Perú in 1543 (in the fleet that brought the new viceroy, Blasco Núñez Vela) as an agent and business partner of Hernando Pizarro. With all the new arrivals, there were far too many claimants to encomienda for the number of indians there were to go around. And the Crown rightly feared that encomenderos would soon be clamoring for greater rights, for title to land and the perquisites of the titled nobility. Such a combination was a recipe for political secession, and the Council of the Indies, moved as well by the moral arguments of Bartolomé de las Casas, voted in 1542 to end encomienda.

The rebellion of the encomenderos led by Gonzalo Pizarro and the killing of the bearer of bad tidings, the viceroy Núñez Vela, are too well known to merit retelling here. Suffice it to note that Hernando de Aldana was one of the Spanish victims of the war, put to death as a suspected royalist by order of Gonzalo Pizarro. Indians also suffered: Juan Colque Guarache carefully relates in his *probanza* the travails brought upon Killaka and Asanaqi peoples as a result of the Spanish civil warfare. In 1548, a respite of sorts came their way in the person of Pedro de la Gasca, the "pacifier" who is credited with the final defeat of the rebels. The defeat came at a high price: Encomienda was reinstated and even expanded. Many encomiendas were divided and redivided to accommodate the maximum number of conquistadors in need of "pacification." With Hernando de Aldana and Francisco Pizarro out of the picture, the Killaka diarchies were reassigned. Puna went to the mestizo son of a notable royalist; Aldana's Killaka and Asanaqi were initially given to a man named Diego de Ocampo, who did not live to see much return. Subsequently, it was divided in half, between two men who had served Almagro in the Chilean venture and had made themselves useful to the royalist camp during the rebellion: don Pedro de Portugal and Diego Pantoja (AGI, Patronato 126, section 6, 1582). General Hinojosa, who had held Awllaka-Urukilla, went on to greener pastures. Until his death by sword thrust during another short-lived rebellion in 1553, he enjoyed a large portion of the Qaraqara federation, perhaps the richest encomienda to be had in the territory (see Platt 1978b). When Awllaka-Urukilla became vacant, it was granted to a follower (and retainer) of the murdered viceroy, a *morisco* (descendant of Muslims converted to Christianity) in flight from lowly status in Castile, named Hernán Vela.[18]

The 1550s and 1560s marked an indigenous awakening to the true nature of the Spanish project. Far more than simply the imposition of state-managed indirect rule to extract tributes and labor services, it aimed to transform indigenous society radically, to annihilate idols, taquies, ancestral mummies, and now even the limited privileges and possibilities that were still granted to the native nobility for mediating colonial policies. What responses to these pressures could Andeans muster? On the one hand, there was the possibility of continued armed resistance, represented in the rebel Inca encampment in Vilcabamba. But their continuing marginality and lack of major successes seemed to close off the military option. On the other hand, caciques began to seek more effective forms of accommodation, turning to Christianity for the moral force and to writing and the legal system for the communicative means to safeguard their positions, using God and king in the courtroom to bring colonizing Spaniards to heel. There was precedent for this option in the active collaboration between mallkus and Incas, which had given the former considerable autonomies and favorable terms in meeting the tributary expectations of the latter. Under the conditions of Spanish colonialism, however, accommodation offered less advantageous terms. Caciques might thus remain in power, but they first had to master Christianity, the legal system which operated through writing, and Spanish ways of registering the past, exercising authority, and transmitting it from one generation to another. They received some help in these endeavors from Las Casian allies and from the "protectors of indians" appointed to Crown appeals courts to represent indigenous peoples before the law. Innumerable lawyers and notaries were also available, at a price. Priests paid special attention to the conversion of native lords. And from 1568, when Jesuits began to organize schools for young indigenous nobles, a new generation gained great advantage in understanding Spanish ways.

Caciques turned to writing and to Spanish law and Christian argument in the same period that Spaniards more seriously began to query the Andean past. Indeed, the intercultural process of chronicling it and of producing probanzas like that of Juan Colque Guarache translated coercive measures of colonial domination into a collaborative, but still power-laden, colonial discourse. All our sources on pre-Columbian forms of social memory are filtered through this double movement of cultural translation. The relatively stable 1550s and 1560s saw an increased priestly presence in the Andean countryside and more attention to the active conversion of Andeans to Christianity; Polo Ondegardo in his role as corregidor of Cusco queried Andeans about the ceque system in order to destroy their wak'as. Realizing that memory was kept in the relationship between people and places and in songdances and libation sequences, Polo outlawed public gatherings in which such drinking, singing, and dancing took place. The more Spaniards learned about how Andeans remembered the past, the more effective they were in forcing them to forget it. Ironically but predictably, effective collaboration on the project of reinterpreting and writing the Andean past was itself but one of the means Spaniards used to colonize it, which is to say, to erase it and rewrite it in their own image. This project might be termed the colonization of Andean narrative. As a result we have no good sources on Qullasuyu mythic narratives or the contexts in which they were told. From the writings of Spanish administrators and the curriculum vitae of native nobles, however, it is possible to paint a somewhat stilted portrait of Qullasuyu diarchies, and of Asanaqi and Killaka, as they existed during the early colony and may have been in pre-Columbian times. Drawing on an administrative report from 1585 (Capoche 1959), Thérèse Bouysse-Cassagne (1978) and Catherine Julien (1983) have mapped out the federations of diarchies that colonial Spaniards recognized before beginning the process of dismantling them (Map 5.1). The division of such groups into the categories of *umasuyu* and *urqusuyu*, "water side" (female) and "mountain side" (male), evinces a pre-Spanish social logic that these authors (and Platt 1987b) explore in greater depth. Both federation divisions and the pan-Qullasuyu uma and urqu moieties likely correspond to Inca administrative units, and possibly also indicate pre-Inca sociopolitical arrangements in Qullasuyu.

KILLAKA AND ASANAQI IN COLONIAL AND PERHAPS INCA TIMES

There has been a significant advance in the understanding of Qullasuyu realities over the past few decades,[19] but given the sparseness of sources, we may never be in a position to describe pre-Inca or, for that matter, Inca-period political-ritual organization. Cusco-centric Spanish chronicles give scarce attention to Qullasuyu realities, and writings like the probanzas of caciques are pitched to official Spanish audiences, careful to remain silent about what they knew they should not say. Platt (1987b) provides a valiant effort to parse from such fragments, with the help of Aymara and Quechua dictionaries, something of what a native political philosophy might have been like.

The fact that most of his and our sources are fiscal and legal (definitions of ownership of property, legitimate succession, tribute owed, etc., all according to Spanish categories) should not lead us to conclude that Altiplano culture was so motivated. On the contrary, Andean thought and the categories which organized it were radically dissimilar to the European. It may not seem so, because caciques[20] learned to manipulate European categories and logics in order to legitimate their rule and protect their own and their subjects' interests in the Spanish legal system,[21] and in so doing were forced to fragment their cultural vision to meet the demands of the radical cultural translation required by the colonial courts.[22]

The cultural progenitors of the K'ulta belonged to a group that goes unnamed in chronicle accounts of the Inca invasion of Qullasuyu. I refer to the diarchy of Asanaqi, which in the best of early colonial sources is subsumed within a people called Killaka. It is quite possible that in the Inca period Killaka too was subsumed within another dual-organized macrofederation, with four-part Killaka paired with another four-diarchy federation called Qaranka (Rivière 1983).

The people of K'ulta today know of a town called Quillacas, and there they celebrate a miraculous image of the crucified Christ, named Tata Quillacas. But Killaka was once the dominant kingdom in a federation including three other kingdoms, wherein the name Killaka, as an unmarked term, could refer to both the highest-ranking part (diarchy Killaka) and the whole (federation of Killaka), as well as to the capital town of both (Quillacas) (see Fig. 5.2).[23]

Today the people of Condo, Culta, Challapata, and Pampa Aullagas exhibit a "historical amnesia" about Asanaqi and Killaka that helps to underwrite the autonomy from such hereditary polities that they achieved during republican times. But colonial caciques were at pains in their probanzas and memoriales to recall to Spaniards the nature of the pre-Columbian social arrangements.

As part of their plea for the rectification of colonial administrative distortions of their realms, the caciques of Charka took great pains to make clear the distinctiveness and independence of the "nations" of the Spanish Provincia de los Charcas. The "Memorial de Charcas" lists them as Charka, Sura, Killaka, Qaranka, Chuwi, and Chicha, "each one different in nation, habits and clothing."

> In our province of Charcas, before the Incas and after them there
> were natural lords of greater than ten thousand vassals and others of
> eight thousand indians and others of six thousand indians and
> vassals. Some of the said lords and gentlemen were superior to the
> other caciques and lords that there were in each nation. . . . And thus
> each one of these lords would have eight second persons and ten as
> well, each [lord] of one thousand indians, and four principales of
> each ayllu of five hundred and of one hundred, and four *mandones*
> [headmen] in each ayllu, each one in his nation of *anansaya* and
> *urinsaya*. And in this order the Incas governed us. (Espinoza Soriano
> 1969: 18)[24]

So Killaka was a "nation" of ten thousand or eight thousand or six thousand vassals (adult male tributaries). To learn more, however, we must turn to other sources. One of the most valuable is a litigation record from the 1560s and 1570s, published by Morales (1977) and Wachtel (1981, 1982), offering useful information on the pre-Columbian Killaka, as well as the institutions through which Incas ruled them. The documents record the struggle between colonial officials and the lords of Killaka, Qaranka, and Sura over the administration of the *mitimas* ("permanent" laborer-settlers from far-flung home regions) placed there by the Inca ruler Huayna Capac, successor of Tupac Yupanqui.[25] Since

Killaka Federation								
Killaka diarchy		Asanaqi diarchy		Awllaka-Urukilla diarchy		Siwaruyu-Arakapi "diarchy"		
alaxsaya	*manxasaya*	*alaxsaya*	*manxasaya*	*alaxsaya*	*manxasaya*	*Siwaruyu*	*Arakapi*	*Marka-Suraqa*
Mallkuqa	Suraqa	Quilana	Yanaqi	Quilana	Taka	Quruqa	Qasa	Quilana
Quilana	Sinaqo	Kallapa	Chankara	Jilasakatiri	Jiwapacha	Suraqa	Chikuqa	Quruqa
Mamanuqa	Sakari	Kawalli	Ilawi	Sullkasakatiri	Awllaka	Sullkakaru	Jilasuqa	Sinaqu
Musquqa	Anqaxuqa	Sullkayana	Sullka			Sinaqu	Sullkaysuqa	Saraqara
Quruqa	Saka		Antamarka	*Urus of Town of Aullagas*		Antuqa	Tauka	Suraqa
Saraqara			Takawa	Urumayu		Quruma	Ari	Mamanuqa
				Suqtita		Chillisawa	Jilakarkasi	Mallkuqa
Uru Ayllus of Killaka		*Uru Ayllus of Asanaqi*		Satu			Sullkakarkasi	
Qua . . . ras		Kullukullu		*Ayllus of Town of Huari*				
Wichaqi		Chiquri		Wari				
				Yuqasa				
				Mallkuqa				
				Quchuqa				
				Chawara				
				Walqa				
				Sullka				
				Ayllus of Town of Salinas				
				Watari				
				Sampari				
				Urukillas of Challacota				

Figure 5.2. Structure of the Killaka Federation, reconstructed from sixteenth- and seventeenth-century documentary sources. Named Uru ayllus appear and disappear from census to census, becoming rare by the end of the seventeenth century. Ayllus found within Salinas de Tunupa (later Salinas de Garcí Mendoza) and within the town of Santiago de Huari are not found within the *reducción* of Aullagas, but nonetheless belong to the "repartimiento" of Aullagas Uruquillas, under the authority of Awllaka caciques. Some of Huari's ayllus are homonymous with those of the Killaka diarchy. Asanaqi ayllus Sullka, Antamarka, and Ilawi are found only within the territory of the reducción of Challapata. Antamarka is likely a former outlier of the Qaranka group of the same name. A few Killaka ayllus were also reduced to Challapata. The diarchy Siwaruyu-Arakapi, within which all Siwaruyu ayllu names are homonymous with Killaka ayllus, became a three-part entity after Vicery Toledo granted lands to Killaka mitima ayllus in the "parcialidad" of Marca Soraga. These Killaka ayllus, whose names were homonymous with Siwaruyu ayllus, were clearly not "of a piece" with the latter ayllus. (Based on information provided in AGI, Quito 45; AGI, Charcas 49; AGI, Charcas 53; AGNA, 9.17.1.4; AGNA, 9.17.2.5; AGNA, 13.18.4.3; AHP, Cajas Reales 18; AHP, Visitas y Padrones, Cuaderno de la visita del duque de la Palata, Repartimiento de Puna)

Inca-owned lands (especially those devoted to religious cult) could be
expropriated for Crown purposes, the proceedings included some relatively detailed ethnographic investigation, producing detailed geographic
and toponymic information along with descriptions of the manner in
which the Incas assigned long strips of land to be worked by particular
ethnic groups within each large *chacara* (field). Such detail enabled
Wachtel to map clearly the distribution of ethnic groups within one of
the chacaras (see Fig. 5.3).

What interests us here is the assignment of the southeast quarter of
the chacara to the Qaranka and Killaka. Each group was assigned four
suyus in this quarter, one strip of land for each of the four diarchic
subdivisions within each "nación" or federation. Among the Charka
lords' accusations against the machinations of Juan Colque Guarache,
the slur that the Guarache mallkus had originally been "of urinsaya de
Qaranka" is suggestive. Perhaps Charka lords were correct in portraying
Guarache as a *mañoso,* a manipulator of the truth who converted service
to the Spaniards into a higher office than his pre-Columbian position
merited. Indeed, consistent grouping of Killaka and Qaranka together in
assigned lands and the fact of their joint suit might also indicate some
kind of formal connection between the two groups (perhaps like that
between the Charka and Qaraqara).[26] Let us focus upon the four
subgroups of the Killaka sector within the Colchacollo field.

The four groups are listed in the document in an unvarying order
(sometimes, in the listing of *suyus* in other *chacaras,* in reverse order):
1. Arakapi de Puna, 2. Killaka, 3. Urukilla de Awllaka, 4. Killaka
Asanaqi. Another of the lists, this one of the suyus of a chacara named
Yllaurco, sheds more light on the Killaka subdivisions. Here Killaka
federation groups occupied the sixth through ninth strips of land across
the valley:

> 6. . . . "aracapi que son yndios del repartimiento de puna"
> 7. . . . "quillacas de Juan Guarache"
> Quillacas 8. . . . "uruquillas de aullagas
> 9. . . . "asanaques que son del repartimiento de quillacas"
> (Wachtel 1982: 226)

The text serves to emphasize the embedded nature of the federation.
The term "Quillacas" appears three times, first as the name of the
federation as a whole; second, as one of four subdivisions, "quillacas de
Juan Guarache"; and third, as the colonial *repartimiento* into which
Asanaqi was lumped with Killaka. Putting aside for the moment this last
usage, the pattern is reminiscent of the use of the term "Charka" to

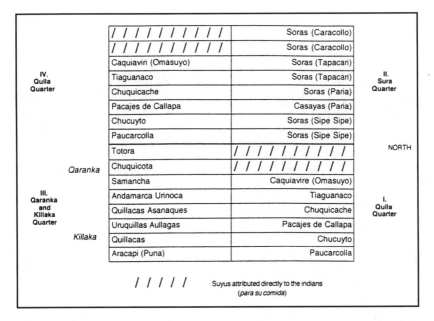

IV. Qulla Quarter		/ / / / / / / / /	Soras (Caracollo)	II. Sura Quarter
		/ / / / / / / / /	Soras (Caracollo)	
		Caquiaviri (Omasuyo)	Soras (Tapacari)	
		Tiaguanaco	Soras (Tapacari)	
		Chuquicache	Soras (Paria)	
		Pacajes de Callapa	Casayas (Paria)	
		Chucuyto	Soras (Sipe Sipe)	
		Paucarcolla	Soras (Sipe Sipe)	
	Qaranka	Totora	/ / / / / / / / /	NORTH
		Chuquicota	/ / / / / / / / /	
		Samancha	Caquiavire (Omasuyo)	
III. Qaranka and Killaka Quarter		Andamarca Urinoca	Tiaguanaco	I. Qulla Quarter
		Quillacas Asanaques	Chuquicache	
		Uruquillas Aullagas	Pacajes de Callapa	
	Killaka	Quillacas	Chucuyto	
		Aracapi (Puna)	Paucarcolla	

/ / / / / Suyus attributed directly to the indians
(*para su comida*)

Figure 5.3. Qaranka and Killaka quarter in the field of Colchacollo (Cochabamba valley), as assigned by Huayna Capac. Suyus were strips of land that transected the Cochabamba valley, running from hilltop to hilltop. Note that the four-part Qaranka Federation and the four-part Killaka Federation were grouped together in the southeastern quadrant of this large field. Sura peoples (including Casayas) divide in a four-part pattern in the northwestern quadrant, with highland peoples (Caracollo, Paria) alternating with valley peoples (Tapacari, Sipe Sipe). "Collas" (Qullas) are also assigned plots according to a pattern, this time duplicated in the northeastern and southwestern quadrants. Note that "Qulla" here designates the peoples of a specific sector of the Inca Qullasuyu, including Qulla people per se (Paucarcolla, Chuquicache), Lupaqa (Chucuito), and Pacax (Caquiaviri, Tiaguanoco, and Pacajes de Callapa). Both Qulla and Pacax included Urqusuyu and Umasuyu sectors. Here the "macro-Qulla" peoples appear to be spatially divided in the field into three Umasuyu groups (Caquiaviri, Tiaguanaco, Chuquicache) and three Qullasuyu groups (Pacajes de Callapa, Chucuito, and Paucarcolla). Possibly, Suras are also divided here by the Urqusuyu and Umasuyu sectors. All the Qaranka and Killaka peoples grouped in the southeastern quadrant, however, apparently belonged to the Urqusuyu macromoiety. (After Wachtel 1982: 212, Fig. 8.2)

designate both the federation of Qaraqara-Charka and one of its component moieties (see Platt 1987b). The Arakapi and "Urukilla de Awllaka" groups were separately assigned to Spaniards in encomienda, torn apart from the greater Killaka federation. Other Spanish administrative divisions also sundered the federation: Core territories of three of

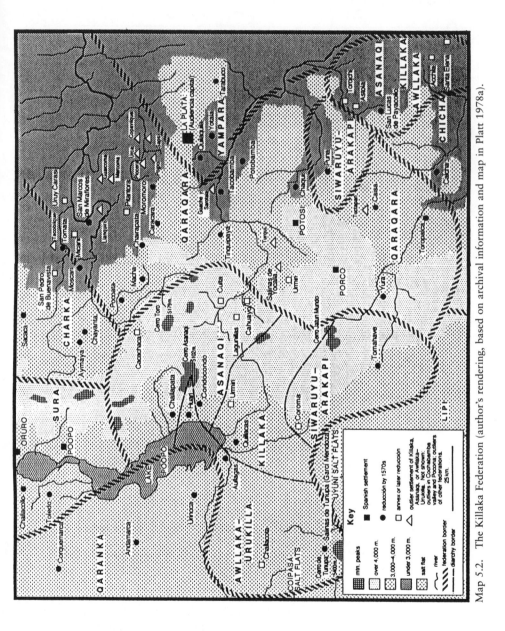

Map 5.2. The Killaka Federation (author's rendering, based on archival information and map in Platt 1978a).

158

the four diarchies of the federation were located around the southern end of Lake Poopó (see Map 5.2), forming a large part of the colonial Provincia de Paria, while the Arakapi of the Repartimiento de Puna, located farther to the east and separated from the rest by other ethnic groups, found themselves incorporated into the colonial Provincia de Porco. But what was the social structure like before the conquest?

Event Chronologies of Colonial Mallku

Our most useful sources for inquiring into the social organization of pre-Columbian Killaka are three successive "proofs of services and merits" (probanzas de servicios y meritos) advanced by don Juan Colque Guarache, cacique principal of all Killaka, during the years 1574–75, and 1576–77, and again in 1580. Like similar probanzas and memoriales (such as the well-known memorial de Charcas produced by Charka lords [Espinoza Soriano 1969]) these documents correspond to the curriculum vitae format of petitions to the Crown, carried out in order to extract concessions from the Audiencia (the subviceroyalty court in the town of La Plata [modern Sucre]) and the king.[27] Their format is very much akin to the probanzas sent in by Spaniards. So too are they like Spaniards' efforts to legitimate and extend aristocratic privilege. They were produced, in other words, by native lords in the process of transculturation as they made themselves into the frontier between their subjects and the Spanish state.

What is remarkable in the proceedings, themselves relatively uncommon events, is that the Killaka lord found it expedient not only to recount his own and his father's considerable services to the Spanish Crown—in expeditions of conquest and "pacification" of rebellious natives, civil war actions, and the regular collection of tribute and administration of Potosí mita services—but also to detail the services of his ancestors to the Incas in *their* conquests, wars, and colonization projects. The questionnaire amounts to an event chronology covering two successive waves of conquest, as told from the vantage of a single ruling lineage within an Aymara-speaking federation. As such, it is also a heroic history.[28] Yet even as it affirms the grandeur of a native noble house and stresses the relative independence and antiquity of the Killaka "nation," this is a distinctly Castilian kind of narrative.

The witnesses in the probanzas represent an impressive array of the important persons of the time,[29] including caciques who were already adults at the time of the Spanish conquest. Since the witnesses were chosen by the claimant and not cross-examined, it is not surprising that

none contradicted Colque Guarache's claims. As a result of the procedure followed, the most interesting material is provided in the questionnaires themselves and in answers based on "eyewitness experience" (*vista
de ojos*) which affirm—and only occasionally expand upon—the information supplied by Colque. By the time of these proceedings (1574–75),
neither Colque Guarache himself nor any of his witnesses could affirm
through "vista de ojos" the first few links of the genealogy, which reaches
back four generations (two generations before Huayna Capac and three
generations prior to the Spanish conquest).

Confirmed in the post of cacique gobernador of the Repartimiento de
Quillacas y Asanaques by Viceroy Toledo just prior to initiating his first
probanza, Colque Guarache claimed for his ancestors the distinction of
being "lords of vassals and caciques of the said parcialidades of Quillacas Asanaques Çibaroyos and Uroquillas and Haracapis" (ATP, Expediente 11, fol. 22r of the first probanza, question 3).[30] They were lords,
that is, of the very same kingdoms as were given lands in Cochabamba
by Huayna Capac.[31] Killaka, Asanaqi, and Urukilla were three diarchies
based around the southern end of Lake Poopó (Lago de los Aullagas).
We shall see that Siwaruyu (Çibaroyos) and Arakapi (Haracapis) together formed a fourth diarchy, centered just south of Potosí and
christened by Francisco Pizarro as the Repartimiento de Puna. Moreover, Colque Guarache continued, these ancestors were such lords even
before the Inca conquest, and recognized no superiors, being legitimately
descended lords of the region, as well as lords who held the *duo*, a
stool-like throne (ibid.).

The first eight questions give Colque Guarache's genealogy—from his
great-great-grandfather to his father—with reference to Incaic succession, despite the fact that question 4 (ibid., fol. 22v of the first probanza)
claims that his lineage predated the Inca conquest of the Killaka. The
genealogy begins with a cacique named Colque (Juan Colque Guarache's
paternal great-great-grandfather), who first submitted to Inca Yupanqui
Inca. Confirmed in his title and possessions, this Colque, says question 5
(ibid.), then aided "Ynga Yupanqui Ynga" in the conquest of the "Chichas
and Diaguitas," in which he acted as "captain general of the people of his
provinces" and was awarded the privileges of using the honorific title of
Inca Colque and of being carried by fifty indians in a litter (ibid.).[32]

The questionnaire's genealogy continues with Inca Colque's son, Inca
Guarache (who succeeded his father during the reign of the Inca "Tupa
Yupanque"), who, in addition to the litter and fifty indians to carry him,
was given ". . . three shirts, one with threads of silver and one of gold

and others with precious stones called *mullu* . . . " (ibid., fol. 7r of the first probanza, question 6).[33] Question 7 continues the genealogy with the succession, during the reign of Huayna Capac, of Inca Guarache's son, called simply Colque, about whom we learn nothing more than that he was succeeded by his son (also during Huayna Capac's reign) named Guarache (ibid., fols. 22v–23r). It was this latter Guarache who, we learn in question 7 was in Cusco at the court of the Inca ruler (Manco Inca, Huascar's successor) when Pizarro arrived in Cajamarca, whereupon Guarache, in company with the Inca (on whose war council Guarache served [ibid., fol. 23r, question 8]), submitted to Spaniards.[34]

We will return to these remarkable probanzas, produced by native lords in the process of assimilating and manipulating not only Spanish law and the Spanish society of orders but also Spanish notions of event chronology. For now, I focus on what these sources can tell us about pre-Spanish relations among native lords and Incas.

References to gifts of rich Inca cumbi cloth and to other perquisites of nobility, such as being carried in a litter, are symptomatic of a key technique of Inca statecraft, delegation of authority through indirect rule, with loyalty in part ensured through a personal relationship of mutual obligation between Inca ruler and native diarchy lord. The account of Killaka and Asanaqi presence in Inca fields in the Cochabamba valley helps to illustrate how mutual obligation between Inca and regional noble translated into access to "ethnic" labor for imperial ends.

Diagnostic of this sort of imperial rule is the personal dimension, which was possible, given the vast territories subject to Inca rule, by virtue of the efficacy of the state's bureaucratic and ritual techniques. Native lords like Guarache were taken as young men to the Inca capital, where they not only learned the "general language of the Incas," the lingua franca Quechua, but were also inculcated in the Inca social calendar, an elaborate historical engine that created as it commemorated a past which now explained and justified the subordination of conquered diarchies and the continued privilege of diarchy lords like Guarache. In effect, the Inca state translated personal obligation between local noble and "his indians" into a form of state labor tax without breaking the personal tie, the give and take of mutual obligation, that continued to make voluntary service for collective ends worthwhile from the perspective of the ordinary householder.

How did the mallku rule? What were the social values (in the absence of a means of absolute coercion) which motivated submission and service to the whole hierarchy of mallkus? That is, what made such submission worthwhile? What was the nature of intra-ayllu relations and authority at that level? In what way were ayllus interrelated within a moiety, and moieties within a diarchy?

In considering such questions for the Asanaqi diarchy and the Killaka federation in which it was enmeshed, it is essential to keep in mind that the "groups" we talk about were constituted by asymmetrical patterns of reciprocal relations among hierarchically ranked individuals. Let us begin at the top and try to account for the superordinate position of the mallku, maintained through his increased access to the labor of household heads. How was this disproportionate access to labor gained?

The first thing to note is that the service given to mallkus was of a voluntary sort. The mallkus had to *ask* for the labor that sustained them, and they had to fulfill certain obligations in return. What is more, the paramount mallku had to ask his subalterns, who in turn asked their subordinates, down to the level at which a local ayllu authority asked the "common" individual to perform a task. Among the "levels" making up society at large, rule was always mediated through a hierarchy of authorities, at ever further levels of remove from the *uta* ("house," or domestic group) itself, which of course had its own patterns of asymmetrical power as well. And "domination," which we might define as the asymmetrically distributed right to expect a prestation of labor service when properly requested, was always couched in the language of the gift and of the reciprocal obligation it incurred. At the very top of the social hierarchy, the federation mallku was personally obligated to the Inca, who refrained from turning the mallku's hide into a drum and gave him rich shirts and other marks of privileged status. Under such terms, the mallku mediated the Inca's requests for labor service (and later, those of Spanish encomendero and corregidor). But what was the return for such services?

From the Inca and the Spanish king, the mallku received rights to sumptuary goods, preeminent social position as expressed in seating and drinking order, and affirmation of his hereditary privilege more generally.[35] But what was in it for the members of an ayllu? The received wisdom of "social contract" theory would suggest that what the domestic group received in return for its labor prestations was a guarantee of limited autonomy, access to land and animals, and defense of its territory from invasion by others. But these were (and are) not Andean terms. Rather, the return for them was (and is) explicable only when one takes account of the nature and shape of social memory and the singularly important role that mallkus and Incas (and later priests and kings) took on in its perpetuation.

Great Inca administrative centers such as Paria and Hatuncolla, through which armies of mit'a workers as well as great maize-laden llama caravans passed and rested on their journeys to and from the fields of the Inca, were also places in which Inca regional administrators dwelled. They were called *kamachik/kamachikuq;* "governor or overseer, or one who commands or rules" (González Holguín 1952: 47).[36] As Morris (1979; Morris and Thompson 1985) has shown for the analogous Inca administrative center of Huanuco Pampa, the officials of such sites did not sit in their elite quarters dryly keeping records and giving commands but from the number of chicha storage jars found there, appear to have presided over what was a kind of Incaic beer hall. Morris concludes that administrative centers served a kind of hospitality function, fêting there, as reciprocal prestation, the laborers who worked for the Inca.

As I have suggested through one of the vignettes with which I opened the introduction to this book, we might be better off conceiving this drinking in more sacramental terms and the rooms in which it was done more as cathedrals than beer halls, for drinking was (and is) a part of serious devotional practice, a corollary of dedicated libations. And libations were simply one part of a whole constellation of sacrificial rites that must have been directed in the administrative centers. It would be impossible here to catalogue the complex system of calendric sacrifices which linked the provinces to the Inca capital, in which cloth, camelids, and the makings of corn beer (the three principal items of sacrifice) were brought into Cusco and then systematically offered to a hierarchy of deities (such as wak'as, themselves "heads" of polities) that radiated from Cusco into the periphery.

Polo Ondegardo describes the most general ordering principal of the empire:

> . . . Among these indians and their way of living . . . the kingdom as
> a whole was divided into parts, that each one was made up of ten
> thousand indians, that they called *uno,* and that each one of these
> had a governor over the caciques and *mandones*—as has been said.
> There was also another more general division, that they called
> Tawantinsuyu, which means four parts into which the whole
> kingdom was divided, called Qullasuyu, Chinchasuyu, Antisuyu,
> Kuntisuyu. This division began from Cusco, from which four roads
> depart, each one towards one of these parts, as can be seen in the
> map of the wak'as. And with this order and division it was easy to
> account for everything, as they did, which I will not describe here or
> recall, but only [mention] so that it is clear that, when it was decided
> in Cusco to bring in 100,000 fanegas of corn, in a moment each

governor knew how much fell to his district and to his storehouses. There were no differences of opinion or quarrels or lawsuits, and each province knew how much fell to each subdivision, so that the accounting began with the headmen and was then distributed to lower levels, so that all was done with great ease. One should not imagine that this distribution was equal . . . rather it was divided among them according to the quality of soils, and in the same way as foodstuff obligations were divided so were those of cloth and animals, by quotas. (Polo Ondegardo 1990: 121–122)[37]

Polo's administrative report, produced to determine how best to collect tributes from indians, reveals a degree of admiration for Inca state efficiency that Spaniards were incapable of maintaining once they began to appreciate just how much of that efficiency of production and administration was directed towards ritual and religious ends, the sort that for Spaniards were idolatrous. That such practices also served as the channels of Andean social memory may help to explain why Spanish chroniclers used so extraordinarily few of their pages to recount them. Let us see what other sorts of interferences occluded Spanish understandings of Inca (not to mention Qullasuyu) pasts.

SPANISH PASTS AND MEMORY TECHNIQUES

There is considerable truth, though not of the literal sort, to the infamous story about the event that sealed Atahuallpa's fate in Cajamarca. Supposedly, the priest Valverde presented the captured Inca Atahuallpa with the Bible (some accounts specify a breviary), explaining that it contained the word of God. Atahuallpa then held it to his ear and, hearing nothing, let it drop to the ground as so much worthless flotsam (see MacCormack 1988a). Through a complex rhetorical maneuver, the account transforms a Spanish legal fiction into an apt moral argument and allegory of colonialism.

Titu Cusi, a rebel Inca of Vilcabamba who in the end capitulated and converted to Christianity in return for rich estates, described the same events from an indigenous perspective. Once he arrived in the plaza and was met my Valverde's delegation, he produced an itemized account from a quipu record of all the damage to Inca properties and looting that Spaniards had carried out, demanding prompt repayment.

Atahuallpa received them very well, giving one of them [chicha] to drink in a golden vessel. When the Spaniard reached out with his hand and spilled it out, [the Inca] was greatly angered . . . ; After that

those two Spaniards showed him . . . a letter or book . . . saying that
it was the *quilca* [the writing] of God and of the king, and . . . as he
had been affronted because of the spilled chicha, [Atahuallpa] took
the letter . . . and threw it down there, saying, "What do I know of
what you give me? Go on, get out of here." (Titu Cusi Yupanqui
1985; quoted in Randall 1993: 73)[38]

For Titu Cusi, the gestures of rejection are analogous, of a kind. What
kind of drinking act does Titu Cusi ascribe to the encounter? Betanzos
tells us that this particular kind of drinking, in which offerer and receiver
drank simultaneously, was especially esteemed among the Incas:

These lords [Incas] and all the others of this land have a custom . . .
of good breeding. It is that if a lord or lady goes to visit another in
their house . . . she has to carry on her back, if she is a lady, a jar of
chicha. On arrival . . . the visitor must set up two glasses of chicha,
one of which he or she gives to drink by the lord being visited, and
the other is drunk by the lord or lady who gives the chicha. Thus the
two drink together. And he who is visited does the same, taking out
another two glasses of chicha . . . and this is the greatest honor that
there is among them, and if it is not done when visiting, the guest
takes it as an affront. . . . In the same way he is affronted who offers
a drink to another, and the other does not want to receive it.
(Betanzos 1987: 72–73)[39]

So the Spaniard's (Valverde's?) spilling of the chicha was a grave
breech of sociality. It was most probably much worse. Titu Cusi does not
specify if libation and dedication were to have accompanied the mutual
drinking, but we may guess that they were. If the act, which Spanish
eyewitness accounts do not describe, actually took place, words of
dedication would have called upon the gods of Andean memory. Andean
drinking made the gods present in an act of communion. Imagine for a
moment that Valverde had presented Atahuallpa with a chalice of
Christ's blood, and the Inca had spilled *that* upon the ground. Valverde's
sacrilege was at least equal to Atahuallpa's (see Randall 1993: 73).

Titu Cusi's account, of course, is as self-serving as any Spanish
description: All seek to foreground the moral virtue of one or another
participant in the fateful event. One thing, though, is certain. Spanish
horsemen, footmen, and a cannon were primed and ready for a surprise
attack on the Inca's immense ceremonial retinue, awaiting the sign of a
dropped handkerchief to spring their deadly trap. Likewise, if Valverde
in fact held forward paper with writing, it was most likely to read out a
text of the *requerimiento,* a brief explanation of Christianity ending in

an ultimatum: If the natives to whom it was read refused to submit to the Spanish bearers of the True Faith on the spot, they would become apostates against whom a just war could be waged. Substituting an unread (and for Atahuallpa, unreadable) Bible for the legal document and active disdain for mere incomprehension, the Spanish chronicler at once marks Atahuallpa for a blasphemer's death and exculpates his executioners and, by extension, justifies the conquest by locating the gulf separating Spaniard from indian in the distinction between the written word and the spoken one (MacCormack 1988a). The gulf between written communication and the imbibed form was yet too wide to be noticed; when Andeans were found to have something akin to writing, it was not in the drunken or sung word and certainly not in sacrificial acts at wak'as along ceques, but in the quipu and, in a way, in the narrative texts that Spaniards would extract from *quipu kamayuqs*.

No matter that the leader of the Spanish expedition, Francisco Pizarro, was himself illiterate: He knew very well the importance of writing for his project, and employed scribes to write the documents he signed (with the aid of a metal template to guide his hand), giving his endeavors the stamp of legality. Like don Quixote, members of the Pizarro expedition, most of whom were of lowly plebeian status in their Spanish home towns (Lockhart 1972), read or listened to readings of chivalric literature. They may not have thought that they too might gain wealth and nobility through the rescue of damsels in distress or the recovery of the Holy Grail, but like don Quixote they knew the value of honor and, with Sancho Panza, no doubt dreamed of finding great treasures and becoming governors of insulae (Leonard [1949] 1992). Yet even the delivery of Atahuallpa's fabulous gold and silver ransom did not necessarily satisfy their desires.

As James Lockhart has pointed out in his study of the (European) men of Cajamarca (1972), only a few immediately returned to Spain with their share of the loot (along with Hernando Pizarro, who went to the royal court to negotiate terms for his half-brother Francisco, to invest some of the capital in Spanish properties, and to line up a contingent of lawyers and business stewards to administer their Peruvian enterprise); most remained, hoping for greater glory. Those who stayed in Perú did so, no doubt, for a variety of reasons. For some, their satchel of silver may still have been too small to guarantee a permanent rise in fortune. All, no doubt, aimed to gain a permanent rise in social estate, moving from their former relatively low social positions into ranks of the aristocracy. And in sixteenth-century Spain, aristocratic status came only with guaranteed rents, best when in the form of tributes paid by vassals. There could be no question that a man who lived on the tributes of vassals was *not* himself plebeian. But vassals could be gained only by a grant from the king. And in the sixteenth century, such grants came as rewards for service to the Crown, especially soldierly service.

All Pizarro's fellow adventurers and business partners therefore depended on a good royal review of their book of deeds. Hernando Pizarro's visit to the king was part of a signally important effort to put a good spin on the chronicling of Francisco's actions. By gaining the status of governor of the Crown's new indian subjects, Pizarro hoped to gain license to reward his men with indian vassals granted in the king's name. Like Pizarro, each of his social-climbing men needed to be written into the empire's event record. Both as a business enterprise and as legally justified imperialism, the conquest required notaries; as a means of rising in the Spanish society of estates, it needed chroniclers.

From long before sixteenth century and in places far from Castile, writing had become a privileged locus of social memory, contract, and obligation. Social status was guaranteed in baptismal records, census lists, and testaments; it was improved through notarized and sworn narratives of personal valor and service, backed up by more official, authorized chronicles and histories. For recollecting the deeds of men long dead (and indeed, of gods) and for transmitting social status from generation to generation, the written document had become essential.

Although respect for letters was deeply ingrained in all conquistadors, including illiterate men such as Francisco Pizarro, it was never more deeply ingrained as in the scribes, notaries, and lawyers employed by men like Pizarro to record every worthy deed and every significant transaction. Yet even men like these, whose livelihoods depended on respect for the written word (and whose pledges of a document's faithful recopying sometimes made or ruined reputations), nonetheless also respected certain nonwritten forms of social memory. Among the conquistadors at Cajamarca, for instance, was a man whose profession was given as town crier (Lockhart 1972), whose services were still required for the legal execution of transactions (like the sale of vassals or the ennoblement of a soldier for his service to the king) that were also written on paper and posted on church doors. The deeds of founding heroes like the reconquest's El Cid, whose struggles and rewards served as models for social-climbing adventurers, were told not only on paper but also in oral epic *cantares*. The life of Christ could be learned by reading the Holy Book, but for most illiterate Spaniards, it was witnessed, in the dramatic *tableau vivant* of commemorations like the *autos sacramentales* of Corpus Christi processions. Indeed, the Church's leading theologians had found ritual to be of critical importance as a teaching tool for the masses. Just so, all good Christians received a weekly history lesson when they participated in the Eucharist, the ritual commemoration of Christ's exemplary self-sacrifice (Rubin 1991). Writing's superiority as historical evidence was tied not only to its context-free nature and its potential for lasting unchanged across generations, but also to the sanctity Spaniards granted to their principal source for history of origins, the Bible, and to links between writing and the authority of God and, hence, of the divinely appointed monarch.

The ritual significance of biblical history and its status as the undergirding of monarchic authority and source for the justifications of the king's claim of sovereignty over indians led rather directly to interest in the indians' relationship to Scripture. When thoughtful scribes and chroniclers of Spanish deeds found time for the task of discovering how an Andean past fitted in with their own, the first source queried, naturally, was the Bible itself. Neither indians nor the Indies are there mentioned, and the more scholarly chroniclers tended to reject the easy explanations that indians either were not men or were descendants of the lost tribes of Israel. The history of Andean indians, then, had to be discovered from the indians themselves. But Spaniards quickly found that native Peruvians lacked writing systems comparable to their own.

In 1492, Nebrija justified the publication of the first Castilian grammar by reminding the Catholic kings that "language is the handmaiden of Empire," a maxim that was never so true as it became a few decades later when the Spanish empire rose to power. The machinery of the first modern empire was fueled by papers produced by an ever-growing stable of professional lawyers and notaries. Fortunately for us, the Catholic kings' state apparatus insisted on punctilious record-keeping, as a result of which many sixteenth-century writings on native Andeans have been preserved for our eyes.

It is worth remembering that most written documents of the period, including the memoriales, relaciones, and crónicas which serve as our sources for appreciating sixteenth-century Andean oral narrative, were intended by their authors to end up in the archive of the Spanish Crown. Its addition to the archive was, indeed, one of the means by which such writing was expected to produce its desired effects. The most frequent of these effects, of course, was the extraction of boons from the king in return for services rendered, which could be expected only when supporting documents were properly preserved and evaluated by a readership made up mostly of state functionaries.

The shelves of the Archive of the Indies are jammed with thousands of "proofs of merit and service," usually containing detailed accounts of services rendered to the Crown by a particular boon seeker (and when possible, his lineal ascendants.) Relaciones were more formal narratives of conquest events, often produced for the same purpose as the probanzas, but composed in a somewhat more distanced and exhaustive format. These in turn provided a primary source for writers of crónicas, accounts in which the composer/narrator fades further into the background and which sometimes tackle material outside the writer's personal experience. Crónicas then became fodder for writers of *historias,* works of a much wider sweep that brought universal history to bear in the interpretation of the material found in crónicas and relaciones. No personal experience was assumed of the writer of a historia, although greater authority was required to presume to write one. Such works were subjected to greater scrutiny, since the breadth of interpretation required of historias could lead their authors into the territory of heresy or sedition. The most authoritative historia, presumably, was that produced by the Crown's official chronicler, whose task it was to decoct from his contradictory sources a reliable official story.

Once validated by publication or by the act of being archived, historias and crónicas authorized new claims on the part of those whose meritorious acts they documented; they are frequently cited and quoted in colonial agents' service records as authoritative proof of an individual's merit, completing the documentary circle. If authorized accounts could help a claimant reap his just reward, they could also, *mutatis mutandis,* become obstacles in one's career path, at least when the acts recounted therein were deemed inauspicious. González Echevarría (1990: 71–87) vividly recounts the lifelong, and fruitless, struggle by the mestizo chronicler Garcilaso de la Vega ("El Inca") to overcome the infamy attached to his father's name by a historical account that described his gift of a horse to the unseated rebel Gonzalo Pizarro on a crucial battlefield.

Under such circumstances, the production of historical narrative was thus freighted with political significance; with questions of honor, wealth, and status at issue, it was also fraught with danger. On the one hand, there was the risk to truth: With so much at stake, writers were inclined not only to embellish their own actions but perhaps also to invent laudable portrayals of sufficiently deep-pocketed others. On the other hand, unfavorable accounts of others' actions could and did lead to prolonged and expensive civil litigation, or worse. Such fears no doubt prompted Cieza, before his untimely death in 1554, to ask his relatives to take care with his still-unpublished writings. These consisted of his account of the Inca empire (which expresses sympathies that might have led to complications, given the developing imperial policies of the day) and a history of the Peruvian civil wars, the accounts of which were career making or breaking for the hundreds of individuals mentioned therein.[40]

RECOLLECTIONS OF ANDEAN MEMORY TECHNIQUES

So writing in sixteenth-century Spain and Perú was inextricably bound up with legal functionality and questions of power.[41] As we shall see, the "field techniques" used by chroniclers of the preinvasion past were themselves conditioned by the techniques and style of the legal deposition and even of inquisitorial interrogation (a confession was also a relación). Indeed, González Echevarría (1990) has rather cogently argued that the legal functionality and archival character of writing in the Spanish empire have been a significant influence on the development of fiction writing in Spanish America from colonial days to the present. Consider, then, that the reporting of Andean oral traditions in our sources is invariably conditioned by the ends desired by our authors, as well as by the strategies of rhetoric and argument they employed in order to achieve those ends.

If such considerations apply to all forms of narrative reportage (and most particularly to the recounting of past events, which is to say, to historical discourse), then they apply in a very special way to written accounts, in Spanish, of oral narratives dictated in other languages. Such accounts were subjected not only to the Spanish author's intentional elisions, supplementations, and reorderings, but also to the vagaries of translation. Yet even if we had been so fortunate as to have inherited the works of a sixteenth-century scribe who had been both willing and able to serve as a direct and invisible amanuensis to Andean raconteurs (and alas, there are no such cases), we would still be faced with difficulties in our efforts to disinter sacrificial meanings from their entombment in letters.

As Polo argued, most products of Andean labor prestations were destined for sacrifices, some of which were carried out on a regular daily, weekly, and monthly basis at shrines in Cusco and in the provinces.

Another such sacrificial ritual was the capac hucha, not a calendric rite
per se but one performed at the accession of a new Inca to the throne.
From each of the provinces of each of the four quarters of the empire,
every polity supplied a set of items for sacrifice, including camelids,
cloth, metals, and children. These were carried into Cusco, where they
were received by the Inca with great pomp and dignity in the main plaza.
In Cusco, the children were dressed in the finest cloth and then sent back
out, along straight lines from the center rather than on the roads, and
great care was taken that every single sacred place received part of the
sacrifice. A child would then be sacrificed to the wak'a of his or her own
polity, in one of several possible forms, including removing the still-
beating heart and anointing the face of the wak'a image with blood,
"almost from ear to ear."[42] In provincial places like Killaka the sacrifices
were directed by a hierarchy of local ritual specialists devoted to the
wak'as' care. Cristóbal de Molina (El Cuzqueño) provides a detailed and
succinct account that merits quotation at length:

> Pachacuti Inca Yupanqui also invented the capac hucha, which was
> done in this way: The provinces of Qullasuyu and Chinchaysuyu and
> Antisuyu and Kuntisuyu brought to this city from each town and
> lineage of peoples, one or two little boys and girls, ten years of age;
> and they brought clothing and herd animals and sheep of gold and
> silver and mullu. And they kept them in Cusco for the purposes to be
> described. And after all this was collected together, the Inca sat down
> in the plaza of Aucaypata, the great plaza of Cusco, and there those
> children and other sacrifices walked around the statues of the
> Creator, sun, thunder, and the moon, which were in the plaza for
> that purpose. And once they had circled them twice, the Inca called
> the priests of the provinces and had them divide the said sacrifices in
> four parts for the four suyus: Qullasuyu, Chinchaysuyu, Antisuyu,
> Kuntisuyu, which are the four parts into which this land is divided,
> and he said to them: "Each of you take your part of these offerings
> and sacrifices, and carry them to the wak'a, and there suffocate the
> children and bury them along with the silver figures of sheep and
> persons of gold and silver, and burn the sheep and rams and cloth,
> and also some small baskets of coca." From Cusco the people carried
> the said sacrifices to Sacalpina, which was one league from Cusco
> where the indians of Ansa received them. And in this manner they
> continued passing them along until reaching the place where the
> sacrifices were to be done, and through this arrangement they were
> carried to the other provinces as well.
>   They performed this sacrifice when the lord Inca began his reign
> so that the wak'as should give him health and he should keep his

kingdoms and lordships in peace and calm, and all should live
without illness into old age. In this manner not a single wak'a, place
of reverence [mochadero], or shrine, no matter how small, was left
without its sacrifice, because it was arranged and agreed in advance
what was to be sacrificed in each wak'a and place. . . .

All these sacrifices were put in the aforesaid place, and then the
priest in charge of the wak'a of Yanacauri, from which they believe
one of the brothers who came out of the cave of Tambo was turned
to stone (and because we treat this fable at length at the beginning of
the "Historia" that Your Illustrious Lordship has,[43] I do not treat it
here, Your Illustrious Lordship may see it there). . . .

And then in all the places, springs, and mountains that where held
in Cusco to be shrines, they threw the sacrifices that had been
dedicated to each, without killing for this purpose any child.

There were so many places to which sacrifices were dedicated in
Cusco, that to write them down here would be very prolix, and
because in the "Relación" of the wak'as that I gave to Your Most
Reverend Lordship, all are indicated, and the manner they sacrificed
to them, I do not put it down here.

And once they were finished with the sacrifices in Cusco, the
priests were sent out with the sacrifices that were to be carried, as I
say. The traveling order with the sacrifices was that all the people
who went with the capac hucha (who by another name were called
Cachaguaes) formed into a flank, somewhat separated from the
others. They did not travel directly along the royal highway, but
without deviating in any way, they walked straight ahead through
ravines and over mountains that they came to until each one arrived
at the place where those who were to receive the sacrifices awaited. . . .

When they arrived at each place destined for sacrifices, the wak'a
kamayuqs, which means "guardians of the wak'as," in whose charge
they were, each received the sacrifice that fell to his wak'a, and he
sacrificed and offered it, burying the sacrifices of gold and silver and
mullu and other things that they used, and the children who fell to
that wak'a, having first been suffocated. The rams, sheep, and cloth
set aside for the wak'a were burned in sacrifice.

Note that not all the wak'as received children in sacrifice, but only
the principal wak'as of lineages or provinces.

And by this order they went walking through all the lands that the
Inca had conquered, through the four districts, and making the said
sacrifices until each one came on his pathway to the ultimate limits
and boundary markers established by the Inca.

They kept such good accounts of all this, and all the sacrifices
destined for each place were so well divided in Cusco, that although
this sacrifice was in great quantity and the places to which they were

sent were numberless, there was never any error or mistake in destination. For this purpose the Inca had in Cusco indians from the four suyus or divisions, and each one kept account of all the wak'as, no matter how small, that there were in the district of which he was quipu kamayuk or accountant, and they were called *willka kamayuq*. . . . (Molina 1989: 120–128)[44]

If such efforts were not enough to interlink the destinies of Inca rulers and conquered peoples, there were other techniques. Once a people like the Killaka federation had been conquered, the Inca practice was to transfer their principal idol as a kind of "hostage" to Cusco, where it was placed in the Qurikancha, the "Golden Enclosure," where the empire's deities dwelled.[45] Subject peoples were thus motivated to contribute their energies to the maintenance of state-supervised ritual practice, which fed their own gods as well as those of Incas.

In the capac hucha, the elevation in rank of a regional mallku went hand in hand with the elevation of his group's chief wak'a. In one of the most detailed descriptions of capac hucha from the perspective of the provinces, Hernández Príncipe (1923: 60–63), another "extirpator of idolatry," reported that the rise in status of wak'a and kuraqa (as mallkus were called in Quechua) was connected with the willingness of the kuraqa to sacrifice his own daughter, after her consecration in Cusco. She was dressed in Inca finery and, after her demise, became an intermediary, through spirit mediums, between her father's people and their own gods. The girl herself was then called capac hucha, as were pieces of fine cumbi cloth (gifts of the Inca) in which the elevated wak'a girl, and kuraqa were now dressed (ibid., 62–63). Thereafter, her cult, along with that of the local wak'as, was directed by a hierarchy of ritual specialists in each ayllu (ibid., 26–46).

Imperial rituals like the capac hucha came to an end with the arrival of Spaniards, although other public rites in Cusco and elsewhere continued unabated for a short while after the conquest. For obvious reasons, don Juan Colque did not report in his probanza of services to Incas and Spaniards the sacrifices that his people had carried out in such contexts. Nor have any complete descriptions of wak'a rites in Killaka territory survived. We know, however, that even when the imperial cult was brought to an end by the radical transformation of social order brought by Spaniards, local wak'as, places, idols, and mummified ancestors, sacred as a group's anchors in the foundational past, continued to receive cult for well over a century after priests began actively to hunt them down and sermonize against them.

Compared with the detailed accounts of seventeenth-century extirpators of idolatry in the diocese of Lima, there are few sources for the
Killaka region (though as we shall see, extirpators were active there too).
Owing to an apparent loss of documents from ecclesiastic archives, there
is but one late sixteenth-century report of a pilgrimage site frequented by
Killaka and Asanaqi peoples (a shrine maintained by a wak'a kamayuq
named Diego Iquisi, dedicated to five idols made of silver), and a
midseventeenth-century discovery by the priest of Coroma (a settlement
belonging to the Siwaruyu-Arakapi diarchy) of three "reverencing
places" and over seventy idols that were still receiving cult from
specialist lineages in 1658 (see chap. 6).

Every province had shrines known as wak'as, some of which were
called (in Quechua) paqarinas, "places of blooming," marking where the
first ancestors had emerged. Once again, Polo provides an account of
how such local shrines were incorporated into empire:

> [In this way the Incas] went for many years without being able to
> lord it over more than the Cusco region, until the time of Pachacuti
> Inca Yupanqui. . . . After [defeating the Chanka] their requisite was
> that of the accounting and inventory of . . . sacrifices, and to oblige
> those who they placed under their dominion to carry them out. And
> they led [their subjects] to understand that the city of Cusco was the
> house and resting place of the gods, and in that place there was no
> fountain or step or wall which was not said to hold mystery, as can
> be seen in each manifest of shrines of that city and the map, that
> from their accounts were more than four hundred and some. All of
> this lasted until the Spaniards came, and up until today they venerate
> them all when no one is watching, and the whole land cares for and
> venerates the wak'as that the Incas gave them. To prove the manifest
> produced from their own registers, I removed many [wak'as] from
> the provinces of Chinchasuyu and Qullasuyu. Because that material is
> inappropriate here, this much will suffice to understand what follows.
> (Polo Ondegardo 1990: 44–45)[46]

A consummate administrator, Polo paid close attention to the nature
of local obligations to the state; in combination with his zeal for
discovering the treasure associated with Inca idols and mummies, such
searching led him first to understand the shrine system of Cusco and then
to seek out analogous systems elsewhere.

Cristóbal de Molina also writes of a map of Cusco's shrines. Like
Molina's account, Polo's full treatise on Inca religion, including the map
of the ceques and wak'as of Cusco, "produced from their own registers,"
has perhaps been lost, but another account (which seems to have been
independently produced) survives. The chronicler Bernabé Cobo (1990)

provides a list of ceques and of the shrines that these radial lines connected; John Rowe (1980) has also published Cobo's list. From them and from allied information on the land claims of the lineage and clanlike social groups of Cusco itself (these were *panakas,* founded by the descendants of embalmed Incas and dedicated to the perpetuation of the Inca's palace and the social relations with peoples he conquered, and ayllus, clanlike groups of the valley's "original" inhabitants), an increasingly clear picture is emerging of an astoundingly complex calendric cycle of commemorative rituals. Through them, these groups recalled the pasts that gave them their shape, land rights, and place in the imperial social hierarchy. Much of that work has been done by Zuidema (1964, 1977, 1989a, 1989b, 1990) and his students (see Fig. 5.4, an idealized representation of the ceques of Cusco), and to date it has most clearly brought into view the ways in which the ceque system served as a form of specialized astronomic and calendric knowledge, linking yearly solar cycles and lunar cycles not only to the calendric timing of agricultural tasks and rituals but also to the deeper past of myth and genealogy, and therefore to the founding events of all the social groups that composed the empire. As MacCormack (1991: 194–195) phrases it, "Apart from exemplifying the political and spatial ordering of Cuzco, and by implication of the empire, the ceque shrines guided worshipers through mythic and historical time. Finally, some of these shrines were also markers of calendrical time."

The specifics of this system, which required a large number of specialist priests and quipu kamayuqs (with their "registers") to function smoothly, are much more difficult to reconstruct from the available sources. Such specialists were queried by Polo and others for practical purposes, to help find mummies and treasures and to understand precisely which idols, shrines, and memories were to be eradicated.

The complex specifics of the system in operation, which harmonized a large number of panaka and ayllu pasts within the Cusco valley and tied these to both the past and the working social arrangements with conquered peoples, led Spaniards to pull their hair. The sheer heterogeneity of Inca social memory, which admitted into a harmonizing whole the multiple origins, repeated and conflicting accounts of "changes of worlds," and relatively autonomous pasts, ritual cycles, and social forms of the empire's diverse social components, was for Spaniards the antithesis of the "future past" they would give to Andeans by bringing them into the single time-line of universal history.

Enough is known, however, to suggest that Inca, and more generally Andean, forms of social memory were "registered" in *multiple* and

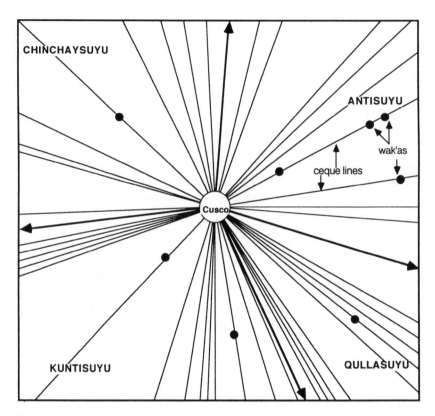

Figure 5.4. The ceque system of Cusco. Forty-one sighting lines radiating from the Coricancha, the "Golden Enclosure" that housed major Inca deities, led to 328 wak'as and divided the lands of Inca panacas and ayllus. Certain other lines (represented by bold arrows), corresponding to astronomic observations, divided the moieties of Cusco and the quarters of Tawantinsuyu, "Land of the Four Parts." Wak'as are placed here arbitrarily. (Author's rendering, based on Zuidema 1964; and Wachtel 1973)

intersecting media. First of all, there were the quipus that so impressed Spaniards as an exact form of record-keeping. Rarely did Spaniards praise other Andean memory techniques, since they seemed inextricably linked to the practices that Spaniards regarded as idolatrous, such as drinking, singing and dancing, and the rites performed at shrines dotting the landscape. Chroniclers continued, however, to single out the quipu as a remarkable and accurate recording device, one that continued to be used well into the colonial period. Guaman Poma illustrates a quipu kamayuq standing amid Inca storehouses. (See Fig. 5.5.) Remember,

Figure 5.5. Quipu kamayuq. The wording at the top translates as "Storehouse of the Inca, *collca*." The wording at the bottom of the page translates as "Storehouses of the Inca." Framed by rows of storehouses (collcas), an Inca ruler, labeled "Topa Ynga Yupanqui," points to a quipu in the hands of a man labeled "Administrator. *Suyoyoc*. Apo Poma Chaua." (From Guaman Poma de Ayala 1980: 309)

however, Polo's revelation that his map of ceques and wak'as was taken from "their registers," referring, no doubt, to quipus. Likewise, the origin narratives that Spaniards sought to use as dynastic chronicles for history making (as we shall see in chapter 6) were most often heard from quipu kamayuqs, who in some way recalled their stories while manipulating quipu cords. The historian José de Acosta was especially impressed with quipus, one of the few pre-Columbian memory techniques still in accepted public use at the time he visited Perú.

> Before Spaniards arrived, the indians of Perú had no form of writing, through either letters or characters or ciphers or little figures such as the Chinese or Mexicans used; but for this they did not conserve the memory of their antiquities any less, nor fail to keep accounts of all matters of peace and war and government. Because in passing traditions from one to the next they were diligent, and the youth kept and guarded what their elders told them as a sacred thing, and with the same care taught it to their own successors. In addition to this care, they made up for the lack of writing and letters in part with paintings such as those of México (although those of Perú were very gross and rough), and in the greater part with quipus. Quipus are certain memorials or registers made from branching cords, on which various knots and diverse colors signify different things. It is incredible what in this way they were able to accomplish, because whatever books may convey of histories, laws, ceremonies, and business accounts, all of this quipus [recorded] so accurately that it is a thing to admire. To keep these quipus or memoriales, there were appointed officials still today called quipu kamayuqs, who were obliged to render all sorts of accounts, just as the public scribes do here, and thus they were given complete faith. Because for diverse genres such as war, government, tributes, ceremonies, and lands, there were diverse quipus or branching cords. And in each handful of these, so many big and small knots, and little strings tied to them, some red, others green, blue, or white. In the end there were so many distinctions, that just as for us by rearranging in various ways twenty-four letters we can construe an infinity of words, so they were able to make innumerable significations of things with their knots and colors. (Acosta 1977: 410–411)[47]

Quipus are well-known to have served as a device for counting and accounting; they were also clearly used to account for the ritual obligations of social groups to wak'as along the ceque to which they were assigned (and which may have served too as a kind of border defining their lands). Quipus could thus be used as a kind of social calendar. It seems likely that in encoding numeric amounts of certain groups' sacrificial obligations to wak'as along ceques, quipus might also have served as iconic representations of ceques themselves; the form of the quipu, a main cord from which a series of secondary cords depend, the latter segmented by groups of knots, itself recalls the shape of the ceque system. Could one have served as the trace of the other? It is an intriguing possibility, and one that provides an alternative to thinking of the quipu as "merely" an arithmetic device or, in some way, constituting a form of writing.

Indeed, there are reasons to think that quipus were icons of ceque systems (cf. Zuidema 1989b). The latter, after all, constituted a topographically inscribed mnemonic system, which projected onto the very landscape the nature of the relationships among the people who inhabited it. And those relationships were figured in relation to the past that landforms embodied, as permanently frozen moments of foundational times. Along a ceque path, certain springs, notable rocks, as well as constructed shrines and idols, which were wak'as, constituted records of event sequences, the results of which were the human groups who remembered them. Yet more, ceques were pathways (in today's Aymara, t"akis, closely related to the colonial Quechua taquies), dance paths that led from one such foundational moment to another, providing a choreographic diagram that wove a series of still-living memories from the past into a narrative whole. Not surprisingly, the song-dances performed on them, called taquies, were also like epics about the creative beings and creational moments that the dance paths connected. To sing and dance was also, then, to enact a story, rehearsing in bodily action the narrative of the body social.[48]

Wak'a figures were embodied, however, in their textile clothing; like humans they became agents capable of social action by being dressed in a social skin (Turner 1980). As extirpators of idolatry discovered, idols might be smashed or burned, but if their clothing, generally the elaborately worked cloth called cumbi, survived, the indians were able to bring the wak'a into being again by clothing some fragment of the old idol in the cloth that identified it.[49] Murra (1989) has highlighted numerous aspects of the role of cloth in the pre-Columbian Andes. Gifts of textiles from lords to subjects were a fundamental expression of the institutionalized generosity by which "common indians" suffered the privilege and pretensions of their lords; mallkus like Guarache of Killaka proudly wore shirts given to them by the Inca. Not just any cloth would do for such gifts: cumbi, which clothed Inca nobles, subordinate diarchy lords, and wak'a idols, was a particularly finely woven cloth, laden with iconographic significance that may have carried references to foundational narratives, origin places, and the gods and ancestors who validated social hierarchy. Although their full significance has not been "decoded," the most elaborate cumbi shirts include numerous figurative or geometric iconographic elements, called tukapus, in checkerboardlike arrays, often arranged in what appear to us as random sequences, suggesting that we might find in them complex messages if we only knew how to "read" them.[50]

In any case, textiles, which were also offered to the gods in vast quantities along with the frequent llama sacrifices and chicha libations that marked out the Andean calendar (Murra 1989), served as yet another medium through which humans ordered their own social relations by calling upon the gods, and hence the past, to intervene in their lives. Franquemont, Franquemont, and Isbell (1992) show how both the learning and production process of iconographic design panels in Chinchero weavings in contemporary Perú take a single form. Both weaving and the task of learning to weave textiles follow a formal process of recursion of minimal units into ever more complex ones, a process which resembles (as we shall see in chapter 7) how libation sequences and embedded hierarchies of social space are conceived and remembered in K'ulta. So it should not surprise us that textile design bands are also a kind of t"aki ("path"), often taking a zigzag form. Embedded within such zigzags in pre-Columbian as well as modern textiles are the frequent design elements called layra ("eye"), serving perhaps as a mnemonic doorway into the underworld and the past, which is sometimes called layra timpu ("eye time"). Likewise a common iconographic motif of the past as well as today is the warawara, the heavenly star that serves as a guidepost along celestial pathways of memory. When provincial lords like Guarache put on the cumbi shirts given them by the ruling Inca, they donned more than an opulent symbol of power; they clothed themselves and the local ancestry that upheld their right to station in the Inca state's more universalist narrative of the past.

Textile "eyes" recall the generalized Andean concept of paqarina, which, as we've seen, were the openings in the earth from which ancestors sprang in pre-Columbian narrated pasts. Into these openings and ushnus, the portals to other worlds that the Incas dug at the center of their ceremonial plazas, quantities of corn beer were poured in acts of remembrance. Spanish chroniclers paid scant attention to the words uttered along with the ceremonial draughts of chicha that Andeans thus shared with gods and ancestors, but as we shall see in part 3, the complexity of twentieth-century Andean poetics of libation dedications suggests that, in pre-Columbian times, drinking and the spilling out of maize beer that accompanied it formed yet another channel of social memory, no doubt congruent with narrated, knotted, and woven "registers."

When Atahuallpa, in Titu Cusi's account, offered to join Valverde in a libational drink, the Inca offered the cleric a vessel called a quero. On surviving examples of such vessels we can see that some of them, at least, bore figurative designs associated with the calendric moments and pasts that their libational use was to evoke (Randall 1993: 108–110, citing Liebscher 1986).[51]

One place where the social memory registers of queros, libations, quipus, and perhaps ceques came together in Qullasuyu was at ancestral tombs, called chullpas. In contrast with the shrines called paqarinas, the ancestral places of emergence such as the Incas' Paqariqtambo, chullpas were places where humans—especially high-ranking mallkus and kuraqas—went into the other world. Portals to the "inner space-time" that Aymara speakers call manxa-pacha, chullpas were potent places of social memory from the very moment of their construction, in which the social ties binding future elite occupants to the groups over which they held sway were given expression.

Witnesses to the probanza of a colonial cacique of Macha in the early seventeenth century, for example, recalled a regionally significant lord named Tata Paria, whose tomb was built by the collective efforts of workers from a multitude of Qullasuyu diarchies. On March 21, 1612, don Felipe Ochani, a principal ("more than one hundred years old") from Ayllu Paro of the anansaya, or upper moiety, of Macha declared that "[Tata Paria was] lord of all the nation of the Caracaras of the said parcialidad [of anansaya], and of the Quillacas, Soras, Carangas, and Chuyes, and all of them obeyed him and he made them come together in Macha, and this witness knew the said Tata Paria very well when this witness was a boy, and saw that the indians carried him on their shoulders like a great lord . . . and all the said nations came together in order to make him tombs . . . " (AGNA 13.18.7.2, 1612, fol. 309r).[52]

From moments like this to periodic rites of commemoration, when the mummies were brought out like the Inca emperors in Cusco and fêted by the members of social groups they had ruled, chullpas served as yet another pivot around which social groups made vivid to themselves the bonds that united them, and recalled their common links to a shared past and destiny. This was in part why the old burial places, as well as wak'as, were so worrisome to Spaniards concerned with the potential reemergence of "countermemories" during a time when Christian priests endeavored to give Andeans a new past.

Polo had warned in 1571 that indians were secretly disinterring the bodies of loved ones buried in churches and cemeteries, moving them to surreptitiously "enclose them in the wak'as, or mountains, or plains, or in old tombs . . . so as to give them to eat and drink at [the proper] times. And then they drink and dance and sing, gathering their relatives and allies to this end" (1916c: 194). Especially in Qullasuyu, and no doubt among the Asanaqi ancestors of K'ultas, as among the Pakax, hereditary lords were placed in tombs "outside the town, squared and tall, in the manner of a crypt, with a stone floor, and covered above with large stones, and painted on the outside with several colors. And they buried the deceased with the best clothing and offered much food and drink . . . " (Mercado de Peñalosa 1965: 339).

Just as mummified ancestors (like wak'a images) were draped with textiles that helped to recall the narrative whose source they embodied, so did above-ground chullpa towers become commemorative emblems. In a survey of numerous painted chullpas in the district of the Qaranka people, Gisbert and colleagues (1996) illustrate how design bands around the tombs' "waist" reduplicate common design elements of elite textiles, including the motif known as the layra, or eye. (See Fig. 5.6.) What is more, just above the narrow east-facing door opening, many such chullpas seem to *have* eyes; a pair of openings formed by queros laid mouth-outwards into the tomb wall. Here it all seems to come together: Gazing upon the chullpa "face," mourners could see into the past (itself suggested by the symbolism of eyes and the layra motif pointing to originary "eye time"), while the still-present deceased peered out at his or her own future and heirs through the every medium of sacrificial drink.

Human beings were not all that originated from and returned to another world through landscape gateways; domesticated and cultivated foodstuffs came with them, and consequently could serve as substitutes for the winking out of life that was otherwise necessary for people to complete their journey fully in space and time back to orginary moments. As many chroniclers noted, some ritual moments required human sacrificial victims to establish a stable conduit for communication between society and the gods. But most of the time, and in far greater quantities, it was domesticated vegetable and animal matter, killed and transformed through human activity (such as butchering, cooking,

Figure 5.6.   Painted chullpa tomb of Río Lauca (Author's sketch of photograph in Gisbert et al. 1996: 33)

brewing, and, in the case of llama wool, spinning and weaving), that enabled humans to conjure up and address the gods of the past.

Especially interlinked were the destinies of humans and llamas, who traveled together from paqarinas in origin times and who travel together to the other world upon death. Still today, in K'ulta, funeral rites include holocaust sacrifices of llamas (and a black dog) to accompany the dead in his or her spiritual journey to manxa-pacha. Accompanied by cloth (a manufactured "social skin" deriving from the animals' natural pelt), corn beer, and coca leaves, llamas were (and are) the sine qua non of sacrifice, in part because Andeans have envisioned llamas as enjoying a kind of social life comparable to that of humans. Guaman Poma illustrates several rituals in which the Inca emperor speaks "llama language," saying "yn, yn," as he prepares to send sacrificial llama messengers to the beyond (Guaman Poma 1980: 292). In some rituals, sacrificial llamas were led to their fates dressed in many-colored woven shirts, gold earrings dangling. They were fed on coca leaves and corn beer, and a quero full of corn beer was placed at their feet. By kicking it over, they participated in the libation offering.[53]

So for pre-Columbian Andeans, llamas were an important way of conceptualizing social power, and llamas as stand-ins for humans became the most suitable intermediaries for bringing the power of the past into the present. Molina (1989: 121) describes llama sacrifices in some detail, as Polo does (1916c). Both also make reference to the importance of human sacrifice on certain occasions. Taking issue with Polo on the existence of human sacrifice (and on many other points), the chronicler known as the Anonymous Jesuit (1879) argues that Polo made a simple error in interpretation, resulting from the fact that terms for age categories of llamas and humans were alike. The Jesuit is no doubt wrong when he suggests that when Polo heard the Quechua word for "child" he misunderstood an Andean's reference to a young llama, called by the same term (ibid., 142–146). But he nevertheless highlights the parallelism between llamas and humans that makes llamas suitable subjects for humans to think about in attempt to change their own social relations. Drawing on the quipus of "Juan Collque, Señor de los Quillacas," as one of his authorities, he adds further depth to our understanding of the importance of the Andean analogy between human beings and llamas that made the latter suitable for sacrifices. Given their pivotal role as a means of crossing the boundary between this world and the other, inhabited by the powerful forces of eye time, we begin to see how sacrifices constituted (and still constitute—see chap. 8) another important technique of social memory.[54]

In the pre-Columbian Andes, then, the past was remembered through its locations in the landscape, the sequence was encoded in woven cloth, in twined and knotted cords, and in the poetically "woven" song-dances and stories whose rhythms were stamped out by footsteps danced in taquies or imagined along t"aki pathways through the landscape that linked the wak'as. A narrative past was also to be seen in a heavenly pathway, the river/road of the Milky Way, along which a series of figures, discerned in the black spaces between the stars as much as in the stars themselves, nightly and seasonally progressed (Urton 1981). Along the bright pathway a man led a llama with its young, pursued by a fox, towards a spring, and just to the side of the pathway, a multitude of heavenly storehouses (*qullqa*) could be seen in the constellation of little stars we call the Pleiades, which they called Unquy. When these store-houses came into view in the first hours of night, they signaled that the time was right to set out on long-distance caravan journeys to stock up on food products to be stored in one's own qullqa. This was unquy mit'a, a time of renewal when certain cleansing rites were performed in Cusco, while crops were dried in preparation for transport and storage.

One might, then, imagine the quipu kamayuq charged with the memory of ceque and wak'a rites with quipu in hand. As his fingers moved along a major cord to its dependent cords and to the groups of knots along them, he may well have mentally traveled the ceque itself and stopped at the wak'as along it. And if myth cycles were themselves tied to the actions of narrative heroes who, turned to stone or spring, still lived as wak'as and breathed life and social meaning into the people who sang and danced to them, then ceque systems and quipus as their twined trace might well have encoded foundational mythic and dynastic narrative.

Recall too some of the other forms of Andean social memory. Mummified ancestors, as actual relics from the past whose acts still reverberated in the cult organization that gave form to living social groups, each had their own stories to tell through ceque and quipu as well as taquies. And the cloth in which mummies, living persons, and stone wak'as were dressed was also rich in iconographic significance, largely still undeciphered. Recall how important these pieces of cloth were in capac hucha rituals, as a kind of "social skin" through which the inner essence of one kind of being could be visibly transferred to another (textiles being made from camelid wool, cloth also provided a link between the human social world and the herds on which humans depended in so many ways). Likewise maize, converted into beer, served as an important medium of social memory. Shared in events of communion with the gods and ancestors and simultaneously with other persons with whom the offerer established or reaffirmed social ties, drinks were given significance by words of dedication to ancestors and gods who themselves, as the defining focal points of social groups like lineages, gave meaning to the human relationships so forged or reaffirmed. A long sequence of libations poured from queros, such as those carried out during virtually all ritual events (requiring the massive quantities of beer that helped drive the imperial system of labor tribute in maize fields) was therefore a means for imbibing the past into the bodies and memories of the libators.

But to what degree were the imperial forms of social memory like those of the provinces? It is once again Polo who describes how the Cusco system of ceques and quipu accounts, linking the present shape and hierarchy of social groups with the past remembered in them, was extended into newly conquered territories. In the first place, there was the Inca administrative practice of seizing and dividing certain lands. This was a necessary complement to the incorporation of subjugated peoples into the sacrificial system of Cusco, by which they were also absorbed into a generalized social hierarchy through their relationship to the Inca who conquered them and to the deities with whom he held court after his death. As Polo explains, the greater part of tribute was itself a labor prestation carried out to feed and clothe the wak'as, and also the laborers themselves, in the process of producing the corn which made the beer subsequently offered up in state-administered sacrifices.

So the Asanaqi people who worked their assigned strips of land in the Cochabamba valley (strips divided by sight lines connecting, one imagines, a set of wak'as, cult to which reshaped the social structure of the groups that participated in these labors) generated corn surpluses that were largely turned to beer; on ritual occasions such as their own celebratory self-sacrifice in performing such labor, they also drank it. The product of tributary herding labors, of course, was cloth, which they came to wear on their backs, just as their mallkus and their wak'as did. So administrative centers and Inca production zones themselves were laid out as icons of the social order of the peoples who worked in them (recall the arrangement of Killaka and Qaranka diarchies into demarcated suyus of the Cochabamba valley). At the same time, Polo suggests with a certain Inca-centrism that it was Incas who provided such mnemonic techniques for the peoples they conquered:

> [The Inca] brought the same order to each town, dividing each
> district into ceques and lines, and established shrines of diverse
> advocations, such as all things that seemed notable like springs and
> artesian wells and *puquios* and large stones and valleys and peaks,
> which they call *apachetas,* and for each thing he placed persons, and
> showed them the order that they should follow in sacrifice, in each
> place and for what end, and he assigned teachers to show them when
> and what kinds of things [to sacrifice]. Finally, although nowhere
> were there so many shrines as in Cusco, the order elsewhere is the
> same; having seen the map of the wak'as of Cusco, in each town, no
> matter how small, they will depict it in the same way and will show
> the fixed ceques and wak'as and shrines, knowing about which is a
> very important business for their conversion. I have proved it in more
> than a hundred towns, and the lord bishop of Charcas [Domingo de
> Santo Tomás] asked if it were indeed so universal. When we went
> together about the business of perpetuity by Your Majesty's order, I
> showed it to him in Pocona [an Inca coca production zone] and the
> very indians depicted for him there the same map, and in this there is
> no doubt because it will be found exactly as I say. . . .
>   Sowing and reaping [the fields] and filling up the deposits that
> were prepared for this purpose were a great part of the tribute that

they gave. Some of it they spent in sacrifices in the town itself and most of it they carried to Cusco for the same effect from all places. . . . It was a huge quantity, because there they had the principal houses of all the gods and in each one many people who did nothing else, and every day each one sacrificed in the plaza and on the hills, and this we see in the general manifest. I do not believe that among any other sort of people of whom we have knowledge is so much, and with so many ceremonies, spent on sacrifices. . . . (Polo Ondegardo 1990: 47–48)[55]

Polo may have been an especially insightful observer of Andean ways and may even have found among them much to laud, but their techniques of recalling the past were not among the Andean traditions he found worthy of preservation. A few chapters later in the same account, Polo returns to the matter of the ceques and wak'a cult:

It is necessary in all the towns to make them depict the map, after showing them the map of Cusco, so that the priest should be well informed of each of these things, as much so that he should understand it and carry out punishments, as to enable him to preach against it and move them with clear reasons so that they understand the illusions and trickery of the devil. (Polo Ondegardo 1990: 102)[56]

One must, in other words, discover the secrets of Andean techniques of social memory in order to force the native to forget. Even in places that were inhabited largely by mitimas, laborer-settlers moved by Inca administrators to important state production zones such as the coca production zone of Pocona, where Polo demonstrated his knowledge of ceque systems to Santo Tomás, memory of the founding acts of ancestors and gods was kept alive. Cristóbal de Albornóz discovered to his horror that Andeans had already rehearsed ways to preserve their commemorations even after the idols had been smashed:

Among these indios mitimas, those who the Inca moved from one place to another, there are other kinds of wak'as. Of great importance and kept most hidden are those of a piece of clothing taken from the *wak'a paqarisqa* of their homeland, which is given to them by the priest or kamayuq of the said wak'a in their land, charging them not to forget the name of their origin and that, in the same way that they had in their homeland, they should reverence and worship their paqarisqa creator. And this they did, taking out this piece of their wak'a clothing in their dances and general taquies. They keep these pieces with great care and have given them service and property. They take and carry them as if they are wak'as: If there are springs in their lands, they bring with them a cup of water, throw it with great ceremony into the springs in the places to which they are transplanted, and give it the name of their paqarisqa with great solemnity, and if it is a stone, they put the piece of clothing they have brought over another stone, and in the same way all the things that they held as paqarisqas. . . .

It must be known that the majority of wak'as, apart from their properties, have clothing of cumbi that they call capac huchas, of the same grandeur as the wak'as. And the first thing one must do so that no relic of the wak'a remains is to procure these capac huchas, because if they remain in their power, they will dress any stone they like with it. (Albornóz 1989: 171, 196)

Not only, then, were occasional rites of rule and sacrificial children called capac huchas, "opulent prestations," so too were the pieces of highly valued cloth, gifts of the Inca, that had traveled the pathways between Cusco and local shrines.

We have surveyed some of the better Spanish sources on pre-Columbian forms of social memory in the Andes. Within a generation after Polo, Albornóz, and Cristóbal de Molina wrote their accounts, investigation into such things became a matter for antiquarianists: No longer performed, most such rites, especially those tied to public contexts and Inca state activities, disappeared into the past, recoverable only through the writings of those closer to the events. This was, of course, precisely the end that our perceptive authors had in mind when they carried out their investigations.

It remains to be seen, however, how Spaniards began the process, not of erasure, but of reinscription of Andean social memory. On the one hand, they sought to drag the narrated Andean past into universal history, which is to say, to reconcile it with biblical narrative. On the other, as we shall see in chapter 6, they began a long process of reshaping Andeans' relationship to time and space, providing an architectural and choreographic substitute for the intimate sacrificial ties that had bound Asanaqi householders to their mallkus and Inca overlords. That substitute would instill in them the good customs, the "*buena policía*," by which they would, for the benefit of their everlasting souls, more readily submit to the Castilians' two majesties, God and king. But first, there was the business of transforming tributary labor organized for a sacrificial system that reproduced Andean social structures into labor that would produce bars of silver, capable of producing and reproducing aristocratic privilege for the conquistadors and the machines of war for the European enterprises carried out on God's behalf by their king and emperor. Let us put such things into context.

In studying the uptake by Spaniards of Inca forms of social memory and the Andean response, we must pay close attention to a pair of interdependent winnowing processes carried out in Spanish minds and writings. First of all, we must examine how a wide gamut of Andean forms of social memory was marginalized or erased by Spanish historians who, in the absence of writing, privileged the spoken word above nonlinguistic communications, and gave special place to kinds of oral narrative that was recognizable to them as dynastic epic, a genre from which early Castilian history was itself drawn. As our chroniclers consider the consequences of the absence of writing in the Andes, they note, here and there, some of the vehicles of an Andean art of memory.

Andean memory had inhered in song and dance, rite and topography, textile designs and painted drinking vessels, as well as in oral narrative. Most such expressive forms soon became suspect and subject to erasure as the vehicles of native idolatry and error. Yet Andean social memory began to wither even before the imposition of systematic persecution. It did so because the conduits of social memory were always and everywhere attuned to the shapes of local social groups and their ways of articulating with the now-collapsed Inca state. A variety of Spanish colonial practices then conspired to reshape the ways in which social groups were constituted, and some brands of social memory were cut loose from their moorings, becoming irrelevant in accounting for the new past (one including Spanish conquistadors and encomenderos) which now haunted Andeans. In such circumstances one might expect a burst of creativity in which new songs, rites, and narratives surge to the fore to recapture the past, or to revise it for congruity with new ways of constituting collectivities. And there was indeed such movement. But it was just here that Andeans slammed full tilt into the barriers erected by the Spanish state precisely as prophylaxis against such creative outbursts: Andean efforts to adapt the tenets and rituals of Christianity to their own ends, or to reshape their narratives so as to account for the Spaniards and their colonial practices (and perhaps to undo them), were subject to the apparatuses of surveillance and discipline characteristic of "the first modern state"; they were censored by Counter-Reformation heterodoxy-sniffers.

Most of the details available to us about pre- and postconquest Andean forms of social memory are written in the censors' books. Captured in moments of crisis, under hostile conditions, and just as a creative burst of innovation overtook somewhat routinized forms of pre-Columbian practice, such records should signal us to be wary, especially in using them as guides to truly precolonial social forms.

Nearly all the sources on Andean culture were produced under inquisitorial conditions, by figures in positions of great power. Polo's study of Inca religion was done while he was corregidor of Cusco; Domingo de Santo Tomás wrote as a privileged cleric, often trusted with high-level administrative responsibilities. And the administrative sources often mined for information on Andean ways—visitas, records of idolatry extirpation, parish registers, notarial records, compilations of Inca narratives, and even grammars and dictionaries of indigenous languages—were all generated as tools for changing native life-ways: calling indians together to be counted, interrogating them and preaching to them, reshaping social subjectivity in baptism, marriage, and funeral, inscribing new links between individuals and property, transforming multiple oral narratives into a single written history, and establishing equivalences between indigenous meanings and Spanish ones. All such sources are marked by the colonial imbalance of power that hyperprivileged Spanish pens to a degree far greater than the discursive imbalances of ethnography.

Not many "ordinary Spaniards" wrote convincingly on Andean topics (most could not write at all), but even when they did, "ordinary Spaniards" were not ordinary in the Indies, but held what often amounted to life or death power over indians. Nonetheless, one relatively ordinary Spaniard is credited with having written the most valuable of the early participant accounts of Andean ways. Pedro Cieza de León traveled the length and breadth of Perú in the 1540s with notebooks in hand, later transforming his writings into the massive *Crónica del Perú*. This is a good place to begin the business of the chapters that follow, on the effects of the active Spanish effort to colonize the Andean past as remembered both in oral narrative and in forms of meaningful action. Next I treat the textualization of the Andean past, specifically the double movement through which Spaniards initially privileged oral narrative as the most "historical" Andean source and then proceeded to transform it, to invade first the logic of epic event-sequence and then the master narrative of universal history.

NARRATIVE CONQUESTS: SPANISH ENCOUNTERS WITH MYTHIC
ANDEAN JOURNEYS

The Spanish chronicler Pedro Cieza de León had arrived in Perú not long after the conquest and led a soldier's life in the northern reaches of South America, far from the splendiferous center of the Inca empire. Having travailed through the period of civil wars that almost immediately broke out among the conquerors after the events of Cajamarca, he must eagerly have taken advantage of an offer from the "great pacifier," Pedro de la Gasca, to carry certain letters to Potosí in 1549. His journey took him to and through Cusco, and everywhere he went, he queried people about themselves and the places he encountered, jotting down notes in his journals that he later revised into a chronicle. At one point Cieza lamented the Andes' lack of writing: "Being so blind about these things, one is led to say how fortunate is the invention of writing, that by the virtue of its sounds memory lasts for many centuries, and news of events spreads throughout the universe. And having readings in our hands, we do not remain ignorant of our desires. But since no writing has been found in this new world of the Indies, we must take our best guess on many things" (Cieza de León 1984: chap. 105, p. 284).[57]

Other chroniclers marveled at the accomplishments Incas were able to achieve without writing, and even praised the Andes' other forms of social memory, from quipu to quero. Almost as asides, they also referred to Inca songs and dances (in which much mythic narrative was imbedded) and to other kinds of ritual commemorative and state theater. But few went so far in their praise as to describe systematically the contents of such memory forms, and those who did (such as Polo Ondegardo, on the ceque system) did so for combined pecuniary and missionary ends, as the first step in confiscating the treasuries of pagan idols and smashing idolatries, as well as erasing idolatry's memory.

The single exception to this rule of erasure was the Incas' orally transmitted accounts of the past that were not to be found in the Bible. Cieza, like Betanzos, Sarmiento, and many other chroniclers, had recourse to oral narrative as the most reliable Inca source for the histories of the Incas they sought to write, histories that would bring Andeans into Europe's and Christianity's universal history. Chronicling the Inca past, that is, was the scribe's contribution to the colonial project. Conquered by the sword, Incas were also to be colonized, it appears, by the pen.

Spanish chroniclers expressed qualms about the process of inscribing native narratives. Virtually every writer of Andean tales worried about the apparent incommensurability of spoken word and written text. One set of concerns derived from the very *orality* of native narrative, which led chroniclers—and even Andeans—to bemoan the absence of writing in the pre-Columbian Andes.

The compiler-author of the Quechua Huarochirí manuscript began this late-sixteenth-century compilation of a provincial oral tradition and account of ritual life with reference to writing: "If the ancestors of the people called Indians had known writing in earlier times, then the lives they lived would not have faded from view until now. As the mighty past of the Spanish Vira Cochas is visible until now, so too, would theirs be. But since things are as they are, and since nothing has been written until now, I set forth here the lives of the ancestors of the Huaro Cheri people, who all descend from one forefather" (Salomon and Urioste 1991: 41–42).

In a footnote, Salomon points out how Quechua verbal usage emphasizes the *"visibility* of the new Spanish mnemotechnology, writing, as opposed to the *audibility* of the endangered oral tradition" (ibid., 42 n. 8; emphasis in original). More difficult to grasp for both Spaniards and Andeans, however, was the contrast between the Spanish emphasis involving two senses, visible writing and audible speech as mnemotech-niques, and the polysensual Andean techniques of social memory. Father Bernabe Cobo, for example, was willing to concede that in spite of their lack of writing, Andeans remembered rather too much: "The most notable aspect of this religion is how they had nothing written down to learn and keep. They made up for this shortcoming by memorizing everything so exactly that it seems as if these things were carved into the Indians' bones" (Cobo 1990: book 1, chap. 1, p. 9).

Here Cobo introduces his account of Andean memory of things he called religious, that is ceque systems and wak'a rites. Such things are not, however, what Cobo regarded as sources of specifically historical knowledge. Where he speaks of history, understanding the term as both reliable record and the recorded event chronology, he finds Andeans at a disadvantage, weighing in with an opinion which both grants reliability to an Andean approximation of writing and denies its value for the historian of antiquities:

> Since the Indians had no writing, the information we find among
> them concerning their antiquities is very meager. Although it is true
> that the Peruvians used certain strings or cords to preserve a record
> of their deeds (as we shall see), nothing was kept on these records
> except what occurred from the time that the Inca Empire started its
> conquests . . . but upon moving from there back, everything is
> confusion and darkness, in which hardly any trace or vestige can be
> perceived that would guide us on an inquiry into earlier times. (Cobo
> 1979: book 2, chap. 1, p. 94)

For these authors, the lack of a writing system is itself linked to both the proliferation and mutability of texts, a multiplication of oral accounts that complicated the chronicler's task. "Here in these provinces of Perú," wrote Cieza, "men, though blind, give great account of themselves, and tell so many fables that it would be harmful to write them down" (Cieza de León 1986: chap. 3, p. 3).[58] Harmful, at least, to both writer's hand and reader's patience. But one wonders if the multiplicity of Andean creation "fables" was not also in some sense unthinkable to Spaniards, from whose perspective an assertion that empire and heterodoxy could be compatible might be interpreted as heresy.

Although Cieza recounts few pre-Inca tales, others were somewhat more forthcoming. Cobo, for example, briefly summarized some Andean origin myths (taken from earlier writers) as a sort of preface to what for him was a more reliable post-Inca narrative corpus. Before beginning this "true" history with Manco Capac's acts in Cusco, he concluded that " . . . they tell a thousand other foolish tales and stories, and trying to write them all down here would be a never-ending task. The ones that I have just told will suffice to show how uncertain and obscure the beginning and origin of the Incas is. But it is customary for true histories to be filled with such fictitious stories, and all those on this subject that the Indians commonly tell point to certain facts . . . " (Cobo 1979: book 2, chap. 3, p. 106).

In a two-step process, writers such as Cobo (and earlier authors like Sarmiento and Betanzos) quickly swept aside the most variable sorts of narrative, those concerned with ancient origins, in order to focus upon less distant stories collected from more reliable sources, the high-ranking nobles of Inca Cusco. The ordinary indians of Cusco, not to speak of the indians of the conquered provinces, were held to be as unreliable in such matters as Castilian peasants. But if descendants of great noble lineages and imperial memorialists, holding quipus in their hands, were admired by a Sarmiento or a Cobo, the compilation of a "true history" nonetheless required careful treatment of informants' testimony, precisely to reduce the multiplicity of native narrative to a single account.

In the manner of an expert witness called by the prosecution, Sarmiento describes the procedures he used to "correct" the stories told him by his Inca memorialists:

> And thus by examining . . . the most prudent and oldest men, to whom more credit is given, I extracted and compiled the present history by showing the declarations of each [witness] to his enemies, or better said to his contraries, since they fall into opposed sides. . . . What is written here has been refined by having contraries check and correct each others' memoirs (all of which are in my power), and finally ratifying them in the public presence of all contraries and ayllus (sworn in by judicial authority), with expert translators and very curious and faithful interpreters (also sworn). (Sarmiento de Gamboa 1942: chap. 9, p. 60)[59]

The technique closely resembles the methods employed a decade before by the extirpator of idolatry, Cristóbal de Albornóz, whose inquisitorial style had successfully extracted confessions from members of the *taqui oncoy* movement of the 1560s (Albornóz 1990). Sarmiento, however, sought confessions, not of idolatrous acts in the present, but of historical memories. There can be no clearer account of the historical method as judicial procedure. As an appointee of Viceroy Francisco de Toledo, Sarmiento used such procedures not only to guarantee the accuracy of his history but also to underscore its admissibility as evidence in the court of public opinion. Thus, he continues: "I have worked so diligently in order to establish the truth in a business as grave as that of proving the tyranny in this land of the cruel Incas, so that all nations of the world should understand the juridical and more than legitimate title, that the king of Castile has to these Indies and to other lands neighboring them, especially to these kingdoms of Peru" (Sarmiento de Gamboa 1942: chap. 9, p. 60).[60]

As Sarmiento was aware, the process required a careful surgery by which narrative was extracted from its context. What he sought to eliminate were discrepancies among the narratives presented by Incas from different ayllus, each with its own "*particulares intereses*" (ibid., chap. 9, p. 59). In so doing, he produced an authoritative account, the authority of which depended both on the judicial nature of his proceedings and upon the depersonalization and decontextualization that they were intended to achieve, in which the battle of informants' antagonistic interests (determined by affiliation to particular social units) would cancel out the distortions in each other's account. The written end product thus might achieve the permanence and hermeneutic closure associated with the printed page. In Sarmiento's case, such closure was also sought to help preclude further dynastic claims by the very men chosen (by virtue of their dynastic claims) as informants! When a long list of myth tellers signed off, in the presence of a notary, to the veracity of Sarmiento's compilation, they also in effect admitted to being the successors of illegitimate tyrants. Or so thought Sarmiento, along with his patron, Viceroy Toledo.

However, as Gary Urton (1990) has demonstrated, Sarmiento's careful inquisitorial procedures were not sufficient to eliminate entirely the "particular interests" of his informants. Among his witnesses was a significant and influential contingent of regional nobles whose claims to noble succession were greatly strengthened by leading Sarmiento to locate Inca origins confidently in a place called Pacaritambo. And so

Sarmiento authorized a single origin point, privileging a particular social group, while he vitiated other origin points and other claims to legitimate power.[61] In spite of Toledo's attempt to prohibit further indian appeals to the Crown, such claims, like those on which Urton draws, were nonetheless made. Following Urton's line of argument, we may suggest that the Spanish desire for a single official story in effect led to the erasure of narrative multiplicity, thereby obscuring one of the features by which Andean narrative traditions differed from Spanish historical consciousness.

Frank Salomon (1982) has argued that the contradiction that ensued from efforts to reduce oral narrative to writing lay in the irreconcilability of Andean and Spanish notions of time and history. Spaniards' perception of historical time as a single, linear, and nonrepeating sequence of events made it impossible for them to recognize, much less understand, the very different perception of historical time current in the Andes, one in which the sequence of episodes in one narrative did not require validation by being fitted into a single master narrative. Contradictions between narratives were of little significance, since each narrative evinced an instance of a cyclic pattern of events. As Salomon also recognizes, however, Spaniards' biblical outlook produced its share of cyclicity; not to speak of the liturgic calendar by which salvation history is played out on a yearly, nay weekly, basis. It is also rather likely that, when an Inca emperor was well established, his own particular lineage-interested past was purveyed as an authoritative story into which subordinate peoples' pasts were supposed to fit. Dynastic struggles or rebellions might then have taken the form of not only a contest at arms but also a battle of histories. Circumstances of dynastic instability, such as the entire period during which Spaniards collected accounts of the Inca past, would then predict the emergence of multiple and contradictory accounts.

Such speculation, however, begs a number of questions. First of all, it rests on the rather dubious assumption that the narratives elicited for the record by Spaniards were, as they assumed, dynastic histories. While they disparaged narratives that competed with biblical event sequences, chroniclers like Sarmiento gave credibility to stories of the succession of Inca kings and their conquests, stories which no doubt struck them as analogous in kind to the postbiblical chronicles of Castilian dynasties. But Zuidema (1990) has argued that stories of Inca rulers were no less a part of an Andean mythical consciousness than clearly "mythic" accounts of cosmogenesis were. For Zuidema, all such accounts had more to do with describing and validating forms of social hierarchy and political relations among their tellers than with historicity. As Salomon suggests:

> In Spain, historians read *crónicas,* and the writers of *crónicas* appear
> to have read *relaciones.* For Andeans, the sources of diachronic
> knowledge were completely different and had never been organized
> on the principles of absolute chronology, cause-and-effect, or
> eschatology. The useful past was embodied in dynastic oral tradition,
> the knot record, the constellation of royal mummies, and the
> spatial-ritual calendar round framed on the system of shrines around
> the Inca capital. (Salomon 1982: 11)

As Salomon notes in the essay quoted here, "Chronicles of the Impossible," which is an analysis of the chronicles produced by the native Andeans who sought to reconcile their own pasts with the conventions of the Spaniards in the latters' very language and writing conventions, such authors had been "formed within a tradition which admitted the concept change-of-worlds (*pachakuti*) and gave humanity multiple, not unique, origins (*paqarinakuna*)" (ibid., 32). It is precisely this latter contrast I would like to emphasize, rather than claims of a fundamental disjunction between linear (Spanish) and cyclic (Andean) notions of time.

Our Spanish chroniclers were clearly disturbed when they found in the Andes nearly as many variations of origin stories as there were storytellers. Their discomfort, I suggest, resulted, not from some vertigo caused by a novel encounter with cyclic time, but from the juxtaposition of empire and narrative heterodoxy. The very multiplicity of the Andean past needed to be homogenized before Andean peoples could be properly ruled by a monarch whose mandate to rule rested on the propagation not only of the true faith but also of universal history. Writing in a Counter-Reformation age of orthodoxy, Spanish chroniclers gathered native narratives precisely in order to colonize the Andean past, to write Andeans into the master narrative that underwrote the Spanish project in the New World and that interlinked the authority of the two majesties (earthly and divine) whose scribes our chroniclers were. It is little wonder, then, that Spaniards so routinely scoffed at the multiplicity of Andean origin stories.

As Spaniards saw it, Andeans' insistence on locating the creation of man in their own local territory evinced an astounding degree of shortsightedness, if not hubris. Many chroniclers were willing to over-look such hubris in the case of the Incas, whose origin stories could be taken as dynastic histories; it is the non-Incas whose stories for the most part failed to merit pen and ink. Let us turn to the "predynastic" Inca narratives that Sarmiento and Cobo recount as amusing prefaces to their serious historicizing work.

Spaniards first learned about pre-Inca times on the Altiplano from the Incas themselves, and only occasionally and incidentally took into account the Altiplano peoples' own views of their past. As do-all empire-building colonizers, Incas saw themselves as civilizers, whose arrival brought light and order to peoples without them. Inca memorialists told Spaniards of the military campaigns by which certain Inca emperors had annexed the warlike peoples of Qullasuyu to the south of Cusco, bringing the benefits of civilization to a previously brutish population. But they also told stories that made certain Qullasuyu places into the very origin places of the early Incas, those who had lived generations before the conquest of Qullasuyu. An island in Lake Titicaca and the site of Tiwanaku, which Incas controlled only after many hard-fought battles against peoples called Lupaqas and Qullas, were nonetheless repeatedly cited in Inca oral histories as their own place of origin, a veritable *axis mundi* far more ancient than the one they created in the imperial capital of Cusco.

The quandary of this conflict of histories, which raises the people and territory of Inca subjects to the ontological (or perhaps, cosmogenic) status of Inca rulers, has fueled a great deal of research and informed speculation about the question of Inca origins, always in conjunction with origins of Altiplano peoples. Unfortunately for students of Qullasuyu, nearly all the explicitly and self-consciously historical material at hand is Inca-centric: gathered directly from Inca noble informants or construed as ancillary to a history of the Inca empire. Apart from fragmentary accounts, no Spaniard attempted to interpret the historical or mythic consciousness of a Qullasuyu group from within its own tradition. Instead, Qulla or Lupaqa stories were curious departures, generally unworthy of the pen, from the more reliable, state-sanctioned accounts of the past that were systematically collected in Cusco. Yet the Inca fixation on Titicaca and Tiwanaku suggests that they may have imported Altiplano perspectives on the past into their own past. Indeed, there are almost no sources in transcribed and translated oral narrative in which Cusco and Titicaca, Incas and Qullas, are not co-implicated.

It is, then, worth our while to survey the fragments of Inca oral history touching on Tiwanaku/Titicaca that have come to us through chronicles produced during the Spanish colony, in light of the more fragmentary accounts of sixteenth-century Altiplano peoples' own oral traditions about their pre-Inca past.

In 1549, Cieza de León traveled southwards from Cusco onto the Altiplano to see for himself this populous and silver-laden territory, which had become famous for its riches even in wartime. Cieza himself had been a participant in conquests in the region of Popayán and in the civil wars that wracked Perú in the decade of the 1540s, and had lived essentially a soldier's life until freed from it by a short-lived peace in the wake of the rebel Gonzalo Pizarro's defeat by the "pacifier" Pedro de la Gasca in 1548. Throughout his travels, Cieza seems to have kept a series of diaries and notebooks which, to judge by the works he drew from them, were written in a blunt and fact-laden style, descriptive, to the point, and free of the literary mannerisms and metaphor of some other authors of his day. In fact, all Cieza's writings read like travelogues, and none more so than part 1 of his three-part *Crónica del Perú* (published in Seville in 1553). Like most travelers of the day, Cieza followed Inca highways, and his travel narrative moves in episodic leaps from place to place along these roads.

As Cieza moved southwards from Cusco into the lands that Incas called Qullasuyu, he followed in the footsteps of the Inca invaders whose conquest narratives move through the same sequence of places: first passing through the land of a people called Kanchi, Cieza proceeded through the lands of Qana, Qulla, and Lupaqa peoples before reaching a narrative resting place in Tiwanaku. These are the peoples whom he most queried about the past and about the curious topographic features and antiquities in their lands. Cieza continued farther south, but his interest in indians and their stories seems to wane as he neared the fabulous mines of Porco and Potosí.

Several factors led Cieza to locate Altiplano peoples as part of a dark past transcended by Inca imperial glories. First of all, there is the narrative flow of his own travel account, which follows an episodic trajectory of its own. Episodes of Altiplano narratives appear only as fragmentary supplements to Cieza's own narrative logic. Yet quite apart from the influence of the book's narrative itinerary, Cieza's response to Altiplano stories of the past is also conditioned by another narrative sequence, the chronology of a biblical universal history against which his informants' pasts are invariably judged. Of special interest to Cieza were episodes from native narrative that rang out familiar notes in his own tradition. Usually unwilling to commit Altiplano oral histories to paper, he relaxes his guard against native *fábulas* and *bulerías* to recount

Andean stories of a deluge: "Many of these indians tell of hearing from their forefathers that in times past a great flood took place (as I wrote in chapter three of the second part). And they explain that their ancestors are of great antiquity" (Cieza de León 1984: 273).[62]

Cieza recounts the myth fragments used by others as evidence of a preconquest Andean evangelization, but he does so only to debunk such theories. He is unwilling to grant that Andeans of the pre-Spanish age had access to biblical truth or the precepts of Christianity. For him Andean accounts of a great deluge could *not* reflect a memory of the true Universal Flood: the multiplicity of Andean languages suggested to him that this Andean flood must have taken place only *after* the division of languages in the tower of Babel, long after Noah's day. Note that Cieza does not doubt the facticity of a universal flood, but simply rejects Andean narrative after comparing its event sequences with biblical ones. Andean flood stories, then, are mere fables. And Cieza derides Altiplano origin narratives at a further remove from biblical truth: "Of their origins they have so many sayings and fables, if they are that, that I should not take time to write them down. Some say they emerged from a spring, others from a rock, and others from lakes, and on their origins one can get nothing else from them" (ibid., 274).[63]

Unfortunately, we can get little more from Cieza's encounters with Andean oral tradition than such scattered references and out-of-context episodic fragments. No doubt the very multiplicity of Qulla origin stories worried Cieza, especially after having collected in Cusco a more homogeneous "great tradition."

Most chroniclers saw fit to locate the beginnings of potentially historical Andean narrative after the emergence of the first Inca king, Manco Capac, from a place called Pacaritambo. In most accounts, four brothers and four sisters emerge (after the flood or after creation elsewhere and an underground journey) from a window on a hilltop "house of origin," or "way-stop of the flowering," as "paqariq tambo" may be parsed. They then proceed on a transformative journey towards the Cusco valley, during which a series of episodes establishes the identity between these ancestral figures and deity-shrines of great importance in Inca religion.

A central feature of this myth is its references to actual topographic features of the Cusco area: The journey of the ancestors established not only a narrative thread by which to unfold the episodic development of its protagonists, but also an actual path, which as a pilgrimage route connected a series of sacred places. Thus narrative sequence marked out a relationship between time and space, which could then be ritually commemorated in calendric sequence by the descendants of these particular ancestors—the Inca nobles who belonged to Cusco's *qapaq ayllu*. Founded in the acts of ancestral beings of primordial times, these sacred places, called wak'as, became the reference points of social groups defined as such precisely through their transitive relationship to the wak'a. The relationship among such groups was then given order with reference to both territory and hierarchy by their wak'as' positions in space and in temporal sequence. Here, in the narrative particular to the noble qapaq ayllu, we have the basis for understanding the significance of the ceque system of Cusco, the coordinated system of such vectors, or transit lines, that radiated from a central point near Cusco's temple of the sun.

As the empire expanded, Incas had to take account of the forms of ritual and cosmological organization that defined the political structure of the groups they sought to bring under state control. That, certainly, is one possible explanation for the equivocal standing of the origin stories emanating from Lake Titicaca rather than Pacaritambo. Whether Incas revered Titicaca because it was an ancient origin place of their migrating ancestors or because it was a powerful shrine among the Qullasuyu peoples they conquered (or in another scenario, simply because it was the alternative origin story of a noble Inca lineage whose story vied for preeminence with Pacaritambo-linked groups) is for the moment irrelevant. Instead, let us focus on the Titicaca stories to see what parallelisms might link these alternative (or consecutive) accounts.

Sarmiento, whose work was carried out as part of Viceroy Toledo's project to transform Andean society, introduces an account of creation in Titicaca/Tiwanaku that multiplies the single creator god Viracocha into a group of four, reminiscent of the four Ayar brothers of well-known Pacaritambo origin stories:

> The natives of this land say that in the beginning, or before the world
> was created, there was one called Viracocha, who created the world
> in darkness, without sun, moon, or stars. . . . And thus he created
> men, like those who live now, in his likeness. And they lived in
> darkness. . . .
> But among these men the vices of pride and avarice arose, and
> they overstepped the precepts of Viracocha Pachayachachi, who,
> indignant, confounded and cursed them.
> And then some of them were converted into stones and others into
> other forms; some were swallowed by the earth and others by the
> sea. And over all of them he sent a general flood, which they called

unupachakuti, which means "water that turned the land upside down." . . .

In the same manner the rest of the nations tell fables about how some from their nation were saved, from whom they trace their origin and descent. . . .

It is said how all was destroyed through an unupachakuti deluge. At this point one should know that Viracocha Pachayachachi, when he destroyed this land as has been told, kept with him three men, one of whom was named Taguapaca, so that they should serve him and help him to raise the new people that were needed in the second age after the Flood. And this is how he did it:

When the Flood was over and the earth dry, Viracocha determined to people it a second time, and in order to do so with greater perfection he decided to raise up luminaries by which to see. To do so, he went with his servants to a great lake, which is in the Collao, wherein there is a island called Titicaca. . . . Viracocha went to that island and commanded the sun, moon and stars to come out and go up into the sky to give light to the world. And thus it was. . . . Viracocha ordered his servants to do some things, but Taguapaca disobeyed Viracocha's commandments. And he, angered by Taguapaca, ordered the other two to take him, to tie him by his hands and feet, and throw him into a boat in the lake. And thus it was done. As Taguapaca blasphemed Viracocha for what had been done to him and threatened to return to take his vengeance, he was carried away by the waters of the river that empties that lake (el Desaguadero), and was not seen again for a long time. This done, Viracocha fabricated in that place a solemn wak'a as a shrine to signal what he had done and created there. (Sarmiento de Gamboa 1942: 48–54)[64]

Sarmiento then relates how the remaining three deities traveled through the other three Inca suyus (Qullasuyu being left to the prodigal son) to create men. Then Sarmiento pauses to relate an alternate version of the story, in which Viracocha creates all men at Tiwanaku, sending nations out from there. These men build the constructions of Tiwanaku as a home for their god (here Sarmiento may refer to the "staff god" of Tiwanaku Stelae; see Fig. 5.7), and when they leave, their languages diverge, as if the ruins of Tiwanaku are some tower of Babel. Drawing on Betanzos' account of a description of a statue of Viracocha that Spaniards saw in Urcos, Sarmiento more bluntly describes Viracocha as a white man of medium height, dressed in a long white robe tied at the waist, and carrying in his hands a staff and a book (Betanzos reports that it was said to look like a breviary).

Figure 5.7. The "staff god" of Tiwanaku, as depicted on the gateway of the sun. Is this the deity who gave rise to Tunupa/Taguapaca, and hence to the miraculous pre-Columbian visitation of the Apostle of the Andes, and finally to the mestizo trader Ekeko? (Author's sketch of drawing in Moseley 1992: 206, Fig. 94)

202

Returning to his original narration, Sarmiento follows Viracocha to Cacha (between Titicaca and Cusco), where he is poorly received by some people there, whom he punishes by calling down from the heavens a rain of fire. He then disappears across the waters of the Pacific, off the coast at the northern reaches of Inca territory. Before he goes, he warns people to beware of false gods who may call themselves Viracocha. Here Taguapaca makes a final appearance:

> Some years after Viracocha left, they say that Taguapaca, who
> Viracocha had ordered thrown into Lake Titicaca in the Collao, came
> back, and that with others he began to preach that he was Viracocha.
> But although initially they held people under their sway, people in the
> end knew them to be false, and ridiculed them.
>   About their creation these barbarous people tell this ridiculous
> fable, and they affirm it and believe it as if they had actually seen it
> take place. (Ibid., 54–55)[65]

Synthesized from Sarmiento's informants' stories in 1572, this narrative already bears the marks of efforts (whether by Sarmiento or his informants, we cannot easily determine) to bring Andean narrative into line with biblical narrative. First of all, there is Sarmiento's own preoccupation with locating (a single) deluge at an appropriate chronological point. But we may also discern an effort to assimilate Viracocha to both the Christian creator and a pre-Columbian apostle. As in Cieza's account of the people of Titicaca, Sarmiento portrays him as a European-like man with the appearance of a priest.

Can we read such accounts as versions of stories told in Qullasuyu? In the absence of sustained texts of Qulla or Lupaqa or Asanaqi origin stories, we cannot know how successfully Incas integrated Qullasuyu peoples' mythic traditions into their own. The only exception to the Inca-centric rule of thumb is the well-known collection of stories (apart from catechetic works, the only extant substantial text in a native Andean language) compiled and written down in Quechua in Huarochirí by, or under the direction of, the Jesuit priest Francisco de Avila around the beginning of the seventeenth century. Although Huarochirí is rather far afield from the peoples of Qullasuyu, reference to it here can serve us in a variety of ways. First, it serves as an example of the richness of local traditions that have been lost as a result of chroniclers' generalized Inca-centric obsessions. More important for the purposes at hand, the Huarochirí corpus, produced by peoples who had been drawn into the clutches of the Inca empire before most of Qullasuyu had, evinces a

surprising degree of autonomy from the Inca accounts. Originary
moments in Huarochirí are local, with scant reference to the Titicaca
area. They illustrate, however, the sort of narrative heterogeneity and
multiplicity of origin places that Inca-centric chroniclers often lamented
for Inca provinces like Qullasuyu, brushed aside so as not to divert
attention from Viracocha and Manco Capac.

Apart from providing accounts of origins differing considerably from
those collected in Cusco, the Huarochirí corpus also admits multiplicity
even within the relatively small district in which the tales were gathered.
Indeed, each ayllu is tied to its own places of creation. Likewise, the
ranking of deity ancestors of neighboring local groups within an
overarching polity is clearly open to question; no collective subject has
achieved narrative hegemony of the sort consolidated in tales told in
Cusco. Rivalry between gods (along the lines of the bad blood between
Taguapaca and Viracocha) is directly linked to rivalries between distinct
ethnic groups who have found together a form of modus vivendi without
a flattening of narrative pasts.

Chroniclers' assertions of narrative heterogeneity in Qullasuyu suggest that a similarly autonomous narrative tradition might have been
found in Qullasuyu, even within a single polity such as the Lupaqa one.
If such narratives were collected, they have not survived. Perhaps,
though, some preconquest and Inca-independent Qullasuyu interpretations of the past still subsist in those Inca stories pegged to the
Tiwanaku/Titicaca axis.

Had an Inca interpretive perspective slighted and demeaned Taguapaca as the "least" member of a "gang of four" culture heroes? Or had
Incas simply transformed one of many alternative creation stories into a
unique event of universal significance, creating an appropriate charter
for state encompassment of divergent and autonomous narrative traditions? Had there been a Qullasuyu narrative tradition in which Taguapaca, in other stories called Tunupa, occupied the highest rank? We
cannot answer such questions.

Let us see, however, how a Qullasuyu mythic tradition, or at least a
Qulla-centric reading of an Inca myth, might have survived embedded
within the accounts of Taguapaca/Tunupa: Two early-seventeenth-
century writers contest the interpretative stance that made Taguapaca an
adequate simulacrum of the devil. Transforming tricksterish ways into
miraculous powers, he radically transforms his struggles with other
mythical heroes when he shifts from a diabolic role to an angelic one. On
the surface, one might not have expected our two revisionist authors, the

priest Ramos Gavilán and the indigenous cacique Joan de Santa Cruz Pachacuti Yamqui, to have shared the same interpretive ground. But the seventeenth century was an age of not only idolatry extirpators but also progressive approximations of Andean and Christian ways of understanding. Shared participation in colonizing discourse motivated both priest and parishioner to seek new narrative theorizations of the past that led to, made sense of, and even justified the manifold tactics and auxiliary colonial impositions that were employed to facilitate conversion.

For both the cleric Ramos Gavilán and the Christianized Qulla noble Pachacuti Yamqui, Taguapaca/Tunupa's tricksterish rebelliousness is no longer evidence of diabolic associations, but of his saintliness. In both accounts, he has absorbed the Christian associations of Sarmiento's Viracocha in the process of being assimilated to Santo Tomás or San Bartolomé as a pre-Spanish evangelizer of indians. Bouysse-Cassagne (1987) and Gisbert (1980), who have studied these stories at length,[66] hold that in spite of the stories' manifest Christianization we can nonetheless discover in them some features of Qullasuyu cosmology, if not of cosmogeny. Bouysse-Cassagne and Gisbert bring a variety of etymological associations and lexicological sources to play in an effort to disentangle Taguapaca/Tunupa, as an Altiplano deity, from the Inca creation synthesis of early chronicles and the Christian synthesis of later ones. (And now see Bouysse-Cassagne's important reanalysis of these myths' derivation from Christian hagiography [In Press]. For yet another perspective and a modern Tunupa tale, see Wachtel 1990.)

Rather than to attempt to peel away the "foreign and imposed" characteristics of Gavilán's or Pachacuti Yamqui's hero trickster so as to reveal the pre-Columbian figure, my aim is to use their accounts to discover a creative moment of intercultural production. We will find that both authors use a tale of Tunupa in the guise of Christian apostle in order to carry out their own creative memory work. As they follow the creative journey of an Andean-Christian martyr whose activities fundamentally transform a prior people and bring a new order into existence, they conjoin two "chronotopic" traditions (of stories in which full human agency is achieved through a transformative journey in space and time) and produce a third, intercultural one, capable of accounting for key features of the colonial order. In this conjoint tradition, the inseparability of "Andean" and "Christian" narratives is central, since clarifying the relationship between them, in particular their temporal or historical relationship, is what the story is all about. The stories of

Ramos Gavilán and Pachacuti Yamqui also, of course, help to motivate subsequent pilgrimage journeys in imitation of the storied "first journey." These too, as we shall see, were means to carry out work in social memory to produce a kind of human agency capable of flourishing under colonial conditions; pilgrimages to Copacabana and other sites of miraculous interfaces between pre-Columbian and Christian worlds reenact an originary narration of the colonial relationship. Work in intercultural social memory is carried out when recapitulating mythic journeys as well as when historicizing them.

CHRISTIANIZING QULLASUYU WANDERERS: TUNUPA AS MARTYRED APOSTLE

Because accounts of the Qullasuyu figure of Tunupa serve as a bridge between the Inca-centric creation stories collected and systematized by Sarmiento and the K'ulta story of Tatala's (Jesucristo's) destruction of the Supay-Chullpas, it is worth our while to linger briefly on the combined Spanish and indigenous effort to discover in Andean myth an account of the Andes' evangelization.

Fray Alonso Ramos Gavilán is best known as the author of the 1621 work (republished in La Paz in 1976) *Historia de Nuestra Señora de Copacabana*. Ramos Gavilán endeavors throughout the book to spread the fame of the miraculous image whose pilgrimage shrine he served, beginning with the destruction of the pagan idol which once stood where the Virgin's temple was erected, and the image's first miracle, the journey from a workshop in Potosí to the spot she selected for herself.

After a long discourse on the disciples' efforts to spread the good news throughout the world, Ramos Gavilán suggests that we should assume that they also reached Perú.

> . . . for there is among the indians a story very consonant with this,
> of having seen a new sort of man, never before known, who
> performed great miracles and marvels. And as some very old indians
> affirm, they gave him the name Tunupa, which is the same as saying
> great Sage and Lord (Matt. 9). And because of his preaching, that
> glorious saint was persecuted and finally martyred in the following
> manner. (Ramos Gavilán 1976: 29)[67]

Here Ramos Gavilán describes this disciple's destruction by fire of Cacha, and relates how the disciple, who wanted to destroy the famous altar and shrine of the Qullas on the island of Titicaca, was set down there from the sky, as if an angel had lifted him up and set him back down by the hair. He arrived during a great fiesta at the shrine of the sun, and began tirelessly preaching against the Qullas' sacrifices. Finally,

... the indians were irritated to such a degree that they cruelly impaled him, running him through from head to foot with a pole that they call *chonta,* made of palm, of a sort that these indians until this day use in warfare as a not little offensive weapon. They have used this form of martyrdom other times as well, as in the case of what they did to the sainted fray Diego Ortíz of the Order of Our Father San Agustín. . . .

After he was dead, they put the saintly disciple on a *balsa* [a reed boat] and threw it into the great lake Titicaca, where it was subject to the providence not of wind or of wave, but of heaven. The old ones say that a violent wind blew the boat and carried it as if by sail and oar, with such velocity that it was cause for wonder. And thus it made land at Chacamarca, where the Desaguadero River, which did not exist before, is now. The balsa's prow made an opening sufficient for the waters to run, and continued sailing on the waters all the way to Aullagas, where as I have said, the waters disappear into the bowels of the earth. And there, they say, the sainted body remained, and each year on one of the holy days, at that time at least, there was seen there a very fresh and green palm, although others say that the palm was seen on a small isle that the Desaguadero River makes near the coast of Chile. . . . Everything is possible on God's earth, but one may still doubt. What I can affirm is having heard of old indians from Copacabana, and especially of one who today serves in the convent to teach reading and singing to the boys of the town, so as to serve the choir and the Holy Virgin, that he heard his ancestors tell that, on that island of Titicaca, the footprints of Tunupa, as they called the glorious saint, are miraculously preserved in the stone. (Ibid., 30–32)[68]

Of course, Ramos Gavilán was a priest, and his account falls squarely within his history of the miraculous Virgin of Copacabana. One would not expect him to relate a Tunupa tale that fails to sanctify the ground on which his temple was built or to prefigure the miracles of the virgin that is today Bolivia's patron saint. This concern leads some analysts to privilege the myth texts offered by the Qulla native author Pachacuti Yamqui, also a favorite source of information on Inca cosmology. It is true that his text is unusually full of native expression missing from the works of Spanish chroniclers. But a close reading of his account of Tunupa reveals another agenda, where temporal priority is tied not only to the problem of sorting out relations between Qullas and Incas, or Qullas and Pukinas/Urus, but also to the problem of Andeans' relationship to Christianity.

Himself a convert to Christianity, Pachacuti Yamqui strives in his 1613 text to demonstrate the essential Christianity of pre-Columbian

Andeans by finding the word of God prefigured in ancestral myth.[69] Thus during his *purunpacha* period, during a time of presolar darkness, the beings of that age, called *hapiñuñus* (whom Pachacuti Yamqui glosses as *demonios*), suddenly begin shrieking, "We are doomed!" whereupon they disappear. "By this," adds Pachacuti Yamqui, "we understand that the demons were defeated by Jesus Christ Our Lord when he was on the cross at Calvary Hill" (Pachacuti Yamqui 1968: 282).

Sometime later, continues Pachacuti Yamqui, an old bearded man of medium height, wearing long shirts and carrying a book, arrived in Tawantinsuyu. Everywhere he went he addressed all as sons and daughters, everywhere speaking the language of natives even better than they. He also performed miracles. He cured the sick by touch alone, and without taking any payment or showing interest in material wealth. "They called him Tonapa Viracochampacachan. Must he then not be the glorious apostle Santo Tomás?" (ibid.).

Coming first to the town of a cacique called Apotampo, Pachacuti Yamqui's Tunupa arrived, very tired, during a festival. The townspeople paid him scarce attention, but fortunately Apotampo treated him well. As a result, Tunupa granted to Aputampu ("lord of the tambo") a staff, through which he taught them almost all of God's commandments, lacking only the name of the Lord our God and his son Jesus Christ. Thus smiling benignly upon the Incas, Pachacuti Yamqui's Tunupa struck down the inhabitants of towns that did not receive him well. In Yamquesupa, his preaching was unwelcome, and the townspeople vituperated him and ejected him from town in his long shirt, book in hand. Tunupa responded by drowning the town beneath a lake. As we've seen, upon the people of Cacha, worshipers of an idol he hated, he visited a scorching fire, "and until this day there are signs of that terrible miracle" (ibid.). In other places, such as Pucara, he turned his enemies into stone.

In a place called Caravaya, Tunupa made a very large cross and carried it on his shoulders to a hill near Carabuco (a town on the northeast side of the lake, where stories of the miraculous cross are still told), and there he preached loudly and shed tears. As a lesson to the people of Carabuco, he made their idol fly like the wind, until it landed, head down and weeping, on a desolate and unpopulated high plain. So the people jailed him and sentenced him to a cruel death. At dawn, with the help of a beautiful slave, he escaped from Carabuco by laying his blanket upon the water. With his new companion he floated away on the blanket, reaching the island of Titicaca. Later, he passed southwards past Tiquina and headed down the Chacamarca River (known by others and still today as the Desaguadero). When he reached Tiwanaku, he found the people engaged in drunken dances, and he preached to them. They failed to respond, and as he left that place, all the people who had been dancing were turned into stone, and one can still see them there. Then he continued until he reached the sea (and from there through the straits until he reached the other sea).[70]

Notice that Pachacuti Yamqui's Tunupa, rather than being impaled by a palm stave, gives a staff to the Incas, presumably the one which, where it sank easily into the earth, marked the Inca's promised land of Cusco. And rather than sailing in a strong wind after his martyrdom, he uses the wind to banish pagan idols.[71] The tricksterish behavior that marked earlier Tunupas or Qullasuyu Viracochas as prefigurations of the devil has been converted into the performance of godly miracles, and his suffering at the hands of Qullas, into an exemplary Christian martyrdom.

For both Ramos Gavilán and Pachacuti Yamqui, Tunupa is associated with a stave or staff: He is impaled by it in one account; in the other he gives the staff to the first Inca, who impales the earth with it and thereby founds the Inca empire. As Urbano (1981: xxx) has noted, his very name also conveys an association with what one might call a vegetable axis. In sixteenth-century Aymara, *tunu* signified the root of large plants and trees (Bertonio 1984), a large-scale variety of *sap"i*, the root of smaller plants. Just so, when K'ulta people pour libations, the liquid is thought to travel to the beings to which it is dedicated, through underground pathways that begin in the *sap"i*, the root, of each altar. In some Aymara dialects, "*tunu achachi*" refers to the most distant male ancestor recalled when pouring libations to the dead, as it were, the "root of the lineage."

Naturally Tunupa's miracles (including the erection of a cross in Carabuco, on the shores of Lake Titicaca) and his subsequent martyrdom at the hands of the natives who were deaf to his preaching (after which he floats downriver) take on new significance as prefigurations of the actions taken during Pachacuti Yamqui's day by Spanish extirpators of idolatry. In effect, Pachacuti Yamqui's act of writing, like that by Guaman Poma and the scribe who recorded, reordered, and commented upon the myth corpus of Huarochirí, has frozen in time an act of mental gymnastics, an effort by a convert to reinterpret the historical consciousness carried by mythic narrative so that it could account not only for relationships among Andean groups through the conflicting agencies of their gods, but also for the now unavoidable and just as hierarchized

Figure 5.8. Guaman Poma's San Bartolomé-Tunupa. The wording at the top reads "Apostol S. Bartolomé." The label on the cross reads "Santa Crus de Carabuco." The note above the kneeling indian reads "Anti Uira Cocha, Colla. Fue bautizado este yndio" (note: resembles item in baptismal register). The wording at the bottom of the page reads "En la

210

relationship between Andeans and Spaniards. To do so required that they go beyond the importation of Christ into their hearts, as the priests urged, and import him into their pasts.

Just so did Guaman Poma locate the miraculous events of Cacha and the origin of the cross of Carabuco in the distant Inca past, identifying the pre-Columbian apostle as San Bartolomé. (See Fig. 5.8.) By establishing and authorizing shrines such as the miraculous cross of Carabuco and the temple of the Virgin of Copacabana, colonial priests actually fostered a new mythic synthesis focused once again on Tiwanaku/ Titicaca. In the end, and still today, this ancient *axis mundi*, home to the ruins of civilization past, serves as a vanishing point of cultural and linguistic difference and, indeed, of time itself: recall how the pretemporal age of darkness ends there with the emergence of a solar clock.

The myths we have surveyed share numerous themes and features. Creative culture-heroes fan out from a central origin point to bring forth multiple ancestors throughout Andean territory from rocks, springs, and hills that thereafter become conduits through which human societies have access to the gods and powers of initial times. The above- as well as below-ground paths through which creators and creation have flowed remain in the storytellers' world as icons of the relationship among founding agencies. As such, they become paths or vectors through which to affirm the identities received as differentia of clothing, language, and

---

Figure 5.8. (*Continued*)
provincia del Collao, de cómo se quemo el pueblo de Cacha. De 1570 años de la santa cruz." (Guaman Poma locates the event 1,570 years before his present, 1612–13, or in the year 40 [see Guaman Poma de Ayala 1980: 1132 n. 92.2].)

Here Guaman Poma (1980: 72) depicts the "apostle of Jesus Christ" San Bartolomé with the pre-Columbian cross of Carabuco. The Qullasuyu apostle faces an indian sorcerer, Anti. In the accompanying text, Guaman Poma reports how San Bartolomé, after his destruction by fire of Cacha, entered a cave to avoid the cold. Anti habitually consulted his idol there. But with San Bartolomé's arrival, the cave demon fell silent. Later, the demon appeared in Anti's dreams, ordering him to avoid the cave. San Bartolomé explained all to Anti, went with him to the cave, and exiled the demon. Then Anti was baptized as Anti Vira Cocha (recalling one of the four Viracochas of Tiwanaku). In memory of this miracle, San Bartolomé left the cross of Carabuco. In this left hand the saint holds a knife, symbol of his martyrdom, having been flayed alive for refusing to abjure Christianity. The cave, contest with the devil, and flaying of San Bartolomé are central today to Potosí's major pilgrimage festival.

Elsewhere Guaman Poma (1980: 606) depicts the saint carrying his own flayed hide. There he argues that the Peruvian miracles of San Bartolomé, the Carabuco cross, Santiago, and Santa María de Peña de Francia should be celebrated as major holy days. (From Guaman Poma de Ayala 1980: 73)

ancestors, and to become reassociated with divinity, through human pilgrimage and through the unseen underworld movement of the substances of sacrifice.

Around the south end of Lake Poopó, at the end of the aquatic axis created by a floating Tunupa, the name still survives in local memory. While the people of K'ulta had not heard of him, he is better known among the descendants of the Killaka and Awllaka. Tunupa has also survived in toponymy. At the extreme south of the territory of the diarchy known as Awllaka-Urukilla, there is a mountain peak bearing the name Tunupa, rising precisely where the waters flowing southeastwards from Titicaca disappear onto the immense salt flats of Uyuni.

Perhaps in the area one cannot find full-blown tales of a Tunupa arising from Titicaca to sojourn southwards, but we shall see in part 3 that elements of the Christianized Tunupa tale have been locally recast, placing his origin in an unknown place far to the east and identifying him, not as an apostle, but as Christ himself. It would be a grave mistake to take contemporary myths for rote copies of pre-Columbian or even early colonial ones. Like all forms of social memory, the value of mythic narrative lies in its adequacy as an account of the origins of contemporary life-ways. Myths of origin must change when the social forms they account for, forms that structure the historical consciousness of their tellers, have changed. And in midcolonial days, Titicaca/Tiwanaku, like the Inca "world navel" of Cusco, was displaced by other destinations in Andeans' actual and imaginary itineraries. Aymara-speaking Andeans called Tiwanaku *taypi q'ala*, the "stone in the center," from which the miraculous image of Copacabana (served by Ramos Gavilán and revered by Pachacuti Yamqui) had sojourned to displace the Inca shrine of Titicaca (site of Tunupa's origin). Although the Titicaca site of Tunupa's departure and Copacabana's shrine would remain an important Andean intercultural pilgrimage site, their new taypi q'ala, destination of frequent and transformative journeys, was to be the frigid silver-mining town of Potosí. And for his part, Tunupa was to be displaced in Andean consciousness by the traveling cultural interloper named Ekeko, for whom Potosí was a lucrative marketplace.[72]

Chapter Six

Colonial Relandscaping of Andean Social Memory

Both Spaniards and Andeans may have likened Tunupa or Viracocha to a Christian apostle, but neither was completely reducible to Santo Tomás or San Bartolomé. As long as the full range of significance of the stories about European apostles and Andean creator deities remained inaccessible to indians and Spaniards, the cross-cultural equivalences established in hybrid stories told by a Pachacuti Yamqui, a Guaman Poma, or a Ramos Gavilán maintained cultural difference even while bridging it. The imbalance of power in the discourse of colonialism, which authorized Spaniards and de-authorized indians, always read the indian back into the Andean, and did so most insistently to the most cross-culturally eloquent Andeans. This was because, of all indians, the most Hispanized and Christian ones presented the greatest danger to the colonial order, which would collapse should the contrast between Spaniard and indian fade away.

By the late sixteenth century, those demoralized indians who had survived three-quarters of a century of epidemic disease, rampant violence, and death in their midst were also subjected to ever more thorough-going missionizing and "civilizational" strategies, and they must increasingly have come to regard colonial rule as inevitable. But in spite of ever more efficient means of Spanish and priestly surveillance, making it more difficult for indians to practice techniques of resistance, to find clandestine corners in which to author themselves in a language

213

of practice unknown to Spaniards, the process of intercultural translation remained a two-way street. Indians were taught abbreviated forms of Christian liturgy and biblical history through a "missionary Quechua or Aymara," by which partly fluent priests translated "San Bartolomé" into "Tunupa," "the devil" into "supay," "hell" into "manxa-pacha." But Andeans, most of whom had little grasp of the Castilian language (much less Latin) and no access to their priests' full texts, were free to interpret San Bartolomé as Tunupa, the devil as supay, and hell as manxa-pacha, endowing each with a range of significance that differed from the Spanish gloss.

Colonialism created metaphoric equivalences through which both Spaniard and indian could gloss a limited range of one another's cultural forms, and with metaphor came license of poetic interpretation. Neither Spaniard nor indian could ignore the equivalences, once established. And indians' interpretive license expired when they usurped the priests' public pulpits and the hearing rooms of colonial courts to declaim interpretations at odds with orthodoxy.

In this chapter I explore the creative tension, often located precisely in a cross-cultural arena of social memory, that has unfolded over roughly four centuries of the power-laden relationship between Spaniards and indians, and between aristocrats and plebeians within (and across) Spanish and indian societies. My story moves in fits and starts, concentrating on moments of the greatest upheaval and change. The first of those moments is the repression of the taqui oncoy movement in the late 1560s and early 1570s, a time when the last vestiges of rebel Inca activity in Vilcabamba also came to an end. That moment of repression, signaling a shift in Spanish attitudes towards the "Andean content" of colonial practice, coincided with the arrival of the reformist Viceroy Francisco de Toledo, who brought a sea change to the strategies employed by the Crown to rule over both colonizing Spaniards and colonized indians.

I then pursue a series of case studies in a hopscotch between the sixteenth and twentieth centuries. For the mid- and late seventeenth century, I query the impact of the civilizational practices that Toledo had implemented, and new ones destined to transform indians' relationship to the land. I suggest that the combined effects of the Counter-Reformation Church and the routines of life within Toledan-era resettlement towns had brought about a simultaneous "destructuration" (Wachtel 1973) and "restructuration" of indigenous life, leading not to "acculturation" but to new kinds of "indigenous" cultures at various cultural frontiers of the colonial world. Jumping ahead a century, I then examine the indigenous rebellions of the 1770s and 1780s for evidence of the full flowering of a colonial interculture, one which made little room for a hereditary native elite. The creative interface in which collective understandings of life were produced, I argue, had by this date shifted definitively from collective practice performed at the cacique's behest, to the saints' festivals and rotative "commoner" councils within Toledo's resettlement towns. Leaping into the postindependence period, I then show how little changed in the early years of the republic, and proceed to describe the impact of late-nineteenth and early-twentieth-century liberalism and its version of a civilizational program based on privatized land tenure and policies aimed towards abolishing collective ownership and town council rights. These had been a hallmark not only of colonial indian society but also of sixteenth- to nineteenth-century Castile, Spaniards' model of "civilization." I conclude the chapter with attention to another moment of revolution and rapid change, the period of 1952 to the present, in which old liberal privatization schemes combined with a renewed vitality of town-based communitarian rights have led to ever-increasing atomization of old collective identities, producing ever-smaller new towns (linked to the state as cantón capitals) on the model of Toledo's sixteenth-century Castilian-style resettlement town.

In my survey of a series of significant moments between the 1560s and the present, my goal is always to understand the implications of transformed social conditions for the reconstruction of the past, which is reborn in ever-shifting forms to help account for ever-shifting realities of life. The first great shift, of course, was the conquest itself and the destruction of the idols, ceque systems, and orderly state—regulated rhythms of sacrifice, to which so much of "political-economic" activity had been oriented. The twilight of the Andean idols also coincided, however, with implementation of certain draconian Toledan policies. For us they are of paramount importance, since (among other things, such as the promotion of Philip II's absolutist state) they did no less than mandate the destruction of Andean social memory and its replacement with other habits of life, another religion, and another "universal" past.

Taqui Oncoy

The late 1550s and early 1560s saw the tightening of the Spanish colonial grip on Andean ways of life. The visitas of the Gascan tasa commission had taken account of those life-ways and had begun the process of their systematic transformation. Encomenderos were now more stringently enjoined to send priests to their indians and to guarantee effective evangelization. Polo's 1559 investigation and destruction of Cusco wak'as and mummies signaled the beginning of similar efforts by zealous priests throughout the countryside.

For a time, pecuniary interest in some cases outweighed the drive to extirpate idolatries and erase Andean memory: "At the beginning of the seventeenth century, a priest overheard a corregidor say that he would not get involved in [caciques'] business, only please them. As long as they provided him with indians, they could live according to any law they liked."[1]

Accusations that priests and colonial officials permitted idolatries, drunkenness, and other sins in exchange for satisfaction of their economic interests are a relative commonplace in colonial archives (see also Stern 1982; A. Acosta 1987). So long as there were priests more interested in profiting from the sale of communion wine than in ensuring that indians fully benefited from the Eucharist, caciques could maintain some control over how they levied labor and in what form they collected tributes, as well as control over a larger "clandestine" space for public libations, taquies, and wak'a cult. But during the period in question, Spaniards increasingly took note of the subtle means by which Andeans kept alive the memory of their idolatrous past. While corregidor of Cusco, Polo had not only investigated and destroyed the ceque system but also outlawed "public and solemn drinking sessions." He nevertheless permitted such drinking "within private houses" (Acosta, quoted in Saignes 1993: 48). This was precisely the opposite of the Inca policy. No doubt Polo's policy, which was seconded by Matienzo (1967: 80), resulted from Spanish views of public drunkenness. It also, however, responded to Spanish conclusions about the linkage between drinking and idolatry. "They drink, dance, and sing all at the same time," Cieza had noted (1984: 84). As Luis Capoche, administrator in Potosí, wrote in 1585: "They are accustomed to drinking in public. Many men and women gather together to carry out great dances, in which they practice the old rites and ceremonies, bringing to memory through their songs the gentile past" (Capoche 1959: 141). Acosta condemned this predilection for drunkenness by referring to an ancient Mediterranean dictum: "Drunkenness . . . leads one to forget all things and, as Pliny says, is the death of memory." It would appear that Acosta disapproved Andean drinking in order to save their memories. But a short while later in the same account, Acosta contradicts Pliny, and suggests that drinking might be prohibited in order to erase memory rather than to preserve it. "They now scarcely conserve any of their old idolatry, apart from the occasion of these solemn drinking and dancing sessions . . . in which in an orderly way they mix epic song [cantares] with wine" (Acosta, quoted in Saignes 1993: 59).

In public gatherings where drink, dance, and song all intervened, caciques had been able to maintain the social memory that had undergirded their authority and given form to society, even in the absence of idols and mummies. Now, however, that nexus had been discovered by the Spaniards, and public space claimed exclusively for Christian performances. And on top of all this, the early 1560s' perpetuity question (during which Polo and Santo Tomás had traveled the countryside explaining perpetuity and, it seems, investigating ceque systems), foregrounded for indians just what was at stake in continued submission to Spanish demands.

Spanish encomenderos had banded together to offer the king a huge payment if he would grant them perpetual title to their indian vassals and, yet more, give them title to land and civil and criminal jurisdiction that Spanish landed nobles enjoyed back in Castile. No doubt with an eye to his fiscal deficits, Philip II was eager to accept, but the Council of the Indies induced him to investigate further the potential consequences and to seek alternatives.[2] It was for this reason that Polo and Santo Tomás traveled the land, explaining to indian caciques the pros and cons of the encomenderos' perpetuity proposal. In Cusco in 1561, a delegate from Santo Tomás outlined the proposal in the most alarming terms, suggesting to the caciques that they themselves, along with their wives, indian subjects, lands, and privileges, were to be sold to Spaniards, like the merchandise commodities Andeans were only just learning about. Perhaps, they would be branded on the face like chattel slaves (AGI, Justicia 434, Pieza 1, January 23, 1563, fol. 9v). On hearing such things, said don Pedro Ochatoma, cacique of the town of Puna Quiguar, "many indians wept, and this witness wept, understanding that it would have to be thus . . . [that] now that I was of God they should sell me" (ibid., 25r).

According to don Juan Guancoyro, cacique of Sallay in the encomienda of García de Melo, ". . . as the said indians heard this, many of them began to weep and to cry out and say that neither before nor after the Inca, never have they been sold; how is it that now they were to be sold, being neither coca nor meat? And thus all gave power of attorney [to petition the king]" (ibid., 17v).[3]

Don Pedro Comsa offered his appreciation of the events: ". . . the said indians felt it deeply and some caciques said that they would first throw themselves into the rivers, or leap from cliffs, before being branded on the face; in the time of Guayna Capac they had never been slaves. Why should they now, being vassals of the king?" (ibid., 23r).[4] The experience induced them to collect funds to produce a counterproposal, an even larger cash offering to the king to *abolish* encomienda.

The possibility of perpetual encomienda disturbed Spaniards as well as indians. The anticipation that all land and indian labor might soon be under the permanent control of a new landed aristocracy led some of the Spaniards in Cusco who lacked encomiendas, along with mestizos and even Inca elites who were not subject to encomienda,[5] to a panic reaction of their own. While the caciques who had assembled to hear the perpetuity arguments signed petitions to the king and returned to their far-flung rural districts, the urban rabble (as citizen-encomenderos sometimes referred to the rest of the urban population) began to stir. Fearful of being left without resources, they reacted to the idea of perpetual encomienda with a revolutionary cry. Thus Cusco in 1561 saw an abortive anti-aristocratic revolt "in the name of liberty, and to the shout of *comunidades.*" Such terms, reminiscent of the rebellion of the commoner-led Spanish towns against nobles and Charles V in 1520–21, led Crown officials to respond swiftly and harshly (AGI, Justica 434, Pieza 1, fols. 2v–3r).

During the early 1560s caciques from many Peruvian provinces responded to end-of-an-era fears raised by the perpetuity proposal by circulating petitions. But not all Andeans were assuaged by sending paper to the state's archive. For at about the same time, Spanish priests discovered in the countryside a very different response, a social movement called taqui oncoy.[6] It has been thoroughly studied by many scholars, beginning with a brilliant analysis by Steve J. Stern (1982: 51–71).[7] Here I draw on such analyses in order to highlight certain features that show how taqui oncoy serves as a bridge not only backward to pre-Columbian Andean realities but also forward to more resolutely Christian forms of Andean contestation of colonialism. Writing about 1573, Cristóbal de Molina provided a succinct restatement of the matter based on an eyewitness account:

> About ten years ago, more or less, there was an irony among the indians of this land, which took the form of a song [*canto*], called taqui oncoy. Since the first person to see the said irony or idolatry was one Luis de Olivera, cleric presbiter, who at the time was priest of the repartimiento of Parinacocha, in the bishopric of Cusco, he puts down here the way that they did it and why:
>
>   In the province of Parinacocha, of the bishopric of Cusco, the said Luis de Olivera, vicar of the province, understood that not only there, but in all the other provinces and cities of Chuquisaca, La Paz,

Cusco, Huamanga, and even Lima and Arequipa, the majority of
indians had fallen into great apostasies, separating themselves from
the Catholic faith that they had received, in order to return to the
idolatry they had practiced in the days of their infidelity. It was not
possible to discover who had started this business, but it is suspected
and assumed that the inventors were sorcerers kept in Vilcabamba by
the rebel Incas. . . . (Molina 1989: 129)[8]

Now, "taqui oncoy" is a compound term which is not glossed in
surviving sources by its actual practitioners. "Oncoy" refers to the
constellation of stars known as the Pleiades, which for Andeans represented storehouses. "Oncoy" also seems to have meant "sickness." We
have already encountered the term "taqui," which meant at one and the
same time "to dance and sing." Literally, then, "taqui oncoy" may have
meant "song-dance of sickness," or "song-dance of the Pleiades." But
while examination of the social movement called taqui oncoy reveal that
widespread epidemic disease may have been an important factor in
motivating the movement, its goals were not exclusively to find a cure
for Andeans' bodily ailments. Rather, taqui oncoy practitioners rejected
Spanish admonitions to cease all customary practice, and insisted on
performing again the song-dances called taquies, in which, through
celebratory song and dance (and also libations and sacrifices), the deeds
of gods and ancestors were recalled and their significance for the present
and future made patent. Taqui oncoy was, then, a struggle over memory.
It was a war of the gods, yes, but also a battle of histories.

So the native "dogmatizers" of this apostasy (suppressed by the
decisive extirpation campaign of Cristóbal de Albornóz, in which
Guaman Poma served as faithful interpreter) danced and sang and strove
to recall the pre-Columbian past to living memory. But many of the
wak'as, as physical entities, had been destroyed and ancestral mummies
burned by activist priests or administrators like Polo. How then to bring
the wak'as back into this world? Taqui oncoy principals preached that,
while idols had been destroyed, the wak'as themselves continued to float
in the air as insubstantial but hungry and vengeful presences. So in 1565,

. . . there were diverse apostasies in various provinces. Some danced,
suggesting that the wak'a had entered their body; others trembled to
the same end, suggesting the same thing; still others walled
themselves into their houses with stones and gave out great laments;
some threw themselves off cliffs, dashing themselves to pieces; yet
others jumped into rivers, offering themselves to the wak'as. All this
until Our Lord, through his mercy, was served to enlighten these
miserable people, so that those of them who were left could see the

foolishness of what had been preached to them. And now they
believe, when they see the Inca [Tupac Amaru] dead, and Vilcabamba
Christianized, that none of that could have happened. Instead,
everything is to the contrary. (Ibid., 132)[9]

The suicidal desperation of the adherents of taqui oncoy certainly
resembles that of the caciques to whom perpetuity was explained in
Cusco just prior to the taqui oncoy events. But the sacrificial nature of
these acts made them, not just efforts to escape from a fate worse than
death, but desperate measures to bring the wak'as back to life. We know
that mitimas, deprived of the wak'as of their homeland, could reconstruct them in their adoptive home by clothing any stone in a fragment
of the original wak'as' cumbi clothing (Albornóz 1989: 171). Here,
however, there is a difference. Believers thought that disembodied wak'a
spirits might help Andeans solve worldly problems by becoming re-
embodied within exemplary humans.[10] That fact, and the extirpation
report that some devotees took the names of Mary and Mary Magdalen,
has led some analysts to conclude that Christian preaching, which had
sought to defeat wak'a superstitions by differentiating between the
world of creation and that of divine spirit, had provided Andeans with a
solution to their own spiritual crisis. And that solution was to grasp hold
of the techniques of social memory, to retake control over what was to
be forgotten and what remembered. Yet doing so in the 1560s, by which
time much of the imperial past had been erased, required a good deal of
innovation. Increasingly, elements of Christian theology and Spanish
mnemotechnics would become useful tools in Andeans' efforts to hold
back the dark tide of enforced colonial amnesia.

Crises and indigenous solutions were also being felt in the day's
largest urban center, the silver-mining town of Potosí. In 1565 the city
council of Potosí sought to abolish the importation of mill-ground flour
to stem the flow from chicha jars. Introducing the theme, the corregidor
Gaspár de Saldana noted,

> ... it is public and notorious ... that ... [the importation of] maize
> flour has caused among the indians and naturales who reside in this
> villa great drunkenness, since it is from ground corn flour that they
> make the *asua* [chicha] that they drink, they make much more than
> they used to, giving them occasion to drink much more than before,
> which is a vice to which they are very susceptible. They are drunk
> almost all the week, from which results much incest and other sins that
> they commit, even homicides, in great disservice of Our Lord and your
> majesty, and a great impediment to their conversion and to the Christian
> doctrine that is preached to them, and it impedes the mine labor for
> which they came here.... (AGI, Charcas 32, item 12, fol. 92r)[11]

In their testimony, several priests of Potosí's indian parishes waxed eloquent on the evils of drink. The very reverend father Frair Alonso Trueno, provincial of Potosí's Dominican community, repeated all the evils referred to above and added more:

> ... many die from their drunkenness and commit other homicides and deaths and hang themselves, and in particular this witness is aware of six indians that died from their drinking, losing their speech and dying naturally, and many others /93r/ lose their speech by the power of medicines and drinks *[bebediços]* that have been given to them, and after having been three or four days without speech have been made to return to themselves. And when drinking I have seen them get up and vomit, and then return to their drink, and one time when I tried to make them stop drinking they wanted to kill me. . . . This witness knows and has seen that it is the principal impediment to their conversion and Christian indoctrination, because every time they are drunk they commit and carry out their old idolatries and rites. . . . (Ibid, 92v–93r)[12]

The canon Juan de Villa Miera, who for several years was priest and vicar of the parish of the Qarankas in Potosí, further specifies the idolatries tied to drunkenness:

> ... This witness . . . has seen the indians who reside there, especially in the doctrina of the Carangas over which this witness had charge as vicar, carry out many and great drunken binges . . . and it seems to this witness that the said drunkenness is an impediment to their conversion and indoctrination, and he has heard from some priests who understand /93v/ the tongue and have long been in this land that, when the indians are drunk in their drinking binges and taquies, they commit idolatries and other rites to the offense of God Our Lord. . . . (Ibid., 93r–93v)[13]

The very reverend father and canon Cuellar de Ocampo adds more:

> ... [They] make sacrifices in diverse ways to their wak'as, and have many other kinds of sorcery, confessing with their confessors, sending *cachas* to the wak'as *hanobicamayos [sic: jampi kamayuqs?]*, and contradicting Christian doctrine. And they practice many other rites and ceremonies and sins, such as women taking one another, and committing various sins of incest, and carrying out the fiestas of *capse pacxi*, and other lesser [festivals] that they celebrate during all the months of the year. . . . (Ibid., 93v)[14]

So in the same period that taqui oncoy was in progress in Huamanga, the indians of Potosí continued to carry out taquies and libation sessions dedicated to wak'as and sacred moments in the pre-Columbian calendar. Given the irregular Spanish effort to represent Quechua and Aymara phonology in Spanish characters, it is difficult to say just what "capse pacxi" might be, but the most likely possibility is sapsi paxsi, "moon" of the "community fields." Cachas, or offerings, sent to wak'as called jampi kamayuqs (caretakers of medicine) suggest that Potosí indians, like taqui oncoy practitioners, sought a cure for the ills that ailed them. And references to medicines and bebediços that caused several days of speechlessness suggest that taqui oncoy's hallucinogen (the cactus called achuma) was also being used. One might have expected theologians to take issue with the loosening of constraint on the imagination produced by all these drinks and medicines, facilitating the devil's work rather than mine owners'. But all the priest witnesses come back in their testimony to the issue of laziness raised by the corregidor. In this colonial context, as Saignes (1993) noted, the operative triumvirate is drunkenness, idolatry, and avoidance of labor.

Elsewhere, in Parinacocha, Andeans were in the process of developing a new interpretation of the nefarious means and goals of the Spanish colonial project, one that provided ever more compelling reasons to flee by one means or another. Again Molina quotes the priest of Parinacocha:

> ... the year seventy but not afterward, the indians held and believed that from Spain they had sent to this kingdom for the body fat of indians in order to cure with it a certain illness for which there was no other medicine but the said body fat. As a result the indians of those times went about very cautiously and kept away from Spaniards to such a degree that they refused to carry firewood, herbs and other things to the house of a Spaniard, saying they did so to avoid being killed there within so that their fat [unto] could be removed.[15] All this was understood to have proceeded from that den of thieves in order to create enmity between indians and Spaniards ... until the lord viceroy Francisco de Toledo undid them and threw them out of there, in which he greatly served God Our Lord. . . . (Molina 1989: 129)[16]

Sober scholars have doubted the existence of a generalized conspiracy linking rebel Incas in Vilcabamba to taqui oncoy (Varón Gabai 1990). All the same, it is worth remembering that certain high Inca priests in Vilcabamba were called by the metonymic designation "ñaqaq," for the blood-letting that they performed as sacrificers.[17] An Andean interpretation of colonialism as an inverted and anti-social form of state-directed sacrifice may reveal, not a Vilcabamba plot, but a way through which non-Inca Andeans appreciated both similarities and differences between Inca and Spanish state practices.

Throughout the 1550s and 1560s, the indigenous peoples of the Andes sought freedom from encomenderos and encomienda and simultaneously managed, by engaging the pecuniary interests of priests and encomenderos, to negotiate a Spanish blind eye to some Andean practices. As with the anti-perpetuity petitions, which sought a form of auto-purchase like that of many towns up for auction in Philip II's Spain, their goal was to become vassals of the king and only the king, paying tribute and performing labor service while conserving as much autonomy and collective self-determination as possible. Ironically, the Spanish policy that emerged from this period of tumult aimed to give them just what they asked for, cast in a distinctly Castilian form.

With the arrival in Perú of Francisco de Toledo as its new viceroy, the colonial order was in for major revamping.[18] Toledo had himself participated in discussions of the Council of the Indies over the interlinked problems of the colony and how best to solve them. Encomenderos were still agitating to gain perpetual title to their encomiendas, and thereby becoming a powerful and difficult-to-control landed aristocracy. Caciques had demonstrated their ambition to defend and expand their own aristocratic privileges. The taqui oncoy movement suggested that the process of conversion was still far from complete, and had also awakened fears of widespread indian rebellion to accompany potential Spanish colonial secessionist movements. And finally, the Crown's perennial shortage of cash and deep indebtedness demanded more Crown control over revenue production, over collection of indian tributes, and over silver production under indian labor. The reforms that Toledo came to Perú to implement led to the utter transformation of the structure of relations among Spanish and indian aristocrats, common indians, and the state; to direct Crown involvement in mining production (especially in Potosí); and to a systematic reorganization of Andean living spaces and life-ways, with profound consequences for Andean social memory.

THE COLONIAL COUNTER-REFORMATION OF VICEROY TOLEDO

By the time Toledo arrived in Perú, taqui oncoy had been ended through harsh priestly repression. But Toledo set to work on other projects, capturing the rebel Inca, moving to suppress the pretensions of the Cusco Inca elite, and beginning a thoroughgoing shake-up of the colonial project. The "Toledan steamroller" was to have far-reaching consequences. It consisted of a massive and thorough inspection tour, a program of forced resettlement of indians into Spanish-style towns, and transformation of both encomienda and *cacicazgo* (native lordship), which brought both encomenderos and caciques down many notches. With Toledo's arrival there was also renewed fervor in the process of Christian evangelization, led by the Jesuits, who, along with Toledo, were to implement the Counter-Reformation strategies of the Council of Trent, displacing the utopian and tolerant Dominicans and Franciscans.

Toledo's mission was prepared in 1567. Philip II had been enamored of the possibility of a major windfall of silver from encomenderos or of indians as a result of the perpetuity "debate," but the Council of the Indies forestalled both outcomes. Its instructions to Toledo were to grant neither the encomenderos the perpetuity they sought nor the indians their wish for an end to the institution. Instead, they devised a subtler plan.

Toledo's policy more strictly enforced the long-standing policy of limiting inheritance of encomienda to two generations; when this term was up, encomiendas were often shifted permanently into the Crown, just as caciques had petitioned some ten years earlier. A gradual form of abolition, it went essentially unchallenged, in part because encomienda itself had lost not only much of its profitability but also its capacity to generate honor, which had inhered in its similarity to Spanish-style *señorío*. Toledo definitively abolished any resemblance to feudal institutions by imposing state intermediaries—provincial corregidores modeled after Castilian Crown administrators—between the remaining encomenderos and their tributes. Encomenderos were now to be paid their tributes from royal banks, after collection by the corregidor. In Spain the Crown had long used corregidores to undercut seignorial powers. In the Indies their intervention between encomenderos and indians turned would-be noblemen into lowly, salaried bureaucrats. A potentially secessionist, landed aristocracy had been eliminated and absolutist ends achieved.

Yet this was not time for indian rejoicing. European diseases, along with the social disruptions of Toledan policies, contributed to a free fall in population: tribute burdens and the new labor levies became correspondingly more onerous. At the same time, other reforms undermined an earlier state of relative indian autonomy in mining operations and, with the new mercury-amalgamation process, made mill and foundry labor deadlier for indian laborers (Bakewell 1984).

Nor did native lords fare well with Viceroy Toledo, for the same Toledan policy that undercut encomendero ambitions attacked caciques' privileges. Caciques became paid state functionaries with few powers apart from collecting tributes and delivering levied labor. At the same time, new arrangements placed them under closer Spanish supervision, by corregidores and more ubiquitous priests, undercutting their ability to use traditional reciprocities to cushion their subjects from the impact of Spanish demands.[19] As Karen Spalding (1984) has argued, the indigenous elite thus tended increasingly to collaborate in the exploitation of their own peoples; when the elite strove instead to resist, it was much more difficult to do so now than it was before.

Toledo's transformations of the tribute and labor regimes undercut encomendero and cacique roles, but were also aimed at a more general transformation of indians. Tribute was changed from a collective obligation to something closer to a head tax, like that of Spain's *pecheros,* payable in silver rather than in goods and services (see Murra 1968; Platt 1978b). To earn that silver, indians were forced to give up their habitual "slothfulness" and go to work for wages. Thus, forced wage labor under Crown direction was made to serve high moral purposes. If the king's conscience was not salved, his authority and pocketbook were.

To the great satisfaction of the growing non-encomendero majority of Spaniards, who had rejected perpetuity because it would have deprived them permanently of indian labor and the rents it produced, Toledo made the levy a state enterprise, with laborers to be given to whoever was able to find the most profitable use for them. The star of mining and milling entrepreneurs suddenly rose. From the territory between Cusco and what is now northern Argentina, the domain of the former Inca quarter of Qullasuyu, nearly fourteen thousand indigenous laborers were to make the yearly pilgrimage to Potosí. A strong factor motivating indians to participate in the mita was the monetization of tribute. To earn that coin, indians would be forced to labor for wages (even for the token wages of the forced labor draft). Such measures were justified as means to encourage industrious behavior among an indolent people; all were part of a more thoroughgoing program to "civilize" indians, to inculcate in them an appreciation of the beneficial effects of proper work discipline, so that they might pull themselves up by their own (store-bought) bootstraps into the capitalist world. They were to learn, in other words, how to conduct social relations and construct social position and obedience to the laws of god and king through the medium of money.

The transition was a difficult one, requiring radical techniques. As Polo noted in his report on the pre-Columbian economy, labor intended for surplus production had always been carried out in festive form, and the bulk of the surpluses had been consumed in collective gatherings, much of it in drink. Surpluses were stored and redistributed to the needy; poverty and hunger of the sort that in Castile resulted from aristocratic accumulation were virtually unknown.[20]

Indians were known for their lack of enthusiasm for wage labor and their fundamental disinterest in money and lack of respect for (Spanish-style) status achieved through its accumulation. But in principal, so were sixteenth-century Castilian aristocrats, who found the wealth and position achieved by bourgeois (which is to say, plebeian) merchants and traders to be ignoble (Bennassar 1979; Góngora 1975; Maravall 1972, 1979, 1984). Old-regime values were living on remittances in imperial Castile even while an industrial (and social) revolution was being forged in northern countries that had not found silver-rich indians. Yet in the colony that provided the silver that kept Castilian aristocrats (and Crown) in silk and cannons (Elliott 1970), merchants and (extractive) industrialists displaced encomendero-style aristocrats on city councils and in state offices. This colonial revolution of the aristocracy did not, however, redeem the value of work or of industry. Indeed, in the Indies, only indians (or to the preference of social reformers like Bartolomé de las Casas, Africans) were thought suitable for the performance of manual labor. *Mutatis mutandis,* in the Indies, to labor was now not only to be a tribute-paying plebeian; it was to be indian. It was therefore critical to colonial Spaniards that indians learn to labor.

Indian "Dukes, Counts, and Marquises" Write for the Archive

In the same period that Toledo's reforms put Castilian-style nobility on a high shelf that encomenderos could not reach, the native elite was in the process of learning what Castilian nobility actually meant. If they were the Indies' equivalent to Castilian dukes and counts, they began to argue, they should be treated as such. So the drastic limitations on their privileges imposed by Toledo came as a special insult. It was to such insults to honor and privilege and to Toledo's deformations in the bounds and hierarchic structure of rule that caciques like Juan Colque Guarache, lord of Killaka whom we have now repeatedly met, responded in their probanzas and memoriales. Just to draw them up, however, these native lords had first to learn new ways of engaging the past.[21] This had to conform increasingly to the canonic chronicled narrative to be useful in the colonial context, in order to, for example, forward a genealogical claim of Inca noble status or, in the provinces, to prove that one's native lordship had been inherited from father to son since pre-Inca times. The latter was necessary because of a Toledan-era anti-Inca policy: To justify his attack on the Inca elite, Toledo drew on the political philosophy that made regicide and conquest morally acceptable in overthrowing illegitimate tyrants. In revisionist Toledan historiography, tyrants are precisely what Incas became. Thus was the legitimacy of the Spanish conquest and title to the Indies affirmed.

Just so does the event chronicle of Juan Colque Guarache's probanza (like those of his contemporaries) reach back through the generations, dating each forebear through linkage to a named Inca emperor until reaching back before Inca times. In one fluid sweep of narrated events, Colque Guarache reaffirms an Inca king list (the Spaniards' temporal frame of reference, carefully constructed by chroniclers), claims to have followed a Spanish-style rule of primogeniture (concealing the more probable Andean pattern of succession, which hinged on birth order and admitted preference for those with ability), and founds his Killaka dynasty in firmly pre-Inca times. Later generations of caciques time and again referred to Colque Guarache's claims, having recourse to the documents that indigenous noble families guarded in archives that have outlived earlier quipu registers. Indeed, one of the most complete later references to the Colque Guarache testimony (also including his will and that of his father, Juan Guarache) is to be found in litigation dating from the early nineteenth century, between noble families seeking confirmation of appointment to a cacicazgo.[22] The expediente (ANB, EC 1804, no. 193) includes genealogies depicted, not as a family tree, but as a genealogical *path* (see Figs. 6.1 and 6.2). Both are drawn by the same interested hand; the noble descendants of Juan Colque Guarache (identified as the first to be baptized, eliding Juan Guarache) are portrayed with their staffs of office, while opponents (the Choqueticlla family, which for several generations had gained the cacicazgo of Killaka) are depicted without them; a particularly ignoble Choqueticlla stands in a separate box, holding out his beggar's cup. Yet in conformity to colonial legal preferences, this early nineteenth-century litigation, begun just before hereditary native lordships were abolished, includes eighteenth-century materials, and in them appear wills, baptismal records copied from parish registers, and bits of other documents dating to the sixteenth century, including recollections from Juan Colque Guarache's probanza. As the colonial relationship between Spaniards and indians matured, the Andean uptake of the written text and its various incarnations as legal artifact seem to have become the shrine of social memory, at least for caciques.

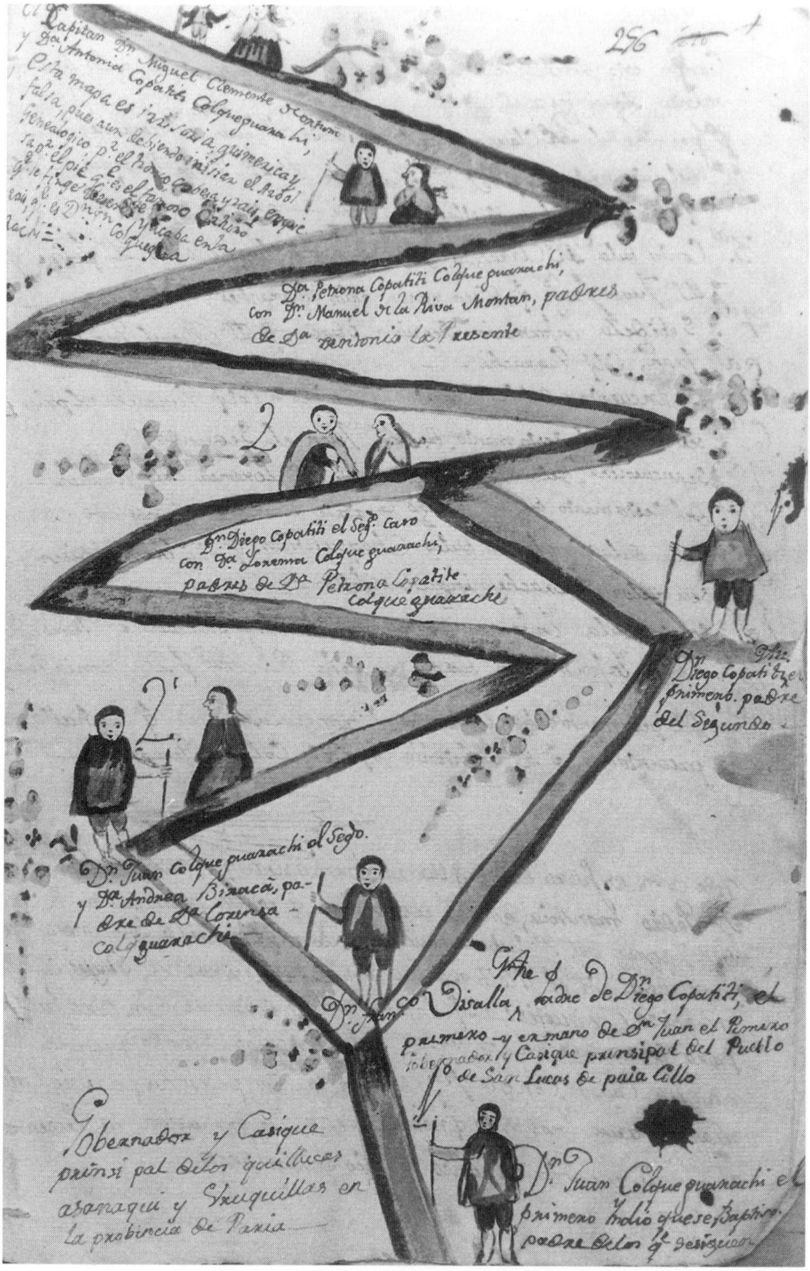

Figure 6.1. Colque Guarache "family path." (From a photograph courtesy of Karen Powers; original in ANB, EC 1804, no. 193)

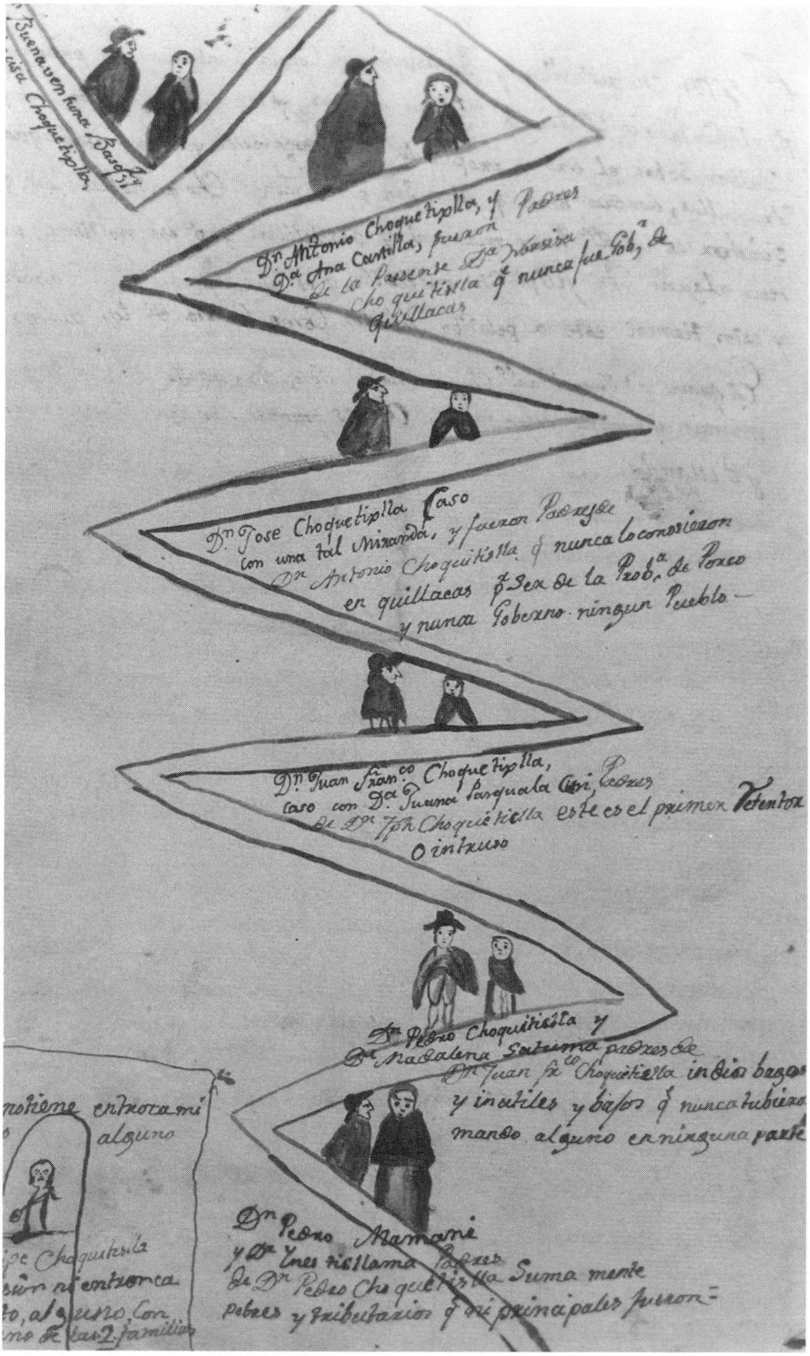

Figure 6.2. Choqueticlla "family path" (with "pathless" beggar Choqueticlla) (From a photograph courtesy of Karen Powers; original in ANB, EC 1804, no. 193)

However, let us not go too far. As an individual and as representative of a generation, Juan Colque Guarache bridged the watershed of the Toledan era. His father may have served as member of the Inca's war council, but was a confirmed Christian by the end of his life, command-ing his kinsmen to bury him in the church of Hatun Quillacas rather than preserve his body in an ancestral shrine. Juan Colque Guarache reports no direct knowledge of pre-Columbian ways, having been too young in 1532 to remember things Andean except in relation to Spaniards. Yet he knew which aged indigenous witnesses to his father's deeds to bring forward in his probanza (as well as which esteemed Spaniards to lend it credibility in the colonial context). He sure-footedly scrambles through the terrain of Castilian legal writing, never letting a single idolatrous or mythic element slip into his genealogy and event chronology. Having learned the Castilian way of writing the past as successive life histories, preshaped for inclusion in crónicas and summa-tion in historias, he must have forgotten, the reader might conclude, his own ancestral mnemonic techniques and ways of construing the past that might contradict the new and politically more useful form. What is more, his entire career as a native nobleman was lived out in Potosí, helping to deliver indian laborers to Spanish silver mines and mills, rather than in Inca Cusco or even in his own Hatun Quillacas. What other kinds of social memory could have survived in such circumstances?

A NEW CENTER OF THE ANDEAN WORLD: MITA* PILGRIMAGES TO POTOSÍ

Toledo's systematic methods for supplying workers to the mines are in many ways novel, but they also redeployed older techniques and logics. The number of mita workers (fourteen thousand) and the Qullasuyu districts from which they came were nearly identical to the mit'a system used by the Inca to work maize fields in the Cochabamba valley, which were now mostly in encomendero hands. Polo had obtained a rich encomienda there, and in fighting a legal challenge brought by the caciques of Qaranka and Killaka, he had learned much about the Cochabamba mit'a. It is quite possible that Toledo's famous mita of Potosí was modeled on that Inca productive system (and perhaps also on the Inca system for providing laborers to the mines of Porco). If Polo was the conduit for the knowledge upon which the Toledan mita was based,

---

*The Spaniards were unable to effect the glottalization in the Quechua and Aymara term "mit'a," which essentially means "turn" or "time." Thus in Spanish contexts, this term is spelled without the glottalization mark.

his writings might also prove useful in understanding the meaning for Andeans of participation in the Potosí mita. Not only had mit'a service to the Inca state in places like Cochabamba been carried out in a festive mode, marked by chicha libations and ritual performances important to both Inca and subject peoples, but also the work process itself came to reflect internal sociopolitical realities of diarchies and federations that participated, including their relative ranking among themselves and their relationship to the state and ruling Inca lineage. On the ground in Cochabamba, the division of fields (with their boundary lines and, we assume, associated wak'as) formed a microcosmic icon of the Qullasuyu quarter of the empire, just as the population and layout of Inca Copacabana reflected the structure of the empire as a whole.

So when Toledo construed the mita in a familiar form, he perhaps inadvertently provided an opportunity for native lords and levied laborers to recoup some features of pre-Columbian ways, most of which Toledo sought in other policies to erase. Such apparent contradiction or waffling is a familiar note in Toledan policies, no doubt because the bottom line of the reforms *was* the bottom line: In the interests of efficiency and profit to the Crown, it was necessary to go with administrative forms that worked, and to get indians to work, Toledo was forced to rely on the native lords they respected.

Just so the mita came to be organized by dividing Qullasuyu into units called *capitanías:* Sixteen large districts, which as Julien (1983) shows are fundamentally the same as the provinces rallied to Inca labors under regional lords, were called to provide workers to Potosí, led by native lords assigned the role of captains of the mita. Juan Colque Guarache's services to the Crown did not lead to recuperation of pre-Columbian-style rule over the greater Killaka federation, which remained divided into distinct encomiendas and repartimientos, but he gained preeminence as captain of the mita of Potosí.[23]

On the surface, it seems to be a job that only status-hungry native nobles could covet. It involved commanding the delivery of forced laborers from all four Killaka diarchies into dangerous and ill-rewarded minework and the day-to-day supervision of those *mitayos* in Potosí. Yet by commanding the delivery of forced laborers from all four Killaka diarchies, Colque Guarache was able to reintegrate his rule, notwithstanding the fact that only two (Killaka and Asanaqi) were under his more direct command, as parts of the Repartimiento de Quillacas y Asanaques. The Awllaka-Urukilla diarchy had long been divested from the federation as a separate encomienda; it had now been incorporated into the Crown. The Siwaruyu-Arakapi diarchy had likewise been sundered from the Killaka federation. With the promulgation of new province boundaries, it now lay in the territory of the Province of Porco, subject to a corregidor different from that of the other three diarchies (which were grouped in the Province of Paria with Sura peoples). All Killaka federation maize lands and coca fields were now located in yet other provinces, rather than being (however unclearly) parts of diarchy-based encomiendas. The territorialization of rule imposed new boundaries and new chains of colonial command that made old land-tenure patterns increasingly difficult to maintain. So the chance to lead mita workers again from all these diarchies, to reintegrate the federation even in microcosmic form within the confines of mine labor, must have seemed a rare opportunity. Indeed, other caciques claiming greater status than Colque Guarache bristled at the insult of *not* being named to such a post.

In his 1576 probanza, Colque Guarache expounded his services in Potosí. Having once gathered up a year's contingent of laborers from their far-flung homes, subordinate caciques sent them to Potosí, transporting food supplies on the backs of llamas that were themselves destined for the table or for the transport of minerals. Toledo had set aside an entire indian parish within Potosí for Killaka and Asanaqi laborers. Streets full of houses were assigned to the ayllus represented in the labor pool.[24] Colque Guarache was proud to have helped pay for the construction of the church of San Bernardo, the Killaka and Asanaqi parish center, where a priest, whose salary their tributes paid, was to work at their indoctrination. Awllaka-Urukilla and Siwaruyu-Arakapi laborers went to their own parish, a neighborhood surrounding the church of San Pablo on the very slopes of the silver mountain to which they had gone since the days of Hernan Vela. Riding back and forth between these parishes on the horse that he was privileged to ride, Colque Guarache ensured that the full contingent of workers gathered on the mountain slope every Monday to await their work assignments. He also seems to have directed work in a series of fields (many of which he or his father had purchased) in the vicinity of Potosí, where mita workers during their periods of rest could recuperate and provide for workers' meals.

In early colonial days the territory of K'ulta and the town itself were no more than pastures and a small annex belonging to the town of San Pedro de Condo, where the native lords of the pre-Columbian diarchy of Asanaqi were installed by Toledo as "caciques gobernadores" with jurisdiction over essentially the same people and territory as they had governed as mallku before the Spanish invasion. So the ancestors of today's K'ulta, who once took their turns working in the Inca silver mines of Porco, were in Toledo's day recruited by the caciques of Condo (and Asanaqi) to be marched off to Potosí. There, they settled into the parish Toledo had set aside for them, San Bernardo, where they were once again beholden (as they would have been in pre-Columbian times when working Inca fields in Cochabamba or Inca mines in Porco) to the highest-ranking mallku of the four-diarchy Killaka federation, Juan Colque Guarache. Although Spanish division of the diarchies into distinct encomiendas and repartimientos, and even into different colonial provinces, began a process of disaggregation of large-scale indigenous social structures, the continued preeminence of the high-ranking Killaka mallku over the mita of Potosí gave Colque Guarache a means of reasserting the significance of pre-Columbian social hierarchy. In the parish of San Bernardo, the children and grandchildren of K'ulta's conquest-era people would be reminded of Colque Guarache's Inca-era stature, even as he oversaw their labors in mine work and in the construction of the cathedral-sized church of San Bernardo or shepherded them into the church for mass.

The details of Colque Guarache's management of the mita and the gruesome conditions of labor and terrible hardships on the Killaka federation population merit greater attention than I will give them here. Suffice it to say that the journey was arduous and the mine work dangerous. Whereas under the Incas Asanaqi and Killaka mit'a workers had traveled to Cochabamba fields and Cusco neighborhoods to carry out labor at the Inca's expense and had made their journey into a sacred pilgrimage, the trip to Potosí was marched to a more somber, funerary dirge. On passing through Inca administrative centers, mit'a workers were invited to pour vast amounts of chicha libations; they sang and danced while performing labors destined to feed their own, as well as Inca, ancestors and gods. This was not the case in Spanish times. Tristan Platt has described a ritual of colonial Pocoata in which mita workers were dispatched as if to their graves, while their relatives mourned their loss with plaintive wails (Platt 1983). So linked did the mita become with death that in K'ulta, until 1978 (more than a century after the mita was abolished), a ceremony marking the departure of youths appointed as mitayos was carried out in the cemetery as part of All Souls' Day. Labor within the Potosí hill of silver that K'ultas call Blood Mountain (a libation name they also give to money) formed an indissoluble whole with the process of mourning and the recollection of ties between the living and the underworld dead.[25]

Yet this shift in the pilgrimage axis linking local group to the state did not entirely displace earlier forms of social relationship through institutionalized generosity or the techniques of social memory that inhered in gifts of food and drink from cacique to "common indian." The very same colonial authors who condemn Andean drinking for the "forgetfulness" it brought on as well as the memories it carried also describe the prodigious drinking that accompanied the Potosí mita. As the largest city of the viceroyalty, Potosí was also the largest marketplace; it was a focal point for the economic pilgrimages of long-distance importers as well as for the export of silver bars. Drawing on García de Llanos' 1603 "Descripción de Potosí" (ANB, Fotocopias, 1603), Saignes (1987) calculates an annual consumption of 1.6 million *botijas* of chicha by a population totaling about eighty thousand adults. At 11.5 liters per botija, total chicha consumption reached 18.4 million liters per year, or 230 liters per adult. Much of this was consumed in *pulperías* and *chicherías*, where mine workers spent their meager salaries. Women and girls also carried jars of chicha to the *cancha* where mita workers gathered on Mondays, leading to the custom of drinking before entering the mines (Tandeter 1981).

No doubt the new Toledan disposition against toleration led to the repression of idolatry-associated drinking in Potosí; they may not have said so, but Spaniards certainly preferred a "secular" drunkenness in Potosí's manifold chicherías to the old "solemn" public gatherings in honor of idols and ancestors. But Spanish policy was not that consistent.

Capoche (1959: 141) gives us another clue about the nature of at least some of Potosí's prodigious drinking: The first to get drunk, he reports, are the caciques and captains of the mita; experts in "feasting and drinking and storytelling," they regaled their subjects with a simulacrum of Inca-period hospitality, and perhaps with a reshaped social memory in libation dedication and oral narrative. Juan Colque Guarache, whose subjects from the K'ulta region came to Potosí and lived there under his authority, was especially well-known for his drinking and storytelling. We may assume that he provided chicha in quantity to the indians of Asanaqi on their arrival in Potosí, as part of the customary redistributive generosity that common indians expected of their lords when they were asked to perform their mit'as. As we shall see, Colque Guarache was also known for his quipus, which the Anonymous Jesuit (1879) cited on matters of pre-Columbian lore, especially in connection with questions of sacrifice. As his will makes clear, Colque Guarache also kept cumbi kamayuqs in his employ to fashion for him the iconographically rich and status-affirming cumbi cloth, which may have carried semantically complex meanings in pre-Columbian days and clearly continued to signify in colonial times.[26] Yet we should not imagine Colque Guarache and other native lords in Potosí attempting to continue pre-Columbian rituals carrying purely "Andean" social memory. Deployed under new circumstances, making patent the meaning of new kinds of pilgrimage and new forms of social hierarchy, in connection with new deities (as well as, we must remember, old ones), drinking and storytelling, quipu accounts and cumbi cloth, and even the llama sacrifices that Colque Guarache explained to a curious Jesuit, necessarily began to carry colonial meanings. For caciques were required to participate and take a leading role in the Christian festivals and ceremonies by which priests sought to inculcate in indians a new appreciation of the relationship between time and society. Just so, Christian bells, prayers, and rituals were now to mark out for indians the time of day, the sequence of days forming the week, and the segmentation of time into monthly and yearly cycles. What is more, the human life career itself was now to be segmented and given meaning in an allegoric synchrony with Christianity's universalist narratives. So native lords like Colque Guarache were given opportunities not only to reintegrate former social hierarchies but also to weave new linkages between economic activity, obligation to cacique and state, and communion with gods and ancestors. Only the gods, the ancestors, the state, and the channels of transmission between them and "ordinary" indians had all been revalorized and transformed, as the nature of tribute and labor obligation had.

Apart from welcoming ceremonies and the prodigious drinking said to have taken place on mine workers' off days, another outlet for chicha sellers was the Christian festivals promoted by those same priests who decried drinking that was outside their public orbit. From the earliest years of mining in Potosí, its festivals had been as lavish as its mines were rich. Arzáns (1965, studied in Hanke 1956–57) describes the production of processional plays during the Corpus Christi celebration of 1608, in which indians played major roles in a representation of Pizarro's defeat of Atahuallpa, and other sacramental plays were also a common part of religious festivities there. Indeed, Toledo's ordinances for life in urban indian parishes specifically required participation in such processions and performances:

> In the festival of Corpus Christi they shall take out their image and
> dance in each parish and go in procession with their cross and flags,

and the brothers of the *cofradía*, with the priest, shall rule them,
examining above all the platform on which the image is carried
[andas] so they carry no idols hidden there, as has happened in other
cities. And before they set out the priest shall tell them in their
language the reason for that festival, so that they understand it and
honor it with the veneration they are obliged to give. (Sarabia Viejo
1986: 414)[27]

While Toledo was swift to condemn public drunkenness, like Polo he
did not prohibit private drinking; and even public drinking was all right
when done in moderation under priestly supervision, precisely during
Christian festivals! This newly created distinction between public and
private spheres, combined with ambivalent ordinances, seems an open
invitation to indians to carry out manifestly Christian rites in public,
glossing them in private, in what was an openly tolerated clandestine
sphere. Which private rites glossed public liturgies, of course, is anyone's
guess. Under such conditions, Potosí became a new taypi q'ala, modeling
now the peculiar asymmetries of the relationship between indigenous
peoples and the Spanish state. Toledo's post-Tridentine concerns for
vigilance and idolatry extirpation, along with his inversion of Incaic
distribution of drinking between public and private spheres and the
always-prominent contrast between productive underground mine labor
(always done in clandestinity) and the aboveground exploitative surplus
extraction by the new entrepreneurial Spanish aristocracy, provided the
grist for some new native interpretations of colonial life, which in
modern forms have been explored by Nash (1979), Taussig (1980), Platt
(1983).

Toledo's changes to the statuses of encomenderos and caciques and to
colonial tribute and labor regimes were dramatic and far-reaching,
substantially altering the colonial equation (while making indians ever
more subject to control by Spaniards, specifically the Spanish state). The
sort of microcosmic model of empire that Incas had established in the
state production center of Cochabamba was reconstrued to model
colonial relations and to fuel the metropole's imperial machinery. It may
appear, then, that to a degree Spaniards had merely displaced Incas at
the head of the empire, leaving old techniques of rule and memory
largely intact. As we shall see, such appearances are illusory. For Toledo's
transformations of authority, tribute, and labor levies were only the
beginning. In the coherent colonialist program he sought to impose,
these changes were to accompany further and more systematically
radical transformations of indigenous society.

INSTITUTIONS FOR THE RESHAPING OF SPACE AND TIME: VISITA, REDUCCIÓN, AND DOCTRINA

The Visita General

In the first three decades of Spanish activity, earnest efforts to evangelize indians had taken a back seat to more practical concerns of looting, battling, and laying claim to the spoils of conquest. By the 1560s Andeans in their rural hamlets were more likely to be rounded up into newly built churches to hear priestly sermonizing, to be baptized, and to be counted in the census visits of Crown bureaucrats. And Francisco de Toledo's "general visit" was the most penetrating and systematic census; it was simultaneously the last state-sponsored direct investigation into pre-Columbian affairs and the most thoroughgoing effort to transform Andean society. Among its consequences, it can be said to have contributed many of the social practices through which K'ultas now constitute their social memory. The process of the visita and the shifts in space and time it brought about thus deserve our careful attention.

The written results of personal inspection tours called visitas have become a favored source for extracting information on Andean states of affairs. Yet as Guevara-Gil and Salomon (1994) argue, the visita was anything but a noninvasive technique of observation. It was a slow-moving, highly disruptive social event, punctuated by a series of rituals, and it was intended to achieve transformative effects. No visita could have been more transformative than Toledo's visita general. Beginning with the usual census taking, which for the common indian involved both trauma and endless boredom, waiting in line to be registered on a list as a subject of a faraway king, this visita went far beyond counting and questioning; it aimed to reshape indigenous society utterly, breaking it up into new collectivities, pushing them into a new and more homogeneous relationship to space and time and to one another.

Following Castilian notions of the kind of living that could be called civil and Christian, repeated royal orders had required that indians be resettled in Spanish-style towns. The title of a royal cédula of 1549 provides a general idea of what the king had in mind: "Gatherings of indians in well-formed towns; year-long posts of mayors and aldermen (AGI, Indiferente 532, fol. 27v).[28]

While some indigenous settlements had already been "improved" by the addition of church and pillory, movement of all indians from scattered hamlets into larger population centers was an enormous undertaking that had not been systematically carried through. Toledo's visita general was to change that. "Visitors" like Pedro de Zárate, who took Toledo's instructions with him to Killaka and Asanaqi territory, were to scout out healthy sites for a radically reduced number of settlements, lay out their plaza and streets, and see that the towns were built and the indians removed to them from their old and remote haunts.

The visitor Pedro de Zárate treated the Repartimiento de Aullagas y Uruquillas, now a Crown encomienda owing to the Awllaka suit against Hernán Vela, to "reduction" in the manner that was also applied in the other Killaka diarchies. From "19 pueblos in a district of 20 leagues," Zárate reduced a total population of 4,851 persons to three new towns. The old Inca tambo of Awllaka became Villa Real de Aullaga (modern Pampa Aullagas), with 824 tributaries. On the opposite shore of Lake Poopó, Zárate founded Santiago de Guari (modern Huari) with a paltry two hundred tributaries. Far to the south, on the edge of the great salt pan of Uyuni, he settled three hundred tributaries and their families in a town he called Salinas de Tunopa (modern Salinas de Garcí Mendoza), recalling an old traveling hero whose name is linked to a mountain thereabouts (Cook 1975: 5).

Zárate visited three of the four Killaka diarchies (now two "repartimientos"). Another man, Captain Agustín de Zaumada, performed a similar task in the diarchy of Siwaruyu-Arakapi, Francisco Pizarro's former encomienda, now called the Repartimiento de Puna. There, 5,968 people who had lived in twenty-eight pueblos were squeezed into two new reducciones, Nuestra Señora de Talavera de Puna with 713 tributaries (modern Puna, located just south of Potosí), and Todos Santos de Quiocalla with 413 tributaries, later renamed Tomahavi (ibid., 23–24).[29] This town was established just south of Killaka and Asanaqi territory, quite far from Puna; the mining center of Porco was located between them.

Turning his attention to the two diarchies of Killaka and Asanaqi, grouped together into the Repartimiento de Quillacas Asanaques, Pedro de Zárate reports the "reduction" of the population, formerly scattered over an immense area in a total of twenty-one old "pueblos," to but four new towns.[30] Each of these "new" towns may already have existed as a settlement, but they were renamed and transformed. The Guarache headquarters of Hatun Quillacas was refounded as Oropesa de Quillacas, and one thousand tributaries were settled there (with their families, totaling about 4,529 individuals). Condocondo, the town near Asanaqi Mountain where lords of that diarchy dwelled, became San Pedro de Condo, with five hundred tributaries (totaling 2,265 persons). It was in this district that a small annex called Santa Bárbara, later Culta, would be founded in the seventeenth century. Nearby, Zárate founded San Juan del Pedroso, which later reverted to its indigenous name of Challapata, settling there some seven hundred tributaries (with families, 3,170 persons). Finally, after what would have been a very long trip, he founded the town of San Lucas de Pabacolla (modern San Lucas), with three hundred tributaries (1,358 persons).[31] The first three towns are all located near Lake Poopó in the Altiplano heartland. San Lucas, however, was located in maize lands far to the southeast, where Killaka, Asanaqi, and Awllaka peoples had long before obtained lands from the Inca in exchange for maintaining forts to defend against Chiriguano invasions. Their presence as a cushion between Chiriguanos and Spanish interests in Potosí was still required.

The Toledan ideal, deriving apparently from an earlier proposal by Matienzo (1967), was to settle about five hundred tributaries in each new town. The numbers in this case do not work out perfectly, but the effect was nonetheless dramatic. Unfortunately only a summary of Zárate's visita has turned up, and no copies of the ordinances he must have established.[32] Only a brief visit to these town suffices to indicate the general plan carried out in each, which closely resembles the "ideal" reducción depicted by Matienzo (Fig. 6.3). In each, a regular grid plan of streets focuses upon a spacious public plaza, on which was built a church with its parish house, a town council hall, a jail, and a "tambo," a house for visiting Spaniards. And along parallel lines and right angles, the indians who were forcibly settled there built their own new homes, also, if surviving examples tell the truth, according to rectilinear principles.[33]

Now, these were not merely new settlements; they came with a new set of institutions and clearly bounded territories. Arbitrarily, visitors decreed which old settlements within the district of a repartimiento would move to what new towns, and the lands pertaining to those that were moved into a new town now fell under the town's jurisdiction. This pattern repeated the manner in which the territory of Castile was segmented, into the *alfóz* districts of Castilian *villas* (Nader 1990). Indeed, nearly all the institutions that Toledo instructed his visitors to establish had precedents in Castilian villas.

Each new reducción town was also called a doctrina, and from the tributes of its new population a priest's salary was to be paid. Such priests, called *doctrineros,* or "indoctrinators," were charged with keeping careful watch over their indian charges, providing frequent instructional sessions in addition to regular weekly (and daily) mass. Above all,

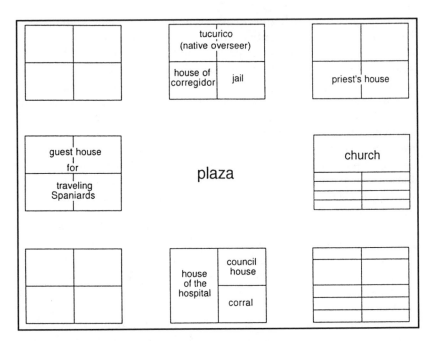

Figure 6.3. Matienzo's 1567 recommendation for the layout of reducciones (Author's rendering after Matienzo 1567, New York Public Library, MS Rich 74, fol. 38r)

of course, they were to make sure that indians left their idolatrous ways behind in the origin communities which they had abandoned.

Toledo's initial project plan, drawn up in Quilaquila (near the City of Silver) on November 7, 1573, urged visitors to take care when caciques begged them to leave more old settlements standing than were absolutely necessary. For reducciones were principally intended to force the indians "to leave the places and sites connected with their idolatries and the burial places of their dead, and for this reason, under every shade of piety, have [the caciques] deceived and continue to deceive the visitors so they are not moved from their old pueblos" (Sarabia Viejo 1986: 281–282). The move, then, was necessary as a technique of amnesia, to distance indians from their past. And active erasure of memory encoded in living space (and commemorative space of burial places) was carried out through demolition. Former homes were to be leveled, along with monuments like burial towers, or chullpas, in which ancestral bones were kept. These were to be thrown together into a common pit and buried. The new towns would have their own cemeteries, located within the church and in its immediate environs. But only Christians could be buried there. Once the old ancestors were gone, new, Christian ones would be left to commemorate in the rituals in favor of the dead that were a specialty of sixteenth-century Catholicism.

This, of course, was preparatory not only to pulling indians into the future but also to giving them another and different past, which is to say, transforming their social memory. But reconstruction of social memory in the Castilian and Christian mold was a complex task, to be performed under constant vigilance lest indians lapse back into their old ways. Indeed, in many ways "vigilance" is the watchword in the Toledan civilization project.

To help the priest round up his parishioners for indoctrination (and to aid in the delivery of tributes and mita laborers), each town was also allotted its own town council, just like those that Castilian villas enjoyed. For Andeans, this was another radical break from the past. The diarchy mallkus had directed their own subalterns, called principales or jilaqatas, of whom there was at least one for each of the subdiarchy units called ayllus. Very likely, such authorities in the past had filled inherited posts, perhaps linked to lineage ritual duties in honor of the ayllu's ancestral mummies, wak'as, and paqarinas. Now, however, the Castilian way was to prevail. The new towns were not only to take the shape of a Castilian town but also to be ruled by a council of officers charged with applying a strict order of behavioral rules.

The record left behind by the visitor and founder of K'ulta's neighbor to the east, the reducción of Nuestra Señora de Belén de Tinquipaya, helps to illustrate the process. When their lands were threatened by invasion by Spanish landholders in 1610, the caciques of Tinquipaya (a reducción into which three separate social groups, the Colos, Caquinas, and Picachuries, were mixed together) produced their copy of the visita performed by one Diego de Sanabria (see Documentary Appendix, part C). On January 15, 1575, Sanabria attested to having completed his visita, carried out at the order of Toledo. His purpose was to "give order in government and good living, a just order like that of the Spanish vassals of His Majesty" (AGI, Charcas 49, fol. 7r). A unique and rich document, his ordinances are divided into two sections, one addressed to the duties of the town council, and the other to the desired transformation in social habits. The layout of the town is not described; it was still under construction in 1575, but mention is made of a plaza, a church, a hospital, and town council offices. One may surmise from references to

"imprisonment" that the town was to have a jail (although "imprisonment" might also refer to stocks), and that delinquents subject to the lash
would have been punished, in Castilian fashion, tied to a pillory like that
erected in Cusco by Pizarro, a picota or rollo (Fig. 6.4).

Inside the town council offices (referred to as the *cabildo, consejo,* or
regimiento) there was to be a locked room and, in it, a lockbox with
three keys. This "community chest" was to contain two chambers: one to
hold the community archive; one in which to deposit moneys from
tributes, salaries earned by mita workers and others who hired themselves out, fines and rents collected in the name of the community, and
profits from the dairy production and wool of the community herd. In
1575 the community herd, endowed through an encomendero restitution payment, consisted of 250 head of cattle and 400 head of Castilian
sheep.

The care of these herds and distribution of meat and profits from
dairy products and wool are elaborately described; indeed, various
works of charity, especially for widows and orphans, are prescribed. So
too are the punishments for those who break the ordinances themselves
or other strictures of moral or natural law that go unspecified. Imprisonment is often mentioned (up to thirty days), along with the cutting of
indians' hair (regarded with special horror by Andeans) and the whip
(not to exceed one hundred lashes in locally decided cases). The nature
of the whip used is carefully prescribed: It should be of cured leather
rather than of rawhide, and should have no more than four "tails," each
no thicker than a finger on a man's hand. Serious punishment was
reserved for perpetrators of serious crimes, who were to be sent for
judgment to Spanish authorities. Only Spaniards were allowed to impose
the death penalty, amputate limbs, or cut off ears.

The ordinances, provided as specific local laws complementing a
variety of other ordinances given and still to be given by Viceroy Toledo,
also specify just how tribute was to be collected from tributaries between
eighteen and fifty years of age, and how laborers were to be levied for
work in mines and urban "plazas." Determining tributes, and indeed
everything involving money, was a matter for the record, but one kept in
the Castilian manner: The first endowment of the community chest
holding the community archive, an archive of written books, was to be
these very ordinances, brought out from the chest by Tinquipaya
caciques in 1610. It was also to hold the *padrones* and visitas of census
takers, by which to guarantee that no one was overlooked or charged
beyond retirement age (when the able bodied began to take turns serving

Figure 6.4.   Punishment at a rollo. The wording at the top translates as "Alcaldes. How the corregidor punishes His Majesty's poor alcalde ordinario." The dialogue written within the picture is: *Corregidor:* "Give it to him." *Whip-wielding slave:* "Bring the two eggs you owe." *Alcalde:* "Ay, for the love of God." (From Guaman Poma de Ayala 1980: 742)

243

the caciques). In conformity with Toledo's instructions to reduce the burden on Spanish appeals courts of "frivolous indian lawsuits," the interrogations of criminals carried out by indigenous authorities was especially *not* to be recorded. The books to be deposited in the community chest were to be account ledgers, wills, and census materials. Social memory of the written sort was distinctly oriented towards preserving a record of the transmission and reproduction of the human, animal, and property forms of colonial capital.

Archives require both authors and archivists, and the new sorts of registers were to be written and deposited (and signed in good faith) by a scribe appointed from among the indians of the town (Fig. 6.5). Yet without administrative supervision, without a town council, there would be no business for a scribe or need for a townhall. Without eliminating the old sort of authority (the caciques principales of the Caquinas and Picachuris, their "second persons," and principales for each of the town's five pachacas [an Inca decimal term for a unit of a hundred tributaries, likely here referring to ayllus]), the ordinances call for the creation of a host of new kinds of authorities.

Each new town was simultaneously a unit of civil administration (reducción) and a unit of ecclesiastic ministration (doctrina). The priest assigned to religious ministrations of the town, the doctrinero, was charged with carrying out stringent measures to convert his flock to Christianity and make sure they did not wander back to old idolatrous ways. Chief among these measures was weekly and sometimes daily preaching, especially to children. But the regular Christian calendar of holy days was also to be observed, and to guarantee properly performed rites and full devotion to Christian beings, several sorts of specialized roles were assigned to indians, ranging from choirmaster and musicians, to mayordomos, alférezes, and other funtionaries of regular cult to the saints. Taken together, they reduplicate the kinds of devotional offices attached to all Spanish churches and the kinds of posts that in Spain belonged to semiautonomous lay confraternities (cofradías) charged with cult to the saints.

On the civil side of things, administration of the community chest, the collection of tributes, levying of laborers, capture and trial and punishment of delinquents, and also services to aid in the indoctrination efforts of the new town's priest were entrusted to a town council, a consejo or cabildo or regimiento (meeting in the building so named), composed of several kinds of offices and numerous individuals. These were to be elected every New Year's Day by the outgoing members of the council. The new council included four *regidores* (aldermen), two alcaldes

Figure 6.5. The cacique at his writing table. The wording at the top translates as "Principales should be examined. The good principal, of Spanish letters and speech, who knows how to make a petition, interrogatory, and lawsuit, and who is not a drunkard, coquette, gambler, or liar, in this kingdom." (From Guaman Poma de Ayala 1980: 718)

245

(mayors), and one alguacil mayor (major bailiff), and two alguaciles menores (minor ones), along with a scribe, a *fiscal* (prosecutor), a schoolteacher, and a majordomo. What is more, each office was to be occupied for one year by men elected to office by the previous year's authorities, new ones replacing old ones like clockwork on January 1 of each year. Toledo's general ordinances specify that no more than half of these posts could be held by privileged relatives of the noble cacique lineages; the rest were to belong to common indians.

The duties of these new kinds of authorities, familiar to Spaniards but novel to those Andeans who had not yet served time in Potosí, were also clearly spelled out in the ordinances of Diego de Sanabria as well as the general and specific ordinances of Toledo (some of these are collected in Levillier 1929; and Sarabia Viejo 1986, 1989). These included all the labors already described and many more as well. Coexisting with the cacique principal of the multi-"ethnic" repartimiento to which this town (along with others) belonged, even meeting jointly with him, they were nonetheless required to report secretly on any misdoings engaged in or denounced by native nobles, especially the usurpation of lands or misuse of indian labor for their personal ends. And although the cacique principal held the tie-breaking vote in council matters, he could not hold sway on any issue if the council was unanimous against him.

In establishing this balance of power, which closely resembled the balance between town councilmen and feudal lords in Castile's seignorial towns (Nader 1990), Toledo struck yet another blow against what he regarded as the overweening power and pretensions of an essentially tyrannical native nobility. The freedom of action of caciques and the town council was constrained further by granting final say on many issues to Crown administrators, especially the corregidores (who in Castilian towns defended the king's interests against both lords and councils). Encomenderos were enjoined from visiting their encomiendas, deprived of indian labor, and effectively eliminated from the equation.

All these changes in Andean rural life can be (and have been) summed up as a new politics of state, massing subjects to control them more efficiently, to guarantee proper deliveries of tribute and labor extending the reach and security of the absolutist Crown. And so it was. Yet the concern for charity, for community property, and for punishment of a wide range of crimes without apparent impact on the king's pocketbook attests to the fact that state control was much more than a matter of collecting tributes. For the sixteenth-century Spanish state, rule in Castile as well as in the Indies meant the extension of the techniques of surveillance and discipline into the most intimate corners of subject peoples' lives. It meant an exactitude and comprehensiveness of observation and recorded representation that had not been seen before among European colonizers. Into the community chest visitors deposited a copy of new rules and regulations, to be observed in a town drawn up by rule and regular pattern. Like Castilians, all indians were now to live in towns with virtually identical structures and institutions; and the detailed censuses and accounts of community chests were also to be carried, along with the observations of regularly repeated visitations, to the capital of the empire. Philip II, under whose lead this *visita general* and similar comprehensive inspection tours of Castile were devised, was also famous for his effort to totalize his realms, to gain a global understanding, represented in maps and painted views (Kagan 1986) and "geographical relations" (Jiménez de la Espada 1965) deriving from Crown questionnaires, displayed and archived in his own "memory palace," the Escorial.

As Timothy Mitchell (1991) has argued for the nineteenth-century colonization of Egypt, peoples and practices that were irregular, unusual, or hidden from view were not susceptible to the totalizing representations required by European modernism and its epistemology, which postulated a positivist mirror relation between sign and referent. Philip II may have operated on prepositivist principles, but his urgency to envision his realms globally from a single Archimedean point led him, like colonizers of Egypt, to force his subjects to become representable, to conform to the units and readily observable identities that his statisticians and geographers required. Andean indians, that is, were to be forced into a homogeneous mold, based on Castilian models.[34]

So far, so good. But to imagine the *reducción* as no more than an epistemological effect, a means of representing subject peoples and therefore the empire, and to insist on the primacy of the visual image as a tool of colonial encompassment is to shunt aside a vital issue. In his work *Colonising Egypt,* Mitchell deploys Bourdieu's (1977) work on the habitus of the Kabyle house to develop a promising approach to understanding colonizers' obsession with reshaping their subjects by reshaping the spaces in which they live. Drawing also on Michel de Certeau (1984) Mitchell also touches on the inculcation of new experiences in time, meant to produce the work discipline required by capitalism.

Once again, nineteenth-century Egypt seems an echo, not of nineteenth-century epistemology, but of the sixteenth-century Spanish

empire. In his 1573 "Instruccíon para los visitadores," Toledo ordered
visitors to lay out reducciones with

> . . . wide and straight streets and blocks, leaving an open space for
> the plaza and a site for the church . . . and a large space for the
> council houses and the offices of justice for alcaldes, and jail with
> different rooms for men and women, and a room for the jailer.
>   Item: You shall lay out the indians houses with doors opening
> onto the public streets, so that no house opens into the house of
> another indian, but that each have a separate house.
>   Item: You shall procure that the houses of indians are layed out
> such that the room of the wife and daughters and maids, is separate
> from that of the male children and other male indians of the house.
> (Sarabia Viejo 1986: 34–35)

So the town plans were explicitly oriented towards the gaze of the
colonial observer, so that behavior regulated in new ways could be
monitored, by the priest and corregidor, but also by the appointed
members of the town council, who had to go out on scheduled circuits of
the town to keep the curfew and guard, mostly, against idolatries, public
drunkenness, and sin, especially of the sexual sort.[35] The disciplining
colonial gaze was to be internalized within indigenous society itself, in
the form of mechanisms for social control oriented towards acts defined
by new logics of "wrong," and also as conscience, to be activated in
confession and directed into penitential acts in public processions.

In Spanish colonial parlance, all that is stated in a few simple phrases.
In the words of the *visitador* Diego de Sanabria, ". . . the reducción of
these indians is made in the town of Our Lady of Bethlehem so that by
coming together they live together in *policía* as Christians, to be better
indoctrinated. . . ." (AGI, Charcas 49, fol. 11v). To live together in
policía as Christians was a straightforward business for Spaniards. The
phrase describes what for them was the taken for granted of life, the
habits and deeply ingrained patterns of thought and practice by which
they *were* Spaniards and Christians. In the sixteenth century the term
"policía" was usually combined with "buena." "Buena policía" can be
glossed as "good customs," but for the theorists of empire who designed
reducciones (where indians were to be reduced to buena policía), it
encapsulated all the aspects of social and civil life that constituted
prerequisites for understanding and living the Christian faith. These
were not easily described in words, precisely because so much was
implicit, habitual, even preconceptual. It could not be explained; it had
to be lived.[36]

Toledo had allotted two full years for the building of each new pueblo, and during that time he continued to solicit advice from Spaniards and indians, and revised and refined his ordinances. While still in Potosí in February of 1573, for example, he had accepted a "memorial" from Juan Colque Guarache, acting as representative of many of the caciques who had brought mita workers to that mining center. Making explicit reference to Colque Guarache and specific complaints, Toledo proceeded to act on them (Sarabia Viejo 1989: 23–33). On March 4, in the introduction to a provision forgiving the indians a half-year's tribute on account of the work time they were investing in the construction of their reducciones, Toledo concisely summarized the reasons for the resettlement campaign:

> Given that the principal effects that have been pursued in the visita general that His Majesty ordered me to carry out in these realms, for which I have come personally . . . is that the natives be reduced and congregate in towns where they can be taught and exercised in buena policía, natural law, and evangelic doctrine, and that they cease their rites, gentilities and abuses that they have practiced up until now, no longer living as barbarians without policía or government, being as they have been so separated from one another in ravines and plains, with neither contact nor commerce with rational people. . . . (Ibid., 85)

If the reducción process was to bring such contact and commerce, something that certainly resulted from the regular pilgrimages of indians to the mines and parishes of Potosí, the visita itself was especially instructive. In another provision issued in Potosí on March 12, Toledo reported that no one might claim ignorance of this particular order, since "at present all or most of the kuraqas and principales of this province [Charcas] and of the Collao and of other parts of this kingdom, and the corregidores of natives, visitors and reducers and other persons. . . ," are gathered together in Potosí (ibid., 36). One might think they were all there to the practical ends of the mining mita, but when Toledo set out on his return trip to Lima some months later, the entire group seems to have accompanied him in a moving viceregal court reminiscent both of the massive caravansary of the Catholic Kings and of the Inca ruler (Rumeu de Armas 1974; cf. Guevara-Gil and Salomon 1994).

During his viceregal progress, Toledo continued to issue and revise ordinances, in some cases radically amending his project, always, it seems, in the midst of a throng of caciques and corregidores and visitors, as well as the usual batch of individual Spaniards and representatives from councils of towns seeking privileges. In June, numerous orders were issued in La Paz; by the middle of July, his papers were signed in the king's encomienda of Chucuito.

In August this movable feast reached Arequipa, from which an especially large number of instructions and provisiones were issued. There on September 10 he gathered together "most of the caciques of the province of Arequipa, Cusco, and Collao" (Colque Guarache and other Charcas lords were also present) to explain to them the meaning of the new ordinances. In simplified language translated, no doubt by the official interpreter, González Holguín, Toledo delivered a speech from a prepared text. Beginning with blandishments about Philip II's benevolent plans for them, Toledo quickly got to the point; he made no bones about the link between reducción and the extirpation of idolatries, and he explained to caciques their special role as models and exemplars of the Christian faith.

> The principal thing that was missing [before reducción] was indoctrination and the priests who might carry it out, and it was impossible to achieve when all lived sprinkled about, so many leagues distance from one another, in so many hidden corners and ravines, and that is why they have been ordered reduced to towns. . . .
> It is convenient that caciques and principales be good Christians and thus be an example for their indians, and help reduce those who have not yet been. And he who does the contrary shall be taken as suspect, and it shall be understood that they have adored and given reverence to the wak'as, and shall be subject to proceedings against them. . . .
> Curacas who give reverence to the wak'as and carry out other rites or superstitions, or know of others who keep and reverence wak'as and do not denounce them, shall be punished. . . .
> The best title for the cacicazgos and their succession shall be that of being the best Christian and of greater ability. And the [office] ought to be given to such an indian, whether from among the legitimate sons [of the cacique] or the other ones, or to another indian in whom these qualities coincide. . . .
> After the matter of idolatries and wak'as, which is such a grave business, no offense is greater than *borracheras* and thus, although His Excellency will not refuse to them what is permitted of the other vassals of the king of Spain, which is to drink, they will be severely punished if they are excessive in their drinking, particularly the curacas, since they can ill govern their indians while drunk. (Sarabia Viejo 1989: 91–95)

In this speech Toledo reiterated the connection between the former dispersed settlement pattern, drinking, and idolatry, and clarified the connection between settled town life, sobriety, and Christian virtue. He also underscored the personal connection between himself and the caciques. Before concluding, he remarked:

> Never before have they seen a viceroy or governor of this kingdom
> walk among them, and they should know that the reason he now
> walks among them is to eliminate the vexations that many persons
> have caused them, such as visitors, scribes, bailiffs and reducers, and
> other persons and royal officials. . . .[37]
> And His Excellency has commanded that justice be done equally
> to indians as to encomenderos. . . .
> [The caciques] must keep well in their memory that which His
> Excellency has said, because if they do not keep to what has been
> commanded and ordered, His Excellency will not forget to have them
> punished.
> Because they are poor, the king has taken them as his vassals, and
> for being so His Majesty takes them as his children.
> For specific business His Excellency will give them audiences, and
> that is the general business he had to say to them. (Ibid., 91–95)

Records survive detailing some of the specific business Toledo carried out through audiences with individual caciques. Juan Colque Guarache, whose intervention had led in Potosí to numerous addenda to the mining ordinances safeguarding indians and especially mita captains from abusive Spaniards, also obtained special treatment in Arequipa. It was not for nothing that the lords of Qaraqara had called him a manipulator.

Colque Guarache's descendants managed to keep hold of noble privilege and the role of cacique governor, but factional disputes, the passing of generations, and the contradictions between Spanish notions of succession to office and Andean ones led to the multiplication of distinct noble houses, tied only to a particular reducción town more often than to its "mother" diarchy. Challenges to them eventually came, however, from new kinds of social groups, led by new kinds of authorities, which were reconstrued, conceived, and enacted within these new, smaller and more "Spanish" spheres of action.

Christian Space-Time Enacted by Town Ayllus and Town Boundaries

After attending to caciques' business and other matters, such as the ordinances of the city of Arequipa (which specify how indian parishes are to be governed and the manner in which Christian festivals and processions should be performed), Toledo issued his "general ordinances for communal life in indian towns" on November 6, 1573 (ibid., 217–266). From these very detailed ordinances and others directed towards corregidores and officials entrusted with judging indigenous crimes, one can clarify just how reducción and doctrina were to achieve the effects of instilling buena policía and hence Christian life.

Far from their old wak'as and burial places the new towns were first of all places of amnesia. But Toledo called upon caciques to remember well his ordinances, and asked priests and town councilmen to instill habit memory of a distinctly Spanish and Christian sort. Toledan ordinances indeed refer to the ringing of church bells to mark out the hours of work, prayer, and rest, and to the adaptation to new calendars and metaphors of old Incaic turn systems for labor levies, now calculated through the use of models of rotation called wheels. But life for indians in the reducciónes was meant to transform the relationship between space and time in more fundamental ways. The Christian calendar that now marked out times for daily mass and indoctrination, weekly observance of Christ's passion, recalling too as a "day of rest" the very sequence and timing of cosmogeny, pointed towards something more than work discipline. The round of festivals in which indians were now to participate constructed the year as a spiraling repetition commemorating Christ's life and death, its cadence sung in Te Deums and beat out in the confessional *mea culpas* leading to eucharistic communions linking the beginning of time to its end. By practices carried out within the space of reducciones, indians were not just to learn but also to become part of a universal history of which Spanish kings and colonial officials could think themselves coauthors.

All this might suggest that the colonial project in Toledan guise was not just coherent and thorough but also fully successful. Yet just as practical concerns (the need to collect tributes efficiently and to rule indian subjects) led Toledo to reinforce the authority of native lords who he otherwise sought to undermine and displace, other exigencies brought important features of Andean society into the very towns that were supposed to undo it. Let us see how the process played out in the favored Colque Guarache's Killaka federation, especially within the diarchy of Asanaqi, the pre-Columbian diarchy that held sway over K'ulta ancestors.

The process of reducción divided the territory of diarchies arbitrarily into the jurisdictions that visitors established for each new town. As they traced new boundary lines and mojones (boundary markers) upon the ground, stringing a conceptual rosary or circular ceque line around each town, they also arbitrarily dissected the social units internal to diarchies. In this way each new town was peopled not only by individuals but also by the ayllus to which the individuals belonged.

Diarchies like Asanaqi were composed of people and the territory they could claim. In fact, the principal landholders were ayllus, each of which seems to have been composed of an assortment of lineagelike entities. Now, like the diarchies that they collectively made up, ayllus held land in discontinuous form, keeping an extension of pastures here and a group of fields there, in such a manner as to have access to a wide range of ecological conditions and therefore of foodstuffs (Murra 1972). As a composite made up of its ayllus, Asanaqi itself was such a discontinuous entity, with a large extension of lands in the Altiplano core territory (in the midst of which other diarchies had claims on small pockets of land), other chunks of territory in far-flung districts, such as in the region of San Lucas on the banks of the Pilcomayo River, and other plots here and there within the districts of the Charka, Qaraqara, and Yampara peoples. In the Cochabamba valley, Asanaqi peoples still stubbornly laid claim to maize fields worked under Inca auspices, though their coca fields in Pocona had been lost.

Even within the highland core territory, small differences in ecological conditions translated into large effects in the crops that could be harvested and animals that could be herded, and so, within the Asanaqi area west of Lake Poopó, each Asanaqi ayllu was an assortment of patches within a territorial quilt rather than a single continuous area. Since visitors established town locations and boundaries according to their own logic rather than any Andean one, their boundaries dismembered the patches of land, and hence the populations, that had composed the ayllus of Asanaqi. Each town thus received the arbitrary assortment of ayllu fragments which held patches of land within the town's jurisdiction.

Just so, San Pedro de Condo, although it had been and remained the capital of caciques of Asanaqi, was not settled by all of Asanaqi's ayllus. Some held no patches of land in San Pedro's new jurisdiction. Asanaqi ayllus lived, farmed, and pastured their animals on lands much more extensive than the relatively small territorial jurisdiction granted to San Pedro de Condo; Asanaqi peoples were settled into other towns as well. Within the territory of the old Asanaqi diarchy, another town was also created, with its own jurisdiction. When the peoples of the lands granted to it were gathered together in their new town, San Juan del Pedroso, today's Challapata, the town obtained a different arbitrary selection of ayllus from the "parent" diarchy of Asanaqi than the town of San Pedro de Condo did. And because the district of Challapata included patches of land worked by Killaka ayllus (and the two diarchies were joined as a single colonial repartimiento), into Challapata were forced not only some fragments of Asanaqi ayllus, but also several pieces of Killaka ayllus, and even an ayllu called Antamarka, which had clearly been an outlier settlement occupied by peoples from the Qaranka diarchy of Antamarka (Fig. 6.6). Of course, since ayllu landholdings and hamlet

Ayllus of Asanaqi and elsewhere[1]	Condo ayllus[2]	Challapata ayllus[3]	Culta ayllus[4]	Cacachaca ayllus[5]	Cahuayo ayllus[6]	Lagunillas ayllus[7]
Quilana	Quilana		Quilana	(Quilana)		
Kallapa	Alax-Kallapa	Kallapa		Kallapa-Araya		
	Manxa-Kallapa					
Kawalli	Alax-Kawalli		Alax-Kawalli	(Alax-Kawalli) → Liwichuku & Jujchu 1		
	Manxa-Kawalli	Kawalli	Manxa-Kawalli	(Manxa-Kawalli) → Jujchu 2 & Kimsa Cruz		
Suilkayana				Suilkayana	Suilkayana	
Chankara	(Chankara)	(Chankara)				
Ilawi		Ilawi	Ilawi			
Suilka Ilawi		Suilka				
(Takawa)[8]		Takawa		(Takawa) → Jujchu 2		
(Yanaqi)[8]	Yanaqi		Yanaqi			
Antamarka[9]	(Antamarka)	Antamarka				
Chiquri (Urus)[10]	(Chiquri)					
Culloculio (Urus)[10]	(Culloculio)	(Culloculio)				
Haparo (Urus)[10]		(Haparo)				
Quisca (Urus)[10]		(Quisca)				
Yuqasa (Awllaka)[11]						Yuqasa
Wari (Awllaka)[11]						Wari
Anqaxuqa (Killaka)[12]		(Anqaxuqa)				
Musquqa (Killaka)[12]		(Musquqa)				
Saka (Killaka)[12]		(Saka)				
Quruqa (Killaka)[12]		(Quruqa)				

Figure 6.6. Towns and ayllus of the Asanaqi diarchy. 1. Ayllus of pre-Columbian diarchies reconstructed from colonial sources (see the sources listed for Fig. 5.2). Territorial interdigitation left varying segments of various Asanaqi ayllus arbitrarily within the boundaries of one or more towns. Not shown: the town of San Lucas in distant valley lands, where Asanaqis were settled along with Killaka and Awllaka ayllus. 2. Condo was a reducción founded well before 1571, when the church required repair. Ayllus Changara and Antamarka have disappeared there. Condo progressively lost jurisdiction over the people and territories of Culta, Cahuayo, and Cacachaca. Since the 1950s, Condo's remaining territory has been fragmented into at least four separate cantóns. 3. Challapata was a reducción founded by 1574, when it was divided into three parcialidades: Ayllus alax-saya Asanaqi, manxa-saya Asanaqi, and manxa-saya Killaka. 4. Culta was a Condo hamlet (Santa Bárbara de Aguas Calientes) by 1591. It emerged as an annex of Condo in the mid-seventeenth century. It became an independent *curato* while still a civil annex of Condo in 1779. Culta became an independent cantón in the mid-nineteenth century. It lost its priest and became a vice-parish of Huari in 1932. 5. Cacachaca (church built in 1612) was an annex of Condo by the mid-seventeenth century. It remained an annex and vice-parish of Condo until becoming a cantón in the 1950s. Since then, a portion of its territory has seceded as Cantón Livichuco. Ayllu Qullana of Cacachaca has disappeared; Ayllus Alax-Kawalli, Manxa-Kawalli, and Takawa gave rise to new ayllus Jujchu 1, Jujchu 2, and Kimsa Cruz (Arnold 1988: 127–131). 6. Masce Cahuayo was founded as a Condo milling center after 1591. It became an annex and vice-parish of Condo by 1645, a vice-curato of Culta in 1779, and a civil annex of Cantón Culta during the nineteenth century, gaining cantón status in the 1960s.

settlements were scattered through the larger territory rather than being of a piece, Condo and Challapata in several cases received parts of the same ayllus. Just so are there ayllus named Kawalli in both towns today, and also in Santa Bárbara de Culta, which fissioned from Condo's jurisdiction in the late eighteenth century.

To collect tributes efficiently and levy laborers, Toledo had left cacicazgos and ayllus in place, but now, in the context of reducciónes, ayllus were to take on a new form. Within the architectural space of each new town, ayllus were assigned particular streets, and so colonially built space itself became a microcosm of a colonially created new social whole. A good example of this process comes from the reducción of Tacobamba, where members of the Asanaqi ayllu Ilawi worked outlier lands. Testimony from 1610 avers that they went to those productive fields to recuperate after serving in the mita of Potosí. In 1573 Juan Colque Guarache had pointed out to the visitor Pedro de Zárate that, if they disoccupied those lands to settle in Condo or Challapata (Ayllu Ilawi had lands in each jurisdiction), they might lose them, so Zárate went to Tacobamba and assigned them a street there (ANB, EC 1611, no. 8, fols. 23r–24v).[38]

So just as the new town plans and boundaries sundered diarchies and town councils cross cut the authority of hereditary lords, "traditional" forms of social organization like ayllus were reintegrated into the towns, but in a partial manner that began the work of undoing the structure of diarchies themselves. And when the social obligations and work duties under the direction of rotative town councils were distributed according to ayllus, as they no doubt were even in the initial construction of the towns, then such work not only enacted the individual tributary's subordination to the council, priest, and state, but also refigured the

---

Figure 6.6. (*Continued*)
7. Lagunillas was a colonial tambo pertaining to Huari by 1574; it became a civil and ecclesiastic annex of Huari in the seventeenth century. With Huari, it was an ecclesiastic annex of Condo during the eighteenth century. Lagunillas became a vice-parish of Culta in 1779 and an annex or vice-cantón of Culta in the nineteenth century, gaining cantón status in the 1960s. 8. Neither Takawa nor Yanaqi (the latter now very populous) are listed as present in Condo in earliest document, but they appear later. 9. Ayllu Antamarka may have originated from the Antamarka diarchy of the Qaranka Federation. 10. These Uru ayllus were short-lived, disappearing from the record by 1645. 11. Yuqasa and Wari of Lagunillas were settled there from the town of Huari for tambo service. 12. These ayllus of Challapata, grouped as the "parcialidad de los Quillacas de Challapata," were originally Killaka diarchy ayllus "reduced" to the new town with jurisdiction over the territory they occupied.

ayllu in terms of these colonial officials and institutions. Gary Urton (1988) provides a visible example of the resulting effects: In the reducción established near the Inca origin place of Pacaritambo, periodic sweeping of the plaza (like festival obligations and other work duties) was divided up among the town's ayllus by dividing the plaza into strips, where each ayllu swept a separate strip and repaired the corresponding section of the plaza's surrounding wall. Over centuries, what was once a single wall came to be clearly divided into stylistically varying segments, visibly "concretizing" the social differences embodied in ayllus.

The most imposing structure in each new reducción was its church, and the most intrusive Spaniard, its priest. With them came a festival calendar and a wide range of social obligations oriented towards the rituals of Christianity. These too came to be divvied up according to ayllu organization, and hence the Christian calendar and the historical theses encoded in its cyclic repetition became another vehicle through which native society was reintegrated around new colonial focal points. From among the local population the priest chose musicians and singers to adorn the mass and to accompany processions of the saint images that came to populate the church. And ayllu by ayllu, as Toledo had specifically ordained for the celebration of urban holy days (and especially for the festival of Corpus Christi, the militant and totalizing procession that expressed the Catholic doxa and underwrote the sovereignty of the Crown, lending the authority of God and king to the social hierarchies that visibly paraded through town in such processions [Rubin 1991]), Andeans played their parts in dramas where religion and politics, the *via crucis* and the social drama of colonialism, were one and the same.

Agents of colonial transformation had traveled the countryside in the visita general, and they left copies of the social forms they inscribed on paper and on human society to ensure that Andeans would periodically recall and revisit such activities. Inspection of the padrones, the census lists produced in visitas, shows one result of Toledo's instructions to visitors: indians were called forth to be registered according to their ayllus, led by their principales. A practical measure to ensure that all were accounted for by the authorities who knew them best, this technique also had the effect of regularly reinscribing ayllu organization within the new towns. Likewise, when priests began to record baptisms, marriages, and funerals systematically in their own registers, they too usually organized their books into sections headed by the names of ayllus, grouped into the moieties to which they belonged. The indexes of the first baptismal registers of Challapata and Condo illustrate precisely this kind of division (Fig. 6.7).[39] The order of moieties and ayllus within

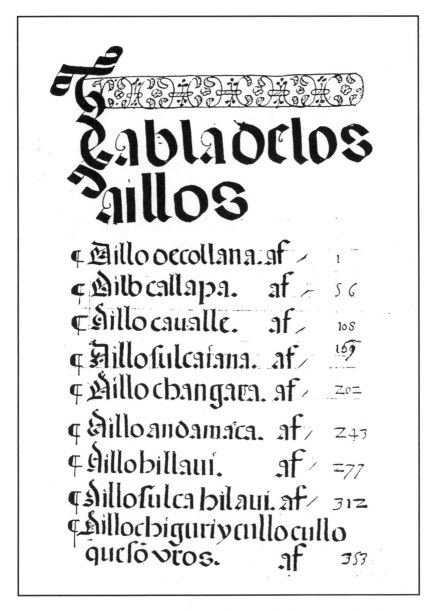

Figure 6.7. Table of contents page of the Libro 1 de Bautismos, San Pedro de Condo, 1571. (Photocopied from the original, formerly in the church of San Pedro de Condo, later transferred to the Archivo Diocesano de Oruro, with permission; also on microfilm in the Mormon Family History Archive)

such documents, we might surmise, may have established the rotational cycles, the "wheels," by which intratown social units took turns at fulfilling the social obligations performed at the behest of town councils as well as priests.[40] Just so did the new obligations within reducción towns and their churches come to provide an armature through which ayllus and moieties, and indeed other Andean ways, were woven into new patterns within the ambit of the colonial state, even as old ways came unraveled.

As we shall see, the integrative powers of such activities, their capacity to weave social wholes out of arbitrary fragments, was to prove decisive in the ultimate defeat of hereditary lords and definitive dismemberment of diarchies as the colonial state was displaced by the republican one. But the process of formation of new kinds of sociality was a long one, marked by struggles between competing kinds of authority, competing registers of social memory, and competing pasts. Given the absolutist nature of the colonial state and the link between Crown sovereignty and the universal history of orthodox Catholicism, we should not be surprised to find that challenges posed by new kinds of authorities to old ones are treated as seditious rebellions, and alternative interpretations of the past as diabolic heresies.

AN ANDEAN PIDGIN BAROQUE: THE COUNTER-REFORMATION
OF INTERCULTURAL HERESIES

Just as Andean men like the mita captain Juan Colque Guarache turned to writing and to Spanish-style registers of the past, such as event chronologies, wills, and the quotidian documents of lawsuit, visita, and account book, they also continued to engage the past through more "traditional" registers. They still told stories, poured libations, and even used quipus. It is more difficult to judge, however, what kind of new past they construed with old techniques. In Potosí, we might imagine Colque Guarache in the process of lubricating with chicha libations the pathways of social transmission that gave them the power to claim his subjects' labor there. And in a diatribe aimed at Polo Ondegardo's account of the Inca past, the Anonymous Jesuit (1879) repeatedly cites for his evidence "the quipus of Juan Colque Guarache" (especially in his effort to prove that Polo had misunderstood Andean testimony on the issue of human sacrifice). Chicha libations were subject to new strictures, and quipus to replacement by the pen and ink of reducción scribes, but both were still in use in the 1570s. Can we judge what they recorded? Records from the previous generation already attest to new contents.

We have seen several examples of quipus in use to report on tribute payments and services to Spaniards in the sixteenth century. Very soon, however, the categories and kinds of social relations registered in quipus underwent considerable change. They recorded goods and new kinds of labors owed to encomendero and priest, carried in very different sorts of journeys to new kinds of places. To accomplish this shift to colonial uses, it was not only the numbers and categories twined in quipu cords and knots that had to change. As a trace of meanings embodied in the landscape, iconically standing with pathways and loci that gave significance to social life, the very logic of the quipu had to change. Ritual journeys and social landscapes traversed in them had to be radically rerouted. Registering how many loads of corn or potatoes had been taken to their encomendero's house, how many families had shifted to the mines of Potosí, how many silver marks had been smelted and delivered to the encomendero, indigenous quipu kamayuqs created a chronotopograph, a map of places in time, of the *colonial* world, not the pre-Columbian one. The pathway of memory in their quipus does not seem to have led to the founding ancestors and wak'as that in Inca times underwrote the tributary order. It led, rather, to the marketplace, to the parish house and church, and to the hearing rooms of the Spanish legal system, from whence it was translated into thin and wavy lines traced on paper, then deposited in imperial archives.

By the 1570s, the process of transformation had progressed yet further. The chronicler José de Acosta, who toured the rural Andes with Viceroy Toledo, reported at length on his observations of quipus (and allied techniques using stones or grains of corn) in use:

> ... It happens today in Perú, that after two or three years of service when it is time for a Spanish administrator to give account of his period in office, the indians come out with their detailed and ascertained accounts. They note that in such a town they gave him six eggs for which he failed to pay, and in this house a chicken, and there two bundles of hay for his horses, for which he paid only so many coins, while he still owes so many others. And in order to do all this, they complete their cross-checking with a quantity of knots and handfuls of cords, and these they take for valid witnesses and certain writing.
>
> I saw a handful of these strings which an indian woman carried and in which was written a general confession of her entire life, and through them she confessed, as I would do with a handwritten paper, and I even asked about certain little strings that seemed somewhat different from the others, and they were certain circumstances required to confess some sins fully.

Apart from these quipus of strings, they have others of small stones, through which they punctually learn the words they seek to know by memory. It is quite something to see certain old men with a wheel made of these stones, learning the Our Father, and with another the Ave María, and another the Creed. They know which stone it is that was conceived of the Holy Spirit, and which one suffered under the power of Pontius Pilate. There is nothing like seeing them correct themselves when they err, for the whole correction consists of looking at their stones. For me, on the other hand, to forget everything I know of choral music, just one of those wheels would suffice. There are usually not a few of these for this effect in the graveyards of the churches.

It is an enchanting thing to see another kind of quipu, using grains of corn. A very difficult account would force a very good accountant to use quill and ink, to see how to fit in so many entries, so many contributions, taking out so many from there and adding so many here, with another hundred little notations. These indians, in contrast, will take their grains and put one here, three over there, and eight who knows where; they pass one grain from here, exchanging three from there, and in effect they come out with their account very exactly made, without even a single accent mark out of place. Much better do they know how to give account and reason of what falls to each one to pay or give than we know how to do with quill and ink and careful checking. If this is not ingenious and if these men are beasts, men are free to judge. What I judge for certain, is that in that business they have great advantages over us. (J. Acosta 1977: book 6, chap. 8, pp. 411–412)[41]

As ingenious as Acosta knew them to be, these mnemonic devices were now being used to recount sins and to remember prayers that themselves contained condensed versions of Christian narratives on which priests expounded at length in doctrina sessions. This was a watershed generation for Andean social memory. The techniques may have remained the same, but the content, the memories, were changing.

The medium had been adapted to carry a new kind of message. Pre-Columbian quipus had not recalled the Hail Mary and the Paternoster or the Christian categories of sin. And as for more narrative, more "historical" media, such as the quipu used to register a sequence of sacred places tied to ancestral events and social boundaries: What past now merited repeated tellings in the context of the Colque Guarache mansion in Potosí? What libations, to what deities, along what ceques, might he have poured there in the presence of the forced laborers who had followed the colonial pilgrimage to the mountain of silver? Once the reducción process had taken effect, many wak'as and burial places had been destroyed, and new channels of social relations focusing on town councils and Christian festivals had become inescapable aspects of experience, these very facts must have been the things most requiring a satisfying historical foundation. As with the narrated past, the past encoded through nonnarrative techniques must have undergone a profound transformation under colonial conditions.

When Juan Colque Guarache died he left behind a detailed will that made restitution for his sins just as the wills of Spanish encomenderos did (ANB, EC 1804, no. 193). He was succeeded by his son of the same name, who had been trained in the Jesuit school for native nobles in Cusco. Surely, this was a different sort of training from that which this pupil's grandfather, Juan Guarache, had taken in Inca Cusco. Juan Guarache would have learned the calendric and topographic intricacies of the ceque system; if Juan Colque "el Mozo," as Capoche called him, knew how to use quipus, we can be sure that the stories he told with them were about Pontius Pilate and Jesus Christ rather than Viracocha and Tunupa. What is more, he may well have done so in Latin, in which Jesuits trained their charges.[42]

As historians or anthropologists of the pre-Columbian past, we must conclude with Murra (1964, 1967, 1968, 1970) that pre-Toledan chronicles and visitas are more trustworthy, providing a clearer view of the Andean past than the colonially transformed narratives of later dates do. Yet when our goal is to understand the emergence and transformation of the colonial world, that very same breaking point in the colonial record becomes significant in other ways. When one learns to read in this record the dramaturgic effects of visitas and the discourses of power and "collective subjectivity" carried out in them and in other colonial procedures (Guevara-Gil and Salomon 1994), this documentary "break" opens rather than closes a scholarly window, granting us a view of how the Andean past came to be transformed through Spanish colonialism and how Andeans increasingly came to understand Spaniards and the colonial experience.

INDIAN SACRIFICES AND INDIAN EUCHARISTS AFTER TAQUI ONCOY

Toledo's execution of the last rebel Inca, Tupac Amaru I, upon the place of punishment erected by Pizarro over the Inca *ushnu* signaled to Andeans the inviability of military resistance to Spanish rule. The inquisitorial techniques of Spanish extirpators of idolatry, unleashed on

Andeans in the wake of taqui oncoy, helped to teach Andeans that the Castilian king and Christian god could not be defeated in an outright war of the gods. But Counter-Reformation disciplines and punishments also served to train Andeans in more inaudible and invisible interpretive tactics.

The result of this concerted repression and increased surveillance was double. On the one hand, Andeans were taught a new difference between public and private activities; their heterodox practices were channeled into clandestinity, where they could be carried out only by small groups of people behind closed doors or on faraway mountain-tops. On the other hand, these private and clandestine practices were simultaneously ever more closely tied to the rituals that could still be carried out in public as large-scale collective performances. Those, of course, were Christian festivities, directed towards the Virgin and the Holy Trinity and towards a host of images that for Spaniards were not idols: the saints and advocations of Christ and the Virgin. Dancing and singing in native languages still persisted, but translated into adjuncts of Christian liturgy. Heterodox meanings could still be parsed in these public performances, especially when clandestine practice was employed as a supplement to public cult. Just so, libation sequences and animal sacrifices were increasingly deployed, in clandestine meetings in the very context of Christian rites, as a means of glossing public liturgic practice.

The transformation of Tunupa into an Andean apostle (Urbano 1981, 1990), like that of the moon into the Virgin (Harris 1986), the thunder god Illapa into Saint James (Silverblatt 1988a), and the sun into Christ (Platt 1987c), was not a matter of Spanish invention alone. Although some priests in an early period of the conversion of indians saw fit to introduce such equations, and other Spaniards, seeking to account for the strange parallelisms they saw between Christian and Andean practices and beliefs, were ready to admit the possibility of a preconquest evangelization, they were just as likely to see the devil behind Andeans' distorted creator gods, confessions, and flood narratives. Certain priests, like Pérez Bocanegra (1631), sought to take advantage of such parallelisms in their efforts at conversion; adapting Andean devotional forms to the worship of Christian divinity, they aimed to interest Andeans in their own indoctrination. Sometimes they succeeded all too well. Just as they strove to transform Andean narrative to strip it of its non-Christian content, missionary priests repeatedly told stories to Andeans, giving greatest emphasis to the redemptive narrative of God's descent into man in the person of Jesus Christ. In spite of Spanish claims to the contrary,

Andeans began to understand and internalize colonial projects of civilization and evangelization, and also to appropriate what they learned for their own ends.

The miracles performed by the Virgin of Copacabana on the site of the Inca ritual center on Lake Titicaca drew Andeans to a now-Christian site that had long before been consecrated as a place of miracles, an Inca shrine in sight of the very place of the sun's (and Tunupa's) birth.[43] But the taquies performed in the new context were radically transformed, as Estenssoro Fuchs (1992) makes plain.

Much as we might like to attribute such facts to the conversion strategies of wily priests, we must also recognize that Andeans themselves were adept at the process of cultural translation. The image of the Virgin of Copacabana was itself the product of an indigenous sculptor's hand, carved in an "Andean baroque" mestizo-indian workshop. In the indian parish of Copacabana in Potosí, indigenous people had already attested to numerous miracles brought about by this advocation of Mary, who often gave aid to indian miners at moments of danger (see Arzáns 1965).

Some Andeans, such as the earnest student of Christian apology and universal history Pachacuti Yamqui, the anonymous compiler-translator of the Huarochirí manuscript, and the itinerant epistle writer Guaman Poma, were active voices indeed in the process of cultural translation (Fig. 6.8). Juxtaposing Spanish and Andean meaning orders in an effort to account for the colonial realities they lived, they actively interwove what had been two incompatible worlds into a single colonial whole. The establishment of translated equivalences of semantic and enacted meanings produced an interculture, but one which under sustained colonial conditions, where an asymmetry of power based on cultural difference was always to be maintained, made complete synthesis impossible, unthinkable to most Spaniards and most indians. On the colonial vanguard, certain intrepid interlopers may have worked to undo difference, to assert, as many caciques did in the 1570s, the essential equivalence of native lordship and Castilian nobility, or (like Pachacuti Yamqui) to laud the fundamental Christianity of Andean religiosity or even (as Guaman Poma repeatedly asserts) the moral superiority of Christianized indians to most missionizing Spaniards.

However, it was precisely at these creative junctures, when Andeans had seemingly appropriated Castilian social forms and Christian liturgy and theology in their own terms, that Spaniards most insistently reasserted difference. When Andeans played an authoring role in Christian

Figure 6.8. Pregunta el Autor: Guaman Poma queries his informants. Here the cultural interloper Guaman Poma, wearing full Spanish dress, questions Inca elders. This one-time aide to Cristóbal de Albornóz, extirpator of idolatry, was well-versed in sixteenth-century Spanish ethnographic techniques, and like most ethnographers was not averse to taking advantage of his relative position of power to gain information about the past. (From Guaman Poma de Ayala 1980: 338)

264

thought and practice, Spaniards insisted on remaining missionary colonizers. Like the Jews and Muslims of Iberia, who posed the greatest threat to Christianity when they converted to it (thus becoming special targets of the Inquisition), it was converted and "acculturated" Andeans who seem most to have worried the extirpators of idolatry and colonial administrators. Especially problematic were those who seemed to usurp priestly authority or Castilian noble prerogative. When they were discovered, they provoked Spaniards to search out the idols hidden behind altars, to question the diabolically heterodox logic of incomplete or "mixed" indigenous Christianity, and to assert the insufficiency of native elites for the honors and privileges of Castilian nobility. And none of these faults was difficult for Spaniards to find. Because colonial Spaniards also "spoke" the intercultural pidgin of colonial discourse, they knew the general location of its "impurities" in advance.

The taqui oncoy movement of the 1560s suggested to Spaniards that too much toleration of indigenous celebratory practices in new Christian contexts did not lead indians to grasp the faith more readily, but gave them opportunity to continue worship of old gods in clandestinity. In the wake of that movement and especially with the arrival of Viceroy Toledo's visita general and the newly strengthened institutions of surveillance that accompanied the process of "reduction," ever more ubiquitous priests turned their attention to sniffing out the heterodox practices of their indian parishioners.

As it happens, Toledo's arrival in Perú with orders to institute a sweeping transformation of the colonial order coincided with another major shake-up that was to affect all regions of the Spanish empire, indeed, all of Catholic Christendom. The Council of Trent called for drastic improvements in the methods by which priests taught doctrine; they were empowered to infiltrate communities of the faithful in an effort, first, to make clandestine heterodox practices and beliefs visible and, then, to eradicate them through strenuous preaching, exemplary punishment, and continued surveillance.

The cause for such extraordinary measures was the spread of heresy, and in particular the Protestant heresies, often in Spain glossed simply as "Lutheranism" for the heretic dogmatizer whose teachings were causing the most serious political crises of the empire. In Castile, another concern was the growing influence of Erasmus, whose suggestions about how the faithful might gain direct and personal contact with divinity (without the mediation of a priest in the Eucharist) had led to a generalized movement called illuminism. Illuminist "cells" had sprung up throughout Castile, gaining adherents within religious convents, but also leading to the emergence of many "third-order" communities. In the late sixteenth century, increasing numbers of ordinary men and, especially, women were induced by dogmatizing priests or nuns to join "irregular" orders, groups of adherents who met privately to share their religious experiences.[44]

Like all practices deemed heretical, illuminism became a special province of the Inquisition, which in 1559 arrested a large group of Erasmians—including some leading citizens—in Valladolid, then the capital of the empire. Santa Teresa of Avila was herself questioned, as was Perú's Santa Rosa of Lima. Many of the suspect came from the ranks of the highly educated and well-to-do, but some of their practices had spread into more popular circles as well. One of Santa Rosa's favorite techniques, self-flagellation, an old form of penitential practice which was also cherished for producing spiritual ecstasy, was a regular part of confraternal processions, although it had not displaced the autos sacramentales that were still a confraternal staple.

In Lima, Santa Rosa's circle of devotees included women of indigenous descent (Iwasaki 1994). Unfortunately for the upholders of orthodoxy in the Indies, indians were by this date no longer in the jurisdiction of the Inquisition. Individual parish priests did, however, report suspect practices to their bishops and archbishops, and by the 1560s special sections within Church archives were being set aside to hold the documents produced in ecclesiastic visits carried out with the express end of extirpating surviving idolatries. Extirpators discovered, however, that clandestine performance of pre-Columbian religious practice was not their only problem. For indigenous peoples in their new towns, influenced by incessant priestly harangues and also by the pomp of Christian ceremonies in which they participated in their hometowns and in the Spanish urban centers where they periodically went to work, had begun their own process of transculturation, selecting suitable pieces of Christian belief and practice and knitting them into their lives in their own manner. Counter-Reformation activities in Perú had to contend now with indian brands of Christian heresy.[45]

Diego Iquisi, Confessor and Wak'a "Doorkeeper," Says Mass

Careful scrutiny of the evidence suggests that taqui oncoy adepts embraced certain ideas taken from Christianity even as they declared a war of the gods. Taqui oncoy was suppressed and religious indoctrination became more insistent, increasing the likelihood of transcultural borrowing. Andeans' aberrant Christianity, rather than their idolatry, became a serious concern.

In the early 1570s, perhaps arriving along with the visita general, a young priest named Hernan González de la Casa took on the Wisixsa diarchy towns of Toropalca and Caisa, where he worked for seven years. At some point during that period, González de la Casa heard reports of an idolatrous cult still practiced within his district, and he set out with his alcalde, scribe, and factor *(fiscal)* to undo it, traveling via a circuitous route to the remote valley of Caltama so as to catch the idolators by surprise. What he discovered seems at first sight quite pre-Columbian. He found a native sanctuary where a native religious leader named Diego Iquisi, identified as a *punku kamayuq,* a "porter" or gatekeeper of a wak'a, was revered as a great sorcerer. In the community of Caltama itself, numerous "pagan indians" lived with their still-unbaptized children. Diego Iquisi, it turned out, performed sacrifices in honor of five idols. Finding the blood and bones of animals and what he believed to be human children, González de la Casa investigated Iquisi's cult. He found that the wak'a, the shrine where the idols were kept, was a center of native *novenas* (calendric rites) and *romerías* (pilgrimage processions). Now, Caltama itself was located near both Porco and Potosí, and Iquisi's five idols were all associated with mines. The principal idol, named Tata ("Father") Porco, was a large chunk of native silver from the mountain and mine of Porco, and the other four were also named for and probably came from mountains with mines. Quite probably, Iquisi had discovered the clandestine home of the idols once kept at the very mines they were named for. Perhaps, he had found the idols by which Manco Inca had lured Diego de Almagro towards Chile in 1535.

Many principal Inca wak'as had already been smashed; cultic centers in Inca administrative sites had largely been abandoned along with the flow of mit'a pilgrims along Inca highways. But whatever the disruptions to pre-Columbian social life elsewhere, these particular idols may still have had currency in the late sixteenth century because of their mining focus. These idols, and Iquisi's cult to them, drew pilgrims from "Cochabamba and the entire district of Charcas, Caracaras, Yanparaes, Chichas, Juras, Visisas, Asanaques, Carangas, and Chuyes" (AGI, Charcas 79, no. 19, fol. 3v), which is to say, from the southern half of Qullasuyu (the northern federations of Qana, Kanchi, Qulla, Lupaqa, and Pakax go unmentioned). A major cultic center, this wak'a was an appropriate clandestine counterpart of the centripetal motion of forced colonial mita laborers. We must ask, however, what kinds of practices

Andeans schooled in reducción Catholicism engaged in under Iquisi's direction.

González de la Casa's discovery and destruction of Diego Iquisi's cultic center is told through references to a *proceso* filed in the extirpation archive of the archbishopric of La Plata, written into his "proof of merit and service." González, rather than Iquisi, is the story's protagonist. Even so, the account contains some unusual details of Andean practice.[46] First of all, pilgrims seem to have come to the shrine for the purposes of divination, to inquire of the gods what their future might bring, and then to carry out sacrifices in conjunction with certain other rites destined to cleanse them of sins and to restore the balance in their relationship to gods so that, we must assume, their futures would be vouchsafed. The testimony of Juan Pérez, an apostolic notary familiar with the extirpation record, fills in further details:

> . . . information that was taken against him and by his confession
> [shows] that he was a famed sorcerer and invoker of the devil, an
> idolatrous priest *[sacerdote]* who confessed the indians, giving
> penances to those he confessed. These he washed in the currents of
> the rivers, taking sand from the river and throwing it over their
> backs, after which their sins were washed away. And he led them to
> understand that he said mass, and that he was empowered to say it,
> and sacrificed sheep and guinea pigs and some children, as witnesses
> say after seeing the bones the priest found. [Iquisi carried out] these
> and other superstitions against our holy Catholic faith, and said that
> he preached to the indians at the command of the devil, with whom
> he said he had communicated, from which there seems to have been
> a great scandal in the entire province of Charcas. To this Diego
> Iquisi, it appears, flocked indians of Charka, Qaraqara, /9r/Chuy,
> Qaranka, Yampara, and Chicha to consult with the demon and find
> out if they would die from their illnesses, or whether their marketing
> and agreements and plantings would come out prosperously or
> adversely. And he led them to have *novenas romerías* [pilgrimage
> processions] to the wak'a, and had them fast and revere it as a god,
> and [likewise] the sun and the moon and the god of the rains and
> lightning bolts. (AGI, Charcas 79, no. 19, fols. 8v–9r)

Even as González de la Casa and his witnesses sought to portray Iquisi and his following as heathens, clear references to Iquisi's usurpation of priestly roles abound. First of all, he was *Diego* Iquisi, certainly a baptized indian. Furthermore, this sorcerer, who somehow "communicates with the devil," also performed confessions, assigned penance, and washed away his followers' sins in the river. Were these Christian practices? One cannot categorically affirm it, since forms of confession and the washing away of "sins" were practiced by pre-Columbian Andeans. But pre-Columbian punku kamayuqs were not named Diego, and did not lead their followers to believe they were saying mass or that they were empowered to do so. For sixteenth-century Spaniards, when any but an ordained priest did such things or made such claims, it was certainly the devil's work, as Iquisi's practice seems to have appeared to his extirpators, constituting a dangerous mockery and a threat to the authority of God and the Church.

In this probanza, witnesses characterized the rites performed in Caltama as confessions, penances, and absolutions, but also as novenas and romerías, rites that to Spaniards were associated with the calendric celebration of miracle-working saints. But these idols were a sort suitable for the smelter. González carted them off and, on the site of the idols' shrine, built an open-air chapel (a *humilladero*) in which indians might adore the crucified Christ. When he gave his deposition, twenty years after the events, the indians were now said to mock their old idols and to adhere devoutly to Christian practice. Things had not been so simple, however, at the time of the events.

When González carried away the idolators along with the idols and their precious ornaments, a mob of indians attacked him and shouted out, revealing at least one of the miracles performed by the greatest of the idols, the silver Tata Porco. They wanted to know why González was taking him away, and threatened to kill González unless he gave back their "Father Porco," the god who had given them victory over the Chicha (in a battle in which Colque Guarache also participated, carried out in colonial times under Martín de Almendras). González survived the rain of arrows and boulders they sent down upon him from above, but nearly died, he tells us, after they poisoned him with a witch's brew of potent herbs. He survived only because an indian woman was able to undo the sorcery with a counterpotion, causing him to vomit up "a knot of worms the size of a hickory nut" (ibid., 3v). González believed in Iquisi's powers if not in those of the idols.

After delivering part of the silver to the royal treasury in La Plata and sending Iquisi before an ecclesiastic extirpation judge, González was promoted to the richer parish of Macha, where he claims to have helped definitively reduce the indians to good customs (and to the tribute rolls). There he helped to build an impressive church and endowed it with precious ornaments, the Christian equivalents of the elite goods found with Iquisi's idols. At the same time, he also gave the indians of Macha (where he had also extirpated idols) suitable Christian replacements for the miracle-working intercessors of idolatrous pilgrimages: He brought them *imagenes de bulto* (ibid., 2d cuaderno), miniature images of potentially miraculous saints, enclosed in wooden boxes (also called retablos), which could be carried in novenas and romerías between the town's church and newly founded chapels in its hamlet annexes. Within a few years, such chapels and saints' images provided the grist for further indigenous experimentation with Christianity.

Miguel Acarapi (alias Miguel Chiri), Indian Christ, Performs the Eucharist with Chicha

Not far from Macha, Viceroy Toledo had created the town of Taco-bamba, where Asanaqi's ayllu Ilavi had been settled on a street. Around the turn of the century, some extraordinary events took place there, recorded in the 1613 probanza of the priest who was sent there to investigate them, one Fernando de Mesa. Like the probanza made by González, this too was a curriculum vita constructed through notarized testimony, the Castilian stuff of event history that led to Crown rewards. As always in probanzas of priests, various important ecclesiastics praise Mesa highly. He had always enlivened his Christian rites with "very good piccolo music and singing" by indians trained to the task (ANB, EC 1613, no. 19, fol. 5v, testimony of Lic. Pedro Ramírez del Águila). What is more, he had passed the Toledan-era exams in both Aymara and Quechua, and because of his linguistic skills had done marvels through his teaching and indoctrination, keeping his indians well practiced in the things of the holy Catholic faith (ibid.). So good was Mesa in his work that the indians of Condo (who knew him through their mitima residents there) had asked the archbishop to assign him to their parish of San Pedro de Condo (ibid., 5v–6r). Fortunately, Mesa was also a curious and energetic man. He was forced to walk about the territory of his doctrina to carry the faith to those who lived in the hamlets (like Ayllu Ilawi's settlement) that the reducción process had left intact (ibid., 2r), and there his curiosity led him to understand the risk in giving indians too detailed an account of the mysteries of the faith.

Mesa had been sent to Tacobamba in the wake of a discovery there, under the watch of his predecessor Father Pedro de Porras, of a very dangerous business. Around 1594, it came to the bishop's attention that, in Tacobamba,

> . . . an indian named Miguel Acarapi, by another name called Miguel Chiri, carried out confessions saying that he was Jesus Christ. And

with this trickery he had attracted many other indians who followed
him in his rites and abuses like disciples. In meeting together they
took and drank the herb called achuma. About eight days ago that
indian died violently when another indian called Juanillo killed him,
because Miguel Acarapi had said that the chicha [they drank] was the
blood of Jesus Christ. The murderer in defense said it was not so,
and stabbed him with a butcher's knife, from which he died. (Ibid.,
21v–22r)[47]

The followers, or "disciples," of this martyred Christ continued to
meet in the countryside, where they buried him

> . . . next to the chapel where before they killed him, they say, he had
> carried out ceremonies leading them to believe that he was saying
> mass. And at present his followers still go to the chapel and tomb to
> that same effect, from which, if there should be any delay in
> punishing and correcting such offenses, some sect might come about,
> damaging to a people who are new to our holy faith. (Ibid., 22r)

In the bishop's commission to Mesa to investigate the matter, he was
instructed to find out who was involved, where it took place, precisely
what doctrine the indians might have been teaching one another,
whether there were teachers, if the teaching was in public or in secret,
and how widespread the business might have been in the surrounding
area. Of particular interest was discovering if such practices were limited
to indians or whether Spaniards might have been involved, and whether
such practices were performed only in drunken meetings or without
drinking (ibid., 21v). Clearly, concern over the emergence of a "sect"
suggests more than the usual worries over indigenous apostasy into idolatry. The problem now was their experimentation with Christianity.[48]

Over the succeeding baroque century of idolatry extirpation and
indigenous uptake of Christianity, references to collectively adored
graven images, widely attended specialist-directed sacrifices to wak'as,
and regionally salient pilgrimage rites gradually fade from the record.
Extirpators in the latter part of the century find no more public wak'a
cults, and for the most part contented themselves with discovering
small-scale superstitions, magical practices, and curing rites, usually
restricted to the private intrahousehold sphere into which sacred drinking had been exiled. Most large-scale rites and regional pilgrimages
performed in honor of graven images were now carried out in churches,
under the leadership of Spanish priests. Yet in these activities, too, even
without declaring themselves to be Christs or claiming to perform the
Eucharist with chicha, Andeans got themselves into trouble.

Foundation of Santa Bárbara de Culta as a Clandestine Confraternity

Until June of 1996, my years of research on K'ulta and Asanaqi had turned up only vague intimations of the origin of the town where I did my fieldwork. In the late seventeenth century, it had been an ecclesiastic annex of Condo, to which Condo's priest traveled to say mass and carry out baptisms, weddings, and funerals once or twice a year. It was once called Santa Bárbara de Aguas Calientes for the hot springs that have since gone cold, and is now called Culta (pronounced K'ulta), say its residents, for the gutturing sound the artesian springs now make. When I asked about the town's origins, I was told that they had something to do with Condo and much to do with miracles wrought by Culta's patron saint, Santa Bárbara. Long ago she had appeared to a shepherd boy, who had seen Santa Bárbara and her sister, Our Lady of Bethlehem, walking in human form downriver from the headwaters of the Aguas Calientes. When the boy saw her, some distance from Culta (about a league away, people say), Santa Bárbara was frozen in image form, while Belén continued walking downriver until reaching Tinquipaya. At a later point, Santa Bárbara was brought to Culta, and though an attempt was made to move her from there, she refused to go.

Now, just uphill from the church and plaza of Culta stands a group of ruined stone houses, arrayed around a small flat area known as Awka Plasa, "Father Plaza." Several people told me that these were the ruins of the original settlement to Culta, which had long ago been destroyed. In construing my own narrative of Culta's foundation, I had set aside the miracle stories, so much like those told of patron saints everywhere, and had imagined the ruins around Awka Plasa to have been a pre-Columbian settlement, burned and destroyed when people of these parts were resettled in the reducción of San Pedro de Condo in the 1570s. New Culta, I supposed, had come into being as a result of the impositions of doctrina-spouting priests, when the population began to recover from epidemic collapse and the lands around Condo had become insufficient. Certainly, the rectilinear layout of the "new" Culta was more akin to the standard reducción than to the haphazard arrangement around Awka Plasa.

Yet a ten-folio document that I ran across in the Archivo y Biblioteca Arquidiocesanos de Sucre in June of 1996 reveals that miracles performed by Santa Bárbara are, for Culta, closer to the truth than any suppositions about high-handed Spanish reducción practices. For in fact Santa Bárbara—or, at any rate, Culta peoples' devotion to her—had everything to do with the destruction of an early settlement as well as with its rebirth, when against the wishes of Spanish priests, Culta rose phoenixlike from its own ashes. Experience with heterodox cults like that of Tacobamba's Miguel Acarapi/Chiri made seventeenth-century priests wary of letting Andeans take Christianity into their own hands. Perhaps that is why members of Ayllu Kawalli bearing the surname of Chiri, who had purchased an image of the saint and constituted themselves as a confraternity, were forced to take their Christian devotions into clandestinity, when successive priests of Condo sought to confiscate their image of Santa Bárbara and demolished the chapels the people had built for her. Their cult cannot be considered a Spanish imposition. To the contrary, the founders of what has become Santa Bárbara de Culta (whose namesakes live on in a Manxa-Kawalli hamlet) struggled for many years for the right to celebrate their saint's image.

According to their later testimony, it was in the year 1616 that don Pedro and don Diego Chiri purchased an image of Santa Bárbara, along with all the accoutrements of the mass, and built a chapel in their hamlet of Junt'uma (or Uma Junto, the Aymara term for Aguas Calientes, or "Hot Waters"). The two men then founded a confraternity of their peers, of which one was *prioste*,[49] and the other, mayordomo. Writing a letter of complaint to the archbishop of La Plata in 1625, the two Chiris[50] explained how they had done all this nine years earlier in the hope that the priest of Condo would come to celebrate the saint's day and perform mass for all those whose fields and pastures in this distant region kept them from easily attending church in Condo. But their priest, far from aiding them in their devotions, had refused to visit the chapel. And what is more, he had confiscated the chalice, paten, saint's banner, and other goods connected with the sacrament of the mass. As a result, the old people of their region were dying without last rites and were deprived of the benefits of their pious works.[51]

Convinced by their arguments, don Pascual Peroches, the provisor and vicar general of the archbishopric, ordered the priest of Condo to return the purloined goods and henceforth to visit the chapel and carry out his duties there, under pain of excommunication. The priest, Gonzalo Leal Vejarano, immediately drafted an indignant response challenging the Chiris' "sinister and false" account and providing a history of Junt'uma confraternal insolence going back to his predecessor's time. Leal's reply of January 16, 1626, begins by asserting that never, since the 1570s foundation of the reducción of San Pedro de Condo, had there been any custom of celebrating the mass in Junt'uma or any priestly obligation to do so.

... in the jurisdiction of this town four or five chapels have been
ordered demolished, so as to reduce the indians to Condo, thereby
avoiding the great borracheras, idolatries, superstitions, incests, grave
faults, and deaths that [the chapels] caused, and in particular in the
case of the chapel referred to in the [Chiris,] petition. Some years ago
the indian referred to in the petition, in order to absent himself from
his town and avoid service and hearing mass there, so as to live in his
infidelity with others like himself, built a chapel. With this pretext,
they thought that the priests would, with bribes, let them live there in
their liberty. Knowing that many sins would be committed there
against God Our Lord, and knowing that the indians who gathered
there did not come to hear mass or receive the other sacraments, my
predecessor Diego Arias refused ever to go to the said chapel to
celebrate mass or any fiesta whatever, even though [the indians]
beseeched him to go. (ABAS, Causas contra Ecclesiásticos no. 5020,
fols. 4r–4v)[52]

When the Kawallis of Junt'uma first built their chapel, Arias had been
ordered to say mass there after the Chiris had obtained an order from
the archbishopric. At that time, Arias had won an appeal and obtained
an order for the destruction of the Junt'uma chapel and transfer of the
image and ornaments to a new chapel in Condo. But Arias had died
before putting the order into effect.

Not long after, taking over the parish in 1616, Leal also fell victim to
the Chiris' sinister ways. He too obtained an order from an ecclesiastic
visitador (Doctor don Pascual Peroches, the same man who in 1525,
now provisor of the archbishopric, favored the Chiris' petition) to
demolish the chapel and confiscate the image and ornaments, so as to
force the Ayllu Kawalli indians to return to Condo. Leal explains what
then happened:

... again these orders had no effect, even though the corregidor of
this district went after the indians, because they fled and hid the
image and the ornaments. And he found that the roof of the chapel
had been removed, and afterwards they had built another chapel a
league farther away. And to accomplish their evil intention, the
indians went before the lord archbishop, don Gerónimo de Rueda,
with a sinister relation and another request like the present one ...
to which I replied with the reasons expressed above, and ... I sent
the lord archbishop the orders and opinion of the lord visitor, and he
responded ... that I should insist that the corregidor burn the
indians' houses and bring them back to their reducción, since it was
in the service of Our Lord. ...

... Yet none of these orders has had any effect, because [the indians of Junt'uma] are the most evil indians of the whole kingdom, *ladinos,* proud, free, and untrustworthy. In the visit that he made to this town, the Lord Doctor Bartolomé Cervantes wrote to the Real Acuerdo about all of this, seeking to remedy it. And in his visita he left ordinances and constitutions [directly addressed to the chapel in Junt'uma] written in the book of this church where other visitas have been recorded. (Ibid., 4v–5v)

At this point Leal introduced a copy of the constitution—an ecclesiastic rule of order—that directly addressed the Chiris' chapel in Junt'uma:

Constitution:

Item: Experience has revealed the great damage and inconveniences that follow when indians have chapels in their hamlets and fields, celebrating in them mass and fiestas. Living in the countryside the indians are at greater liberty to carry out their borracheras, cantares, and taquies, to the dishonor of our Catholic faith, and carrying out the said fiestas does notable damage to their conversion and the faith that is taught to them. I [therefore] order and command that the said priest not celebrate mass in such chapels, nor any festival whatever pertaining to their confraternity or any other saint, unless such fiestas are carried out and celebrated in this town of Condo or in Huari its annex. . . . (Ibid., 5v)[53]

In other words, argued Leal, the 1625 order commanding him to perform mass in Junt'uma was a grave miscarriage of justice, contradicting the repeated opinions and policies of the archbishopric and its visitors that under no circumstances should indians be allowed to build chapels or celebrate saints in the countryside.

The constitution written into a Condo parish book and priestly denunciations repeatedly refer to borracheras and *hechicerías* (sorceries), but no evidence of such practices is actually forwarded. Clearly, the ritual practices the priests actually sought to stamp out, and of which they have explicit evidence, involve the construction of chapels, foundation of confraternities, celebration of saints' fiestas, and requests for priests to visit them and celebrate the holy sacraments. Priests were able to justify the stealing of saints' images and destruction of Christian chapels by interpreting indian acts and requests as cynical maneuvers and indian faith as false. Apparently, the Kawallis of Culta used Christian devotion as a convenient cover behind which to conceal their pre-Columbian practices.

Readers inclined to celebrate indigenous resistance to Christianity may be tempted to disbelieve what the Chiris themselves say and to take as gospel the Spaniards' insistence that the Chiris of Ayllu Kawalli built their chapel in Culta only to gain the freedom to continue with their "idolatrías, borracheras, taquies, and hechicerías." Indeed, the sacrifices, t"akis, and other shamanic practices that are today associated with cult to Santa Bárbara in Culta might be taken as evidence in support of the priests' arguments. But one has only to witness streams of tears from the eyes of today's Kawallis as they kneel in prayer before the image of Santa Bárbara to understand that their Christianity is in no way cynical. It is as earnest as it is heterodox.

Just such heterodoxy was the target of Counter-Reformation practices often attributed to decisions of the Council of Trent. When common people began to interpret Christianity for themselves, without proper guidance by priests, and even to believe that through their own faith and deeds they might gain direct contact with God, they strayed onto the primrose path of error and heresy that Satan was ever preparing for them and that had led the followers of Luther, Calvin, and Erasmus to join satanic sects. Therefore good Catholics of the Spanish empire were to be subjected to heightened levels of priestly surveillance. As secular sodalities which often operated without priestly interference, Spain's confraternities, riddled with heterodox devotions to local patron saints, were a special target of the Spanish Counter-Reformation. From the Church's perspective, too many within such groups had followed Erasmus' advice to develop a personal relationship with God through private devotions, challenging, as the breakaway Protestants did, the Church's monopoly over eucharistic and confessional intercession between God and the faithful. The premier institution for safeguarding Christian souls from such errors and heresies was the Inquisition, which held sway over Spaniards of both the Old World and the New. But the Inquisition lacked authority over indians. The latter could not be fruitfully accused of heresy. *Their* lapses could be redressed only by first classifying them as idolatry or witchcraft, there being no other way to justify destruction of their chapels and confraternities.

We must be careful, then, as we seek to interpret the priestly denunciations of Andean sorceries and idolatries, to remember that Spaniards were predisposed to find pre-Columbian practices lurking behind apparently Christian indigenous practice. Even when the "superstitions" described by idolatry extirpators lack any sign of Christianity, it is more prudent to suspect their ability to recognize Andean Christianity than it is blithely to accept conclusions based on prejudice, a tendancy towards essentialism, and juridical expedience. Nonetheless, idolatry extirpators sometimes did describe details of practices that still resonate with ethnographic accounts of Andean religiosity.

A case in point is an extirpation record from 1649, quoted in the 1658 probanza of another priest (AGI, Charcas 96, no. 11), this time one who worked in the Siwaruyu and Arakapi town of Coroma. Located just south of Quillacas and Condo, Coroma is home to llama caravaners who routinely travel through Culta on their way to maize lands in the vicinity of Tacobamba. Encountering three mochaderos, sacred reverencing places, and more than seventy small idols, some of which had been "inherited among the indians for 60 years," the priest sent for an extirpator of idolatry, who is said to have produced a proceso more than two hundred folios in length.[54]

None of these extirpations was carried out by the Inquisition, but the extirpators nonetheless followed inquisitorial policies. Using repeated interrogation of suspects held incommunicado, they ramified their suspect list by eliciting accusations of third parties, who were then also questioned about their friends, relatives, and co-conspirators. Such techniques cast an ever wider net of surveillance over the dark sea of clandestine practice, but, rather than pulling all heterodox practices up into the daylight, forced them into ever deeper waters. Sacred sites were destroyed, sorcerers punished, and evangelization carried out with renewed fervor. Even so, sacrifices and libations at sacred places in the landscape, like local cult to saints at scattered hamlet chapels, continued unabated. Perhaps Andeans thus learned to differentiate orthodox and acceptable Christian devotions from "idolatries, superstitions, and sorceries." But at the same time, heterodox practices, whether directed towards mountain deities or saint images, were forced underground in intimate proximity to one another.

By the later seventeenth century, the Church began to ease up on such surveillance. Chapels in Culta, Cacachaca, Lagunillas, and Cahuayo were formally recognized, and the priest of Condo was required to visit them on a regular basis, with no hope of legally avoiding the arduous journey. Not indigenous peoples' resistance to reducción, but their stubborn insistence on replicating the institutions of reducción and on celebrating their very own patron saints finally won the day. A combination of factors even led priests to aid and abet the sprouting up of hamlet chapels, new annex towns, and indigenous cult to the saints. On the one hand, priests fattened parish revenues by collecting rich fees from alférezes and mayordomos and came to depend on the subsidy known as *ricuchico,* a banquet of foodstuffs such fiesta sponsors delivered to the priests along with their payments of silver and wax and incense. Such payments were increasingly subject to limits set by bishops, fee scales known as *aranceles.* When priests charged more than published aranceles allowed, as seems to have frequently occurred (ricuchico was always prohibited but usually collected anyway), they opened themselves up to their parishoners' accusations of corruption. By the mid-seventeenth century, accusing indians of idolatry or meddling with their saints' cults or residence patterns could lead to costly litigation.

Along with such practical reasons for tolerance, a general lessening of priestly credulity occurred at the end of the seventeenth century. The activities of the Peruvian "extirpation of idolatry" fell off sharply in this period, just as the Inquisition's prosecution of witchcraft did in Europe (Caro Baroja 1965: 20 1ff.). An increasingly rationalist mentality made the Catholic clergy less likely to believe in the efficacy of "witchcraft" or the presence of Satan in indigenous popular religiosity; they were more inclined to regard any straying from orthodoxy as harmless superstition. Prosecutions for superstitious practices by the end of the seventeenth century were as likely to be carried out by the state as by the Church. And rather than trying to prove that indians involved in heterodox cult had made pacts with Satan or worshiped the golden calf, the prosecutors found a more effective accusation: that these indians, like some modern television evangelists, had defrauded the credulous. In seventeenth-century civil and ecclesiastic trial documents, we see sorcerers transformed into flimflam men. Such was the fate of Martín Nina Willka, a cofradía-founding devotee of the Virgin of Copacabana, and either a native *jilsa* (prophet) or an *embustero* (con artist).

Martín Nina Willka and the Dove of the Holy Spirit

In the 1670s a man named Martín Nina Wilka, from the region of Kanchis, escaped during his mita pilgrimage to Potosí in order to adopt a new home, a place where, as one among a growing legion of *forasteros,* he would be exempt from mita and subject to smaller tribute payments. But such escapees did not run off to uncharted territory; they settled into the lands of already established reducciónes and sought out the protection of local caciques (see Powers 1991). With such escapees, caciques and town councils were able to strike private deals, among which, most likely, working of community lands and fulfillment of obligations to the community might have loomed large. Nina Willka, who settled in a hamlet outside the town of Mohosa, not far from the old tambo of Paria, seems to have specialized in carrying out religious obligations. In 1680 they got him into serious trouble when he practiced them, on trip to Oruro, in the indian parish of that mining city. Caught up during the alcalde's nightly rounds, some of Nina Willka's clients denounced his practices to the city's civil authorities, and an investigation was carried out, after which he was tried for being an embustero, a con artist, and for his "superstitious practices" (AJO, Leg. 1680–82). Nina Willka's crime involved devotion to a miniature image of the Virgin of Copacabana, a devotion which he habitually practiced as the founder of a chapel in his hometown, surrounded by local members of the virgin's confraternity. According to his testimony, he had taken on his obligations after having made another sort of pilgrimage, a religious one, to the temple of the Virgin of Copacabana on the shores of Lake Titicaca, to honor the very same image that Ramos Gavilán (chronicler of Tunupa/Santo Tomás' journeys) had served. Nina Willka had gone there with an injured leg, and had in good Castilian fashion made a promise to serve the virgin if he were cured. Because his leg immediately and miraculously healed, he purchased a miniature wooden image of that virgin contained in a wooden box known as a retablo, to take home, where he kept his promise. To render her appropriate cult, he founded a small chapel near his home and a cofradía—a confraternity or "brotherhood"—to organize cultic practice, as was quite usual in those days.[55] The size of the following that his particular devotions drew, however, was not so usual. Going essentially unnoticed in his adopted home, his practices came to light because, after his image had been damaged, he brought it to Oruro to be repaired by an image maker in the artisan district of Oruro's indigenous parish. Apparently in need of funds, he also opened up a miracle business in the house where he was lodged.

His practice, as extracted from many participants and witnesses, was this: Assembling his disciples at night within his chapel or in the house of one of the faithful, he set the image before the altar, with a crucifix in front of it and two candles burning, and then for some hours led his assembly in the standard prayers of the rosary. For this purpose he kept several rosaries hung over one arm of the cross, while over the other he draped several scourges of the cat-of-nine-tails variety, very much in vogue after the publication of hagiographies of Santa Rosa de Lima (canonized in 1670), who had used such measures to achieve ecstatic union with the heavenly host. He then led devotees in penitential self-scourging while they continued to pray. Participants describe how he then fell to the floor in a trancelike state for some time. When he arose, he doused the candles and began to ring a small bell kept with the saint's image. It was then that, in the darkness, the sound of flapping wings was heard. This, Nina Willka explained, was a dove, the Holy Spirit. And when it had descended, fluttering about and even brushing against some of the participants, it brought with it the voices of Jesus and the Virgin. Nina Willka would speak with them, asking them questions, and they, as oracles, answered questions posed to them, and even aided the faithful to communicate with and help to save souls in hell.

At least, that is how his actions and words are described in the Spanish of the trial transcript. But Nina Willka normally spoke with his devotees, and with God, in Aymara, which the trial record does not preserve. I must ask, What Aymara words would have glossed his activities? Almost certainly, "hell" would have been rendered as "manxa-pacha," the underworld where, indeed, Aymara souls (and the preconquest beings called Chullpas) dwelled. And what Aymara term might have been translated as "Holy Spirit" or "dove"?

For what his judges took to be a form of ventriloquism and for "bilking" his followers of payments for his services, Nina Willka was condemned to two hundred lashes, public shaming (he was ridden around town backwards aboard an ass), and a term of forced labor served in a Potosí bakery, after which he was remanded into the custody of a priest. There was, however, sympathy among his followers. During his trial, the people of his neighborhood were overheard to say that his prosecutors and indeed the whole city, for their crimes against God, were to be punished, destroyed by a rain of fire (recall the destructions wrought by the Viracochas, Tunupa, and the Titicaca saints Tomás and Bartolomé upon inhospitable unbelievers). For, according to witnesses, this Nina Willka (whose name means, in Aymara, "solar fire") was held to be a jilsa (literally, "our brother" or "our elder"). The trial interpreter added that "jilsa" also means "holy man, saint, or prophet." Indeed, the trial record was entitled "proceso de jilsa"; apparently, the term was well enough known to constitute a generally understood category of offense.

Rather than for heathenism, Nina Willka was tried for being a little *too* Christian, that is for usurping priestly authority. Though he, a rude indian operating in ruder circumstances, was prosecuted as a fraudulent prophet, there was in fact very little difference between the practices he carried out and those that brought other would-be prophets of the same period, such as Santa Rosa, to sainthood. The principle difference between them, perhaps, lay in their qualifications for sainthood: Santa Rosa had been a virtuous Spanish woman, properly enclosed and bound by the rules of a religious order. No ordinary mortal, and especially no indian, could hope to be considered so virtuous.

Let us sum up. The cases of Diego Iquisi, Miguel Acarapi, Culta's Chiris, the idolatrous indians of Coroma, and Martín Nina Willka span a century of priestly evangelizing, indian mita pilgrimages, and Counter-Reformation extirpations of idolatry. This was a century during which indigenous religiosity as well as Spanish responses to it underwent sometimes dramatic and often subtle changes. Mass pilgrimage centers devoted to non-Christian idols gave way to an unholy combination of public devotions and pilgrimages to saints' shrines and to continued but clandestine performance, within the private sphere, of rites for miniature "idols," the many *mamas* or *conopas* that later extirpators (like that of Coroma in 1649) found buried within indian houses. One might conclude with Serge Gruzinski (1993; also see Bernand and Gruzinski 1988), who has studied similar phenomena in Mexico, that by the end of this period native religion and the social forms in which it was imbedded had been effectively destabilized, or, in Wachtel's (1977) terminology, "destructured." Likewise, early indigenous attempts at transculturation, efforts to actively reinterpret and manipulate Christian teachings and practices to indigenous ends, outside priestly control, were suppressed. Nina Willka did not, as his predecessors had done, pretend to usurp the priest's role of performing the miracle of the Eucharist. Although his oracular practices were thought excessive and superstitious, his efforts to seek the intercession of saints were just the kind of religiosity granted to laymen by the Catholic hierarchy, and brought to indians by priests like González de la Casa in the form of portable images replete with miraculous hagiographies taught in native languages.

At the same time, the century saw a sea change in Spanish reactions to such practices. Diabolic sorceries with real effects (like the witchcraft perpetrated on González de la Casa) gave way to misguided superstitions and phony flimflammery. As students of the European Inquisition have noted, churchmen's faith in the reality or effectiveness of witchcraft gave way in the same period to more "rational" theses about human gullibility. The devil was no longer everything he had once been cracked up to be.

For a variety of reasons—among them the spread of a new rationalism among Spaniards, a more pragmatic *modus vivendi* between priests and indians, the general waning of the evangelic mission in the colonial project, and above all, perhaps, the disappearance of large-scale collective rites devoted to non-Christian idols (most of these adduced by Duviols 1977, 1986; Silverblatt 1987)—campaigns against idolatry and native superstitions faded away by the end of the century. There is also, however, another way of looking at this business. Rather than lamenting the destruction of authentically indigenous ways, one might well conclude that Andeans learned how to negotiate the distinction between public and private spheres that Spaniards taught them about in the architecture and ordinances of buena policía; they successfully discovered the times and places when unorthodox practices might remain private and clandestine; they learned the limits of their authority in the conduct of Christian practice. As hand fits glove, they had, in Certeau's terminology (1984), devised tactics of resistance fitting the strategies of domination imposed upon them.

It is nonetheless true that the forces set in motion by repartimiento and reducción, as well as by doctrina and extirpation, led to the progressive disarticulation of indigenous social forms. Tawantinsuyu fell to the Spanish sword; federations, diarchies, and, finally, native hereditary lordship fell to Spanish institutions and Christian practices. Another sort of repeatedly enacted colonial pilgrimage ritual, the circumambulation of territorial boundaries, contributed to this disarticulation or "destructuration," but also to the successful synthesis of new social forms through which transformed indigenous societies more effectively defended themselves under colonial as well as republican conditions. Let us see how portable saint images placed in chapels like those of Miguel Acarapi, the Chiris of Culta, and Martín Nina Willka became the cultic foci of new kinds of indigenous collectivities.

COMPOSICIONES AND BOUNDARIES: CIRCUMAMBULATING NEW POLITIES

Escape from the mita pilgrimage to settle as an outsider in another people's territory was not an option exclusive to men like Nina Willka. Throughout the seventeenth century, forasteraje, the process by which indians avoided mita and high tribute payments by negotiating terms with the caciques of adoptive provinces, had become a nightmarish problem for Spanish administrators. The percentage of fully vested "original" inhabitants of mita districts fell precipitously, and numerous administrators sought to resolve the issue, whether by returning escapees to their homeland or simply converting them by fiat into mita-owing "originals." This matter has received much historical attention (see

Powers 1991). The issue that I would raise, however, is the significance of this massive movement of indigenous migration to social memory. Clearly, permanent migrants seeking to dissolve their former social identities within a new social context would have sought to enmesh themselves quickly in their new territory and reducción, rather than always referring to the homeland's ancestors or wak'as. The most straightforward way of harmonizing in the seventeenth century was to participate in the ritual system centered in church and town. This is the case because that same century saw the ever clearer demarcation of intertown boundaries, a rapid increase in the number of land wars and lawsuits between towns over those boundaries, and the progressive erosion of the coherence of diarchies and, therefore, of the authority of hereditary caciques. It was also a period during which the turn system called mita was complemented (or, in the eyes of mita administrators, undermined) by increasingly complex turn systems for sponsoring (and paying for) the celebration of Christian calendric festivals. And newly arriving forasteros also linked themselves to the calendric life of the reducción by founding their own hamlet or household saint shrines, linking hamlet to church through the procession path by which their miniature "token" images might visit the full-size "type" image kept in the town's church. Possession of such images provided a private context linked directly to the public one. As a result, thousands of Nina Willkas, perhaps not all so entrepreneurial, carried out heterodox rites in honor of saints. Given the degree to which the collective groups defined by reducción life defined themselves through the participation in buena policía and *cristiandad,* this was the only way—a much more generalized and transportable one than genealogical ties to immobile and particular wak'as—to join a new community. By the end of the seventeenth century, ritual systems established to honor saints had, indeed, become a principal means by which town-based social groups defined themselves.

The establishment of hamlet chapels like those of Culta's Chiris went hand in glove with a process that some analysts have cited as evidence of the failure of reducción and doctrina: Almost from the very moment that reducciones were completed, indians began to return to their scattered rural hamlets, initially, perhaps, as caretakers of fields and herds for which town ordinances had made provision. Yet the fact that newly repopulated hamlets seem always to have contained chapels in which were carried out Christian activities (heterodox or not), even (or especially) in the absence of the priest, suggests that priestly teachings had made a profound impact rather than a slight one. During the seventeenth and eighteenth centuries, an ever growing number of such hamlets were granted the status of "annex." Given a church and a patron saint and constructed along rectilinear reducción lines, annexes became legitimate hamlets and obtained their own councils as well as periodic visits by the priest of the "mother" parish. That is how places like Santa Bárbara de Culta, Vera Cruz de Cacachaca, and La Concepción de Cahuayo, all within the ambit and under the political and ecclesiastic umbrella of San Pedro de Condo, came into being. All of them had already existed as hamlets of annexes by the end of the sixteenth century; Culta was raised to the status of independent doctrina, with a permanently resident priest, in 1779, when Cahuayo became *its* annex.

If the division of diarchies into town districts had arbitrarily sundered one territory into many, willy nilly severing fragments of ayllus from one another and binding the pieces into multiple new wholes, the seventeenth- and eighteenth-century expansion of fully vested reducciones and doctrinas considerably advanced the process, leading to an increasing number of squabbles over the increasing number of borders. Likewise, the possibility that annexes might be promoted to independent town and doctrina, thus obtaining a full town council and the legal protections that ensued, along with a resident priest, no doubt led to a general rise in envy, pretension, and factionalism. At least that is how we may interpret the precipitous rise in litigation over lands and boundaries during the period, by town against town and by town against cacique, in addition to some perhaps very injudicious proceedings, carried out in the 1590s, the 1640s, and periodically thereafter, known as *composiciones de tierras*.

It was such procedures that gave rise to the older kernels within the encrusted document that Pablo Choquecallata showed me in Cruce, and which had led to the Asanaqi cacique's use of his visita fragment in litigation with the people of Tacobamba.

A hybrid legal text, Pablo Choquecallata's document had been created when successive generations of, first, caciques and, then, town councilmen called on old documents they considered to be land titles. Sometimes, they had the documents in their own possession, but often they traveled to archives, as cantonal authorities still regularly do, to get copies of documents previously submitted in litigation. The modern notary's transcription of sixteenth-century handwriting is flawed, sometimes finding modern entities like "cantones" in a sixteenth-century text and often muddling dates, but it progressively improves when it reaches the pages added in 1647, 1695, 1711, 1746, three dates in the nineteenth century, and two in the twentieth. The document records a long series of legal actions on the part of indigenous authorities to defend their territory, and serves as witness to the progressive separation of a once-unified polity into multiple fragments, which again sought to act in concert in the 1940s.[56]

The first and earliest item in that document dated from 1593. It is the record of an auction conducted by Fray Luis López, bishop of Quito, as one small contribution to the general sale of indian lands that was called *composición*. In effect, cash-hungry kings ordered people like Fray Luis to inspect the countryside, seize all "excess" and unused lands in his name, and then sell them off to the highest bidders to improve the Crown's cash flow. Applied in Castile as well as in the Indies, *composición* was for "unoccupied" land the equivalent of the Castilian sale of villas (such as the one purchased by auction by Awllaka encomendero Hernán Vela) for settled places.

In this case, a huge swath of the highland extension of Asanaqi lands had been declared vacant, including the entire region of Culta and Cahuayo. At auction, the highest (in fact, the only) bid of seven thousand pesos came from the cacique gobernador of the Repartimiento de Asanaques, an man named Taquimalco. Composiciones led to ambiguous titles, sometimes appearing as private property and sometimes recorded as communal lands. Understanding the possibilities, Taquimalco had purchased a separate title to an extension of the well-watered land "Masce Caguayo," within which hot springs, salt mines, and the strong-flowing Cachimayo River were all combined. In the early seventeenth century, he petitioned for license to construct water-driven flour mills there (one of which, incidentally, is still used to grind corn into flour). In 1647, one of his grandsons, who had become a cleric of minor orders (an unordained priest), had this property recorded as a private hacienda. Almost immediately, the Taquimalco still in office as cacique petitioned for *amparo*, Crown protection against land invasion by his own cousin as well as by the peoples of Tinquipaya. Producing the title from the 1593 composición, the Taquimalco caciques also sought protection from the Crown representatives in process of again claiming vacant land for composición sales. Successful in their efforts, the Taquimalcos this time achieved a *deslinde y amojonamiento*, confirming their title not only to the Culta and Cahuayo region and the *finca* of Masce Cahuayo (centered on the flour mills), but also to the entire territory of the Repartimiento de Asanaques. With a land judge, they walked the perimeter of these lands, naming the boundary markers, mountain peaks, and rock piles called mojones, which the land judge read out from an original amojonamiento dating to the visita general of the 1570s. Into each mojón, the judge inserted an inverted bull's horn containing a copy of the amojonamiento (later documents specify use of a clay pot).[57]

Present-day jilaqatas still circumambulate their territory each year after taking office, following a path defined by some of the mojones listed in the 1646 document. But Taquimalco's border pilgrimage did not circumscribe only the territory of K'ulta, dividing its lands of the town of Culta from those of Cacachaca, Challapata, Condo, Lagunillas, and Cahuayo; Taquimalco's mojones included all these territories within a single district that divided the "Asanaques de los Taquimalcos" from peoples it calls "Tinquipayas, Machas, Pocoatas, Jucumanis, Aymayas, Carangas, Quillacas, and Urmiris." The late-twentieth-century town councilmen to whom I read the document were puzzled by its references to hereditary lords and a vast realm called Asanaqi.

In fact, interpretation of such documents was already problematic by the end of the seventeenth century, owing to the fact that visitors and composición judges sometimes took money and provided titles as many as three times for the same bit of land, for three different classes of buyers. A cacique governor like Taquimalco claimed title to the territory of all Asanaqi. But caciques and town council alcaldes from Challapata, and from annexes like Santa Bárbara de Culta and Cahuayo, also clamored for titles to the lands within their town jurisdiction (Diego de Sanabria, remember, had established a string of such mojones around Tinquipaya). As a result, later land litigation is rife with conflicting claims backed up by conflicting colonial titles.

Many such documents still survive in the paper bundles transmitted every New Year's Day from outgoing town council members to incoming ones; others have become part of the personal patrimony passed from father to son. In K'ulta, it is a rare privilege for a historian or ethnographer to be shown such jealously guarded documents; Pablo Choquecallata was the only one to open up his kitchen archive to me. I have nonetheless seen copies of many more composición documents; hundreds if not thousands of them have been copied into the property ledgers of republican fiscal archives as proof of ownership, in efforts by town councils to avoid alienation of their lands at the hands of the Bolivian state. In Derechos Reales, the active judicial office within the Corte Superior de Oruro, people of that city come to search for old title deeds, and on any given working day so do groups of rural authorities come in search of their own land titles. Between the 1880s and the 1960s, the town councils of all the town districts cut from Asanaqi diarchy territory have brought titles to be copied into the record. Some date from the 1590s, but most record composición sales carried out in 1646–47 by one José de la Vega Alvarado, signed always by a scribe named García Morato.[58] His signature is affixed not only to the land titles granted to diarchy caciques and to town councils, but also to those delimiting the separate territories of *"parcialidades"* within those towns (the "Asanaques de Challapata" obtained separate title from the parcial- idad called Quillacas de Challapata), to annexes like Santa Bárbara de Culta and Cahuayo, and even to the individual ayllus *within* those annexes, each of which paid separately for the paper safeguarding their nested and contested claims to firm borders: In the 1647 composición, for example, Vega Alvarado declared certain lands belonging to "Quil- lacas de Urumiri" to be vacant. They were purchased by the Taquimalco governor of Condo "para sus indios del ayllu Yanaque." The sale set in motion a struggle over the new boundaries that continues to this day, and it established mojones and legal title for Ayllu Yanaqi.[59]

Territorial circumambulations, called amojonamientos, were not just practical acts of land division; they were also ritual pilgrimages. Accom- panying the land judge, a whole host of authorities moved en masse along sight-lines connecting mojones. At each one, the judge was to send for the authorities of the social groups on the other side of the line; discussions over the history and proper placement of each mojón then ensued, and are sometimes recorded in the documents.

One seventeenth-century cacique of Challapata underscored the deep historical significance that was attributed to mojones. Domingo Choque- callata, perhaps an ancestor of Cruce's don Pablo, argued that the mojones of Asanaqi had been originally established by Huayna Capac himself. Almost certainly they were traced or retraced in the 1570s by Toledo's visitor Pedro de Zárate, and again the 1590s by the bishop of Quito, and in the 1640s by José de la Vega Alvarado. At each of these moments, however, a hierarchy of authorities would have been present; mojones marked out not only diarchy boundaries but also those of the moieties and ayllus within them. So boundary pilgrimages were more than an enacted discourse between the authorities of distinct diarchies, working out the differences between them as well as shared obligations to the state that granted such boundaries. Each "level" of authority within a diarchy carried out its own sort of boundary pilgrimage, circumambulating a portion of Asanaqi territory. In their boundary pilgrimages, many sorts of social groups moved along pathways that coincided at some mojones with other groups of the same order: Sometimes, alcaldes from a particular ayllu of one town, say Ayllu Kawalli of San Pedro de Condo, might have encountered the alcaldes representing Ayllu Kawalli in Challapata. What had been a single ayllu before reducción boundaries were established had now become two, each with representation in a town council capable of asserting its rights against the other. Boundary pilgrimages around reducción jurisdictions not only fragmented the diarchy of Asanaqi but also caused the fissioning of its component parts. As in the process of cell division known as mitosis, each "daughter" ayllu gained its own authorities and its own boundaries, but unlike biological reproduction, the daughter ayllus sometimes shared some of their mojón boundaries, and the resulting territorial and social units were reduced in size. At other points along its border, a town ayllu's mojón also marked a diarchy boundary.

These different sorts of mojones may have looked the same, but the social action carried out at or because of them took different shapes and had distinct consequences. When a disagreement erupted between two patrilines within a single ayllu belonging to a single reducción, the dispute would be settled by the ayllu's own authority. If the squabble involved a fight between hamlet patrilines of two different ayllus, say Kawalli and Ilawi of Challapata, it might be resolved through the mediation of Challapata's council as a whole. But when a land fight between two small groups erupted over one of the new mojones dividing the now distinct parts of the formerly entire Ayllu Kawalli (and this mojón also divided one reducción from another), the resulting fights and litigation now involved two distinct sets of reducción authorities, each with a land title. Under the leadership of the two councils, the multi-ayllu populations within each came together to confront those of the other town. Such actions reinforced the legitimacy of reducción councils while undercutting that of the old diarchy mallku. This was especially true when the diarchy lord, say that of Asanaqi, residing in San Pedro de Condo, took the part of his own reducción against, say, Challapata. Yet at a different point along the border of Ayllu Kawalli of Challapata, another mojón separated its lands from those of an ayllu belonging not just to a different reducción but to a different diarchy. Differences over that sort of mojón led not to further fragmentation and fission but to fusion: A fight between Ayllu Kawalli of Challapata and Ayllu Laymi of Chayanta typically escalated, first, to a battle between reducciones and, then, when each called upon old allies, to a dispute between diarchies, which thus repeatedly came back into existence as something more than a cacique's tax-collection district. Eventually, the rancor and longevity of intradiarchy disputes led the reducciones of Asanaqi to autonomy, driving Asanaqi out of existence and, with it, any remaining sense of common destiny. The people of Challapata and Condo became to one another Nuers and Dinkas, rather than members of sister towns with a common ancestral past.

Another document, an early-twentieth-century title kept by K'ulta authorities and copied in the 1970s into the departmental tax registry, includes pieces of another of the composiciones of Vega Alvarado. Although nineteenth-century interpolations are mixed into this document, it illustrates the issue at hand. Its list of mojones delimits the lands of a single ayllu of K'ulta, Manxa-Kawalli, from those of Ayllus Qullana, Alax-Kawalli, Yanaqi and Ilawi of the same town, and from Ayllu Sullkayana of Cahuayo as well as from the territories of Tinquipaya and Macha. One mojón is singled out for special mention:

> ... arriving at Pachuta which is a hill they ask to serve as a mojón of
> both Ayllus Kawalli and Qullana, and from there continuing through
> a very long plain towards the east, to the hamlet of Tolapampa, and
> continuing towards the east along a little river to the mojón called
> Quintiri, and then to a rock called Pairumani, and from there
> continuing to Cruz Pata, and again continuing to Churicala, which is
> the mojón where from time immemorial each one planted his vara,
> and from there to Chiaraque ... (Archivo de Hacienda, Prefectura de
> Oruro, "Protocolización ...)[60]

The "planting of varas" was a ritual act without other documentary exemplars from colonial or republican times, and I was unable to find out if the act continues to be performed as part of the annual boundary rituals that still recapitulate the border pilgrimages of Huayna Capac or Spanish composición judges.[61] Whether they were placed there by hereditary caciques or by town council authorities, the act underscored the connection between sacred boundary pilgrimages and the legitimacy of the authorities who represented the collectivity as a whole, or in this case, it seems, the authorities of the competing social groups that came together and sometimes clashed over just such landmarks. These cross-cutting and intersecting boundary pilgrimages both reflected and created rivalries and factional disputes, between social units of the same kind (say, ayllus within the annex town of Culta) and between those that directly challenged the legitimacy and efficacy of another's authorities and rights.

By the late seventeenth and early eighteenth centuries, diarchies like Asanaqi were riven with such disputes; the boundaries around Asanaqi as well as those that dissected it into townships became the fault lines of colonial destructuration and restructuration. Asanaqi was legally still a single "continent," but one now made up of numerous "plates" pushing and straining against one another, creating "rings of fire" defined by the mojones, where social struggle sometimes created volcanic heat. At times, as Tristan Platt has shown (1987b), even fighting between social groups, carried out as a ritual tinku, served to fuse them together as constituent parts of a larger social whole; but sometimes escalating ritual battles led to ch'axwa, wars where the victors took the spoils and defined themselves, not as complementary to their opponents, but as autonomous entities.

Mojones had more than just a practical value as boundary markers, and the violent confrontations that sometimes took place over them were also more than just "senseless violence." Both were (and continue to be) meaningful in other ways. Mojones were sacralized as sites of social memory, recalling the link between present social groups and the founding generations. Likewise, the blood that was shed at these places of intersection of ayllus, moieties, and diarchies took on a sacramental or sacrificial caste. Certainly, the mojón where the lands of Condo, Challapata, Huari, and Lagunillas met was one such sacred place: Not a rock pile, that mojón was the actual peak of the mountain—and god, now called mallku—named Tata (Father) Asanaqi, a being who is still offered the blood of sacrificial victims.

Furthermore, boundaries were also pilgrimage routes defined by a sequence of mojones resembling a string of pearls (or perhaps a rosary, or a succession of subordinate cords dangling from the master quipu cord). As such they were t"akis, pathways of social memory. So the disputes and litigation and land wars that broke out with increasing frequency along these transit lines were more than just fights over land; they were struggles over the definition of social groups and the legitimacy of the authorities who led them. They were also historical arguments, performed through mnemesis in the act of circumambulation and by reference to documents in the courtroom. The victors in such struggles were the authorities who were best able to rally their followers, perhaps by making the mojón-to-mojón boundary pilgrimage broadly meaningful to their constituents. One might guess that a cacique of a formerly great diarchy called Asanaqi, bearing the name Taquimalco (or t'aki mallku, "lord of the path"), ought to have come away with all the honors. But honorific names, once perhaps titles but now surnames, were legion in the Altiplano. What was more vital in obtaining the consent to be ruled that constitutes legitimate authority was to be able actually to constitute authority by perpetuating and leading the kinds of t"akis, song-dances on ritual pathways, that were possible in the colonial world. As local-level tribute collectors, justices of the peace, mediators in local squabbles, and organizers of community activity, entrusted with distributing usufruct land rights to townsmen and with regular patrolling of each ayllu's and each town's boundaries, the alcaldes and regidores and alguaciles of the town councils were well positioned to do just that. As we shall see, their authority was reinforced by their mastery of other sorts of t"akis, ritual paths defined with reference to the churches and chapels and portable saints by which divine power was now incarnate and able to walk upon the earth. The authority of town councilmen was underwritten by the saints. Town councilmen, rather than the hereditary lords, were the heirs to the religious leadership enjoyed by the innovators in social memory Diego Iquisi, Miguel Acarapi, the Culta Chiris, and Martín Nina Willka.

FESTIVALS OF REBELLION: GENESIS OF AN ANDEAN "REVOLUTION
OF THE COMMUNITIES"

By the early eighteenth century, councilmen in the town of Asanaqi territory regularly drew upon composición titles and references to town rights granted by Viceroy Toledo when they began to challenge the authority of the caciques of the old diarchy-based social units called repartimientos. Following Toledo's ordinances, one year's regidores, alcaldes, and alguaciles were to elect those of the next year, and parcialidades and ayllus within the town were to take turns occupying the offices. But what were the criteria for election to office? And on what basis, other than mere legalism, was the authority of town councilmen taken to be legitimate by other town inhabitants? In addressing such questions, we enter the vexed arena of debate over the historical development of fiesta-cargo systems.

Twentieth-century ethnographers have recorded the existence of fiesta-cargo systems throughout Spanish America. From rural Chiapas to rural Bolivia, town council officers are chosen, not by popular election, but by the performance of specific periodic duties connected to saints' festivals. The resulting interlacement of religious and civil offices into fixed sequences constituting fiesta-cargo careers (see Fig. 4.1) seems to be a very widespread but exclusively colonial phenomenon. There is no direct Castilian model for the straightforward merging of civil and religious posts into individual career sequences. In Castile, religious festivals were organized and underwritten by associations known as cofradías, "confraternities" or "brotherhoods," each of which was devoted to a specific saint or advocation of Christ or the Virgin.[62] Within the urban context in Spanish America, the Spanish model predominated; artisan guilds as well as voluntary associations were organized as confraternities, whose memberships paid fees and costs for processions and masses in honor of their saintly patron. In rural reducción communities, however, confraternities did not generally take this urban form. Instead, the confraternity devoted to each image seems to have included the whole community in its membership. The term "cofradía" may not be entirely appropriate to describe the institutional structure that resulted. For just as each parcialidad and ayllu was to take its turn providing officers to the town council according to a fixed rotational system, so do rural festivals in honor of saints seem to have been sponsored.

Under the priest's direction, three kinds of "sponsorship" offices were filled each year for each of the festivals celebrated in any particular community. Across Spanish America, terms and festival posts varied; in the Charcas area, however, they were quite consistent, most likely owing to the control exerted by the archbishop of La Plata over the number and kinds of festivals celebrated in rural doctrinas.[63] The most costly festival post was that of alférez, the individual chosen to carry the saint's banner in the procession. Mayordomos were charged with the care of the actual saint's image and with organizing the carrying of the image during the procession and the costs associated with its direct cult (provision of candles, incense, etc.). In colonial San Pedro de Condo, the third post was that of the *mayordomo de afuera,* the "outside mayordomo." Here we have the origin of the K'ulta festival post known simply as *p"wira,* or fuera. These individuals were charged with paying cult to a saint and keeping a miniature image of that saint, an imagen de bulto, which spent each year in a different hamlet chapel, coming to visit the matrix church during the saint's day itself.[64] The superstitious and heretical cults of Miguel Acarapi and Martín Nina Willka were closely related to legitimate practices introduced by doctrina priests.

The documentary record does not enable us to say just when the turn systems regulating the allotment of religious festival posts merged with those distributing town council offices.[65] This is so in part because such fused systems were clandestine; there was no provision for them in colonial law. Indeed, K'ultas still maintain the public fiction of town council election; they tell neither priests nor subprefects about the complex rotational systems by which alcaldes, jilaqatas, and alguaciles are automatically "elected" a specific number of years after sponsoring the last in a career of saints' festivals. As complex as their turn system is, they do not write it down. The pattern of moiety alternation in each office and the orderly, interwoven succession of civil-ritual careers are the stuff of *un*written social memory. Historians are unlikely to find written records of merged systems in archives.

If we begin with the question of not *when* but *how* civil and ritual posts came to be merged, answers are more forthcoming. In each reducción, both kinds of authority were supervised most closely by a single individual, the Spanish priest, who was charged in Toledo's ordinances with making sure that obligations of all sorts were fairly distributed among the reducción's constituent units. Priests knew the hierarchic order of such units through their parish registers, just as town councilmen knew them through padrones locked in the community chest, and more permanent scribes or quipu kamayuqs knew them through one or another accounting technique. We might speculate, then, that inhabitants of towns construed the two kinds of rotational systems (and those regulating other duties such as service in tambos and turns in the mita) by the same principles. Ultimately, they may have been harmonized within a single mnemonic order simply for the sake of mnemonic efficiency. Why keep elaborate and perhaps contradictory records, when all the social groups within the reducción knew which formal duties and obligations fell to them by simply knowing who came before and who after, according to their position in the kind of turn sequence Spaniards thought of as a wheel?[66] If the reader finds it difficult to imagine how a simple mnemonic system might keep track of three kinds of festival sponsors for each of several festivals, various town council posts, and their rotation between moieties and among the moieties' constituent ayllus (and even among the patrilines within ayllus), turn to the modern K'ulta examples in chapter 8, carried out entirely without the intervention of priest, state authority, or written record.[67]

The best evidence for the colonial emergence of fiesta-cargo systems comes from litigation records, trial transcripts, and administrative reports from the period of the 1780s rebellion. Such evidence reveals that hereditary lords in the Charcas region were more often targets of rebel violence than leaders of it. And as many students of the rebellions have noted (most provocatively, perhaps, Szeminski [1987]), priests were usually spared by rebels who, according to an earlier generation of scholarship, were engaged in an anti-Spanish millennial movement (see Lewin 1957; Rowe 1954). Why did priests, unlike corregidores and the caciques who collaborated with them, enjoy immunity from immediate execution by rebels? The answer is that priests, like saints, had become a fundamental part of the new order. As Nancy Farriss so aptly put it for the Yucatán, priests had become not so much directors of Christian cult in which indians participated as a kind of honored part of the hired staff, required for certain functions in the indians' own cosmos and polity-sustaining ritual system (1984: 343).

More evidence for the centrality of this reducción-based ritual-political order comes from descriptions of the actual fighting in late-eighteenth-century uprisings. For Andeans contrived to use performances of Christian festivals to overwhelm their enemies in a Trojan horse manner; arriving in traditional moiety groups to perform a ritual battle in the saint's honor, moieties united to transform what normally was a ritual battle between them into a rout of Spanish observers.[68] The first to die in late-eighteenth-century revolts, however, were native lords, targets of the social groups that now defined themselves through festival sponsorship in reducciones. Festival processions, of course, were organized by alférezes, mayordomos, and mayordomos de afuera. If we suppose that it was by taking on such roles that individuals were subsequently "elected" to town council posts, the two sorts of leadership, exercised through the township's usual means of "collective self-representation," led rather directly to events such as the following.

The case of the 1774 rebellion of San Pedro de Condo is instructive. In that year, a mass of indians descended upon the house in which the caciques of the town were sleeping. The cacique gobernador Gregorio Feliz Llanquipacha and his brother Andres (the cacique's "second person") had taken over the lordship from the Taquimalcos in the late 1740s. More than twenty-five years after claiming the hereditary posts, the two brothers were held by Spanish officials to be apt and capable. But apparently they had failed to impress their own subjects with the legitimacy of their rule. When members of the mob began to pelt their house with stones, the brothers emerged from the doorway, threatening rioters with a gun. In those days only one shot could be fired without a lengthy reloading process, so shooting one of a large and riotous crowd was not a wise move. Pelted by sling-thrown stones, the brothers fell to the ground, where rebel women finished them off.

Soon after the events, Crown authorities began to search for and arrest the culprits, many of whom had fled to distant maize outlier lands in the multi-"ethnic" valleys of Chayanta. The suspects, it turned out, came from a single ayllu, Sullkayana, most of whose members lived around Condo's annex (and former Taquimalco redout) of Cahuayo. When asked to explain their motives in the murder, they gave a strange reply: According to the testimony of the accused assassins and witnesses (including the cantor of the local church), the murders resulted from an affair concerning the local priest. According to these accounts, the murderous crowd had just finished accompanying the priest to the edge of the parish, from which they believed he had been expelled by the moiety lords. Outraged and pained that they had to lose "such a fine priest, who had done them so much good," there was nothing left but to avenge the insult (ANB, EC 1781, no. 83, fol. 76r).

So the "common indians" of an annex town—and from a single ayllu, that of Sullcayana—had assassinated hereditary lords of the Asanaqi diarchy, defending a priest who was at odds with the native elite. In the aftermath of the violence, the widows of the slain men (one of these women being named Colque Guarache) fled to valley lands that they had converted into private estates. With no heir yet of age, the Crown appointed interim governors. At this point descendants of the Taquimal-cos (who now called themselves Fernández Acho, and produced an entire genealogy of that lineage without using the name Taquimalco) litigated to regain the cacicazgo of Condo's urinsaya, or lower moiety; they lost to a man claiming descent from Colque Guarache (ANB, EC 1775, no. 165). In September of 1776, the "común de indios de Condocondo," led by the town's alcaldes (joined by the alcalde of the annex of Culta), filed a complaint against the interim governor "Luis Barachi" (no doubt Luis Guarache) and also against the corregidor's "cobrador de repartos," a Spaniard who the corregidor had delegated the job of collecting payments for the forced sale of mules (ANB, EC 1777, no. 139; the corregidor's appointment of alcaldes is attached). The leaders in the revolt claimed that the cacique governor charged two pesos more than the proper rate. The corregidor responded that the instigators were all notorious for their involvement in the Llanquipacha murders. One of them, indeed, had publicly told the widows of the slain caciques that he would drink chicha from their skulls (ibid., 20r).

Two months later, the situation heated up. The lieutenant of the corregidor had dispatched to Culta the "cacique cobrador" Luis Colque Guarache along with a Spaniard sent to collect reparto debts. On November 5, the people of Culta mutinied. Announcing that they had learned from Juan de la Cruz Choque (one of the litigants over the cacicazgo of Challapata) that they legally owed only half the tribute and reparto debt, they stood firm against the authorities' arguments. Finally, men and women together attacked the two men, throwing them to the ground and then dragging them about the territory until they managed to escape by a night-long mule ride (ibid., unfoliated pages). When they reached Challapata, however, news had preceded them, and they were forced to retreat to the province capital of Poopó.

The whole picture now begins to emerge: Native lords had become heavily "hispanized" functionaries of the colonial state, acting as the right arm of corregidores by collecting tribute and mita laborers and helping corregidores collect payments for the mules and cloth they forcibly sold to indians. Denouncing such abuses, the priests became yet further allied with the "commoner" authorities who had sprung up from below, the town councilmen, whom Toledo had intentionally set up as a counterweight to native noble pretensions. There were reasons, too, why priests encouraged the support of "common indians": The Bourbon Crown had made corregidores and their native lord allies into their tools in an effort to "secularize" the state (Farriss 1968; Penry 1993). Encouraged to denounce the excessive burden of festivals imposed by priests, as well as the numbers of indians whose service in saints' festivals exempted them for a year from mita duties, corregidores and caciques initiated countless legal actions against priests, including the priest of Condo. Striking back, priests throughout the region aided preparation of commoners' denunciations of corregidor and cacique abuses.[69]

Rebel violence against Spaniards and native lords ran rampant through 1780 and, by early January of 1781, had infected the city of Oruro, where creoles with an independence project of their own planned to make use of indian violence to rid themselves of peninsular Spaniards. The plan backfired when masses of indigenous rebels failed to make the subtle distinction between Spaniards born in the Indies (criollos) and those born in Iberia *(peninsulares)*; surviving creoles fled town disguised in the clothing of their indian servants (Cajías de la Vega 1987). Many of the rebels came from the town of Challapata, where not long before both the cacique governor and the province's corregidor had been slain (ibid.). But a Royalist army approached from the south, soon to end both the abortive creole independence movement and a siege of La Paz by rebel forces led by a former sacristan named Tupac Catari. Challapata leaders learned of the army's advance and sent out letters to rally reinforcements. One such letter was then intercepted by the priest of Santa Bárbara de Culta:

> To the cabildo [council] of Colpacaba: To the principal lord I give
> certain news . . . that all those of Peñas and Hurmiri have been
> driven away. They say that more than two thousand soldiers have
> done harm, and that another such number is on its way via Chichas.
> We will be encircled. They would arrive tonight without fail to
> depopulate us, leaving not one of us in the entire province. And thus
> for God's sake, having seen this, take and give the news to all, to
> Culta, Cahuayo, and Lagunillas, and to all the hamlets, to come with
> all fury and the greatest urgency, in the manner of soldiers, without
> even an hour's delay. And I beseech by Holy Mary that all come,
> come what may, all the commons as one. God Our Lord will help
> us. . . . Challapata. Changara. (ANB, SG 1781, no. 42, fol 1r)

The circular was written by a would-be cacique of Challapata, a man
named Chungara, who hailed from that town's "parcialidad urinsaya de
Asanaqi," and his information was good.[70] A large army was indeed on
its way. The priest of Culta noted that the circular was addressed to the
senior alcalde of Culta, one among the councilmen (and festival sponsors) with whom Chungara had allied himself in his hometown in a
struggle with the cacique governor of that town's upper moiety, who was
soon killed. The worried priest, hoping, it appears, to be recalled to the
safety of Potosí, attached a letter with his own observations and sent the
two missives with a young indian letter carrier to the intendant and
governor of Potosí, Jorge Escobedo.

> Culta, February 18, 1781. My companion and lord. I do not know
> how to ponder the difficulties I live with in this curacy, since daily
> there is trouble with these indians who wish to live without God or
> king, making themselves into judges of their own causes without any
> veneration of God or his ministers. I attribute it all to the great
> rapacity with which they have acted until today, taking lives and then
> robbing them of all they have had.
>
> I have some news that the priest of Condo expressly wants to
> leave for that villa [Potosí] to take refuge, because the indians have
> tried to move against him, giving three motives. The first is because
> he had hidden a Curaca whom they wanted to kill.[71] The second is
> their suspicion that he intends to turn them over to the soldiers. And
> the third is because they are certain that the silver of don Diego
> Cosido is in the hands of the priest. And moved by that interest they
> want to carry out this inhumanity, and they themselves have
> proffered such words, in this curacy.
>
> On the eleventh of this month there was a wedding, and the next
> day an end-of-year [anniversary of death], in which many of our
> indians gathered together, and some from Macha and Tinquipaya.

And among them they read out a circular letter written by a principal of Challapata (it is attached) and sent to this curacy, as Your Mercy will see, and after those of this place read it, they convoked those of Tinquipaya, begging them to go to Challapata, [saying that] if not they would be lost. The next day the alcaldes of our curacy went out, and gathered up many of the indians, and sent each one with two or three slings, sticks, and other things for their defense.[72] On the same day, the eleventh, the indians were speaking in their gatherings, saying that the priest of Macha had turned over the keys to the church so they might be on the lookout, preventing any of the Spaniards or Cholos or other people among their contraries, by any means from taking refuge there in the church. (ANB, SG 1781, no. 42, fols. 2r–3r)[73]

At this point, the priest began dramatically to report indian speech in the first person:

In the same way that the priest of Macha has offered us, shall be carried out here, and will come out to defend us as the above-mentioned priest has offered, similarly giving us the equity of weddings, and that all things should cost 13 reales, following the letters of favor that our departed Catari sent us, which have been usurped by the priest here who has come out against us, making us pay the tasa. He should not do this, but should defend us, but all will be seen to. (Ibid., 3r)

Catari's "letters of favor," perhaps invented or at least written down by the priest of Macha, Merlos, were the privileges he claimed to have won from the viceroy in the new viceregal capital of Buenos Aires, to which Catari had gone on foot to pursue his claim to the post of cacique. The king, he reported to his indian followers, had decreed a reduction of tribute and had abolished certain ecclesiastic fees, but corrupt colonial administrators had hidden the king's merciful orders. Indians here accused the priest of Culta of hiding these measures. Our priest then continued on the issue of Catari's letters, providing some personal proof that the people of Culta also credited their existence:

We have been given news that the curacy of Macha is without priest, helper, sacristan or singer, because all of them have become fugitives for what they have seen. They have also told us that they will not give *mithanis, pongos,*[74] or any other things, following the letters of favor written by Cathari. And in fact when I went to carry out the election of alférez and mayordomo in the annex of Cahuayo, they gave me no pongo or mithani, and kept me in the dark, dying from the cold and the other things they did. (Ibid., 3r)

In the midst of regionwide upheaval and danger, this Mercederian priest continued on with the election of festival sponsors such as alférez and mayordomo, and complained of the indians' lack of attention to his personal comfort. Yet he waxed most eloquent on the matter of an unaccustomed indian insolence:

> On the 15th, Godfathers' Thursday [just prior to Carnaval] while I was going to marry some of my little parishioners [*filqueritos*] I ran into three indians who had been elected by our alcaldes, but had been in surplus.[75] One of them approached me to ask what news I had of the soldiers. And I, as if ignorant of everything, answered that I knew nothing at all. But this was not sufficient. Giving me some blows on my left side, he told me that I had hidden all within my heart, and that I did not wish to let them know anything. And with these demonstrations, they said good day, and went away very contented, with their wives. . . .
> . . . preserve Your very important Mercy many years, who my affection desires, and of your parents, to whom I give care of my heart. Your faithful companion and sure chaplain, Joseph Balzeda. (Ibid., 3r–3v)[76]

Escobedo's reaction to the letter was panicky. Noting that he had news of risings in Yura and Puna, towns near Potosí, where caciques had been assassinated by their subjects (ibid., 7r; see also Rasnake 1988a), Esobedo sent threatening letters to the indians of Yocalla and Tarapaya ("buffer" towns between Potosí and rebellious Culta and Tinquipaya), suggesting that by joining the rebels they would lose their fields and herds and wives.

Once we realize that council authorities and the means of social articulation within reducciones were deeply implicated in Christian practices that required priestly participation (so deeply implicated that alcaldes continued to carry out elections of festival sponsors even during the height of rebellion), then many of the otherwise problematic features of rebellion fall neatly into place. The local-level leadership of alcaldes and alguaciles in rebellion events, the murder of so many native lords, and the sparing of priests, while corregidores and other Spaniards were routinely executed, all make sense if we regard the rebellion as a kind of Andean "revolution of the communities," more like that 1520s Castilian revolt than like a neo-Inca movement. Rebels, as Penry (1996) convincingly shows, did not act in the name of Incas or diarchies such as Asanaqi. Instead, organized through many intercommunicating town-based public spheres, they acted as collective bodies defined by the

300 PART TWO. HISTORICAL PATHS TO K'ULTA

names of their towns. It was not the indians of Asanaqi who rebelled against Spanish and cacique misrule, but "El común de indios de Condo," "El común de indios de Challapata," and a host of other commons led by rotative town councilmen and festival sponsors.

Perhaps local authorities and festival sponsors were not central to each town's "self-definition." What made the rotation of such officials so important that they were still being appointed on schedule even at this moment of special danger, just when everyone anticipated major rebel actions and Spanish repression? The answer lies in the nature of indigenous authority as well as the fighting tactics. The legitimacy of rebellious town councilmen was directly connected to their rotation schedules and the festivals in which they participated. The latter also provided the most effective channel for mobilization. In September of 1780, at a time when the Catari revolt was getting under way, the coronel of the militia of the mining town of Aullagas (not the town in the Awllaka diarchy, but another in the province of Chayanta) reported that Spaniards' problem there was what might happen in a fiesta: "Rumor has it that the assault of this mining town is planned for the twenty-ninth of this month, which is the day of the celebration of the feast of the patron, the archangel San Miguel, with the indians' plan being to come to the feast for their customary rock throwing between those of the towns of Pocoata and Macha, uniting on this occasion to do away with all Spaniards and mestizos who are the objects of their insolence" (AGNA 9.5.2.1.).

As Szeminski (1987) has shown, Tupac Amaru, the great rebel leader in the Cusco area, claimed to be on a mission from God, and promised continued loyalty to both God and king.[77] Colonial Spaniards, however, deserved to die, because they were apostates. Having turned against the faith they professed, they had become obstacles in indian efforts to lead good Christian lives. Priests were to be spared and the faith saved in a revitalized "Spanish" colony under indian leadership. This was a "purification" movement, aimed at the corrupt and unworthy native lords and Spanish administrators who had failed to open their ears to their subjects' pleas and had hidden away in their hearts the justice of God and king.

How genuine were these Andean professions of the faith? The Spaniards of the day easily dismissed them. For them, "indian" and "Christian" were mutually exclusive terms. The Spanish chronicler of Tupac Catari's siege of La Paz recorded many acts of apparent Christian devotion among the rebel forces, but took them all for a mockery of the faith (see Diez de Medina 1981). Christian indians would not, after all, insolently challenge colonial authorities; buena policía involved not just orderly Christian ways but also submission to Crown authorities. Tupac Catari erected an altar in sight of this chronicler at besieged La Paz, and had his captured priests say daily mass and lead processions during Christian holy days. This rebel leader, formerly a sacristan rather than a cacique, also sought advice from a portable oracle, a miniature image of the Virgin of Copacabana.[78] To us, if not to our chronicler, the sincerity of Tupac Catari's devotion was dramatically proved in an event witnessed by one of the priests he kept in his company: When the rebel leader heard two of his own indian lieutenants mock the Virgin of Copacabana, the patronness of the campaign and the image in his retablo, he had them summarily put to death at the same scaffold where Spanish prisoners were hanged.[79]

Even before the sacristan Julián Apaza became the rebel Tupac Catari, his namesake predecessors had already established a pattern of action and express motive that is a far cry from millennial revitalization of pre-Columbian ways. In the Bourbon era of "enlightened" reform, priests may have seen new state policies as an attack on Church prerogative and purse. But indians and, especially, town councils (and the occasional, usually marginalized cacique who retained close ties to priest and church) regarded attacks on festival cycles as a threat to their ritual means of articulation as collectivities and as a challenge to the techniques and calendric institutions in which social memory was now embedded. From this vantage, it is easier to explain why so many rebel actions took place during Christian festivals, often actually *through* ritual processions. The custom in which the moieties of the Chayanta province mining town of Aullagas threw stones at one another during their celebration of San Miguel's day is a case in point: The ritual battle known as tinku had been transposed into a processional moment when Spaniards, in *their* festivals, played out dramatizations of the defeat of Satan by the archangel, or of Moors by Christians. Blood let during such Spanish and indian "holy wars" had a sacramental quality. In the Aullagas case, the structure of the ritual itself dramatized the relationship between town moieties and ayllus, Christian God, and Spanish king (see Platt 1987c). This was precisely the moment in which new kinds of polities crystallized around "common indian" town councils and in which the saints of the Church might redefine their relationship to leading figures of the colonial world. Through such acts, town councils displaced hereditary lords, towns supplanted diarchies, and saints' rites, dominated by common indians rather than by native lords, took the place of now-prohibited public "idolatries" through which native lords had once reciprocated for their subjects' labors with generosity in collective rituals. By the end of the colonial era, indigenous social memory had definitively shifted along with the channels of authority and boundaries of salient social collectivities.

By the 1790s, hereditary lords were about to become a thing of the past. Successful repression of the 1780s rebellions enabled authorities of the Crown, whose end was also in sight, to appoint new and more loyal caciques. They also, however, continued to reduce native lord pretensions, a process reinforced from below, while hereditary caciques exerted always less influence over ever-shrinking territories. In San Pedro de Condo, the surviving son of the murdered Llanquipacha cacique governor was now of age and regained the cacicasgo for his family. But Lucas Feliz Llanquipacha oversaw the final days of the Repartimiento de Asanaques and even contributed to its definitive rupture.

In 1792, a very characteristic sort of Andean squabble ended up in the courtroom, to be decided by colonial judges. According to the initial report, a denunciation and petition for Crown amparo (protection) brought by the cacique gobernador of Challapata, it all began when a peaceful hamlet of Challapata citizens was suddenly overrun in a violent raid by indians from the Condo annex of Cacachaca. The Qaqachakas had burned the Challapatas' houses and then demolished them to their foundations. The Challapata authority, one Ambrocio Miguel de la Cruz Condori, governor of the Ayllus Sullka, Antamarka, and Chankara (which is to say, of Asanaqi lower-moiety ayllus that had been settled in Challapata), had then produced a copy of the 1593 composición title (with its references to Toledo's mojones) to prove that the lands were within his territory, as a descendant of the legitimate caciques of the Repartimiento de Asanaques. But when it came time for the accused raiders to give their side of the story, Lucas Feliz Llanquipacha stepped into the fray. Declaring in his opening remarks that "his subjects" from the Condo annex of Cacachaca had indeed carried out the raid, he argued that it had been entirely justified. Since the land was within the jurisdiction of Condo, his indians were entitled to evict trespassers. To back up his arguments, he too produced a set of land titles, this time, the amojonamiento of the reducción San Pedro de Condo (ANB, EC 1792, no. 108).

Not only did Llanquipacha interpret his own documents, but in well-practiced Spanish and careful legal language he also undid his opponent's interpretation of the documents. The Challapata cacique, he suggested, had misread history. The boundaries he had cited were those of the Repartimiento de Asanaques as a whole, not the separate and much smaller area of Challapata as a town-district. The larger and more embracing territory was from a bygone era, having no legal standing under mid-eighteenth century circumstances.[80]

An ever-increasing number of border wars marks the definitive separation of the collateral lineages of caciques created through Toledo's appointments. More and more, competing lineages of caciques were also litigating over rights to cacicazgo. Increasingly unlike the "original" native lords from whom they claimed descent, and ever more conscious of the similarity of their prerogatives to those of Spaniards, such caciques, draped in silk and using lawyerly language in elegant Castilian, rankled like Spaniards at insults to their honor carried out by insolent "plebeian indians."[81]

It was just about this time that the term "cacique" came into use in a new way, applied no longer to hereditary nobility but to members of rotative town councils. In Santa Bárbara de Culta the term is first used in this way in 1797 (displacing the term "regidor"), when such a cacique and other Culta natives (including many Mamanis) once again insisted that they were being overcharged for tributes (ANB, EC 1797, no. 25). This time the collector is their very own *cacique cobrador,* rather than a cacique gobernador from Condo. The *subdelegado* of the Partido de Paria responded that he had arrested Culta's cacique for delivering a written demand drawn up by Mamanis and for lacking five hundred pesos of tribute. He concluded that he could not release the cacique lest the indians be encouraged in their insolence,

> . . . especially the indians of Culta and Peñas, who are the most
> perverse in all the realm, and the most seditious and rebellious,
> without subordination to the /6r/ judges, and not just me, but to all
> my predecessors. The cause is not having been punished for all the
> iniquities that they committed in past years. (Ibid., 5v–6r)

At the end of the document, the *"protector de naturales,"* a kind of court-appointed public defender, added his evaluation of the K'ultas:

> There is not the least doubt that the unhappy indians of Culta are the
> most unfortunate of all those in this vast partido, short on land, with
> ridiculous resources, with the exception of the little they can make of
> their everyday activities, although always full of misery. The richest
> one owns a hundred llamas, and one or another poorly constructed

shack; the most gallant is draped in rags. I offer Your Grace a
succinct description with physical speculations, so that he may see fit
to decide what his invariable insight judges to be in accordance with
Law and Justice. Doctrina de Culta, February 9, 1797. José Anselmo
Alarcón. (Ibid., 7r–7v)

LIBERALISM AND ETHNOCIDE: FROM LAND PRIVATIZATION TO
CANTONIZATION AND THE LAW OF POPULAR PARTICIPATION

After creole Spaniards achieved a direct hegemony over their "half-caste"
and "indian" labor force, becoming in the process simply "creoles"
differentiated from the rest not by being "Spanish" but by being "white,"
the principles of Bourbon liberalism were enshrined in more thoroughgoing socioeconomic theses. Just as colonizing Spaniards had done, they
sought to "civilize" the indians whose collective forms of land tenure and
adherence to a nonaccumulative subsistence economy seemed the greatest obstacle to national progress, always measured in terms of the
industrialized nations of the Northern Hemisphere.[82]

In republics like Bolivia, the liberal solution to the "indian problem"
took several forms. Some recommended the physical elimination of
indians, known as the American solution (carried out in Argentina);
others proposed to dilute unsound indian stock through immigration by
white Europeans. Less draconian proposals sought to civilize the indians,
beginning with the cancellation of communal land tenure and the
introduction of private and alienable titles. In a more principled variation on the auctions of seventeenth-century composiciónes, the republican state seized lands collectively and inalienably possessed, and once
again sold them to the highest bidders. In theory, private enterprise
would then work its magic, leading to capital improvements, increased
productivity, and the promotion of industry. Through a process of land
seizure known as *exvinculación,* the nineteenth-century republican state
abolished the entities known as ayllus and demanded that all indigenous
communities register property in an alienable form.[83]

As Tristan Platt (1982a, 1984) has shown, nineteenth-century political necessities led creoles to ally themselves with the interstitial "mestizo" sphere; the latter gained political power at the expense of combat-
ive town councils. And even though places like Culta were too barren for
large haciendas, the favor shown to mestizos gave them room to extort
what good lands there were for their private uses. This was the manner
by which a "nonindian" political and economic elite came to impose
itself over indian town councils in towns like Culta. The post of

corregidor, once a provincial colonial post reserved for Spaniards and creole-Spaniards, was miniaturized and imposed in every rural town as master of the town council. The republican state's new provincial administrators, subprefects, invariably preferred creoles or mestizos to occupy this post.

This new rural elite, the figurative (and often literal) heirs of colonial caciques, came to impose its will over the rotative indian town councils of former reducciones, forming a new privileged class known collectively by the old Castilian term "vecinos." Recall that in the 1550s, only encomenderos were entitled to the status of vecino in Spanish-dominated cities like Potosí and La Plata. And only vecinos enjoyed full civil rights. Once reserved in the urban setting for Spaniards alone, the term and its attendant privileges now fell, in rural indigenous towns, to those whose "mixed blood" racial status and relation to capital (as private owners of shops and lands) made them the rural vanguard of "civilization and progress." Indigenous persons, however, did not see things that way.

Corcino Pérez and the "New Caciques" Movement in the Towns of Asanaqi

In 1868 Corcino Viscarra, "Cacique de Culta, cantón de la subprefectura de Paria," appeared before a judge in Potosí, where he had found a copy of the Taquimalcos' 1593 and 1646 composición titles, copied into a 1698 document:

> . . . for years we have been perturbed in the possession of the lands
> of Culta that as originarios we possess, by the originarios of
> Tinquipaya. But divine providence has restored our tranquility, with
> the discovery of the titles that accompany this in fifty-two folios. In
> them it can be seen that our interests had purchased the lands of
> Culta and the mills for the sum of seven thousand pesos. Thus we are
> hacienda owners, not colonos, and we can dispose of our acquisition
> as owners, and neither the government nor particular individuals may
> impose unfair duties upon us, nor usurp even a hand's breadth of
> what our money purchased. So that with the said titles we may make
> use of our rights, we ask that the notary don Miguel Calvimontes
> provide us a complete transcript of the accompanying fifty-two folios,
> with approval of the *fiscal*. As the representative of the community of
> Culta, that is what I ask of you. Potosí, August 5, 1868. Corcino
> Viscarra. (Choquecallata document)[84]

No republican governmental officials seem to have taken Viscarra's briefly stated assertion of ownership seriously.

By 1880, when ayllu and council authorities came before state officials to complain, they represented entities now called ex-ayllus and ex-comunidades, and their chances of success were even less. In that year, members of the town council of Challapata gave power of attorney to a local man, one Juan Mamani, to carry *their* composición titles (copies from a different source) to the Bolivian Senate. Mamani's argument, like Viscarra's before him, was that the townspeople of Challapata had already purchased private title during colonial days. They therefore had no need of new land titles, and sought exemption from the exvinculación process. The Senate returned the petition and suggested that it be presented to the land boundary judge of the province. These efforts were not the local invention of Challapata or Culta leaders. Hundreds of other ex-communities tried similar maneuvers with their colonial titles during the 1880s, many of which ended up in the books of the Derechos Reales archives kept in each Bolivian department.

Viscarra's document, however, somehow got into the hands of a very creative jilaqata cobrador, a tax collector–council authority, who represented Ayllu Sullkayana on the town council of San Pedro de Condo. Corcino Pérez, as the jilaqata was called, personally carried Viscarra's documents to the Bolivian capital in 1894, but not before writing his own testimonial to accompany them and obtaining power of attorney from Condo and many other nearby towns to represent their collective interests. Pérez' astute and passionate arguments, preserved now in the typescript obtained by don Pablo Choquecallata in 1942 from an Oruro archive, deserve publication on their own merit. What makes them truly exceptional, however, are the powers of attorney that Pérez obtained. Signed by the entire town councils of Condo, Cahuayo, Culta, Cacachaca, Huari, and Lagunillas, these *poderes,* issued by towns that for the preceding century had sought recognition of the boundaries that divided them, granted Pérez the right to act in their *collective* interest. Pérez' arguments to these town councils must have been just as compelling as his *memorial,* directed to the president of the republic and actually received by the Senate before being buried in a judicial subcommittee.[85]

He begins by summarizing the Taquimalco titles and repeating Viscarra's assertion that the inhabitants of the territory so demarcated are hacendados rather than colonos, and should be exempted from tributes and other impositions demanded only of indians. Then quoting articles of the Bolivian constitution and civil code, and the "principles of political economy," he explains why the president should listen to the demands of the "indigenous class, who have been humiliated since colonial times and even more since our emancipation" (ibid., fourth item). In his last paragraph, Pérez calls upon the president's patriotism and rephrases tenets of liberalism:

> Sixth. Because of indigenous oppression, this caste prospers neither in its property nor in its intellectual enlightenment, which is the waning of our nation, and at the same time deserving of the compassionate gaze by which other states criticize us. It is therefore necessary for the supreme government to carry out this passage to civilization for the good of our republic, raising up this oppressed caste, which cries out before its misfortunes, notwithstanding the fact that its strong arm is that which carries out agricultural production and the most difficult and arduous labors. Founded in this and other reasons that are too many to enumerate. . . . Sucre, October 21, 1894. Corcino Pérez. (Choquecallata document, 1894 petition of Corcino Pérez; see part F of the Documentary Appendix for the full text and the original Spanish)

Nevertheless, Pérez does enumerate them, in another petition addressed to the Senate in the following year. This time, he seeks a Senate vote to approve a budget to pay salaries of land judges who might reaffirm the boundaries laid out in the Taquimalco titles. Pérez continued with a litany of neocolonial abuses ranging from overly high tribute charges, to *postillonaje,* road repairs, mine labors, and personal service performed for corregidores (who by this date rule over every town council). Rounding out this second petition, Pérez finally reveals the extent of the "hacienda" his titles demarcate and, in a rising crescendo of sarcasm and cynicism, practically threatens regionwide rebellion:

> Finally, I have said that this *solicitúd* is founded in the public good, because verifying the boundaries, recognizing and reactivating borders and mojones [of Condo], and those of the cantóns that neighbor it, Quillacas, Tinquipaya, Macha, Pocoata, Ucumani, Chayanta, Laimes, Tapacarí, Peñas, Huancané, Isla Morato de San Agustín, Puñaca; (so many cantóns, and even within the parcialidades that make up each one) [this measure] would prevent the killing of the indigenous race that is carried out under the pretext of rebellions that are invented in calumny. Such calumny is enough excuse [for our oppressors] to jail and shoot the indigenous race, from which they are harmed much more than by epidemics.
> They would have much to say, Supreme Lord, but there they are now demanding justice at the feet of Your Lordship's throne. So

much innocent blood and so many tears have been spilled as a result of a simple calumny thrown out by covetous ones, who want even the poor indians' rags. All this has resulted from the never well enough damned laws of the authorities, voted without consultation, understood even worse, and cruelly executed.

I will not molest the Sovereign Lord with other reflections. It is enough to say that I demand justice in favor of the indigenous race of Cantón Condocondo, asking them to vote the quantity of money sufficient to pay for the commissioners who might practice the above-mentioned operation. And it should be entrusted to a person even middlingly honorable, with even an atom of sense, and perhaps a little patriotism and morality.

Moreover, in the name of all and every one of the propertied indigenous people of the Department of Oruro, I entrust what has been expressed to the Sovereign Señor, about the fact that indigenous people are not obliged to pay the tax of postillonaje, solely to the interest of the corregidores, ordering the immediate return of lands that have been taken under the pretext of postillonaje.

Given that the indigenous race of Bolivia deserves some consideration and justice, given their ignorance, timidity, and defenselessness, and above all the wealth they produce and develop for all the ciphers of society and of the republic, which cannot escape the penetrating wisdom of the Sovereign Lord, for these reasons we also seek the naming of commissioners to validate our property titles to the boundaries and mojones given long ago. I wait in the name of those I represent. Let justice be done. Sucre, October 12, 1895. Corcino Pérez. Seal of the secretaría of the National Senate. (Choquecallata document, 1895 petition of Corcino Pérez; see part F of the Documentary Appendix for the original Spanish)

Seeking the *revivamiento,* the "resuscitation" of the boundaries of Asanaqi (and beyond—Huari and Lagunillas, former settlements of the Awllaka diarchy not encircled by Taquimalco's mojones), Corcino Pérez was one among many *apoderados* (representatives given power of attorney) of the late nineteenth and early twentieth centuries who tried similar legal ploys to safeguard their lands from "covetous" creole and mestizo latifundistas and vecinos (see Condori Chura and Ticona Alejo 1992). In 1899, an indigenous captain in the Bolivian civil "war of the capitals," a man from Nina Willka's Mohosa, who happened to be named Zárate Willka, refused to lay down his arms when the war was ended, leading an indian army against the very enemies Pérez cites. Other widespread rebellions against the rural oligarchy followed in the

1920s (little studied in the Asanaqi region). Unforeseen effects of massive mestizo and indian mobilization in the 1930s Chaco War, combined with the arrival of trade unionism and socialist platforms, led in the early 1940s to the emergence of indigenism, which had a realpolitik side in the National Indigenous Congress called by President Villarroel in 1942. It was in that year that Pablo Choquecallata, a survivor of the Chaco War and then leader of the work gang for the construction of the Pan American Highway in its Culta extension, became Culta's delegate to Villarroel's National Indigenous Congress. The congress came to an abrupt end when Villarroel was assassinated by a joint mob of Communists and Falangists, but the experience likely galvanized the spirit of solidarity that had earlier given rise to daring efforts like those of Corcino Pérez.

In 1952, mine workers, indigenistas, and a wide array of left-of-center activists took control of government in the revolution forged by the Movimiento Nacionalista Revolucionario, devoted above all to nationalization of mines and oil fields. Promulgation of the Agrarian Reform Act, however, had not initially been a high priority of government. It became so when indigenous peoples mobilized on a grand scale, once again laying siege to the city of La Paz. The Agrarian Reform Law established a means by which indigenous communities could recuperate lands usurped by hacendados, and legally undermined the nonindian rural oligarchy (the town vecinos) by turning over election of cantonal corregidores to the councils of ayllu alcaldes, jilaqatas, and alguaciles (or to the "peasant unions" that began then to emerge). Revolutionary or not, the MNR government's agrarian reform allowed seizure of hacienda lands only by granting private (but nonalienable) titles to individual "peasants" (as indians were now officially called). Peasants were also to be pulled into the national project through universal education and mandatory military service, through which men like Manuel Mamani have learned to speak, read, and write Spanish, and to read the Civil Code and instigate petitions to the government. Such petitions are legion, in part because the revolution was not an indigenous project and did not truly aim to empower rural people. The Napoleonic state structure by which the power of national government filters down to the department and province through presidential appointees, rather than upwards through elected local representatives, remain in place. Under this patrimonial authoritarian state, only those local communities that can find a direct link to government coffers can hope to gain the development aid they seek.

Cantonization

Since shortly after independence, there has been great advantage to those
towns that have been designated as province capitals, for they became
the seat of state authority in the person of the subprefect, who presides
over a provincial courthouse and jail and, often enough, has access to
state patronage money. "Advances" and infrastructural improvements
came first to the country's capital and then to the department capital, but
at least something also came to province capitals, even though that
something has often included a battalion of soldiers. Such capitals were
the first to get schools when the 1950s nationalist revolution brought
them into the countryside, along with other icons of national culture,
including medical posts, electricity, and a dependable water supply.
Provinces are in turn divided into sections, and these into cantóns, most
of which began as reducciones and their districts. Now, cantón capitals
are too far down the hierarchy to have received much benefit from state
and party patronage—most is siphoned off in department and province
capitals—but they are in a better position to obtain schools and other
development aid than the dependent towns and hamlets within the
cantón's jurisdiction are. Not surprisingly then, there is much fervor in
the countryside to achieve the status of cantón capital, and among
cantóns to become the head of a new province.

During ethnographic fieldwork I first learned of the business of
cantonization very indirectly, when I asked why all of K'ulta's ayllus did
not participate in most of the festivals in Santa Bárbara. Don Manuel
explained that this was no longer possible owing to the outbreak of
serious interayllu fighting in the previous few years. Ayllu Qullana had
entirely withdrawn from meetings and now attended only the patron
saint feast of Santa Bárbara. Even then, the council routinely requested a
detachment of soldiers to help maintain the peace during that important
festival.

A few years earlier, he explained, a traditional ritual battle, which has
for centuries been fought as part of that saint's fiesta, had gotten
seriously out of hand. The usual controlled fighting, which is called to a
halt with the first serious injury or death, had suddenly become out-and-
out warfare. Dynamite had been thrown, houses burned, and several
deaths had occurred.

Difficulties in maintaining the ritual order were the result of another
dispute that had erupted in 1968. In that year the authorities of Qullana
petitioned the government for the status of cantón; this is not possible
without a roadhead for a capital town, so they laid claim to a piece of

land on the Pan American Highway where they might build their town. Their claim to the land, however, was disputed by the ayllu neighboring them, Alax-Kawalli. The town that Qullanas had sought to build was Palqa, just a few kilometers from Cruce. When they started work on their new town, a land war ensued, in which hundreds of fighters participated. Each of the two principal parties called upon their allies. To the sound of cattle-horn battle trumpets, numerous skirmishes over a period of four days produced many casualties on the pampa that lies between Cruce and Santa Bárbara. The Qullanas had been joined by a handful of allies from two other ayllus, Ilawi and Yanaqi, which together with Qullana had formed K'ulta's upper moiety. But they also called upon men from the territory of Macha, from hamlets near Qullana's northern border. Alax-Kawalli on the other hand (in whose territory Cruce is located) drew large numbers of allies from Manxa-Kawalli (to which the Mamani belong). In addition to standard-issue slings and macelike weapons of leather and stone, knives, axes, and picks also came into play, along with a few rifles dating to the 1930s Chaco War.

According to don Manuel and the corregidor, the Qullanas were roundly defeated and were saved an even greater thumping by the fact that Alax-Kawalli leaders had run short on provisions for their soldiers (the principals in a land war are expected to feed the soldiers who heed their call). In Cruce, however, vecinos told a different story, insisting that the fighting, clearly visible from the highway, was ended after a few days by a detachment of soldiers sent from the barracks in Challapata.

Much later, in 1988, I was to find the Qullanas' petition for cantonization filed away in an office of the prefecture in Oruro. It contained a map of their boundaries, drawn up by a certified land judge, and an architect's plan for their new cantonal capital. In filing their petition, the Qullanas had also incorporated themselves as a peasant union, a sindicato. They were the first ayllu in the area to have done so. Filed with their cantonization petition was an appeal for *amparo administrativo:* Qullana authorities had sought emergency military support, alleging that their new town (now visible in the ruins of Palqa, where I had been greeted with stones) had been burned and demolished in an unprovoked Alax-Kawalli raid. In their denunciation, the Qullanas named the principal promoter of violence against them: none other than the septuagenarian founder of Cruce, my friend Pablo Choquecallata (Archivo de Hacienda, Prefectura de Oruro, Expediente de Amparo Administrativo, 1968). In the same office, I also saw a petition from Alax-Kawalli authorities, including the always progress-minded Pablo

Choquecallata, seeking to transform Alax-Kawalli into a cantón head-quartered in Cruce (ibid., Expediente de Proceso Administrativo, August 20, 1987). What is more, Ayllus Ilawi and Yanaqi had also begun the costly process of seeking cantonization.

So apart from Ayllu Manxa-Kawalli, in whose territory Santa Bárbara is located, all the ayllus of Cantón Culta had begun efforts to secede from the union, joining a trend that is far advanced in the rest of the Altiplano. Furthermore, cantonization is but one of the mechanisms of fragmentation that push rural communities towards ever greater atomization. Since the late 1950s, some of these same groups, but also smaller fragments of ayllus such as patronymic hamlets, have had recourse to the office of the Agrarian Reform to settle land disputes with their neighbors. What they seek, in essence, is a semi-private kind of land title. In 1980 in the archive of the Agrarian Reform in La Paz, I saw three requests for visits by surveyors and land judges that were then under consideration for the district of Ayllu Manxa-Kawalli alone.

There was little talk about either sort of petition in K'ulta territory. Although a Qullana jilaqata once showed me his architect-produced plan for Palqa (when trying to convince me to become his ayllu's factor in La Paz), Pablo Choquecallata never mentioned his petition to me. Nor had Manuel Mamani ever told me that he and some (but not all) of his brothers and cousins had filed in the Agrarian Reform office for private title and a deslinde defining their lands. They did talk about differences and fights, raids and land wars, but always prefaced by accusations against their contraries for stealing land, stealing people (by convincing a patriline from a neighboring ayllu along their border to switch ayllu affiliation), or stealing saints' images or church bells to outfit a new cantón capital church. Ayllu Yanaqi, which is already divided into upper and lower moieties, took an image of San Antonio from Santa Bárbara's church to place in the oversized hamlet chapel on the town square of their planned capital town. I do not know if cantonization or Agrarian Reform petitions were involved, but the Alax-Kawalli people of the former tambo of Thola Palca had in the mid-1970s tried to carry away the image of Guadalupe and one of the bells from Santa Bárbara's church tower when they built their own church. However, a series of natural and personal disasters there convinced them that they had angered the saint, and they returned both items within a few weeks.[86]

The cantonization process provides one key to unlock the secrets of the cultural synthesis that has emerged from the old reducción fiesta-cargo system under republican circumstances. Just as local authorities must undertake to defend local interests, procure a more advantageous interface with national society, and generally serve as intermediaries with the state apparatus, only those who are properly constituted may legitimately play this role. In K'ulta, which has not yet undergone massive conversion to Protestantism, authorities are made, not elected, through a nearly lifelong ritual process that legitimates them. In seeking cantonization, the authorities involved in drawing up the petition may appear to the outsider to be undercutting the ritual order, by withdrawing from a more embracing ritual political order. At the same time, this process of community fissioning signals that the promoters of cantonization, acting as representatives of the constituent groups of Cantón Culta that are now seeking autonomy, believe that the collective interests of their fragment of the cantón will be better served standing alone as a whole, directly dealing with the Bolivian state.

In the 1960s Cahuayo, which had been relegated to the status of annex to Culta since the end of the eighteenth century after their unsuccessful bid for independence of action in the 1774 murder of the Llanquipachas, also became a cantón capital (ibid., Expediente de Proceso Administrativo, September 23, 1966). Citizens of Cahuayo then went on to commit the ultimate rebuke of both Culta and Condo; when census takers arrived in the 1976 census, they declared themselves inhabitants of the department of Potosí and were so recorded. Seeking to hark back to an earlier time, when the main road between Potosí and Oruro passed close to Cahuayo before reaching the tambo of Lagunillas, the Cahuayos sought a new road project that would link them to a major thoroughfare and leave Cruce and Santa Bárbara de Culta marginalized. Hundreds of such petitions are filed away in Bolivia's archives.

Does all this mean that the sociocultural order bound up in the ritual politics of Cantón Culta is a dying world, in the process of acculturation? If so, it is difficult to understand why each of the seceding ayllus has sought to reproduce key facets of that order on a reduced scale.[87] To meet state requirements they draw up a grid-plan capital town with corregimiento, church, jail, and school, located on a serviceable road: A cantón capital, it turns out, must have all the features of a reducción. Furthermore, petitions uniformly emphasize the "progressive" mentality of their promoters, directly engaging the state's aim of "civilizing peasants." At the same time, local, rather than state, mandates reproduce moieties in each new cantón candidate, along with a system that concatenates ritual sponsorships and political offices. While the cantonization process underlines the seceding group's lack of commitment to the previous manifestation of the ritual-political order, its reinscription into a more circumscribed social space with the same kind of cultural features characteristic of the old, larger one proves to be a reaffirmation, rather than a rejection, of its commitment to the values that motivated participation in their ritual-political synthesis in the first place. It cannot be denied, however, that cantonization continues a process of atomization of indigenous social formations, at the encouragement of state authorities, that began in the distant colonial period with the process of reducción.

To explore these facts adequately, however, we must plunge more deeply into the forms of social memory by which the people of Cantón Culta's would-be daughter cantones apprehend the significance of such transformations.

Part Three

Social Memory in K'ulta:
A Landscape Poetics of Narrative,
Drink, and Saints' Festivals

Chapter Seven

Telling and Drinking the Paths of Memory
Narrative and Libation Poetics as Historical Consciousness

In the literary artistic chronotope, spatial and temporal indicators
are fused into one carefully thought-out, concrete whole. Time, as
it were, thickens, takes on flesh, becomes artistically visible;
likewise, space becomes charged and responsive to the movements
of time, plot, and history. This intersection of axes and fusion of
indicators characterize the artistic chronotope.
— Mikhail Bakhtin, "Forms of Time and of the
Chronotope in the Novel"

T″AKIS OF MODERN LIFE: HISTORY AND SOCIAL MEMORY IN K′ULTA

In part 2, I traced the outlines of a history that, since it is drawn from
writings emanating from and addressing non-K′ulta frames of reference,
we might call a history of K′ulta but not a K′ulta history. I have sought
to illustrate the profound impact of colonial policies and of incorporation into an overarching state upon the life-ways of the people of this
corner of pre-Columbian Asanaqi territory. At the same time, I have
tried to suggest the degree to which sociocultural forms have been in
motion over a longer time span. Asanaqi was not a stable, objectlike
entity that survived over many centuries. A pattern of social relationships, Asanaqi has been reborn in many incarnations in relation to rising
and falling states and empires. Sometime around the transition from
membership in the Spanish colonial empire to the Bolivian national state,
Asanaqi simply ceased to exist, in spite of the efforts of men like the
nineteenth-century Corcino Pérez to resurrect something like it. Colonial
and republican civilizational measures and techniques of rule gave
preference to other sociopolitical forms: the colonial towns and councils
from which daughter polities have arisen from Asanaqi's ashes. The

317

people of K'ulta do not regard K'ulta as a reincarnation of Asanaqi. For them Asanaqi is a mountain, a powerful mallku, and also San Pedro, guardian of heaven's gate.

Some brands of K'ulta social memory tell a story very different from the one I have laid out in part 2. To defend themselves against the insults of colonial and republican states that excluded indians from political participation so as to exploit them, the people of K'ulta might have been expected to give themselves a glorious pre-Spanish past, to imagine themselves the descendants of powerful primordial beings with continuing secret powers that can be used to resist invading and foreign interlopers. One might expect it, because that is precisely how Andeans have been regarded by late-twentieth-century elite nation builders in need of a "natural citizenship" that only indians seem to possess (Abercrombie 1992). In a logic derived from colonial missionaries and administrators, urban "nonindians" imagine "indians" to have access to ancient earth deities through magical and fundamentally non-Christian techniques inherited from the pre-Columbian past. In this way of thinking, indians occupy a timeless world that preserves uniquely Bolivian customs from the depredations of imperialist and transnational modernity. So far, K'ultas' past does not respond to the needs of nation builders, but helps to account for the social realities K'ultas must live; their past provides keys to understanding their present situation, including the hegemony of Christianity and the creole-dominated state, the continuing centrality of the powerful distinction between indians and nonindians in Bolivian social life, *and* the primordial powers that nonindians impute to indians.[1]

In part 2, I depicted how pre-Columbian techniques of social memory, all of which construed social time and space as a sequence of places and moments along pilgrimage itineraries, were reshaped along colonial pathways that made sense of changing contexts of social life. I also discussed the progressive uptake in the countryside of the cultural forms, themselves serving social memory, that Spaniards called buena policía and Christianity. Yet the reorientation of tribute pilgrimages away from wak'as and Cuscos and towards mining centers and markets, the shift from wak'a cults to the cult of the saints, and the reinscription of native social groups within the cyclic calendar of Christian universal history did not eliminate all Andean techniques of social memory; they only gave those techniques new content. The processes of reducción and doctrina, the formation of annexes with their own churches and festival calendars, and the provision of new boundaries through composiciones and amojonamientos made town councils and the rituals that undergird them into the successors of hereditary nobility and social forms of diarchies. Even in the current wave of this continuing fragmentation of rural social formations, that of cantonization, ayllus and moieties continue to be essential features of rural life, reinscribed in each new town and cantón through the performance of calendric rituals founded in a colonial cultural synthesis.

K'ultas preserve old documents and forge new ones in their petitions to the state, but rarely do such documents make explicit reference to the techniques of oral transmission and customary ritual action through which they also bring the past to bear on the present. Those kinds of social memory can be discovered and understood only by engaging in the kind of face-to-face social relations that forged them.

While trying to arrange my first interview with the septuagenarian patriarch of Cruce, don Pablo Choquecallata, I saw him engage in one of the libation sessions that the people of K'ulta call memory paths. During that first interview, don Pablo also had recourse to another genre of historical memory, the narrative of the past we call myth and that for K'ultas is a form of t"aki, another pathway. K'ultas value "eyewitness" testimony, but reaching back beyond the individual lifespan to find deeper truths, they resort not to suspect hearsay but to primary sources. Written documents containing colonial land titles are one such locally respected source, and as we saw in part 2, don Pablo himself engaged with the documented past notwithstanding his lack of letters. Old truths, however, are not only recorded on paper. They are present in customary action sequences, rituals such as structured libations, sacrifices, and commemorative events, as well as in another "customary" form of sequentially coded information, mythic narrative. In the present and following chapter, my goal is to provide an account of such living K'ulta ways of construing and using the past.

A few cautions may be in order. I describe here the varieties of narrative, libation sequence, and sacrificial saints' rites through which processes of life and death, the human life cycle, and longer social cycles involving marriages and feuds are harnessed to deeper pasts. Being a written account, this can never provide more than a partly adequate understanding of ways of knowing that reside in practice and daily habit as much as in verbal narrative. At the same time, the memory forms I describe are neither long-term cultural survivals from the preconquest past nor "traditional" practices about to be lost forever. The give and take of cultural discourse, the continuous transformation of individuals and groups and their continuous reinvention of their own pasts within multiple contested arenas of culture and memory, ensure that what I describe here is ephemeral rather than stable. Written and published, my account freezes out of time the enacted social memory of specific peoples during what, in the larger scheme of things, is but one brief moment in the stream of transformative social process which it helps to shape and by which it is shaped. Culta was reborn as a saint cult center and cofradía sometime before 1616, became an official civil and ecclesiastic annex of the reducción Condo later in the seventeenth century, and achieved independence as an autonomous doctrina (encompassing Lagunillas and Cahuayo) in the late eighteenth century. Becoming a cantón including those other groups in the nineteenth century, it ceased to be a parish and then lost jurisdiction over its own annexes in the mid-twentieth century. Accompanying each of those historical conjunctures, the patterns of collective practice carrying social memory have been overhauled, and the past has been revised to account for a new present and a new social formation.

The complex fiesta-cargo system I freeze on paper here, integrating only two of the five ayllus that less than thirty years ago were woven into it, and the reduced scale of border pilgrimages that has ensued from these secessionist movements should be enough to indicate the irritability of social memory and its institutional frameworks, which are as fragile and inventive as the people who create them in the process of creating themselves. Today, Cantón Culta is in the process of fragmenting into yet further autonomous social entities, just at a moment when a rising tide of conversion to Protestantism, only now underway within K'ulta territory (since completion of my most recent extended fieldwork there), begins to sweep away the mythic narratives, saints' festivals, sacrifices, and libations of alcoholic beverages that are at the core of the techniques of social memory I describe here. Even so, certain techniques of social memory are in K'ulta surprisingly stable. And all of them (including Protestantism, which is the "path of Jesus") take the name t"aki. What does the term now mean?

The term "t"aki" is applied to a variety of phenomena, from paths on the ground by which people travel on foot, to oral narrative, and to various kinds of individual and collective sequences of fiesta-sponsorship careers. All these things are t"akis because they are sequential strings of action in movement which begin, subjectively, in one place and time and end in another: They may all be conceived as kinds of travel itineraries. By examining the several forms of t"aki in K'ulta, we may discern the outlines of what might be called a K'ulta poetics, which is at the same time a way of encoding social process and of transforming young and unformed K'ultas into fully adult social agents. As we shall see, today's t"akis may be quite different from the taquies of yesteryear, but they are the locus of a contemporary Andean history.

Chief among the means by which K'ultas recall, address, and manipulate the past in the present are three forms of t"aki: narratives (and also songs); libation sequences, called amt'aña t"akis, "paths of memory"; and p"ista t"akis, "fiesta paths" or fiesta-cargo careers. All such t"akis are actual channels of social transmission with both spatial and temporal coordinates, through which K'ultas make their lives into meaningful journeys. In the opening epigraph, Mikhail Bakhtin's application of Einstein's theory of relativity to the analysis of narrative also applies nicely to the organization of space and time as itinerary in K'ulta t"akis.

Forwarded in an effort to understand the novel as it has developed since *Lazarillo de Tormes* and *Don Quixote,* Bakhtin's "chronotope" mirrors K'ultas' interpretation of human life as moving patterns in space and time. It has precedents in the pre-Columbian borracheras, taquies, and ceque systems and in many features of social memory that can also be found in Iberia. But I am only incidentally concerned with tracing the etymological or derivational history of K'ulta myths, libation sequences, sacrificial rituals, and festival careers. I am much more interested in understanding the fact that K'ulta people categorize all of them as kinds of t"akis, "pathways." T"aki may be described as a poetic category of exceptionally broad scope, encompassing all the techniques that K'ultas use to transmit social memory.

I begin with the most familiar of such vehicles, oral narrative, through which K'ultas understand the social implications of the most distant and encompassing structure of space and time, that of the cosmos at large. We will then see how a narrower range of living spaces, from the structure of the house to that of the town of Santa Bárbara de Culta, is given meaning in relation to more universal processes.

K'ultas deeply value mythic narrative, not because it places foundational moments outside history (regarded as the flow of contingent events shaped by human action), but because mythic events are not contingent, and none is the exclusive product of autonomous human action. The most "rote" form of memory in K'ulta, mythic narrative is relatively immune to the distortions of untrustworthy and interested individual reporting. It is also valued as the most generalizable *topos* of socially significant space-time. It sets out the ways in which human activity can be given meaning as episodes in living narrative, as parts of a larger and more encompassing story, a universally salient history.

THE NARRATED PAST: THE SOLAR-CHRIST DEFEATS THE SUPAY-CHULLPAS

Don Pablo Choquecallata enjoyed recounting stories of his own life experiences, and it was from him that I first heard tales from the days when animals as well as mountains could speak. He told me the story of how the condor wooed and kidnaped a young shepherdess, carrying her to his high cliff where she languished on a diet of rotten meat. He recounted the time that fox (*lari*) took a ride on condor's (mallku's) back to a banquet in heaven, but ate so greedily that the condor could not carry him home. Braiding a rope, fox tried to climb back down to earth, but could not keep himself from insulting some parrots that flew past; they cut the rope with their beaks, and fox fell down upon the hard earth, whereupon his overstuffed belly burst open, giving to earth the heavenly seeds of maize, potatoes, and beans, which had not grown there before. Don Pablo also told the tale of the mountain Wila Jaqe (Red/Blood Man), who in a competition with Turu (another nearby mountain), had ended up with vicuñas as his lot, while the deer had gone to Turu.[2] Pointing up at the hillsides, where exposed sedimentary layers were bent and dislocated from the geological processes that made these mountains, don Pablo told me that there was evidence enough that the mountains had once moved about.

Events of the time before time, what K'ultas call layra timpu, are significant because such stories convey information about the significance of this past for the present. Indeed, for K'ultas, the past *is* present. Also called layra, the past may be seen lying open like a book in the landscape and social space of the living. "Layra" can also refer to origin places, specifically mountaintop springs from which herd animals sprang and, in the Kaata case described by Bastien (1978: 174), the place to which human souls return. K'ultas also add the term "layra" as a qualifier (in variation with the term "laq'a," "dust") to the most remote ancestors in a genealogy, the generation of the *layra* (or *laq'a*) *jach'a*-mothers and fathers, forming the apex of genealogies, from whom each person traces his relationship with kin and therefore, applying K'ulta's rules of the prohibited degrees of marriage, can work out whom he may marry. In the mountain-as-body metaphor recorded by Bastien (ibid.), the well-springs of human existence are the eyes of the mountain god on which the community is located.

After hearing several stories about layra timpu, I asked don Pablo about the early days when men first lived in K'ulta territory. The story he told me then resonates with tales of Tunupa and Viracocha, yet also provides a local setting and local meanings for another tale repeated thousands of times by Spanish priests, that of Christ's passion. The tale's protagonist, Tatala, also known as Jesucristo, is an old and bearded stranger who was ill-received on his arrival in a settlement of primordial men known as Supay-Chullpas. Widely told throughout the Bolivian highlands, this story is given pride of place in my considerations upon the position of oral narrative in contemporary social memory. Many other narratives of the kind that K'ultas call *kwintu* are just as widely known and often told, but "Tatala-Jesucristo and the Supay-Chullpas" more clearly helps to understand the dialogical origins of the structures and processes of space-time that frame all contexts of K'ulta social action.[3] Rather than continuing here with don Pablo Choquecallata's recension of the story, I turn to a version told by a man renowned for his storytelling and other varieties of poesis.

September 1, 1982. We are sitting around a small table that I have carried into the house, on which a tape recorder whirs, illuminated by a single candle. Smoke rises from a cooking fire in the far corner of the dark house, where doña Basilia stirs a pot of corn mush over a clay stove. Every now and then, she adds some sticks to the fire. The pungent smoke rises up towards the rafters and seeps out through the roof thatch. Three small children lie in a row on the bed nearby, listening to nighttime stories they have heard many times before, though not in these circumstances. Don Bartolomé warms to his storytelling. The children, and even the usually serious doña Marta, inspired him with their giggling when the wily and philandering but hapless fox lost his penis in the denouement of the last story. I ask again for the story of Tatala, which I heard a few days before while don Manuel worked at his loom in the llama corral outside. Ari, ari (yes, yes) . . .

Jesucristo-Tatalantix Supaytinsi-Chullpantix
Tatala and the Supay-Chullpas were enemies, they say. The Chullpas chased Tatala, a foreign, old man, and finally were able to kill him because they were many and he only one. They buried him in the earth and put thorns [*ch"api*] on top. They waited, then went away. Later they discovered that he had escaped. They caught him and buried him again, this time putting a large stone on top. They waited and waited, but when they left, again he escaped. They went after him. While following his trail, the Chullpas asked some other people if they had seen the fleeing old man. These people pointed out the ashes of his cooking fire, and from the ashes' appearance the Chullpas believed that he was long gone. [Here don Bartolomé explains that this is a deceit in which the ashes, from a bush called *sak'a sunchu*, only appear to be old.] Exactly at this point the

Chullpas became frightened. They learned (or remembered) that it had been foretold that the old man would conquer them if he got away. Frantically, they built strong houses; and since Tatala had gone off to the west, they built all with doors facing east, to protect themselves from the heat and light of Tatala's fire. Tatala rose into the sky as the sun from the east, and the Chullpas died in their houses, burned and dried up by the heat. To this day, one can see their remains, and the sun, Tata Awatiri, continues to travel across the sky. Some of the Chullpas, however, managed to escape by diving under the water of Lake Poopó. That is why there are still some Chullpa people alive [that is, the Chipayas and Urus Moratos].[4]

History of a Myth

The contexts which produced tellings of (or references to) the story may help to locate it within the K'ulta symbolic universe. Told not just to pass the time, this story provides a sometimes satisfying explanation for some otherwise disturbing facts. Pablo Choquecallata told it when I asked where the first K'ultas had come from. Others usually avoided responding to this question, deferring it to others. "The schoolteachers must know", "It must be from Adaneva" (though no one seemed to know that story); "The layra jach'a talas must have known." I was often told that *I* must know better than they. Most often this and other stories were drawn upon or even told in their entirety to answer other, less loaded sorts of questions.

K'ultas are aware that their ancestors must have existed before the arrival of the Spaniards, and yet that idea establishes the ancestors as non-Christians, like the babies who die unbaptized, who are *moros* (deriving from the Spanish term for Moors); K'ultas find this conclusion unacceptable, since it links them to a class of wild and disorderly humans who belong to the past (and continue in the present as hunter-gatherers on Lake Poopó). Chullpas, unlike Tatata, did not keep herds or understand cultivation. They were not *jaqi*, persons who live as rule-governed human beings. How can such non-jaqi be ancestors of K'ultas, whose lives are governed by the processes that Tatala's defeat of Chullpas set in motion? When asked if they are descendants of conquered Chullpas, K'ultas firmly deny it. They are aware that their origin story does not specifically recount the arrival of the first K'ulta person or even the first jaqi, and some K'ultas therefore make reference to Adaneva stories (though none knew the story) to fill in the gap.[5]

K'ultas hold the myth's Chullpas in low esteem—just as Aymaras, Incas, and Spaniards regarded the Urus of colonial days—because of what they do (living by hunting, fishing, and gathering of "wild" foods) and what they do not do (cultivate or herd). As such, they are consistent with Bertonio's characterizations of the hunting Choquela people in the Lupaqa area (1984: book 2, 89), as well as of the larilaris who, like foxes (laris) and wife givers (laritas), live through hunting and occupy the pampa and puruma (open and uncultivated space). Like Urus, Choquelas, and Larilaris, the Supay-Chullpas lack social hierarchy and order, living "outside of town" and without submitting to authority (ibid., 191).

Another time I heard the story told was while sitting in Manuel Mamani's llama corral as he wove woolen cloth on a treadle loom, which as we shall see is another social process made possible by Tatala. I had been asking about the plants that I found growing wild around Vila Sirka, some of which, I had been told, are edible but not usually eaten by people. They were chullpa foods. In the corral I noticed many small plants that looked to me like miniature potato plants; when I pulled one up, I found some very small tubers that looked all the world like miniature potatoes. And so they were. Don Manuel explained that, like the other wild foods he had told me about, people did not eat them, apart from children at play and desperately poor and starving folks. Like other uncultivated and undomesticated plants and animals (which are edible but not food), K'ultas presume these to be the food sources of the Chullpa people, who did not know how to cultivate and herd. Don Manuel then told the Tatala versus Chullpas story. Questions about the origin of the sun also led to this story, for Jesucristo *is* the sun.

If we view the myth not only as a colonial history qua history but also as a philosophy of conquest and the identity transformation it entails, it would seem that the conquest pushed unbaptized dead (such as the diarchy lords who were buried in the "chullpa" tombs the myth describes) into the past that in Tunupa and Viracocha stories preceded their transformative journeys, that of the "orderless" age of natural beings who existed in a state of natural and cultural lawlessness. If that is so, then Jesucristo here takes on the world-transforming role once granted to Tunupa and Viracocha. As told today, the Solar-Christ and Supay-Chullpas story makes no room for today's K'ulta people to claim pre-Christian ancestors.

As long as we seek in it an account of historical events or the genealogies of its tellers, this myth is problematic and apparently antihistorical. A Christ figure (with some un-Christlike characteristics) is already present at the beginning of time. Rather, he makes time; like another god who divided the land from the waters and the earth from heaven, calling up light with his words, Tatala did so through his struggle with Chullpas.

How can a story that does not refer to fully human (jaqi) ancestors of its tellers account for their origins? I suggest that K'ultas' ambivalence about their origins and their unwillingness to trace their ancestry either to Chullpas or to Tatala express the colonial contradiction at the heart of the story, and that the contradiction itself and the story's method of resolving it explains K'ultas' ontology. Our historical investigation revealed that those interred in chullpas were K'ultas' actual pre-Columbian ancestors (or at least ancestors of the hereditary lords whose legitimacy expired with the colonial period). Incessant colonial preaching insisted that those who had died without baptism were condemned permanently to hell, which Spaniards' glossed as "manxa-pacha": The process of translation laid one conquest and succession of epochs over another. Pre-Columbian ancestors were pushed into the pre-Christian, diabolic space of pagan Romans and perfidious Jews who, in Spanish accounts of Christ's passion, tried and failed to kill Christ. Such preaching assimilated the pre-Columbian dead to the idolatrizing, pagan antithesis of enlightened Christianity and buena policía. The pidginized intercultural discourse of missionary Christianity then facilitated the equation of Christ (whose radiance and enlightened teachings Spaniards portrayed in straightforwardly solar terms, such as Christ's radiant halo and the sun-shaped monstrance in which the consecrated host was displayed) and the sun (in whose golden brilliance and glittering rays pre-Columbian Andeans had envisaged their redemption from a disorderly and watery past). The equation of Christ and the sun, and of pagan Romans or Jews and the warring and unreciprocating people of *awka-pacha* (era of warriors/rebels) or purunpacha, was Andeans' way of understanding the cataclysm of conquest, reducción, and conversion to Christianity. It is true that Christ's radiant, solar powers have much in common with those of Viracocha and Tunupa, but like the miracles of Ramos Gavilán's or Pachacuti Yamqui's Tunupa/apostle, those powers are Christian ones—heterodox, perhaps, but accessible only through the intercession of saints, the mass performed by consecrated priests, and some truly heretic practices through which Andeans have learned to perform their own Eucharists in clandestine chapels.

Narration of Cosmic and Calendric Process

The story's Chullpas live in a cool, dark, and wet place; they are well-supplied by the self-generating foodstuffs which sprout in their moist and fertile domain. Such characteristics link the Chullpas with both nocturnal and hydrophilic creatures like K'ultas' mythic foxes, and also with a space that still exists, the underworld domain of manxa-pacha. The Chullpa realm, however, is not yet manxa, an "under" or "inner" domain, because their world is spatially undifferentiated, just as it lacks the alternating segmentation of experience into days and years that we call time. As a result, there is no change and no death in the Chullpa world. Those things come to Chullpas only through their struggle with Tatala.

In their initial encounter with him, the Chullpas take the initiative, striving to "kill" him and to encompass him within a tomb. But people incapable of change and to whom death is unknown cannot hope to kill death's very master.[6] Nor can they enclose him in their tomb, since they are exceptionally inept at activities involving the division of space into inside and outside, a kind of dimensionality that their world lacks.

After Tatala's resurrection from the Chullpas' tomb, he escapes their pursuit precisely through his control over temporal process. The deceit of the ashes in his first trick, and in other recensions his second trick involves a maize crop.* These Chullpas may know the "how" of fire and of harvesting foodstuffs, but it is Tatala who controls the "when" as well as the "where." So when Chullpas once again try to make enclosures, building "strong houses" in which to hide, they place the doorways opposite the direction in which Tatala has gone, facing the east. However, Tatala does not reverse course, but continues around, completing a circuit and completely encompassing the Chullpa domain. By doing so, he reduces Chullpas to dimensionality and, more specifically, to an interior and inferior space enclosed within the exterior and superior space that he himself represents. The Chullpas may have built strong houses, but once again they fail to enclose space properly: Their east-facing doors expose them to the desiccating heat and light emitted by Tatala when he emerges at the eastern horizon in the very first sunrise. Completing his circuit, Tatala makes enclosure possible for the Chullpas, but within tombs rather than fortresses. The changeless, dark, and damp Chullpa life-way becomes untenable on the dried surface of the earth. So, too, does Tatala bring Chullpas' unchanging timelessness to a close. When he completes one circuit of his pathway he begins another, repeating his journey on a regular schedule that segments the seamless

*In Pablo Choquecallata's version of the story, the Chullpas, while chasing Tatala, encountered a man harvesting his maize field. When they asked him about the old man (Tatala), he reported simply that such a man had passed through the field when he was sowing it. What the Chullpas did not know was that Tatala had caused the crop to grow and set fruit just by passing through.

flow of the Chullpa era into the days, seasons, and years of cyclic
alternation. Time brings change and death to the Chullpas. A few dive
beneath the standing waters into the depths of space that is now both
past and "interior," and Chullpas are relegated to the dark night of
manxa-pacha.

Just as Tatala does not remain always in the sky, the Chullpas did not
entirely disappear. Their dried bones, relics of the layra timpu that is
now the past, can still be found in their tombs, which are the burial
towers of pre-Columbian hereditary lords that archaeologists call
chullpa tombs (Fig. 7.1). These are still powerful and dangerous forces in
K'ulta's landscape. Touching such bones causes a swelling infection;
exposing them to the sky can lead to prolonged drought.[7] Living
descendants of the Chullpas who dove into the waters, the Urus Moratos
and Chipayas of the Lake Poopó region, are themselves powerful
sorcerers, sought after for certain kinds of magical effects. And beneath
the surface of the earth, in the dark and watery manxa-pacha, autogenerative powers that cause seeds to germinate and rains to fall must still
be called upon to make use of Tatala's heat, light, and seasons for
agricultural production, as well as for the reproduction of herds and
humans. Chullpa powers must also be regularly banished when the
growing season is over.

While Tatala triumphs in the myth, both he and the Chullpas are
relegated to opposed otherworldly zones, outside this earth and the
horizontal space in which the initial action of the myth takes place, and
into a vertical (and spherico-concentric) opposition in complementary
and mutually exclusive realms. As constituted in the denouement of the
myth, Tatala's journey takes place simultaneously in both horizontal
space (east to west) and vertical space (first above to below [his
interment in the tomb], then below to above [his escape]). It is in this
form that Tatala recapitulates the journey along the path towards and
away from the Chullpa's realm every twenty-four hours (in setting and
rising again), as well as every six months (in ceding to the rains and then
overcoming them).

As agents in the story of cosmogeny, Tatala and the Chullpas carry
out their struggle as a social drama, and so cosmological bodies and
events continue to be invested with the creative agency and subjectivity
of the people who tell the story. As gods (or analogues of gods, for the
Chullpas provide but a "natural" model for the caretakers of herds and
crops, which can be "controlled" only through the intervention of
Tatala), the forces described in the myth become the ultimate sources of

Figure 7.1. A chullpa tomb. (From E. George Squier, *Peru: Incidents of Travel and Exploration in the Land of the Incas* [New York: Harper and Brothers, 1877], vol. 1, 243)

social power and limits to human action; that is, they become a humanized nature. Outside the direct control of human agency, the cyclic alternations set in motion by the mythic struggle are those to which human social processes must conform. That does not stop humans, of course, from trying to conform alax-pacha and manxa-pacha powers to their own purposes.

Thus the rhythms of rites of passage are attuned to the change of seasons, with funerary rites beginning at the start of the rains (Todos Santos period, about November 1) and carrying through to the beginning of the harvest (carnaval). During that time the dead, allied to the watery and autogenerative underworld but not yet fully committed to it, remain nearby to quicken the growth of crops, the birth of herd animals, and the successful rotation of the authorities (see Harris 1982; Rasnake 1988b). K'ultas mark the rainy season in a variety of ways, including musical performance. From November 1 and 2 (All Saints' and All Souls' days) to the beginning of Lent, they play recorderlike *t'arkas,* flutes that are considered "wet" instruments and that play melodies composed by deities of rivers and waterfalls, to which the dead and rains are attracted. Once the end of carnaval (and the growing season) comes, however, t'arkas must be put aside, replaced by "dry" wind instruments such as panpipes. Marriage rites, as well, are tied to this schedule, taking place just after the carnaval ban on mandolinlike *charangos* and panpipes has been lifted, and after the dead have been dispatched to the netherworld.

In the workings of the seasons, however, we already see that the alternation between Tatala and the time of the Chullpas is no simple opposition: each realm also incorporates, as a subordinated element, a reflection of the power of the other. Thus alax-pacha is also inhabited by the moon, the sky's version of the feminine underworld, while the underworld has its gods of above in the high mountains. In diurnal alternation the relative values of above and below are partly inverted, as the darkness and cold take over alax-pacha and the sun warms the netherworld on his journey "inside." Similarly, the time when the sun is at the height of his power (rising higher and remaining longer) is precisely when the warmed earth most needs to be watered, and the dead help to bring this about, along with the intermediary saints who are called upon for just this purpose. In the dry and cold season, when K'ultas travel to the low-lying and wet, feminine valleys, the reverse process takes place. The dead keep the rains in manxa-pacha, so that the weakened sun remains sufficient to dry the surface of the earth. Now twenty-four-hour cycles come into play. The alternation of long and freezing cold night with sunny and dry days provides the conditions that enable men to "domesticate" cosmic processes to transform their "wet" crops into storable dry forms. Intentionally applying to their foods the process that Chullpas once underwent against their will, K'ultas lay out potatoes and strips of meat upon the ground for several days and nights. Freezing hard during bitter cold nights and thawing in the desiccated daytime, such foodstuffs (along with corn still on the ear) are freeze-dried, producing the dried corn, beans, ch'uñu, and jerked meat that become K'ultas' sustenance for the rest of the year. The original pattern of social process established in primordial times becomes the basis for the processing of foods.[8]

None of these processes is fully within human control, however, and it behooves humanity to call upon just those aspects of each zone which are nearest its opposite in order to bring a measure of success to their endeavors. To channel Chullpa powers, and for that matter Tatala's, K'ultas call upon a whole host of messengers and intermediaries associated with one or the other realm, and especially upon certain beings who are both humanlike and practiced in mediating the divide between the seen and the unseen: the human dead and the saints. With both, living persons share some affinity; communication with either helps the living reach into the heavens or underworld to tap into their powers. As minor refractions of sun and moon (and unbeknownst to K'ultas, as exemplary but now-dead persons in heaven), the saints are capable of descending to the earth in controlled or uncontrolled forms. As emissaries of persons, they are palpable images capable of moving in horizontal, social space, while as agents of unmediated vertical contact between the above and below, they may strike in the form of lightning.

Likewise in manxa-pacha there are the mallku, the condor peaks who, most like Tatala, look down on this world from lofty heights and are capable of rising into the sky in the form of predatory birds in order to confer with the saints. Establishment of control over the relationship between these opposed forces, in fact, requires the human regulation of the interaction of saints and mallku, whether through shamanic sessions in which the two confer or through fiesta rites in which the saints' images on earth (and the hierarchy pertinent to alax-pacha) communicate with the space and time of manxa-pacha across ritual paths (themselves icons of the paths of the cosmogeny's antagonists) which make alax- and manxa-derived diagrams of social process into icons of one another.

K'ultas understand the human life cycle and all social processes in relation to the path of the sun, Tatala's t''aki, by which ordering processes of layra timpu are endlessly reenacted.[9] To gain some control over such processes in social life, indeed, to be human, people must conform the spaces in which they live to the vertical, horizontal, and concentric coordinates established in the Tatala-Chullpa struggle. Social action gets its most fundamental meanings from the east-to-west, inside-to-outside, and male-to-female coordinates according to which all social space and social time is built. Many of those coordinates also coincide with reducciones and the kinds of orderly activities carried out to the patterned-time rhythms of buena policía.

SPACE-TIME IN THE CONTEXTS OF EVERYDAY LIFE

The daily routines of K'ulta life take some of their significance from already-understood contexts of social space and social time; they perform the rigorously structured and nonroutine activities that we call rituals in order to have an impact on their relationships with those contexts, changing the contexts or aspects of their identities. To do either, social space and social time themselves must first be constructed, hewn from the building blocks provided by the Tatala-Chullpa struggle. To set up an independent household, and thus take the first step on the "great fiesta path," a fiesta-cargo career that provides the itinerary of a lifetime, the house must first be built.

Unlike the proposed cantón capital, which must follow an abstract representation embodied in an architect's plan in order to meet the criteria of "townness" established by the state (thus also meeting the entry requirements of modernity, which is what the state hopes to bring about by promoting such petitions), the K'ulta house does not result from implementing a preconceived and abstract plan or model.[10] K'ulta home builders follow no architect's plan, but K'ulta houses are nonetheless as similar to one another as if they did. That is because the proper sort of house emerges directly from K'ultas' familiarity with the proper spatial and temporal coordinates of the activities that take place inside and outside a house, and because the kinds of social relationships that make a new house can be properly conducted only when the house takes the shape those relationships give it.

The space within the house is divided into opposed domains (see inset in Fig. 3.1). To the right as one enters there is a raised sleeping platform (and near it, a raised altar). This end of the house is pata (a raised, flat place), and it is here that men and boys sleep or pour libations. At the other end of the house (to the left as one enters the door) is a low floor and (if there is not another building for this) the fireplace for cooking.

This is a pampa (a low, flat plain), where women and girls sleep (on the floor), cook, and pour *their* libations.[11]

When libations are performed, the pampa, with the addition of a woman's lliqlla (carrying cloth/shawl), becomes the women's altar, while the raised altar of the pata end of the house (with a man's poncho) becomes the men's altar. Because most houses face the north (seeking in this Southern Hemisphere region the maximum of sunlight through their doors), the men's end of the house is on the west side, and the women's on the east.

To achieve this end K'ultas do not need to lay out their houses according to a plan with cardinal directions indicated on it, because the pouring of libations is one of the ritual acts that accompany the construction of the house. All libations must be carried out while men sit at raised altars facing the east and while women, a few yards away, sit upon the ground facing the west. So in performing the rituals of house building, the orientation of the house takes shape through the orientation of its builders, who always include a married couple with children and two complementary groups of construction workers, the husband's patriline brothers and the wife's patriline brothers. The house, that is, is a product of the social relationships brought into being through marriage. First of all, there is the complementary relationship of husband and wife, whose attributes and activities also shape the house. But since land in K'ulta is transmitted only through men and residence is prescriptively patrilocal, the house is built within the confines of the husband's patrilineal hamlet, among the houses and patios and corrals of patriline mates with whom the husband shares his surname. These conform a landholding corporation, a fighting unit when it comes time to defend land claims, and a collective body that engages in relations through marriage and saints' festivals with other patrilines (see Map 4.1). The house, that is, also takes form as a relationship between groups, that of the husband and the patriline from which the wife comes.[12]

As an enclosed space, the house expresses the gendered relationship of the couple who occupy it, by virtue of its replication of the structure of cosmological process originally established in the Tatala-Chullpa relationship. It is a feminine, flat, and open space, a pampa, gendered precisely by being enclosed with vertical and masculine walls. Beneath the floor, its builders bury a ritual bundle granting the house and its altars "roots" that reach out to the uywiris and mallkus of husband and wife. The floor and its altars become, then, a feminine entity called *iskin mamala*, "corner mother," in reference to the house corners where walls meet. Foundation stones, called *inkas*, are then laid in place, helping through their connection with "Inca" times (referring to layra timpu rather than to Incas of Cusco), when stones could move of their own volition to ease construction. Walls are raised with adobes. When they are completed, the unroofed house receives the blood of sacrificed sheep in a *wilancha* like that performed when Santa Bárbara's church was refloored. At a later ritual, roofbeams and thatch are installed. Walls and roofbeams are given masculine attributes; the house as a whole is then called by the ritual name *kuntur-mamani tapa*, "condor-eagle nest." It is, like the home of great flesh-eating birds, a nest, an enclosed nurturing space (consequently also called *tapa mamala*, "mother nest"), in which male and female generative powers are combined, linking past generations to future ones. The house is, then, the cosmos in miniature, manxa-pacha defined by its enclosure within alax-pacha walls and roof.

The corral and house patio are also built forms, which recapitulate the cosmographic structure of the house on a larger scale. They are like houses in being enclosed spaces to the degree that they are walled, and thus are also partly feminine forms (*jira t'alla*, "dung female," and *uta uyu* or *uta anqa*, "house corral" or "house outdoors"), but unlike the house they are open to the sky (and to direct contacts between alax and manxa). Within the patio, a stone altar with stone bench constitutes a collective libation space where all members of the patri-stem group with houses on the patio (brothers and cousins) address the uywiri and mallku they share. Each hamlet is composed of multiple patio groups; one of these is usually recognized as the *jach'a misa*, the "great altar" built by the hamlet's apical patriline ancestor.

Outside of the patio and house entrances, a series of additional enclosed spaces are reserved for herd animals. Corrals should ideally open to the east, and in the seating arrangements in ch'allas there the men are again assigned the west side, against the corral wall and associated with it. Women sit again on the ground in their enclosed pampa, this one made of dung. Again the men face the east, and the women, west. The patio configuration is much the same, though here the raised (pata) men's altar backs up against the house on the west side of the patio. Women sit in the midst of the eastern pampa space, the open space, facing the men.

The order of the cosmos is given only through such opposition, always framed in terms of a struggle or process, and so the relationship of women to men is thought to be one of complementary opposition, through which the cosmogenic model is made to order social life. As a kind of *yanani* (a pair), like *llantirus* (lead llamas), men and women, as husband and wife, are mutually necessary in order to bring the mutually exclusive realms towards which they are oriented to bear on human affairs. K'ultas carry out all their rituals in gender parallel, men libating male deities, altars, animals, and souls, while women libate the feminine realm, so that men's and women's ch'alla paths proceed apace.

The human life cycle also conforms to the process described in the Tatala-Chullpa myth. When they are born, infants are like wild animals and Chullpas, eating naturally produced, unprocessed, and uncooked food.[13] In the human life cycle, people originate from an enclosed yet undifferentiated pre-manxa-pacha space, and only by stages along a path of progressive differentiation do they come to internalize the formal hierarchizing attributes of social process which make them finally human.

After death, they must follow a similar but inverse path. Provisioned by their mourners for the journey with llantirus and every kind of cooked and uncooked food, they follow the sun's path to the west, and finally enter the mountain of souls, a manxa-pacha place where the rhythms of life invert those of this earth.

The dead are dispatched for a return journey to the underworld on two separate harvesttime occasions, both linked to Christian moveable festivals. Men are sent packing on the Monday before carnaval Tuesday, and women on the Monday before Easter. I was able to participate in only one such event, when Virgilio Mamani, while carrying out festival duties in his father's place, sent his father away for good.

In the midst of many other rituals associated with carnaval, Hilarión Mamani came back for a final visit through the intercession of his tullqa. Hilarión's sister's husband arrived in Vila Sirka early on Monday morning and took the dead Hilarión's best suit of clothes and hat out to Vila Sirka's jach'a misa, the "eldest" patio altar in the hamlet. Atop the altar he set up a wooden cross, pouring libations over it, dedicating them to Hilarión's bones. The cross then became the dead man's bones: the tullqa (the dead man's sister's husband, then in his sixties) used it as a mannequin, dressing it in Hilarión's clothes. When it was finished, the widow and her son Virgilio joined the other Mamanis at the altar amidst a great deal of lamentation and tears, each one taking a turn speaking to and drinking with the image of Hilarión as if he were actually present, and finally presenting him with plates heaped with food for his last supper. As the *alma cargo* of a ritual sponsorship in progress, Hilarión wore a bread crown (a *pillu*) atop his hat; his mourning relatives were clothed in black capes and ponchos for the event. I took my turn drinking with Hilarión, and offered him a pack of cigarettes, an act for which his widow thanked me. At the time, however, the image that came to mind was Guaman Poma's drawings of ch'allas to the sun (Fig. 7.2; see also Fig. 5.1, p. 142). Not long after his last smoke, Hilarión rather

Figure 7.2. Drinking with the sun. The wording at the top translates as "June. Hacaicusqui." The word at the bottom of the page is "qusqui." The words within the drawing translate as "Drinks with the sun in the fiesta of the sun." Here Guaman Poma depicts the Inca ruler sharing a drink with the sun. The Inca drinks from one quero

suddenly announced (through the voice of his tullqa helper) that it was time for him to leave. The tullqa then removed the bread crown and gave each mourner a piece; we were to eat it as quickly as possible while the tullqa carried Hilarión's image away. A few moments later, however, Hilarión reappeared. The tullqa had dressed himself in Hilarión's clothes and was carrying the whip that belonged to Hilarión as a former alcalde. Bursting upon the group of mourners, he began to shout and scold, striking each one with the whip. "Stop your crying," he told us in an authoritative voice. "Take off your mourning clothes, and think of me no more." When the assembled Mamanis began to remove their black mourning clothes, Hilarión then announced that he was leaving, never to return. Having become Hilarión, the dead man's wife taker now rushed about picking up the black ponchos and shawls, the bits of uneaten bread, and several plates of food. With a last goodbye and a stern order not to follow him, he rushed away from the altar, out of the patio, and onto the western path leading away from Vila Sirka, until after a few hundred yards he disappeared behind some rocks. There, he would remove the clothing by which Hilarión had returned to life, make a bonfire, and burn all that he had taken with him. Other relatives then held back Hilarión's widow and son, keeping them from following him to manxa-pacha. Placing piles of cacti on the path, they then barred the dead soul from any change of heart.

The western path taken by Hilarión leads towards manxa-pacha, the destination of the dead. So, too, does the preferred path taken by all "naturally cooked" (digested and/or rotting) substances and the diseases that yatiris transfer from a person to a ritual bundle to be carried out of the hamlet. All such things are said to have a bad or fetid smell, to be *t"uxsa,* in contrast with the sweet smell of the incense bundles that are offered on the eastern path to the rising sun. Thus the solar path, when projected onto horizontal space, becomes an icon of the narrative sequence which produced the fundamental oppositions of the cosmos and of the social processes thereby produced.

Figure 7.2. (*Continued*)
while another, on the ground before him, reaches the sun in spirit, which the Christianized Guaman Poma depicts as the action of a demon. In the accompanying text, Guaman Poma explains: "This month they carry out the moderate fiesta of Inti Raymi, and they expend much in it and sacrifice to the sun. And in the sacrifice called *capac ocha,* they buried 500 innocent children, and much gold and silver and *mullo.*" (From Guaman Poma de Ayala 1980: 220)

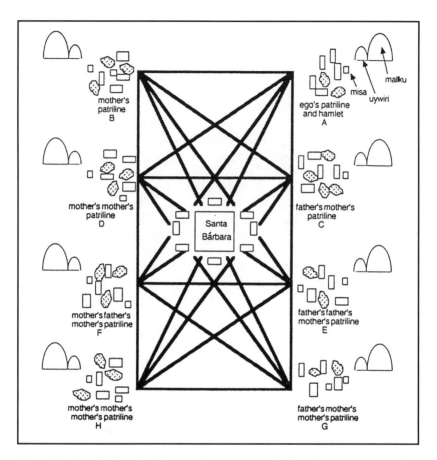

Figure 7.3. Patriline-hamlet paths, marriage journeys, ch'alla pathways. Here patriline-hamlets, which in reality are widely scattered through K'ulta territory and connected by meandering pathways, are shown connected by straight-line paths. At the upper right, ego's patriline-hamlet (A) is linked by a t''aki (a path, shown here as a horizontal line) to his or her mother's patriline hamlet (B). This is the path taken when a male ego serves his larita (mother's brother) in subservient tullqa roles. Ego's father's mother's brother (C) and mother's mother's brother (D) are also laritas to him. All eight patrilines are origin-homes of ancestors recalled in ch'alla t''akis performed at the male sponsor's altar; the male sponsor's wife toasts an identical pattern of ancestral patrilines, but all eight should be different patrilines from those libated by her husband. These patrilines correspond to patronyms listed by a prospective bride and groom when determining whether or not their marriage is proscribed. Actual visits from kinsmen in life-crisis rites, from pillu carriers in fiesta-linked rites, and from miniature images in fiesta exchanges follow paths and include stops at samarayañas, "breathing places."

Libations are thought to travel underground from the "roots" of the misa, where they are poured to the roots of the entity libated. Conceptually, ch'allas reorder the landscape genealogically, beginning with the concentric hierarchy of misa, uywiri, and mallku of ego's own patriline. Successive libations reach ever further back in time, ending in the patrilines of the generation of ego's great-grandparents. Although ego is prohibited from marrying

All the built forms discussed so far are both alax and manxa entities, with a lower inside and a higher outside. K'ultas construct their life-world from complementary opposites. But if the opposites are of the same kind (features defining a divided whole), they are not unranked, and the hierarchy of conquest penetrates even the household. The alax wall (which is the elaborated, built part of a house, corral, and patio) defines the unelaborated low and feminine by enclosing it, giving cultural order to the "natural" or "wild" form of feminine space, the pampa, or plain.

At the level of the whole hamlet, however, the pampa (a feminine space in contrast with the masculine hills and mountains that surround it) is not what is *inside* the hamlet space of houses and patios, but the wild and unordered space *outside* it. From this perspective, the hamlet itself becomes an alax entity, while the surrounding territory becomes manxa space. This fact inverts the concentric hierarchy established through Tatala's journey and serves to demarcate what, on this earth, is human and "cultural" from what is animal and "natural." At the same time, the boundary around the hamlet separates what is not yet whole (the partial, solely manxa beings, foodstuffs, and social processes from outside the hamlet) from the locus of production of the whole, where such items are transformed through the solar-derived process of cooking and herding.

The pampa also separates the hamlets of distinct patrilines, but is crisscrossed by footpaths linking one hamlet and one patriline to another. These become pilgrimage pathways along which patrilines engage one another as groups during several stages of marriage rituals (house building being one of them). In rites connected with the exchange of saint images and sponsorships, the paths are the routes taken by exogamous patrilines in order to appropriate the sources of the manxa-type generative power, which they cannot themselves produce: wives(Fig. 7.3).

Figure 7.3. (*Continued*)
someone bearing any of these eight patronyms (or from the corresponding patriline-hamlets), ego's children will not recall patrilines E, F, G, or H in ch'allas. Ego's children will likely travel to them in courtship visits during the carnaval season. The same hamlets, or rather the corral altars, caretaker hills, and mallku mountains connected with them, are recalled when libating the origin places of herd animals.

All interhamlet pathways conceptually converge at the town of Santa Bárbara de Culta. Each patriline travels to its house there for litigation, baptisms, weddings, funerals, service on the town council, voting, and payment of taxes. For major festivals, contingents from several patrilines allied through intermarriage and reciprocal festival duties, having visited during the year, merge together as they near the town. Miniature images held in hamlet chapels also travel to town to visit with the corresponding "main" image in the church. Likewise libations to patriline place deities converge upon Churi Asanaqi, the hierarchically superior mallku-mountain of Santa Bárbara. (Author's rendering)

Marriage and Predation

Owing to the nature of incest prohibition and marriage rules, the men of
a patriline must seek wives elsewhere, just as the sisters and daughters of
patriline men must find husbands with different patronyms from their
own. In fact, marriage is prohibited not only with those who share the
same patronym but also with all those who share any of the patronyms
and matronyms of the grandparental generation. This corresponds to the
prohibition of marriage with any descendant of one's eight great-
grandparents. Since one's proposed spouse must then libate eight patronyms (and patrilines), sixteen distinct patrilines must be recalled. This is
clearly a tall order, since Ayllu Manxa-Kawalli, for example, has only a
few more patrilines than the required minimum. If all marriages were
ayllu endogamous (which they are not), it would be almost certain that
the remaining, permitted patrilines would have been prohibited to the
prospective couple's parents. After casting sisters and daughters out of
the patriline for four generations, the patriline brings its female descendants back into the fold in the fifth generation.[14] To ensure that the rule
is adhered to, every stage of the long and drawn-out marriage rites,
including the initial betrothal stage, is accompanied by libation sequences poured to the bride's and groom's ascending ancestors,[15] thus
tracing a mental journey backwards in time along most of the paths that
connect patrilines and link them through marriage.[16]

When memory fails the prospective bride or groom, they may have
recourse to the birth records kept by the registro civil, where one can
find out what one's great-grandmother's patronym was. Sometimes, it is
an unpleasant discovery, and genealogical amnesia is the best measure to
keep the marriage intact. K'ulta's registro civil told me of several
occasions when written social memory was best forgotten; with suitable
recompense, he was able to lose the evidence.

There is great force to patrilineal biases in K'ulta, in which most
hamlets correspond to a single patriline.[17] Genealogical memory tends to
falter beyond the grandparental generation apart from one's direct
patrilineal ascendants. Don Manuel Mamani, for example, could remember the names of seven ascending ancestors in the male line (father,
father's father, etc.); all of them had lived in Vila Sirka. His wife, doña
Marta Cariri, recalled only four ascendant male ancestors of her
patriline. But just as many North Americans do, don Manuel had
difficulty recalling the matronym of either of his grandmothers. Doña
Marta, in contrast, knew the matronyms of her grandmothers and of
their mothers as well.

Of course, the deeper genealogies, of patronymics or matronymics, often collapse several generations into one. All the Mamanis knew the name of the first Mamani in K'ulta, but different individuals placed him at different degrees of remove, and none went back far enough in time to account for the Mamanis who, in the late 1770s, had pummeled the unfortunate cacique gobernador of Condo. Ancestors that far back, the forgotten ones, are nonetheless still libated, because they form a vital part of the *mujuts kasta,* the "seed line," which defines membership in the patriline. Likewise, distant matrilineal ancestors, whose names must be forgotten so that marriages can occur, are nonetheless recalled as "generic" ancestral beings of the *wilats kasta,* the "blood line."

All K'ultas are aware that in the deep past, usually, in fact, only five or six generations back, mujuts kasta and wilats kasta fade into one another; all members of the ayllu, in the end, are "blood" relatives, related to one through the substance that, in the K'ulta theory of conception, is the woman's contribution to reproduction. Women, who concern themselves more deeply with recalling the transmission of cloth, pottery, and herd animals from mother to daughter, remember more matrilineal connections than do men, to whom the main rights of inheritance are to patriline land. To this degree, Arnold's (1988, 1992) assertions about the importance of matriliny as a complement to patriliny have much merit, notwithstanding the fact that in reality, both mujuts kasta and wilats kasta, as forms of genealogical reckoning, are constructed according to patrilineal principles. In K'ulta, the blood-line genealogy traces kin related to one through one's mother; emphasis even in women's libations to ancestors is upon *their* patrikinsmen, who of course constitute a different patriline from that of their husband.[18]

There is even more merit to the matriliny argument when we turn to the genealogies of herd animals rather than those of humans. Corrals, like houses and patios, are also built upon "roots" that connect them to the ancestral hill and mountain caretakers of animals. Since, unlike lands, herd animals are passed from mother to daughter, a genealogical litany of the animals' guardian deities does recall matrilineal transmission.

Yet parallel transmission of moveable property through a female line is, after all, a matter of degree, since men also inherit animals; likewise the notion that the ayllu is a kind of circulating connubium in which patrilines are linked through transmission of blood does not erase the probability that ayllus were once also conceived as clanlike "super" patrilineages, linked together through a shared ancestral paqarina.

Evidence for the latter claim (quite apparent in the Huarochirí myth corpus) comes from the Aymara term that Bertonio's seventeenth-century dictionary reports for the Quechua term "ayllu": "*hatha*," meaning not only the social form Quechua speakers called ayllu but also "seed." "Hatha" seems to have had nearly the same range of meanings as today's "muju." At one time, "ayllus" were, as patrilines are today, conceived in terms of shared *male* generative substance (and perhaps also female blood). And regardless of how strong matrilineal ideas might be, they do not in the end mitigate the primacy of patri-biases in everyday life. Such biases grant to men, not to women, positions of authority on the town council, and make land, houses, and fiesta-cargo careers into patriline property: A widow does not inherit her husband's fields or her husband's ritual career, which pass to a son if one is available and, if not, to a brother or patri-nephew of the dead man. A widow without children is sent packing unless she remarries within the patriline.

K'ultas conceptualize authority itself in a manner that underscores the biased gendering of political life. As we shall see, men become authorities within the hamlet, *jiliris,* only by first being equated with the lead llamas of the domesticated herd, the llantirus (Sp. *delanteros*), that is, by domesticating and leading other human beings, beginning with his wife, who forms the nucleus of a man's herd. Internalizing Tatala's encompassing qualities as "our father shepherd," pascal lamb, and herder of men, a new husband draws his wife into the patriline in order to reproduce it. The fact that authorities should be thought of as herders is itself ironic, since men regard the role of actually taking animals to pasture as a demeaning and feminine activity. Men's herds are human ones, and their herding is domestic and collective politics in a patriarchal vein.

Of course, all this is a matter of perspective. The man who gathers a wife, herds, inlaws, and a ritual following may become a domesticator of the wilderness, a herder of men, for his patriline mates, but he is a wild predator to those whose sister and herd animals he takes. Likewise, the debt incurred by taking a wife transforms the woman's brothers into predators, bent on stealing from their new brother-in-law's flock of sisters.

To a newly married man, his wife's male patrikin become larita, a term that also means "fox." The animal reference notwithstanding, it is a term of respect, and a man is permanently indebted to his laritas. Laritas call the man who marries their daughter or sister tullqa. Every time the wife's brother or father carries out an important ritual task, the tullqa must aid his laritas in the most subservient ways; he can never fully undo the sting of his theft of their daughter and sister, remaining permanently indebted.[19]

Harris (1982) reports a house-thatching ritual among the Laymi (a people who border Qaqachaka just northwest of K'ulta) that makes explicit the complementary forms of predation played out between patrilines. The groom dons a costume made of a dried condor, transforming himself into a mallku. He then dances, carrying his wife's brother, his larita, on his back, recapitulating the mallku's journey with larita to heaven, from whence larita fell with the seeds of domesticated crops. From one another's patri-centric vantage, each is a wild predator on the other's "herd," even while both seek the powers of heaven. Of course in this instance, the one who has succeeded in domesticating a wife is the groom, the condor, while the fox's efforts backfire.

Sister exchange is a relatively common form of marriage alliance in K'ulta, so in real life the predatory larita sometimes exacts vengeance on his sister-stealing tullqa by taking away his tullqa's sister in marriage. The two men (and women) then enter into a completely reciprocal relationship, each alternatively serving the other as subordinate tullqa and demanding service as larita. Each as larita will carry on his back the other, in the form of a condor. Since all the same-generation men and women within a patriline are classified as brothers and sisters, and since the most common form of sister exchange is of the classificatory type, the reciprocal relationship of debt and obligation (or predation and vengeance) established by marriage is as much an interpatriline affair as it is an interpersonal one.

There are many opportunities for men to win the hearts of women from other patrilines in the collective interpatriline visiting of marriage rituals and saints' festivals. From the vantage of young people, the best of all are the nighttime courtship visits that take place during carnaval, when patriline entourages visit the hamlets of their contraries for competitive singing and dancing and a good deal of sexual play. In all such visits, each patriline seeks to use their superior "metaherding" powers, gained through their efforts to emulate Tatala, to "domesticate" the women of other patrilines, turning the unruly predation of Chullpa times and the wild forces of the pampa to the purpose of reproducing the regulated life of the patriline household and hamlet.

I have surveyed how hamlet/patriline settlements are interconnected through paths of social transmission made manifest in every practical and ritual act within household and hamlet social space. It remains to point out that each house in the hamlet is also endowed with a patron saint, a miniature image called a *riwusyun* (again, from Sp. *devoción*). So in addition to the underground channels linking household roots to the patri-stem group's uywiri (hill) and the patriline's mallku (mountain), aboveground pathways lead from each house to the hamlet chapel (called, in Aymara, *pukara,* a term once applied to hilltop fortresses). Within it, the hamlet/patriline as a whole keeps its patron saint, also one of the "imagenes de bulto" first introduced by doctrina priests. From every hamlet chapel, a straight ritual pathway, made (like the famous Nasca lines) by clearing away stones and plant life, leads to and up a nearby uywiri, ending at an altar (called the saint's *silu,* from Sp. *cielo,* "heaven") and a stone-built tower topped by a cross (much like the humilladero erected by González de la Casa atop Diego Iquisi's wak'a shrine) (Photograph 7.1). Just as in the town of Santa Bárbara, the hamlet's patron saint is celebrated by an annual festival. Sponsoring that festival is the first task incumbent on a newly married couple while they progress towards full adulthood and an independent household. Such sponsorship is a step on another kind of path, the jiska p"ista t"aki, "small fiesta path," which leads to full adulthood and to authority within the hamlet. All male members of the hamlet/patriline may consider one another "brothers," jilata, but some brothers, by participating in the hamlet festival system, become "elder brothers," jiliri, leaders of the patriline. That is when they begin the jach'a p"ista t"aki, the "great fiesta path," traveling the road that leads to the church and the town council office, and perhaps to the status of jilaqata, the highest-ranking of all the elder brothers.

The first step in such a life career, however, presupposes that one knows how properly to carry through another sort of t"aki, the "path of memory" embarked on through drink. Only then can one begin to plumb the sacrificial logic by which men are able actually to grasp the powers of Tatala to transform themselves first into herders and agriculturalists and concomitantly into herders of men.

AMT'AÑ T"AKI: "PATHS OF MEMORY" TRAVELED IN DRINK

In his foundational journey, K'ulta's Solar-Christ episodically confounded a timeless and immortal humanity with tricks of time and space, and created the very fabric of space-time with which modern humans must contend. His original itinerary became the t"aki, or path, through which as the sun he continues to move. Human society is now inextricably bound up in the cyclic alternation of night and day, and the

Photograph 7.1. A dance group at a hilltop silu altar. Young men of Sikuyu Hamlet and accompanying sisters doff hats while saluting the hamlet chapel and its image of the Virgin of Purification. They play a tune on octave-graded panpipes. Behind them, a flower-bedecked cross juts from a stone pillar atop the hill, which serves as the saint's silu (from Spanish *cielo*, "heaven"). A cleared processional path links chapel and hilltop. Near Sikuyu Hamlet, Ayllu Manxa-Kawalli, Cantón Culta, February 2, 1980. (Photograph by author)

spiraling cycles of warm rainy season and cold dry season, of life and death. I have tried to show how critical to K'ulta social life are the myriad ways of trying to regain control over the processes that Tatala set in motion. In the first place, they must ensure that the patterned activities of social life conform to Tatala's rhythms. And like a mythic Inca who was able to lasso the sun to lengthen the day, they also seek to manipulate those rhythms to serve social ends. That is possible because Tatala, as master of social space and social time, is also a social being, who can be convinced to accept the prestations that incur obligation towards the humans who offer them. Likewise, the very alternations produced by the original battle between Tatala and the Chullpas left the latter a critical role to play. They killed Tatala, but like Tunupa at the hand of Viracocha, he never did die. In the same way the Chullpas, who did not know death, came insistently back to life, and their dark and autogenerative powers, ruled by Tatala's clock, must also be engaged in social relations with humans (through the dead and in the darkness) if they are to gain control over the temporal patterns on which the processes of life now depend.

Like Tatala, K'ultas must become masters of time, and this is possible only by mastering the relationship between the present and the past. For K'ultas, the past is located in space, in the relationship between encompassing heavens (alax-pacha) and the hidden under or inner world (manxa-pacha). As we have seen, it is also clothed in the architecture of their life-spaces and embodied in the features of the local landscape. For the people of K'ulta, the story of Tatala and the Chullpas provides a key to the past. As a travel narrative, it is itself a form of t"aki, an episodic sequence of interactions that describes the temporal dimension of space and of human life. As such, the story is a narrative icon of the original journey remembered through it. This, and all, oral narrative is remembered and shaped by poetic rules of composition, character development, and plot, all of which are embodied in the social space-time established by the sun's movement along his itinerary, which is the primordial t"aki.

In K'ulta, the road one travels through drink is not that of amnesia but of its opposite, memory. That drinking alcoholic beverages should serve as a mnemonic technique is surely at odds with the commonplace in so-called Western culture that one drinks in order to forget. Even those perceptive sixteenth-century Spaniards who recognized the link between borrachera and idolatry had difficulty imagining drink as a memory technique.[20] Nevertheless, sequences of libation dedications, or toasts, that are pronounced in the moment of throwing back one's drinks are called amt'añ t"akis, memory paths.[21] To understand drinking in the Andean countryside, we must take stock of the way that a shot of aguardiente (or, as the K'ultas pronounce this Spanish term, awarinti) becomes a measure of meaning.[22]

Ch'alla in K'ulta

In K'ulta and throughout the countryside, solitary and secretive drinking is exceedingly rare, in contrast with drinking in cities and among town vecinos. Drinking is instead most often associated with collective ritual events, in which the sharing of alcoholic beverages is an important medium of reciprocity, a sign of hospitality, and in sum a significant medium of organized social interaction. Rather than taking the form of the occasional drink shared informally among friends, drinking in K'ulta usually involves extraordinary outlays of time, effort, and funds. It is almost invariably done "for something," in a ritual context in which drinks are almost always dedicated and offered to divinities. Drinks do not, however, simply mark birthdays, Friday nights, formal occasions, and holidays, as they may in the city, but serve to bring to mind the distant past, reinforce the sense of self, family, genealogy, and mark out the organization of the cosmos and man's place in it. They do so through the ch'alla form that is fundamental to all kinds of ritual in K'ulta. Ch'allas provide the structuring backbone which gives sequential form to the llama sacrifices that mark out virtually every ritual context, from naming ceremony to funeral, and from curing rite to saint's festival.[23]

A ch'alla, essentially, is a libation involving the partial spilling (or flicking from the finger tips) of a liquid upon (or towards) a sacred altar or other deity. But that is not the end of it. The place of libation itself then becomes a channel through which additional ch'allas reach more distant beings. Nor are libations simply poured out: a few words of dedication direct the libation to its final recipient. The drink is therefore a kind of offering, one type among many.[24]

It is late evening of the Thursday before carnaval, 1981. With Virgilio Mamani and his cousin don Bartolomé, several other senior Mamani men, and their wives, I enter Virgilio's father's house in Vila Sirka. Virgilio's father, who died the previous year, had nearly completed a long career of festival sponsorships and town council posts and, had he lived, would have been preparing to sponsor his last festival in the coming month of December, in honor of Santa Bárbara. Fiesta careers, however, are inherited. So Virgilio is preparing to take his father's place to complete the career. Since he is unmarried, his mother will accompany him. We enter the house in order to carry out the ch'alla sequence of uywa ispira t''aki, the "memory path of the herd vespers." His mother begins by lighting a pair of charcoal braziers, pouring an incense mixture onto the hot charcoal, and encircling the inside of the house, enclosing it within ritual time. Don Bartolomé and his wife, doña Basilia, prepare two quantities of alcohol diluted to 80 proof with water. Onto the misa on the right side of the house, Virgilio places a poncho, and in its center, a coca cloth. Next to the coca he places his father's varas, wrapped in an ancient vicuña scarf, and a bull's horn pututu.

The menfolk take seats around the altar, while Virgilio's mother and doña Basilia sit upon the floor on the left side of the house, around a woman's carrying cloth and a quantity of coca leaves upon it. Several other Mamani men and their wives take their respective seats. Now Virgilio and his mother give each participant a double handful of coca leaves, received in open palms and transferred to each one's ch'uspa. Several then exchange their coca ch'uspas, touching the other's bag to the floor and saying "Tata Santíssimo taki," or "Tata Mustramu Awksa taki" ("for Our Holy Father Sun"), dedicating the chew to the God whose trials on a Thursday, before his Friday death, make this his day. (The suffix "taki"—which is unaspirated, differentiating it from "t″aki," "path"—indicates "for" in the dedications.) Then don Bartolomé and doña Basilia get down to business, each with a can of alcohol and a small tin cup.

Finally, the amt'añ t″aki session is underway. Like any other, the session begins with a single ch'alla. Don Bartolomé begins by filling a tiny silver cup with his alcohol mixture. He then dribbles a few drops at each of the altar's four corners. Then, just prior to drinking the remainder of the cup in a single draught, he says the words "Iskin Mamala Misa taki." He then refills the cup and hands it to Virgilio, who repeats don Bartolomé's action and words. In the hierarchic order of age and social privilege (I am next, reflecting the eminence the Mamanis have bestowed upon me as a wealthy outsider), the rest of the men seated on stones behind the altar then repeat the words and acts.

"Kuntur mamani tapa misa" refers to the very altar (misa) at which we sit, belonging to the house, the "altar of the condor-eagle nest." Subsequent ch'allas are then dedicated to the altar's "root," the channel of transmission connecting the altar below the ground to other sacred places, and then to a whole hierarchy of deities located elsewhere, beginning with Janq'u Nasa Uywiri taki "for the herder hill [named] White Nose," the deity inhabiting the hill that stands close to Vila Sirka, sacred to all the Mamanis of the hamlet. Next the cup makes the round again, this time dedicated to Pirwan Tata Mallku taki, or Churi Asanaqi Kumprira taki, alternate names for one and the same mountain deity, the mallku, "male condor," or kumpira, "he of the peak," who goes by two names, Pirwan Tata, "Father Storehouse," and Churi Asanaqi, "Asanaqi the son." This is a mountain near both Vila Sirka and Santa Bárbara of higher rank than a mere uywiri; all Mamanis of K'ulta revere him as their mallku.[25]

While the men carry out these libation offerings, which prepare the way for dedications to many more sacred beings, the women are not idle. Seated behind their altar cloth, facing the men, they pour their own ch'allas, led by don Bartolomé's wife, doña Basilia. They follow the same sequence of gods, but their words are not precisely the same. Ch'allas must always be performed in gender parallel, and women pour not to the male misa, uywiri, and mallku with whom men share their drinks, but to those beings' female counterparts, iskin mamala misa t'alla taki, Janq'u Nasa Uywiri T'alla taki, and Pirwan Tata Mallku T'alla taki: "for the corner mother lady," "for the lady of White Nose Herder-hill," and "for the lady of Father Storehouse Condor-peak."

When don Bartolomé, acting in the specialist role of wasu wariri ("he who passes the cup") gives me the alcohol cup, and I intone the words "Pirwan Tata Mallku taki" while pouring out a few drops, I enter into a complex social relationship. The alcohol has been provided by Virgilio, acting as alma cargo, stand-in for his dead father's ghost, who is the sponsor of the rite. Mediated by don Bartolomé as "drinking path" specialist, I also enter into a relationship with the alter and its root, which receive and transmit the liquid offering, via underground channels, to a thirsty being, the "uywiri of White Nose Hill," who lives within the hill.[26] This libation, then, involves four persons (wasu wariri, ghostly ritual sponsor, the latter's stand-in, and myself as pourer) and a variable number of gods and their intermediaries. Indirectly, since libations *must* be carried out in gender parallel, the performance also links each pourer with his or her opposite-gender complement, the opposite-gender sponsor (in this case, Virgilio's mother), and each of the opposite-gender consorts of libated gods, beginning with those that have been built into the house, patio, or corral.[27]

Such social relations are indexed by gifts, beginning with the sponsor's prestation (through the specialist server) of the cup of alcohol to the pourer. The pourer then passes the gift on to the gods through the mediation of the altar and its root. This kind of gift is *paq"ara* (literally, a "flower" or "blossom"), which incurs a debt of obligation in the recipient(s) of the gift, who must reciprocate at some point in the future. The gift is also often itself a reciprocation of a prior obligation. Just as the pourer becomes obligated to the sponsor for the gift of alcohol, the inverse is true; the sponsor is obligated for the pourer's participation in the ritual, without which the sponsor's obligations to the gods may not be sufficiently met. By participating in the rite, the sponsor and pourer become (or reaffirm) their roles as ayni to one another, coparticipants in a gifting relationship, and both seek to establish (or reestablish) a similar relationship with the gods. Gods receive liquid alcohol "flowers," but return the debt in another kind of flower: crops, newborn herd animals, and power over men.[28]

In this schema an offering to a god is made through an exchange between persons. Conversely, exchange between persons is understood as a form of exchange between people and gods. Similarly the hierarchy of gods is called upon to pass the offering on up the line and deliver the return in reverse order (rather than in a disruptive direct form such as lightning or hail or disease). K'ultas explained to me that their aim is to provide control over generative forces that the ethnographer might prefer to interpret as biological, meteorological, and social processes. This kind of fetishized understanding in which relations among persons are objectified in the cosmos at large, however, is not mere mystification, because it in fact makes expressible the cultural ordering which gives specific form to the relations of social production that themselves produce the participants in the rite.

A ch'alla, however, never travels alone; it is always soon followed on the altar and down the gullet by a seemingly endless caravan of similar drinks.[29] But there is more to the sacrificial bargain than mere quantity. Ch'allas are not a haphazard business, but a precisely performed sequence of dedications.

CH'ALLAS IN SEQUENCE: AMT'AÑ T"AKI AS TEXT AND PERFORMANCE

Ch'allas occur individually only as elements in rigidly adhered to sequences, unwritten "scripts" which mandate the order and recipients of a long series of libations. Each kind of ritual occasion demands a specific ch'alla sequence. K'ultas call such sequences *umañ t'akis* (drinking paths), or amt'añ t"akis (*amt'aña*, "to remember," + *t"aki*, "path/ road," = "path of memory").

It would be impossible to catalogue here all the *kinds* of ch'alla sequences practiced in K'ulta, much less the actual contents of such sequences. A description of just the sequences forming part of a single fiesta performance would severely tax the reader's patience. Suffice it to note that there are specified sequences for each stage of a sacrifice, as well as for other subparts of fiesta performance. There are sequences connected with the calendric rites associated with agricultural and herding tasks, with the duties of civil authorities, with warfare, with healing and other forms of shamanism, with each of the steps of each of the marriage rites, and with a whole set of funerary rights, just to name a few. Such sequences are remembered as idealized or abstract conventional forms (lists of generic deity types like misa, uywiri, and mallku that correspond to the purposes of a particular rite; in practice, the generic deity types are always replaced in performance with particular named "tokens" of the type (such as Janq'u Nasa, Pirwan Tata, etc.). Which specific deities will be named hinges on the social identity of the sponsor and his wife and the place of performance.

Certain ch'alla "paths," like the other ritual action sequences with which they are associated, form "modular" segments that are inserted into a particular rite when called for. For example: all rites of passage, including the fiesta, are built from the stages of llama sacrifice, and each stage of the sacrifice has a corresponding ch'alla path to accompany it. Thus, whether in a marriage or a saint's feast, the segments dedicating the animals to be killed (uywa ispira), slaughtering the animals (qarwa k"ari), and dedicating the meat of the feast (*ch'iwu*) will be carried out. Within each sequence, too, there are lower levels of segmentation. All begin with ch'allas to the altar, root, uywiri, and mallku of the sponsor and place of performance; each of the above also includes dedications to gods of the herd animals. Uywa ispira includes a long sequence dedicated to the ancestral dead, as the memory paths of funerary sacrifices do. As abstract sequences of kinds of gods, animals, foodstuffs, and ancestors (and of the gods and sacred places associated with each), the modular segments are well-known throughout K'ulta, but the "personal names" of such gods, places, and dead ancestors vary. The performances of two brothers would be very similar, but each one would begin with a different house or corral altar, and the social ties that come through their wives would also differ.

UYWA ISPIRA T"AKI: THE "HERD VESPERS PATH"

Seated next to Virgilio Mamani in his father's house, I had begun the first few ch'allas of uywa ispira t"aki. Always performed when preparing for a llama sacrifice,[30] it is a complex and lengthy poetic form. Figure 7.4 shows the sequence of ch'allas that I reconstructed from notes, partial tape recordings, and repeated attendance at Virgilio Mamani's uywa ispira rites, which he had to perform every time he prepared to sacrifice llamas in fulfillment of a festival obligation. Rather than recounting the personal names of gods and ancestors, which are often the actual words spoken, I present for purposes of analysis the names of the *categories* of gods and genealogically reckoned kinship to which K'ultas have recourse when they do not know the personal name or place-name in question.

Note well, however, that I list here only those libation dedications performed *at the men's altar.* Seated on raised benches or stone seats,

			Libation dedications	Free translation
I	A	1	iskin mamala	"corner mother": the house itself
		2	misa	"altar/table": altar of the house
		3	uywiri	"one who nurtures": household caretaker hill
		*4	kumprira [or mallku]	mountain peak/condor: patriline deity
II	B	5	jira t'all mispa	"manure plain" altar: altar of the llama corral
		6	yanan jira t'all mispa	conceptual "twin" of llama corral altar
		7	ch"itan jira t'all mispa	altar of sheep corral
		8	yanan ch"itan jira t'all mispa	"twin" of sheep corral altar
		9	jira t'all misa uywirpa	caretaker hill of llama corral altar
		10	yanan jira t'all misa uywirpa	"twin" of caretaker hill of llama corral altar
		*11	jira t'all misa kumprirpa	peak of llama corral altar
	C	12	warmin jira t'all mispa	altar of wife's corral[1]
		13	warmin jira t'all uywirpa	caretaker hill of wife's corral
		*14	warmin jira t'all kumprirpa	mountain peak of wife's corral
	D	15	mamalñan jira t'all mispa	altar of mother's corral[2]
		16	mamalñan jira t'all uywirpa	caretaker of mother's corral
		*17	mamalñan jira t'all kumprirpa	peak of mother's corral
	E	18	taykch'in jira t'all mispa	altar of wife's mother's corral[3]
		19	taykch'in jira t'all uywirpa	caretaker hill of wife's mother's corral
		*20	taykch'in jira t'all kumprirpa	mountain peak of wife's mother's corral
	F	21	jach'a malan jira t'all mispa	altar of grandmother's corral[4]
		22	jach'a malan jira t'all uywirpa	caretaker hill of grandmother's corral
		*23	jach'a malan jira t'all kumprirpa	mountain peak of grandmother's corral
	G	24	warmin jach'a malan jira t'all mispa	altar of wife's grandmother's corral[5]
		25	warmin jach'a malan jira t'all uywirpa	caretaker hill of wife's grandmother's corral
		*26	warmin jach'a malan jira t'all kumprirpa	mountain peak of wife's grandmother's corral

Figure 7.4. Men's ch'allas of uywa ispira and qarwa k"ari. This reconstruction of a performance sequence is based on repeated participation, tape recordings, and interviews. In actual performance, many of the deity types (uywiri, kumprira/mallku) are replaced by secret "personal names" of the hill and mountain deities invoked. In qarwa k"ari, the initial sequence begins with "jira t'all misa," the alter within the llama corral. In qarwa k"ari, section K, deities of the vegetable foodstuffs are replaced by the

352

			Libation dedications	Free translation
III	H	27	llantiru awki	Sp. "delantero"/Ay. "awki": father herd leader
		28	yanan llantiru awki	"twin" of father herd leader
		29	t'amap llantiru awki	father herd leader's herd
		30	waynapat llantiru awki	father herd leader's young male offspring
		31	paq"arap llantiru awki	father herd leader's "flower": newborn offspring
		32	llantir awki mispa	father herd leader's altar
		33	llantir awatir uywir mispa	altar of father herd leader's shepherd uywiri
		•34	llantir awatir kumprir mispa	altar of father herd leader's shepherd peak
		•35	llantir samirpa	herd leader's "breath giver" (stone icon)
		•36	llantir muntu	herd leader's "mountain" (underworld)
	I	37	sariju	ram
		38	sariju paq"arapa	ram's newborn offspring
		39	sariju mispa	ram's altar
		40	sariju awatir uywirpa	ram's shepherd caretaker hill
		•41	sariju awatir kumprirpa	ram's shepherd peak
		•42	sariju samirpa	ram's "breath giver" (stone icon)
	J	43	lumpri awki	father bull
		44	yanan lumpri awki	"twin" of the father bull
		45	lumpri paq"arapa	bull's newborn offspring
		46	lumpri mispa	bull's altar
		47	lumpri awatir uywirpa	bull's shepherd caretaker hill
		•48	lumpri awatir kumprirpa	bull's shepherd peak
		•49	lumpri samirpa	bull's "breath giver" (stone icon)
IV	K	50	awiyaru	Sp. "aviador": provisioner hill of foodstuffs
		51	yanan awiyaru	"twin" of provisioner hill god
		52	paqulakutan awiyaru	"golden hair" awiyaru: provisioner deity of corn
		53	tuña t'iris awiyaru	"doña Teresa": patron/provisioner of potatoes
		•54	almasina	Sp. "almacén": storehouse or shop

Figure 7.4. (*Continued*)

cooked-food sequence known as ch'iwu t"aki, interrupted by the delivery of cooked llantiru "heart" and the frolicking of the jañachus, the male sponsor's sons-in-law (or his sisters' husbands) dressed in llantiru pelts.

The numbers preceded by * designate dedications that are also libated in puro from the sponsors' bottles. During qarwa k"ari, k'usa (chicha) libations are carried out between lettered segments. Every item in practice terminates with the suffix *taki*,

353

			Libation dedications	Free translation
V	L	55	mayruwiri	spirits of recent dead (named in dedication)
		56	mayruwir jach'a tala	spirit of grandfather
		57	mayruwir jach'a mala	spirit of grandmother
		•58	mayruwir awksa	spirit of our father (apical patriline ancestor)
VI	M	59	surti	Sp. "suerte": luck
		60	yanan surti	"twin" of luck

Figure 7.4. (*Continued*)

meaning "for," which has been omitted here. Some items here include the infixed *pa,* as in "mispa taki," "for his (or her) misa," indicating nonpresent entities pertaining to named others.

Regarding the translations followed by superscripts: [1]"Wife's corral": that of her patriline; her father's. [2]"Mother's corral": that of her patriline; mother's father's corral. [3]"Wife's mother's corral": that of the wife's mother's patriline; wife's mother's father's corral. [4]"Grandmother's corral": usually that of ego's paternal grandmother, perhaps maternal. Reference is to her patriline; father's mother's father's, or mother's mother's father's corral. [5]"Wife's grandmother's corral": usually that of the wife's father's mother's father, sometimes the wife's mother's mother's father corral. Altogether, these corral libations refer to corrals of the closest six (sometimes eight) patrilines of husband's and wife's ascending kindred, which will be invoked to proscribe patrilines the couple's children may not marry.

adult men arrange themselves around a tablelike altar in an order of seniority and status. Women, on the other hand, sit down a few yards away around a cloth laid upon the ground (or house floor). As in all libation paths, uywa ispira ch'allas are carried out in gender complementarity: men pour ch'allas to male beings while women carry out a parallel performance, pouring to female ones. Working as a team, the man and woman who act as libation specialists ensure that the two groups remain synchronized, pouring to gendered *pairs* of gods. Gender complementarity in performance, that is, mirrors the fertile and generative complementarity of action they seek from the gendered landscape and past. Now back to the men's altar, where I dribbled away many hours in libations.

Since every participant should pour (or blow) a libation for each of the gods listed, while sharing a single small cup, the herd animal vespers path takes several hours to complete. At irregular intervals, there are short breaks to refill the pail of alcohol or the sponsor's bottle. Between major segments (indicated in the figure by uppercase alphabetics and roman numerals), the master of ceremonies pauses, setting down the cup in order to pass to each man present some coca leaves from a clothful kept on the altar. These are also the moments that the sponsor of the ceremony chooses to offer a drink from his bottle of *puro*. Dedicated always to the highest-ranking mountain gods, this 97 percent pure cane alcohol (from which the dilute awarinti is made) is unadulterated firewater, potent stuff for powerful gods. Not present in the uywa ispira context, but critically important during other memory path libation sequences, are libations of home-brewed corn beer (Sp. "chicha," called k'usa in Aymara), offered during these same breaks between awarinti cup "stanzas," but to saints and gods of the sky rather than to earth deities and ancestors. On receiving proffered coca or a bottle of alcohol, each guest utters not only a dedication but also thanks, *yuspagarpan* ("God will repay you").

The memory path begins, not with the most distant and unfamiliar beings, but with those very close at hand. The first libation is always for the place of performance itself, here, the house altar: kuntur mamani tapa misa or iskin mamala misa. The next one is for the personal guardian hill (uywiri) of the sponsors (and their house) and the mallku or kumprira to which that uywiri is subordinate.[31] Each compound or group of households, corresponding to a sibling group around their father's homestead, has its own uywiri,[32] whereas there is only one kumprira for the entire hamlet. This first set of ch'allas (segment A, group I) moves outwards from low and nearby to high and faraway beings. Like a series of concentric circles, these ch'allas provide a mental map of the relative inclusiveness of embedded social groups, ranging from the household itself to the compound and patriline hamlet. From the sponsor's alcohol bottle, further and more inclusive rings of social and territorial inclusion are marked out by naming the great mallku peaks of the Ayllu Manxa-Kawalli as a whole, the sum of ayllus that is K'ulta, and the distant peak of Tata Asanaqi, to which the major mountain gods of K'ulta and many other towns and cantóns are subordinate. At the women's altar, meanwhile, a very similar series of events unfolds, naming the female counterparts or companions of these mountain deities. The sponsor's wife does not innovate here by naming the uywiris and mallkus of her own patriline, which are not "connected" to the altars of her husband's house, compound, or patriline; instead she names the t'allas, the plains that are the wives of her husband's sacred mountains and also the places where her animals now graze and crops ripen.[33]

Back to the awarinti cup, the master of ceremonies, wasu wariri, once again begins his rounds, carrying to each man a cup to be dedicated to one of a long series of deities specific to corrals and herd animals (segments B–G, group II; and H–J, group III).

Segment B refers to the corrals attached to the sponsors' household, including the altar of their male llama corral (5), the altar of the "mate" of the male corral (that is, the female llama corral) (6), the male sheep corral altar (7) and its mate (8), and the uywiris and kumprira (9–11) which correspond to them. The last are sometimes, but not always, the same as the humans' uywiri and kumprira; but because animals are pastured in many areas, they have need of more caretakers, not always well known by the animals' herders. The term for corral, "uyu," is not employed in these ch'allas. Instead, as in many ch'allas, K'ultas prefer a respectful ritual name: jira t'alla, meaning "dung-lady/plain."[34] Women pour their ch'allas not to altars, but to the t'allas themselves.[35]

The progression of segments B–G (within group II) moves from the corrals of the sponsors of the rite outwards (and backwards in time) to genealogically receding branches of herd ancestral deities. As such the intersegment order recapitulates the internal ordering of each segment, but in inverse form: The first item within each segment is a single particular, subordinated to an encompassing form (uywiri) which, in segment A, relates the household to other patri-stem households, and the uywiri is subordinated to a kumprira, which encompasses all hamlet/patriline uywiris. Within segment B, differentiated corral altars and uywiris (note the plurals) of already hierarchically evaluated types of animals (first camelids, as an unmarked form, and then corrals marked "sheep") are encompassed by a single kumprira. In the hierarchy of corrals, then, the corrals of reference (of the sponsors' herd) "encompass" more numerous ascending-generation herds and sets of corresponding territorially dispersed deities belonging to the landscapes of other patrilines, other ayllus, and sometimes (since people occasionally buy animals at the fair in Huari) other regions of Bolivia, beyond the reach of the mountain Tata Asanaqi.

Segments H–J (within group III) are dedications to the animals themselves, rather than to their corrals, and at the same time dedications to the animals' own deities (that is, the deities of the pastures on which they graze, which often lie in collective, interpatriline and interayllu lands). The herd animal segments each begin with libations to the animals, starting with the most esteemed mature animal and progressing downwards in age hierarchy. This is most pronounced in segment H: The camelid sequence is always more developed than those for other, less favored animals. Llantirus (and *lumpris,* "bulls") appear with yanani (partner) repetitions. Llantirus are the lead male llamas of the herd, those that "go before," as the Spanish origin of the term "delantero" suggests, and like yoked bulls, they should always travel in pairs. Item 29, *tama llantiru awki taki,* refers to the herd (tama) which the llantirus define through their totalizing practice of "leading."[36]

The hierarchic movement of items 27–31 progresses, then, from the dominant adult males, to the herd they lead, to the subordinate young who will eventually replace them. The sequence also points towards one desired result of the sacrifice it anticipates, which is the increase of the herd, through the reciprocation of the "flowers" given to the gods (drink and sacrifices) in the form of newborn animal "flowers."

Items 32–36 of the llantiru sequence form a subset which is analogous to the last four items in both the ram and bull sequences (segments I and J) and yet differs in having an extra term. The progression from misa to uywiri to kumprira repeats the form of each previous segment in the performance, but we see the deity form samiri for the first time. Samiris take two forms, collapsed here into a single entity. The term is derived from *sama,* "breath" (*samaña* = "to breathe"; *samaraña* = "to rest"), which when made agentive with the *-iri* suffix becomes "one who [gives] breath." The first type of samiri is large boulders vaguely animallike in shape, high in the mountains, which are kinds of ideal types of ancestor forms.[37] Second, a samiri is the locally more common equivalent of an *illa,* the miniature stone figurine in animal form which is kept buried in the corral with llama ear pieces from yearly marking rites of carnaval time. Both samiri forms are repositories of the life-principle of animals, which is carefully nurtured with the aid of the animals' ultimate owners, the uywiris and kumprira.

Item 36 stands out as unique among uywa ispira libations. Muntu or llantiru muntu is the most mysterious of all the deity forms, because no one is quite sure where or what it is. While all conceive of it as a mountain, which as the ultimate source and repository of great herds encompasses the llamas' kumpriras, it does not lie within K'ulta territory.[38]

Each category of animal herd (and especially the camelid, as represented by the llantiru[39] is thus treated as analogous to human society, as if it has its own set of deities, like the human ones libated in segment A. In some cases, sponsors actually name specific place deities (associated with particular pastures) here, sometimes enumerating several for each category, sometimes giving the dedication in the plural.[40]

What is important here is that in the very enumeration of animal types as internally hierarchic (in terms of age) they are related as a herd through a hierarchy of encompassment, making them like humans and gods. One of the goals of the rite is precisely to establish an equation between humans and herd animals, who are prepared for sacrifice through uywa ispira.

Next in the ch'alla sequence come the lumpris, "bulls," which have no corrals.[41] Finally, segments K–M refer to neither human nor animal place deities. The beings of segment K control the production of nonanimal foodstuffs, beginning with the general form *awiyaru*, from the archaic Spanish verb "*aviar*" ("to provision"). These are uywiri-like deities at the heads of valleys producing the bulk of vegetable food that K'ultas eat. Virgilio here names the deities corresponding to the valleys to which he travels during the dry season. Items 52 and 53 name the awiyarus controlling corn (referred to metonymically as *paqulakutan*, "golden hair") and potatoes (*tuña t"irisa* from Santa Teresa, being both patroness and ritual name for potatoes). Item 54, *almasina* (Sp. *almacen*, "storehouse"), recalls the store where it was purchased.

Once sponsors have remembered the animals and foodstuffs, they turn to long-dead ancestors. In the performance of segment L, Mamanis called to the deceased by personal names (when they remembered them) rather than specifying what kind of relative they were. In other circumstances, for memory paths performed in other contexts such as marriages and death rituals, they may be drawn out to a much greater genealogical depth, back to the *laq'a jach'a*, "great-dust," generation, which is to say back to the apex and limit of memory and genealogical significance. In the context of a festival sacrifice like this one, it is forbidden to ch'alla those who have been dead for less than three years, for whom funerary rites are still ongoing. Recent dead are addressed only on Mondays (the day of the dead), during which no part of nonfunerary sacrificial rites may take place. In any case, the dead are remembered, like the corrals, in progressive backwards steps from most recent to most distant, the mayruwiri.[42]

The final segment of the sequence, segment M, is more of a request than a dedication, and terminates all ch'alla sequences: "for luck" and "for the yanani of luck" (*surti*, from the Sp. *suerte*)[43] addressing the imponderable factor (the *genius vocati*) which makes performance of rites such as this productive for some but not for others. To paraphrase one Mamani, "For some people the fiesta is not their luck, and no matter what they do their children die and their herds do not increase." These have to seek their luck in other places, through other rituals engaging other pasts.[44]

By the end of the sequence, all present (with the partial exception of don Bartolomé and doña Basilia) were quite drunk. But all had nonetheless engaged in a mental journey, following an itinerary progressing ever further from the immediate concerns of the household, branching out into ever more distant realms. The ch'alla path organizes space concentrically, focusing always on the specific altar of performance and the social unit indexed by it. Recapitulating the internal hierarchy of inclusion of each segment, the progression of segments (and of major chunks of segments) also forms a concentrically focused hierarchy of inclusion (see Fig. 7.3).

As illustrated in Fig. 7.4, the ch'alla sequence moves from deities specific to Virgilio Mamani (rather, to his father), to those shared with all Mamanis (segment A), to Virgilio's corrals (segments B–G), to the realm of herd animals and their faraway pastures and hill protectors (segments H–J), the more distant sources of vegetable food (segment K). Outside K'ulta and its ecozone, ch'allas then continue to the ancestral "other world" (segment L), and finally to "luck" (segment M), that which is furthest outside Virgilio's control and understanding.

As a "path of memory," this sequence of libation dedications describes a series of places across the territory, recalling the actual channels of social transmission which, like a journey, have both spatial and temporal coordinates. As a single itinerary, a path with a beginning and an end, it also integrates spatial and temporal hierarchies into a single order, moving simultaneously across territory and back in time.

The most encompassing form of metaphoric equation in this ch'alla poetics is achieved through its recursive stanzalike structure, which like poetic devices, make it possible to equate seemingly unlike entities and to imbue one kind of hierarchic logic with the sense of another kind. The sequence "misa, uywiri, kumprira" describes a vertical hierarchy of inclusion, one that conforms as well to the principle of patrilineal descent through which K'ulta's patronymic groups define themselves. Thus a single apical "ancestor" mountain controls and encompasses all its "lower" descendants. At the same time, however, the relationship among animals' corral deities moves in hopscotch fashion across K'ulta landscape, expressing the *matrilineal* links which multiply the number and horizontal reach of salient kumpriras. Finally, in the latter segments of the sequence, distance is not correlated with genealogical depth or encompassing height, but with categorical difference. The realms of the awiyarus, city merchants, ancestral souls, and even of luck are all extrasocial in a more profound manner than the animals and the genealogically and vertically ordered gods are. Each is also lower, more dangerous, less subject to control.

To grasp fully the kinds of metaphors brought about by equating distinct forms of hierarchy, we must turn to the correspondingly distinct cosmic levels that are juxtaposed in the performance of amt'añ t"aki. During this uywa ispira t"aki sequence, all libations are poured in water-diluted cane alcohol by don Bartolomé and doña Basilia, acting as awarint wasu wariris, "aguardiente cup servers." All the deities libated belong to the underworld realm of manxa-pacha. But this particular memory path is only part of the larger sequence that accompanies the llama sacrifice and frames the fiesta performance.

While libations were in progress, Virgilio and his mother set to work preparing an incense offering that would link the ch'allas of uywa ispira to other parts of the sacrifice.

The Q'uwa

The *q'uwa* is a burnt incense offering made at several junctures during fiesta performance, as on many other occasions during the year. The heads of all herding households prepare and burn q'uwas as part of major calendric rites, and also at full and/or new moons. A special q'uwa is offered by sponsors at the new moon immediately preceding the fiesta proper and at the full moon immediately following it. During the actual fiesta (the named rites commencing with uywa ispira and ending with *ch'iwuru* [from *ch'iwu uru*, "meat/dark cloud day"]), two q'uwas are burned by the sponsor:[45] The first of these is prepared in the sponsors' home, by the male sponsor's tullqa assistants, during the performance of uywa ispira ch'allas, and burned by the sponsoring couple at dawn of *qarwa k"ari uru* ("llama cutting day"); the second, prepared in the sponsors' town house during *ispiras* (the night before the feast), is burned at the dawn of *p"isturu*, the saint's day itself. The preparation is the same in each case, as is the name of the place in which the q'uwa is burned, called the q'uwaña.

The centerpiece of the q'uwa offering is a pair of miniature llamas (called, as one might expect, *llantirus*, the highly prized lead males of the herd), which the sponsors' assistants sculpt from a llama's dried pectoral fat while the sponsors and ch'alla-eligible adults finish their uywa ispira libations. Such fat, called *untu*, is burned during many other ritual events as well, and is, along with the blood of the *paxcha* (the "spurting of blood" in the sacrifice), the part of the llama given directly, through destruction (as opposed to human consumption), to the gods of the sky.[46]

When finished, the figurines are "made to flower" (*paq"arayaña*), as the sacrificial llamas will be during the coming day. The sponsor's assistants decorate the figurines' ears and back with the flower tips of an aromatic herb which is itself called q'uwa. Around these figures are placed twelve coca leaves, twelve coca seeds, a sprinkling of sugar, cinnamon, and other aromatic spices from the valleys. When incense is added (both chunks of copal and pressed cakes in the form of charms, purchased in the city), the offering array is complete.

The offering is made at the break of dawn, in a spot always located on a hillside to the east of the settlement; these spots differ from household to household and are kept secret. The q'uwaña is often the same place as the *asintu* is buried, which is a place where herd fertility offerings are made during the "open earth" rituals of early August and February. Aside from being located to the east of the hamlet or town, the q'uwaña should also receive the rays of the rising sun, to which it is dedicated.

Just before sunrise, the male sponsor is roused from his sleep by his assistants. He carries his prepared q'uwa bowl, with its special array of aromatic and inflammable ingredients, and, after a few ch'allas, he dumps the contents into a pile of burning coals, when the first rays of morning sun appear on the eastern horizon.

The burning of the q'uwa prefigures the sacrifice (also a pair or pairs of llantirus) to come, but it does more than that. Not only are the q'uwa llantirus icons (diagrammatic representations) of the "real" llantirus, as are the yanani in the chicha-drinking vessel and the samiri llantiru buried in the corral; q'uwa llantirus are, in addition, metonymic icons, made from a part of a llantiru that is its generative substance. Making the q'uwa llantirus entirely from this substance and other inflammable and aromatic substances also makes the sacrifice (here, if not in the killing of flesh-and-blood animals) a holocaust offering.[47] The significance of the untu as male generative substance also points to the meaning of the sacrifice as a whole, as an offering of the "patrilineal" force by which the fertile llantiru creates and circumscribes a herd. This is the very kind of generative encompassment, of course, of which the sun (Tata Awatir Awksa, as he is called while the fragrance of the untu and incense rises) is the origin and prototype.

On the day following uywa ispira, Virgilio and his mother would sacrifice four llamas, the select llantirus, in the male-llama corral just outside the sponsors' hamlet house. This event, known as qarwa k"ari, "llama cutting," is carried out during a much longer ch'alla sequence, one that takes several hours to complete. The memory path of qarwa k"ari repeats the basic structure of the uywa ispira t"aki but elaborates it further. First of all, ch'allas are interrupted not only by ch'allas from the sponsors' puro bottles, but also by other ch'allas poured in corn beer, and are directed to Christian-inflected deities (Christ, the Virgin, and the saints).

Qarwa k"ari libations in cane alcohol are always accompanied by libations in chicha, the home-brewed corn beer called K'usa in Aymara. Prepared in advance, the chicha arrives at the corral where qarwa k"ari libations are to be performed in large jars. Another pair of serving specialists, the k'usa wasu wariris, make ready to serve the chicha at breaks in the alcohol ch'allas between major segments. Everyone present then receives two or three large servings of this maize beer in a special vessel. In contrast with the libations performed in alcohol, directed towards underworld beings, chicha libations are offered to the gods of alax-pacha, in other words to the Lunar-Virgin, the Solar-Christ, and the saint in whose honor the sacrifice is performed. Through the orchestrated concatenation of libations directed by these two specialists, the beings and attributes of alax-pacha and manxa-pacha are given distinct diagrammatic sensibility and differently mapped onto the local terrain. As we shall see, the interrelationship of alcohol and chicha libations serves to address the colonial asymmetry of power, within which the people of K'ulta have carved out a space for themselves.

CORN BEER AND CANE LIQUOR IN A CONCATENATED COSMOS

Most amt'añ t"aki performed in saints' feasts and rites of passage include libations in chicha as well as in cane alcohol, and kinds of libation liquids are in complementary distribution with kinds of sacred beings.

Nowadays it is only the sky gods who receive the endogenous form of libation liquid, fermented k'usa, "chicha." This locally manufactured drink, extremely time-consuming to make, is thus reserved for the more "Christian" of gods (Photograph 7.2). In the past, before the colonial availability of distilled liquor, the byproducts of chicha manufacture were also used for libations; chicha was at one time subdivided into its sedimentation strata for different classes of deities.[48]

While it may be ironic that the drink of pre-Columbian Andean gods was assigned to the sky deities of Christianity, it is doubly ironic that a

Photograph 7.2.   Brewing chicha. A woman stirs a pot of chicha during fermentation. Yucras of Vintu Hamlet engaged in the enormously labor-intensive process of chicha brewing in preparation for festivities connected with Eleuterio Yucra's Guadalupe tayksa t"aki fiesta career, which he inherited from his brother. Vintu Hamlet, February 1980. (Photograph by author)

363

type of distilled spirits—a frequently proscribed drink for indians—
became the drink of choice for the prohibited, clearly "non-Christian"
gods. Of course, since both kinds of spirits (hard liquor and mountain
gods) were prohibited, they came to occupy the same clandestine space.
Too, the very strength of distilled spirits, which colonial administrators
regarded as dangerous in "indian" hands, may have made it particularly
appealing for libations to the gods who had been pushed underground.
The sixteenth-century practice of Miguel Acarapi/Chiri, however, suggests another interpretation. The sacramental beverage par excellence,
chicha, became the indians' communion wine used in their own versions
of the mass.[49]

In some phases of sacrifice and fiesta performance, such as qarwa
k"ari, most of the ch'allas of uywa ispira are repeated with the inclusion
of alax-pacha gods, libated in pure alcohol (puro) from the sponsors'
private bottles, as well as in chicha. Indeed, puro and chicha are offered
to a whole array of church-associated sacred places, such as the church
tower (called turri mallku) and its gender complement, the plaza (*plasa
t'alla*), the saints' "seats" and altars in town, as well as the altars on top
of the hamlet uywiri and the "*niño*," a cross-topped pillar in front of the
hamlet chapel. All of these, alongside the sun, the moon, and the saints,
are given puro as well as chicha.[50]

Chicha/k'usa, is served by the k'usa wasu wariri from a large "cup,"
for the libation of sky deities. These deities both reside in and constitute
alax-pacha, the upper or outer space-time which dominates and encompasses manxa-pacha. They are, of course, also the deities of conquest,
simultaneously of culture over nature, human beings over animals, the
present over the past, and of Spaniards over indians. The sun is the most
distant and foreign agency, a latecomer who became the first cause of a
new order wrought in his struggle with the old, but, like the moon, is
more distant and less accessible to humans, who must make offerings
insubstantial (smoke, breath, etc.) for them to reach alax-pacha. In this
respect the celestial gods are quite unlike those of manxa-pacha, which
are everywhere perceptible in the landscape: Layra timpu, the time when
Christ and Chullpas, mountains and animals, freely moved about the
earth, now lies frozen in the landscape in the residues of these beings'
activities, directly visible to the eye (layra). Substances offered and
poured out to the gods of the landscape flow, like rivers, away from the
here and now and into the past. Only the saints, who are refractions of
the Solar-Christ and Lunar-Virgin, are embodied on this earth, and it is
through them that offerings to alax-pacha pass. Saints' images are also

the channels through which alax-pacha powers descend to the realm of men. As such, they are like embassies of alax-pacha, through which the vertically assigned attributes of gods can be reworked as horizontal relations among social groups. Just as the dead mediate to the living the powers of the manxa-pacha Chullpa realm, the saints stand between living humans and the gods of above. Both, of course, are also conduits through which people gain access to the powers of the past; they are emissaries of history.

In the ch'alla sequences of qarwa k"ari and ch'iwu (the commensal banquet at which the llamas' meat is eaten), all three kinds of libation are concatenated into a single order of performance. Just how complex any particular performance will be hinges on whether or not it includes another patriline, ayllu, or moiety among its collective participants.

The uywa ispira sequence by itself lacks chicha because it is performed in a house and because it is a "private," intrapatriline (not to say intrahousehold) affair. *Inter*patriline rites (and phases of rites) take place at the outdoor altars of the sponsors' house patio (and the jach'a misa of the apical hamlet founder). Libations in chicha, puro, and diluted alcohol are concatenated in these contexts because they involve a relation between structural opposites (groups evaluated as complementary inverses, like the levels of the cosmos), in which the discourse between them is conceived in terms of that between cosmic levels. In rites like marriage ceremonies and saints' festivals, where the relationship between patrilines is precisely the issue at hand, one group always plays the role of host, and the other, that of visitor. In an oppositional confrontation that sometimes includes ritual violence, the meeting of patrilines is something like a sporting event: Hosts play visitors, who are treated with a certain circumspection as potential enemies or predators, but in the expectation that the visit will be reversed in the future. In the final marriage rites, for example, wife givers visit the patriline hamlet of wife takers, sealing a pact which is fundamentally asymmetrical and which creates a social debt to be repaid in kind when the shoe is on the other foot. The entire group of a wife's patriline brothers becomes for the husband's hosting patriline a pack of marauding foxes, intent on stealing away a replacement for their lost sister. One group's act of alax-pacha-style "herding" is the other group's act of manxa-pacha predation. So relations between patrilines, whether in sealing a bond of marriage or in exchanging a saint's image, themselves reflect the fundamental oppositions of cosmogenic process.

Figure 7.5.   Turu wasu (chicha drinking vessel). This bowl, eleven inches in diameter with yoked bulls at the center, is carved of wood. When filled with chicha, the bulls stand in a "lake," amidst the abundance they help to bring people. (Author's sketch)

A fitting symbol of this discourse is to be found in the wooden bowls used for chicha libations (Fig. 7.5). These vessels are called *yanan turu wasu* (or k'iru; "quero," as Spaniards wrote the term). At the bottom of the turu wasu is a matched pair (*yanani*) of carved wooden bulls, yoked together. A less common but even more esteemed alternate form, the *yanan llantir wasu,* contains a pair of llamas. Whether bulls or llamas, the figures bear a marked resemblance to two other miniature forms (both llantirus): the untu (chest fat) figures standing in their q'uwa (incense) bowl, which are burned and sent to alax-pacha at dawn in the q'uwa rite as an advance on the blood sacrifice to come; and the illa (also called samiri), the stone figures of llamas and alpacas which are buried (with llama ear pieces) during carnaval-time llama-marking rituals in the center of the male-llama corral. When it is filled with chicha, the turu wasu or llantir wasu becomes a lake (*q'uta*) in which the yanani stands immersed. The camelids are held to have originated in miniature "illa/samiri" form in highland springs (which are layra, "eyes,") and, as passageways to the underworld river (doorways to layra timpu), and when the chicha is drunk from the bowl, the pair of animals within appears to emerge from such a spring. Such miniature animal pairs, then, serve as iconic signs of the complementary opposition of like but opposed social units. In qarwa k″ari ch′allas this becomes explicit, when *llantirus* (that is, the paired sacrificial victims) are addressed as *tinkur awkis*, "fathers [who go] to tinku."[51]

Signifying fundamentally "a meeting of opposites," tinku is applied to a range of phenomena, such as the meeting (that is, forking) of rivers or of branches on a stem (see Urton 1984; Platt 1987b). The most salient use of the term here is perhaps its application to a form of ritual battle which constitutes a central element of many rites. While actual ritual fighting occurs only in the ritual center town in moiety-level fiestas, it is also implicated in all interpatriline rites (including marriage ceremonies) where the musician-dance groups exchanged by patrilines appear as "platoons" of warriors prepared for fighting and for the "sacramental" spilling of human blood.

Both the implied tinku of interpatriline rites and that to which the paired llantiru victims are sent represent, simultaneously, the meeting of opposed social units and the conjunction, in sacrifice, of otherwise opposed cosmic zones. But while the conjunction may appear at first sight to be between balanced, complementary opposites, it always has the character of the conquest and subsummation of one unit by the other, just as the presence of "Christian" deities in the sky, enclosing "indigenous" gods of the below, brings these opposed realms into an asymmetrical but complementary relationship.

To substantiate such claims, I must turn to a closer view of festival sacrifices and to the human careers, the *p″ista t′akis*, that form through cult to the saints.

Chapter Eight

Living on Tatala's Path
Uses of the Past in Sacrifice and Antisacrifice, Saints' Festivals, and Sorceries

THE GREAT FIESTA PATHS

In the previous chapter we saw that the forms of houses and hamlets and constructed architectural spaces are built from the stuff of meaningful social activity. As gendered persons and social groups like patrilines construe themselves in alignment with Tatala's path through the heavens and a transformative relationship to Chullpa forces, the spaces of daily life and the social processes played out in them become microcosms of cosmic processes. As meaningful action within the hamlet is made to conform to the values which Tatala's action gives to social space, the goal of human society and of each social actor is to replicate the actions of the sun, whose taming of the disordered and wild nature of the previous age made cultural life possible. Thus domesticated food and drink and the fruits of the womb are dedicated to the sun and his realm, always facing the direction from whence the initial order came, while feces, death, decay, and disease are relegated to the west, towards the end of Tatala's path, the future past where generative but fetid manxa-pacha forces are predominant. Social time and social space are played out in a single arena, in tune with a single primordial sequence which is also the lay of the land.

It is also true, however, that these carefully maintained microcosms in social space-time are isolated in the midst of the wilderness: Not only the west but the whole periphery (the pampa or puruma) is still the domain of natural forces and presocial beings (including laritas, wife givers, and potential wives who come from other patrilines and hamlets beyond the pampa) which must continually be constrained and transformed by human activity to reproduce human society. The wild space outside the hamlet is most "disordered" in the uncultivated, unfenced empty spaces (which are also vaguely defined borders) between patriline lands. Yet these spaces are crossed by ritual paths on which people walk (and which they re-create through ch'alla performances) in the repeated intergroup visits of marriage rites and festival pilgrimage.

Marriage is but the first step along what is also a kind of "path" along which individuals become most like the shepherd of men who resides in the sky: authorities over the ayllu and the polity as a whole. This is the jach'a p"ista t"aki, the "great fiesta path," spanning the life career of a couple (and household), from the dawning of the power to unify a herd to the twilight of its dispersion (which is frequently at death, when the persons are sent packing to the west and the underworld with the setting sun, and both herds and lands are dispersed to children).

Paths have beginnings and ends, which are at the same time earlier and later points in a sequence, and likewise fiesta sponsorship or civil office, as a step on a career path, is also a moment in an alternation: The incoming sponsor or authority takes over for an outgoing one, who is a step ahead on his own career path. The coming year's sponsor, called a *machaqa* ("novice"), just starting on his path (that is, of his year of performance, which is the saint-centered analogue of the sun's "year-path"), is always later than and subordinate to this year's, and the groups in whose stead the rite is sponsored are similarly ranked. As the alphas and omegas of fiesta sponsorship, the new and old sponsors of a fiesta stand in a relation very like that of east and west as directions on Tatala's path, and consequently as alax to manxa, "above to below," "outside to inside."

Ayllus and moieties emerged as defined entities of K'ulta (as opposed to being mere parts of Asanaqi ayllus and moieties) out of the rotative-exchange practices through which town council authorities and fiesta sponsors came to be constituted. But the mechanism by which such social units have been constituted is also a kind of historical engine, applicable at more than one level of polity and thus capable of redefining parts as wholes wherever it is applied.

In the present moment of local political and ritual life, four of K'ulta's five ayllus are in various stages of secession from the rest in search of cantonization and autonomy. Each of Ayllus Qullana, Yanaqi, and Ilawi has independently initiated its own system of rotative fiesta sponsorship (and its own internal moiety division) through which the authorities defining them as polities are now produced. Alax-Kawalli, which initiated a cantonization petition (promoted by Pablo Choquecallata) in 1987, for the present still participates in a reduced system of festival alternation with Manxa-Kawalli. Until recently, the two had together formed K'ulta's lower moiety; today they are its moieties, participating together in a complex system of alternation and rotation of town council posts (three for each ayllu) and festival sponsors (three each for five collective festivals). All told (including more minor posts like numerous posts of *alcalde escolar* and the prestigious sponsorship roles that cap a career), members of the two ayllus fill over forty separate civil and ritual offices every year. A three- to four-year rest separates different posts in a single individual's career, so over a span of three years we might very conservatively estimate that 150 of the two ayllus' approximately 600 adult married couples sponsor a feast or occupy a town council post.[1]

Although K'ulta's fiesta-cargo system—centered on the town of Santa Bárbara—has been periodically restructured and is essentially ephemeral rather than an enduring tradition, the present two-ayllu system nonetheless presents itself as a stable order projected well into the future. The sponsorship roles of five different major saints' feasts are interlaced with council posts in a predetermined order of rotation and alternation that is fixed for years in advance, well beyond the point that current political-ritual arrangements are likely to last. Figure 8.1 illustrates the system over a period of years for which I have adequate information. From another perspective, what are concatenated are four different types of ritual careers, in each of which an individual occupies an office or feast sponsorship role every three or four years, in a fixed order.[2] An individual who enters one of the two careers leading, after several religious cargos, to the post of alguacil will eventually (after more religious cargos) reach the post of jilaqata. As it happens, the two jilaqata careers are also called tayksa t"akis, or "our mother paths," since each involves sponsorship of major roles in female saint fiestas. One who wishes to become jilaqata-mayor must carry out the highest-ranking (and also longest and most costly) career, Santa Bárbara t"aki, which takes over twenty years to finish.

Entering a great fiesta path is incumbent on any man who wishes to be well respected in his hamlet and ayllu. A man who has finished his career is also said to be "finished" or complete as an adult, a pasado and

	JILAQATAS						ALGUACILES					
Year	Name	Hamlet	Age	T"aki	Last fiesta	Whose t"aki?	Name	Hamlet	Age	T"aki	Last fiesta	Whose t"aki?
1973	Zacharías Carata	Paxsi Kayu	70	G.	fuera G. 1970	his own	**Benedicto Carata***	Paxsi Kayu	36	S.B.	mayordomo Corpus 1971	his own
1974	Antonio Quispe	Chiyuta	60	S.B.	fuera S.B. 1971	his own	**Zacharías Yucra***	Vintu	34	G.	mayordomo S.Andres 1972	his own
1975	Hilarión Mamani	Vila Sirka	60	G.	fuera G. 1972	his own	Luis Carata	Paxsi Kayu	41	S.B.	mayordomo Corpus 1973	his own
1976	Bentura Anco	Chipana	40	S.B.	fuera S.B. 1973	his own	Tomas Mamani	Vila Sirka	37	G.	mayordomo S.Andres 1974	his own
1977	Juan Canaviri	Q'asa	50	G.	none	heir to father's brother	Urbano Canaviri	Q'asa	38	S.B.	mayordomo Corpus 1975	his own
1978	Donato Mamani	Janq'uyu	25	S.B.	fuera S.B. 1975	heir to father	Cayetano Carata	Paxsi Kayu	45	G.	mayordomo S.Andres 1976	his own
1979	Rufino Vazquez	Sikuyu	55	G.	fuera G. 1976	heir to father's bro's son	Alejandro Yukra	Vintu	48	S.B.	mayordomo Corpus 1977	his own, heir Eleut. Yucra
1980	Eduardo Mamani	Chikuyu	32	S.B.	fuera S.B. 1977	heir to father	Daniel Carata	Paxsi Kayu	25	G.	none	heir to father's brother
1981	Bernardo Yucra	Vintu	50	G.	fuera G. 1978	his own	Casiano Carata	Paxsi Kayu	45	S.B.	mayordomo Corpus 1979	his own
1982	**Benedicto Carata***	Paxsi Kayu	45	S.B.	fuera S.B. 1979	his own	Mariano Lia	Kayuma	45	G.	mayordomo S.Andres 1980	his own
1983	**Zacharías Yucra***	Vintu	43	G.	fuera G. 1980	his own	Andres Quispe	Chiyuta	43	S.B.	Mayordomo Corpus 1981	his own

G. = Guadalupe   S.B. = Santa Bárbara

Figure 8.1. The concatenation of alguacil and jilaqata authority posts, and the braiding of "our mother" great fiesta paths, among hamlets and patrilines of Ayllu Manxa-Kawalli, 1973–83. *Here Benedicto Carata and Zacharías Yucra, alguaciles in 1973 and 1974, respectively, also appear at the bottom of the "Jilaqata" column in 1982 and 1983. In 1985, the 1975 alguacil, Luis Carata, became jilaqata, and so on. Yearly alternation of Guadalupe and Santa Bárbara t"akis is shown in the "T"aki" column, and the "Last fiesta" column indicates the role, festival, and date of the fiesta most recently sponsored by each man. Career paths are heritable; in the "Whose t"aki?" column, note that some authorities inherited their careers from others. The two alcalde posts and their respective "our father" great fiesta paths are likewise concatenated and braided.

jach'a jiliri (great elder-brother), whose voice commands respect in public decision making and who is regarded as having thus gained the full capacity for oratory and myth telling, maximally free from constraint. Boys and young men may be shamed in such contexts; when before a gathering of "finished" men, they are supposed to be "fearful," which is to say fearful of being called *yuqalla,* which is not only a reference term for young boy but also a powerful insult for young men. Spoken to a man's face, the term is an open invitation to fight and (along with other terms comparing adversaries to women and their roles in both domestic and sexual life) is hurled with great frequency during actual fights. Thus it is no small matter that a man who has not embarked on a fiesta career is also thought to be of little weight among his peers and is called (usually behind the back) a yuqalla.

Unless they leave K'ulta (or nowadays, become Protestants), even those couples who do not take up a "great fiesta path" will undoubtedly sponsor saints' festivals during their lives. First of all, of course, there is the weekly cult to the riwusyun image that rules every house. Next, the patron saint of the hamlet's chapel demands sponsorship, which rotates among a hamlet's households and is often the first extrahouse sponsorship engaged in by a newly wed couple. Many patriline hamlets, however, also engage in limited festival systems with other patrilines, alternating in sponsorship of a single "miraculous" saint image, which then takes turns residing for a year in each patriline hamlet's chapel. These kinds of festival alternations are considered extensions of the "small fiesta path," but they also include many features of the great path. Often, patrilines that have become deeply intermarried choose to enter into such a festival system in order to maintain the kinds of group-to-group visits that characterize weddings, after incest prohibitions prevent them from further exchanges of women. When they do so, the asymmetrical (but reversible) relationship of wife giver to wife taker is supplanted by other forms of alternating asymmetries, more akin to moiety rites. This, no doubt, is how moieties within groups like Yanaqi and Ilawi have come about.

Even within the great fiesta path, in which sponsorships and council posts alternate between Manxa-Kawalli and Alax-Kawalli, visiting among intra-ayllu patrilines is required. Two years in advance of his own sponsorship year, during the "rest" period between major sponsorships or council offices, an "entering" sponsor must visit the hamlet of his ayllu's "standing" sponsor. Such visits are extremely complex. Suffice it to note that within the ayllu, numerous patrilines thereby enter into a relationship of structured opposition, but also alliance. In these carnaval-time visits, which double as interpatriline courtship rites, such future sponsors must also erect a kind of maypole in their patio, a flower-covered pole called a *jurk"a*. There the subordinate couple, two years prior to their year of sponsorship, travel to the patio of the dominant couple (who are in their year of sponsorship) to bring a banquet and place pillus, crowns of flowers and bread, on their heads.[3] The crowns and the banquets are reciprocated, but the dominant role is to receive a visit, not to go on one. As far as festival sponsorship goes, the visits are received only by the novena and alférez of Santa Bárbara, the fuera and alférez of Guadalupe, and the fuera of San Andres (sponsorships in each of the four paths). But since standing council authorities, couples who have recently completed marriage rites, and sons at the moment they receive their inheritance from a deceased parent also erect such poles and receive visits from future civil authorities of the same ayllu, in-law patrilines, and godparents, very many interhamlet paths are traveled by visiting groups during the carnaval visiting season.

These visits are not individual affairs; rather, they are between patrilines. The pillu-carrying sponsors-to-be bring with them the meat of two sacrificed llamas, a quantity of food, and a large dance-warrior group, who in this rite are called the soldiers of Santa Bárbara and carry mock rifles and flags in special dance formations. The host group also puts up a dance group, and the two carry out a competition which is not supposed to end up in real fighting. The pillu-carrying duties of the presponsor also correspond to the responsibility to provide a dance group (and warriors) when the sponsor who receives the visit actually "passes" his fiesta. (It was during such a visit that I first met the simulacrum of Hilarión Mamani, Virgilio's dead father and novena for the year his mannequin hosted a visit and wore a crown of flowers brought to him by the following year's alférez of Santa Bárbara. A few hours later, Hilarión's ghost set off on the westward path to manxa-pacha, bequeathing his fiesta path to Virgilio.) So in any given saint's fiesta in the town of Santa Bárbara several groups of allied patrilines within each ayllu converge on the town along their ritual paths, brought together by the crosscutting obligations among sponsorship roles and career types.

Of the three sponsors in a Guadalupe fiesta, two (the mayordomo and the alférez) are from one moiety, while the fuera comes from the opposite moiety. Mayordomo, as the most subordinate role, is required to assist in the alférez's sponsorship, and his own patio and patriline thus tend to become overshadowed by those of the alférez, just as the machaqa sponsors, with the dance groups they must bring, join the activities and dance groups of this year's sponsors from their own moiety while they oppose the old sponsor (of the same type) from the opposite moiety.

During the course of the fiesta, these same-ayllu groups (which have "practiced" their musicianship and joint battle formations during the previous carnaval) merge into a single "army" for a ritual battle against the opposite moiety's congregation. When they merge, they become something other than an army and something other than patrilines: they are unified as a single herd and ayllu and are addressed by the sponsor (whom they call father herder and lead male llama) as his "herd."

All the sponsors and future sponsors converge together on the town of Santa Bárbara during the feast of the patron saint, joining Santa Bárbara's sponsors in massive conjoint ayllu-moiety groups. Each separate patriline must acknowledge the "passing" of the sponsorship from finishing sponsor to entering one, after which the ayllu-moieties as wholes face off against one another in ritual battle, enacting their own dance of encompassment. Kulta society as a whole and all its parts reflect the continuing import of the cycle set in motion when Tatala battled the Chullpas.

Sequences of a Saint's Feast

Within the context of these multipally concatenated and ranked alternations, each type of sponsor (mayordomo, fuera, alférez)—and for each type, both the outgoing and the incoming sponsor—performs a segmented set of ritual duties. The duties of one sponsor very much resemble those of another, but they are differently timed in a complex interweave. A fiesta is segmented, first of all, by space and movement: Sponsors carry out initial and concluding ritual acts in the hamlet, bracketing the central rites performed in the town. Second, a single sponsor's fiesta duties are divided into discrete chunks of action as large as a full day's events. The names of such stages of fiesta performance suggest that the sequence of major segments follows the logical and temporal order of two partly overlapping llama sacrifices. Named segments of the fiesta corresponding to parts of a sacrifice (which are also carried out on many other ritual occasions) are uywa ispira (dedication), qarwa k"ari (killing), and ch'iwu (banquet, distribution). Other major segments of the fiesta reprise these steps in condensed or expanded versions. Within each major chunk there are more numerous named events, and these are further subdivided. Within qarwa k"ari, for example, there are subsegments called q'uwa, paq"arayaña, tinku, paxcha, ch'iwu, jañachu, and qurpa, each of which recurs in other segments within the fiesta.

Some kinds of named ritual action (again, those which are parts of a sacrifice) are repeated several times during the fiesta. Thus there are four events qualifying as paq"arayaña, two q'uwas, three performances of the ch'allas called ch'iwu, and so on. The multiple and overlapping repetition of the sacrificial sequence establishes stanzalike formal parallelisms, which repeatedly mirror in microcosm the overall structure of the fiestas as a whole. Sacrifices are carried out again and again, but the identities of sacrifier, sacrificer, victim, commensals, and deities of dedication, differ in each case.[4]

A fiesta performance in K'ulta lasts from four to six or seven days, depending on issues of scheduling.[5] Regardless of the number of days involved, a fixed set of named ceremonies must be performed in a determined order and in specific localities. From one perspective, a fiesta works through the symbolic relations between hamlet and town by the staging of events: Libations are performed for the herd and hamlet deities, and some llamas are sacrificed in the hamlet; then the ritual participants become pilgrims in a sacred journey to the town, where more sacrifices are performed, banquets given, a battle fought, and sponsorship relinquished. Finally, a reverse pilgrimage takes place, bereft of the foodstuffs expended in the town, and final libations are poured to the hamlet deities.

Such a scheme divides fiesta rites into public (town centered) and private (hamlet centered) types. Only the former are likely to be observed by outsiders. Without close familiarity with fiesta sponsors, nonparticipants will systematically misunderstand the meanings of town events (determined in relation to hamlet ones). The corollary form of structured miscommunication results from interpreting only the clandestine practice as an authentic indigenous meaning world.[6] The colonial situation created a divided space and communicative barriers between public acts and clandestine ones; the observer who takes the part for the whole is deceived by the legacy of colonialism, constitutive now of postcolonial predicaments and the interpretive debates of folklorists, ethnographers, and historians, and of indigenistas and indianistas.

The Unifying Metaphors of Herding and Sacrifice

Sacrifice is not only a secret practice tied to herding and hamlet, but is also absolutely fundamental to the fiesta performance as a whole. Indeed, the stages of sacrifice structure the division between hamlet "privacy" and town "publicity." *Uywa ispira uru*, "animal vespers day," when the sponsor makes dedications in his hamlet house, comes first, followed by *qarwa k"ari uru*, "llama cutting day," when animals are ceremonially killed within the hamlet corral. After a journey with the llama herd and patriline to town, in a reprise of the food-laden return from valley caravan trips, comes the more public *marka qarwa k"ari uru* or *wallpa k"ari uru*, "town llama cutting day" or "chicken cutting day," actually a second llama sacrifice, perhaps reduced to a chicken slaughtered when a zealous priest is around. Finally, there are *p"isturu*, "fiesta day," and *ch'iwuru*, "meat/cooked 'heart'/shade/black cloud/ llama young day." The first two days and last half-day of the feast are those performed in the hamlet. Consequently, the casual (outsider) observer of public events in the town is unlikely to see the festive banquet, drunken boisterousness, and saint image–related ceremony as

Fiesta day	Liturgical moment	Time	Saint image	Sponsors	Llantirus	Q'uwa llantiru figurines	Tulqas as jañachus	Dancer-musicians
Uywa ispira day one (in hamlet)		P.M.	paq"arayaña (textiles)			paq"arayaña 1 (q'uwa leaves)		
		dawn				paxcha 1 (burned)		
		A.M.			paq"arayaña 1 (yarn)			
Qarwa k"ari day two					paxcha 1		paq"arayaña 1 (llantiru pelts)	
(in hamlet)							paxcha 1 (feigned)	
		noon			ch'iwu 1			
caravan to town	romería	P.M.			paq"arayaña 2 (tinku outfits)			
		A.M.			paxcha 2 (tinku)			
Wallpa k"ari day three		A.M.			ch'iwu 2		paq"arayaña 2 (llantiru pelts)	
	pasacalle	noon					paxcha 2 (feigned)	
(in town)	(ispira) vespers	P.M.				paq"arayaña 2 (q'uwa leaves)		
	(alwa)-alba	dawn				paxcha 2 (burned)		
P"isturu day four	limusna waku	A.M.						paq"arayaña (feet and bronchia)
	procession and mass	A.M.						
(in town)	(qurpa: throw bread)	P.M.		paq"arayaña (gift textiles)	qurpa banquet (inter-patriline)			
		P.M.						tinku/paxcha (ritual battle)
Ch'iwuru	(isi turk"a)	A.M.	paxcha (clothes off, gives blessing)	"tinku/paxcha" (pass to machaqa)				
day five caravan to hamlet	romería	A.M.		paq"arayaña (saint's clothes)			paq"arayaña (saint's clothes)	paq"arayaña (saint's clothes)
(in hamlet)		P.M.			qurpa banquet (patriline ch'iwu)			

Figure 8.2. The fiesta as sacrifice: concatenated event sequence. The days and names of the fiestas, as well as the locations of activities, are indicated in column one. Column two describes the corresponding "official" liturgic sequence (the items not within parentheses), all of which may be completed if a priest is present for the fiesta. Approximate time of day is shown in column three. Columns four through nine display the concatenation of "actual" and "metaphoric" stages of sacrifice experienced by all principals of the fiesta: At two separate moments llantirus are "made to flower" (paq"arayaña), "made to flow" (paxcha), their "hearts" are eaten (ch'iwu), and their meat is divided and eaten in a banquet (qurpa). One set of sacrificial acts takes place in the hamlet, and the other in the town. This dual sacrifice is also experienced by small llama-fat figurines of llantirus and wife takers (tullqas); the saint image, sponsors, and dancer-musicians undergo a single sacrificial sequence, each predicated on the other. Yet more complex forms of concatenation link one sponsoring couple's event sequence to those of other sponsors in the town, as well as to other-ayllu machaqa sponsors who will replace them: Machaqas begin a full sacrificial sequence one day later than sitting sponsors. The liturgical sequence performed when a priest is present also involves a metaphoric sacrifice with its own stages of dedication, consecration, and consumption.

integral parts of an imbedded pair of llama sacrifices dedicated not only to the saint and Christian deities of the town but also to a plethora of underworld deities and ancestors tied to the altars of the hamlet.

Repeated and more intimate participation in fiestas, which for me was possible only after staying in Vila Sirka for over a year and gaining the friendship and trust of Mamanis, who were drawn to me by their own frontier leanings,[7] revealed that each of the named days of the fiesta is segmented into a multitude of named ceremonies, the majority of which are also connected with sacrifice. The sequenced metaphors of fiesta rites (see Fig. 8.2) establish the formal equivalence of llamas, persons, saints, and gods, expressing their analogous powers in terms of their exercise of hierarchic control (such as "herding"). It is by metaphorically transferring such powers from distant sources into themselves, through herd animals and saint images, that K'ultas create themselves as herder authorities and as fully formed human adults. Having located the originary sources of human agency in processes of long-past events, they must bring that past (fortunately for them located just around the corner, in the landscape that holds their memory of it) to bear on the present in order to take control over the way the future will unfold. Saints' festivals and sacrifices are for them a means of "writing" a history that supports their present projects and the futures such projects build.

A JACH'A P"ISTA PERFORMANCE: THE EVENTS OF GUADALUPE, SEPTEMBER 1982

In September of 1992 I returned to K'ulta, forearmed with the knowledge that another Mamani would then carry out a sponsorship role as the fuera of Guadalupe. This time it was the turn of Tomás Mamani to fulfill his festival obligations.[8] I had not seen much of Tomás during carnaval of 1981, when Virgilio and his father's mannequin, as that year's novena of Santa Bárbara, were visited by the 1982 alférez of that festival, because Tomás had gone on a visit to the hamlet of the 1981 sitting fuera of Guadalupe.

Having prepared quantities of chicha and amassed large amounts of corn and wheat for the coming banquet, Tomás and his wife carried out their uywa ispira memory path on the night of September 6, two days before the saint's day of September 8. Through the night, they had prepared their q'uwa bundles, containing miniature pairs of llantirus made of fat and the aromatic q'uwa herb, and had burned them at dawn at their secret q'uwaña place on the slope of their household's uywiri hill.

Early in the morning, when I arrived to accompany them, along with Bartolomé Mamani and his wife, Basilia, who had been asked to serve as wasu wariri libation specialists, Tomás and his wife, Petrona Gómez, prepared to carry out the memory path of qarwa k"ari, that of "llama cutting," in the corral where they kept their male llamas. Qarwa k"ari libations are very similar to those of uywa ispira, although they begin with a ch'alla to the corral altar and its t'alla "mate" rather than to that of the house. In contrast with uywa ispira libations, qarwa k″ari also includes chicha, and therefore much more attention to the gods of the sky and the saint to whom the fiesta is dedicated. Since during qarwa k″ari the llamas that provide the meat of the festival banquet are actually killed in the definitive moment of sacrificial offering (uywa ispira and the banquet in town being other parts of the sacrifice as a whole), the focus in qarwa k″ari libations is very much upon the animals that are killed, the *tinkur llantir awki,* the "father (awki) caravan leaders (llantiru) who go to ritual battle (tinku)."[9] As in uywa ispira, libations recall animals, animals' altars, and the herd's ancestry through a listing of corrals. But there are also ch'allas to the animals' patron saints' towers (in chicha), especially to San Antonio, who is patron of the male herds. At their altar, women drink ch'allas for Guadalupe, who is a patroness of the female herd. In addition, chicha is poured and drunk for the Solar-Christ and Moon-Virgin, for their attributes and those of the saints such as lightning, and for the saints' altars upon the hamlet's mallku hill. As the ch'allas proceed, there is also a good deal of talk, mainly about the llamas and their individual histories.

During qarwa k″ari of 1982, Tomás Mamani's larita (his father's sister's husband) arrived in the corral somewhat late, well after the corral had been dedicated by encircling it with incense braziers, and after the men's altar had been consecrated with libations to jira t'all misa, "the altar of dung lady plain," as they call the stone corral altar, surrounded by a thick layer of dried llama manure. At the women's altar, Tomás' wife, Petrona, had poured the first libation to jira t'all misa t'alla, the women's altar laid out flat on the ground, around which the women sat on the thick mat of dried llama dung.[10] Tomás' father's sister's husband was immediately inserted into the seating order next to Tomás himself (that is, second in line), and given a rapid series of ch'allas to catch up with the rest of the group. In the ch'alla performance, each participant must drink for each entity libated, so Bartolomé moved around the men's altar (Basilia did the same a few yards away) proffering drinks and coaching the drinkers on the libation dedication accompanying each one, in a fashion known as *wasu muyuyaña* ("encircling with the cup").

Paq″arayaña and Paxcha (Making Bloom and Spurting Blood)

Interruption, competition, and joking are all built in to qarwa k″ari. When the elders had begun the wife's and mother's corral sequence, the service personnel, including Tomás' *tullqas* (the husband of one of his sisters, accompanied by a younger brother and another young man who

Photograph 8.1. Making llamas bloom, María Colque and José Mamani. Vila Sirka llama corral, carnaval 1980. (Photograph by author)

is godson to Tomás), decorated the herd of llamas, which still huddled together within the corral, impatient to get out to pasture, by sewing colored yarn through the animals' ears, an act referred to as paq"arayaña (see Photographs 8.1 and 8.2).

Photograph 8.2.   Paq"arayaña: making the herd bloom. Manuel Mamani prepares to sew paq"ara, "flowers" made of colored tufts of yarn, into ears of a llama. The rest of the herd awaits the same fate, while women, facing west, pour libations at their altar. Hidden from view by the llamas, Mamani men sit at their raised stone altar, facing east, a few yards beyond the women. Mamani corral, Vila Sirka, 1980. (Photograph by author)

When all had been thus decorated, including female llamas and the alpacas brought to the corral for this purpose, Tomás pointed out four llamas that would be killed, and his tullqas tied their legs and pushed them down in a kneeling position. Tomás' young daughter then drove the other animals out of the corral while Tomás and Petrona threw bowls full of *ch'uwa* (a clear liquid byproduct of chicha manufacture) over their backs.

While the corral libations were in progress, the tullqas pacified the bound llamas. They gave the llamas coca to chew and chicha to drink by pouring it into their forcefully opened mouths, calling the chicha the animals' lake ("so that the chicha does not run out") and referring to the coca as their grass ("so that the pastures flourish").

Photograph 8.3. Paxcha: Alax-Kawalli musicians play a dirge in a Culta patio, honoring sacrificed llamas. A pair of llantirus (herd leaders) have just been dispatched in the paxcha ("flowing") after this sponsoring group's arrival at their hamlet house in Culta. Culta, September 1982. (Photograph by author)

When the corral sequences were finished, the llamas to be killed were directly libated in pairs, with ch'allas for tinkur llantir awki, the "herd-leader father [who goes] to tinku," and for his yanani, the second such llama. Just before killing them, the tullqas held up to their noses a special bag of coca, so that the tinkur awkis would breathe their life into it, "and their color/pattern type will not die out in the herd."[11] Then, in a moment called the paxcha (flowing), the tullqas pulled back the llamas' heads and quickly cut their throats through to the bone, making sure that the blood spurted toward the rising-sun side of the corral (see Photograph 8.3).[12]

While the blood flowed out, Tomás (who up until this point had been leading ch'allas at the men's altar) scooped up handfuls of blood and smeared it across the faces of each paq"arayaña and paxcha participant, in an act reminiscent of Inca sacrifices when blood was smeared on the face of the wak'a idol, "almost from ear to ear." Flicking some drops of blood towards the sunrise point on the horizon, Tomás dedicated the flowing blood to the sky deities Santisima Mamala (Moon-Mother) and Tata Awatir Awksa (Sun-Father Herder).[13] The Solar-Christ thus partook of a K'ulta Eucharist and of the llama blood, which here, as we shall see, stands for the sacrifice of himself, in which Tomás was engaged. Chicha ch'allas were then given again for the patron saints of the herd and for the sun and moon. While the animals lay upon the ground and tullqas began to butcher them, a dance group of Mamani youths approached the corral and began to play a dirge on their panpipes, ending on their knees in an open circle outside the corral.

Death and Resurrection of the Tinkur Awkis

After spilling the blood of the sacrificed llantirus, the tullqas and other low-ranking followers (such as unmarried sons, younger brothers, etc.) butchered the carcasses as quickly as possible. Meanwhile, the men at their altar inside the corral began the ch'alla list called ch'iwu (again, meaning "meat," "shade," "black rain cloud," and "llama progeny"), which is directed to the deity-guardians and "ideal types"[14] of all forms of foodstuffs and to every desired type of herd animal (not including, however, terms for sterile males or, at the men's altar, females).

At the same time, Petrona's assistants, collectively called *yuqch'as* ("daughters-in-law," though they included unmarried Mamani girls along with young Mamani wives), took away the animals' *chullmas,* or "hearts" (in our anatomical terms, the lungs and liver), and stomachs, and rushed to cut up and boil the organs as swiftly as possible.[15] At this point the continuation of the ch'alla, the butchering of the llamas, and the cooking of the "heart" were all carried out in a kind of competition, in which Petrona's assistants sought to interrupt the ch'alla as quickly as possible with the presentation of small bowls of cooked pieces of liver and lung (rather, semicooked, this being how the women win this particular competition) at both men's and women's altars. After the plates of ch'iwu, they served bowls of potato and stomach soup. With this, the ch'alla was interrupted, and we all ate our portions, awaiting the next interruption.

The "Infertile Studs" (Jañachu)

Moments after the chullma was served, that is, while we were still eating the internal organs (and vital essence) of the tinkur awkis, a pair of tullqas burst into the corral wearing llama bells and the pelts of the sacrificed llantirus, still including the heads and feet. Bleating like frantic llamas, they began attacking and mounting all present in feigned llama mating. After some minutes of raucousness and laughter, Tomás and Bartolomé pacified these "human llamas," newborn members of Tomás' herd, giving them paired draughts of chicha and mouthfuls of coca, saying, "Here is your lake, here is your fodder," just as they had done to the animals before killing them. The jañachu, as the ersatz llamas are called,[16] were then driven out of the corral by Tomás' whip- and sling-wielding younger patriline brothers. Not far away, these herder-assistants captured the tullqa-llamas, throwing them to the ground. Feigning the action of cutting their throats, they then pretended to sacrifice the tullqa-llamas, who had become a humorous kind of "anti-llantiru," and had relieved the sponsors' sense of loss after having killed a significant number and valued part of their herd.

At this point, Tomás and Petrona and their wasu wariris began the ch'iwu ch'alla list anew from the beginning, this time to be carried through to the end without further interruption. During the second and complete performance of the ch'iwu ch'alla path, the sponsor's dance group, now including the tullqas, formed again and circled the corral. Once finishing the ch'allas in the corral, Tomás and Petrona returned to their patio altar, where they hosted a repast for their followers.

Hamlet-to-Town Pilgrimage

On the afternoon of the same day, the assistants of Tomás and Petrona loaded their llama troop with all necessary provisions. Dressing the lead llamas, the llantirus, with articles of human clothing, the entire entourage then began a pilgrimage to the ritual-center town of Santa Bárbara.[17] The entire herd had already been "made to flower" with colored yarn in the ears, and the lead males were adorned in significant items of mature men's dress (taken from the sponsor and his close followers), such as long scarves, coca bags (ch'uspas), charm bundles (carrying cloths worn by men around the waist, containing a supply of coca and items bringing luck in travel and fighting), and, topping it all off, monteros, battle helmets in the conquistador style. The overall effect of these adornments is the same as that which caravaners strive for on the last leg of their return trips from the valleys, similarly laden with foodstuffs, after yearly winter expeditions for provisions. It is not dissimilar to the effect of the image of Ekeko for city folks. But it also continues the metaphoric equation of humans and llamas, granting to the living llantirus a status like that which Tomás is in the process of achieving. Later on in the fiesta, these metaphoric transfers of leaderly qualities become yet more apparent, for Tomás will become a llantiru of the human herd.

On the journey from the hamlet to the town of Santa Bárbara, in this case a short one, Tomás as fuera carried the sacred miniature retablo image of Guadalupe that he had kept in his hamlet chapel all year, now wrapped in numerous weavings (in this case, women's outerwear lliq-llas). After an entire year of caring for the saint in their hamlet, Tomás and Petrona prepared to give the saint high honors, before handing it over to the incoming sponsors from Ayllu Alax-Kawalli.

Following one of the six (major) ritual paths which enter K'ulta from outlying hamlets, they stopped every now and then in order to place the image upon a series of sacred stone altars for "rests" and special libations.[18] At each stop their band of musician-dancer-fighters played a tune on their panpipes, dancing in a circle around the altar, image, and libation-pouring sponsors and elders.[19] The members of the dance group dress as for battle, wearing monteros, heavy shoes or boots, and matching jackets.[20] Though they do not partake of the sponsors' libations, they do perform alcohol libations according to their own special ch'alla lists while they accompany the sponsors from hamlet to town and back again. Throughout the fiesta, they play at numerous appointed moments, becoming a fighting unit in the tinku, or ritual battle. We have seen that these dance groups "practice" their perfor-mances during the previous year's carnaval rites, in which they play an instrument called a t'arka while also in military guise. In the sponsors' own hamlet and in the journey to town, the dancers are those recruited from the sponsors' patriline and subordinate individuals. Arriving in town, however, they will be challenged, and then joined, by the dance group of the entering sponsor who visited with pillus in the previous carnaval. The joining of same-ayllu sponsors and dance groups, when they converge on the town along their individual paths, is an important aspect of fiesta rites, leading, among other things, to a tinku (a term which also refers to merging paths or rivers, as well as to intermoiety battles).

Town Qarwa K"ari (Wallpa K"ari) and Ispiras

When the entourage arrived in town, they proceeded to their hamlet's house, on a patio shared with other Mamani hamlets. As some of the helpers unloaded the caravan herd, and Tomás and Petrona rather unceremoniously poured some quick libations upon the patio altar there, while the tullqas sacrificed more llamas, without the benefit of a full ch'alla performance.[21] Accompanied by the Mamani dance group, they all then proceeded on a round of visits in the temporarily lively and well-peopled town, giving special ch'allas to the church tower and plaza[22] and paying special visits to the council office and the houses of the occasionally present vecinos.

In the town qarwa k″ari, ch′allas are conspicuously fewer and more haphazard. There are very few of the numerous alcohol libations for uywiris and mallkus (such as those performed in the hamlet qarwa k″ari; in their place there is a decided predominance of chicha libations directed towards the more "Christian" saints and sky gods. Receiving special attention are the highest, most universal alax-pacha gods, Tata Awatir Awksa ("Our Father Shepherd," referring simultaneously to the sun and to Jesus Christ), and Santisima Tayksa (or Paxsi Mamala), "Our Most Holy Mother" (or Moon-Mother), referring to the moon and to the Virgin Mary, whom K′ultas regard as Tatala's wife.

This contrast between hamlet ch′allas, emphasizing the manxa-pacha mountain deities, and town ch′allas, emphasizing the alax-pacha sky deities, no doubt reflects the proximity of the town to the saint's residence and the more encompassing quality of the performance and the authority to which this proximity leads. It also, however, seems a product of priestly surveillance and the Counter-Reformation practices that bifurcated the Andean cosmos along lines resembling the division between "Spaniard" and "indian." K′ultas are well aware that outsiders (such as the priest, visiting provincial officials, and the enterprisers who come to fiestas for commercial purposes) regard rites to the mountain gods as sacrilege, and they willingly mislead such observers about the purposes of town libations.[23]

But we need not imagine that the hamlet-town contrast results from an intentional effort to keep local practice clandestine. My interviews with don Bartolomé suggested that wasu wariris recall their "paths" as generic kinds of hierarchies, which take specific shape according to the place of performance. In the town, altars are connected to saints' paths, not to patriline uywiris and mallkus; likewise there are few corrals in town, and none that are consecrated with ritually active altars. Thus the corral sequences get short shrift in the town performance, while other segments of the "type" list are greatly expanded (that is, those pertinent to sky deities and to the extrapatriline hierarchy of mallkus). Nor is Tomás Mamani's town patio altar connected directly to the Mamani uywiris and mallku, but to uywiris and a mallku of the town, which are shared by all K′ultas and are thus of a considerably higher rank than the others.

The "type" ch′alla sequences boil the particularity of the gods of distinct contexts down to their essentials; the result amounts to a narrative diagram of the hierarchy of gods and also the channels of social hierarchy. Thus this mnemonic device serves to reproduce the underlying and resultingly shared understanding of social-cosmic structure, and to equate metaphorically the hierarchies of hamlet and town, creating a basis for linking local and global orders.

Formal Visiting in the Town

Once the town qarwa k"ari has been completed, a round of formal visits begins. The displacement of manxa-pacha deities from the context of the Christianity-dominated town implies an encompassment of the hamlet (and local, "indigenous" uywiris and mallkus) by the hegemonic forces of town-centered alax-pacha. So too, formal visits in the town foreground an imbedded set of subordinations: The patriline is subordinated to the ayllu-moiety; each moiety is subordinated to the other; and all participants are subordinated to the town's symbolic state representatives.

During formal visiting, Tomás and Petrona and their followers proceeded from altar to altar through the town, stopping to pay homage to their hamlet's places in the town; then to the church and its male turri mallku (tower peak/condor); to the corners of the female plaza (the plasa t'alla); to the altar of the saints on the slope above the church, a stone table carved out of the living rock that is called Inka Misa; to a series of altars associated with town government; to the former parish house, kitchen, and corrals; and then to the office (and its altar, an adobe desk) of the corregidor, who, along with his jilaqatas, alcaldes, and alguaciles, waits there for the sponsors' homage. In Photograph 8.4, don Bartolomé Mamani serves as wasu wariri during visits of the town in the fiesta of Santa Bárbara, 1979. After this, the entourage visited the altars of the two occasionally resident outsider-storekeepers. Finally, the dancer-musicians and the sponsors visited the compounds of the other sponsors in the town.

The town as a whole is a kind of condensed diagram of the social space of the whole of K'ulta, with separate neighborhoods divided among K'ulta's ayllus, and a line running diagonally east to west through the plaza separating the former moieties. Visits along the altar-to-altar paths in the town therefore become icons of visits (and the relations thereby construed) among patriline-hamlets during the rest of the year. The intersponsor visits, which are initially among sponsors of the same ayllu-moiety, recapitulate carnaval pillu visits between patriline hamlets. Once same-moiety sponsors have merged their dance groups and coordinated their activities, however, the oppositional and hierarchic form of intramoiety (and interpatriline) visits is generalized to the inter–ayllu-moiety level, during which the schisms among intra-ayllu patrilines are nullified. During the latter visits, the year's authorities (sometimes accompanied by armed soldiers or, as in the fiesta of Santa Bárbara in 1979, by the province's subprefect with his pistol)[24] wield their whips and strive to keep order.[25]

During the night before the feast itself, called ispiras, the sponsors, important guests, and young people drink and dance around bonfires in the plaza, with jula-jula groups of each sponsor encircling their sponsors in multiple and separate formations. Merging of the groups is avoided, because the tinku between conjoint groups from each moiety should not take place before the saint's mass (of the following day). Those ayni contracted for the service roles spend the night preparing quantities of

Photograph 8.4. The fiesta of Santa Bárbara: dancing in the plaza before tinku. Notice the matching jackets and the cowhide and lard-tin helmets. Visiting merchants hawk their wares (mainly foodstuffs) around the plaza. Patriline dance groups merge into two opposed moiety groups, striving to outplay and outdance one another. When jostling leads to individual fights, dance groups become fighting platoons, moving onto the nearby plain, called tinku pampa. Santa Bárbara de Culta, December 4, 1979. (Photograph by Mary F. Dillon, used with permission)

food for the following day's feast. When public dancing in the plaza breaks up (when the firewood is depleted or the cold too intense), the sponsors and libation specialists repair to their house to prepare another q'uwa, an offering to be burnt at dawn, this time on the uywiri to the east of the town. The authorities independently prepare similar q'uwas of their own. Young people, meanwhile, break up into small groups and couples, dancing through the streets most of the night, singing popular Quechua love songs to strummed charangos.

P"isturu (Fiesta Day)

P"isturu is the day of the fiesta proper. On this day, the events held to be most important (and of most interest to noncentral participants and observers) take place: the formal transferral of sponsorship from old to new alférezes and mayordomos (the fuera transfer takes place the next day); the banquets offered by the sponsors of both moieties; the ritual battle; one of two annual tasa collections (held by the assembled authorities at Kawiltu Misa ["kawiltu" from Sp. "cabildo"]); and, if the priest comes to town (a rare occurrence apart from the patron saint's feast of Santa Bárbara), a procession around the plaza of the principal saint image (normally kept in the church), and a mass held in its honor. If the priest is present, p"isturu is also a day of numerous weddings, baptisms (and other rites of compadrazgo), and funeral masses.[26]

P"isturu opens with a predawn performance of the q'uwa, followed by ch'allas at Inka Misa, Kawiltu Misa, and the sponsors' (and authorities') town patio altars. While the q'uwa burns, the dance-musician groups of each sponsor proceed from their patios to the church door for a formal visit, known from Spanish liturgies as alwa (Sp. *alba*, "dawn"): As dawn breaks, they play a solemn tune, hats off and facing the rising sun. After this the group visits the patio of each sponsor in turn. While playing a song, the visiting group is given (by each sponsor in turn) a bottle of alcohol and the cooked ribs (*pichu*) of one llama. The musicians then return to their own sponsors' patio for breakfast.

Kawiltu Kupraña (Tax Collection)

During the festival of Guadalupe (and again at a minor festival in January, reflecting colonial custom), council members lead a special ceremony, that of tax collection. At about ten in the morning, the authorities (who have received visits from the musician-dancers and accompanied the sponsors on their round of visits) begin their own round of conjoint visits. Assembled jilaqatas, alcaldes, and alguaciles tour the town while blowing their bulls'-horn trumpets (pututus), calling the gods and the members of their ayllus to attend the kawiltu misa. Beginning with the church tower, the authorities (carrying bundles of varas wrapped in vicuña wool scarves) proceed to Inka Misa, then visit the patio of each sponsor, where they both present and receive ch'allas while their vara bundles and pututus rest on their sponsors' altar. Finally the authorities arrive at Kawiltu Misa, where they begin their own ch'alla sequence specific to tax collection.[27]

When the authorities are ready to receive payment, they set off a pair of dynamite charges. When the sponsors and their followers enter the patio in which Kawiltu Misa is located, they are presented with more ch'allas of alcohol and chicha and asked to libate the great mallkus by the authorities, who act as their own wasu wariris. Again, a women's altar has been laid out opposite Kawiltu Misa, and the sponsors join the authorities (and authorities' wives) behind their respective altars, jointly receiving tasa payments. Authorities and honored sponsors are here addressed by tasa payers as tata awatiri and tata awki ("father herder" and "father-father"), and when each man pays his tasa, he is addressed by the authorities as llantiru, and dances around the altar and the authorities, braying like a llama and blowing a pututu taken from the altar.

Recently married young men paying for the first time are accorded special respect and may carry a patriline vara as they dance. As part of a kawiltu performance (both here and during the other collection on January 20), the authorities name the following year's sponsors, again giving special homage to those who are just beginning their jach'a p″ista career (who are the same young men paying for the first time).[28]

While the payment takes place, all the musician groups play (each their own tune) and dance simultaneously, crowding the kawiltu patio. Each dancer wears his montero, now decorated with greenery from the molle (pepper tree), for this performance (as well as all performances to follow). Meanwhile, the assistants of the fuera and alférez erect tents over the (men's) altars of their patios, in preparation for their banquets.

Kiyun, Bandera, Qurpa, and Procession

When the tax collection is finished, in the early afternoon, each sponsoring couple and their retinues proceed to the church, where more ch'allas are poured. If the priest were in town, he would begin saying mass at this time, and the procession would shortly follow. Normally, however, there is no priest and no (major image) procession. The sponsors nonetheless enter the church with their small images, which they place in front of corresponding saint elder while the dance groups play on their knees just outside the door. Lighting candles and llama untu for both large and small images (which visit one another briefly before another year-long separation), the sponsors offer incense and ch'allas of sugared tea and ask the saints for a blessing. From the alcove behind the image, the fuera (and other male sponsors) takes a kind of velvet flag on a pole, called a kiyun (Sp. *guión*, "guide"), as a symbol of his sponsorship of the rites of the major saint image. Sponsors' wives receive a small white flag called a *pint"una*.

When the sponsors emerge from the church, with their standards and miniature images (and the major image, if the priest is present), the church bells are rung and all go forth in a procession around the plaza, stopping with their image bundles and standards to pour ch'allas at each corner of the plaza. As they finish this circumambulation, with musicians dancing in circles in the center of the plaza, their assistants throw miniature loaves of bread (qurpa) from the tower into the plaza, which those in the assembled crowd, including pilgrims from afar who have come to pay personal devotion (related to shamanism) to the saint, scramble to pick up.

"Qurpa" is a term with many meanings, most of which seem related to hospitality functions.[29] On the one hand it refers to a guest, and on the other, to a meal served a guest or to a banquet (such as that which the sponsors will soon serve). Here it refers to the small loaves which sponsors' assistants throw from the top of the turri mallku. It is quite possible, as Tristan Platt (1987c) suggests, that the act is also an allusion to the myth of origin of cultigens, which burst from the stomach of the overstuffed fox (who the mallku condor could not carry) when he hit the ground on his return to earth after a banquet in heaven. The profusion of small round loaves may also allude to the self-multiplying host (which in the countryside is not given to participants of the mass).[30] Thus the sacrificial sacrament is linked to the sacrificial communion about to take place in the sponsors' patios.

Ilija (Election) of Machaqa Sponsors

After the procession and qurpa, each sponsor proceeds with his standard to the patio of the incoming machaqa sponsor of the same sponsorship role. Here they mark the formal "election" (*ilija*), already prefigured in the authorities' nomination, by receiving two large (two- to three-liter) gourds of chicha for each participant, which must be dedicated to the saints and then passed by sponsors to their followers, who each say words of dedication and then drink. Not long afterwards, the machaqa sponsors visit the patio of this year's sponsors, and each is given a meaty, cooked shoulder blade (*kallachi,* which is the charango of the suitor-fox in another myth of the trickster cycle) from the sacrificed llantirus.

The (Qurpa) Banquet(s)

Once they had finished ch'allas and visits of ilija, Tomás and Petrona (like the other sponsors) served a banquet at their patio altar. Announced by the concussions of a few sticks of dynamite, the banquet drew a large crowd. Descending on the meal, the sponsors' *arkiri* ("followers"), the authorities, and the opposite moiety contingent assembled. If the sponsors meet expectations, enough food is distributed so that all are sated and carry home hats and ponchos full of excess food. The sponsors will be condemned if the food and drink do not exceed the appetites of the crowd.[31] This feast must demonstrate a generosity of spirit and an ability to constitute a congregation of followers, to lead and subsume and contain, akin to that of the gods they celebrate (Photograph 8.5).

Photograph 8.5. Women and children await the banquet. The fiesta of the Exaltation of the Cross, Santa Bárbara de Culta, September 14, 1979. (Photograph by author)

Paq"arayaña of Sponsors

After serving the high-ranking guests, Tomás and Petrona moved to one side of the patio and began to dance to the accompaniment of their dancer-musician group. This began a ceremony called paq"arayaña, like the decoration of llamas' ears before the hamlet qarwa k"ari. This time, however, it was not yarn sewn into the ears. Instead, Tomás and Petrona's close followers—especially their cohamlet residents, brothers and sisters, and other Mamanis, but also their tullqas and subordinate helpers—gave their thanks by dunning Tomás and Petrona with gifts. With each gift, Tomás and Petrona served the giver a pair of especially large cups of alcohol, called t'inkas.

Gifts—called paq"ara ("flowers")—were invariably articles of clothing such as ponchos or lliqllas, or other woven or twined goods such as blankets, carrying bags, belts, llama-hair rope, or slings. These were draped over the sponsoring couple's shoulders. In the act of "making the sponsors flower," participants make an explicit as well as implicit reference to the paq"arayaña of the llamas before their sacrifice.

The equation is accomplished, in part, through the name of the rites: "paq"arayaña" also carries the connotation of "making fertile," and "paq"ara" is the ch'alla term for newborn camelids. But the most explicit equation of sacrificial llamas and sponsors is in the terms of respect by which giver and receiver address one another at this moment. In drinking the t'inka, the gift givers called Tomás llantiru and awatiri (and called Petrona llantir t'alla and awatir t'alla, the female counterparts of the male terms), and the sponsors responded by addressing givers as *tamaña* ("my herd").[32] When the paq"arayaña and the serving of food at the sponsors' altars are finished, the whole crowd moves on to other patios to yet further, equivalent banquets.

Town Ch'iwu and Jañachu

Once back at their own patio, Tomás and Petrona presided over another round of ch'iwu events (reduplicating the corral events of the hamlet qarwa k"ari. This time, however, the libations were begun within the privacy of their town house, and it was there that the ch'iwu (the boiled liver and lungs) was eaten. Afterwards, they began the ch'alla sequence ch'iwu t"aki, preparatory to a secondary banquet eaten by their helpers. Again the meals are interrupted by the appearance of the wild and uncontrollable jañachu.[33]

The Tinku Battle

During the feast of Guadalupe, Ayllus Alax-Kawalli and Manxa-Kawalli engage in the ritual battle known as tinku (or ñuwasi). Though these may be quite serious in their consequences, such battles are regarded as mere practice sessions for the Santa Bárbara tinku, in which the two Kawalli ayllus merge to face Ayllu Qullana, which as of 1982 still participated in this festival.

In many ways the tinkus of K'ulta are less formally organized than those of neighboring Macha (reported in Platt 1978a). The authorities make a show of trying to break up individual fights, though some secretly plan (with feast sponsors) for the organized fighting which often follows fist fights. Though often precipitated by a series of individual-to-individual fights in and around the plaza, the face-off between upper and lower Kawalli fighters takes place on a small plain just above the town. Most fighting is by the dancers, well prepared with helmets, shoes, and padding under their clothes. As the fiesta progresses, the dancing takes on increasingly aggressive forms, and while all sponsors visit the church tower and authorities, their dance groups (swollen by the addition of late-arriving members) compete in wide and menacing circles, with increased jostling when the two circles meet. When fighting actually breaks out, the groups—joined by other nondancers—rush to the tinku pampa. Here the battle elevates from individual fist fighting to an affair of strategy, in which the two sides rush one another in turn and hurl rocks—often provided by wives and sisters—with their fighting slings, while elders (and women in particular) shout encouragement to their side and hurl insults at the other.[34]

I was unable to witness fighting on the tinku pampa. Once the subprefect began firing his pistol to stop the plaza melee, panicked food sellers jammed into our house seeking protection, and my friend Manuel Mamani pushed me inside as well. Insisting that this was dangerous business for me to watch or photograph, he locked us all in, so when night fell along with a hail of stones, we settled into a huddled mass to sleep. He was certainly correct that it is dangerous business, since the immediate object of each side is to cause serious injury or death to a member of the opposed group and, if possible, to rush in and drink some of a fallen enemy's blood in a coup de grâce. We have seen that such events have also become strategies of rebellion; vecinos in larger towns know what they are doing (and why) when they arm themselves behind well-closed doors. The battle ends with nightfall, serious injury, or fatality, not to be repeated until the next major fiesta.

Ch'iwuru or P"wiruru (the Day after P"isturu)

The final day of ritual action in the town is a short one. Sometimes called ch'iwuru (day of meat/cooked"heart"/young/dark clouds) and sometimes p"wiruru ("day of the fuera") because the central acts are carried out by the outgoing and incoming fueras, the day is given over to preparations for the return trip to home hamlets and to the passage of the saint's image from the old sponsors to the new ones, all of which is usually accomplished before midday.[35]

After breakfast, Tomás and Petrona prepared to send their retablo image of Guadalupe on a journey into the territory of Alax-Kawalli as their last public ritual act (which is the first one for the incoming sponsors). At first sight, the act is straightforward enough: Outgoing sponsors demonstrate to the incoming ones that the image and all its possessions are intact, hand it over, and then all leave town. But a closer look reveals that the saint's passage, in a rite called *isi turka* ("changing/exchanging of clothes"), is structurally parallel to that of other fiesta events. Once again, it is a form of sacrifice.

Isi Turka

Fundamentally, the ceremony of "clothes changing" is a sequence of acts among three parties: the outgoing fuera couple and their followers, the incoming (machaqa) fuera group, and the image which is passed from the former to the latter. During a round of ch'alla visits to the tower and plaza, in which Tomás as fuera carried the sacred bundle one last time, some of his lower-ranking aides loaded the assembled herd and headed off on the return trip to Vila Sirka. The elders, the wasu wariris, and most others remained behind for a while to assist in the image's last rites. When their ch'allas were finished, Tomás, Petrona, and their retinue returned to their patio and laid out a new misa on the ground between the men's and women's altars.[36] Laying the saint bundle on the altar, they served another form of ch'alla,[37] meanwhile carefully removing each piece of "clothing" that covered the image box of the saint.

The first articles to go were a dozen lliqllas and ponchos, the iconographically complex outerwear items worn by adult women and men (and made by women), which had been wrapped about the image box (just as Tomás and Petrona had been draped in such items as paq"arayaña gifts during the banquet). When all of these were removed (and lay beneath the wooden box containing the miniature image), the box was opened and the saint's possessions were laid out and counted. These consisted, first of all, of a large number of miniature items of clothing (patterned on local dress), from among which fueras dress the saint image itself.[38] There was also a small box containing the saint's money, consisting of bills and coins (primarily antiques) and receipts from priests for festival masses, added to the pot over many generations. Then with much reverence, Tomás and Petrona undressed the image itself.

After they had completely disrobed the image, they prepared an incense offering, like the *supliku* of a lurya misa. The placed two plain ceramic bowls filled with burning embers on each of a pair of small planks of wood. The bowls on one plank (that to the right, facing the saint) were dedicated to the Solar-Christ (Tata Awatir Awksa), and the left-hand pair of bowls were dedicated to the Moon-Virgin (Santisima Tayksa). Then, kneeling together before the image (Tomás on the right, Petrona to his left), each held a plank and raised it repeatedly while assistants sprinkled powdered incense and small pressed incense cakes over the coals and smoking untu. As they raised the planks, the couple intoned dedications to the saint and again to the gods of the sky, in the usual gender parallel form (so that the left-hand bowl on the husband's plank was dedicated to the yanani of each of the deities of dedication, while the right-hand bowl of his wife was for the yanani of the feminine counterparts of Tomás' dedications). Asking for a *bendición* ("blessing"), they put the incense bowls down and each touched a corner of their own outerwear garments (poncho for the man, lliqlla for the woman) to the exposed image, through which the blessing passes. Then the sponsors' followers repeated the same procedure, always in pairs.[39] When the Mamani group finished this procedure, they waited in silence while those in the machaqa group took their place.

When all had finished receiving the image's blessing, the machaqas tallied the articles by type and compared this with a list kept in the saint's money box.[40] Finally, the machaqas replaced the saint's clothing; first the miniature clothes, then, adding the ponchos and lliqllas provided by their followers, they rewrapped the image's box in a new set of outerwear. While the image was being dressed, Tomás and Petrona sorted out the outerwear textiles in which the image had been wrapped for the previous year, and draped them over their own shoulders and those of close followers who had lent the weavings to begin with.

Pilgrimage from Town to Hamlet and Final Ch'iwu Meal

At this point the transaction was complete. The saint's annual pilgrimage had brought patrilines and ayllus to the town where their interrelationship is articulated, and now she sent both groups on return journeys to their home hamlets. Draped in gift cloth, Tomás and Petrona led their followers back to Vila Sirka, some of them wearing the saint's clothes and all having received the saint's benediction and a touch of lurya.[41] On arriving back home, Tomás and Petrona marked the end of their year of sponsorship in a final and private ch'alla and banquet (called ch'iwu). Like the first of these ch'allas and meals carried out in the corral, the final ch'iwu ch'alla is directed towards the local deities of patriline and hamlet, rather than the shared ayllu and moiety deities of the town. When the meal was finished, the fiesta was over. Another year or so would pass before Tomás and Petrona began the ritual duties connected with the next step on their great fiesta path. In 1985, that step made Tomás Mamani a jilaqata of Ayllu Manxa-Kawalli.[42] In the meantime, the hamlet and patriline rallied on the fiesta paths of other couples.

GODS, MEN, AND LLAMAS IN HERDING AND SACRIFICE: POETICS
OF A K'ULTA EUCHARIST

Two aspects of the fiesta performance deserve our immediate attention. The first is the priority given to sacrifice in both word and deed. The second, related to the first, is the expression of a profound identification between the journeys and powers of person, llama, saint, and gods above, developed through the formal parallelism between the segments of the feast and made explicit through the repeated use of a special set of honorific terms.

A single sponsor's performance includes two complete llama sacrifices. One sacrifice begins in the hamlet and is concluded with the distribution of meat in the town; the second begins in the town and is concluded with a meal in the hamlet. Such counterpointed sequencing and repetition of the stereotypic acts of sacrifice play a crucial role in establishing the meanings and achieving the desired ends of a fiesta. (See Fig. 8.3.)

Why carry out two concatenated llama sacrifices (interlaced with those of machaqa sponsors) in such a complex form? A preliminary step in answering the question hinges on recognizing the differences between the town and hamlet gods to whom the sacrifices are dedicated, and the different character of the "communities" established through the distinct banquets. Focusing exclusively on llama sacrifices, however, is to miss the point, for the herd animals and herding metaphors serve to express sacrifices of persons, saints, and, yes, of Jesucristo. Llama sacrifice grants K'ultas access to the power of the Eucharist.

Not only does a sponsor sacrifice his llamas (which are killed by his wife takers), but he also symbolically sacrifices his own followers. In the jañachu he offers up his tullqas in their llama disguises. Then the

Role	Dates	Main Duties	Other Duties
Escolar	School year	Supply bread to schoolchildren.	Assist teacher in 6 de Agosto pageant.
Mayordomo of San Andres	Nov. 30, '62 to Nov. 30, '63	Perform sacrifice for festival; reside for six weeks in Culta; care for image, perform twice-monthly cult; care for saint's "goods."	With alférez, make arch (arku) for church during fiesta of Santa Bárbara (Dec. 4); maintain until Jan. 1.
Machaq alguacil (alguacil elect)	Jan. 20, '64 to Jan 20, '65	Attend quarterly común wilara sacrifice for varas with sitting authorities.	In carnaval 1964, carry flower crowns (pillus) to that year's alguacil during carnaval.
Alguacil	Jan. 20, '65 to Jan. 20, '66	Attend council meetings; serve as bailiff and jailer under jilaqata; attend ayllu festivals; round up disputants; walk mojones with jilaqata.	During carnaval 1965, erect jurk"a pole, perform sacrifice, provision feast, and receive pillus from next year's alguacil.
Machaq fuera (fuera elect) of Guadalupe	Sept. 8, '70 to Sept. 8, '71	Perform sacrifice; supply provisions and dance-group tinku platoon to accompany 1971 fuera; attend 1971 fuera mid-year cult.	In carnaval 1971, perform sacrifice, provision feast, and carry pillus to standing alférez of Guadalupe (of Exaltación t"aki).
Fuera of Guadalupe	Sept. 8, '71 to Sept. 8, '72	Perform cult to image in hamlet on new or full moons; perform sacrifice; supply provisions and dance-group tinku platoon for 1972 fiesta.	In carnaval 1972, erect jurk"a pole, perform sacrifice, provision feast, and receive pillus from machaq fuera of Guadalupe.
Machaq jilaqata menor (jilaqata elect)	Jan. 20, '74 to Jan. 20, '75	Attend and assist in quarterly común wilara sacrifices for varas led by 1973 jilaqata.	In carnaval 1974, perform sacrifice, provision feast, and carry pillus to sitting jilaqata of ayllu.
Jilaqata menor	Jan. 20, '75 to Jan. 20, '76	Sponsor quarterly común wilara sacrifice for varas; attend weekly council meetings; collect tasa; walk mojones in ritual journey; carry varas to Condo for San Pedro fiesta; mediate disputes; attend ayllu fiestas.	In carnaval 1975, erect jurk"a pole, perform sacrifice, provision feast, and receive pillus from machaq jilaqata of same ayllu.
Alférez of Corpus	June '77 to June '78	Perform sacrifice and provision feast; lead procession; with Corpus mayordomo, erect arku in Culta church; maintain to Jan. 1.	
Machaq novena (novena elect) of Santa Bárbara	Dec. 4, '79 to Dec. 4, '80	Perform sacrifice and supply provisions and dance-group tinku platoon to accompany 1980 alférez on Dec. 4, 1980.	In carnaval 1980, perform sacrifice, provision feast, and carry pillus to standing alférez of Santa Bárbara (of Santa Bárbara t"aki).
Novena of Santa Bárbara	Dec. 4, '80 to Dec. 4, '81	Perform sacrifices and provision feast on Dec. 4, 1981; provide dance-group tinku platoon to join other Manxa-Kawalli groups.	In 1981 carnaval, erect jurk"a pole, perform sacrifice, provision feast, receive pillus from both machaq alférez and standing fuera of Santa Bárbara (both Santa Bárbara t"aki).

Figure 8.3. The principal duties of a single career path (Guadalupe tayksa t"aki), as illustrated by the career of Hilarión and Virgilio Mamani. The sequence does not include hamlet-level and interhamlet duties of the "small fiesta path" or other principal life-crisis rites of the human social career as a whole from birth to after death. Such rites entwine individuals in relations of mutual obligation from the moment an infant is named, through marriage, house building, first tasa payment, participation in dance groups of both one's own patriline and that of the larita, and duties performed in spirit and in effigy after death. Although duties were carried out by Virgilio Mamani after Hilarión's death in 1978 (with his mother in 1980 and with his new wife in 1981), Hilarión was present in effigy through the carnaval of 1981.

subordinate, not-yet-adult dancers are offered in the tinku battle, in which their blood is spilled upon the plaza and the pampa. In return, the sponsors' own followers make them bloom by draping over their shoulders the "social skin" made of the animals' pelts, even as they exclaim that the true sponsors of the feast are the mallkus and Tatala himself, whose herds are men. Finally, all together sacrifice the saint's image, "making it bloom," removing its "clothing," and receiving the substance of the mediating power it represents.

The identification of man and llama begins during the rites of qarwa k"ari in the sponsors' village corral. Here the male sponsor honors the herd when his assistants decorate the animals' ears and backs with spun and died yarn and then asperse them with ch'uwa (clear chicha), an act called paq"arayaña.

Subsequently the sponsor's wife-takers, his sisters' or daughters' husbands, are transformed into "human llamas" and demand that they themselves receive paq"arayaña, or at least part of it (the ritual food and drink). So the sponsor's control over the herd is explicitly equated with his control over a class of men, through the similitude established by what amounts to an exchange of "pelts": The tullqas, being an effeminized and laughably ineffectual kind of men, express their adolescent sexuality in the clothing of the jañachu, the weak and "laughable" alpaca stud. The llantirus of the herd, which are soon to be sacrificed in earnest, are subsequently dressed in the clothing of an admired class of men, the tinku fighters, for their entrance into town.

Complicating matters is the sponsor's equation with the llama, though unlike his wife-takers he becomes the llantiru (by being addressed as such beginning in the hamlet festivities). During the banquet of p"isturu, he and his wife are again equated with llamas during their own paq"arayaña. Thus the male sponsor is identified with the sacrificial victim and with the role of herd leader. But if he is the sacrificer in the corral, who is the sacrificer of the sponsor? The answer must be *the gods,* especially the sky gods (but also the major mountain gods), who are the herders of men (awatiris). Indeed during the ch'allas just prior to the ritual banquet, followers exclaim that "the sun is sponsoring the fiesta" or "the saint is sponsoring the fiesta" or "the mallku is sponsoring the fiesta."

However, the sponsor is also addressed, during his paq"arayaña (as is the jilaqata during many of his rites, such as the kumun wilara), as "awatiri" (herder). As such, he usurps the place of the god (who, as herder of men, should be the one to sacrifice them). Acting *in loco dei,* the sponsor symbolically sacrifices certain categories of followers. He is the sacrificer of the jañachu, of course, but also of the not-yet-adult men of the patriline.

In their roles as dancers, musicians, and warriors, the accompanying group of young men (who also come to the feast prepared for courtship), along with the tullqas, become the sponsor's human herd. And in the tinku, they are compared to the tinkur llantir awkis, the sacrificial llamas "who go to tinku." The llamas are, of course, killed and their blood and fat offered to the gods. In the tinku, the dancer-musician-fighters seek to injure or kill an opposite-moiety fighter, not to offer the blood to their gods, but to scoop it up and drink it, inverting the direction of sacrifice.

In the distribution of meat during the day of the banquet, this equation is again stated in the nature of the dance group portion. In what constitutes the return of the sacrificed llamas in the form of the dance group, the sponsors drape the boys' shoulders with the feet and tracheas of the sacrificed llamas, all the better to sing and dance, run and shout.

The "sacrifice" of the wife-takers (as jañachus) and the young men of the male sponsor's own patriline (as an unspecified type of llama) marks both as members of the herd of which the sponsor is at once the lead male (the llantiru) and the herder (awatiri). So the sponsor takes both the role of the ideal sacrificial victim in the human herd, the llantiru, and that of the sacrifier of that herd, the awatiri, and especially of Tata Awatir Awksa, "Our Father Shepherd," which is to say the Solar-Christ, Tatala. His dual role is consistent both with the social function of the authority, who must mediate between the group and state authority by being simultaneously a member of both orders, and with a vision of the nature of the internalized hegemonic relationship between the state and its associated sky gods, on the one hand, and K'ulta society and *its* local, underworld animal-herding gods, on the other.[43]

In the final "sacrifice" of the fiesta, as the last act carried out in the town, the fuera gives up the image to the following year's fuera, from the opposing moiety. In this rite, the spatial configuration of participants neatly recapitulates both social and cosmic orders. Like the llama which gives up its blood and fat to the gods, its "heart" and breath to humanity, and its pelt and body parts to "human llamas," the saint gives up its blessing after being symbolically butchered. The sponsors and their followers then go home to their hamlet dressed in the clothes of the saint.

People thus dressing in the clothing of the gods refers us back to other exchanges of clothing in the feast. Remember that the llama herd comes to the ritual-center town dressed in the clothes of men; the sponsor's human herd (typified by the jañachus) dresses in the clothing of llamas; the sponsors (like the saint image) dress in the transformed pelts (weavings) during their paq"arayaña. All are iconic indexes of the raising of the clothes givers to the honored status of sacrificial victim and an appropriation of certain of their substances and/or qualities by the wearers. In the last instance, the sponsors' followers return from their tinku with the opposite moiety, dressed in the saint's clothes, in a transformed state, embodying the power of mediation enacted in the fiesta's transformation of human control over llamas into authorities' control over men.

The ancestral wak'as and mountain gods that were once "created" by clothing them in precious cloth and the sacrificial pilgrimages construing social memory still persist in K'ulta, but the visible, tangible, and portable manifestations of the mountain gods and the ceque paths of the pilgrimages have been taken over by the saint images and pathways to churches and chapels. Saints now serve as the intermediaries through which people can speak with the gods, whether those inside the mountains or the heavenly shepherd of men. And it is only through being clothed in the "skin" of the saints that men become authorities capable of bridging the gap between the gods of the conquerors, the K'ultas, and the mountains.

Making use of saints' dual powers to travel horizontal pathways linking social groups and vertical ones bridging the gap between the here-and-now of this earth and the distant-and-past creative journey of Tatala, K'ultas appropriate for social use the agentive and transformative power they attribute to the god of conquest, who first harnessed Chullpa powers to the seasonal round and not only brought agricultural and herding life-ways to men, but also made human life itself a journey leading to death. By appropriating Tatala's powers, K'ultas lay claim to control over their own destinies. To do so, they have understood those agentive powers as a relationship between space and time, laid out on the landscape on which they live.[44] The practices they must use to control their destinies are historical ones.

Colonial and postcolonial state domination is (and has long been) an inescapable reality, made into an integral part of peoples like those of K'ulta, and not only as an external force impinging on the territory at its political-center town. It is a truism to say that without the forces of alax-pacha, there could be no human society as envisioned in K'ulta and no manxa-pacha to oppose itself to the gods and men of the conquest. But much more fundamentally, such polities have internalized the form and processes of conquest into their very hearts; the relationship of adult to child, man to wife, father to son, elder to junior, wife giver to wife taker, all are construed in terms of the imposition of a form of hierarchic control appropriated from without, as a species of self-conquest. This is never so explicit as in the relationship between men and women, in which men make themselves into privileged "encompassers" of other men (and women) by claiming the status of herders, even while they label the arduous labors of actual herding as unworthy "women's work."

No doubt, as Denise Arnold (1988) insists, women have their own ways of inverting the value system so that they come out on top, just as men have done vis-à-vis the colonial and neocolonial forces of the state. Such forms of symbolic amelioration of gender asymmetries are very much worthy of study. But as the (mostly male) activists of Bolivia's "indian nationalism" might respond, there is no amelioration like taking hold of tangible political power.

In K'ulta, political power and that of effective human agency, of which political office is a special case, are achieved by taking a historical turn, bringing the struggles of founding moments to bear on those of today. Every K'ulta likens himself (and in a different way, herself) to the ancestral hero Tatala, seeking to embody the powers that make self-determination, a fully human existence, and effective political action possible in daily social life. This would not be possible without the commemorative monuments engraved on the landscape that link their personal life-stories and political struggles with those of their antecedents and provide pathways that help to recall, and to make palpable and manipulable, the historical logic of conquest that established the concentric asymmetries of power in which K'ultas are enmeshed.

INVERTED MEMORIES: FROM K"ARISIRIS TO PROTESTANTS

Not all K'ultas are entirely convinced by the sacrificial ways of doing history that I have described. Some, especially younger men like the textile trader-turned-truck driver I had met in Cruce and Julián Mamani, whose efforts to turn the past to his private benefit sent him to jail, were positively cynical about the old ways. This does not mean, however, that they no longer believe in miracles—only that the miracles they seek now require rites more like the ones their fathers condemn as evil sorceries. This is especially true since the mid-1980s, when prolonged ecological catastrophe devastated the crops and herds of the Altiplano and led massive numbers of K'ultas to emigrate temporarily or permanently to mining centers, cities, and, especially, to coca production zones. The mining sector also collapsed in this period, so the high wages available for the job of treading coca leaves (mixed with kerosene) into the first stage of refining cocaine were especially welcome. When K'ultas move to cities, mines, or coca zones, and consequently forsake their herds and fields in favor of wages, the beautifully elaborated poetic order

equating men and llamas ceases to convince. New circumstances require
new ways of understanding how man makes himself. Migrants need not,
however, invent themselves from scratch, for centuries of sustained
intercultural contact in the cities have generated a creolized culture,
replete with thousands of native "speakers," out of the former fruitful
miscommunication of cultural pidgin.

I introduced some of these notions in chapter 2, in reference to the
witches' market of Sagarnaga Street, the magical miniatures of the La
Paz Alasitas fair, and the figure of a commodity-laden mestizo Ekeko.
Other related examples are well described in the literature of mining
beliefs. Miners, who are union or guild organized and celebrate festivals
in honor of the patron saints as rural ayllus do, have no uywiris or
mallkus linking their homes to fields and pastures, for they have no herds
or crops. Instead, they dig in the earth for minerals. Deep inside the
mines, as Nash (1979), Taussig (1980) and Platt (1983) have extensively
documented, miners also pour libations and sacrifice llamas to manxa-
pacha beings called *tios*, revered as devil-shaped statues. The tios
resemble nothing more than the uywiris in their most dangerous,
human-form incarnations, capable of seducing the unwary towards a life
of ease that drains them of their life-substance. So too do tios strike a
bargain with miners, granting them mineral wealth in exchange for
frequent tribute, but also taking their pound of flesh. Tios can be kept in
check, however, by paying heed to the mine's patron saints (a practice
that goes without much comment in the cited analyses). In the mines and
the cities, "Christian" deities of the above and "chthonic," diabolized
indian deities of the underworld appear as caricatures of their rural
counterparts, stripped of all subtlety and cast into a stark Spanish versus
indian opposition.

That being so, it is no surprise that tios, like Ekeko and a host of new
chthonic shrines associated with urban patron saints, all demand tribute
on precisely Tuesdays and especially Fridays, when traditionalists in
K'ulta refuse to sacrifice llamas. In K'ulta, these days are saxra, "evil,"
days, when sorcerers work their dark spells, the kind that cause harm
rather than cure it. Men like the textile trader I had met in Cruce, whose
goal was to accumulate capital and avoid sharing it out among his
patriline mates, are suspected of just such sorceries. Gaining through
mysterious methods forms of wealth that are mysterious in themselves
(resting, not on harnessing the productive capacities of Chullpa powers
through Tatala labors, but on exchanging commodities) cannot be
explained other than through the use of inverted forms of ritual

production. My wealthy young friend in Cruce was certainly thought to have "gone to the dark side" in order to accumulate his wad of hundred dollar bills; and for abrogating the fundamental principles of sociality, he was also called q'ara, an insult meaning "naked" or "culturally peeled," that is, lacking in the social graces of a proper jaqi. In all truth, it must be said that K'ulta suspicions about his having practiced antisocial witchcraft were entirely correct.

The young man, who is today a vecino living in some other town, exiled from K'ulta but more fully integrated into "national culture," confided to me that he has found a productive "secret," one which I witnessed in another textile trader's storeroom. Forsaking the household riwusyun intercessor that most K'ultas keep, miniature saints' images, these young men (as I noted in chapter 4) have taken skulls of their own ancestors from the cemetery, and now pay them a gruesome cult exclusively on Fridays, in imitation of the urban and miners' preference. In between trading trips, they keep their dollars locked in the jaws of their skulls, each of whom is addressed by a personal name. I was able to learn little more about these practices, which are widely condemned within K'ulta, but which also may be a wave of the future. In a treatise on the practices of powerful yatiris in the La Paz region, however, Tomás Huanca (1989) reports a very similar practice. There, the skull-riwusyun is purposely collected from the burial place of known, evil individuals, whose terrible sins make them condenados, souls who shift uneasily between embodied and disembodied form, permanently wandering this earth with no hope of entering heaven. Our capitalist practitioners, it seems, hope to harness and control the condemned soul so as to invest their money with spirit (very much like Taussig's Cauca valley cane cutters). Huanca's yatiris, however, use the skulls' malevolence to inflict damage on their clients' enemies in a form of sorcery that in K'ulta is also frowned upon.

From a K'ulta purview, both commit an even more fundamentally antisocial act. No matter whose skulls they are, removing them from the ground and exposing them to the sky risks bringing about a punishing drought, presumably because Tatala recognizes in them his old Chullpa enemies, in need of yet another desiccating blast of fire. To make money into capital, in other words, is to unbalance the generative powers of the K'ulta cosmos and to impoverish one's kinsmen. This, at least, is how a greedy kinsman chooses a path that makes him a stranger. How, then, do K'ultas understand strangers and interlopers like ethnographers, priests, urban market intermediaries, and textile traders who come from elsewhere, possess no lands or herds, and draw on fat and inexplicable bank accounts? My own explanations of my source of support, a "research fellowship," were never regarded as satisfactory. Some K'ultas, I was to discover, had their own theories about how I prospered without, apparently, doing a lick of productive labor.

Q'aras and K"arik"aris: Capitalism and Vampires

Not long after Easter of 1980, Mary and I ran out of supplies, money, and health, and returned to La Paz for a break from fieldwork. We were gone for about three weeks. I had wanted to return in time for the preparations for Corpus Christi, one of K'ultas five festivals, and we made it back in plenty of time. But something had changed the demeanor of my Mamani friends.

It did not take long to get to the bottom of the problem. Just before our departure from K'ulta, a Carata man, one of this year's mayordomos, had arrived in Santa Bárbara to carry out his duties as caretaker of the church and its images. During our absence, he had suddenly and mysteriously died one night while engaged in libations and incense offerings to Santa Bárbara with some visiting yatiris. Now, the Caratas are the patriline that had sought a warrant of arrest against my Mamani hosts in Vila Sirka for having murdered one of their men during a festival fight. Clearly this feud now played into what happened next. It does not, however, explain it away.

There being no reasonable explanation for his death, the Caratas threw the blame on me. I was, they said, a k"arik"ari or k"arisiri, literally a "cut-cut" or "fat cutter." This is a well-known sort of demon in K'ulta: Many have said that the priest is one; others have reported suspicions about certain schoolteachers, Cruce vecinos, and marketeer interlopers in the territory. This being a widely understood and very serious accusation, I had a good idea from the literature of what was meant and the sort of trouble I was in. In most of the cases I knew of where ethnographers (and often archaeologists) had been so accused, they had been forced to flee, sometimes fortunate to get away with their lives. That is because k"arisiris are so terrifying to K'ultas and hated by them that the guilty party must be killed. A k"arisiri, in essence, is a being capable of putting ordinary humans into a trance and then magically removing their very life force, leaving the victim no memory of the event and no scars as evidence of the crime.[45]

We have already encountered an early k"arisiri scare, in Molina's parroting of a priest's 1570 report from Parinacochas, when indians accused Spaniards of stealing their body fat. There, the term used was "ñaqaq," a word that also means "one who cuts," but which additionally designated the Inca priest who actually put sacrificial victims to the knife. The difference when applied to Spaniards was the use to which such fat was supposedly put: It was said to be sent to Spain, where it was transformed into holy oil.

Nowadays, k″arisiris, whose name also recalls an association with sacrifice (qarwa k″ari), turn the substances they magically remove from healthy rural people into money, deposited in banks. Although k″arisiris have a decided preference for the fat that adheres to internal organs, especially that around the kidneys, they do not limit themselves to fat. Their appetites also run to blood. As it was explained to me, the blood of city people is "bad." So to maintain their vigor, they must periodically exchange their blood for that of a healthy person. Rather than seeking a transfusion in a hospital, k″arisiris go straight to the source, performing a blood exchange with their stupefied victim, in which the victim receives the exhausted and bad blood and gives up the potent blood of the countryside.

Body fat and blood: No doubt the reader has noticed, as Gose (1986) brilliantly deduced by combining Bastien's (1978) account of the circulation of sacrificial substances and ethnographic descriptions of k″arisiris, that the substances involved are precisely those that contain the generative power that is Tatala's due in festival sacrifices. K″arisiri practice, that is, amounts to a terrible and antisocial manipulation of the logic of sacrifice. Whereas festival sponsors symbolically offer themselves to Tatala by metaphorically equating themselves with the llantirus that are killed, the k″arisiri takes the god's portion, not of a metaphoric human body, but of a real one. The k″arisiri performs a travesty of the herders' Eucharist and takes vital generative powers out of the proper form of circulation among gods, men, and animals, in order to produce an antisocial kind of wealth that cannot sustain itself, but must be periodically renewed through additional knifery.

Don Manuel explained this to me in some detail so I would be forearmed when the Caratas made their move, which was very soon. I was dumbfounded. I had in fact been far away from K'ulta when the death took place, but no alibi could save me here. K″arisiris can become invisible, so my absence proved nothing.

The situation was no joke. Mamanis informed me that a group of Caratas had come by Vila Sirka just a few days before, and they had kicked down a few Mamani doors and thrown some sticks of dynamite.

They promised to come back until they found me. The very next day I saw one of the Carata men in Santa Bárbara. He made the sign of the knife across his throat and told me that I would be "butchered like a llama" for my crime. I had to do something, and ethnographers' traditional reticence in reporting these kinds of experiences gave me no clues as to what I should do. Fortunately, I still had friends on the town council, and that was my recourse. Acting on the advice of Manxa-Kawalli's jilaqata and alcalde, I made a formal *denuncia* before the corregidor, demanding that the Caratas come forward to explain their threats of violence. Council officials advised me to take the denuncia to Challapata and to bring the subprefect, and his gun, back with me. Instead, I got his signature on my *demanda,* to lead the Caratas to believe that friends in high places might come to my aid. When I returned from Challapata, the council issued an arrest order and brought some fifteen Carata men from their hamlet to the council office, where we faced off under conditions more to my liking than a lonely interhamlet path.

While I was not actually tried for blood- and fat-sucking witchcraft, the Caratas did repeat their accusation, which I roundly denied. I too accused them of trying to get at the Mamanis through me. Finally, the corregidor summoned the registro civil, who wrote out an acta de buena conducta, a routine measure when no outright resolution of a dispute is forthcoming. The document that I signed, along with the Carata men, promised that whoever engaged in any recurrence of violence would face a fine of five thousand pesos (just the amount that had sprung a Mamani from jail where he had been held for killing a Carata). The document itself was not reassuring. More to my liking was the formal apology ceremony that ended the session. Following the corregidor's instructions, each of the Carata men knelt in front of me and apologized for any unintentional affront while shaking my hand and clasping me around the shoulder. When they were finished, it was my turn to do the same, and the event came to an end.

I have been back to K'ulta many times since then, and only once has this business with the Caratas been problematic. Of course, I avoid taking the long path from Cruce to Santa Bárbara, which passes through the Carata hamlet in an isolated and rocky little valley. And on one visit, when I discovered that the Carata man who had promised to cut my throat was jilaqata of the ayllu, I saw fit to cut my stay short. Fortunately for me and for the feuding K'ultas, such roles rotate to other patrilines every year.

As a person enmeshed in the logics of wages and commodified social relations, I will always be an interloper in places like K'ulta. Joining the ranks of K'ultas who are themselves alienated from the brand of social memory expressed in fiestas, libations, and stories of Tatala, I will also remain a q'ara, a "culturally naked" person devoid of essential knowledge of proper human sociality, suspected of inverting "traditional" K'ulta methods of undoing the sorcery of history with its memory.

However, from my perspective, and indeed from the perspective of disaffected K'ultas who convert to Protestantism or become vecinos in other towns or proletarianized migrants to the city, sacrificing to tios in search of money and commodities, my own techniques of social memory are not inversions of someone else's, but a means to my own personal, social, and historical ends. As for sixteenth-century Spanish chroniclers, my effort to encompass and inscribe a history of K'ulta and K'ulta histories can also be construed as insidiously colonizing and imperialist, even though I turned down K'ulta offers to settle there as a store-owning vecino. Whether or not we claim any special ethnographic authority or scientific objectivism, however, we all seek to understand ourselves in the mirror of our encounters with "others," even when we construe those encounters as pasts or as histories. Let us then take stock of the relationship among the many kinds of social memory I have surveyed.

Chapter Nine

Conclusion
Ethnography and History of
Social Memory and Amnesia

*Our very laws were made by our conquerors; and whereas it's
spoken much of chronicles, I conceive there is no credit to be
given to any of them; and the reason is because those that were
our lords, and made us their vassals, would suffer nothing else to
be chronicled. We are now engaged for our freedom; that's the
end of parliaments, not to constitute what is already according to
the just rules of government.*
—John Wildman, *Putney Projects*

ORALITY AND LITERACY, ETHNOGRAPHY AND HISTORIOGRAPHY

I have sought in this book to bring about a cohabitation (if not a
marriage) of historical and ethnographic sources and methods, so as to
write a history of K'ulta and also account for K'ultas' history. Using the
concept of social memory, I have also aimed to question tacit assump-
tions about the supposed gap between oral and written culture that has
helped to shape the disciplinary divide between anthropology and
history. I have not used the term "ethnohistory" to characterize my
enterprise, precisely because the term tacitly routinizes the antinomy
between orality and writing, anthropologist's interview and historian's
source, that I seek to question. Rather than referring to "another people's
way of doing history," along the lines of other "ethno" anthropological
specialties (such as ethnobotany, "another people's knowledge of
plants"), "ethnohistory" has simply served as a label for the ghetto into
which we place the pasts of peoples without writing. It has long been an
anthropological ghetto, populated by book chapters on the precolonial
situation. "Ethnohistory" has not often been used to label the study of
myth and cosmology (apart from the approach of a few who treat them
as oral sources of objective chronologies), because these are the opposite

408

of what historians often regard as their own object of study. Historians have long thought themselves to be debunkers of myths rather than students of them.

Although today various postmodern turns among historians have led them to seek out the "secret" and unchronicled stories of subordinated peoples, dominated classes, and patriarchally silenced women in various places in the world and many points in time, devising, in order to do so, innovative approaches to documents (those of social and cultural history, for example) such as I have tried to use here, they have still not often turned their attention to peoples without writing. Even less often are historians terribly interested in the distinct ways of interpreting the past in which the past peoples they write about may have engaged. No matter what inroads the various postmodernisms have made into the profession, the discipline of history remains that of objectivism, and the historian's work is judged by the adequacy of his or her writing as a representation of "what actually happened," or at least "what was actually written."

In one way at least, historians and ethnographers have long engaged in similar means of laying claim to disciplinary authority, means of a sort that have of late come into question in both disciplines. Historians play on the duality of the term "history" to suggest that their line of work, writing history, is a relatively unproblematic business of providing an account of history in the commonsense meaning, the "what really happened" of the past. Anthropologists, in contrast, use the term "ethnography" to describe both what they write and the process of fieldwork through which they learn about the subjects of their writings. Playing on this slipperiness in comparable ways, historians and ethnographers grant themselves authority (underwritten by university degrees) to make pronouncements on the truth or empirical factuality of "what happened" or "what they were actually like." Through such techniques, both sorts of scholar have long evaded fundamental questions about the politics and partialities that underlie their work.

These are the ruminations, the reader should recall, of a symbolic anthropologist who found himself turned into a historian. Neither my historian colleagues nor my anthropologist ones will perhaps find my disciplinary (transdisciplinary?) transgressions amusing. There are some good reasons for the existence of disciplinary specialization. There are also, however, good reasons to work on disciplinary frontiers.

There is no arguing, though, the degree to which written and unwritten pasts supplement as well as challenge one another, or at least challenge disciplinary boundaries. When I, as an anthropologist, began to talk seriously about working in archives to supplement understandings of the past gained through ethnography, a prominent historian advised me to cease and desist. Orally transmitted memory, he told me, is unreliable as a historical source after the passage of only a few generations, perhaps only one. If I was interested in history, he said, I should gather oral accounts of the past, especially that known to my interlocutors through personal experience, the results of which might then be collated with documented facts by a professional historian.

Regardless of the admonitions of such disciplinary gatekeepers, I have found that writing about the past using documentary sources and writing about ethnographic presents on the basis of talk and observation are in many ways not only complementary projects but also similar ones. The kinds of nonwritten social memory that I foreground in my ethnography, imbedded in ritual acts and formulaic speech and grounded in meanings lived in the social landscape, do not often leave written traces. The colonizing state demanded writings for its archive, and subordinated peoples were duly represented there. But the colonial self was divided into public and private, canonic and clandestine. So colonized peoples' most successful contestations of the colonial project remained largely uncharted. They could not be understood on the basis of the official public "text" of orthodox practice, but only by "reading" their hidden and mostly nonverbal commentaries. K'ultas do not interpret the Eucharist through sacrificial metaphors, incorporating into themselves Christ's powers, for the benefit of priests and other outsiders. They do so for themselves.

There have been many pitfalls in carrying out my project, not the least of which is the fact that what I write is itself a representation with scholarly pretensions, although not necessarily objectivist and scientific ones. I have nonetheless made sure that readers know I was actually present in K'ulta, striving through text and photographs to establish my ethnographic authority (as one who was there, who saw and experienced and can therefore provide a reliable report), just as I have cited archives and quoted from documents, grounding historical interpretation in solid (tangible, seeable) evidence. Regardless of my disclaimers, these are standard objectivist credentials. To demystify such pretensions at least in part in the ethnographic sections of the book, I have taken a reflexive turn, remaining on the scene in my accounts so that readers may judge the adequacy of my account and recognize its origins in discourses and power-laden social relations, rather than in antiseptic observation.

My reflexive turn in history required a somewhat different approach. I have described in a few cases my relationship to the documents I quote or cite, but demystifying the process of historical interpretation and writing is more difficult.[1] The historian's work methods, such as the process of determining what constitutes an acceptable topic, the selection of documents for analysis, and the determination of what is relevant or irrelevant to the topic, are all easily concealed from the reader; historical representation is no more transparent than ethnographic representation, although questions of ethics are less of a problem when one's sources are dead.

Rather than subject the reader to what would be a very dry and one-sided account of my dialogues with documents (but see Photograph 9.1),[2] I can only aim to make clear what interested and politically loaded goals informed my research and writing. I do, though, call into question the specifically historical consciousness and historical projects of those who *wrote* my sources. And so I queried interests and power-infused projects of Spanish chroniclers, and also the Spanish, indian, and in-between "informants" and authors of curriculum vitae reports that are sources for us as they were for chroniclers. One of the reasons I did so was to highlight the potential distortions and lies of which we should be wary. But I also sought to uncover the ways that their understandings of the past and of history interfered with or precluded the possibility of portraying Andean pasts and ways of doing history.

I have reached the conclusion that Spaniards' insistence on attending only to oral narrative as historical source for understanding an Inca past led them to ignore, apart from brief, superficial, and usually disparaging accounts, the techniques by which Andean social memory was largely kept. For Spaniards, history was the Word, on the one hand, grounded in the authority of the Church and the empire and, on the other hand, grounded in language, specifically in written language. They could not be expected to understand readily the significance of histories recorded in three dimensions, in the warp and weft of textile design and in the fingering of quipus, and replayed in the polysensual experience of singing, dancing, drinking, and sacrificing.[3]

I have tried to characterize how such techniques might have been used by ancient Andeans, and what kinds of meaningful pasts might have been conveyed by them. There may be little to go on, but all is not lost. If one cannot unearth in colonial documents much information on pre-Columbian pasts that has not been mangled in the process of the cultural translation into written Spanish, one can focus on the process of

Photograph 9.1.   A historian in his microfilm: author and documents in the archive. In the top frame, the author reads a document in the archive, which is also the chambers of the juzgado de Poopó and the anteroom of the jailhouse. The photograph was taken with the author's camera, in use for microfilming documents, by a resident ethnographer studying hamlets of Urus Moratos along nearby Lake Poopó. Urus Moratos named themselves for the seventeenth-century scribe who wrote land titles they found in this archive, like the composición title in the bottom frame. The document is a colonial record of a boundary pilgrimage between mojones, dividing Uru lands from those of Sura peoples. Archivo del Tribunal de Poopó, September 1982. (Photograph of author by Darwin Horn; photograph of document by author)

412

cultural translation itself, which is to say, on the genesis of the colonial interculture that is still very much alive in the Andes. Crossing the border between orality and literacy (or rather, between polysensual pasts and the visual ones of writing) was my goal in the chapters of part 2. By doing so, I sought to foreground neither "pure Andean" nor "pure Spanish" cultures and histories, but rather the history of the border culture that resulted from the colonial encounter and the new pasts that it produced.

HISTORICIZING THE COLONIAL AND POSTCOLONIAL FRONTIERS

Portraying the long-term interplay and complicated development of forms of social memory belonging to colonizers and colonized is an arduous task, especially when considering that our sources for understanding preinvasion systems of social memory are the writings of men who sought to erase Andeans' memories, to rewrite the Andean past in their own image. Although not entirely successful from their own point of view, Spanish missionaries and administrators did alter Andeans' modalities of social memory. They did so by substituting Spanish statist forms for Inca ones; by transforming the relationship between native lords and native "vassals"; by moving Andeans about, regrouping them and resettling them into new kinds of living spaces, with new coordinates of time and space regulated by tribute schedules, markets, forced labor, transport cycles, and ritual calendars; and by interposing between indigenous people and the recognized realm of the sacred a new set of powerful intermediaries, the parish priests who oversaw much of the day-to-day transformation of indigenous life. In fits and starts, rather than as gradual progression, the kind of social group that shaped itself by construing its own past went through successive reductions in scale (for the most part, a progressive shrinking as earlier and larger-scale formations were fragmented and reconstituted through new kinds of collective practice in new kinds of settlements). Another important factor in this process of fragmentation and reconstitution was the vast trauma of the colonial demographic tragedy, since even before Spaniards arrived in Tawantinsuyu and the lands of the Asanaqi diarchy, European diseases had begun a massive attack on the Andean population. By the early decades of the seventeenth century, at which time the last of the pre-Columbian Andean memory specialists were dying of old age, epidemic disease had also killed more than half, and perhaps as much as three-fourths, of the total population. As Andeans began to regroup within reducciones, often those to which they had fled the weight of mita and tribute to become forasteros, demographic collapse and the succession of generations contributed their share to a cataclysm that brought in a new era, with its own shape in space and time. Colonial "indigenous" groups were then reformed vis-à-vis new nexes of collective articulation: "Indians" constructed themselves as members of collective social groups through new kinds of activities, in new sorts of places, according to new calendars.

When the boundaries and modalities of the social life undergo radical transformation, so will the shape of the past which gives that new social life its significance. If we could appreciate Andeans' accounts of their past at several points along the trajectory in time that begins for us in 1532 and ends in the present, we should expect them to differ from one another, perhaps in the extreme. Extinct social formations do not inscribe their genealogies in the consciousness of their members. Instead, the members of surviving social groups have had to come to grips with the past that could account for and reproduce new circumstances, new kinds of articulation with new sorts of states. Indeed, the single most pressing historical problem for the first several postinvasion generations must have been to account for the Spanish conquest itself, to understand a past that now included demographic collapse caused by Old World diseases, the destruction of pre-Columbian forms of large-scale social cohesion, the smashing of the old gods by Spanish priests, who brought new notions of divinity, and the continuing cataclism of colonial and neocolonial domination.

To the degree that Andeans succeeded in their efforts, they did so by beginning to share with Spaniards new techniques for interpreting the past and some of the critical topoi of Spanish and Christian social memory. Through their colonial relationship, Spaniards and indians came to share a limited vocabulary of concepts, deployed in recognizably similar social spaces. They could recognize one another's saints' rituals and communicate through a mutual cultural pidgin that named the acts and gods they apparently held in common. And certain indigenous people who moved permanently into colonial cities, adopting specifically urban dress styles and other practices, came to share with locally born Spaniards not only a term of identity (the former, in colonial Potosí, were termed *indios criollos;* the latter, *españoles criollos*) but also a creolized culture. Indeed, the shared understandings, produced by colonial practices, of clandestine meanings (indians' sorceries using saints' images being one example) led creoles to indian shamans when they needed to undo colonial sorceries (see Taussig 1987).

The social situation that gave rise to Andean pidgin and creole cultures developed during a historically particular moment for both Spaniards and indians. Sixteenth-century Spanish society was in the midst of a struggle between state-sponsored orthodoxies and "popular" heterodoxies over precisely which "doxa" (collectively construed systems of belief and practice) were to be tolerated. Popular resistance to state efforts to homogenize collective practice led to clandestine practices, which, here and there, came under the harsh light of inquisitorial surveillance. Within this Counter-Reformation situation, certain ingenious methods of veiling cultural critique from absolutist censors produced the narratives of the Spanish Golden Age and the flowering of the novel. It is ironic that the form the novel then took, called the picaresque, should have been that of a story of travel foregrounding the deeds of the narrator. It is also ironic that, as González Echevarría has argued (1990), this novelistic strategy should be modeled on the *relación* and legal deposition, the colonial curriculum vitae composed for the archive, through which authors both Spanish and Andean sought legitimation of their actions and rewards from the king. Full of boastful swagger and countless lies, hundreds of thousands of pages of such petitions, personal reports of heroic deeds in service of the king, cram the shelves of the Archivo General de Indias.

On the basis of such models, the fiction writer (and the philosopher and social critic) could purvey damning social criticism only by putting it in the mouths of madmen and the most pitiful criminals, all duly punished and cured in the denouement. Repression of dissent, then, would seem to be the midwife of creativity. Cervantes' fellow sufferers in the Indies, subject to the scrutiny of their local parish priests, did not have regular recourse to the pen or any compulsion to revise books of chivalry. The colonial Counter-Reformation, however, targeted indigenous resistance to the king's civilizational program and especially frowned on the misuse of Christian practice, deemed the devil's work. Such repression did not dim but rather heightened Andeans' creativity as cultural critics.

As a result of this colonial "pidgin culture of the Baroque" (Maravall 1987), town-based native societies have reproduced a bifurcated cosmos, in which "Spanish-Christian" forms are apparently distinguishable from "pre-Columbian–indian" ones. Yet they did so, not to mock Christianity, but in order to be Christians in their own way. In K'ulta, libations to mountain and hill deities, poured in alcohol, are strongly associated with relatively closed and private contexts, while libations to sky deities, such as Christ and the Virgin, are fully developed in the most open and public

of ritual contexts. Likewise, the eucharistic mass, procession and banqueting associated with the most publicly visible portions of patron
saints' festivals form but part of a larger indigenous liturgy, one that
includes closed sessions that frame the public processions, priest's mass,
and public banquets within the named phases of llama sacrifice. This
sort of bifurcated or interwoven ritual order provides fuel for the
interpretive stance that I called the "thin veneer" resistance paradigm, in
which the more public and "Christian" aspects of the total performance
are regarded as token kowtowing to the power of Church and state
authorities and institutions, while a native culture and cosmology are
preserved, intact and fundamentally continuous with pre-Columbian
cultural traditions, behind the scenes in clandestine form.

I hope to have shown just how mistaken such conclusions are. While
they register an essential feature of Andean societies, both urban and
rural, creole and indigenous, they fail to recognize what is most
characteristic of the Andes' intertwined postcolonial intercultures, which
is precisely the creative tension in the relationship between putatively
distinct prior, conquered underworlds and later, conquering heavens.
There can be nothing more "purely Andean" than the efforts of people in
the Andes, whether rural or urban, Spanish, indian, or in between, to
understand that relationship or to find ways to make use of it.

Once we accept that all parties in the colonial and postcolonial social
context are frontier practitioners, then what were barriers to
investigation—the evasions, miscommunications, lies, and buried truths
of documentary sources, or the analogous distancing techniques encountered by the ethnographer in search of clandestine cultures—are transformed. No longer barriers to "what truly happened" or "true indigenous culture," they become keys for understanding. K'ulta authorities
struggled to keep me close to the realm of public events and orthodox
practices because their role is to mediate K'ulta and the world outside.
Likewise the natural-looking snapshot photographs that I hoped to
make were rejected by K'ultas, who did not refuse to be photographed
but aimed to control the representation by elaborately preparing for
stiffly posed portraits. I caught informality only by my own clandestine
practices and by aiming at children. The division of their practice
between public and clandestine constitutes the colonial and postcolonial
frontier. While I was once frustrated by the difficulty of getting past it, of
"being let in," it now seems that the process revealed the frontier and
that the frontier is the essence of K'ulta culture. The same might be said
for the difficulties encountered by historians when they seek "truly

Andean" culture in colonial documents but find that everything has been tainted by asymmetries of power, by the intrusion of Christian and Spanish practices and points of view, and by the interested and archival orientation of writing and recording techniques. Yet practices of colonial inscription, such as census visits, relaciones, trial testimonies, reports of extirpation of idolatry, and the writings directed to Spanish authorities by "transcultural" frontier authors like Guaman Poma or Pachacuti Yamqui did not just distort prior Andean social realities; they were the techniques that brought colonial social realities into existence. By practicing a more reflexive ethnography and reflexive history, we transform the obstacles to investigation into the investigation itself. They are frontier scholarly practices for frontier societies.

POSTCOLONIAL SOCIAL MEMORY AND (POST?) MODERNITY

In pilgrimage centers dedicated to miraculous saint images, one may find the Andean shamans of a type called *ch'iyar yatiri* (see Platt 1992). The ch'iyar yatiri (literally, *yatiri,* "one who knows," *ch'iyara,* "darkness") brings his client into a darkened house. There, after pouring libations and burning incense, the lights are put out. The shaman then advises his clients "to feel themselves not to be Christian," and begins blowing upon a sort of stone whistle and ringing a little bell. Soon the beating of wings is heard in the room—the mallku (not a hereditary lord from the past, but a male condor from the mountain peaks) arrives and, through the mouth of the shaman, intones the words of the mountain god in answer to the client's questions.

In a way, the ch'iyar yatiri's ventriloquism is triple: Not only does he mouth the words of an unseen god through the mouth of a condor that he has created in the minds of his clients; he also gives voice to the image of indian powers that his clients confer on him: Indians are the legitimate heirs of a race of pre-Christian beings and of forces of natural production, genesis, and wealth. In the popular urban view, they are maximally "other" mediators of cosmic realms, upon whom Christianity and civilization have been unsuccessfully foisted. Indians are said to worship the pachamama, a pre-Christian earth goddess, and the mountain gods, the mallkus. It is only through coercion, it is often said, that they also pay lip service to Christian beings.

The ch'iyar yatiri's invocation to "feel yourself not to be Christian" points his clients towards the interpretation to which they are already inclined. This is never so clear as in the urban pilgrimage centers, where, on the margin of town, Kallawayas and ch'iyar yatiris ply their trade, on the edge of the folkloric festivals and carnaval processions linked to miraculous patron saints in which city people nowadays carry on a patriotic strut, costumed as indians in homage to their nation's original citizens (Photograph 9.2). Such postcolonial passions will be the subject of another book, but it is worth bearing in mind that the indigenous past has become a critically important theme not only for scholarly books but also in the identity projects of decidedly nonindian Bolivian national elites. Nowadays, candidates for political office must do more than kiss babies to attract sympathy and votes; they must costume themselves as "authentic wild indians" and burn incense bundles at the urban shrines of indian earth gods. Sometimes they even hire yatiris and Kallawaya practitioners to aid them in their quests for political power.[4]

The ch'iyar yatiri's injunctions urge us towards the temptations of a former anthropological romance. But taking his advice leads us into an archaizing endeavor, that of understanding indigenous presents through attention only to pre-Columbian indian pasts. Published ethnographies along these lines have played into the hands of a progressivist Bolivian elite search for a heroic—and still living—ancestral culture, an antique, mystical-magical, nature and use-value–bound moral economy of signs, that can serve as a native foil against which to highlight rational, civilized, and capitalist assertions of modernity. Frontier shamanism like that of the ch'iyar yatiri, carried out in the pilgrimage centers where the Andean interculture has developed its most effective pidgin language (one that foils communication while seeming to enable it), may well provide Bolivian city folks with the stuff of an anti-imperialist, anticolonial, and locally grounded national identity. All this has led to some positive outcomes, especially a new (though relative) degree of tolerance by national elites for indigenous cultural difference. Much understanding, however, is thereby sacrificed. By taking up a reductionist vision of the indigenous present—denuded of Christian and Spanish elements— urban elites in fact revalorize their old prejudices, now celebrating the assumed difference that they used to abhor. Celebration, of course, is preferable to the ethnocidal policies engendered by past abhorrence.

Seeking to separate colonizing and colonized cultures analytically in the Bolivian context undermines the possibility of understanding to what degree all participants in the long-running colonial and postcolonial encounter have internalized one another. From the rural and indigenous side of things, I hope that I have demonstrated that K'ultas are a historical product of colonial and postcolonial discursive contests, even

Photograph 9.2. Oruro kindergarteners on parade in tinku dance costumes. Oruro, August 1988. (Photograph by Mary F. Dillon, used with permission)

as the Counter-Reformation or baroque interplay between cultural surveillance and clandestine secrecies presupposed and reinforced a bifurcated cosmos that historicized the colonial situation itself, with opposed indian and nonindian, wild and civilized, and Supay-Chullpa and Tatala-Jesucristo as its separate temporally divided parts.

There is a point-by-point correspondence between the jilsa practice described in the 1680 case of Martín Nina Willka, who helped his clients, through recitations of the rosary and suitable Christian discipline, to call upon the dove of the Holy Spirit in order to communicate with Christ and the Virgin, and the pilgrimage-center ch'iyar yatiris' practice, admonishing their clients, Christians all, to feel themselves not to be Christians, in order to converse with mountain gods through a condor. Such practices, like the K'ulta sacrificial Eucharist, are kinds of frontier sorceries deployed to sunder, like the flash of lightning, the barriers in space and time that otherwise hinder the project of taking control of personal and collective destinies. Taken together they illustrate the critical role played by colonial and republican agents of the state and Church in maintaining authorial control over the collective practices that shape social memory: To a large degree, the wak'a kamayuq Diego Iquisi, the "indian Christ" Miguel Acarapi/Chiri, the jilsa Ninan Willka, and the founders of Santa Bárbara de Culta were condemned for the heresy of trying to usurp that authority. Ironically, today the ch'iyar yatiri survives without undue repression, and indeed prospers in urban and pilgrimage-center contexts, precisely because his practice is explicitly *dissociated* from Christianity. The systematic interrelation between the contemporary progeny of the colonial clash of Spanish and indigenous ways might be said to constitute a Bolivian metaculture. Understanding it requires us to treat the fuzzy foundary between Spanish and indian, "national" and "ethnic" cultural realms, as the object of analysis rather than an obstacle to it.

As an ethnographer-cum-historian I have sought to sew together tidbits of personal experience, the "eyewitness" testimony of K'ultas, documents from the past, and some understandings of national (and nationalist) trends in Bolivia and the facts of international globalization to provide a portrait of the historical currents that traverse K'ulta territory and, like the region's highways and llama caravan trails, have left K'ulta (and of course, Cruce) at a crossroads.

The highways that have diverted K'ultas from old llama-caravan journeys lead to urban markets and migrant settlements, and also towards national (and hence global) forms of social memory. Regardless of its specific content, these tend towards kinds of individualized subjectivity: that of the individual citizen whose rights stem from membership in the only collective subjectivity that is now globally salient, the national state erected on the basis of "popular sovereignty"; and that of the consumer within the now global capitalist marketplace. "Indianist" movements such as the Movimiento Revolucionario Tupac Katari, whose Aymara-speaking candidate became vice-president of Bolivia, have become palatable to old elite-dominated parties, not only because the changing electorate and the appeal of populist candidates necessitated an expedient alliance, but also because they have not become separatist movements.

The indigenismo to which some Bolivian elites turned in the 1940s as the basis for a new kind of patriotism has indeed helped to engender a cross-caste and cross-class romance, along with the literary romances that Doris Sommer calls foundational fictions (1991). It has also fostered a level of respect for indigenous peoples that was unimaginable a century ago. But that respect, even adulation, is a corollary of increased indian engagement with the national state and participation in national culture (expressed and generated through electronic media, national transportation systems, the ubiquitous spread of commodity culture, and massive rural-to-urban migration). It is in this context that the politically sponsored urban pageants (derived from old Catholic festivals and pilgrimages) in the 1980s and 1990s have increasingly admitted and actively encouraged first the representation (by nonindian urban guilds) and then the self-representation (by "folklore" groups imported from rural communities) of the Bolivian nation's indigenous traditions. The state, that is, has fostered respect for the nation's *indigenous* past, just as the local media and messages of the social memory of rural collectivities have been progressively displaced by mnemonic techniques—history books, parades, and monuments—recalling the *nation's* past.

However, the postcolonial historical sorceries of Bolivian intercultures are in no imminent danger of disappearing. Ritual action is capable of transforming the relationship between context and human subjectivity and, consequently, of transforming the ways in which messages can be interpreted and by whom. Like the poetics of action employed by Diego Iquisi, Miguel Acarapi/Chiri, the Chiris of Culta (Junt'uma), Martín Nina Willka, the festive rebels of 1781, or the indigenous communities that now travel to urban pageants and dramatize their llama sacrifices to show city folks the country's true heritage, such nonverbal techniques of memory, rather than the textual blips that flow across computer screens or the thin and wavy lines that cover this paper, are best suited for carrying out revolutionary transformations of the past, of the kind that grant their practitioners control over the circumstances of the present.

From my point of view, when doing social and cultural history, it is sufficient neither to document the political and economic exploitations of the colonial situation nor to treat that situation as a discursive event full of talk and symbols.[5] Instead we must work to understand how Spaniards and indians of the colonial situation, and the creoles and rural peoples of the postcolonial one, have themselves used history to understand and represent their power-infused relationships, because their understandings and miscommunications in the end helped to shape the colonizers' projects as well as colonized peoples' replies to it.

Documentary Appendix
Notes
Glossary
References
Index

Documentary Appendix

A. FRANCISCO PIZARRO'S GRANT OF ACHO AND GUARACHE TO HERNANDO
DE ALDANA

. . . I give you in deposit in the province of the Aullagas 823 indians:
260 indians with the cacique Acho in this manner:
  a pueblo they call Acalvo with the principal Gualca, 38 indians;
  and in another [pueblo] called Berenguela 18 indians;
  and in another they call Millme 53 [indians], with the principal Colque;
  and in another they call Pisquero, 9 [indians];
  and in another they call Yana, 29 [indians];
  and in another they call Callapa, 16;
  and in another they call Taparo, 37;
  and in another they called Yanaque, 21;
  and in another they call Pucuro, a field [chacara] of the said cacique, 3;
  and in another they call Yanaqui, a field of the said cacique, 21;
  and also another pueblo called Sacina, with a principal Acho, with 14 mitimaes,
    of Aullaga who are near the settlement of Chuquisaca.
Indians and pueblos of the cacique Guarache: 560 indians in this manner:
  In a pueblo called Quillaca 174 [indians];
  and also close to the said pueblo of Quillaca, 30 who are fishermen;
  and also another pueblo of the said Guarache called Sacari, with the principal
    Talare, 33 [indians];
  and another pueblo of the said cacique, they call Guamanoca, and the
    principal Condor, with 21 [indians];
  and another pueblo called Sacachapi, with the prinicpal Caya, 19;
  and another they call Caya, with the principal Caya [*sic*], 33;
  and another pueblo called Liocari with the principal Mollo, with 12;
  and another pueblo they call Quilla with the principal Ururo, with 26;
  and another pueblo they call Sinago, with the principal Copavilca, 14;
  and near this said pueblo of Sinago another, 14;
  and two *estancias* of the said cacique, one of them called Pachacaio and the
    other Andaraque, with 11 [indians];
  and a pueblo called Guaçarapapi, with the principal Toma, with 28;
  and another pueblo called Sogara, with the principal Caquia, with 20;

425

and another pueblo called Caracara with the principal Salcacho, 9;

and an estancia of the said cacique they call Llallaua, with 5;

and another estancia of the said cacique called Saco, with 6;

and another pueblo they call Hu Usca, with 40 and 9;

and another pueblo called Aparo, with 47;

and a garden [*chacara de sementeras*] they call Samancha, with 5;

and another pueblo they call Hu Urca, with 10 mitimaes who prepare food.

In the province of Paria, sixteen leagues from Paria a pueblo called Xigona, with the principal Chichina who commands 13 indians, apart from the 25 indians who the cacique Caligoana has there;

also 8 indians in an estancia called Molo in the province of Caracara, with a principal named Acho. It is a maize field.

Also 25 in a pueblo called Urca, apart from those who the cacique Quita also has there;

and also a village [*una aldea*] they call Conacona which is near Chuquisaca, with a principal named Chilaca;

and also an estancia they call Tuisamo, four or five leagues from Chuquisaca, 3 indians subject to Guarache;

and here nearby a village they call Piusera, with 9 indians subject to Guarache;

and in another village they call Aye, 6 indians subject to Guarache;

and also in a pueblo of mitimaes from Aullagas called Sacasaca, 39 indians with the principal Copagallo, subject to Guarache;

And also in the Moiosmoios a pueblo which is of Tirique called Suere, with 62 [indians];

and in another village next to this pueblo, 32 indians;

and in another pueblo they call Viroviro, 42 indians who are subject to the cacique Ylla.

The original Spanish is as follows:

. . . yo vos deposito en la prouinçia de los aullagas 823 yndios:

260 yndios con el cacique Acho en esta manera:

un pueblo que se dize acaluo con el prinçipal gualca 38 yndios

y en otro que se llama berenguela 18 yndios

y en otro que se dize millme 53 con el prinçipal colque

y en otro que se dize pisquero 9

y en otro que se dize yana 29

y en otro que se dize callapa 16

y en otro que se dize taparo 37

y en otro que se llama yanaque 21

y en otro que se dize pucuro chacara del dicho caçique 3

y en otro que se dize yanaqui chacara del dicho caçique 21

y mas otro pueblo que se llama sacina con un prinçipal acho con 14 mitimaes de aullaga que estan junto al asiento de chuquisaca

Indios y pueblos del cacique Guarache: 560 yndios en esta manera:
En un pueblo que se llama quillaca 174
y mas çerca deste dicho pueblo quillaca 30 que son pescadores
y mas otro pueblo del dicho guarache que se llama sacari con el principal talare con 33
y otro pueblo del dicho cacique que se dize guamanoca y el prinçipal condor con 21
y otro pueblo que se llama sacachapi con el prinçipal caya con 19
y otro que se dize caya con el principal caya [*sic*] 33
y otro pueblo que se llama liocari con el prinçipal mollo con 12
y otro pueblo que se dize quilla con el principal uroro con 26
e otro pueblo que se dize sinago con el prinçipal copauilca con 14
y çerca de este dicho pueblo sinago /11r/ otros 14
y dos estancias del dicho cacique que la una dellas se llama pachacaio y la otra andaraque con 11
e un pueblo que se llama guaçarapapi con el principal toma con 28
y otro pueblo que se llama sogara cn el prinçipal caquia con 20
y otro pueblo que se llama caracara con el principal salcacho con 9
e una estancia del dicho cacique que se dize llallaua con 5
y otra estancia del dicho cacique que se dize suco [or saco?] con 6
y otro pueblo que se dize huvsca con 40 y 9
y otro pueblo que se llama aparo con 47
y una chacara de sementeras que se dize samancha con 5
y otro pueblo que se dize hu vrca con 10 mitimaes de hazar comida.
y en la prouinça de paria diez y seis leguas de paria un pueblo que se llama xigona con el principal chichina que los manda 13 yndios sin los que alli tiene el cacique caligoana que son 25
y mas 8 yndios en una estançia que se llama molo que esta en la prouinçia de caracara con un principal que se llama acho es sementera de maiz
y mas 25 en un pueblo que se llama Vrca sin los que tiene aqui tambien el cacique quita
y mas vna aldea que se dize conacona con vn principal que se llama chilaca que estan çerca de chuquisaca
e mas vna estançia que se dize tuisamo [or trusamo?] a quatro o cinco leguas de chuquisaca 3 yndios subjetos a guarache
y aqui junto vna aldea que se dize piusera con 9 subjetos a guarache
y en otra aldea/11v/ que se dize aye 6 subjectos a guarache
e mas en vn pueblo de mitimaes de avllagas que se llama sacasaca 39 yndios con el prinçipal copagallo sujeto a guarache.
y mas en los moiosmoios vn pueblo que es de tirique que se llama suere [or sulre] con 62.
y en otra aldea junto a este pueblo 32 yndios

y en otro pueblo que se dize viroviro 42 yndios son sulgetos al cacique ylla. (from encomienda title, Cusco, 1539: Francisco Pizarro to Hernando de Aldana; copied into AGI Charcas 53, item 1, Charcas, 1622: "Memorial de don Diego Copatete cacique principal de los indios Quillacas y Asanaques")

B. JUNTAS DE INDIOS EN PUEBLOS FORMADOS; ALCALDES HORDINARIOS, REGIDORES CADAÑEROS [TITLE IN MARGIN].

Al Presidente e oydores del nuevo reyno de granada, que platicado con los perlados de las provincias subjectas aquella audiencia horden en lo que vieren que conviene sobre si converna que se hagan pueblos de casas juntas en las comarcas que los yndios eligeren y sobre que aya alcaldes hordinarios y regidores cadañeros entre ellos e otras cosas:

El Rey

A nos se a hecho relaçión que al bien de los naturales de esas partes e a su salvaçión convernía que se juntasen e hiziesen pueblos de muchas casas juntas en las comarcas que ellos eligiesen, porque estando como agora estan cada casa por si e aún a cada barrio, no pueden ser doctrinados como convernía ni promolgarles las leyes que se hazen en su benefiçio ni gozar de los sacramentos de la Eucarestía y otras de que se aprovecharían y valdría estando en pueblos juntos e no derramados. E que en todos los /28r/ pueblos que estuviesen hechos e se hiziesen era bién que se criasen e proveyesen alcaldes ordinarios para que hiziesen justicia en las cosas ceviles y tanbién regidores cadañeros de los mismos yndios que los elijesen ellos los quales tuviesen cargo de procurar el bién común y se proveysesen ansý mismo alguaziles y otros ofiçiales necesarios como se haze a costumbre hazer en la provincia a de Tascala y en otras partes y que tanbién tuviesen cárçel en cada pueblo para los malhechores y un corral de conçejo para meter los ganados que les hiziesen daño que no tuviesen guarda y que se les señalase las penas que llevare y que se persuadiese a los dichos yndios que tuviesen ganados al menos ovejunos y puercos en común e en particular y que tanbién en cada pueblo de yndios uviese mercados y plaças donde oviese mantenimientos para que los caminantes españoles o yndios pudiesen conprar por sus dineros lo que oviesen menester para pasar su camino y que se les devía conpeler a que tuviesen rozines para alquilar o para otros usos e que a todo los suso dicho devían ser los dichos yndios persuadidos por la mejor y más blanda e amorosa vía que ser pudiese pues hera todo en su provecho y beneficio y visto por los del nuestro consejo de las yndias queriendo proveerse lo fue acordado que devía mandar dar esta mi çédula para vos e yo tove lo por bién por quanto vos mando que veays lo suso dicho y platicado çerca de todo ello con los perlados de las provincias subjetas a esa audiençia poco a poco ordenéys sobre ello lo que biéredes que conviene fecha en Valladolíd a nueve días del mes de otubre de mil e quinientos y quarenta y nueve años Maximiliano la reyna por mandado de su magestad sus altezas en su nombre. Juan de Samano. En las espaldas estan seys rúbricas y señales. (AGI, Indiferente 532, fols. 27v–28r)

C. CHAPTERS AND ORDINANCES FOR THE TOWN OF OUR LADY
OF BETHLEHEM,

which is in Tinquipaya, province of Caquina and Picachuri, for the indians and vecinos and those who live and stay in the said town and the other towns subject to the /7v/ province of Caquina and Picachuri, as follows:

Firstly, that each year on New Year's Day the alcaldes who have been named in the said town . . . shall meet jointly with the regidores and the alguacil mayor and the cacique principal, and through their votes shall elect another two alcaldes, four regidores, one mayordomo, and one alguacil mayor and two minor ones, and a scribe, a teacher of children, and a prosecutor. And once elected the alcaldes, regidores, and alguaciles shall be sworn to do, use, and exercise their duties well and faithfully in His Majesty's name, always favoring the poor and orphans and widows and needy, well looking after the republic and its business. And the other officials, the mayordomos, scribe, schoolteacher, and prosecutor of the town . . . shall be sworn in by the alcaldes and regidores and alguaciles. . . . And if any of them or all for a year or more can find no other capable persons, they may be renamed as many times as they like.

Item: That no alcalde or regidor may be named again for three years, until the fourth year or later, after he has once been alcalde or regidor.

Item: That when equal votes occur for one of the said offices, the cacique principal may elect the one he likes.

Item: The said alcaldes may judge all and whatever matters as alcaldes ordinarios, in civil cases, without creating procesos or writing anything down, giving aid and favor always to widows and orphans as have been said.

Item: That in judging civil cases involving fields greater than two *almudes* of maize seed, after carrying out an investigation with witnesses inform the corregidor of the City of Silver or Potosí, or whatever judge of *naturales,* so long as the corregidor judges and sentences.

Item: That in the case of gold or silver mines exceeding twenty pesos in value, after investigating with witnesses inform the judges or corregidores so that they may judge and sentence.

Item: That the said alcaldes of the said towns named below have jurisdiction over whatever criminal case, such as deaths or injuries to members, and the imprisoned delinquent or delinquents when sufficient investigation of the case has been completed, shall be taken and delivered to the justices of the City of Silver or the Villa of Potosí, if there is no corregidor or judge of naturales.

Item: That in criminal cases where given commission to intervene, [you] may not cut off limbs or pull out earrings of any delinquent indian, no more than to molest them with imprisonment not to surpass thirty days in jail, or shave the heads of such delinquents. For those condemned to a lashing, they may not be given more than a hundred lashes, and the whip shall have no more than four tails, and be made of cured, not raw, leather. And each branch of the whip shall not exceed in width one of the four of the hand, understood that the four branches be as thick as the fingers of the hand.

Item: That a chest of three keys within a locked room in the houses of the cabildo, and the chest shall have a box in one part where papers, prohibitions, visitas, tribute lists, census books, and any other writings that ought to be in a book in an archive.

Item: In the other part of the chest under three keys, shall be kept whatever silver there is that shall be collected from each of the indian residents of the said town to pay their tribute.

Item: The three keys shall be kept by one alcalde, one regidor, and a mayordomo.

Item: Each six months when half the tribute is to be collected, a new book shall be made, keeping track of the visita that remains in your power, of the ages of each one; and the boy who reaches eighteen years shall be told to look for his tribute so that he can pay it at the first semester's collection as well as in the second. And inform the old man who completes fifty years of age that he does not have to pay tribute six months hence, nor any other tribute or service, except what comes to him as his turn of the wheel along with the other old men who are able to walk or serve in whatever service owed to the curacas and principales.

Item: Likewise keep a book of great account and reason of the indians who are given for service in the plazas of Potosí and Porco and for mercury or mines, so that one or more indians do not go to serve twice, before the wheel turns through all the tributary indians.

Item: That those indians who must serve in the said plaza, mines, or mercury [works] shall carry food enough for the said month and may not collect the wages they may have earned without the presence of their principal, so that all they may have earned may be gathered together and carried to the chest and handed over to be put inside by those who keep the keys, and the scribe writing in the book the names of each indian and what each deposits in the said chest.

Item: That if some indian among them collects some silver that he earns and spends it, unless he is sick or has another great need, the said alcaldes shall punish him so he does not do it again.

Item: If in the service of the tambo or tambos in their charge, keep account and reason as in the other services of plazas and mercury.

Item: If any mines are discovered in the lands and province of Caquina and Picachuri, of gold or silver or *soroche* or other metals, the said alcaldes shall give for them some indians to work for wages, and of whatever they earn keep account and reason as with the other wages.

Item: And if in the ordinances that His Excellency [Toledo] has made for the mines, it happens that indians may own mines, then the said alcaldes and cabildo in the name of their town may own mines for the said town and council, and put indians into them to work them and take out metals with which to pay their tribute.

Item: The said alcaldes and officials, curacas and principales, take great care to execute and carry out the ordinance that His Excellency has given out about forests, and carry out the penalties therein.

Item: That the animals owned by the community, which are 250 head of cattle and 400 of Castilian sheep, the said alcaldes and officials of the council take great care to assign men to guard them, and take great care with them. And the said cowboys and shepherds shall remain a full year keeping watch over the said herds, and from the fruit and multiplication that from them is taken, the herders' tributes for each semester shall be paid.

Item: Whatever is left over of the increase in the herd shall be sold, or moneys that are obtained from the said increase, cheeses, milk, or butter, be placed in the chest of three keys, and from it shall be paid the tributes of sick indians and those who were unable to work for the six months of the semester, and in the same way help other poor indians with the said silver, such as those who have many children, or those who have little strength to work and search out the tribute they owe.

Item: From what remains of the said silver, after this help has been given, take account that it is distributed among all the other indians of the community, to forgive that which they are obliged to pay of the tribute, and in this account and reason the priests may be greatly charitable.

Item: From the increase of the said herds, take for the poor and sick and needy some meat, by whatever order the priest of the said doctrina gives.

Item: Every year shear the sheep and divide the wool among the widows, old women, and orphan girls, and for other necessities, and from that which is left make storage sacks to be sold for your tribute.

Item: The alcaldes and regidores shall name as mayordomo an old indian who does not pay tribute, to stay in the hospital to take in the sick and poor to be cured, providing the said hospital with all that is required, before all other things of the fruit and increase of the said herds.

Item: For the service of the holy church the said alcaldes shall take great care in the order given to them by the priest who shall have charge of the town and doctrina. And the said service shall be from among the children of the principales and those of some rich men, and they shall walk to school serving by their turns of the wheel the said boys, of whom some of the older ones shall be taken, after the said town is built and completed and has been populated, so that after having taught them song and music they shall serve in the church, officiating at mass when the priest wishes to perform it sung.

Item: The alcaldes and regidores shall take great care to make sure that neither the curacas or principales take the fields and lands that some indians have, or that they do them any other damage or injury, nor give them work taking advantage of the said indians, more than that which they are given and assigned for service.

Item: That the said alcaldes within their jurisdictions, may take charge of cases within their purview not only of the indians and vecinos of their town, but also over any other indian, mestizo, or mulato, up to the point of capturing them and sending them prisoner and well guarded to the justices of the City of Silver and Potosí, and in the same way they may take charge of any and whatever indians who are within their territorial limits and mojones, and of any other repartimiento with yanaconas who are in or reside or pass through your said province.

Item: Whatever pecuniary penalties that the alcaldes collect may be applied in thirds, one part for the work of the church and its ornaments, another part for the hospital, and the other part for the town's public works.

Item: The said alcaldes shall give account to the cacique principal of the said towns, and in his absence to his second persons, of any criminal or civil suit of consideration that there may be among the indians, and shall do as he commands if one of the other judges of the said towns agrees with his opinion.

Item: The said alcaldes may remedy and take charge of any aggrievement that any of the five principales of the five *pachacas* [an Incaic unit of one hundred tributaries] causes to any indian, whether civil or criminal, and may capture and punish him in the manner already declared. And if the delinquent is one of the second persons, except the cacique principal, without investigation of the case may be caught and sent before the justices of the City of Silver or the corregidor of the said city or the Villa of Potosí.

Item: If the said accusation of crime or quarrel or complaint is made by or against the curaca principal, without investigation and secretly one of the regidores shall go to the said justices and apprise them of it so that they might send for the said cacique and punish him.

Item: In all the things that come before the government of the said province and town, if the cacique principal wishes to enter the cabildo he shall be supreme in proposing any business, and if it is his wish, one alcalde or one regidor shall be supreme above the other votes and opinions, except in the election of the officials, in which it shall be as has been said.

Item: In the absence of the cacique principal and when the second person is in town, he shall have the supreme vote as the cacique principal.

Item: The cacique principal or the second persons shall take care if some indian or powerful principal does not wish to obey any of the alcaldes over whatever misdemeanor or case he has done or committed, and may see to the capture of the said indian or principal to be punished in conformity with justice.

Item: The minor alguaciles with the prosecutor shall take care to see what babies are born to bring them before the priest to be baptized.

Item: The said prosecutor and bailiffs shall bring all the people on the festival days they must keep, and the other days of the week that men, women, young boys, and young girls are obligated to go to doctrina.

Item: The said prosecutor shall take care in manifesting to the priest and telling him who is living in sin [*amancebados*] so they may be punished.

Item: The said prosecutor and minor bailiffs shall take weekly turns making sure that boys and girls come to doctrina in the afternoon and morning in the order that the priest gives them for it.

Item: No person whether Spaniard or of any other quality or condition may take lands and fields that at present are left in the towns that by my order have been depopulated, so that they may come to live in the said town of Our Lady of Bethlehem, which are the following towns:

Caquina	Saruquira	Antora
Yanane	Chiquibi	Tactari
Picachuri	Omaca	Guayrarusa
Tomoro	Tantaqui	Toroma
Tulala	Torcopaqui	Locroma
Entacalla	Torcosasale	Colo
Ancoma	Pinapina	Coapalla
Guacale	Coloyo	Soycoco
Coayapo	Quirula	Yurina
Puchula	Ynroynro	Salama
Yaguacare	Aucaqui	Quinemiquisi
Sabelico		

Item: If it seems convenient to sell some of the said lands and fields because they are too far away or for any other reason, the caciques may not sell them unless the alcaldes and regidores meet together in council and seek license for it from His Excellency and the Royal Audiencia, and if this is not done, the sale shall be void.

Item: The cacique principal of this town, jointly with one of the alcaldes and regidores, shall within six months from now divvy up to each tributary indian and to the old indians and the poor and widows, all the lands and fields that they might need, for planting maize as well as potatoes and other seeds, and they may not sell them to any person. And the said lands of each indian shall be divided from the other and marked with mojones, to the judgment of the cleric priest who shall be there.

Item: If some necessity should arise that the community pay some silver in favor of the community, let there be no collections for it except by the license of the Royal Audiencia or of the corregidor of the city, rather take what is needed from the fruits and rents of the said herds, when license is given to such effect.

Item: The caciques and principales shall not occupy the male and female indians by taking them along to the City of Silver or to Potosí or to any other place, and if it were necessary let them be from among those who have been assigned in service and from among no others.

Item: None of the said caciques principales shall send any of the said indians anywhere with letters or messages, and if such messengers are necessary for the good of the republic, they may not do it for charity, and the master will be Lope de Mendoza, and for this reason they must be free from tribute and they must be given the salary that the caciques and alcaldes and regidores and the scribe of the council see fit, and I order that it be taken from the rents of the community goods.

Item: The said alcaldes and principales shall take care to have trees and fruits of this land, and those of Castile, planted in their lands, so that there be gardens and orchards to help with sustenance, since the land is appropriate for it.

Item: The alcaldes of each one of the towns shall whip all and any indians who plant in their lands, of the [indios quitas] or yanaconas of any Spaniard whatever, unless they are paid ten loads of any seeds of maize, potatoes, or other seeds that are sown and harvested by means of a loan or lease.

Item: The said caciques and alcaldes of the said pueblo of Our Lady of Bethlehem shall convince and compel and command their indians to give and serve the Spaniards who are lords of fields and herds who might be in their province, renting themselves to them or working for the wages that His Excellency has ordered, by days and weeks or by the year. And the said alcaldes shall make comply and provide to the said Spaniards all the service or wage workers they might need, under pain or privation of the said office.

Item: Those of Caquina shall have twenty indians on that of Marquez and Yanamier twenty houses [sic] as the lord president and judges have ordered; and those of Picachuri ten, understood without the women or children, because they die, and in the same way those of Picachuri shall have five old men in a house and shack in Ancoma, so that they might guard the lands and fields, and they shall be changed as the priest sees fit and gives them license. Diego de Sanabria.

Ordinances for Good Customs

And because the reducción of these indians is made in the town of Our Lady of Bethlehem so that by coming together they live together in policía as Christians, to be better indoctrinated, the following must be kept:

From here on there shall be no gatherings in drunkeness, apart from some festival days with the license of the priest of the doctrina, and before the sun sets the fiesta must end, under the penalty that His Excellency shall set.

And the caciques and principales may not ask for nor take female indians to have as their concubines, or sleep with them, under the penalty of the chapter above.

And because of the custom that no /12r/ indian wishes to marry a virgin without first lying with her, and without which they will not marry, neither the priest of the doctrina nor the cacique shall consent to this, subject to the said penalty.

And because they name each child in conformity to their rites and auguries that they keep from the time of their infidelity, giving to some the name of the moon and to others, of birds and serpents and animals and stones and mountains, the first name that the father or mother hears at the time of the infant's birth, I order that they give no name to their children except for the name of their parents or grandparents, subject to the same penalty.

Item: The female indians tend to bind their infants with threads and belts about the head, from which they die. I order they not do so, subject to the said penalty.

Item: I command that no indians keep dogs in their houses, apart from the caciques, and that all be killed.

And the said scribe shall take care to keep the ordinances above, and the tribute lists, publically each six months, when it is wished to pay tribute and all are gathered together, and they shall write it down in faith.

Item: Because the indians have their own herds, and for a single sheep in the field they put a child of theirs to work to guard it, it is a great deal of work. I command that the cabildo and regiment name each year one indian to guard all the privately held animals, or two or more as necessary, to whom salary shall be assigned from the community goods, giving account of it to the corregidor.

In the service of the tambos, keep the order that will be given by His Excellency.

Item: Every day, eat in the plazas as has been ordered and notified in conformity with the instruction that on this matter His Excellency has given, and under the said penalties, and the priest that shall be is charged with carrying out this ordinance, as well as the others that are made in favor and utility of the republic, and in works of charity that might be done as obligation in service of God Our Lord and the good of the republic.

All of which ordinances the said lord visitor made and declared, by virtue of the commissions of His Excellency, for the good government, Christianity, and policía that have been declared, all of which keep and ensure they are kept and carried out just as is contained in each and every one of them, caciques under pain of privation of their offices, and alcaldes subject to head shaving and whipping, and the other indians subject to the penalties that the alcaldes and caciques shall wish to give. And he signed in his name, Diego de Sanabria, by order of His Mercy Rodrigo Garçcon, scribe of the visita. (AGI, Charcas 49, fols. 7r–12v)

D. EXTIRPATION REPORT OF PRIEST HERNÁN GONZÁLEZ DE LA CASA
(LATE SIXTEENTH CENTURY)

... While I was priest of the towns of Toropalca and Caisa I heard about a wak'a [scribe writes "guaca"] and shrine in the town of Caltama where all the indians of this province sacrificed infants, guinea pigs, sheep, and other animals and carried out many superstitions, for their illnesses as for the weather, invoking the god of rains and lightening, and pretending to say the mass. The one who did this was a great sorcerer named Diego Iquisi. In order to go secretly I walked twenty leagues to this wak'a, at great risk to my life, and taking with me my alcalde and scribe /3r/ from the town, and my factor. More by divine than human work I took away from the wak'a five idols. One, of *tacana* ore, was called Porco, devoted to the mountain and mines of Porco, and the others were called Cuzcoma, Chapote, Suricaba, and Aricaba, all the names of mountains where there are mines and shafts of silver and lead. I took away some silver items from the service of the other idols, and small pieces of silver and *chanbis* and *taracas* and *chipanas* and *queros,* much cloth and things made of feathers, *guascas* and *chuces* and *macno* [all ceremonial and decorative objects] and pelts of sheep of diverse colors, and other things and the clothing of the other wak'as, and trumpets. All of which was offered to the other idols. And with the alcalde and scribe I made an inventory of all this and carried it to this royal audience as attested by the proceso that is in the office of your secretary Juan de Lossa. And having taken away the said wak'a, I returned to my town with twenty-four male and female unfaithful indians, and forty-three boys and girls three and six and eight years old, still unbaptized. And on fording the river more than one hundred indians came at me trying to kill me, shooting many arrows and throwing boulders down upon me. In the space of a single league they made me swim across the river fifteen times. Close to death, I was hit in the leg by an arrow, and they followed me down the river more than a league from one shore to the other, while all the while I carried the wak'as and other things I had found without leaving anything behind. /3v/ They threatened to kill me unless I gave them their father [the wak'a Tata Porco] who had given them victory over the Chichas. Why was he being taken away? And in effect they did try to kill me, giving me herbs from which I was at the point of death, until an indian women cured me with a drink [*bebediço*] of other herbs, and I vomited up a sack of worms like a hickory nut. I brought all these things to this royal audience, and half of it was placed in the royal treasury without costs, all of which I paid. I have spent much in all this, and at the same time I have removed from the said town and from that of Macha many other wak'as and idols and pillus [crowns] and other superstitions for which I punished 175 persons who had apparently been confessed by the other Diego Iquisi and for being idolators. And for this the said Diego Iquisi has been thrown into the hospital.

In that place they adored the said wak'as, carrying out novenas and the penances required by their confessions, and sacrificing sheep and guinea pigs and a three-year-old child. In all of this I have served our Lord and his majesty and the general good of this entire province, since they came to the wak'a in pilgrimage from Cochabamba and the entire district of Charcas, Caracaras, Yanparaes, Chichas, Juras, Visisas, Asanaques, Carangas, and Chuyes, and ending it as I did the adoration and idolatry ceased. [In that place] I built a humilladero with the holy cross, where our Lord is adored and given reverence, and it has been to the great utility and advantage of the naturales, who have been disenchanted from their blindness. At present they mock the said idols and wak'as. Also, I am an Old Christian *hijodalgo,* son of Hernán González, chief master builder of the holy church of Toledo and of its archbishop, and of Juana de Alvarado, native of the town of Linpias in the mountains [of Vizcaya] where I have my house. (AGI, Charcas 79, no. 19, fols. 2v–4r)

E. CIRCULAR LETTER TO ALCALDES OF K'ULTA, 1781

Al Cavildo de Colpacaba: Al Señor Principal doy la noticia fijo, que llego el propio con la noticia que los havía arrastrado de todos de los de Peñas y Hurmiri, una lástima dise que havían hecho los soldados más de dos mill quinientos. Otros tantos disen que vienen por arte de Chichas, nos veremos rodeados para esta noche llegarían sin falta a despoblar a todos nosotros, sin que quedemos ninguno todos de esta provincia, y asi por Dios, Vista esta tengan y den noticia a todos hasta Culta, Cabayo, y Lagunillas, a todas las estancias, pasara a toda furia con maior empeño, como a modo de soldado sin demora ni una ora, y suplico por María Santísima bengan en todo caso todos los comunes a comforme nos ayudara Dios Nuestro Señor, sinco de por muchos años [*sic*]. Challapata. Changara.

—[marginal note] Es su origen de la esquela dirigida al Alcalde mayor deste curato.

—Culta dies y ocho de febrero /1v/ de ochenta y uno. Compañero y señor mío. No se como ponderar los sobresaltos con que en este curato vibo, pues diariamente tenemos nobedades con estos yndios que quieren vibir sin Dios, ni Rey haciendose jueses de sus proprias causas sin ninguna veneración a Dios, y sus Ministros, y todo lo atribuio a la summa rapina con que ellos hasta la ocación presente han vibido quitando vidas y de estos robandoles quanto han tenido.

—Siertas noticias tengo de que el cura de Condo, tiene ánimo expreso de hirse para esa Villa, a refugiarse, por que los yndios han querido dar abanse contra el poniendo por objeto tres motibos. El primero el haver ocultado a un Curaca a quién quicieron quitarle la vida. El segundo tener ellos sospechas, de que los quiere entregar a los soldados, y el tercero tener ellos sertidumbre de que la Plata de don Diego Cosido, para en poder del predicho cura, y mobidos de este ynterés quieren haser esta inhumanidad /2r/ y estas palabras han proferido ellos mismos en este curato.

—El día onse de éste hubo un Casamiento, y al día siguiente un cabo de año a donde se juntaron muchos de los yndios nuestros, y algunos de Macha y Tinquipaya, entre los quales se leyó una esquela, escrita por un principal de Challapata (que ba adjunta con esta) a este curato como V.M. [Vuesa Merced] la berá, y despues de haverla leydo los de este, combocaron a los de Tinquipaya, rogándoles bayan para Challapata, y que si no se berían perdidos. Al día siguiente salieron los alcaldes de nuestro curato, y juntaron muchos de los yndios, y los despacharon a cada qual con dos o tres jondas, palos y algunas otras cosas para su defensa. En el día mesmo onse hablaron los yndios en sus bureos, diciendo que el cura de Macha les havía entregado las llaves de la yglesia para que estos estubiesen a la mira, por si acaso se dentrasen los españoles, ó cholos ó demas gente, que en sus contras fuesen, para que de estos de ningún modo pudiesen refugiarse, en la yglesia. /2v/

[Here the priest begins reporting indian speech:] Así mismo harán aqui y del mesmo modo que nos ha ofrecido, el cura de Macha executaran aquí, y saldrán a defendernos como nos tiene ofrecido, el predicho cura haciendonos semejantemente la equidad de los casamientos, que todas las cosas importarán trese reales, según las cartas de fabor que nos embió nuestro finado Catari, las quales nos ha usurpado el cura de aquí y ha salido en nuestra contra, poníendonos exfuerso y que nosotros paguemos la tasa lo que el no debía de egecutar, antes a defendernos, pero de todo lo verá.

—Nos han dado noticia como el curato de Macha se halla sin cura, ayundante, sacristan ni cantor, por que todos ellos se hallan fugitibos por los que han visto. También nos han dicho que no pondrían mithanis, pongos, ni demas cosas según las cartas de fabor escritas por Cathari, como de facto haviendo ido a haser la elección de alféres y mayordomo al anejo de Cavayo, no me pucieron pongo ni mithani, y me /3r/ tubieron a obscuras, muerto de frio y otras cosas que executaron.

—El día quinse Jueves de Compadres haviendo estado yendo a casar algunos filqueritos, encontré con tres yndios, quienes havían sobrado de los electos de nuestros alcaldes, y el uno de ellos se acercó a preguntarme que noticias havía tenido de los soldados. Yo como ignorante de todo, respondí no saber cosa alguna. No bastó esto, sino dandome algunos golpes en el lado del corasón, me decía que todo lo tenía ocultado dentro de mi corasón, y que no quería a abisarles cosa alguna. Y con estas demostraciones, se despidio, y se fueron mui contentos todos con sus mujeres. Y del mismo modo que los antecedentes.

—Remito a V.M. los treinta y tres pesos los que se han juntado, pues no hemos tenido más entradas, por que todas las personas que han muerto han sido pobres, y estas repentinas, y no nos queda, ni a un medio para nuestro gasto.

—Estimare a V.M. me haga el fabor de atendérmelo al Niño /3v/ que ba a esa cosilla hasta el inter de que se sociegen los yndios o que V.M. se benga, y al mismo tiempo, si alguna cosa se ofreciese en mi casa pues no tengo otro alibio en esa sino el de V.M. y sus padres.

—No se han podido conseguir las Plantas de Lampasos por que los yndios de Cavayo, no se hallan en el lugar, sino en Challapata.

—Estimaré a V.M. procure quanto antes embiarme al yndio y abisarme de su determinación, pues como le tengo dicho del sobresalto con que bibo en este curato, que no beo ora como poder estar en su compañía, y permita su Dibina Clemencia, se sociegen quanto antes estos para que nosotros vibamos sirbiendo a nuestra Patrona Señora de la Mercedes, a quien ruego prospere la importantísima de V.M. los muchos años que mi afecto decea y de sus padres, a quienes de corasón me encomiendo. Su fiel compañero y seguro capellán, Joseph Balzeda. . . . (ANB, SG 1781, no. 42, fols. 1r–3v]

F. CORCINO PÉREZ' PETITIONS TO THE PRESIDENT OF BOLIVIA

1894 Petition

Señor President of the Republic. With the attached titles and powers of attorney I seek exemption from the indicated tax. I, Corcino Pérez, in my name and as the proxy (*apoderado*) of the *comunarios* of Condocondo, before you through the worthy office of the Señor Minister of Hacienda, say with respect: Because of the oppression they suffer with the weight of taxes illegally and unconstitutionally imposed upon this unhappy race, the clamor of the communities does not cease. Our laws have been written but for us are not executed. Because of this, knowing today the enlightened judgment of the Constitutional Government that rules us, we come before your saving protection, so that recognizing the legitimacy of our property in the lands and mills that belong to the community of Condocondo, we be excused from the taxes that, supposing us to be tributaries, have been made to fall upon us, especially the territorial tax, known by the name of tribute. And to this end we base ourselves in the following reasons that we shall lightly now formulate.

First. The community of Condocondo through its principal and representative don Francisco Javier Taquimalco, acquired the property of the lands of Condocondo and the mills of Masce by the cash payment of nine thousand strong and assayed pesos, in simultaneous auction and composición, according to the titles that in forty-one folios accompany this. They are most clear and conclusive, and consequently our right to free property is unquestionable, just as that of all other citizens, in just title as required by article 1,517 of the Civil Code, by which we have possessed it now for almost four centuries.

Second. If this is the case, we exercise over these properties the clear and full right conceded by article 289 of the Civil Code, and tribute like the other obligations that do not fall to the rest of the citizens, are no more than *gavelas* that have no reason to exist, and are based upon no legal disposition whatsoever.

Third. Apart from our legitimate property, accredited by titles, as we have demonstrated, the article of the laws of July 21, 1871, October 5, 1882, and July 3, 1883 has declared and recognized the ownership of lands by their indigenous possessors, with the notorious circumstance that properties composed before the Spanish Crown, by the payment of money, unlike those who do not have these titles, have been recognized as free property, and consequently only those who have not obtained composición are tributaries. So apart from the title, we are supported by the said laws.

Fourth. In consequence, any tax, especially the territorial tax, is an unconstitutional gavela contradicting fundamental principles and statutes of articles 14 and 16 of our fundamental letter, in part because the said tax has no legal foundation, and in part because it has no foundation in equality, falling solely as it does on the indigenous class, who have been humiliated since colonial times and even more since our emancipation.

Fifth. The imposition is even resented as antieconomical, because if [tributes] on indigenous properties were thus transformed into the free exercise enjoyed by the rest of the population, they would produce double or triple the income for the state, because desert places would become towns, and these would not only enlarge the republic but would produce more wealth and more taxes, enriching their owners and consequently the nation since according to the principles of political economy, the wealth of the citizens constitutes that of the state.

Sixth. Because of indigenous oppression, this caste prospers neither in its property nor in its intellectual enlightenment, which is the waning of our nation, and at the same time deserving of the compassionate gaze by which other states criticize us. It is therefore necessary for the supreme government to carry out this passage to civilization for the good of our republic, raising up this oppressed caste, which cries out before its misfortunes, notwithstanding the fact that its strong arm is that which carries out agricultural production and the most difficult and arduous labors. Founded in this and other reasons that are too many to enumerate. . . . Sucre, October 21, 1894. Corcino Pérez. (Choquecallata Document; see note 84 of chap. 6)

The Spanish Original:
    Señor Presidente de la República.—Con los adjuntos títulos y poder pide la excención del impuesto que indica.—Corcino Peres, por mi y como apoderado de los comunarios de Condocondo, ante usted por el digno organo del Señor Ministro de Hacienda respetuosamente digo:
    Que es insesante el clamor de las comunidades, por la oprecion que sufren, con el peso de los impuestos que graviten sobre esta infeliz raza, ilegal e inconstitucionalmente; pues nuestros leyes han quedado escritas sin ejecución para nosotros y por esto conociendo hoy la ilustrada justificación del Govierno Constitucional que nos rige, acudimos ante su protección salvadora para que reconociendo la legítima de nuestra propiedad en los terrenos y molinos que pertenecen a la comunidad de Condocondo, se nos exocere de los impuestos que en el supuesto de ser tributarios, se ha hecho pesar sobre nosotros; especialmente el impuesto territorial, conocido con el nombre de tributo, y para ello nos fundamos en las siguientes rasones que ligeramente pasamos a formular.—
    Primero.—La comunidad de Condocondo por su principal y representante don Francisco Javier Taquimalco, adquirió la propiedad de los terrenos de Condocondo y los Molinos de Masce con dinero de costado de NUEVE MIL PESOS fuertes ensayados, en remate y en composición a la vez según lo acreditan los títulos que en fojas cuarentiuno acompaño que son los más claros y concluyentes, siendo por consiguiente incuestionable nuestro derecho de propiedad libre como la de los demás ciudadanos, justo título con que poseemos desde ahora cerca de cuatro siglos, requerida por el artículo mil quinientos diecisiete del Código Civil.—
    Segunda.—Si esto es cierto, ejecmos sobre esas propiedades, el derecho claro y nato consagra el articulo docientos ochentinueve del mismo, y el tributo así como las demás cargas que no son comunes como a los demás ciudadanos, no son sino gavelas que no tienen racón de ser, ni descansen sobre disposiciones legales alguna.
    Tercera.—Además de nuestra propiedad legítima, acreditada con títulos, como llevamos demostrado, el artículo de las leyes de treintiuno de julio de setentiuno, cinco de octubre del setenticuatro, así como la ley de veintitres de noviembre del ochentitres, confirmando las resoluciones de veintiuno de octubre

del y tres de julio del ochentitres, han declarado y reconocido la propiedad de los terrenos en fabor de los indígenas sus poseedores, con la notoria circunstancia que las propiedades Compuestas ante la Corona de España, mediante el pago del dinero, a diferencia de los que no tienen esos títulos, se ha reconocido de propiedad libre, y por consiguiente no ser tributarios sino los que no obtuvieron la composición; luego además del título, estamos amparados por las citadas leyes.—

Cuarta.—Por consequencia de cualesquier impuesto especialmente el territorial es una gavela inconstitucional contra los principios fundamentales, estatuidos en los artículos catorce y diesiseis de nuestra carta fundamental, tanto porque dicho impuesto no se funda en ley, cuanto porque no descansa en ley, cuanto porque no descansa también el la igualdad, haciendose gravitar tan sólo sobre la clase indígena, que vive humillada desde el coloniaje y continúa aún más desde nuestra emancipación.—

Quinta. Hasta de anti-económico se resiente el gravamen, porque suprimido este las propiedades de los indígenas, entrando en el ejercicio libre como las demás, produciría el doble o triple de los ingresos para el Erario; porque de lugares desiertas, se constituirían en poblaciones que no sólo engrandeserían la República, sino que producirían más riquesas y más impuestos, haciendo ricos a sus propietarios, por consiguientes a la Nación, porque según los principios de Economía Política, la riquesa de los ciudadanos constituye la del Estado.—

Sexta. La opreción indigenal, hace que esta casta no prospere ni en sus propiedades ni en su ilustración intelectual, que es la mengua para nuesta Nación, y la mirada compasiba a la ves que critica de los demás Estados. Se hace ya nesesario que el Supremo Govierno dé este paso de civilización en fabor de nuestra República y levante esta casta oprimida, que gime en vista de su infortunio, no obstante de que su braso fuerte es el que se emplea en las producciones agrícolas, en los trabajos más fuertes y árduos. Fundado en esto y a otras rasones que sería larga enumerarlos, a usted por el Organo de la secretaria de Estado, pido que en atención a nuestro legítimo derecho de propiedad, se sirva de declarar la excención del tributo y demás gavelas con que está gravado el indígena. Si así se modificara el presupuesto aumentará.—

Sucre octubre treintiuno de mil ochocientos noventicuatro.—Corcino Pérez.—Sello del ministerio de hacienda e industria.—Sucre, octubre treintiuno de mil ochocientos noventicuatro.—Vista el señor Fiscal del Distrito.—Firma ilegible.

1895 Petition (English translation on pp. 307–8)

Finalmente he dicho que se funda esta solicitúd en el bién público, porque verificado el deslinde, reconocimiento y revivimiento de los linderos y mojones con los cantones primero colindante—Quillacas, Tinquipaya, Macha, Pocoata, Ucumani, Chayanta, Laimes, Tapacari, y Peñas, Huancané, Isla Morato de San Agustín, y Puñaca—con tantos cantones, y aún entre las parcialidades que componen a cada uno, se evitara tanta matansa de la rasa indígena bajo el pretexto de sublevación que inventa calumniosamente, cualquier afecto a la cosa ajena, bastante esta simple calumnia para balear y encarcelar a la rasa indígena a la cual se diesma mucho más que con las epidemias. Mucho tendrían que decir Soberano Señor, pero allí estan demandando justicia ante los pies del trono del Señor, tanta sangre y tanta lágrima inocentemente vertidas; y sólo mediante una simple calumnia propalada por los codiciosos, aún de los androjos de los pobres indígenas, a que ha dado lugar las nunca bién maldecidas leyes de las autoridades, inconsultantemente votadas, peormente comprendida y cruelmente ejecutada.

No molestare al Soberano Señor en otras reflecciones. Bastante decir que demandando justicia en mayor fabor de la rasa indígena del Canton de Condocondo, pidiendo se vote la cantidad de dinero, suficiente para dotar a los comicionados que deben practicar la operación arriba mencionada que debe encomendarse a persona, siquiera mediante honrada, siquiera de un átomo de justificación, y que siquiera tenga un poco de patriotismo y moralidad.

Además, impetro la declaratoria que expresa del Soberano Señor, a serca de que los indígenas no estamos obligados a pagar el impuesto de postillonaje, en sólo provecho de los Corregidores ordenandose a la ves la inmediata devolución de los terrenos, coactivamente de que se nos ha cobrado, con el pretexto de postillonaje; y todo cada uno de los indígenas propietarios del Departmento de Oruro.

Puesto que la rasa indígena de Bolivia cree merescan alguna consideración y justicia, atenta su ignorancia, timidéz e indefensa, y sobre todo por la riquesa que produce y desarrolla para todas las cifras de la sociedad y de la República, cual no se escapa de la sabiduría y penetración del Soberano Señor. Por lo expuesto pedimos también se sirva ordenar a los comicionados para que con vista de nuestros títulos de propiedad de los linderos y mojones antiguamente repartido. Espero a nombres de mis causantes. Será justicia. Sucre, doce de octubre de 1895. Corcino Pérez. Sello de la secretaria del senado nacional.

Notes

PREFACE

1. In this anthropological-ethnohistorical vein of the influence and training of John Murra and Tom Zuidema, one might also mention (without being exhaustive) the works of Albó (1975, 1976, 1979, 1980, 1987, 1991, 1992, 1994; Albó, Greaves, and Sandoval 1983; Albó and CIPCA team 1972); Allen (1988); Bastien (1978); Bouysse-Cassagne (1975, 1978, 1987, 1988); del Rio (1989); Earls (1969, 1971); Gose (1986, 1991); Harris (1978a, 1978b, 1978c, 1978d, 1980, 1982, 1986, 1987); Isbell (1977, 1985); Mannheim (1986, 1991); Mayer (1977, 1982); Rivera Cusicanqui (1978a, 1978b, 1986); Urton (1981, 1988, 1990, 1994); and Wachtel (1973, 1977, 1978, 1981, 1982, 1990, 1992, 1994). The work of John Rowe (1945, 1954, 1980) and students (especially Julien 1982, 1983, 1995), has also enlivened cultural-historical debate.

Historians have also contributed their share. Among those who have fruitfully tempered materialist leanings with cultural interests on Andean topics, see Bakewell 1984; Barragán 1990, 1992, 1994; Choque 1979, 1986, 1992; Cook 1975, 1981; Cook and Cook 1993; Duviols 1973, 1976, 1977, 1986, 1993; Langer 1989; Larson 1988; Lockhart 1968, 1972; MacCormack 1984, 1985, 1988a, 1988b, 1991; Mallon 1992a, 1992b, 1994; O'Phelan Godoy 1985; Pease 1973, 1977, 1978, 1992; Powers 1991; Ramírez 1987, 1989; Rostworowski de Diez Canseco 1981, 1988a, 1988b; Spalding 1974, 1984; Stern 1982, 1987, 1993; Varón 1982, 1990; Varón and Jacobs 1987; Zulawski 1995. Literary scholars have also fruitfully contributed. See Adorno 1982, 1986, 1992; Mignolo 1993, 1994.

2. Throughout this book, I have chosen to render terms from the Aymara language in the orthography devised by the linguist (and my Aymara teacher in La Paz) Juan de Dios Yapita (1968). I continue to use the official cartographic and state-recognized spellings of proper names, such as towns and persons. I thus contrast "Culta" (as the name of a town and cantón) with "K'ulta" (as the autodenomination of a local group of some of the people living in the town's territory and as the name of that wider "ethnic" territory, or ayllu, itself.

For more difficult cases, such as the names of historical persons or deities reported on in chronicles who never themselves wrote or chose an orthographic

443

convention, I have adopted the most widely used spellings (Huayna Capac rather than the presumably more "correct" Wayna Qapax).

Quechua orthographies differ from Aymara ones, and, while in some cases I have chosen a linguistically correct spelling over chronicled spellings (e.g., *wak'a* instead of *huaca* or *guaca*), to avoid confusion I have in a few cases chosen to render frequently used and widely known Quechua and Aymara terms in their Castilianized forms. *Ceque, quipu, taqui(es),* all Quechua words in the uses reported here, become homographs of different words in Aymara when rendered in current Quechua orthographies. For readability and simplicity, I have also followed the convention of using the Spanish *-s* for the plurals of Quechua and Aymara terms.

For the same reason, and also to avoid making Aymaras appear to speak in "dialect," I use Spanish orthography for most Aymara borrowings from Spanish, for example, *puro* (for pure cane alcohol). For its relative transparency I use *chicha* for the Aymara *k'usa*. Some terms have developed new colonial meanings distinct from pre-Columbian ones. *Pongo,* a house servant, derives from *punku,* door; colonial *yanaconas* were different from pre-Columbian *yanakuna;* in Potosí the *mita* was quite different from pre-Columbian *mit'a* turn systems. In such cases orthographic distinctions can help to clarify the phenomena referred to.

Yapita's orthography describes Aymara phonology with the consonant *j, l, ll, m, n, ñ, r, s, w,* and *x*. The consonants *p, t, k,* and *q* are further subdivided by differentiating nonaspiration, aspiration, and glottalization—for example, *p, p",* and *p'*—providing a total of seventeen distinct consonantal sounds. Three vowels, *i, a,* and *u,* and the pseudovowel *y,* suffice to render vowel sounds, since more rounded *o* and more open *e* vowel sounds are effects of proximity to the back-of-the-throat *q* consonants.

3. This was the linguistically essentializing term that I had then used for certain "natives."

4. Later return trips in 1981, 1982, 1988, and 1990 provided new experiences and insights into some of those matters.

5. In attending specifically to the clash of colonizing and colonized peoples' social memory, I have given short shrift to the ethnohistorical project of reconstructing from various sources an account of the social forms of a precolonial people. Indeed, that was the goal of the historical portions of my dissertation (Abercrombie 1986). Readers specifically searching for a detailed account of the social organization of the Killaka and Asanaqi peoples, pasted together from *visitas,* parish records, *memoriales,* and lawsuits, may find it there.

CHAPTER 1. INTRODUCTION: FROM RITUAL TO HISTORY AND BACK
AGAIN, TRAJECTORIES IN RESEARCH AND THEORY

1. Spellings of *capac hucha* (sometimes joined as a single word, as in *capacocha*) vary in colonial sources and in the scholarly literature. Without actually hearing the term pronounced, it is difficult to determine how to spell it

correctly according to one or another orthographic convention. Distinct Quechua orthographies would in any case produce different possible spellings, and some of these would produce homographs of Aymara terms used elsewhere in the text. This is also true with other Andean terms known mainly from colonial texts, such as *ceque* (sight line or ritual path), *quipu* (knotted cord mnemotechnic), and *taqui* (song-dance). None of these terms is used today by Quechua speakers for the kinds of signification mentioned in colonial texts. I choose therefore to maintain the most commonly accepted colonial spellings of such terms rather than to make arbitrary and possibly confusing orthographic choices. For consistency I spell the term "Inca" with a *c* throughout the text, both when referring to the empire and generic people and when the term is a constituent part of proper names, which I spell according to modern Spanish convention.

2. I have drawn this vignette from a number of sources, including my own imagination. Asanaqi and Killaka subjects undoubtedly served mit'a (turns of service) to the Inca, but their precise duties (apart from service in the Inca fields of Cochabamba) are unknown. Guarache was in Cusco at the time of the Spanish invasion, where he was close to Manco Inca (supposedly as a member of Manco's war council), but no document suggests when or under what circumstances Guarache first went to Cusco. Guarache was indeed awarded *cumbi* shirts by the Inca emperor, but ascribing the event to a change-of-status ceremony during Huayna Capac's investiture or royal visita, or during periodic *capac hucha* rites is mere speculation (see analyses of capac hucha in Duviols 1976, Rostworowski de Diez Canseco 1988a; of Inca royal visits and the comparable ritual effectiveness of Spanish visitas in Guevara-Gil and Salomon 1994.) Likewise, it is impossible to say with any exactness that Asanaqi mit'a workers would have stopped in Jatun Qulla (excavated by Catherine Julien [1983]) on their way to Cusco, or have performed the sorts of libations I describe. The idea comes from the work of archaeologist Craig Morris (1979; Morris and Thompson 1985) on another Inca administrative center, Huanuco Pampa, where *chicha* was consumed in quantity within the elite structures that might have been thought of as the formal work spaces of high priests or ranking Inca bureaucrats.

3. One of three probanzas produced by Colque Guarache in the mid-1570s, this *curriculum vita* in question-and-answer format is published in Espinoza Soriano 1981 (from the original in AGI, Quito 45). Another almost contemporary Colque Guarache probanza, with significant but not startling variations, is located in the Archivo del Tribunal de Poopó (see chapter 7).

4. The pouring of *ch'allas* during amt'añ t"aki sessions is always carried out in gender parallel, where men, sitting on benches or stone seats, pour libations to male beings, while women, seated directly on the ground, pour to female beings. The performances of men and women may be complementary, but their position in space (high versus low, east-facing versus west-facing) also underscores and reproduces a gendered asymmetry of power. Gender complementarity is

explored in depth in Harris 1978c, 1978d, 1980, 1986; and in Arnold 1988, 1992, 1993; Arnold and Yapita 1992a, 1992b; Arnold, Jiménez, and Yapita 1992; and is treated historically in Silverblatt 1987.

5. I provide a description that is a composite sketch drawn from my participation in many such performances in Vila Sirka over the period of 1980–82, during which I was usually given an honored place at the men's altar.

6. My understanding of Julián's case derives from my participation in courtroom proceedings and from access to the expediente that I enjoyed after becoming part of it. I also discussed particulars with Julián and his wife at considerable length. Sent by Julián to K'ulta to round up his kinsmen as additional character witnesses, I learned another side of the story (see concluding chapter).

7. Interview with don Pablo Choquecallata (a pseudonym, as are all names I provide here for the people of K'ulta), October 1979.

8. Very forthcoming and proud of his efforts on behalf of Cruce, Pablo Choquecallata spoke with me on many different occasions between 1979 and 1982, and again in 1988, by which time he was in his early eighties. He never mentioned his prominent role in forwarding cantonization petitions by which Cruce—and Ayllu Alax-Kawalli—strives to secede from Cantón Culta (originals in the Archivo de Hacienda and Archivo del Instituto Geográfico Militar, Prefectura de Oruro). Nor was he forthcoming on the murder accusations leveled against him for destroying a nearby settlement that members of Ayllu Qullana had begun to build as their proposed new town and cantón capital (Archivo de Hacienda y Tesoro, Prefectura de Oruro, Expediente de Amparo Administrativo, 1968). See chapter 6 for details.

The Choquecallata document is a typescript made by the notary Eloy Lascano of Oruro in March 1962, from an earlier transcription that cites the ADRO, Provincia Abaroa, Libro de Propiedades, 1945, no. 8. It is laden with copyist's errors. Many other copies of the 1593 and 1646 *composición* titles are also in existence (though without the nineteenth- and twentieth-century accretions described here), including those presented in 1757 by the caciques of Challapata in their denunciation of the Condo indians' raids on their hamlet, and by the Condo cacique Llanquipacha in his reply and counteraccusation in the same litigation expediente. Rotative authorities of Challapata, Condo, Culta, and Cahuayo independently submitted the same titles in defense of their lands during the late nineteenth and early twentieth centuries, which were then copied several times into the bound and dated property registers located in the Juzgado de Derechos Reales, in the Corte Superior de Oruro.

9. Connerton draws especially on Halbwachs 1925, 1941 (republished in Halbwachs 1994). Other recent works in the arena of social memory include: Gillis 1994; Hobsbawm and Ranger 1983; Hutton 1993; Le Goff 1992; Nora 1984. For the Andes more specifically, some recent works mining this vein are: Arnold, Jiménez, and Yapita 1992; Boone and Mignolo 1994; Burga 1988; Flores Galindo 1987b; Rappaport 1990, 1994; Saignes 1993. Many of these authors pay respects to Yates 1966.

10. I thank Florencia Mallon for pointing this out to me.

11. Indeed, the very sixteenth-century Spaniards who scorned uncertain Andean oral fables and lamented Andeans' lack of writing, even as they strove to construe a certain written history of the Andes from the confusions of native myth, placed the certain foundations of the most vital aspects of their lives in extrahuman activity: that of Divine Word. In an era when most of the Castilian population remained illiterate and, indeed, when theologians agreed that literacy provided untutored minds access to texts they could not correctly interpret, the teaching of correct doctrine and well-ordered life-ways was generally consigned to sensual techniques, to bodily habit and public performance, constrained within controlled public spaces open to the censorial gaze of the Inquisition and its familiars. An instructive case is the fate of Menocchio, the late-sixteenth-century miller from the Friuli whose wide-ranging but poorly disciplined reading enabled the devil to lead him into heresy and eventually to the stake (Ginzburg 1982). Far better for him had he left letters alone and depended on the pedagogy of liturgical ritual for his instruction in history (which is to say, the tenets of the faith). At the very least, the twentieth-century reader of his foibles might interject, the omnipresence of the Inquisition and dangers inherent in frank discussion of religious matters ought to have led him to keep his own counsel.

What Menocchio seems not to have learned, either from his illiterate artisan comrades or from the society of aristocratic and clerical literati to which he did not fully belong, is what Maravall (1987) termed the "culture of the Baroque." Radical social critiques could be safely articulated in this Counter-Reformation context only by clothing the wolf in sheep's skin, by simultaneously becoming clandestine and taking the outward form of the opposite of social critique, defense of orthodoxy. Thus much of the "popular religiosity" condemned by the Church hierarchy as dangerously unorthodox moved into the sphere of still fervently "Catholic" but difficult to parse clandestine practice; the literati found that they could still publish social critiques so long as they cloaked those critiques in distancing tropes, as the mouthings of madmen like Cervantes' Quixote, the ridiculous conversations of dogs miraculously and temporarily graced with the power of speech, or the confessions of pitiful criminals such as the eponym of *Lazarillo de Tormes*.

12. MacCormack 1991 (also Bilinkoff 1989) explores the philosophic and theological arguments which accounted for how the devil regularly made use of the imagination, the very means by which men could understand divinity, to lead them astray.

13. In this reformulation of the project that I began so long ago, I draw on various semiotic approaches to culture and the linguistic turn towards pragmatics (some precursors: Silverstein 1976; Hanks 1990; Parmentier 1987), along with Bourdieu's (1977, 1979) analogous retargeting of "cultural coding" from linguistic abstraction to the plane of embodied and practiced habitus. I also draw on the results of the collective enterprise of interpreting Gramsci's theses on the interplay of culture and power, through the now well-worn concepts of hegemony and counterhegemony (see especially Comaroff 1985; Comaroff and

Comaroff 1991, 1992). All these sources help in conceptualizing how intersubjective orders of meaning arise in lived experience, are deployed in habitual practice, challenged in contests of power, and put at risk in contingent events (Sahlins 1985). Above all such theoretical schemata, I here prefer the notion of social memory, meaning context-linked enactments of collective meanings, whose authority lies in its supposed source in the past. Traditions may be invented (Hobsbawm and Ranger 1983), but social memory inevitably denies that invention, rooting the specific nature and privileges of subjective identities, that to us are contingent, in given rather than invented sources and authorities, that is, in primordial tradition. I thus focus on such collectively validated practices as oral narrative and ritual, but I take these as the products and producers of collective authorship, of social groups, and assume that social memory covaries along with the shape of the social formations to which it pertains. All histories (both ritual or mythic, and written kinds) are shaped by the political and personal concerns of their authors, in order to reflect or validate, challenge or revise, the lived meanings of present social worlds. As Steve J. Stern has recently argued (1993), there can be no such thing as a dispassionate and objective historical work, only works by authors who *believe* themselves to be without causes. To this degree, I take written and nonwritten forms of social memory to be alike.

14. Anthropology's historical turn has been deftly reviewed by Biersack (1989); Faubion (1993); Hunt (1989); Kellogg (1994). The anthropology of history is treated as part of the discipline's theorizations of time in Munn 1992. Product of a larger discipline-centered critique of structuralist and "culturalist" theoretical constructs, which were (unlike the myths and rituals that provided their grist) kinds of antihistorical windmills, anthropology's interest in history (now waning as "posthistorical" paradigms of internationalization and globalization move to the fore) bore little direct relationship to history's ethnographic turn. The latter, taken especially by historians with a bent for "history from below," has been an effort to portray from fragmentary sources the life-world, or "culture," of some group or class who had been erased from official chronicle. Paradoxically, history's "ethnographic turn" has tended to favor closed semiotic models of culture. For an overview, see: Burke 1991; Cohn 1987; Desan 1989; Sharpe 1991.

15. Sanctified by divine law, positive science, or the law of the marketplace, imperialist and nationalist projects presuppose teleological trajectories towards which their subjects and citizens should aim.

CHAPTER 2. JOURNEYS TO CULTURAL FRONTIERS

1. Because of its proximity to La Paz, to the Peruvian rail line to Juliaca, and to Lake Titicaca, and perhaps also because of the strength of the hacienda system (by which ethnographers, archaeologists, and travelers more generally were once guaranteed a position of power on the Altiplano), the Titicaca area has been host

to a long series of ethnographies, beginning with Bandelier 1910, Tschopik 1951, La Barre 1948, and continuing through Buechler and Buechler 1971, Carter 1964, 1968, 1977; and a crop of newer work by scholars such as Barstow 1978; Crandon-Malamud 1993; Collins 1988; etc. As of 1979, only a handful of works by Platt (1978a, 1978b, 1982a, 1982b, 1983, 1984, 1987a, 1987b, 1987c) and Harris (1978a, 1978b, 1978c, 1978d, 1980, 1982, 1986, 1987) had pushed the Aymara frontier south of the Titicaca Basin. Since then, considerably more has been published, and an influx of scholarly interest in Bolivia (fed by the scholarly flight from a dangerous Perú) has dropped large numbers of anthropologists and historians upon Bolivian territory. Complementing the extensive ethnographic and historical work by Harris and Platt on the Chayanta and Macha territories, the early and mid-1970s produced a number of studies on the Altiplano and its valleys in the Departments of La Paz, Oruro, Potosí, and Chuquisaca. See, for example, studies of Pakax/Pacajes (Albó and CIPCA team 1972), Chipaya (Wachtel 1978, 1990, 1994), Qaranka/Carangas (Rivière 1982, 1983), and Lipes and Atacama (Martínez Cereceda 1991). Field research in the late 1970s and early 1980s produced ethnographies/ethnohistories of Awllaka/Aullagas (Molina Rivero 1986a, 1986b; West 1981a, 1981b), Yura (Rasnake 1986, 1988a, 1988b; Harmann 1988), Pakax/Pakajes (Albó 1992; Choque Canqui 1979, 1986, 1992; Rivera Cusicanqui 1978a, 1978b, 1986; Rivera and Platt 1978), Jukumani/ Jucumani (Godoy 1990), Calcha (Medlin 1984), Yampara (Barragán 1994), and Challa/Quirquiavi (Izco Gastón 1992). More recently, work has been carried out in and on Sakaka/Sacaca (Zorn 1996), Quntu/Condo (Sikkink 1994), more on Macha (Torrico, n.d.), Sura (del Río 1990; del Río and Gordillo 1993), Qaqachaka/Cacachaca (Arnold 1988; Arnold, Jiménez, and Yapita 1992), Tarija (Langer 1989; Presta 1995), and a group calling itself Jallqa (Martínez 1992). Much more ethnographic fieldwork is currently underway or being written up on Pukwata/Pocoata, Tinkipaya/Tinquipaya, Murumuru or Ravelo, San Lucas, and no doubt other areas in the Departments of Oruro, Chuquisaca, and Potosí.

2. On the Aymara language, see Hardman 1981, 1986; and Hardman, Vásquez, and Yapita 1975, 1988. Aymara dialectology is explored in groundbreaking work by Briggs (1993). The shift since colonial days towards Quechua, especially in mining centers and along major transport routes, has been documented by Albó (1979, 1980). Earlier shifts from formerly widespread languages called Puquina, Uru, and Uruquilla are studied by Torero (1987, 1990, 1992) and Wachtel (1978, 1990). Early colonial language distribution attested in a colonial source is described by Julien (1983) and summarized on a map by Bouysse-Cassagne (1975).

3. There is a growing literature on such domestic service, especially for the cases of La Paz and Lima. On La Paz, see Gill 1994.

4. On the Tupac Catari siege, see Diez de Medina 1981; and Szeminski 1987. On liberalism as ethnocide, see Platt 1984. Indigenous rebellion in the aftermath of the "War of the Capitals" is treated in Condarco Morales 1966. The 1920s rebellions have as yet received little attention, but see Platt 1987a; and Langer 1990.

5. There is a large literature on the revolution wrought by the Movimiento Nacionalista Revolucionario (MNR). See the bibliography in Klein 1992.

6. See Klein 1992. I was able to follow the progress of two such blockades over the radio from K'ulta.

7. Kallawaya practitioners have received much attention. Among others, see Bastien 1978; Girault 1987; Rösing 1990. As yet, however, the urban "magic" system has not been adequately described. Ubiquity of first-Friday ceremonies and brisk business in "mesas" in markets of Bolivia (see Martínez 1987) warrant much more study, especially as such practices gain in public respectability and visibility as the indianista star—and the value of indian magic—rises in national politics.

8. One may also find the tools of nearly every imaginable trade, certificates of mastery of trades, papal dispensations for divorce, papers granting husbands license to commit adultery, and, of course, mini household appliances for those hoping to acquire some of the goods available in Miamicito. Alasitas has yet to find its definitive ethnographer. It is a folkloric extravaganza in La Paz but can be found in other highland cities and in the countryside (where beans and stones stand for money and bulls).

9. The vecinos of Cruce and of Santa Bárbara are frequently asked to become the godparents of campesino children and the patrons of campesino marriages. To be sure, the resulting obligations of *compadrazgo* and *padrinazgo* oblige campesinos to offer their produce and animals to their *compadres* and *padrinos* at "reasonable" prices, putting vecinos in a position to supply their stores and restaurants (as well as kitchens) cheaply, and to "bulk" rural products for profitable resale in urban markets. Relations of obligation, however, cut both ways. Padrinos must be generous in providing gifts to their godchildren in the context of certain rites of passage, and will certainly come to lack in new godchildren if they are overtly exploitative. At the same time, godchildren and campesino co-godparents often call upon their vecino padrinos and compadres to reciprocate by providing loans of urban commodities in times of need, by giving support during festival sponsorship, and by offering hospitality at critical moments. Thus when K'ultas travel to Huari for its annual fair, most have a place to stay in the households of vecino compadres or padrinos who come from there.

10. Nowadays one Aymara speaker may also apply the term "q'ara" to another when the latter is perceived as having adopted urban values by, for example, hoarding cash to buy a truck and thereby refusing to participate in expected generalized reciprocal relations.

11. In an idealist indigenista moment, I heard a few vecinos refer to themselves as part of a more embracing *nación mestiza,* thereby adopting, for self-conscious and politically charged motives, a dual heritage that they most often deny through their usual strenuous efforts to distance themselves from indios and cholos.

12. It is all too easy to hypostatize the supposed social categories of indio, mestizo, and criollo, and to imagine them as clearly bounded and castelike strata in a society born of colonialism, in which degree of privilege correlates

inversely with race or national origin. Such a view of Bolivian social stratification is overly simplistic even for the sixteenth century, and tallies very poorly with what I was able to observe in Cruce. One might more carefully rethink such terms as ethnically tinged markers of social class drawn from the language of race. These terms were first applied, however, fully two hundred years before doctrines of racial difference became fashionable in nineteenth-century Bolivia (see Abercrombie 1996). Analysis is complicated by the fact that the other terms that are used to euphemize, supplement, or displace them, such as "campesino," "cholo," and "vecino," carry meanings from distinct arenas of signification like "relationship to the means of production," "level of cultural intermediacy," and "civic status vis-à-vis state-recognized municipality."

13. For Cruce's vecinos, "ethnic/class" identity is also relative. Some vecinos hail from the town of Huari, and when they return there, where they own herds and work the soil, they become campesinos to the wealthier and more "criollo" vecinos of that town. If they are not very careful with their dress and language when they travel to the larger cities, they are likely to be taken for migrant cholos, thus merging with those, back in Cruce, with whom they would contrast themselves. The line separating vecinos and campesinos in Cruce is extremely thin and highly permeable. The categories meet at a point of indeterminacy. This fact does not free the relationship between them from conflict; on the contrary, it only seems to intensify the relationship in a continuing struggle for self-definition. Although cultural differences, along with levels of economic means, are much wider between the highest and lowest urban strata, a similar story might be told of its cholos, mestizos, and criollos.

14. The most celebrated (or lamented) case of textile sales was that of the ritual textile bundles of Coroma, partly recovered through the extraordinary efforts of Bolivian anthropologist Cristina Bubba.

15. Since the fieldwork period of 1979–81, Cruce has notably "progressed." It now has two one-room churches, if Protestant ones, both run by Aymara evangelists. Another few restaurants also line the highway. The Catholic church has responded by regularly dispatching a group of catechist nuns to Cruce, to augment the priest's yearly visits. In addition, Cruce has obtained the cantón's first rural *posta sanitaria,* where a nurse practitioner dispenses first-aid and vaccinations. A new Saturday market has also drawn the town's first artisan, maker of *ujutas* (rubber tire sandals), and its first *chicherías,* two bars that sell a drink that was formerly available only in the festival context. Another addition is a transit policeman, who mans a new *tranca* (a "toll booth" where travel permits are inspected and truck cargoes sometimes searched for contraband).

CHAPTER 3. THE DIALOGICAL POLITICS OF ETHNOGRAPHIC FIELDWORK

1. When I asked don Manuel to draw a map of K'ulta territory, he placed Santa Bárbara at the center, dissected by the east-west highway and north-south caravan trail. The Pan American Highway follows the route of an older road

built for mule-drawn wagons sometime during the late nineteenth or early twentieth century. An earlier east-west road, with gradients too steep for either wagons or motor vehicles, bypassed Santa Bárbara to the south, just as the new highway bypasses it to the north. I have walked sections of the older road, which passed through Lagunillas on its way west to Condo rather than to Challapata. To the southeast, it may well have led to Porco rather than to Potosí. Sections of this now unused road are clearly Incaic, forming a still-unsurveyed east-west link in the Inca road system studied in Hyslop 1984.

2. This was one of many *samarayañas,* "breathing" places where people and gods pause on their pilgrimages to and from Santa Bárbara's church.

3. A young couple dressed in city finery were hustled across the plaza towards the office by a large group of angry people, jostling and insulting the unlucky pair until they were inside the office and the corregidor asked for quiet. It turned out that they had recently been married in Potosí and had returned to collect their belongings before setting out on a life together elsewhere. This had been a mistake, for the young man's belongings were in a house that was still occupied by his old wife, whom he sought to replace with this new one. His own patriline kin had taken the newly weds captive and had been joined in the plaza by his first wife's kinsmen. The couple received a terrible tongue lashing, punctuated by pushes and slaps, until finally the corregidor called a halt to the proceedings and sent for the new wife's kinsmen. The bigamist was thrown into the town's tiny one-room jail (the only building in town made entirely of stone), while two of the authorities dragged the young bride towards the church. In the thirty paces between the town hall and the church, women in the crowd managed to tear her newly bought cholita outfit to shreds. While the authorities waited for further interested parties to arrive (such as the second wife's kin from a distant hamlet), we were admitted to the meeting room.

4. The cemetery was moved from the churchyard as a result of an eighteenth-century hygienic policy.

5. The vast majority of the identity cards I saw on this occasion belonged to men, though many women also carry them. What I found most noteworthy was the profession by which most had chosen to be identified. A small minority of men had elected *agricultor,* "farmer," whereas the great majority chose to be identified as *commerciantes,* "businessmen." The few dozen women whose cards I handled, on the other hand, were almost evenly divided between *pastora,* "shepherdess," and *tejedora,* "weaver."

6. Since election results have been published, however, it is not remiss to note that local balloting heavily favored Siles Suazo and his Union Democrática Popular party. A minority of votes went to Victor Paz Estenssoro and the Movimiento Nacionalista Revolucionario. Both of these men had occupied the presidency before, and their left-leaning political movements had been centrally important to the national revolution of the 1950s, with its expropriations of mines and oil fields and its peasant union–forced agrarian reform act. Voting confirmed continuing sympathy for the changes in rural life that had resulted from that revolution.

7. By formal interview, I mean extended private discussions, seated at a table with tape recorder and notebook, in which I had prepared extensive lists of questions in advance. The most extensive discussions were with don Manuel Mamani of Vila Sirka, over a period of nearly ten days. At don Manuel's insistence, these interviews were both remunerated and carried out far from K'ulta territory. His insistence on remuneration, at a rate based on (but higher than) the daily wage in the mine work he has periodically undertaken, was supported by sound argument: Ten days of continuous questioning would be difficult and would take him from other productive labors. In particular, it cut into his planned long-distance trading trip. He preferred to do the interviews away from K'ulta to avoid the prying ears of his countrymen, who might think him involved in unscrupulous dealing or become envious (of his payments and ties to influence). Precisely the same argument was forwarded by don José Camino of Lakachaka (Ayllu Manxa-Kawalli), with whom I spent five less fruitful days. In both cases, interviews were carried out in rented rooms in La Paz. Don Manuel and I encamped for ten days in a somewhat seedy hotel room. Across the hallway, a textile trader from Tarabuco engaged in deals with a hippy-capitalist exporter. All of us shared the bathroom with twins from Colombia, dwarves born without legs, who paid for their room with the proceeds of their begging on the main street of La Paz. We ate together in the market and a few times in classier restaurants (after don Manuel convinced me to buy him better-quality clothes and a pair of coveted soccer shoes, so he would not feel ill at ease). Don Manuel took time off on market days to spend some of his pay, mostly on high-quality alpaca pelts.

I twice obtained the consent of don Pablo Choquecallata, founder of Cruce, to tape-record his storytelling, under almost formal conditions. Don Bartolomé Mamani, the *yatiri* who officiated in several ch'allas I had attended, also sat for many hours with me, helping to reconstruct the ch'allas I had missed once too many had been poured. Since he insisted on pouring and drinking a small shot of alcohol every time he pronounced the words of a libation, tape recording proved essential in these sessions. Here interviews were made possible by goodwill and long-term reciprocal indebtedness rather than by wages. Both men preferred to work after dark and behind closed doors, for the same reasons that don Manuel and don José had chosen to travel to La Paz.

8. In an ideal year, planting in late September and early October is followed by the return of the rains from November through February, then harvests in April. In May, crops of bitter potatoes, the only variety that does well in the cantón's high-altitude fields, are processed into a freeze-dried form called *ch'uñu,* which can be stored for years. Strips of meat are also freeze dried at this time, producing *charki* (from which the term "jerky" comes). But rarely is there an ideal agricultural year in Cantón Culta. Hail storms, late or early freezes, and poorly timed or insufficient rains make farming an unusually risky business. What is more, none of the cantón's lands are suitable for maize farming, and only a few sheltered spots sometimes permit the harvest of a small crop of the much-appreciated *janq'u imilla* ("white girl") or *ch'yar imilla* ("black girl")

varieties of potato. Broad beans and onions can sometimes be grown within the shelter of the walls of roofless houses, and quinua is also planted in small quantities. A variety of barley that does not reach maturity here provides animal fodder, useful when standing hail keeps llamas in the corral.

9. Challapata hosts the Ranger Battalion, U.S.-trained "red berets" famed for Che's execution.

10. I once witnessed the signing of another such acta in a wrongful death suit that was settled without recourse to supracantonal authorities. Later, I myself was to sign such a document.

CHAPTER 4. STRUCTURES AND HISTORIES: K'ULTA BETWEEN GODS AND STATE

1. So sacrosanct are local jurisdictions that authorities in Cruce and Santa Bárbara twice stamped my passport with cantón and vice-cantón rubber stamps. Other permission papers quickly accrued a collection of such stamps, signatures, and thumbprints, the likes of which are also part of all petitions to provincial, departmental, or national governments.

2. As an administrative unit of the Bolivian state, Cantón Culta is one among the dozens of cantóns that make up the next highest administrative division, the province, under the political leadership of a subprefect. Several such provinces make up the Department of Oruro, administered by a prefect in the department capital of Oruro. From shortly after Bolivian independence, Cantón Culta belonged first to the Provincia de Paria, derived directly from a colonial province. After the War of the Pacific in the last quarter of the nineteenth century, Paria Province was subdivided. Along with Condo, Huari, and Challapata, Culta became a cantón of the Provincia Abaroa, with its capital and subprefect located in the town of Challapata. In 1984, Huari (then capital of the second section of the province) obtained approval of its provincialization petition, becoming capital of the breakaway Provincia de Atahuallpa. Condo and the cantóns that had broken away from it (including Condo K, Urmiri, Culta, and Cahuayo) were charted to join the new province. Resisting the secession of Huari (which, with its brewery, is the principal tax base of the region), Challapata (supported by several hundred Qaqachaka fighters) marched on Huari and bloody fighting (and legal oppositions) ensued, settled finally by the Bolivian Senate. Cantón Culta has remained in Provincia Abaroa, while Cahuayo, in theory still part of Provincia de Atahuallpa, has declared its allegiance to the Department of Potosí.

3. Both prefect and subprefect are presidential appointees and, as such, loyal members of the ruling party or coalition of parties. The vast majority of government financing for cantonal, provincial, and departmental projects, such as road construction and provision of water and sewer lines, electricity, health services, and development loans, has until recently been funneled through the department's and province's appointed officials. Given the state's scarcity of resources and the appointed nature of departmental and provincial offices, it is

not surprising that most such money has been spent on projects in the department capital, with some spin-off funding to the provincial capitals from which subprefects hail. Very little funding has made it to rural cantóns, most of which, like Culta, lack electricity, running water, and most other municipal services. Recent populist politics and the new Law of Popular Participation have lately funneled more development funds into the countryside, but their true impact has yet to be seen.

Apart from their administrative duties (which include control of police forces, collection of taxes, etc.), these appointed officials also serve as judicial authorities of second resort. The subprefect's office in Challapata is also a juzgado, and the subprefect there dispenses a certain amount of summary justice, hearing cases brought before him by the town councils of the cantóns of his jurisdiction.

4. Cantón Culta (spelled per maps and state documents according to Spanish orthographic convention) is the social unit and territory understood vis-à-vis its relationship to the state and its formal incorporation as a unit of that state (just as Santa Bárbara de Culta is a recognized cantón capital). Ayllu K'ulta (spelled in Aymara orthography as pronounced in that language) is that very same social group, as it is sometimes locally understood and constituted, and the territory the group claims and occupies. The two are essentially synonymous. Both Cantón Culta and Ayllu K'ulta were composed of five constituent ayllus: Qullana, Alax-Kawalli, Manxa-Kawalli, Yanaqi, and Ilawi. Both units are still undergoing processes of fragmentation. For a period of time in the past, Ayllu K'ulta was also divided into moieties, wherein Ayllus Alax-Kawalli and Manxa-Kawalli together constituted K'ulta's lower moiety (*manxa-saya*), while Qullana, Yanaqi, and Ilawi joined forces within K'ulta's upper moiety (*alax-saya*). During the period of fieldwork, only Alax-Kawalli and Manxa-Kawalli participated fully in all political and ritual activities of Cantón Culta/Ayllu K'ulta. The two ayllus now engage in cycles of alternation and ritual battles making *them* into moieties. The distinction between Ayllu K'ulta and Cantón Culta is an analytic one, not clearly made by the people of the place, but it is not merely heuristic, since in the past Cantón Culta included what are now Cantones Lagunillas and Cahuayo, although these were conceived of as made up of major ayllus distinct from the five ayllus of Ayllu K'ulta. According to Platt (1987b), neighboring Ayllu Macha remains a coherent maximal ayllu (subdivided into constituent moieties and major and minor ayllus), notwithstanding its division into multiple cantones, though this would appear to be an unusual case.

5. During my time in K'ulta I have witnessed council-directed collective labor to repair the church, build a new house for the local schoolteacher, repair the access road to Santa Bárbara, and build the posta sanitaria in Cruce. I also saw collective action to block the Pan American Highway in national strikes that brought down military dictators in 1979 and 1982. Formerly, council-led labor levies were also responsible for construction and repair of the main highway where it runs through K'ulta territory, but such work is now undertaken with heavy machinery by state-paid road crews.

6. Both the authority and mediating powers of the council are, however, limited. Individuals against whom substantial evidence of adultery, incest, theft, or murder has been advanced are well advised to leave town, to avoid the swift and terrible justice that local "posses" mete out in such cases.

7. To satisfy the subprefect, the successful candidate for corregidor must speak Spanish, and this becomes an important concern in seeking candidates. But other criteria also come into play. As a result, perhaps, of long experience with abusive and peremptory corregidors, the post-1952 system of corregidor election undermines that official's potential power and legitimacy. In the cases I know of, candidates were on the young side and had not participated in the legitimacy-inspiring fiesta-cargo system. While they presided over meetings as chair, they lacked authority to override the collective weight of the council and tended literally to rubber-stamp the decisions of their seniors, the assembled jilaqatas, alcaldes, and alguaciles.

8. A frequently broadcast radio spot that year consisted of a few minutes of breakers washing over a beach, followed by a solemn pledge to recover "*nuestro mar.*"

9. Inscribed on the base of a statue to Abaroa's memory in Oruro, the dictum is the subject of a running joke based on the word play sometimes attributed to Abaroa himself. "Que se rinde su abuela" is officially interpreted as "Let your grandmother surrender," but can also be parsed as a vulgar taunt on the basis of extended meanings of "surrender."

10. The dance of choice was the one called *caporales,* a favorite of Oruro's *carnaval* procession that is regularly performed by the children of that city's elite high school. Derived from another dance, the *negritos* (a dance of slaves and slave drivers), caporales are exclusively whip-wielding slave drivers dressed in brilliantly sparkling colors, but bereft of slaves.

11. The term "supay" was apparently applied in preconquest times (and by speakers of Quechua) to a category of ancestor (see Harris 1982; MacCormack 1991, Taylor 1980). Used by early missionaries to translate "Satan" or "devil," "supay" acquired some of the qualities Spaniards ascribed to "devils" and "demons." K'ultas also accept "supay" as a designation for the presolar people called Chullpas, relegated to the underworld by the first rising of the Solar-Christ. I later learned that the libations I was told were dedicated to "some supays" were actually poured for uywiris, mallkus, and t'allas (feminine, flat plain dieties). Telling the outsider that these were superstitions performed for demons served to "diabolize" the performance, simultaneously distancing the speaker from such activities, raising him towards the cosmopolitan status of the hearer, and validating the outsider-hearer's presumed preconceptions of indian ritual practices, thus closing the door on further inquiry. Yet indirectly, the characterization of indigenous gods as supays also categorized them correctly, since, like some deceased ancestors, Supay-Chullpas and uywiris and mallkus are powerful beings from the past, still present in the underworld. Here we see how differing interpretations of the same acts, events, and numinous beings can thus

appear to overlap on a higher level of abstraction, producing a structured system of limited communication that I shall call cultural pidgin.

12. Long-festering rivalries and feuds and competing claims to land are often brought to a head when patronymic groups appear en masse to cultivate and fence new fields in long-fallowed parcels. Given the length of fallow, opening lands that have not been cultivated for generations, often in *puruma* areas considered "no man's land," are especially likely to lead to such disputes.

13. Several members of dancing and fighting groups in the festivals of Guadalupe and Exaltación told me that these were mere rehearsals compared with the ritual battle of Culta's patron saint feast of Santa Bárbara.

14. I later discovered that, fearing a major fight between Qullana and the Kawallis, the corregidor had also asked for soldiers to provide a "peace-keeping" force during the festival of Santa Bárbara.

15. Similar rhetoric and specific recommendations for change can be seen in regulations for orderly town life laid down in the *ordenanzas* of Viceroy Francisco de Toledo (see chap. 6 and part B of the Documentary Appendix).

16. Don Bartolomé was also an accomplished and admired storyteller, whose versions of Aymara myths I have chosen to present here. Doña Basilia's narrative skills were employed elsewhere as a frequent leader of wedding songs and songs to the animals (on which see Arnold and Yapita 1992a, 1992b).

17. Some forms of cultural analysis insist that every class within a system such as Bolivia's shares common cultural ground. Maybe so, but the scope of shared cultural knowledge may be broad or narrow, and interpretations of apparently shared terms of symbolic actions may still differ considerably. "Speaking" in a cultural pidgin, everyone in the country understands roughly that Supay is to indian as Christ is to creole elite, but they do not understand it in the same way or with the same implications. As a kind of language, pidgin has the advantage of making communication possible, bringing speakers and participants of two or more distinct languages and cultures into conjunction for certain circumscribed ends, which lately have included the building of "creole" national cultures. Such a "cultural pidgin" exists, of course, because the intercultural communications of today have a history, dating back to the first moments of the Spanish invasion of this part of the Andes and to the mutual accommodations reached by Spaniards and indians in the colonial situation, and by creole elites and indigenous campensinos in the postcolonial one.

18. For an indication of where I would take this argument, see Abercrombie 1991, and for first installments on a study of the emergence of a "mestizo-cholo" cultural zone in which the cultural pidgin of the Spanish and indian frontier is a native language, see Abercrombie 1992, 1996.

19. The term "discourse" here must be expanded, of course, to include the history of violence and oppression to which the people called indians were subjected, as well as the active and passive and the overt and hidden forms of resistance in which they have engaged (see Abercrombie 1991).

20. Another version of the story has it that Santa Bárbara was walking down from the headwaters of the Pilcomayo with her sister, Belén. When a young boy saw the two of them, Santa Bárbara was frozen into image form, while her sister continued on downriver to the town of Tinquipaya, where she is venerated as Our Lady of Bethlehem.

21. On Inca stones in nearby ethnic groups, see Platt 1978a; and Arnold 1992.

22. A rich source of data on the symbolism and ritual of the tata reyes (as well as of the fiestas of authority in general) is to be found in Rasnake 1988a.

23. K'ulta is part of the fluid linguistic border between Quechua and Aymara. In nearby Macha and Tinquipaya, in the Department of Potosí, Quechua is now most often spoken in the home. Although almost all K'ultas speak Aymara in the home and in ritual contexts, the majority of men have learned Quechua as a second language, necessary in their trading lives for dealing both with Quechua-speaking valley peoples who grow the produce they need and with the Quechua-speaking vecino elite of many towns, cities, and mining centers. Young K'ulta men also spend time working as miners, as ore carriers in mining communities, and lately as "treaders" in the processing of coca leaves into "pasta." Since their opportunities for travel to such places are generally fewer and come later in life, K'ulta women are less frequently fluent in Quechua. The increasing prevalence of Quechua has led to an unstable process of linguistic borrowing, especially of certain kin terms and comparative adjectives. For example, "yes" in K'ulta is most often the Quechua *ari,* rather than the Aymara *jisa,* which sounds old-fashioned to K'ultas.

24. In 1993, none of the jilaqatas of Condo's former annexes arrived for the fiesta of San Pedro (Lynn Sikkink, personal communication, September 1993).

25. At the end of a week-long process of obtaining the permission of the priest (in Huari), the town council of San Pedro de Condo, and Condo's mayordomos, who agreed to let me see the books (kept in a beautifully worked and painted colonial sacristy), I had a total of two hours with them. I had also obtained permission to microfilm some of these books, but my camera batteries died at that moment. Along with Culta's parish registers, dating from 1778, these books were collected by order of the bishop of Oruro into the new Archivo Obispal in the mid-1980s, where I consulted them at greater length in 1992. Many of these registers can be consulted in microfilm in the Family History Centers operated in the United States by the Mormon church. My thanks to Family History Center staffs in Menlo Park, California, and Homestead, Florida, for help in 1989 and 1991.

26. Hot springs are rather common in the Bolivian highlands. There are still hot springs within K'ulta territory, about an hour's walk south of Santa Bárbara. Elsewhere, in Poopó, site of the colonial archive of the Provincia de Paria, hot spring baths help compensate for research conditions.

27. See G. Martínez' (1976, 1983) analyses of place deities (including uywiris) of Isluga, west of Killaka territory, in present-day Chile.

CHAPTER 5. PATHWAYS OF HISTORICAL COLONIZATION: STORIES OF AN
ANDEAN PAST FROM THE ARCHIVES OF LETTERS AND LANDSCAPES

1. On the significance of town life in Early Modern Spain and the three-way struggle among townsmen, Crown, and señores, see Font Rius 1954; Guilarte 1941; Hinojosa 1903; and Nader 1990.

2. On the Buen Retiro palace see Brown and Elliott 1980; Philip II's effort to catalogue and map both his Castilian and indian realms produced not only increasingly standardized census taking and visitas but also the *Relaciones Geográficas* of both areas (Jiménez de la Espada 1965; N. Salomon 1973).

3. It is arguable that the development of this "first modern state" (Maravall 1972) ushered in the first blush of the "modernity" that, for Timothy Mitchell (1991), came two centuries later with the rationalism and full-blown positivist epistemology that led French and British empire builders to model their colonies on the representations they had first created in nineteenth-century universal expositions.

4. On the old-regime values that motivated conquistadors, see Góngora 1975; Leonard [1949] 1992; and Lockhart 1972. Elliott (1970) underscores the difficulty for Spanish state building posed by the combination of municipal autonomy and noble pretensions.

5. Hemming (1970) provides the best overall account of the Spanish conquest of the Incas. Barnadas (1973) gives greater attention to the invasion of Charcas, of which Julien (1995) offers an insightful reinterpretation.

6. "La primera y principal causa por do atavaliva, señor de dicha provincia, se prendiese" (AGI, Indiferente General 422, fols. 206v–207r).

7. Guarache's son Juan Colque Guarache insists that this act of submission took place in Cajamarca, which is unlikely, since Spanish chroniclers place Manco Inca's submission to Spaniards on the outskirts of Cusco.

8. Summarized by MacCormack (1991: 71); paraphrasing Estete (1924: 54–56).

9. The Spanish original:

> Era tanta la gente y . . . era tanto lo que envasaban en aquellos cueros, porque todo su hecho es beber y no comer, que . . . dos vertederos anchos de hueco de más de media vara que vertían por debajo de losas en el río que debían ser hechos para la limpieza y desaguadero de las lluvias . . . corrían todo el día orines de los que en ellos orinaban; en tanta abundancia, como si fueran fuentes que allí manaran; cierto, según la cantidad de lo que bebían; y la gente que lo bebía no es de maravillar aunque verlo es maravilla y cosa nunca vista. . . . Duraron estas fiestas más de XXX dias arreo; donde se gastó tanto vino de aquello, que si hubiera de ser de lo de acá, según lo que él valía, era muy poco todo el oro y plata que se tomó para comprarlo.

10. Polo describes the form of split inheritance (see Conrad and Demarest 1984: 116ff.) that helped to impel Inca expansion as well as to reshape social memory periodically:

> It was no small affliction, although infrequent, the service that these gave to the Inca when he succeeded as lord in the kingdom, because, as has been written, [he inherited] none of the service of his predecessor, not even the clothing that in the course of his life had been placed in the deposits of Cusco, nor his utensils of gold and silver . . . nor anything else that he held as his own. Instead, all this and his servants remained for the corpse, for the support of which they made fields and had great expenses. . . . (Polo Ondegardo 1990: 110)

The Spanish original:

> No era pequeña pesadumbre, aunque se hacía pocas veces, el servicio que éstos daban al Inca cuando sucedía por señor en el reino porque, como está dicho, el servicio de su antecesor ni en la ropa que en el discurso de su vida se hallaba en los depósitos del Cuzco, ni en su vajilla de oro y plata . . . ni en otra cosa que él tuviese por propia, sino que todo esto y la gente de su servicio quedaba para el cuerpo, para el cual y para el servicio se le hacían chácaras y tenían gran gasto.

11. The act of possession:

> En el asiento de Porco termino e jurisdicción de la Villa de Plata provincia de los Charcas veynte e çinco dias del mes de septiembre de mill y quinientos y quarenta años ante el Magnífico Señor Pedro de Ansures teniente de capitán general de la dicha Villa de Plata e alcalde ordinario della por Su Magestad etcetera. E por ante mi Juan de Grazeda escrivano público de la dicha Villa paresció presente Hernando de Aldana vezino de la dicha Villa y dixo que no embargante que el tiene la posesión de los yndios de aullaga a siete años y más por çédula del señor marques don Françisco Piçarro governador /12r/ por Su Magestad que agora hazia e hizo presentaçión de la çédula desta otra parte contenida e pidió a su merçed le meta en la posesión de todos los yndios caciques e principales e pueblos en la dicha çédula contenidos. . . .
> E luego el dicho señor capitán aviendo visto la dicha çédula dixo que metía e metió al dicho Hernando de Aldana en la posesión de todos los caciques pueblos e yndios en la dicha cédula contenida según y como o por su señoría le es mandado y en señal de verdadera posesión e por posesión le dió y entregó a Guarache cacique prinçipal e a Tarache hijo que dixo ser de un prinçipal natural del pueblo de

Quillaca y el dicho Hernando de Aldana reçibió en si la dicha
posesión. . . . AGI, Charcas 53, item 1, fols. 11v–12r, Sept. 1540,
Porco, Posesión de Hernando de Aldana por Per Ansures; copied into
"Memorial de don Diego Copatete caçique prinçipal de los yndios
Quillacas y Asanaques," 1622)

The scribe notes Aldana's claim of prior possession of part of the "aullagas,"
of which the indians received now are the "other part." "Aullagas" here refers,
not to the diarchy of Awllaka, but to the entire Killaka region as the "provincia
de los Aullagas," after the Lago de Aullagas (now Lake Poopó). This designation
has led to much confusion in encomienda lists of the period, in which Aldana is
often misidentified as *Lorenzo* de Aldana, Hernando's relative and *encomendero*
of Paria (Sura peoples).

12. The first Spanish expedition into Qullasuyu was led by Francisco
Pizarro's partner-turned-rival Diego de Almagro, accompanied by a looting band
of Spaniards on an ill-fated expedition to Chile. Almagro's small group of
Spaniards had been joined in their expedition by a large contingent of indian
allies led by Manco Inca's brother Paullo and the high priest of Cusco, Vilaoma.
The expedition received provisions and reinforcements from native lords of
Qullasuyu, and in particular from Guarache, mallku of the four-diarchy federation called Killaka. As his son Juan Colque Guarache attested, his help was vital
to this expedition into southern Qullasuyu, because on a southward journey the
storehouses of the Inca tambo of Awllaka afforded the last dependable supplies
before reaching inhospitable desert regions.

13. "Cotapampa" is likely a Hispanized rendition of the local Aymara
compound term *"q'uta-pampa,"* meaning "lake-plain" in Spanish, and is trans-
latable to the Quechua *"qucha-pampa,"* rendered in Spanish orthography as
"Cochabamba." Barnadas disputes this, opting for a highland site of the same
name (1973: 34–35).

14. Apart from already-cited sources in Cieza, Betanzos, and caciques'
memoriales, my account of the Spanish invasion of Charka comes largely from
Barnadas 1973; Barragán 1994; and Hemming 1970.

15. In assigning native lords and their subjects to Spaniards, Pizarro must
have relied on information provided by the lords themselves, coupled with
testimony of Spanish participants in the 1538 invasion of Qullasuyu. Hernando
and Gonzalo Pizarro had learned enough about the territory in their reconnais-
sance, after their victory at "Cotapampa," to claim labor sources in the vicinity
of the Inca silver mines at Porco.

16. A descendant of a native lord named Consara (or Cuysara), present at the
surrender, claimed that this mallku was the first to have surrendered to the
Spaniards. As mallku of the Charka people, a group of hereditary lordships that
formed half the Qaraqara-Charka federation, Cuysara was a man of great local
stature, favored by the Incas and granted major privileges and power. It is
probable that his counterpart, mallku of the Qaraqara portion of the federation,

was of even greater stature in Inca times. Yet Cuysara's quick action in surrendering first led the Spaniards to name the entire region after his group, as the "province of Charcas" (Espinoza 1969: passim).

17. See part A of the Documentary Appendix: Francisco Pizarro's Grant of Acho and Guarache to Hernando de Aldana. Marti Pärssinen (1992) argues that pueblo lists such as this were read into Spanish documents from quipu accounts. But the irregularity of the account, which seems to mix place-names with the names of social groups and which does not add up to the totals given in the grant, suggests otherwise.

18. I am currently working on a detailed study of Vela's relations with Awllakas and his similar difficulties with the vassals he purchased in Spain with his indian silver. Vela's troubles were set in motion by La Gasca, who inserted a clause in some of his encomienda grants that fed suits over restitution:

> ... [The caciques] and the rest of the indians subject to them you shall treat well and procure their conservation, asking from them moderate tributes *such that they well can give. And if you should exceed in it apart from being punished you shall be ordered to return the excess as part of the payment that in the future shall be owing to you,* in conformity with the limits to be put on the tributes that the said indians shall owe.

The original Spanish:

> ... a ellos y a los demas yndios a ellos sujetos los trateis bien y procureis su conservaçion pidiendoles tributos moderados /3v/ *y tales que vuenamente los puedan dar con aperzevimiento que si en ello ezediecedes allende de ser penado se vos mandar a tomar la demasia en parte de pago para lo que adelante ovieredes de aver* comforme a las tassaziones que de los tales tributos que huvieron de dar los dichos yndios se hiziera. (four-folio item inserted in AGI, EC 497-C, Pieza 23, 1560 [unpaginated]; emphasis in original)

19. See especially the forthcoming volume of source materials and essays on the Qaraqara-Charka federation (Tristan Platt, Thérèse Bouysse-Cassagne, Olivia Harris, and Thierry Saignes, eds.). Much of this advance is, of course, due to the efforts of scholars who have heeded Murra's admonitions (1968, 1970) to seek out the relatively uncontaminated data of bureaucratic and administrative reports. Guevara-Gil and Salomon (1994) suggest that such reports should also be regarded as descriptions of rituals of rule, which created the very social realities that they recorded.

20. The term "cacique," imported by the Spanish from the Caribbean into the Andes, was applied to indigenous authorities who might otherwise have been titled kuraqa (Quechua) or mallku (Aymara). "Cacique" displaced Andean terms, obliterating the finer Andean distinctions of hierarchy.

21. On this point see Spalding 1974, 1984; Stern 1982; and Rivera Cusicanqui 1978a.

22. See the stricture offered in Salomon's essay (1982) on the insoluble contradictions inherent in these early attempts to bridge the cultural gap between the Andean and Spanish worlds: "They necessarily speak partly through ideas and myths not their own, and partly through those that are too much their own to be readily conveyed in a foreign vehicle" (32).

23. As among the Macha, members of present-day "ethnic groups" such as K'ulta (Culta), Wari (Huari), Challapata, or Quntu (Condo) may at times refer to their society as an ayllu (Ayllu K'ulta, for example). This usage corresponds to Platt's term "maximal ayllu" (1978a: 1082). Similarly, the component moieties of each group may be called ayllus (Platt's "major ayllu"), as are the variable number of theoretically endogamous social groups within each moiety (Platt's "minor ayllu"). I use the term "ayllu" only for the named minor ayllus of each diarchy (and now of town-based "ethnic groups"). It is possible that "ayllu" (or an Aymara equivalent, such as the term "*hatha*," found in Bertonio's Aymara dictionary [1984]) may have been used in historical times to refer to diarchy moieties, diarchies, and federations as well. I use these last terms because the historical record lacks differentiating indigenous terms.

"Ethnic group" is another problematic term. The most frequent usages in Andean studies apply the term to the class and racial category of indian (versus mestizo, white, etc.), to language groupings (Quechua versus Aymara ethnic groups), to the boundaries of sixteenth-century diarchies or federations (Lupaqa versus Killaka), or other groupings easily identifiable by observers as "ethnically distinct" because of clothing styles and so on. As a label for self-defined social groups, the term may be preferable to the also frequently used and vague term "community." I choose to use the term "rural social groups" for peoples like K'ulta or Macha.

24. The original Spanish is as follows:

> Lo otro. En nuestra prouincia de Los Charcas, antes de los ingas y
> después de ellos solía hauer señores naturales mayores de a diez mil
> vasallos y otros de a ocho mil indios y otros de a seis mil indios y
> vasallos otros dichos señores y caualleros eran superiores de los
> demás caciques y señores que hauia en cada nación. . . . Y ansí cada
> uno de estos señores solían tener ocho segundas personas y diez
> también de a mil indios y cuatro principales de cada ayllu de a
> quinientos y de cient indios y cuatro mandones en cada ayllu cada /
> uno en su nación de hanansaya y Hurinsaya. Y en esta orden
> governaron los ingas.

25. Colonial encomiendas had separated the mitimas (and their lands) from their native highland groups of origin. The result of the litigation was the affirmation of the rights of the highland lords over their indians and some of the

Inca-administered lands. Toledo allotted to Juan Colque Guarache, as part of the "tasa y servicio," "los Yndios que reciden en el valle de Cochabamba le han de sembrar coger y beneficiar una cementera de anega y media de Maiz . . ." (AGNA, 9.17.2.5., fol. 126r). The lands allotted to the Qaranka and Killaka—called "la Chulla"—were in periodic litigation until at least 1771 (see ANB, EC 1771, no. 143).

26. Qaranka and Killaka may have formed a dual federation on the scale of the Qaraqara-Charka federation.

27. There are some small differences between the partial copy of the 1574–75 probanza which I found in the Archivo del Tribunal de Poopó (ATP, Expediente 11, 1574–75) and that used by Espinoza (AGI [Sevilla], 1575, "Primera información hecha por don Juan Colque Guarache, . . ." [as cited by Espinoza; actually AGI, Quito 45]).

The second probanza, completed in 1577 and also published in part in Espinoza Soriano 1981, repeats much of the information available in the first while providing some new data (AGI, Quito 45, 1576–77, "Segunda información . . ."). In quoting the first probanza, I have preferred to use my own transcription of the ATP version where possible, because it was either an original or a late-sixteenth-century copy. The original encomienda grant is found in a scribal copy of early documents in a seventeenth-century memorial presented by a grandson of Juan Colque Guarache (AGI, Charcas 53, item 1).

Fragments of a questionnaire for yet a third probanza, dated 1580, were inserted and then retained in an eighteenth-century document produced in an effort (by a member of the Choqueticlla line) to seek the return of the papers from an "outsider" to whom they had been loaned (ANB, EC 1792, no. 42; also see ANB, EC 1804, no. 193).

Juan Colque Guarache was succeeded by his brother, don Francisco Visalla, ". . . caçique prinçipal y capitan (en la Villa de Potosy) de los yndios del Repartimiento de los quillacas y asanaques que subçedio en lugar y como hermano ligitimo de don Juan Colque Guarache diffuncto . . ." (ANB, EC 1588, no. 5, fol. 2v). In June 1575, after the completion of the *tasa*, Toledo had appointed Visalla, at the request of his brother, to the post of cacique of San Lucas and his brother's *segunda persona* (the Provisión was copied into the 1588 document).

28. I refer to the concept as developed by Sahlins (1985). Speaking of the Maori chief (but also of the divine king and divine chief in general), Sahlins writes: "The chief's marriages are intertribal alliances; his ceremonial exchanges trade; as injuries to himself are cause for war. Here history is anthropomorphic in principle, which is to say in structure. Granted that history is much more than the doings of great men, is always and everywhere the life of communities; but precisely in these heroic polities the king is the condition of the possibility of community" (35–36).

29. Witnesses for the first *interrogatorio* included three caciques and fourteen Spaniards. The second questionnaire (as identified by Espinoza [1981: 228]) included four indian and eleven Spanish witnesses.

30. The full text of questions 3 and 4 of the interrogatorio:

3—Yten si saven [etcetera] que antes y en el tiempo del ynga los antepasados y predeçessores del dicho don Joan fueron señores de vasallos y caçiques de las dichas parçialidades Quillacas Asanaques Çibaroyos y Uroquillas y Haracapis los quales no reconoçieron superior ni menos subçedieron en el dicho caçicasgo por titulo de merçedes sino por subçession como dicho es y asi mesmo fueron señores de duo antes y en el tiempo del ynga y despues aca que era los ynsigma de los cavalleros y como tales fueron allidos y repartados contribuydos libres ni compelidos a ofyçios ni cargos digan lo que saven.

4—Yten si saven [etcetera] que antes del dicho ynga gozavan de las dichas libertades /22v/ hasta Colque su predecessor que fue el que dio la obediençia al ynga el qual le confyrmo lo que tenia de antes que fue por el ynga Yupanque ynga el qual conquisto la dicha provinçia de los quillacas digan (ATP, Expediente 11, 1574–75, fols. 22r–v)

31. The interrogatorio of Juan Colque Guarache's second probanza, pursued in 1576–77 (Espinoza 1981: 252ff.), presents, in the first question, a different list of groupings subject to the cacique principal:

1. Primeramente si conocen al dicho don Juan Colque Guarache, cacique principal del repartimiento de los Quillacas y Asanaques y de los Saracapis [*sic*] y de Puna y Yucasa y Guare, y que ansí lo fueron sus padres y abuelos por le venir el dicho cacicazgo por justos y derechos títulos de línea reta de Huno Mallco, que quiere decir señor de salua [que es] como duques, condes, marqueses en los reinos de España.

32. It is certainly possible that these lords had had the Inca title of unu mallku, "lord of ten thousand households," bestowed upon them, as question 1 of the second questionnaire claims. As of 1574, when counted in the Toledan visita (after significant demographic decline), the Killaka federation was still populated by more than twenty thousand souls. If we assume that four-fifths of the population had died in the years following the conquest, Juan Colque Guarache's father may have ruled the approximately 100,000 individuals necessary to have deserved the title of unu mallku. Nonetheless, question 2 of the second questionnaire, in which the term is defined as "señor de cinco mill indios," casts doubt on the centrality of the decimal terminology to the conception of authority in this group of (mostly Aymara-speaking) diarchies (Espinoza 1981: 252). All four indigenous respondents to this questionnaire, however, corrected the error in their answers to this question (ibid., 258–265).

33. The original reads: " . . . tres camisetas la una de chaperia de plata y otra de chaperia de oro y otras de piedras preçiossas que llaman mollo. . . ." Responding to question 6 of the questionnaire, the octagenarian cacique of Moromoro (today's Ravelo), don Pablo Humoro, revealed his familiarity with such sumptuary gifts:

> 6—A la Sesta pregunta dixo que este testigo era criado del dicho
> guayna capa que le aderoçava las plumas que se ponía e vio que un
> dia el dicho ynga llamó antesi al dicho Colque Guarache ynga y en
> señal de amistad e por querrelle mucho en presençia de este testigo le
> dio tres camisetas de su vestir el qual las rreciviió y en aquel tiempo
> lo suso dicho era negoçio muy señaldo y esto dize a la pregunta.
> (ATP, Expediente 11, 1574–75, fol. 7r; cf. also Espinoza 1981: 242)

Nevertheless this same Pablo Humoro—spelled "Humiro" in Espinoza's copy from a different MS (Espinoza 1981: 241)—raises some questions about the veracity of Juan Colque's genealogy. Presumably in a position to know, he made it clear in his response to question 5 that the individual who received the shirts was " . . . el abuelo del dicho don Juan, padre de su padre . . ." who had gone with the Inca in the conquest of Chichas, and upon his return had come " . . . en andas y a el llamavan todos Inga Guarache Colque . . ." (ibid.).

34. Up to the point at which Guarache (Juan Colque Guarache's father) became *Juan* Guarache, the names in this genealogy appear to alternate: Guarache succeeds Colque succeeds Guarache succeeds Colque. I cannot explain this regularity. Note, however, that these names appear to be honorific titles, and were certainly not surnames. Secondary sons of the Juan Guarache (and of Juan Colque Guarache) were given different names altogether, a practice which continued (among the commoners, especially) into the first half of the eighteenth century.

35. An excellent survey of such signs of authority is found in Martínez Cereceda 1995.

36. "Kamachik" is the Quechua form (spelled here in the seventeenth century lexicographer's orthography) of what in Aymara is *kamachiri* (formed from the root *kama*, plus the causative *-cha* and the "agentifier" *-iri*), "one who causes to be ordered/obliged/accomplished," applied to figures of authority from the father in the household, to the "elder brother" of the hamlet, to the highest authorities of the ayllu. We will see in part 3 that it is the kamachiris who make sacrifices, as well as the sacrifices that make kamachiris.

37. Polo Ondegardo 1990: 121, "De la orden que los indios tenían en dividir los tributos y distribuirlos entre si." The Spanish original:

> Entre estos indios y su manera de vivir, es notorio que todo el reino
> estaba dividido por partes, que cada una era de diez mil indios, que
> llaman uno, y de cada uno de éstos había un gobernador sobre los
> caciques y mandones—como está dicho—allende de otra división más
> general, que llamaron éstos Tahuantinsuyo, que quiere decir cuatro

partes en que todo el reino estaba dividido, que llamaron Collasuyo,
Chinchasuyo, Andesuyo, Condesuyo, la cual división empieza desde
el Cuzco, del cual salen cuatro caminos, cada uno para una parte de
éstas, como parece en la carta de las huacas, y con esta orden y
división era fácil tener cuenta con todo, todo, como ellos la tenían, la
cual no se pone aquí ni hace memoria de ella, sinó solamente porque
se entienda que en estando acordado en el Cuzco que se trajese cien
mil fanegas de maíz, en un momento sabía cada gobernador cuanto
cabía a su distrito y a los depósitos de él sin diferencia ni porfía ni
pleito, y cada provincia cuanto cabía a las parcialidades, empezando
la cuenta por las cabeceras y luego se iban distribuyendo por
menudo, de manera que todo se hacia con la facilidad que está
significado y no se ha de entender que la distribución de esto era
igual . . . sinó que estaba repartido conforme a la calidad de la tierra,
así el pan como la ropa y ganado, por cotas. . . .

38. The Spanish original:

[Atahuallpa] los resçivio muy bien y dando de bever al uno dellos
con un vaso de oro de la bevida que nosotros usamos, el español en
resçibiendo de su mano lo derramó, de lo qual se enojó mucho . . . ;
y despues desto aquellos dos españoles le mostraron . . . una carta o
libro . . . diziendo que aquella hera la quilca [escritura] de Dios y del
rey e . . . como se sintio afrentado del derramar de la chicha
[Atahuallpa] tomó la carta . . . y arrojolo por ay diziendo: "qué sé yo
que me dais ay, anda bete."

39. The Spanish original:

. . . tienen una costumbre . . . be buena crianza estos señores e todos
los demás de toda la tierra, y es que si un señor o señora va a casa de
otro a visitarle . . . ha de llevar tras sí se es señora un cántaro de
chicha y en llegando . . . hace estanciar de su chicha dos vasos y el
uno da a beber al tal señor que visita y el otro se bebe al tal señor o
señora que la chicha da y ansi beben los dos y lo mismo hace el de la
posada que hace sacar ansi mismo otros dos vasos de chicha y da el
uno al que ansi le ha venido a visitar y él bebe el otro . . . y esta es la
mayor honra que entre ellos se usa y si esto no se hace cuando se
visitan tienen por afrentada la persona que ansi va a visitar al otro y
esta honra no se le hace de darlle a beber y excúsase de no le ir más
a ver y ansi mismo se tiene por afrentado el que da a beber a otro y
no le quisiera rescebir. . . .

40. Cieza asked that, apart from the colorful travel account of part 1, the
remainder of his writings be held for a period of fifteen years before possible
publication (Pease, Introducción, p. xx, in Cieza de León 1984). Another

colonial chronicler, Agustín de Zárate (Polo Ondegardo's brother) succinctly described another danger inherent in the act of writing:

> No pude en el Perú escrivir ordenadamente esta Relación (que no importára poco para su perfección) porque solo averla allá començado, me huviera de poner en peligro de la vida, con Maestre de Campo de Gonçalo Piçarro, que amenaçaba de matar á qualquiera que escriviese sus hechos, porque ententió que eran mas dignos de la lei de olvido (que los Athenienses llaman Amnistia) que no de memoria, ni perpetuidad. (Zárate 1862, quoted in González Echevarría 1990: 73 n. 69)

41. Another indication of which is rather forcefully preserved in the writings of Bernabé Cobo. Like Acosta, Cobo found the Andean knotted-cord records, or quipus, to be their closest approximation to writing. To demonstrate the system's praiseworthiness, Cobo related an anecdote in which a quipu served the role of state's evidence to prove the identity of an indian guide who, years before the trial, had murdered a Spaniard (Cobo 1979: 253–255).

42. Compare this practice with the *larita's* (mother's brother's) role in the Sucullu vicuña sacrifice (Bertonio 1984: part 2, 323), and with the annointing of the sponsor's aides in K'ulta sacrifices (see chapter 8).

43. Molina refers to his "Historia de los Ingas" manuscript, now presumed lost.

44. My translation. The original Spanish:

> La Capacocha ynventó también Pachacuti Ynga Yupanqui, la cual hera desta manera: las provincias de Collasuyo y Chinchaysuyo y Antisuyo y Contisuyo trayan a esta ciudad, de cada pueblo y generación de jentes, uno o dos niños y niñas pequeños, y de hedad de diez años; y trayan ropa y ganado y ovejas de oro y de plata de mollo. Y lo tenían en el Cuzco para el efeto que se dirá; y después de estar todo junto, se asentava en la plaza de Aucaypata el Ynga, que es la plaza grande del Cuzco, y allí aquellos niños y demás sacrificios andavan alrededor de las estatuas del Hacedor, Sol, Trueno y Luna que para el efecto ya en la plaza estavan. Y davan dos bueltas, y después de acavado, el Ynga llamava a los sacerdotes de las provincias y hacía partir los dichos sacrificios en quatro partes para los quatro Suyos: Collasuyo, Chinchaysuyo, Antisuyo, Contisuyo, que son las quatro partidas en que está dividida esta tierra; y les deçía: 'Vosotros tomad cada uno su parte de esas ofrendas y sacrificios, y llevadla a la principal huaca vuestra, y allí las sacrificas; y tomádolas, llevavan hasta la guaca, y allí ahogavan a los niños y los enterravan juntamente con las figuras de plata, de ovejas y de personas de oro y plata; y las ovejas y carneros y ropas lo quemavan, y tanbién unos cestillos de coca. La jente del Cuzco llevavan los sacrificios ya dichos

hasta Sacalpina, que será una legua del Cuzco y ado los recevían los yndios de Ansa. Y desta manera yban entregándolos hasta donde se avían de haçer los sacrificios; y por esta horden los llevavan a las demas provincias.

Hacían este sacrificio al principio que el Ynga señor empeçava a señorear para que las guacas le diesen mucha salud y tuviese en paz y sosiego sus reynos y señorios y llegase a biejos, y que veviese sin enfermedad, de tal manera que ninguna guaca, ni mochadero ni adoratorio, por pequeño que fuese, no quedava sin recevir sacrificio, porque ya estava diputado y acordado lo que en cada guaca, lugar y parte, se avía de sacrificar. . . .

Todos los sacrificios ya dichos se ponían en el lugar ya dicho, y luego el sacerdote que tenía a cargo la guaca de Yanacauri de do ellos se jatan quedó echo piedra Ayarcache, uno de los quatro ermanos que dicen salieron de la cueva de Tanbo, y porque en la fábula que desto tratamos al principio de la Historia que Vuestra Señoría Ilustrísima tiene, traté largo dello, no lo trato aquí; allá lo podrá ber Vuestra Señoría. . . .

Y luego en todos los lugares, fuentes, y cerros que en el Cuzco avía por adoratorios, hechavan los sacrificios que para ellos estavan dedicados, sin matar para esto ninguna criatura.

Heran tantos los lugares que dedicados tenían para sacrificar en el Cuzco, que si se ubiesen de poner aquí sería mucha prolijada, y porque en la Relación de las guacas que a Vuestra Señoría Reverendísima di, están puestos todos de la manera que se sacrificauan, no lo pongo aqui.

Y así concluydo con lo que en el Cuzco se avía de sacrificar, sacauan los sacerdotes con los sacrificios que se avían de llevar, como ya está dicho, la horden del camino con los sacrificios, era que toda la jente que con la Capaccocha que por otro nombre se llama Cachaguaes, yban hechos un ala, alguna cosa apartado los unos de los otros, sin ir por camino real derecho, sino sin torcer a ninguna parte, atravesando las quebradas y cerros que por delante hallavan hasta llegar cada uno a la parte y lugar que estavan esperando para recevir los dichos sacrificios. . . .

Y así llegados a cada parte y lugar, los que auían de hazer los sacrificios, los guacacamayos, que quiere decir 'guarda de la guacas', y que a cargo las tenían, reçevía cada uno el sacrificio que a su guaca cavía y los sacrificava y ofrecía, enterrando los sacrificios de oro y plata y mollo y otras cosas de que ellos usavan; y las criaturas, aviéndolas ahogado primero, las que aquella guaca cavían, quemavan en sacrificio los carneros, corderos y ropa que la cavían.

Es de notar que no a todos las guacas sacrificavan criaturas, sino sólo a las guacas principales que provincias o generaciones tenían.

Y por esta horden yban caminando por toda la tierra que el Ynga conquistada tenía, por las quatro partidas, y haciendo los dichos sacrificios hasta llegar cada uno por el camino do yba a los postreros limites y mojones que el Ynga puesto tenía.

Tenían tanta cuenta y raçón en esto, y salía tan bien repartido del Cuzco lo que en cada parte y lugar se avía de sacrificar, que aunque hera en cantidad el dicho sacrificio y los lugares do cavía de hazer sin número, jamás avia yerro ni trocavan de un lugar para el otro. Tenía en el Cuzco el Ynga para este efecto, yndios de los quatro Suyos o partidas, que cada uno dellos tenía quenta y raçón de todas las guacas por pequeñas que fuesen, que en aquella partida de que él hera quipocamayo o contador, que llaman uilcacamayo.

45. Polo Ondegardo, who as corregidor of Cusco in 1559 investigated Inca religious practices, comments on this technique of rule:

> . . . each conquered province gave its principal idol and placed it in the city of Cusco, along with the very body of the lord who had conquered it. And thus all the bodies and the idols were in that great hall of the house of the sun, and each idol had its servants and expenses in women. . . . I was much surprised by it, since the Romans did the same, keeping the principal idol of each conquered province in that house that in Rome they called the Pantheon, which was later made into a church, and very appropriately was given the advocation Omnium Santorum [All Saints]. (Polo Ondegardo 1990: 85–86)

The Spanish original:

> . . . todas las provincias que se conquistaron dieron el ídolo principal y se puso en la ciudad del Cuzco, el cual estaba con el mismo cuerpo del señor que le había conquistado, y así todos los cuerpos y los ídolos estaban en aquel galpón grande de la casa del sol, y cada ídolo de estos tenía su servicio y gastos en mujeres. . . . me causó gran admiración por la misma orden tuvieron los romanos; y así tuvieron los ídolos de todas las provincias que conquistaron el principal de cada una en aquella casa que llamaban en Roma panteón, que después se hizo iglesia y muy a propósito se le dio por advocación Omnium Santorum.

46. The Spanish original:

> . . . Así con este título anduvieron muchos años sin poder señorear más de aquella comarca del Cuzco hasta el tiempo de Pachacutec Inca Yupanqui. . . . Después [de conquistar los Chancas] siempre su título fue esto de la relación y inventariada el día más generoso de

sacrificios y obligar a ellos a todos los que metían debajo de su domino, y dar a entender que aquella ciudad del Cuzco era casa y morada de dioses, y así no había en toda ella fuente ni paso ni pared que no dijesen que tenía misterio como parece en cada manifestación de los adoratorios de aquella ciudad y carta que de ellos manifestaron que pasaban de cuatrocientos y tantos; todo esto duró hasta que vinieron los españoles, y hasta hoy se hace veneración a cada uno cuando no los ven y toda la tierra guarda y venera las huacas que los incas les dieron y yo por sus mismos registros para ensayar la manifestación saqué muchas de las provincias de Chinchaysuyo y Collasuyo. Por que ésta no es la materia que tenemos presupuesto, basta esto cuanto a este artículo para entendimiento de los demás.

47. The Spanish original (I have modernized the orthography):

Los indios del Pirú, antes de venir españoles, ningún género de escritura tuvieron, ni por letras ni por carácteres, o cifras o figurillas, como los de la China y los de México; mas no por eso conservaron menos la memoria de sus antiguallas, ni tuvieron menos su cuenta para todos los negocios de paz, y guerra y gobierno. Porque en la tradición de unos a otros fueron muy diligentes, y como cosa sagrada recibían y guardaban los mozos, lo que sus mayores les referían, y con el mismo cuidado lo enseñaban a sus sucesores. Fuera de esta diligencia, suplían la falta de escritura y letras, parte con pinturas como los de México, aunque las del Pirú eran muy groseras y toscas, parte y lo más, con quipos. Son quipos, unos memoriales o registros hechos de ramales, en que diversos ñudos y diversas colores, significan diversas cosas. Es increíble lo que en este modo alcanzaron, porque cuanto los libros pueden decir de historias, y leyes y ceremonias, y cuentas de negocios, todo eso suplen los quipos tan puntualmente, que admira. Había para tener estos quipos o memoriales, oficiales diputados que se llaman hoy día quipo camayo, los cuales eran obligados a dar cuenta de cada cosa, como los escribanos públicos acá, y así se les había de dar entero crédito. Porque para diversos géneros como de guerra, de gobierno, de tributos, de ceremonias, de tierras, había diversos quipos o ramales. Y en cada manojo de éstos, tantos ñudos y ñudicos, y hilillos atados; unos colorados, otros verdes, otros azules, otros blancos, finalmente tantas diferencias, que así como nosotros de veinte y cuatro letras guisándolas en diferentes maneras sacamos tanta infinidad de vocablos, así éstos de sus ñudos y colores, sacaban innumerables significaciones de cosas. (Acosta 1977: 410–411)

48. "Ceque" is a Quechua term from colonial sources, for sight lines and paths that radiated from Cusco and connected wak'a sites. The colonial Quechua term "taqui" (pl. "taquies") labeled song-dances akin to Spanish cantares, epic poems sung while dancing, which narrated the deeds of gods and ancestors. Such deeds were tied to specific places, such as the wak'a shrines found along ceque paths, and taquies were likely performed while dancing along such paths, in conjunction with festivals honoring gods and ancestors at their wak'a sites. Thus if the system of ceques was a kind of abstract social map projected onto the landscape as paths, taquies contained the oral narrative performed while moving through that landscape. The modern Aymara term "t"aki," which is used both for paths on the landscape and for narrative sequences such as the myths and libation performances which give voice to paths and take the mental shape of a journey across the landscape, covers the semantic ground of both the colonial Quechua terms "ceque" and "taqui."

49. "It must be known that the majority of wak'as, apart from their properties, have clothing of cumbi that they call capac huchas, of the same grandeur as in the wak'as. And the first thing one must do so that no relic of the wak'a remains is to procure these capac huchas, because if they remain in their power, they will dress any stone they like with it" (Albornóz 1989: 196).

50. On tukapus see Harrison 1989: 60–62, who cites additional sources. Also see Cummins 1994: 188–219, who advances a subtle argument similar to that presented here on the Andean use of quipus, textiles, and queros in recollecting the past and bringing it to bear on the present.

51. See, however, the interpretive cautions of Cummins (1994: 205–211) and accompanying illustrations.

52. The Spanish original: "[Tata Paria fue] señor de toda la nacion de los caracaras de la dicha parcialidad [de anansaya] y de la de los quillacas soras carangas y chuyes y todas ellas le obedecieron y las hacia juntar en Macha y este testigo conocio muy bien al dicho Tata Paria siendo este testigo muchacho y vio que le traian en onbros de yndios como gran señor . . . y todas las dichas naciones se juntaron para hacelle sepulturas . . ." (AGNA, 13.18.7.2, 1612–19, fol. 309r).

53. See discussion in MacCormack 1991: 173–181, and references there.

54. According to Cobo, "The sacrifice of domesticated animals was valued and esteemed second only to that of humans. And sacrifices were made only of the domestic animals, not of wild animals. The reason they gave for this is that sacrifices should be made only of those animals that were raised [by the Indians] and not of the others that were born and raised on their own" (Cobo 1990: 112).

Cobo goes on to dispute the labor theory of value that he here ascribes to the Incas, by saying that hunting wild animals is clearly more work than raising domesticated ones. What Cobo missed, the Old Testament Yahweh was able to make clear (as does Valeri 1985): Domesticated animals participate in human society, and are therefore more apt to bridge the gap between humans and gods.

55. The Spanish original:

[El Inca] en cada pueblo puso la misma orden y dividió por ceques y rayas la comarca, e hizo adoratorios de diversas advocaciones, todas las cosas que parecían notables de fuentes y manantiales y puquios y piedras hondas y valles y cumbres que ellos llaman apachetas, y puso a cada cosa su gente y les mostró la orden que habían de tener en sacrificar cada una de ellas . . . ; finalmente, aunque en ninguna parte fueron tantos los adoratorios como en el Cuzco, pero es la orden una misma y vista la carta de las huacas del Cuzco en cada pueblo por pequeño que sea la pintarán de aquella misma manera y mostrarán los ceques y huacas y adoratorios fijos, que para saberlo es negocio importantísimo para su conversión, que yo la tengo ensayada en más de cien pueblos, y el señor obispo de las Charcas [preguntando] el si aquello fuese tan universal, cuando vinimos juntos al negocio de la perpetuidad por mandado de Su Magestad, se lo mostré en Pocona y los mismos indios le pintaron allí la misma carta, y en esto no hay duda porque se hallará como digo sin falta. . . .

[F]ue una gran parte del tributo que daban el sembrarlas y cogerlas y poner lo que se cogía en los depósitos que para esto estaban hechos, parte de lo cual se gastaba en sacrificios en el mismo pueblo y lo más se llevaba al Cuzco para el mismo efecto. . . . [E]ra una grandísima cantidad, porque allí tenían las casas principales de todos los dioses y gente mucha en cada una que entendían en otra cosa, y cada día sacrificaba cada uno en la plaza y en los cerros, que cierto ver en esto la manifestación general, no creo yo que se halla en ningún género de gente de la que tenemos noticia que tanto ni con tantas ceremonias gastasen en sacrificios. . . .

56. The Spanish original:

Es necesario en todos los pueblos hacerles que pinten la carta y viendo la del Cuzco luego lo hacen, que al sacerdote le quede noticia de cada cosa de aquellas en particular, así para la que entienda y haga castigar, como para predicarles contra ella y moverlos con razones claras a que entiendan las ilusiones y engaños del demonio; que es negocio que por ser general va mucho en él y es gran fundamento para su edificación y conversión.

57. The Spanish original: "Por estar estas cosas tan ciegas, podemos dezir, que bienauenturada la inuención de las letras, que con la virtud de su sonido dura la memoria muchos siglos: y hazen que buele la fama de las cosas que suceden por el vniuerso: y no ignoramos lo que queremos, teniendo en las manos la letura. Y como en este nueuo mundo de Indias no se ayan hallado letras, vamos a tino en muchas cosas."

58. The Spanish original: "Acá [en estas provinçias del Perú] aunque çiegos los honbres [dan más] razón de sí, puesto que quentan tantas fábulas que serían dañosas si las oviese descrevir. . . ."

59. The Spanish original:

Y así examinando . . . los más prudentes y ancianos, de quien se tiene más crédito saqué y recopilé la presente historia, refiriendo las declaraciones y dichos de unos a sus enemigos, digo del bando contrario, porque se acaudillan por bandos. . . . Y estos memoriales, que todos están en mi poder, refiriéndolos y corrigiéndolos con sus contrarios, y ultimamente ratificándolos en presencia de todos los bandos y ayllos en público, con juramento por autoridad de juez, y con lenguas expertas generales, y muy curiosos y fieles intérpretes, también juramentados. . . .

60. The Spanish original: "Hace hecho tanta diligencia, porque cosa, que es fundamento del hecho verdadero de tan gran negocio, como es el averiguar la tiranía de los crueles ingas desta tierra, para que todas naciones del mundo entiendan el jurídico y más que legítimo título, quel rey de Castilla tiene a estas Indias y a otras tierras a ellas vecinas, especialmente a estos reinos del Perú."

61. Among the quipu kamayuq gathered in Cusco by Cristóbal Vaca de Castro in 1542 were two individuals from Pacaritambo named Callapiña and Supno, who portray Manco Capac as something of a con artist. His father, they assert, was a lord in Pacaritambo, and the Inca claim to priority as sons of the sun was nothing more than a politically motivated lie (Vaca de Castro 1929: 6–12).

62. The Spanish original: "Muchos destos Indios quentan que oyeron a sus antiguos, que ouo en los tiempos passados vn diluuio grande, y de la manera que yo escriuo en el tercero capítulo de la segunda parte. Y dan a entender, que es mucha la antigüedad de sus antepassados. . . ."

63. The Spanish original: ". . . de cuyo origen quentan tantos dichos y fábulas, si lo son, que no quiero detenerme en lo escreuir: porque vnos dizen que salieron de vna fuente: otros que de vna peña: otros de lagunas. De manera que su origen no se puede sacar dellos otra cosa."

64. The Spanish original:

Dicen los naturales de esta tierra, que en el principio, o antes que el mundo fuese criado, hubo uno que llamaban Viracocha. El cual crió el mundo oscuro y sin sol ni luna ni estrellas. . . . Y así crió, los hombres a su semejanza como los que agora son. Y vivían en oscuridad. . . .

Mas como entre ellos naciesen vicios de soberbia y codicia, traspasaron el precepto del Viracocha Pachayachachi, que cayendo por esta transgresión en la indignación suya, los confundió y maldijo.

Y luego fueron unos convertidos en piedras y otros en otras formas, a otros tragó la tierra y a otros el mar, y sobre todo les envió un diluvio general, al cual ellos llaman uno pachacuti, que quiere decir "agua que trastornó la tierra." . . .

Y así de esta manera las demás naciones tienen fábulas de como se salvaron algunos de su nación, de quien ellos traen origen y descendencia. . . .

Dicho es cómo por diluvio uno pachacuti todo fué destruído: es, pues, ahora de saber que el Viracocha Pachayachachi, cuando destruyó esta tierra, como se ha contado, guardó consigo tres hombres, el uno de los cuales se llamó Taguapacac, para que le sirviesen y ayudasen a criar las nuevas gentes que había de hacer en la segunda edad después del diluvio; lo cual hizo de esta manera.

Pasando el diluvio y seca la tierra, determinó el Viracocha de poblarla segunda vez, y para hacerlo con más perfección determinó criar luminarias que diesen claridad. Y para lo hacer, fuése con sus criados a una gran laguna, que está en el Collao, y en la laguna está una isla llamada Titicaca. . . . A la cual isla se fué Viracocha y mandó que luego saliese el sol, luna y estrellas y se fuesen al cielo para dar luz al mundo; y así fué hecho. . . . Y como Viracocha mandase algunas cosas a sus críados, el Taguapaca fué inobediente a los mandamientos de Viracocha. El cual, por esto indignado contra Taguapaca, mandó a los otros dos que lo tomasen; y atado de pies y manos, lo echaron en una balsa en la laguna; y así fué hecho. E yendo Taguapaca blasfemando del Viracocha por lo que en él hacía, y amenazando que él volvería a tomar venganza dél, fué llevado del agua por el desaguadero de la mesma laguna, adonde no fué visto más por muchos tiempos. Y esto hecho, Viracocha fabricó en aquel lugar una solemne guaca para adoratorio en señal de lo que allí había hecho y criado.

65. The Spanish original:

. . . Y al cabo de algunos años, que el Viracocha se fué, dicen que vino el Taguapaca, que Viracocha mandó echar en la laguna de Titicaca del Collao, como se dijo arriba, y que empezó con otros a predicar que el era el Viracocha. Mas aunque al principio tuvieron suspensas las gentes, fueron conoscidos al fin por falsos, y burlaron de ellos.

Esta fábula ridícula tienen estos bárbaros de su creación y afírmanla y créenla, como si realmente así la vieran ser y pasar.

66. Also see Urbano 1988, 1989, 1990 and references therein.

67. The Spanish original: ". . . pues tan consonante es a esto, lo que entre los Indios se trata, de que se vió un hombre nuevo y jamás otra vez visto, el cual hacía grandes milagros y maravillas, por lo cual le pusieron por nombre (según afirman algunos Indios antiquísimos) Tunupa, que es lo mismo que decir gran

Sabio, y Señor (Math. 9). Pues aqueste glorioso Santo por su predicación fue
perseguido y finalmente martirizado de la manera que se sigue."
    68. The Spanish original:

> . . . Con las quales los Indios se iritaron de suerte que le empalaron
> cruelmente, atravesándole por todo el cuerpo una estaca, que llaman
> ellos chonta, hecha de Palma, de que estos Indios usan hasta hoy en
> la guerra, como arma no poco ofensiva, forma de martirio que han
> usado otras veces, como se ve en el que hicieron al Santo fray Diego
> Ortíz de nuestro Padre San Agustín. . . .
>   Pusieron pues al Santo Discípulo después de muerto, en una balsa
> y echáronle en la grande laguna de Titicaca, a la providencia no de
> los vientos, ni de las ondas, sino del cielo. Refieren pues, los antiguos
> que un recio viento sopló en la popa de la balsa y la llevó como si
> fuera a vela, y remo, con tanta velocidad que ponía admiración; y así
> tocó en tierra de Chacamarca, donde ahora es el Desaguadero que
> antes de este suceso no le había y la abrió con la proa de la balsa,
> dando suficiente lugar, para que las aguas corriesen, y sobre ellas fue
> navegando hasta los Aullagas, donde como arriba queda dicho, se
> hunden las aguas por las entrañas de la tierra, y allí se dice, quedó el
> Santo cuerpo y que cada año en una de las Pascuas, o por aquel
> tiempo, se veía allá una muy fresca y verde Palma, aunque otros
> afirman se ve esta Palma en una isleta que el Desaguadero hace
> vecina a la costa de Chile. . . . Todo es posible a Dios, aunque yo no
> le vendo por indubitable. Lo que puedo afirmar es haber oído a
> Indios ancianos de este asiento de Copacabana y en especial a uno,
> que en el mismo convento sirve hoy día para enseñar a leer y cantar
> a los muchachos del pueblo, para ministerio del Coro y servicio de la
> Santa Virgen, el cual dice, que oyó a sus antepasados, que en la
> misma isla Titicaca, quedaban impresas en las peñas las plantas de
> los pies del Tunupa, que así llamaban al glorioso Santo, por ser
> milagroso.

    69. Pierre Duviols and César Itier have recently suggested, in the introduction
to a new transcription of Pachacuti Salcamayhua's text (1993), that the whole
constitutes a kind of homework assignment produced for his missionary teachers. Drawing on a preaching manual, Duviols also convincingly argues that
Pachacuti's famous and much republished drawing of the gods of the Qurikancha temple in fact constitutes a representation of a *retablo* used by priests to
depict (in the native's own categories) the works of the God's creation in heaven
and earth that the misguided mistake for gods in themselves.
    70. Summarized and paraphrased from Juan de Santa Cruz Pachacuti Salca-
mayhua 1968: 282–284. Also see Urbano 1981: 19–22. The foregoing analysis
has benefited greatly from MacCormack 1991.

71. For Pachacuti Yamqui, the aquatic axis from Titicaca to Aullagas seems of little concern. And it is unclear what he intends to convey by his comments on Tunupa's final destination. Does the Apostle Tunupa's journey downriver to the sea, and then through the *straits* to another sea, refer to a passage through Lake Poopó and then to the salt pan of Uyuni (where a mountain named Tunupa now stands)? Or is this a way of sending an apostle from the Pacific through the Straits of Magellan into the Atlantic, to reach the Old World only after preaching the gospel in the new one?

72. Ekeko is certainly an appropriate figure for veneration by the traders who now plied their caravan routes along old pilgrimage axes (Glave 1989). On the relationship between Tunupa and Ekeko, see Ponce Sanjines 1969. In his 1612 Aymara dictionary, Bertonio links the two figures: "Ecaco, 1. Thunnupa: Nombre de uno de quién los indios antiguos cuentan muchas fábulas: y muchos aún en ese tiempo las tienen por verdaderas: assí sería bien procurar deshacer esta persuasión que tienen, por embuste del Demonio" (1984: part 2, 99).

CHAPTER 6. COLONIAL RELANDSCAPING OF ANDEAN SOCIAL MEMORY

1. Balvi, "Memoria sobre las reducciones y mita," La Paz, 1609, ADI; quoted in Saignes 1993: 49; my translation.

2. Encomendero requests for perpetuity had been incessant; the king lit the fuse to perpetuity fireworks in a *cédula* of 1556, when he ordered that perpetuity be immediately established (AHN, Sección de Diversos, Docs. de Indias, no. 145). The first Las Casas–Santo Tomás memorial on the matter arrived at court in late 1560 (ibid., no. 152; catalogue note cites presentation in corte at end of 1560 or before February 7, 1561). The king asked the Peruvian viceroy's advice in early 1561 (ibid., no. 171). Santo Tomás reinforced his opinion a year later (ibid., no. 181).

3. The original Spanish: " . . . como los dichos yndios lo oyeron muchos dellos encomençaron a llorar y a sentirse e a dezir que antes ni despues del inga nunca an sido vendidos que como avian de ser lo agora que ellos no heran coca ni carne para que los ovyeresen se vender e ansi dieron un poder todos."

4. The original Spanish: " . . . los dichos yndios syntieron mucho e algunos caçiques dixeron que se hecharian antes en los rrios aver se herrados en la cara e despenarse e pues que en tiempo que heran de Guayna Capa nunca avian sido esclavos que porque lo avian de ser siendo vasallos del rey. . . ?"

5. Non-encomienda Inca elites in Cusco had joined with the anti-perpetuity effort, fearing that they might lose their own aristocratic privileges should encomenderos become a landed aristocracy. Don Juan Tambo Uscamayta, Inca of Cusco, testified that he initially balked at joining with this contradiction of perpetuity, because " . . . la perpetuidad se entenderia con los demas yndios que estan encomendados y no con ellos que heran libres y los susodichos anton ruiz lengua e gonçalo de monçon dixeron que el mesmo avia de ser de ellos que de los otros e ansi dieron poder . . . " (AGI, Justicia 434, piece 1, fol. 14v).

6. The term "taqui" (in its colonial usages) has been recently scrutinized by Estenssoro (1992).

7. See also Spalding 1984: 147ff., and the superb analysis of Varón Gabai (1990).

8. The Spanish original:

> Abrá diez años, poco más o menos, que huuo una yronía entre estos yndios desta tierra y era que hacían una manera de canto, al qual llamavan Taqui hongo, y porque en la provincia de Parinacocha, un Luis de Olivera clérigo presbítero, que a la saçón hera cura del dicho repartimiento que es en el ovispado del Cuzco, fue el primero que vio de la dicha yronía o ydolatría, él pone aquí de la manera que lo hacían y por qué. . . .
>
> En la provincia de Parinacocha, del ovispado del Cuzco, el dicho Luis de Olivera, vicario de aquella provincia, entendió que no solamente en aquella provincia, pero en todas las demás provincias e ciudades de Chuqicaca, La Paz, Cuzco, Guamanga y aun Lima y Ariquipa, los más dellos avian caydo en grandísimas apostacías apartándose de la fe católica que avían recevido y bolviéndose a la ydolatría que usavan en tiempo de su ynfidelidad. No se pudo averiguar de quien uviese salido este negocio, más de que se sospechó y trató que fue ynventado de los echiceros que en Uiscabamba tenían los Yngas que allí estavan alcados. . . .

9. The Spanish original:

> Durante esta tiempo obo diversas maneras de apostacías en diversas provinçias, unos baylavan dando a entender tenían de la guaca en el cuerpo, otros tremblavan por el mesmo respeto, dando a entender la tenían también; otros se encerravan en sus casas a piedra seca y davan alaridos, otros se despedaçavan y despeñavan y matauan, y otros se hechauan en los ríos ofreciéndose a las guacas, hasta que Nuestro Señor, por su misericordia, fue servido alumbrar a estos miserables y que los que an quedado dellos y an visto la burlería que se les predicó y creyan con ver al Ynga muerto y a *Uilcabamba* de cristianos y ninguno de lo que se les podía aver sucedido, antes todo al contrario. (Emphasis in original)

10. Molina's account puts it this way: " . . . que ya bolvía el tiempo del Ynga y que las guacas no se metían ya en las piedras, ni en las nuves, ni en las fuentes para hablar, sino que se yncorporan ya en los yndios y los hacían ya hablar y que tuviesen sus casas baridas y adereçadas para si alguna de las guacas quisiese pasar en ella" (Molina 1989: 130–131).

11. My translation. The Spanish original:

> . . . Es publico e notorio . . . que . . . la harina que se haze de maiz se a causado en los yndios y naturales que rresiden en esta villa grandes

borracheras porque como hallan el maiz molido de que hazen la açua
que beuen hazen mucha mas cantidad della de la que antes solian
hazer lo qual es ocçasion y causa de beber mucha mas cantidad que
solian que es biçio que esta en ellos muy arraigado y estan casi toda
la semana borrachos de que se sigue muchos ynçestos y otros delitos
que cometen y aun omiçidios en gran desseruiçio de dios nuestro
senor y de su magestad y es grand ympedimiento pa su conversion y
dotrina cristiana que se les predica y ara la labor de las minas que
fue el efecto para que aqui fueron venidos. . . .

12. The Spanish original:

. . . muriendo muchos de sus borracheras y cometiendo otros
omiçidios e muertes y ahorcandose asi mismos y en particular a
enterrado esta testigo seis yndios que de su borrachera sea muerto
quitandoseles la habla y muriendo naturalmente y a otros muchos
quitandoseles la habla a poder de medeçinas y bebedizos que les a
dado auiendo estado tres o quatro dias sin hablales a fecho boluer en
si y los avisto estar beuiendo y levantarse y gomitar y tornar a beuer
y vn dia por les quitar este testigo la borrachera le quisieron
matar. . . . Sabe este testigo y a visto que es el prençipal ympedimiento
para su conversion y dotrina cristiana por que todas las vezes que
estan borrachos cometen y hazen sus ydolatrias y rritos antiguos. . . .

13. The Spanish original:

. . . Esta testigo . . . a visto a los yndios que en el rresiden
espeçialmente la dotrina de los carangas que este testigo tubo a cargo
siendo vicario hazer a los yndios muchas y grandes borracheras . . . e
que le paresçe a esta testigo que las dichas borracheras es
ympedimiento para su conversion y dotrina y a oydo dezir algunos
sacerdotes que entienden la lengua y antiguos en la tierra que los
dichos yndios estando borrachos en sus borracheras y taquies
cometen ydolatrias y otros rritos en ofensa de dios nuestro señor. . . .

14. The Spanish original:

. . . hazer sacrifiçios en diversas maneras a sus guacas y otras muchas
maneras de hechizerias que tienen confesandose con sus confesores
enbiando cachas a las guacas hanobicamayos [sic] contradiziendo la
dotrina cristiana y otros muchos rritos y cerimonias que usan y pecados
asi como tomandosse las mugeres los vnos a los otros y cometiendo
diversos pecados de ynçesto y para hazer las fiestas del capse pacxi [sic]
y otras menores que celebran en todos los meses del año. . . .

15. Such fears, which echo modern beliefs about fat- and blood-sucking
witches (see the concluding chapter), may seem improbably superstitious. But see

Wachtel 1994, and listen to Bernal Díaz on some conquistador activity in Mexico: " . . . with the unto of a fat indian, from among those we killed there, who was opened up, we cured our wounds, since there was no oil" ("con el unto de un indio gordo de los que allí matamos, que se abrió, se curaron los heridos, que aceite no lo había") (Díaz del Castillo 1964: 177).

16. The Spanish original:

> . . . el año de setenta y no atrás, de aver tenido y creydo por los
> yndios que despaña avían enviado a este reyno por unto de los
> yndios para sanar cierta enfermedad que no se hallava para ello
> medicina sino el dicho unto, a cuya causa en aquellos tiempos
> andavan los yndios muy recatados y se estrañavan de los Españoles
> en tanto grado, que la leña, yerba o otras cosas no lo querían lleuar a
> casa de Español, por dezir no los matase allá dentro para les sacar el
> unto. Todo esto se entendió aver salido de aquella ladronera por
> poner enemistad entre los yndios y Españoles . . . hasta que el señor
> visorey don Françisco de Toledo los deshizo y hechó de allí, en lo
> qual sirvió Dios Nuestro Señor mucho.

17. In the words of the Anonymous Jesuit, "Nacac, carniceros ó desolladores de animales para el sacrificio" (1879: 170).

18. Discussion of Toledan projects from various angles can be found in Bakewell 1984; Fraser 1990; Spalding 1984; and Stern 1982; among others.

19. Stern (1982) shows how such cushioning, before Toledo, was possible in part by private deals struck with encomenderos.

20. Polo's argument condemning this productive system (even while marveling at its efficiency) is itself a marvel of sixteenth-century sophistry. To paraphrase Polo liberally, he concludes that in taking from each according to his ability and giving to each according to his need, the Inca system had been guided by Satan himself, depriving Andeans of sufficient opportunity to witness poverty and hunger, and therefore to practice the cardinal virtue of charity (Polo Ondegardo 1916b [June 26, 1571]: chap. "Del servicio de las huacas"). Polo knew well the importance of charity for Castilian Christians, who, given some Castilians' love of money and accumulation, had no end of opportunities to feed the poor and bury the destitute. (On the practice of charity within Spanish confraternities, see Flynn 1989.) Fortunately for Andeans (as Polo would have it) the brusk changes introduced by Toledan reforms restored to them the conditions under which the virtue of charity might develop.

21. We have seen in chapter 5 how Spanish chronicler-historians like Sarmiento (in the service of Toledo) used inquisitorial techniques to carry out a systematic inscription (and transformation) of the Andean past, reducing multiple channels of social memory to narrative alone, and then forcing narrative multiplicity into a single homogeneous and written text. For later, antiquarianist chroniclers (and twentieth-century historians), this kind of deformed product of

Spanish narrative colonization *became* the Andean past. Insofar as the chronicling process was itself a colonial ritual with real effects in the world of power relations, it came to transform Andeans' visions of their own past.

22. The litigation record was found in the ANB by the historian Karen Powers, who kindly made the citation and a partial transcription available to me.

23. First of all, the federation had once been moiety organized. Following the southern Andean custom of diarchic organization at both diarchy and federation levels, a counterpart cacique, only slightly less elevated in stature than Guarache, should have been in command of the federation's lower moieties. Indeed, in Hernando de Aldana's possession ceremony of 1540, there had been a second native lord from Killaka. Apparently, Colque Guarache or his father Juan Guarache had somehow pushed this lineage into the background, for they are not heard from again. (The same process seems to have taken place in the Asanaqi diarchy and in Awllaka-Urukilla. Only in Siwaruyu-Arakapi was a pair of lords consistently named after Toledan days.)

24. The acts of foundation of these parishes are in ANB, ALP Minas, tomo 125. Surviving parish registers prove that some diarchies remained intact in their parish microcosms into the eighteenth century.

25. Of course, as Olivia Harris (1982) shows, the seasonal return of the dead from the warm and watery underworld to the surface of the earth, between All Souls' and Carnaval, is essential for germination and growth of the crops. Taussig (1980) argues that miners' devil beliefs are a transmutation of agricultural sacrifices to mountain gods, generated by miners to help them understand the nature of their alienation as newly proletarianized wage laborers, recently arrived at an exchange-value world from a use-value subsistence economy. Contesting Taussig, Platt (1983) argues that the analogous ties between agriculture and the dead, and between mineral (and money) production and the *tio-supays* of the mines, form a single, fundamentally "Andean" whole and are to be found (at least since early colonial days and perhaps since pre-Columbian times) in both mining camp and rural countryside; when colonial mitayos journeyed to Potosí they called their destination the *chacara del rey,* the "king's field." From the perspective developed here, however, they appear as contextually varying theses on the colonial and postcolonial situation, which has included at least partly alienated wage labor (supplemented by other kinds of relations of production) since the establishment of the Potosí mita. As an interpretation of the intercultural conjunction produced in intercultural contexts, it is neither specifically Andean nor Spanish in origin, but is generated by and addresses the relationship between the two.

26. See the Colque Guarache will in ANB, EC 1804, no. 193. Claims for the communicative content of certain kinds of cumbi cloth, such as the shirts given by Incas to certain provincial lords (like Juan Guarache, Juan Colque's father) appear in Harrison 1989: 60ff.; and Cummins 1994: 198ff. Further sources are cited therein.

27. The Spanish original:

En la fiesta de Corpus Christi saquen sus andas y danza en cada
parroquia y vayan en procesión con su cruz y banderas y sus
hermanos de la cofradía los ríjan y el sacerdote con ellos,
examinando ante todas cosas las andas que llevan por que no lleven
excondidos algunos ídolos, como se les han hallado en otras
ciudades, y el sacerdote antes que salga les diga en su lengua la razón
de aquella fiesta para que la entiendan y honren con la veneración
que son obligados.

28. See the Documentary Appendix, part B, for full Spanish text.

29. Evidence that Quiocalla became Tomahavi and that its ayllus (and those
of nearby Coroma) belong to Siwaruyu and Arakapi is in the 1683 visita of the
Repartimiento de Puna (AHP, Cuaderno de la visita . . .).

30. I draw here on the summary published by N. D. Cook (1975) and an
unpublished "tasa" (as such summaries were called) located in AGNA, 9.17.2.5.
These summaries vary in the level of detail provided for particular repartimientos. Another unpublished tasa is to be found in AHP, Cajas Reales 18.

31. Zárate gives a total of 11,526 persons in the repartimiento de Quillacas
y Asanaques, and a total tributary population of 2,545 (he rounded tributary to
pueblo numbers). By simple division, those numbers give 4.5 persons per
tributary. I have multiplied each town's tributary population by this reasonable
figure to estimate total populations of each town.

32. The Toledan visita of Tiquipaya has been published by del Río and
Gordillo (1993).

33. The classic on reducciónes is Málaga Medina 1974. More recently, see
Fraser 1990.

34. As Fraser (1990) has argued, towns of the Indies were built from scratch,
more or less all at one go. As a result, they in fact became much more regular and
alike than the actual towns of Castile were, which after all had long histories and
Visigothic as well as Muslim pasts, leading to irregular plans (though with all the
structures and institutions established in indian towns).

35. See Sarabia Viejo 1989: 236 ("Que los alguaciles ronden de noche y
hagan tocar la queda," in the "Ordenanzas generales para la vida común en los
pueblos de indios," Arequipa, November 6, 1575).

36. On the concept of buena policía, see Lechner 1981; and Fraser 1990.

37. Here Toledo anticipated Guaman Poma's lament: "Free me, Jesus Christ,
from fire, from water, from earthquake. Jesus Christ, free me from the authorities, the corregidor, the bailiff, the magistrate, the investigators, the visita judges,
the teaching priests . . ." (Guaman Poma, quoted in Mayer 1982; Guevara-Gil
and Salomon 1994).

38. When the lands were under attack again in 1592 (owing to the process of
composición), the cacique principal of the Asanaqi, don Diego Malco, named the
fields and the hamlet Chiucori, which belonged to Ayllu Ilawi in Tacobamba

territory, and (no doubt from his community chest) produced the visita document itself, the only part of the Zárate visita that survives. Zárate conducted his house-by-house survey of "the site and town of Chiucori" on May 28, 1573, and produced the "padrón of the indians of this said repartimiento . . . visiting the houses and indians of the ayllu called Hilavi, of Anansaya, in the following manner. . . ." Zárate goes on to list fourteen men of tributary age, the names of their wives or concubines and children, the animals they possessed, and their current whereabouts. All but four of the men were absent, mostly in the mining centers of Potosí, Guariguari, or Porco (ANB, EC 1611, no. 8, fols. 25r–28r). In 1610 Juan Colque Guarache "el Mozo" was still involved in the suit.

39. Condo's "book one of baptisms" was begun in 1571 by "Father Peñalosa." Initial pages are all written and decorated in a fine gothic hand, beginning with page one, a depiction of the crown, keys, and other emblems of San Pedro. I first took notes on this volume in Condo itself in 1980. Since then it and other parish registers have passed into the Archivo Obispal de Oruro.

40. Some church posts, however, were not initially rotative in nature. Into Condo's 1571 baptismal register were bound ordinances from a 1575 ecclesiastic visit requiring appointment of mayordomos to take charge of church ornaments. As of a visita in 1580, two men appointed were still mayordomos (AOO, Libro 1 de Bautismos, San Pedro de Condo, fols. 374r–378r). The same register records a meeting of the town cabildo (written by an indigenous "*escribano del pueblo*") when this priest left the parish. At this time the priest turned over responsibility for safekeeping of church property to the collected authorities (along with the two mayordomos).

41. The Spanish original:

> . . . hoy día acaece en el Pirú, a cabo de dos y tres años, cuando van a tomar residencia a un corregidor, salir los indíos con sus cuentas menudas averiguadas, pidiendo que en tal pueblo le dieron seis huevos, y no los pagó, y en tal casa una gallina, y acullá dos haces de yerba para sus caballos, y no pagó sino tantos tomines, y queda debiendo tantos; y para todo esto, hecha la averiguación allí al pie de la obra con cuantidad de ñudos y manojos de cuerdas que dan por testigos y escritura cierta. Yo vi un manojo de estos hilos, en que una india traía escrita una confesión general de toda su vida, y por ellos se confesaba, como yo lo hiciera por papel escrito, y aún pregunté de algunos hilillos que me parecieron algo diferentes, y eran ciertas circunstancias que requería el pecado para confesarle enteramente. Fuera de estos quipos de hilo, tienen otros de pedrezuelas, por donde puntualmente aprenden las palabras que quieren tomar de memoria. Y es cosa de ver a viejos ya caducos con una rueda hecha de pedrezuelas, aprender el Padre Nuestro, y con otra el Ave María, y con otra el Credo, y saber cuál piedra es que fué concebido de Espíritu Santo, y cuál que padeció debajo del poder de Poncio Pilato,

y no hay más que verlos enmendar cuando yerran, y toda la
enmienda consiste en mirar sus pedrezuelas, que a mí para hacerme
olvidar cuanto sé de coro, me bastará una rueda de aquellas. De esta
suele haber no pocas en los cimenterios de las iglesias, para este
efecto; pues verles otra suerte de quipos que usan de granos de maíz,
es cosa que encanta. Porque una cuenta muy embarazosa, en que
tendrá un muy buen contador que hacer por pluma y tinta, para ver
a cómo les cabe entre tantos, tanto de contribución, sacando tanto de
acullá y añadiendo tanto de acá, con otras cien retartalillas, tomarán
estos indios sus granos y pornán uno aquí, tres acullá, ocho no se
dónde; pasarán un grano de aquí, trocarán tres de acullá, y en /292/
efecto ellos salen con su cuenta hecha puntualísimamente, sin errar
un tilde; y mucho mejor se saben ellos poner en cuenta y razón de lo
que cabe a cada uno de pagar o dar, que sabremos nosotros dárselo
por pluma y tinta averiguado. Si esto no es ingenio y si estos
hombres son bestias, júzguelo quien quisiere, que lo que yo juzgo de
cierto, es que en aquello a que se aplican nos hacen grandes ventajas.

42. When Juan Colque the Younger took over his father's role in Potosí, he
came dressed in Spanish-style silks, but without his father's knowledge of
Andean ways or his grandfather's personal experience of Inca society. Luis
Capoche, a Spanish bureaucrat reporting on the labor system of Potosí's mines in
1585, said this about the young Colque Guarache:

Don Juan Colque el Mozo, natural de los Quillacas, es capitán de los
asanaques y quillacas, del partido de Urcusuyu de esta provincia de
los Charcas. Ha oído gramática en el colegio de la Compañia de
Jesús y anda vestido a nuestro modo, con mucha seda. No se hallan
bien con el los indios, así por el traje que para sustentarlo es
menester robarlos, porque no es cacique, y también porque no
entiende el estilo y usanza y costumbres de su gobierno, ni trata a los
indios con afabilidad. Diéronle este cargo por ser hijo de un indio
paramucho y que había servido mucho a Su Magestad. Al presente
está con los soldados de los chiriguanaes, que fué por capitán de los
indios que llevó el factor Juan Lozano Machuca. Tiene por sujetos a
estos pueblos: . . . [Puna; Quillacas y Asanaques; Aullagas y
Uruquillas]. (Capoche 1959: fol. 52v)

43. On the pre-Columbian image of Copacabana and its displacement by the
Virgin, see Bouysse-Cassagne 1988; Gisbert 1980; MacCormack 1984; Urbano
1988, 1989, 1990.
44. Essentially, illuminism entailed the imposition of strict self-discipline,
involving fasting and other privations (such as sexual abstention), self-inflicted
discomforts including flagellation, wearing a crown of thorns and a sackcloth
shirt, and especially long hours of prayer, all done in order to induce a

heightened state of spirituality, one that freed the imagination to serve as God's channel to man. Of course, from the Church's perspective, this was an exceedingly dangerous practice. Outside the direct mediation of cautious priests using theologically approved ritual, direct communication with God was itself a Protestant act. But more to the point, private nonconventual worship outside priestly control led to heterodoxies and heresies. Also, opening the imagination to divine truth also opened it to diabolic purposes, and only priestly supervision could ensure that the illuminists practitioners had not been misled by the great deceiver.

Erasmianism and its offspring illuminism themselves derived from the Thomist philosophy of cognition and imagination elaborated by Aquinas from Aristotelian principles (summarized in MacCormack 1991, see esp. pp. 17–49). Aquinas also explained, however, why consecrated priests were the only ones who should access the divine power of human imagination for use in that central rite of the faith, the Eucharist: "Although the priest was only human, he repeated Christ's words by virtue of his institutional power. Accordingly, the consecration of the Eucharist, and by implication eucharistic visions, exemplified a social order in which priests exercised divinely delegated functions in a hierarchy of authority that descended from god via the priesthood to laypeople. Theology, philosophy, and social order, religion and politics, went hand in hand" (ibid., 35).

The Eucharist was also, of course, the centerpiece of Spanish Christian social memory, an act of commemoration capable of bringing the effects of past acts (themselves future directed) into the present and its future (see Rubin 1991). It is no wonder that the priestly authority, embodying the very logic of the eschatological history upon which the king's authority rested, needed ever to be guarded by exerting control over the independent exercise of unruly imagination.

45. As MacCormack suggests, however, the situations of Castilian as opposed to indian religious innovators may have been susceptible to the same subtle means of distinguishing divine from satanically inspired imaginations, but those means were not brought into play equally in the two parts of the empire. MacCormack argues that, in the face of indians great numeric preponderance in Perú, the unfamiliarity, the total otherness of indian culture, came to displace the need for a careful tweezing of truth from lies that was an inquisitorial specialty in cases of Castilian heterodoxy. "When Spaniards confronted Andean people, therefore, the familiar scale of nuances that had served in the peninsula to distinguish truth from error, and god from demons, collapsed into a consolidated sense of a difference that was total" (1991: 48).

Other forces also militated against nuanced interpretations of the indigenous imagination, especially when indian practices seemed to approximate or borrow from Christian ones. The maxim that religion and politics go hand in hand was never so true as in the colonial situation, where the cultural difference that was total translated into the contrast of social estate. There could be no tributes or forced labor from successfully converted indians, who would in theory gain the rights of any Crown subject along with their civilization and Christianity. To serve God by preserving the empire, and to preserve the empire by maintaining its colony, indians had to remain fully "other."

46. This probanza (AGI, Charcas 79, no. 19) was found and partly transcribed by Thierry Saignes and further transcribed and photocopied by me. A full, corrected transcription is to be published (with notes by Tristan Platt) in Platt, Bouysse-Cassagne, Harris, and Saignes, eds., in press. See a partial translation in part D of the Documentary Appendix.

47. These events are studied in Saignes 1993: 65; the document is to be published entire in Platt, Bouysse-Cassagne, Harris, and Saignes, eds., in press. Separately, the priest Pedro Ramírez del Aguila, who had served in Tacobamba, also reported an indian Christ there (1978: 135).

48. Thierry Saignes (1985b: 436–439) reports authorities' suspicions that Juan Colque Guarache was involved in such activities, also in the vicinity of Tacobamba, where the priest Pedro Ramírez del Aguila reports that Colque had been found with a gathering of five thousand indians. Ramírez del Aguila's concern was that this gathering was somehow related to "messages" directed to indians from Francis Drake, the great "Lutheran," reported amidst other panic-filled claims by coastal authorities. Since no other sources confirm Colque Guarache's involvement in any such matter, I conclude that this was more likely preparation for one of Colque's efforts in the Spanish war against the Chiriguanos.

49. The term "prioste" seems to be an alternative for "alférez."

50. The "dons" before their names suggest that they were hereditary lords, perhaps principales of Ayllu Kawalli, although a noble house by the name of Chiri appears in no other documents. Note that they share this name with Miguel Acarapi, for whom Chiri was an alias. See Thierry Saignes' discussion of the significance of these names (both common in K'ulta territory) vis-á-vis shamanistic practice.

51. ABAS, Causas contra ecclesiasticos, no. 5020: "Condo, liçençia para capilla, 1626," 10 fols. My thanks to Dr. Josep Barnadas, director of the Archivo y Biblioteca Arquidiocesanos de Sucre, for his help in locating the document. The Chiris' letter:

> Don Pedro Chiri prioste y don Diego Chiri mayordomo y de los demás fundadores de la cofradía de Santa Bárbara del Pueblo de Condocondo. Digo que en la estancia de Uma Hunto tengo mis haçiendas de chacaras y ganados de ella en la qual abrá nuebe años poco más o menos que con asistençia del cura del dicho pueblo fundamos la dicha cofradía con los cargos y condiçiones que por ella consta para fundalla se lleuo liçençia del ordinario y con ella se a continuado hasta oy dia. Y sin embargo de que en la dicha confradía y yglesia donde esta fundada tiene todo rrecaudo para celebrar el culto diuino, sin que les falta cosa alguna comprado a nuestra costa, el padre Gonçalo Real Vejarano nuestro cura que es al presente se

rretiene en sí los ornamentos y todo lo demás necesario y no quiere continuar en la celebrazión de la dicha cofradía ni acudir a la dicha estancia a cuya causa muchos de los yndios biejos que ay poblados en las dichas tierras carezen de los sacramento de la confissión y se an muerto sin ella ni tampoco oyen misa por auer faltado esta buena yntroduzión y para que no se deje de consiguir tan buena y pía obra.

A V Md. pido y supplico me mande despachar Racaudo en forma con penas y aperçiuamentos para que el padre cura continue en la dicha obra pía, pues demás de ser seruicio de dios esta a sido para el bien de los naturales y que así mesmo buelba todos hornamentos calises y las demás cosas que tiene en su poder pues no le perteneçe por ningun derecho sino a la dicha cofradía por ser suya que en ello reçiuiremos bien y merced con justicia que pedimos. (firmas: don Pedro Chiri/don Diego Chiri)

E vista por su merced mando se notifique al beneficiado Goncalo Leal Uejarano cura de Condocondo guarde la costumbre que ay en la çelebraçión desta cofradía y en acudir a la administración de los santos sacramentos a esta estancia [*sic*] y buelba a los yndios [entre renglones = mayordomos] los ornamentos que della obiere lleuado so pena de excomunión mayor sin dar lugar a que los yndios buelban a quejarse. (firma = Doctor Pasqual Peroches. Ante mi, Paulo Garzes) (Ibid., 1r–1v)

52. The Spanish original:

. . . que an sido quatro o çinco capillas que en la jurisdiçión de este curato abiase mandaron derribar y rreduzir los yndios a este dicho pueblo por evitar las grandes borracheras ydolatrías susperstiçiones ynsestos graues pendençias y muertes que dello se causauan como en particular lo ay en aquel sitio donde esta la dicha capilla contenida en el pedimiento, la qual pocos años a el yndio contenido en el por ausentarse de este su pueblo y no acudir al serviçio del ni oyr missa y bibir en su infidelidad con otros tales como el lebantó una capilla para que so color de ella los dejasen bibir allí en su libertad pensando que con dádibas los curas los dejarían y así Diego Arias su antesesor conosiendo y sabiendo los muchos pecados que allí se cometían contra dios nuestro señor y que los yndios que allí se juntaban no benían a oyr missa ni ser administrados de los demás sacramentos, no quiso jamás a yr a la dicha capilla a çelebrar ni hazer les fiesta alguna aunque le rresalaban para ello mucho. . . .

53. The Spanish original:

. . . y no tubo effecto aunque el corregidor de este partido fue por ellos a caussa de que se huyeron y escondieron la ymajen y ornamentos y la dicha capilla hallo destechada y después hizieron otra capilla una legua más adelante y por conseguir su mal yntento, ocurieron al señor arcobispo, don Gerónimo de Rueda, con relaçión siniestra y otro pedimiento como el presente a lo qual . . . rrespondío . . . por las caussas que ban espresadas, y . . . le ynbió el mandamiento y pareser del dicho señor visitador . . . y le rrespondió . . . que ynstase con el corregidor quemase las casas a los yndios y los trajese a su rreduçión pues hera seruiçio de dios nuestro señor. . . .

. . . y porque lo uno ni lo otro no a tenido effecto a caussa de ser los yndios más malos que ay en este rreyno ladinos soberbios y libres y que no puedan ser abidos, el dicho señor doctor Bartolomé Serbantes en la visita que hizo en este dicho pueblo por constarle de todo lo que de si suso ba dicho escribió al rreal acuerdo para que lo rremediase y prebiniendo el rremedio para lo de adelante dejó ordenado por obra de bisita escritpo en el libro de esta dicha yglesia donde se an fecho las demás visitas unas constituçiones y ordenansas. . . .

[marg. izq. = constituçión] Yten por quanto se a bisto por espiriençia los grandes daños e ynconbinientes que se an seguido y siguen de tener los yndios capillas en sus estançias y chácaras y celebrar en ellas missa y fiestas y que con mayor libertad los yndios estando en el campo hazen borracheras cantos y taquies en desonor de nuestra ffee cathólica y bienen aser las dichas fiestas en daño notable de su conbersión y ffee que se les enseña, ordeno y mando que el dicho cura no çelebra missa en las dichas capillas ni haga fiesta alguna de cofradía ni otro sancto alguno sino que las dichas fiestas se hagan y çelebren en este pueblo de Condocondo o en el de Guari su anejo, y si las dichas capillas tubieron bultos ymajenes y ornamentos los traygan y rredusga a la yglesia de este dicho pueblo de Condocondo en que ponga todo cuydado como negocio que tanto ymporta al augmento de la ffee de los naturales.

Y en quanto a la capilla de Sancta Bárbara que estaua fundada en la estançia de Huntuma se cunpla y guarde lo ordenado y mandado por el Señor Doctor don Bernadino de Almança arzedecano de La Plata visitador general que fué de este arçobispado, derribando la dicha capilla hasta sus simientos y se traje el bulto de la sancta y sus ornamentos y se acaue el edifiçio de la capilla de la dicha sancta que esta enpesada a deficar [sic] en este dicho pueblo y en ella se çelebre la fiesta de la sancta y en el campo con apersebimiento que haziendo lo contrario se le hara cargo en la visita.

Y los curacas e hilacatas del ayllo caualle que tienen sus estançias en el asiento de Huntuma traygan la jente a çelebrar la dicha fiesta de la dicha sancta y los traygan a misa todos los domingos y fiestas suyas y que asistan en el pueblo para que así el cura bean si estan doctrinados y los doctrine y enseñe y los mesmos curacas derriben la dicha capilla y traygan los sanctos y ornamentos que obiere y lo

cumplan todo so pena de çinquenta asotes y de cada dies pessos [*sic*]
corrientes aplicados a la fábrica de esta sancta yglesia con
apersebimiento que no cumpliendo con lo aquí ordenado en la visita
que subçediere a ésta se yrá a executar a su costa y serán castigados
con mayor rrigor como a cónpliçes de los delictos superstiçiones y
hechizerías que en el dicho asiento de Huntuma se cometen contra
dios nuestro señor y nuestra sancta ffee cathólica y mando que estas
hordenansas se notifiquen al cura y curacas. La qual dicha
constituçión es como se contiene a la letra de su original y está
firmada, Doctor Bartolomé Basques Cerbantes y rrefrendadada [*sic*].
Ante mi Gaspar Martín notario, y el dicho benefficiado Gonsalo Leal
Vejarano dió por su rrespuesta todo lo que de suso ba declarado. . . .

54. Yet the most interesting detail is difficult to interpret: Coroma natives also adored certain "heads" in the manner of skulls with sculpted and painted facial features and certain sculpted figures of horses, one of which was endowed with a horn protruding from its forehead "in the manner of a unicorn." I cannot explain the unicorn or horses, but the skulls with artfully reconstructed faces resemble certain of the "mummified" ancestors revered in Cusco. In modern Bolivia, they also resemble the skulls adored as "riwusyun" (from Sp. "devoción"), bones of those whose sins make them condenados, condemned to wander this earth (for a detailed account of such rites, see Huanca 1989). They are addressed as oracles for divination, especially for nefarious purposes, and usually on the "evil" days, Tuesdays and Fridays, when sacrifices to Tatala (Christ) or to the moon (the Virgin), or libations to the ancestors in "heaven" (or rather, in manxa-pacha, the underworld) are not performed. In K'ulta the term "riwusyun" also refers to miniature saint images kept in nearly every domestic unit.

Like the extirpation records detailing the Diego Iquisi and Miguel Acarapi scares, this proceso has not been found. When taken together, however, they amply support the argument that extirpation campaigns had not been limited to the archbishopric of Lima, as some scholars have suggested.

55. In the same year Oruro authorities tried still another man for very similar practices. Domingo Ramírez, who advertised himself as an "*hilsa*," directed his devotions to an image of the Virgin of Guadalupe, and the holy spirit that descended into him conveyed the words of "Our Lord and the Virgin and the glorious apostle Saint James" (AJO, Leg. 1779–82). Ramírez had erected his chapel in the hamlet of Guaguaxasi, in the doctrina of Paria, from whence he had been brought under guard. There may have been a connection between Ramírez and Nina Willka; Ramírez had once been punished by the priest of Mohosa for carrying his rituals there. The ubiquity of hamlet chapels and images entirely under indian control became a more general concern of both civil and ecclesiastic authorities at about the same time.

56. For their indigenous content, Gruzinski (1993) studies faked "*títulos primordiales*" in Mesoamerica. Apart from documents such as the one shown to

me by Cruce's founder, I came across no further colonial "títulos" in K'ulta comparable to the often recopied and reworked documents described by Joanne Rappaport for the Paez. Nor did any K'ultas I met seek to synthesize ancestral myth and colonial documents into a coherent founding narrative. And although I did meet men in Challapata and Condo who claimed to own large collections of titles, I was not able to convince them, in my brief sojourns in those towns, to show them to me, much less produce an exegesis. On a foray into the archives of the prefectura de Oruro, however, I found a fragmentary colonial title, dating from the Vega Alvarado composición of 1647, that had been submitted in prosecution of a land claim by none other than don Manuel Mamani. Having lived on don Manuel's patio for over a year and in his house for months, I was surprised to find that he had kept this document from me. Such documents are a sacred business indeed.

57. The bull's horn, incidentally, also serves as a trumpet called pututu, an emblem of authority and the instrument through which ayllu members are called together to defend their lands, whether by paying tribute or through battle.

58. Morato, it seems, may have given his name to the social group created from the Urus of Lake Poopó, who call themselves Urus Moratos.

59. Most probably that ayllu was once the lower moiety of Asanaqi; today it is one of the ayllus of Santa Bárbara de Culta (ADRO, Provincia Abaroa, Libro de Propiedades, 1931–33, part 27, fols. 38–40).

60. The document was poorly copied from an earlier document from the council archive by the cantón's corregidor in 1914 before being deposited in an Oruro archive in 1970. It was carried to Oruro in an effort by don Manuel Mamani to defend certain lands from incursions by Ayllu Qullana by none other than my host in K'ulta, who never made mention of the document's existence.

The Spanish original: " . . . llega a Pachuta que es un morro y pide sirve de mojón de ambos aillos Cahualli abajo y Collanas, de hay sigue por una pampa muy larga rumbo al Este al lugar de Tolapampa, y sigue al Este por un riachuelo al mojón llamado Quintiri sigue a una roca llamado Pairumani, de hay sigue a Cruz Pata, prosigue a Churicala que es el mojón desde tiempo inmemorial que hay plantaron sus varas cada cual, de hay Chiaraque . . ."

61. Colonial varas, or staffs of authority, are still carried by the jilaqatas, alcaldes, and alguaciles of K'ulta. Often tipped and banded with silver, they were also a Spanish emblem of authority. They are usually also still made of chonta palm wood, as the staff carried by Tunupa was or that carried by Manco Capac, which, when plunged into the fertile earth of Cusco, defined an Inca promised land; varas also complexly resonate associations deriving from both Spanish and Andean sources. Called tata reyes (king fathers) when ritually addressed or libated (Rasnake 1988a), they now synthetically embody external sources of power from which that of council members emanates.

62. An excellent overview of sparse European literature and a history of confraternities in Early Modern Spain is Flynn 1989. Christian (1981) surveys rural religiosity in New Castile, drawing upon another of Philip II's totalizing questionnaires.

63. Few studies of the merger of civil and ritual hierarchies have been published for the Andean area. Chance and Taylor (1985) and Farriss (1984) for the Mesoamerican area provide useful guides to the methodological and historiographic problems encountered. Rasnake (1988a) and Platt (1987c) are among the few studies of the phenomenon in the Charcas region. For Peruvian cases, Celestino and Meyers (1981) provide a comparative study of cofradías, mostly within larger towns, where they more strongly resemble the Spanish and urban model. Varón (1982) suggests that the cofradía was a principal means by which ayllus were (re)articulated within reducción communities. See also Hopkins and Meyers 1988.

64. In 1756, when an "indio principal" of Condo's ayllu Sullcayana, named don Joseph Guarcaia, brought a complaint against his parish priest, ten festivals were celebrated there.

> . . . Digo que en el dicho mi pueblo tenemos dies fiestas entabladas desde muchos años como son el Nombre Santo de María, San Miguel, San Francisco Xabier, San Salbador, Nuestra Señora de Candelaria, la Resurrección de Nuestro Señor, la fiesta de Corpus, San Pedro, Santa Rosa, y la Natividad de Nuestra Señora, y en cada fiesta se ponen tres indios, dos mayordomos, y un alferes, y estos contribuien de limosna ciento y catorse pesos que en todas las fiestas se exercitan treinta yndios con más otros gastos que hasen, de lo qual quedan pobres y enpeñados de manera que quedan peresiendo deviendo y vendiendo quanto tienen y no tienen con que pagar sus tributos: con más otras dies fiestas que tienen en los sinco anejos que tiene el dicho pueblo quedan de limosna en unos anejos quareinta [*sic*] y quatro y en otros treinta y tres con más otros gastos que tienen en las dichas fiestas por lo qual mucha gente del dicho pueblo se ban ausentando y consumiendo por no tener con que pasar las dichas fiestas por que quedan enpeñados deviendo y vendiendo quanto tienen; y lo otro los derechos d—— dos de los entierros casamientos y olios sin atender al Real Aransel dispuesto por sinodales de este Arsobispado y a las Reales Cédulas que su Mages /1v/ tad que dizque asido servido de despacharnos como a miserables vasallos de su Cathólica y Real persona de veinte y nuebe de Junio del año próxssimo pasado de setecientos sinquenta y dos. . . . (ANB, EC 1756, no. 41, fols. 1r–1v)

65. I suggest that merged fiesta-cargo systems reached something like their modern form during the late seventeenth to mid-eighteenth centuries. The convincing work of S. Elizabeth Penry (1996) focuses precisely on this conjuncture for both San Pedro de Condo and towns in the colonial province of Chayanta. On the 1780s rebellion in the Charcas region, see also Arze 1991; Cangiano 1988; Cajías de la Vega 1987; Hidalgo 1983; O'Phelan Godoy 1985; Penry 1993; Serulnikov 1988, 1989; and Thomson 1996.

66. In Tinquipaya, the visitor Sanabria specified how alcaldes should assign certain children to the service of the church: " . . . serving by their turns of the wheel the said boys, of whom some of the older ones shall be taken, after the said town is built and completed and has been populated, so that after having taught them song and music they shall serve in the church, officiating at mass when the priest wishes to perform it sung" (AGI, Charcas 49, fol. 9v [see the Documentary Appendix, part C, for full text]).

67. Chance and Taylor (1985) survey the received wisdom on fiesta-cargo systems in Mesoamerica, suggesting that it has been predisposed to opposite conclusions (such systems are said to give evidence of acculturation or of cultural resistance) because of a serious historiographic flaw: modern fiesta-cargo systems studied ethnographically have been contrasted with pre-Columbian social forms to find survivals or the lack of them, without first historically investigating the successive intermediate forms of the colonial period. The issue is fruitfully taken up in Carmagnani 1988; Farriss 1984; and Penry 1996.

68. The strategy is widely reported in local-level rebellions in both countryside and city. Spalding (1984) analyzes a 1750 conspiracy in Lima, where rebels planned to use weapons carried in an auto sacramental during the festival of San Miguel to attack the viceregal palace. The link between festival and rebellion is well attested among the many eighteenth-century revolts summarized in O'Phelan Godoy 1985.

69. Many such priest-instigated or -aided suits by commoner indians against corregidores and hereditary lords are recorded in AGNA, 9.14.8.7 and 9.14.8.8. See AGNA, 9.36.6.1, for the involvement of a loyalist descendant of Juan Colque Guarache (through the San Lucas collateral lineage), who gained a cacicasgo in Chayanta for his role in fighting 1781 rebels.

70. Chungara and his ancestors had engaged in many disputes with the caciques of the "parcialidad de los Asanaques de anansaya." See ANB: EC 1738, no. 62; EC 1743, no. 9; EC 1759, no. 139. In January of 1781, Challapata rebels, led by Lope Chungara, killed the corregidor of the province of Paria, along with the anansaya cacique (Cajías de la Vega 1987).

71. This was almost certainly Lucas Feliz Llanquipacha, surviving son of the murdered Gregorio Feliz Llanquipacha (see below for the son's difficulties with his "plebeian" indians in the 1790s).

72. Note that it was the alcaldes who mobilized rebels.

73. The priest of Macha, one Gregorio Joseph de Merlos, was later tried as a rebel collaborator and accused of having personally written Catari's correspondance.

74. Mitanis and pongos were kinds of personal servants that the town council supplied to the priest.

75. Apparently the alcaldes presented the priest with a roster of candidates for festival posts, from which he chose the "lucky winners." These three men had not been given festival duties.

76. See text of Spanish original in part E of the Documentary Appendix.

77. The studies of a landmark reanalysis of late-eighteenth-century Andean revolts (Stern 1987) have questioned earlier interpretations of revolt as messianic or millenarian movements or as patriotic anti-Spanish movements foreshadowing independence. Stern's introduction provides a masterful overview of the literature.

78. His portable image and shrine were similar to the image through which, a hundred years earlier, Nina Willka had communicated with Christ and the Virgin. Such images can still be seen in today's commercialized Ayacucho-style retablos, available in Miami shopping malls, and in the imagenes de bulto kept in every house and hamlet chapel in K'ulta.

79. Between 1680 and 1780, sponsorship of rituals devoted to saints within merged cofradía–town council frameworks had become the centerpiece of polity formation, and it is likely that a systemic division of labor—or division of the cosmos on cultural lines—was also in place, one that gave priests control over authorized ritual performance relating to the Eucharist and the word of God, and left indian fiesta sponsors control over unauthorized, indeed increasingly clandestine and cryptic, ritual forms pertaining to the sacred beings of the underworld (Nina Willka's souls in hell), as preconquest or "heathen" indian ancestors, lurking just below the surfaces visible to priests, are considered to be.

80. What is more, the Challapata cacique, named de la Cruz Condori, claimed descent from the Taquimalco lineage of hereditary lords, based in Condo rather than in Challapata. The Llanquipachas had managed to displace the Taquimalcos in the cacicasgo of Condo only a few years before, claiming descent from Martín Pacha, a cacique named in the tasa of the visita general of the 1570s. The Llanquipachas did not present a full genealogy to prove their link to Martín Pacha; by the mid-eighteenth century, such proof was not necessary to gain office, only the approval of the corregidor. The Taquimalcos, for their part, claimed descent from one Acho, perhaps the man named in Pizarro's encomienda grant to Hernando de Aldana.

81. The phrase belongs to Lucas Feliz Llanquipacha (ANB, EC 1792, no. 108).

82. For this rapid summary I draw from Klein 1992; and Platt 1984. It should be noted that nineteenth-century Spain saw the application of precisely the same sort of policies, known there as *desamortización*. In Spain, liberalism meant the confiscation of lands pertaining to "dead hands": the common fields, forests, and pastures owned collectively by council-led towns, and the vast properties owned by the rentier class, including the Church and absentee noble landlords. Over the course of the nineteenth century, the corporate towns of Spain lost most of their communal lands; the Church and some great noble families lost their feudatory titles. Yet between theory and practice there were difficult obstacles.

In their own history, Castilian townsmen had never seen servitude such as that which nineteenth-century liberalism brought to indians, at least until becoming *"peones"* on the nineteenth-century private estates into which their former commons had been transformed.

83. Although many lands were stolen from indigenous communities, the project was not successful. On the one hand, indigenous communities put up concerted resistence. And on the other, privatization of indigenous peoples' land often meant the establishment of great latifundios where a new *hacendado* class, rather than investing in machinery, retained as pongos the very same indians who had formerly held the lands (Klein 1992; Larson 1988; Platt 1982a, 1984; Rivera Cusicanqui 1986). Warm and irrigated fields in the valleys where Killaka and Asanaqi peoples still maintained access to croplands were also attractive to the growing ranks of neocolonial latifundistas (Platt 1982a). As a result, the nineteenth century saw the progressive loss of Altiplano peoples' rights to valley lands.

84. The original Spanish:

> Corcino Viscarra, Cacique de Culta, cantón de la sub-prefectura de Paria, ante usted me presento y digo: Que hace años que hemos sido perturvados en la posesión de los terrenos de Culta que como originarios poseimos, por los dichos originarios de Tinquipaya; más la divina Providencia nos ha restituido la tranquilidad con la imvención de los títulos que en fojas cincuentidos acompaño, por ellos se ve que nuestro interés habian comprado los terrenos de Culta y los molinos por la summa de siete mil pesos; así pues somos hacendados, no cólonos, podemos disponer de nuestra adquisición como propietarios, y al Govierno y los particulares, no pueden ni imponernos gravámenes, ni usurparnos un palmo de los que costó nuestra plata; a fin de que con los títulos mencionados podamos hacer uso de nuestro derecho pedimos que el notario don Miguel Calvimontes nos franquee un testimonio integro de los títulos que acompañamos en fojas cincuentidos, y sea con sitación Fiscal. Es lo que a usted pido como representante de la comunidad de Culta. Potosí, agosto cinco de mil ochocientos sesentiocho. Corcino Viscarra. (Choquecallata document, unpaginated)

This document is a typescript that was made by the notary Eloy Lascano of Oruro in March 1962, from an earlier transcription. There, "ADRO, Provincia Abaroa, Libro de Propiedades, 1945, no. 8" is cited as the source. I could not locate that original.

85. See the text of Pérez' petition to the president of Bolivia in part F of the Documentary Appendix.

86. One of the Agrarian Reform petitions for deslinde and amojonamiento (the same procedure that Challapata caciques sought in the mid-eighteenth century and for which Corcino Pérez had lobbied in the nineteenth century) that I briefly saw in La Paz had been submitted by two neighboring patronymic hamlets of Ayllu Manxa-Kawalli.

87. As Xavier Albó (1975) has noted for the much more atomized Lake Titicaca region, the struggle between tendencies towards factionalism and group solidarity visible in cantonization conforms to structural features inherent to contemporary "Aymara culture" itself.

CHAPTER 7. TELLING AND DRINKING THE PATHS OF MEMORY:
NARRATIVE AND LIBATION POETICS AS HISTORICAL CONSCIOUSNESS

1. K'ulta social memory, that is, serves K'ultas rather than indigenistas, folklorists, or the Bolivian state. In the conclusion of this book, I pursue the question of whether the heroic past and timeless cultural stasis imputed to indians by Spanish missionary priests and creole folklorists may yet serve indigenous interests as indigenistas gain a voice on the national political scene.

2. For a collection of such stories from Qaqachaka, see Espejo Ayka 1994; and for perceptive analyses of stories about *sallqa,* wild animals, see Arnold and Yapita 1992a, 1992b; and Yapita 1992.

3. For a more detailed analysis of the myth, see Dillon and Abercrombie 1988. Much of the substance of the present analysis derives from the collaboration that produced this coauthored article.

4. This free translation of "Jesucristo-Tatalantix Supaytinsi-Chullpantix" was made by Mary Dillon and the author from a version I tape recorded in an interview with a K'ulta research consultant in September 1982. It conforms well to versions heard in other contexts (also in K'ulta, in 1979 and 1980). The myth is well-known and widespread in the area, often told, as other myths are, after dark within the home and during rest breaks in collective labor.

5. Arnold (1993) reports such a story from Qaqachaka, and asserts that Qaqas do accept descent from Chullpas. Arnold takes exception to the treatment of the Tatala versus Chullpas myth presented in Dillon and Abercrombie 1988, asserting that in Qaqachaka territory, Tatala may be called Jesucristo, but their Christ bears little resemblance to the Christ of the priests. Of course, as Arnold insists, Tatala is also the sun. I disagree, however, that Tatala's solar associations make him a fundamentally non-Christian figure. Preferring one of his names and certain of his qualities over other names and qualities to advance theses on cultural resistance is a time-honored Andeanist tradition. From my point of view, it seriously underestimates Andeans' abilities of intellectual synthesis and, like colonial extirpators, refuses to grant Andeans (such as Miguel Acarapi, Martín Nina Willka, or Tupac Catari) the interpretive space by which to suit Christian doctrine to their own ends.

6. In a myth of these presolar times from Huarochirí, such autochthones are clearly immortal (Salomon and Urioste 1991).

7. That is why elders are so concerned about the practices of their textile-trading sons, who rob such tombs for valuable cloth and artifacts and take skulls from them (also sometimes from the cemetery or from older, colonial graves found in the churchyard).

8. Freeze-drying is one of the techniques that Murra (1984) has lauded as the "domestication of the cold," since it facilitates transport and long-term storage. In the manufacture of freeze-dried potatoes (ch'uñu) and meat (charki), the central process takes advantage of the alternation between the extreme cold of night and the temperate daytime temperatures and low humidity resulting from the strong solar radiation at Altiplano altitudes. Water released from tissues

through freezing is pressed out and then evaporates. Compare this with the transformation of the Chullpas from wet- and dark-loving, "natural" men into desiccated corpses, inhabiting their own kind of long-term "storehouse."

9. Space does not permit discussion of the heavenly path which appears when Tatala sets at night. The Milky Way is also conceived as a path (and as the river that carries manxa-pacha moisture to the heavens, from which it may fall as rain). As a t″aki, the Milky Way is a pilgrim's path, traveled by man and llama (who are trailed by a fox), on a neverending journey between food-production zones and highland storehouse, represented in the qullqa, the storehouses that K'ultas see in the Pleiades (see Urton 1981). It is no coincidence that it is through observations of the Pleiades that K'ultas determine when it is time to prepare their caravans to valley production zones and begin the process of freeze-drying.

10. On the contrast between house building as implementation of a plan and a product of social enactment, see the classic analysis in Bourdieu 1979. Mitchell (1991) amplifies Bourdieu's discussion and applies it (with perhaps too much insistence on enlightenment origins) to the study of the "modern" epistemology of colonial states.

11. This does not mean that east is feminine and west masculine; on the contrary, ch'alla performance demands that men face the east and women the west, and the space is correspondingly inverted to allow for this. Such inversion corresponds to the inverted recursion characteristic of the cosmos as a whole, in which each pole incorporates a subordinated aspect of its opposite.

12. House construction rites have been the focus of many Andeanist ethnographies. See Arnold 1992 for a detailed analysis for Qaqachaka.

The complementary and hierarchic relationships between these groups are ritually expressed in the specific building supplies and construction tasks allotted to each; the house as an end product expresses in great detail the social relations that brought it into being as a place of human activity. They are expressed in the names, uses, and meanings of all the house's component parts, from foundation stones to walls and corners to roofbeams. Indeed, even before construction begins, the house is invested with social life, given "roots" through which libations that are poured within may reach the ancestral dwelling places of the lineages that have been conjoined in husband and wife.

Once the house is completed, its walls and door define a relationship between inside and outside that also carries social meanings. In Aymara, "house" is "uta," and the open space outside its door is "utänqa" ("house-outside") usually an enclosed patiolike space shared with other houses belonging to the husband's patriline.

13. The *sucullu* rite described by Bertonio, which makes the infant's larita the one who brings the infant into humanity (by naming him), does so through a kind of "natural" sacrifice, equating the larita to the predator/hunter-gatherer and anointing the infant, as a wild equivalent of the herd llama, with vicuña blood. It was in this rite, as Bertonio noted, that the infant was first given gender-marked clothing to wear, with vertical stripes worn by boys, and

horizontal stripes by girls. In K'ulta the same contrast in alignment of striped outer garments is still a strongly marked form of gender definition (Bertonio 1984: book 2, 323).

14. This logic conforms to the Inca marriage rules analyzed by R. T. Zuidema (1977).

15. Let us consider the implications of a serious invocation of the four-generation exclusion, both when applied through patronymics and when applied through strict genealogizing. Manxa-Kawalli and Alax-Kawalli are both endowed with more than the necessary sixteen plus one patronymics required, and so the patronym exclusion rule may well work for a prospective couple. Of course, there is also the complicating factor of ayllu exogamy, which in my calculation occurs in nearly one in four marriages. In fact, K'ultas were universally adamant that there was no need to marry within the ayllu. There is a slight preference, however, which was explained quite pragmatically. Serious land wars, and indeed ritual battles which in K'ulta are called ñuwasis, are generally fought between ayllus rather than within them. Marrying within the ayllu, then, is a way of avoiding situations in which one might be forced to go to war with one's affines. At the same time, it becomes considerably more difficult for a husband or children of a woman to claim usufruct rights to her father's, or patriline's, land if the wife and mother are from another ayllu, or even worse, from another cantón, than if she share's the husband's and children's ayllu affiliation. Of course, on the other side of the coin, a daughter who chooses to marry a complete outsider presents very little problem. Apart from these practical inconveniences, I was assured, there is nothing wrong with ayllu exogamous marriages, and many were pointed out to me when I raised the issue.

Still, most marriages in K'ulta, perhaps 80 percent all told, *are* ayllu endogamous, with the least endogamous hamlets being those near ayllu borders. What accounts for this? Simply put, young men and women in K'ulta most often marry a partner with whom they have fallen in love, after a prolonged period of courtship. Courtship takes place most often in festivals and in furtive meetings in the hills, where young men become wandering minstrels singing love songs to pretty shepherdesses, and the latter flash invitations to their suitors with the mirrors hanging on their clothes (an action that has the advantage of frightening away possible ghosts). Endogamy results from propinquity rather than prescription.

16. It should be noted that the custom of tracing lineage through surnames was imposed by Spaniards, who found it difficult to convince Andeans to accept their practice of name inheritance. Before the 1730s, padrones and parish registers show that few Andeans apart from hereditary lords (who were forced to demonstrate their genealogical rights) gave their name to their children.

17. There are some exceptions: a few hamlets have more than one patriline "neighborhood," whose lands are kept distinct from one another; some patrilines, like the Mamanis, occupy several hamlets while remaining a single unit for the defense of land rights.

18. Clearly, muju contrasts with wila in many ways. Muju, which means "seed" as well as "semen," is repeatedly planted over the generations in a single spot, in the hamlet and lands that are passed from father to sons. Wila, on the other hand, is a circulating, generative substance. Rather than being rooted to a single place, it moves throughout the territory along well-worn channels of transmission, linking the mosaic of patrilineal hamlets and, ultimately, unifying them as a single ayllu. Both kinds of generative substance are critical not only to human well-being and reproduction but also to communication between human and nonhuman realms. As we shall see, it is blood and three forms of muju—semen/seed, breath, and congealed seed in the form of visceral fat—that give both humans and herd animals their vitality and that Tatala receives in great quantity in K'ultas' brand of eucharistic sacrifices.

19. Although the etymology of "tullqa" is unclear, the final marriage ritual, performed as a relationship between two patrilines, illustrates that wife takers are also conceived as a kind of wild predator, as a mallku (condor). Arriving en masse at the groom's hamlet, the bride's patrikin are all welcomed as laritas. In turn, they address members of the groom's patriline as *ipalas,* a term for a father's sisters. The groom's patrikin have meanwhile completed a sacrificial sequence and have prepared most of the elements of a banquet they will serve to the arriving pack of "foxes." For their part, the laritas bring a quantity of stones to the feast. Along the path that connects the two patriline hamlets, they select certain flat and rounded stones of a sort that can often be found on riverbottoms. Those chosen are said to be fox's kinsmen from *layra pacha,* a time when (as one story recalls) fox challenged his cousin, stone, to a downhill race and ended up suitably flattened. Even today, K'ultas say, the only way to kill a marauding fox is to throw this sort of stone at him. So the wife-giving laritas bring their wife takers precisely the ammunition needed to drive them away. The stones, however, have another purpose. The wife will henceforth use them for a certain sort of ritual cooking, beginning at the moment they are received. The groom's kin build a bonfire, and the laritas put the stones into the flames. Later they are dropped into a pot (often a wooden one) to cook a special stew called *qala p"iri,* prepared without a cooking fire, a cooking method that might well date to preceramic times. When the stones become hot, laritas and ipalas, couples from the bride's and groom's patriline, leap over the bonfire in a wedding dance, during which they tease each other in song. The laritas sing: "Nax apasjapini-may. Kullaknan chukt'añapar chukt'askapinitaw" (I shall take you away. In my sister's seat you shall be seated). The ipalas then reply: "Atxasmati janipi atxasmati" (Shall you? I think you shall not) (Arnold 1988: 483–484). Seeking to reverse the relationship that has made them into foxes, the laritas hope to take wives from the groom's patriline, and often they do just that.

20. Europeans and North Americans commonly regard alcoholic beverages as a social lubricant, the disinhibiting qualities of which help to ease the awkwardnesses of some social situations—hence the folk theories that give rise to arguments of functional utility.

21. In pondering the meaning of drinking in the Andes, I leave aside the theses on high-altitude hypoglycemia that have for decades plagued the study of Aymaras, and the supposed genetic susceptibility to alcoholism by which some scholars characterize all Native Americans. Such arguments, along with the steam engine functionalism of "safety valves" and "stress release," have often been adduced to account for drinking patterns among rural Andeans. But because consumption of alcoholic beverages in the countryside is quite uncommon outside ritual contexts, ethnographers of highland Andean drinking have begun to move beyond such determinisms to pursue, not the question of what makes Andeans drink, but what meanings they make by drinking. For the most detailed account of contemporary Andean drinking, see Meyerson 1990.

22. Like coca and coca chewing, drink and drinking in the Andes have received a great deal of anthropological (and more recently, historical) attention. The late Thierry Saignes (1987, 1993) brought together a significant part of the surviving Spanish colonial considerations of indian drinking. From Tschopik 1951 and La Barre 1948 to Buechler 1980 and Carter and Mamani 1982, and from Allen 1988, Bastien 1978, and Harris 1978d, to Meyerson 1990, Platt 1978a, 1987b, Randall 1993, Rasnake 1988a, and Urton 1981, to mention but a sample of ethnographic sources, the ch'alla form of Andean ritual drinking has been repeatedly foregrounded, to the point where it has become a leitmotif of Andean cultural practice. In none of these sources, however, are extensive libation sequences actually described. An exception to the rule is to be found in Tomoeda 1985. Also, Arnold 1988, 1992, invokes Yates's *Arts of Memory* to explain amt'añ t"aki as a mnemonic technique. Arnold also invokes the Greek technique of drinking a potion of the goddess Mnemosyne in preparation for a journey to the land of past generations. My analysis of ch'alla practice hinges on information gathered under circumstances that might seem to make a mockery of ethnography's scientific pretensions. Seeking to understand the meaning of drinking while becoming drunk foregrounds the pitfalls of participant observation as a field technique; the more I participated, the more disorganized my observations became. But it is not possible to gather information about ch'allas without in fact drinking them. Without the collusion of don Bartolomé Mamani, the yatiri and libation specialist of Vila Sirka, where I lived during most of my fieldwork, who agreed to make my servings small, my observations on ch'allas would have been reduced to a few spare paragraphs. Don Bartolomé's private reprises of his ch'alla performances, carried out with alcohol but in the presence of notebook and tape recorder, were also crucial. My own limitations as observer required that I use mechanical memory techniques to remember later my own (prompted) libation dedications; under proper performance conditions I could not remember later portions of long K'ulta "memory paths" long enough to jot them down in my notebook.

Fortunately, libation specialists like don Bartolomé have practiced techniques that enable *them* to name long sequences of beings, uttering them into the present from the past in which they dwell. As we shall see, historical conscious-ness can indeed reside in practices leading to unconsciousness.

23. I do not mean to gloss over the serious consequences of drinking to excess even in ritual contexts. This was brought home to me when, in 1980, I more than once helped to bury young men who had died, apparently, of alcohol poisoning during fiestas.

24. Not all K'ultas are allowed to carry out these offerings. Only adults (which is to say, married individuals or those long beyond the usual age of marriage) should chew coca or drink alcohol or chicha, and children (and marriage-age single youths) remain on the periphery of the ritual performances in which these substances are used for offerings.

25. I simplify here. Each of these libations is also paired with a dedication to the yanani, a "helper" or "spiritual double," of the altar, root, uywiri, and mallku.

26. *Uywa* = "domesticated grazing animal"; *uywaña* = "to care for" or "raise." Adding the agentifier *-iri,* "one who," we have "one who raises," or "caretaker of herds."

27. Following local convention, I always sat at the men's altar. My under-standing of women's ch'allas is therefore necessarily limited. Doña Basilia and don Bartolomé always tried to remain closely synchronized, so that male and female deities and ancestor pairs received their drinks apace. One might perhaps produce an adequate, if not full, list of women's uywa ispira ch'allas by adding the term "t'alla" to each of the place deities in the men's sequence. And when they arrive at ch'allas for the deceased, women pour for dead women and reaffirm not only the matrilateral links in the men's patriliny, but also the female sponsor's lines of matrilineal transmission, those through which most of the herd animals were transmitted. This is where men's and women's libation paths truly diverge. For no matter how far back they go in their genealogizing, men's patrilineal ancestors travel very little distance in space: they are firmly rooted to the male-transmitted patriline territory and to a narrow set of uywiris and a single mountain mallku. The matrilineal links elaborated in women's memory paths, however, reach far and wide across the territory, jumping each generation back to the territory and gods of a different patriline, and making reference to a wide range of mallkus. Ties through men are exclusive; those through women, inclusive, reaching out to embrace the ayllu as a whole.

A full analysis of the significance of gender in memory paths would have to account both for the respect and honor accorded to those women who complete a fiesta path with their husbands and for some striking inequalities. For in spite of the importance of complementarity in this symbolic schema, women's sponsorship is nonetheless culturally subordinated to that of men. In K'ulta a fiesta career, like territory, is the collective and inalienable property of the patriline. If a man is widowed, he can carry on with his fiesta career with or without a new wife, but unless a widowed woman remarries one of her deceased husband's patriline brothers and the latter inherits his brother's career, she forfeits the fiesta career.

The processes associated with women—cooking, the bearing of children, and caretaking of the herds—may themselves require the intervention of alax-pacha forces to civilize and cultivate manxa-pacha ones. But in men's purview, their festival internalization of Our Father Shepherd's (Tata Awatir Awksa's) transformative and encompassing powers is at least in part done so that they can "domesticate and cultivate" women, and therefore reproduce the patriline and their own privileged roles in it. In the cultural synthesis evinced in K'ulta's cultural poetics, gender domination becomes inseparable from that of colonial domination.

28. Newborn animals and first fruits are themselves referred to as "flowers" in libations.

29. It is true that becoming intoxicated, which not everyone wishes to do, is a necessary part of rites and is itself an offering of the body (Saignes 1987). Intoxication is but a visible sign of repletion, of having become filled with so many offerings. On the one hand, copious drinking of libations calls forth an attribute of the god (that of boundless containability, all-encompassing completeness), while on the other, one sacrifices one's body in repletion to index the generosity and earnestness of the sponsor, which is otherwise suspect. The demonstration of both repletion and surplus (as there should always be more than enough food and drink to satiate all participants in a rite) also points to the desired return for the sacrifice, which is the gods' help in providing just such plenty. As the sponsor thus takes the place of the gods in provisioning this demonstration of bounty, so also is it incumbent on ritual sponsors (as well as their assistants, and in particular the libation specialist wasu wariris, "cup bearers") to imbibe more and longer but nonetheless remain sober. It is bad form should a sponsor become incapacitated before the conclusion of a rite (and worse, in consequence, should his wasu wariris "forget" their paths). Of Andeans, the sixteenth-century Anonymous Jesuit chronicler remarked: "They hold in great esteem those who can drink much and still keep their heads," a maxim that remains true today (1968: 176). The mallkus of the colonial period were capable of great acts of consumption. As Capoche put it while describing mita captains like Juan Colque Guarache: " . . . they are the first to get drunk . . . and are so fat and heavy they cannot get around" (1959: 140–141, quoted in Saignes 1987).

30. Llamas must always be sacrificed in pairs, and given uywa ispira, qarwa k"ari, and ch'iwu ch'allas, apart from certain exceptions which preclude these ch'allas, such as: wilara (when the animal and its blood are offered to dedicate an architectural form or symbol of office, and head, feet, pelt, and bones are buried in the salient mallku mountain); funerary sacrifices, in which the blood must be consumed by the mourners, and the head, feet, pelt, and bones burned for the use of the dead person in his or her journey; and healing sacrifices, in which the animal explicitly represents the patient and is given his disease before being given to the gods in lieu of the person. Sacrifice of but a single animal is acceptable in all these exceptions, and in all but funerary rites, sheep (or lesser animals, when the occasion is slight) may be substituted. For more detail see Abercrombie 1986; see also Van Kessel 1992.

31. "Mallku" and "kumprira" are alternate terms for a single entity, the god of high mountain peaks. The condor is one form which the kumprira may take when "outside" his mountain chamber.

32. The number of uywiris in a hamlet corresponds rather well to the genealogical depth of focal ancestors linking households. Nonetheless an elder son, forming a new household "neolocally" within the hamlet, may create his own uywiri. Thus a profusion of uywiris in a hamlet may index social schisms as well as genealogy. On uywiris and other genius loci in the Aymara-speaking Chilean Andes, see Martínez 1976, 1983.

33. Only adult, which is to say married, women with children and separate houses participate in the drinking and dedication. All present share in the status of having come from other patrilines, linked to other uywiris and mallkus. The female sponsor, however, also serves puro from a bottle to the major mountains of the ayllu and beyond, shared by all women present.

34. As we shall see "t'alla" is qualified by deity-type terms or names to give the "wife" of the deity. In the center of town, the male tower is coupled with the plaza before it (plasa t'alla) as a "married" couple. Here the term refers to the flat area enclosed by corral walls, which is, of course, covered in a deep layer of dry dung, used for cooking fires and fertilizer.

35. Segments C–G within group II also dedicate hierarchies of corral deities (misa, uywiri, and kumprira), but this time, of corrals from which the sponsors' household herd derives. The progression is the same as that used in wedding ch'allas, beginning with the "wife's corral altar" of origin, that is, her father's corral altar, and progressing through the wife's mother's, father's mother's, and wife's mother's mother's corral deities, all from the perspective of the male sponsor. If the sponsor has not inherited his father's corrals, these will also be included, between B and C, as jach'a jira t'alla, "great corral." In wedding ch'allas, however, the deities of persons and patrilines are given, not those of corrals.

36. Items 30 and 31 progress downward in age status, waynapat being a not-yet fully grown male (similar to the human youth term "wayna" or "maxta"), while "paq"ara," "flower," refers to the newborn animal. One might argue that the more elaborated recognition of camelids reflects their greater similarity to human beings, or rather creates a greater similarity.

37. K'ultas told me that a few patrilines in K'ulta have their own samiris of humans, which these lines ch'alla after their own kumprira in sequences corresponding to segment A, but I was unable to confirm it.

38. Some say that muntu or llantir muntu is "near Yura" to the south and west, while others believe it to be very far to the west, that is, not on this earth at all, but in the land of the dead. What matters is that it exists as a space (inside the mountain) within which great herds are kept. Though it is analogous to the muntu (or *mayruwiri qullu*, "ancestors' mountain") which is given libations in funerary sacrifices, consultants were very ambivalent about making the analogy explicit, because the dead and the uywiris must not be "mixed." A paramount extra-K'ulta mallku known as Tata Kusqu ("Father Cusco") is also sometimes

said to be located somewhere to the southwest, but others associate it with the former Inca capital, and yet others think it to lie in the "other world," under and behind, where the sun goes at night.

39. Both llamas and alpacas are subsumed within a single category by metonymic inclusion of the entire herd of camelids in the term "llantiru." "Llantiru" in its more restricted use signifies only the leader(s) of the herd, those which are especially honored (and given bells to wear) because they actually take the lead (and unify the herd) when going to pasture or on caravan trips. While the uywa ispira ch'alla sequence presented here is the most commonly heard form, some performances nonetheless differentiate llamas and alpacas (*"ulu"* in K'ulta Aymara), in a separate segment (after segment H in group III), as *ulu llantiru, ulu llantir waynillu,* and *ulu llantir paqʷara.* Nonetheless, they remain assimilated to the llantiru type, which prototypically corresponds to llamas.

40. Mamanis were unsure whether the ram's uywiri was the same as that of its corral. Unlike the human deities, in which knowing their names is crucially important, the specifics of the animals are not always attributed (they are, after all, the *animals'* gods).

41. The exclusion of bulls from corrals (which they could in any case knock down in short order) is undoubtedly also related to the fact that, unlike other esteemed herd animals, they neither produce wool nor carry loads. Instead, pairs of bulls symbolize a bountiful agricultural labor force and production, and as a result cattle are libated even when a household has none. I estimate that there are on the average fewer than one pair of bulls per hamlet in all of K'ulta.

42. I am unsure as to the etymology of "mayruwiri." On the one hand it may be a frozen composite of *"mayura"* (from Sp. "great/elder") + *"uywiri."* See also an entry in Bertonio's dictionary: "Mayruru, vel Marmuru: Kidney, and also the best of the wool; and of the earth" (1984: book 2, 220).

43. In a fiesta performance, as with other rites in which musicians and dancers participate, another wasu wariri is contracted in order to serve special libation sequences (in alcohol) related to music and dance, as well as to fighting, since dance groups are also battle "platoons" at times.

44. Initially I thought the term was used to signify certain metal (copper?) balls, also called *surti* or *surti wala* ("luck ball/bullet"). These are thought to be the product of lightning strikes, and are used by shamans (who are "called" to their profession by being hit by lightning) to "call" their awukatu familiars.

45. Other q'uwas are burned during the fiesta by the visiting authorities, as part of their duties.

46. Since untu is held to be a form of solidified, stored male essence (a form of muju, or "semen/seed"), and blood the female contribution to conception, we see that the gods of alax-pacha are favored, in q'uwa and paxcha, with the generative aspects of the llama's body.

47. Although consultants did not freely make this connection, one might also see this holocaust at the emergence of the sun as a reference to the initial sunrise, which burned the autochthonous beings in a sacrifice, making herding and cultural life possible.

48. In the sixteenth to eighteenth centuries, Aymara lords made use of their herds to become great market intermediaries, and one of the products thus transported was wine in quantity (see Murra 1977).

49. While both dilute cane alcohol and chicha are served to participants by memory path specialists, the sponsors themselves serve pure cane alcohol from small bottles. In the uywa ispira sequence of Fig. 7.4, asterisked items receive puro from the sponsors' bottles (while also receiving cups of dilute awarinti). Puro, that is, goes to the mallku/kumprira, the samiri, and to muntu mountain, which is to say, to the most powerful and predominant manxa-pacha powers. What these deities have in common is genealogical depth as links between disparate households and herds, as well as height, dominating the multiple and partial uywiris and misas under their purview. It is appropriate that the sponsor should present pure alcohol directly to the pourer, since ritual sponsors in all the events calling for libations of mallkus are themselves traveling a path, leading them towards kinds of totalizing activities like those of the highest mallkus. Indeed, rituals like this one aim precisely to transfer successively to sponsors the attributes of leadership that are possessed by the gods.

50. There are also preparatory ch'alla sequences performed by the sponsor and his wasu wariris and the service personnel (*tispinsirus*) in charge of alcohol and chicha supplies. Upon opening a new can of alcohol, the first ch'allas are for the "factory" which produced it. For chicha, the first ch'allas address the storage vessels as a "lake," that the chicha should be as much.

51. The concept of tinku is treated well and at length in Platt 1978a, 1987b.

CHAPTER 8. LIVING ON TATALA'S PATH: USES OF THE PAST IN
SACRIFICE AND ANTISACRIFICE, SAINTS' FESTIVALS, AND SORCERIES

1. Some of these couples, say a hundred of the total, will have completed their careers and be exempt from further duties, while others (perhaps fifty to a hundred) have not yet set up independent households or are still engaged in hamlet-level festivals so have yet to begin a "great fiesta career." So our of 450 "eligible" couples, at least a third are in the midst of a career at any one time. Not all will complete, or even begin, a jach'a p"ista civil-ritual career, but there are no patrilines or hamlets without representation in the career system.

2. Such sponsorship rotation systems were at an apogee in scale in the late eighteenth century, when diarchy and federation ties among reducción towns were played out in macrocycles which included several towns. Visits of K'ulta jilaqatas to Condo for the feast of San Pedro are most likely a remnant of such a macrosystem centered in the former diarchy capital, when sponsorship roles in Condo may have been part of the investiture of annex council officers. Such complex regional systems are best recorded for the province of Chayanta in 1793–97 (see chapter 7, and for the 1770s, see Platt 1987c). Fiesta systems which unite highland polities with valley outlier kinsmen are still in existence, such as that by which authorities of Ayllu Qullana are chosen today.

3. Among fiesta sponsors, pillu carriers are as follows: During the year before receiving the sponsorship, the fuera of Guadalupe carries pillus to the present year's alférez of Guadalupe. In the following year's carnaval, the same fuera (now in his year of sponsorship) receives pillus from the -1 year alférez of Guadalupe (a different man from the same ayllu). This exchange, of course, is between role types of a single saint, but corresponding to the Guadalupe jilaqata path and the Exaltación alcalde path.

The -1 novena of Santa Bárbara takes pillus to the year's alférez of Santa Bárbara, and the following year the novena (now a sponsor) receives pillus from the -1 alférez of Santa Bárbara. This exchange is between sponsorship roles of Santa Bárbara, but between men in the two jiiaqata paths.

The -1 fuera of San Andres takes pillus to the same year's alférez of Guadalupe and receives pillus, the following year, from the -1 alférez of Guadalupe. Here the exchange is between saints and between the two alcalde paths.

Finally, two of the lowest-ranking sponsors take pillus *during* their year of sponsorship, without receiving return visits: the mayordomo of Guadalupe (in the Exaltación alcalde path) carries crowns to the same year's alférez of Guadalupe, while the mayordomo of Santa Bárbara (in the Santa Bárbara jilaqata path) carries pillus to the same year's alférez of Santa Bárbara, in the same Santa Bárbara jilaqata path.

4. Along with the poetic device of recursion and imbedding of microcosmic icons in macrocosmic form, other poetic forms are also employed. Metaphoric, metonymic, synechdochic, indexical, iconic, and symbolic signs amplify, modify, and refer such parallelisms to a wide range of extraritual referential orders, reorganizing them in a totalizing metacommunicative form. In combination, the symbols and metaphor-making structures of fiesta ritual establish equivalences and disjunctions with the power to affirm, create, and transform the social identities of participants as their roles in the progression of sacrifices are transformed.

5. Monday (*mayruwiri uru*) is considered the dead's day and is reserved for funerary rites. Tuesday, Thursday, and Friday are called *awksa uru,* "our father day," but only Thursday is considered truly propitious for male saints' feasts and sacrifices. Tuesday and Friday are the *saxra uru* ("evil" or "secret" days), thought most appropriate for sorcery and for rites to the mining gods of money. Friday is also called *qinsa milakru,* "three miracle day," when Tata Mustramu (the sun), Tata Exaltación (Exaltation of the Cross, also called Tata Killaka), and Santiago (Saint James) are unified in a kind of trinity. Wednesday, Saturday, and Sunday are *tayksa uru* (our mother day), of which only Sunday (the day of Mama Rusario) is considered relatively unpropitious. Consideration of the qualities of these days is always brought to bear on scheduling for collective work, travel, and ritual, and each deity form is given coca dedications during its day.

6. On urban and mining frontiers, ethnographers' efforts to get past mine entrances and showy fiesta pageantry to the hidden sacrifices to tio-supays of the

mines and associated earth shrines (as, for example, in Nash 1979, taken up [along with Bastien 1978] by Taussig 1980) seem to blind them to the constitutive relationship between such clandestine practices and the public cult of miraculous saints carried out in the light of day, such as the devotions to patron saints of mines organized by mine workers' unions, and those to city patron saints by confraternities and folkloric brotherhoods. But this is the subject of another book.

7. In a way, both the ethnographic goal of gaining deep insight into hidden practices and the aid in that project afforded by inquisitive and ambitious (and semi-alienated) frontier spirits like Manuel Mamani and Pablo Choquecallata mirror the productive link between the inquisitorial project of extirpators of idolatry such as Cristóbal de Albornóz, who investigated the idolatrous secrets of the taqui oncoy movement with the aid of Guaman Poma. So modern ethnography reduplicates some of the very strategies by which clandestine realms were investigated (at the moment they first began to appear) and became more deeply entrenched.

8. A cousin of Virgilio, Tomás had married a Jallqa woman in his father's adoptive home, where he had grown up. Arriving in distinctive Jallqa clothing styles, Tomás and his wife, Petrona, changed into K'ulta costume before beginning their ritual duties. Both Virgilio and Tomás regularly returned to their grandfather's birthplace of Vila Sirka, driving their llama herds before them, in order to perform the duties that made them K'ultas and guaranteed their rights to Mamani lands.

9. They are not likely, however, to actually *be* the lead llamas of the herd, which are too valuable for sacrifice. Although K'ultas would not consider substituting vegetables or noncamelids for the required llamas (unlike the Nuer, who substitute cucumbers for oxen), they do substitute sterile females or old and weak males for sacrifices that take place in the hamlet. They are, however, concerned about appearances during public sacrifices in the town, and the animals killed there are actually males and generally strong and large ones at that. Whether male or sterile female, however, the animals killed are called llantirus.

10. Used for fertilizer after several years of composting, llama dung is in the form of small dry pellets, which are used as fuel in cooking fires. On the symbolism of jira t'alla, see Arnold 1988.

11. Manuel and Bartolomé Mamani told me that the coca bag used for this purpose is kept aside for use in the sacred bundles, which all herders bury in the corral during herd fertility rites of ear-marking carried out during carnavales.

12. I point out again that a pair of llamas must be killed together, rather than only one. But in a major fiesta, much more meat than this is needed for the banquets to follow, and two to five pairs of llamas will actually be killed.

13. All consultants agreed that the entire rite of qarwa k"ari must be scheduled so that the paxcha takes place before midday, while Tatala's strength is rising (and he is on the ascending part of his path), rather than in the

afternoon, when Tatala begins to sink into the feminine manxa-pacha (and is outshined by Paxsi Mamala, "Moon-Mother").

A different procedure is employed in the sacrifices performed as part of mortuary rites. For these events, in which the blood must be collected in its entirety (to be cooked in corn meal and eaten by mourners), the animals are killed while standing, by inserting a knife between the neck vertebrae. Blood is then collected in the animal's thoracic cavity by severing the aorta while the heart still beats. In the case of mortuary sacrifices, the killing should be done *after* noon, on a hamlet's western path.

14. By "ideal type," I mean that a ritual name for each foodstuff is used, in some cases a metonymic reference to the food item, in others the name of the saint thought to have special power over the item. The deity-guardians of foodstuffs include the valley-area mountains called *awiyaru* (from the sixteenth-century Sp. noun *aviadora*, "provisioner").

The cup used to serve ch'iwu ch'allas is different from that used in other alcohol ch'allas: it is larger and, if available, is a miniature copy of the wooden bowls used for chicha ch'allas. These have a pair of llantirus or *turus* ("bulls") carved in the bottom.

15. I use the word "heart" here advisedly, notwithstanding the fact that the organs which are cooked and eaten in the corral are the liver and lungs. When confronted with an actual carcass and the organs in question, the term "chullma" was unhesitatingly applied to the liver and lungs, which are considered the seat of the *animo* (Spanish term for "soul") and *samana* (an equivalent Aymara term which also means "breath"). My K'ulta consultants also insisted that "chullma" translates into Spanish as "*corazón*" (= the English "heart"). I believe that the vehemence behind this translation derives from the cultural importance of the roughly equivalent "figurative" meanings of "chullma" and "corazón," which are used interchangeably in poetic discourse, love songs, and prayer to approximately the same effect as "heart" is used in English popular music. When rechecking the meaning of "chullma" with consultants on two separate occasions (and with an array of internal organs present to index), I was unable to convince them that the blood-pumping organ was a corazón. It took a Spanish-Aymara dictionary, referring to the action of the heart and translating it in the physiological sense as "*lluqu*" (the Aymara term for the pumping organ) to convince (rather, astonish) them that only my Aymara, not my Spanish, was faulty.

16. "Jañachu" may literally be parsed as "sterile" (*jani* = "not," *achuña* = "to produce," as in young, foodstuffs, etc.). It is also a term which is applied to stud male alpacas, which are thought to be weak and less likely to breed successfully than male llamas. Jañachus thus seem to differ categorically from the strong llantiru males, which should be sacrificed. Indeed, the relationship of jañachus to llantirus is much like that of the sponsor (who is also a strong, fertile, lead male) to his tullqas (who are dependent, effeminized subordinates) and of the eldest brother to the youngest brother.

17. Usually the llama herd precedes the sponsor's entourage by up to several hours. However, even with frequent stops for ch'allas along the way, the sponsors and their followers often overtake the slow-moving llamas before they arrive at their destination.

18. Names of these rest stops are numerous, but several are recurrent: The most common is samarayaña (lit., "place to breathe"), but *q'asa* (a toponym referring to a saddlelike depression between hills, often passes with views of other sites or of the town) is also frequent.

19. Between Todos Santos (November 1) and the end of carnaval (March-April), the band plays carved, wooden, recorder-type instruments called *t'arkas*. During the t'arka season (a period when, as Olivia Harris [1982] asserts, the dead have returned from manxa-pacha to reside in the highlands and aid in crop growth), the ukelelelike charangos (on which love songs are played) are put aside. A rite at the end of carnaval enacts the throwing down of t'arkas (and the jurk"as, or maypoles) and the renewed playing of charangos.

20. The jackets are made of homespun, in the style worn by all K'ulta men. What differs is the color and design (width of stripes, size of checks, etc.). Most young men (those known as maxtas, in particular) own a set of such jackets— one in a style particular to the hamlet, the patriline, the wife's and mother's patrilines, and one in the most "generic" of styles (such as the common brown-white-black jackets with small pinstripes or checks) particular to the ayllu.

The group has its own structure, composed, ideally, of maxtas (mature but unmarried males) who are the sponsors' patriline mates, plus (when free of other duties) his tullqas and *sutiyuqas*, "godsons." The *jula-julas* are led by a "captain" (or "mayura"), who "herds" the dancers with whip and sling, and they are accompanied by a pair (or pairs) of unmarried "daughters," called *mit'anis*, who may be real or classificatory daughters of the sponsors.

The organization of the dance group appears related not only to the generalized military form common to many aspects of ritual sponsorship (and deriving in part from the nature of a sixteenth-century cofradía organization) but also to the organization of local contingents of laborers on their way to the Potosí mita. Until abolished in the nineteenth century, local men were "taken" to the mita by appointed mita captains, and were accompanied by wives or women chosen to serve them while in the town. A now-defunct rite performed during Todos Santos' festivities until 1977 (and described to me by various individuals) made the connection between fiesta dance groups and the mita more explicit: In that rite, those who served as jula-julas in the year's fiestas participated in a kind of race (from the cemetery to a pass on the path to Potosí), in which, paired with unmarried girls, they carried large stones to a large apacheta on the pass. When they returned, they were "married" in a mock ceremony by a mock priest, with mock European officials looking on. Partly as a result of a series of especially violent intermoiety battles (between the assembled "dance" groups of maxtas), and partly because, as one collaborator put it, "no one knew why it was done any longer," the rite was abolished in 1978, during a general reshaping of the Todos Santos ritual which now keeps the moieties and ayllus apart by scheduling them to arrive on separate days. Three large stone monuments remain, however, on the trail to Potosí, as a reminder of the abolished rites.

21. The town sacrifice, qarwa k"ari, is sometimes referred to as wallpa k"ari (rooster cutting) because of the former practice of killing chickens on arrival for use as gifts to the priest. Since 1932, however, there has been neither resident priest nor need for gift chickens in K'ulta.

22. They also ch'alla an altar just above the plaza which is a large rectangular boulder in the hillside, called Inka Misa. The altar is not so much associated with the Incas as given the ritual name for building (and fighting) stones: it is thought to be the saints' principal altar outside the church, connected to the saints' *silu* altars in the subordinate hamlets, just as the hamlet Pukara chapels and their *niñu* "towers" are connected through their roots to the church and tower of the town.

23. Indeed, during the performance of the first fiesta that I witnessed in K'ulta, I asked another (K'ulta) observer what was happening at a stone altar (Inka Misa) on a nearby hill where a crowd had gathered. He replied that the "indios" were drinking to the "supays." The latter term translates as "devils" in the usage of city dwellers, who apply the term to all the mountain deities; locally, the term is applied to the dangerous and destructive forms sometimes taken by neglected mallkus. These may take the form of a vecino or city person in order to capture the unwary indian's spirit, or they may try to strike nasty bargains with the avaricious. In this, the local supay closely resembles the frequently reported *wamani* of the Quechua Ayacucho area (see, for example, Earls 1971; Isbell 1985). It must be added that the individual who, in speaking to a stranger-outsider (myself), distanced himself from devil-worshiping indios (a term which is always disrespectful in use) later proved to be fully involved in a fiesta career of his own.

24. In 1979 the subprefect used his pistol during p"isturu of Santa Bárbara, trying to stop a fight that was rapidly escalating into a tinku in the town plaza. After firing all six shots into the air to no avail, he got into his jeep and fled the town.

25. When the evening of the day before p"isturu approaches, the same-ayllu sponsors (with their own and their borrowed dancer-musician groups giving musical accompaniment) carry out ch'allas for their respective images and then, at their patio altars, prepare the money to be paid to the priest for the mass. After a set of ch'allas in the patio, all the sponsors together visit the kitchen (now collapsed) of the parish house, repeating (if the priest is not present) the ch'allas of this rite, called *limusna waku,* "collection of the alms."

Limusna waku takes place regardless of whether a priest is present, and the money is held for a future mass, sometimes in the nearby town of Challapata. The ch'allas for limusna waku, interestingly, for the first time in the fiesta include libations to the gods of money: *Wila Qullu* ("Blood Mountain," the famous mountain of Potosí and source of silver), *wanku* ("the bank"), and the *tiu* (Sp. *tio*, "uncle"), who is a malevolent form of mallku presiding over the extraction of minerals from the mines. Apart from their performance in the town, especially in connection with the priest's exactions, such ch'allas are thought to be dangerous and best restricted to rites for the increase of money, normally performed during the saxra days of sorcery (Tuesdays and Fridays).

Individuals who are successful in marketing transactions involving money (which most exchanges for foodstuffs do not involve) are thought to practice secret rites for these infernal deities in their homes on a periodic basis, rites which always involve inversions: Money that is capital is thought to be kept in the mouth of an ancestral skull stolen from the cemetery, which is wrapped and stored with unbaptized (and dried) human fetuses, and their rituals bringing life to this money are supposed to be held always on the saxra days of sorcery.

26. Because the priest—during the research period, part of the regular clergy of the *obispado* of Oruro—normally gives but one mass a year in K'ulta, on the day of Santa Bárbara, and is not present for the fiesta of Guadalupe, it would be inappropriate to enter into great detail about his activities here. I offer but a few comments: The priest lives in his central parish, in the brewery town of Huari (part of the former Awllaka-Urukilla kingdom), from whence he makes yearly trips to Culta, Lagunillas, Cahuayo, San Pedro de Condo, and Cacachaca. On his arrival in the town of Culta (by jeep) the day before p″isturu of Santa Bárbara, the priest sets up a table in the plaza, where he receives gifts (of foodstuffs, including chickens) and collects payments for his ritual services. These amount to a considerable sum, since most K'ultas wait until this day to carry out church weddings and baptisms, ask for masses for the dead, and pay for masses to the saints of the great and little fiesta careers of the area. In 1979, the priest collected over a hundred payments, averaging a few dollars each. All the masses paid for, of course, are taken care of in a single actual mass, at the end of which the weddings and then baptisms are performed en masse. Apart from these trips to the ritual-center town, he also may give masses at settlements on the road, such as the crossroads (and district school center) town of Cruce Culta (located some thirteen kilometers from Santa Bárbara), and the settlement (with church) of Thola Palca, the location of a former tambo in Alax-Kawalli territory. The priest is both feared and respected, and the services he performs are considered essential. On another day when the priest's presence is thought crucial (but when he is never present), during Easter, a set of stored vestments are used to make a local man into an ersatz priest for the recitation of prayers and the "walk of the cross" performed at that time. The importance of the priest's function seems to make the severity of the priest's admonitions against local custom (delivered in sermons when he does come) more acceptable for K'ultas. The fact that the sermons are delivered in formal Castilian Spanish, a language (and register) most K'ultas do not understand, must also diminish their effect.

We must, of course, find it ironic that the indigenous deities (or transformations of them, those associated with money and mining) find their most satanic forms only in closest proximity to the town, church, and priest. Yet as we shall see, the priest, and indeed all outsiders and the mining centers and cities where they come from, are thought to be particularly apt at an insidious form of this "devil worship" in which the sacrificial victims are not llamas but rural people.

27. Ch'allas presented by authorities, whether at sponsors' altars or at Kawiltu misa, have a different character from those of fiesta sponsors, because only authorities are entitled to give ch'allas to the great extra-K'ulta mallkus, to which the mallku of K'ulta is subordinated. K'ulta's premier mallku is named Pirwan Tata ("Father Storehouse," because of a rock formation on its peak) and Churi Asanaqi ("last-born son" of Asanaqi, the predominant mallku of Condo, former capital of the Asanaqi kingdom). The ch'alla path of *kawiltu kumpraña,* of course, also includes the gods of money, which the authorities begin to collect from their "subjects" when they have finished their own ch'alla sequence.

28. Most of those "named" to sponsorships, of course, are already in the midst of their careers, and the date of their sponsorships has long been predetermined.

29. One meaning of "qurpa" is "boundary stone," which I take to be a homonym.

30. In towns with a resident priest (which K'ulta lost in the 1930s), the feast of Corpus (which is in honor of the host) includes a procession of the host, kept in a solar-form monstrance which K'ultas regard as the image of Tata Mustramu (who is Christ as well as the sun).

31. Following an order of hierarchy, the servers hand out small bowls of *lawa* (a wheat or maize porridge), boiled maize, soup, quinua, potatoes, and meat (and sometimes exotic dishes such as rice or lentils) to the whole congregation, along with ground chili peppers as a condiment. As in the serving of ch'allas, men serve men from supplies at the men's altar, and women serve women from bowls at the women's altar. Especially honored individuals (the authorities, those who have finished their careers, and elders in general) sit in rank order around the altar, and are served first and given select pieces of meat (such as long rib bones). Less senior, married adults sit nearby, still within the confines of the patio, and are served next. Finally, the sponsors' aides serve the younger people, unmarried individuals and children, who often sit or stand outside the patio and have been excluded from participation in ch'allas. The cooks, food servers, jula-julas, and other contracted ayni are fed in a later meal.

32. As I have explained, these are the same terms by which authorities and ayllu members address one another during tax payment (kawiltu) and during the *kumun wilara* (the "blood for the community"), a sacrifice for the benefit of the ayllu which the jilaqata performs when he takes office.

33. First, the sponsors' tullqas again don the pelts of the sacrificed llamas. Shortly thereafter, they are chased by their mock shepherd into the patios of the other sponsors in the town for visits. Similarly, the jañachus of other sponsors visit the fuera's patio. One cannot placate these jañachus, however, with individual servings of chicha and coca. Instead, an altar is set up on the ground

(between the sites of the men's and women's patio altars), and a large bowl of chicha and quantity of coca are placed there, as if they were supplies for a libation series. The jañachus drink and eat on all fours, and then are driven out of the patio. When the fuera's own jañachus return from their cavortings, they are again mock sacrificed by their "herder" (who, carrying a whip as well as a sling, resembles a cross between authority and herder). Only after this interruption can the helpers' banquet be served and the ch'iwu ch'alla sequence be finished.

34. It must be added that the line between tinku (a controlled form of fighting) and ch'axwa (a more unrestricted sort that may also occur outside calendric feasts and for the control of territory) is not always clearly drawn. As Platt has pointed out for the Macha case, long-standing feuds (usually over land) may be prosecuted in fiesta tinkus in which one group plans in advance to exceed the bounds of tinku and engage in ch'axwa. Whether in tinku or ch'axwa, vengeance for previous losses plays a crucial role in the motivation of fights. As we have seen, the term for vengeance "ayni" is the same as is used to describe the exchange of labor prestations. In addition, it is used to refer to the exchange of sponsorship which takes place during the fiesta, to coparticipants in the gifting relationship therein, and to those who sponsors tap for service roles in the fiesta.

35. Indeed, the other sponsors may leave town before the fueras perform their final rites.

36. That is, the isi turka misa was, on two occasions I witnessed, placed in approximately the same spot that the jañachu misa was placed during the previous day's rites. It may be that the exact location is unimportant, so long as it is not on either men's or women's ch'alla misas. The seating arrangements which I observed, however, seemed to point to the significance of gender attributes of patio space in the placement of individuals around the isi turka misa. The first time that I saw isi turka, the rite was carried out in the church itself, and with the opposite moiety's mayordomo standing in for a no-show fuera couple. Afterwards, the image was left in the church in the care of the mayordomo until it was reclaimed (the next day) by the machaqa fuera.

37. As is also the case within the church (but not within the hamlet "chapels," or pukaras, which also contain saint images), the ch'allas of isi turka are done neither with chicha nor with alcohol. Rather, the liquid poured and drunk, called chuwa (a term otherwise referring to the clearest, top-skimmed part of a newly brewed vessel of chicha), is a sort of sugary tea.

38. Each saint, of course, has its own special characteristics. All have some attributes of herders, and carry small slings and the like. Male images (such as San Andres) may possess a number of miniature war helmets, coca pouches, and so on. The main saint images, located permanently in the church, tend to have fewer articles of indigenous clothing but possess other things which the miniature images lack. The main image of Guadalupe, for example, owns a herd of "toy" (under six inches tall) llamas and alpacas. All main images also possess small metallic balls (from pea to cannonball size), which are the concrete token

of saints' gifts of power to shamans. When a man chooses to reject the calling, the ball, called surti wala (used by yatiris to call his familiar spirit/saint when needed as an intermediary between himself and the gods) is returned to the saint from whence it came, during a rite called lurya misa (the "glory mass" or "lightning altar").

39. If an individual is not accompanied by an opposite-gender companion, two men may kneel together with the higher ranking (that is, usually the elder) kneeling on the right side.

40. The number of articles counted should be greater than those counted the previous year, because fueras are expected to give gifts to the image (during the twice-monthly clothes-changing which is part of their yearlong sponsorship). With each item enumerated, the machaqas' wasu wariris serve a round of chuwa (sugared tea), which has been provided by the outgoing fuera couple.

41. Machaqas begin in the first qarwa k"ari rite of their sponsorship (the uywa ispira dedications having been performed before their trip to town).

42. The 1982 fuera of Guadalupe became jilaqata in January 1985, and finished his jilaqataship on January 20, 1986, following the established timing of career sequences. As jilaqata, his first duty was a visit to each household within the ayllu, "begging" them with gifts of coca and alcohol to come to the kawiltu (also his installation) on January 20 in order to pay their tasa. In between the rogation of payers and the payment itself, he also had to perform a kumun wilara sacrifice for his vara and his new ayllu-wide herd, followed by a full circumambulation of his ayllu's mojones.

43. The authority's duality not only resonates with the internalization of imposed structures (and reproduction of hegemony), but also indicates the degree to which such domination is thereby resisted: cooptation (and the sacrificial knife) cuts both ways. Thus it is illuminating to contrast the perceived role of the ritually established local authority with evaluations of their direct counterparts, the state- and church-sanctioned, non-K'ulta figures to whom the K'ulta leaders must pay obeisance. For these outsider authorities are also understood in terms of sacrifice, but a nefarious and uncontrollable sort of sacrifice akin to sorcery: they slyly steal (through a kind of invisible surgery) the body fat and blood of indigenous people, and transform these substances not only into increased vitality (at the expense of the victim) but also into specie, through their own network of ties to the more insidious (aspects of) mountain gods.

The notion that the llamas of sacrifice are substitutes for human victims (which is explicitly stated in healing rites) implies that humans are appropriate sacrificial victims, and if the Spanish-associated sky gods are herders of men, then one might assume that men are their proper offerings as well as offerers. Human sacrifice was indeed part of the Inca imperial rites known as capac hucha, and the possibility of the sacrificial use of humans remains ever present. As it was the foreign, dominating Incas who required such sacrifices of their subject polities, so it is representatives of the foreign, dominating state who are thought to carry out such sacrifices in the present day. Nowadays, however, one does not volunteer victims, but the sacrificers nevertheless obtain them through magical means.

44. At first blush, the relationship of the town, as the locus of state and alax-pacha intervention and of social domination, to the hamlets, in which manxa-pacha gods are "surreptitiously" honored, seems clearly to be one of formal vertical hierarchy, so that town is to hamlet, as above is to below, as outside is to inside, as whole is to part, and as center is to periphery. But by quarantining the sky gods and state apparatus within the town, surrounded by the space of hamlets, and incorporating the sky gods' hierarchizing power within the elder brothers and father-herders of the patrilines and ayllus, the poetic devices of the fiesta performance reverse the direction of encompassment and domination. This, it might be argued, is a fundamental kind of resistance, a sort that can be practiced by any people who seek to define themselves as an independent collectivity while being dominated by an unyielding colonial or postcolonial power.

45. See the excellent overview of the k"arisiri and ñaqaq literature in Wachtel 1994. My first encounter with the literature was the first-person account of Liffman (1977), the publication of which was at that time heroic. I am also indebted to Stuart Alexander Rockefeller (1995), who shared with me his perceptive analysis.

CHAPTER 9. CONCLUSION: ETHNOGRAPHY AND HISTORY OF SOCIAL MEMORY AND AMNESIA

1. It is curious that historical practice is routinely regarded as "humanistic," and ethnographic work is regarded as a social "science." Historical work follows disciplinary norms using sources that others can hope to read for themselves; history is repeatable and falsifiable, and can (and, indeed, does) make stronger claims to being an objective endeavor; anthropology may be based on first-person observations and experiences, but they are unique and unrepeatable, and hence eminently subjective ones.

Of course, the very notion that the historian's goal is to construct a single "reliable" narrative of the past has come into question. "What happened" at any point in the past was already a matter of interpretation and contention for those people actually involved; the accidents of which interpretations were then inscribed on paper and which papers survived the slings and arrows of preservation always leave the historian with fewer contradictory interpretations to work with, sometimes misleadingly suggesting that fully disinterested accounts (truth) can be separated from interested ones (lies).

2. A capricious friend captured me with my own camera between frames of a document I was microfilming in the Archivo del Tribunal de Poopó which at that time was the anteroom of that town's juzgado and jail.

3. I thank Sabine MacCormack for suggesting to me the ways that experience with the two-dimensional memory device of writing interfered with Spaniards' comprehension of Andean multidimensional memories.

4. During a recent election campaign, a La Paz television station hired a panel of Kallawayas to predict for their audience the election outcome.

5. See the recent controversy about "colonial discourse" in Mallon 1994; Seed 1991.

Glossary

Alphabetic order has been modified to accommodate the Spanish letter and phoneme *ch* and the Aymara phonemic distinction between unaspirated, aspirated, and glottalized forms of *ch*, *k*, *p*, *g*, and *t*. Glottalization is marked by a single prime following the consonant; aspiration, by a double prime. Unaspirated consonants are unmarked.

Alax-Kawalli (Ay.).   A K'ulta ayllu, formerly of the lower moiety.

alax-pacha (Ay.).   Upper or outer space/time; upperworld; heaven.

alax-saya (Ay.).   Upper moiety; equivalent to Quechua *anansaya*.

alcalde (Sp., from Arabic).   "Mayor"; one of the three civil authority types in K'ulta.

alférez (Sp., from Arabic).   Standard-bearer, lieutenant; fiesta career post.

alguacil (Sp., from Arabic).   Bailiff, constable; *jilaqata's* assistant, town council role.

alma cargo (Sp.).   "Soul sponsor," one who inherits a dead man's fiesta-cargo status.

amt'aña (Ay.).   To remember.

amt'añ t''aki (Ay.).   Fixed sequence of libation dedications; lit: "path of memory."

anansaya (Q.).   Upper moiety.

arkiri (Ay.).   Followers who give gifts to a fiesta sponsor.

awarinti (Ay., from Sp. *aguardiente* [*agua ardiente*, "burning water"]).   Diluted cane alcohol.

awatiri (Ay.).   Herder (one who herds).

awayu (Ay.).   Carrying cloth, shawl; also, *lliqlla*.

awiyaru (Ay., from Sp. *aviadora*, "provider").   *Uywiri*-like deities at the heads of valleys producing the bulk of vegetable food eaten in K'ulta.

awki (Ay.).   Father.

awukatu (Ay., from Sp. *abogado*).   Lawyer, intercessor.

ayllu (Ay.).   Polity self-formulated through ritual.

ayni (Ay., Q.).   Reciprocal aid, labor exchange; revenge; persons owing or owed aid or revenge.

516

cabildo (Sp.). Civil offices, town council; altar where tribute is collected; tribute district. See *kawiltu*.

cacique (Sp., from Caribbean term for "chief"). Used generically in place of local words for "chief."

cacique cobrador (Sp.). "Collecting cacique," a role *jilaqatas* fill as tax collectors.

capac hucha (Spanish orthography [spellings vary] for Quechua *qapax jucha[?]*). Inca rite of human sacrifice and reordering of regional shrines; opulent prestation.

ceque (*siqi?*) (Q.). A sight line or straight path leading from a center point (in Cusco, the Qurikancha temple) outward, connecting sacred sites (*wak'as*) and serving as a pilgrimage or dance path.

cofradía (Sp.). Sixteenth-century Spanish religious and military confraternity.

corregidor (Sp.). Royal/state authority in province (sixteenth century); cantón authority (modern).

corregimiento (Sp.). Province of *corregidor's* jurisdiction (colonial); offices of cantón (modern).

cumbi (*qumpi?*) (Q.). High-quality warp-patterned textiles; clothing for nobility or *wak'a* images in pre-Columbian times.

chakra (Ay.). Field.

charango (Sp.). Mandolinlike instrument played during the dry season, used by young men in courtship.

chicha (Sp., from Taino). Corn beer. (Ay. *k'usa;* Q. *asua*).

chullma (Ay.). "Heart," metaphorically; lit.: liver and lungs.

Chullpas (Ay.). Autochthonous people of presolar age; preconquest tombs.

chuñu (Ay.). Freeze-dried potatoes.

ch'alla (Ay.). Libation.

ch'arki (Ay.). Freeze-dried meat.

ch'axwa (Ay.). Land war.

ch'iwu (Ay.). Meat, shade, black rain cloud, llama progeny.

ch'uspa (Ay.). Textile bag for carrying coca.

doctrina (Sp.). Colonial Spanish ecclesiastic district with resident priest.

encomienda (Sp.). Grant of indian labor and tribute to a Spanish conquistador.

fuera (Sp., derived from colonial *mayordomo de afuera*). P"*wira* in Aymara. Fiesta sponsor of intermediate rank; caretaker of portable saint image.

Ilawi (Ay.). K'ulta ayllu, formerly of the upper moiety.

ipala (Ay.). Father's sister (male ego), husband's sister (female ego).

isi (Ay.). Clothing.

isi turqa (Ay.). Clothes-changing ritual, in which the innermost of twelve textiles covering a saint image is rotated to the outermost position.

iskin mamala (Ay.). "Corner mother," house deity.

jach'a jiliri (Ay.). "Great elder brother," one who has completed a fiesta career.

jach'a misa (Ay.). "Great altar," patio altar of a founding ancestor of hamlet/patriline.

jach'a p"ista t"aki (Ay.).   "Great fiesta path"; fixed concatenated sequence of festival sponsorships and terms of civil office conforming an individual career.

jañachu (Ay.).   Male alpaca. Etymology, "sterile male"? Lit., stud male alpaca; term applied to *tullqas* during their ritual role as mock llamas.

jilaqata (Ay.).   Highest-level authority of a major ayllu; also called *cacique*.

jilata (Ay.).   Brother.

jiliri (Ay.).   Elder.

jira t'alla (Ay.).   "Dung plain," libation term for "corral."

jisk'a p"ista tak"i (Ay.).   "Small fiesta path," a fiesta-cargo career.

jula-jula (Ay.).   Octave-graded panpipe; dance group playing such instruments.

jurk'a (Ay.).   Pole covered with flowers and erected in carnaval rite.

kamachiri (Ay.).   One who commands or rules.

kamayuq (Q., Ay.).   Specialist, such as the *quipu kamayuq*, a specialist in keeping records with the *quipu*.

kasta (Ay., from Sp. *casta*, "lineage").   Descent; kindred figured through mother (*wilats kasta*) or father (*mujuts kasta*).

kawiltu (Ay., from Sp. *cabildo).*

kumprira (Ay., from Sp. *cumbre*, "peak").   High mountain deity.

kumun wilara (Ay.).   "Bloodletting, aspersion for the community"; sacrifice to dedicate the staff of authority.

k"arisiri (Ay.).   "Fat cutter"; also *k"arik"ari*. (Q. *ñaqaq, likichiri*).

k'usa (Ay.).   Corn beer, *chicha*.

k'usa wariri (Ay.).   *Chicha* server.

laq'a (Ay.).   Dust; tasteless food.

larita (Ay.).   Wife giver; mother's brother, wife's brother, father's sister's husband.

layra timpu (Ay.).   An earlier age, a time long past; lit. "eye space-time."

limusna waku (Ay.).   Fiesta sponsors' payment to priest for mass.

llantiru (Ay., from Sp. *delantero*, "leader").   Lead llama of herd.

lurya (Ay., from Sp. *gloria*, "glory").   Heaven; lightning; product of contact with the sacred.

lurya misa (Ay.).   Rite aimed at channeling *lurya* away from those who have come purposely or accidentally into excessive contact with saint image or who have offended a lightning-associated saint.

machaqa (Ay.).   New, novice; incoming fiesta sponsor.

mallku (Ay.).   Mountain peak, mountain spirit, condor; hereditary authority (pre-Columbian).

mamani (Ay., Q.).   Falcon; Inca province below the level of quarter empire.

mama t'alla (Ay.).   Town plaza.

Manxa-Kawalli (Ay.).   K'ulta ayllu, formerly of the lower moiety.

manxa-pacha (Ay.).   Under or inner space-time; underworld.

manxa-saya (Ay.).   Lower moiety; equivalent to the Quechua *urinsaya*.

maxta (Ay.).   Youth, marriageable young man.

mayordomo (Sp.). Post in fiesta-cargo career, in charge of church key (Ay. *mayurt"umu*).

mayruwiri qullu (Ay.). Mountain of souls, ancestors' mountain; also called *muntu*.

mita (Sp., from Ay., Q. *mit'a*, turn of duty). Coerced labor system of colonial period.

mitimas (Q., Sp.). Permanent settlers from far-flung home regions, resettled by the Incas.

mojón (Sp.). Boundary marker, usually a rock pile, pillar, or notable feature of landscape.

muju (Ay.). Semen, seed.

mujuts kasta (Ay.). "Seed line"; lineage figured through paternal and patrilineal links, or ascending kindred through father; the patriline.

muntu (Ay., from Sp. *mundo*). World mountain, afterworld, underworld abode of dead humans and/or herd animals.

niñu (Ay., from Sp. *niño*, "child"). Cross erected at hill-peak altar, or *silu*, belonging to a saint image; also, front pillar of a *pukara*, a hamlet chapel.

ñuwasi (Ay.). Ritual battle; lit. "knuckler." Also *tinku*.

padrón (Sp.). Locally produced census list.

pampa (Ay.). A plain.

paqarina/pacarina (Q.). Origin place, place of ancestor's emergence. Paqariqtambo: rest house of emergence, origin place of Inca myth. Probably related to or derived from the Aymara *paq"ara*.

paq"ara (Ay.). "Flower, bloom."

paq"arayaña (Ay.). "To make bloom"; the action of decorating llamas before sacrifice; adorning sponsors with gift textiles.

pasado (Sp.). "Passed"; one who has completed a fiesta career. (Ay. *pasaru*).

paxcha (Ay.). Flowing, spurting; moment in llama sacrifice when throat is cut.

pillu (Ay.). Flower or bread wreath; crown.

pongo Colonial and modern Spanish and Aymara term for a form of domestic labor service owed by indigenous tenants of haciendas to their patrones, by extension from pre-Columbian *punku kamayuq* ("door keeper").

principal (Sp.). Colonial term used for *ayllu jilaqata*, and for past *cabildo* officeholders.

probanza (Sp.). Service report in form of curriculum vita backed up by sworn witness testimony, presented to Spanish Crown in an effort to gain privilege or position.

pukara (Ay.). Fortress; hamlet chapel.

puna (Q.). High-altitude zone suitable for pasture and bitter potato production. (Ay. *suni*).

punku (Ay.). Door.

puro (Sp.). Pure distilled cane alcohol. (Ay. *puru*).

q'ara (Ay.). Naked, incompletely dressed; fig., culturally peeled; an insult reference term for nonindians (mestizos, criollos, Europeans, and, sometimes, traitorous indigenous people).

qarwa (Ay.). Llama.

qarwa k″ari (Ay.). Llama cutting, part of the llama sacrifice.

quero (*q'iru?*) (Q.). A pre-Columbian and colonial painted or incised wooden or metal vessel for drinking *chicha*.

qullana (Ay.). K′ulta ayllu, formerly of the upper moiety.

qurpa (Ay.). Miniature loaves of bread thrown from the church tower during a fiesta; banquet.

q'uwa (Ay.). Resinous herb used for incense; *q'uwana,* incense offering including this ingredient.

reducción (Sp.). A new town within which a scattered population of indians was to be concentrated.

repartimiento (Sp.). Term replacing *encomienda;* colonial administrative district.

samarayaña (Ay.). Places to catch one's breath along a ceremonial route between hamlet and town; alternate "resting" years of a ceremonial career.

samiri (Ay.). Deity form, "one who gives breath": (1) a high mountain boulder that is an ideal type or ancestor form; (2) miniature stone figurine in animal form that is the repositor of the life principle of animals.

Santisima Paxsi Mamala (Ay.). "Holy Moon Lady," Holy Mother, the Virgin, the moon.

sap″i (Ay.). "Root" of an altar, house, church tower, or mountain deity.

segunda persona (Sp.). Second in command; Spanish designation for the indigenous lord of the lower moiety.

silu (Ay., from Sp. *cielo,* "sky"). Hill-peak altar of a saint image.

subdelgado (Sp.). Nineteenth-century authority, replacing colonial *corregidor;* twentieth-century subprefect.

sucullu (Bertonio) or *sukullu* (Ay.). Naming rite.

suni (Ay.). High-altitude zone suitable for pasture or bitter-potato production.

supay (Ay.). Devil or evil spirit (meaning was forged in colonial period).

surti walas (Ay.). Metal or stone balls belonging to shamans and saints.

-taki (Ay.). Nominal suffix added to recipient of action or gift.

tama (Ay.). Herd.

taqui (pl. *taquies*) (Q.). In colonial texts, refers to songdances, glossed sometimes by Spanish *cantar,* epic poem, in which narratives were sung while dancing, sometimes along *ceque* lines, which were ritual pathways connecting sites of memory across the landscape. Colonial observers associated *taquies* with *borracheras,* drunken meetings, and regarded both as vehicles through which natives preserved memories of their heathen past. Compare with modern Aymara *t'aki.*

tasa (Sp.). An assignment of tribute resulting from a census.

Tata Awatir Awksa (Ay.). "Our Father Herder"; Jesus Christ, the sun.

Tata Exaltación (Ay.). The Exaltation of the Cross. Also, Tata Killakas.

Tata Mustramu (Ay., from L. [?] *mostramo,* "soliform monstrance"). The sun.

tata rey (Ay. *tata,* "father," and Sp. *rey,* "king"). Libation term for *vara,* "staff of office."

tinku (Q.). A meeting of opposites; ritual battle (see *ñuwasi*).

tullqa (Ay.). Wife taker: man's sister's or daughter's husband.

turri (Ay., from Sp. *torre,* "tower"). Alternate term for *mayordomo.*

turri mallku (Ay.). Church tower.

t'aki (Ay.). Term with a gamut of meanings linking chronological sequence and landscape. Most prosaically, "path" or "trail," but modified in a variety of compound terms, it appears to be an ethnopoetic category akin to English "narrative."

t'inka (Ay.). Ceremonial pair of repayment drinks, ceremonial return gifts.

t'uxsa (Ay.). Rotten, smelling of decay.

t'arka (Ay.). A type of flute played during the rainy season.

untu (Ay.). Llama fat from the chest cavity.

urinsaya (Q.). Lower moiety.

urqu (Ay.). Male; (Q.). mountain.

Urus (Ay.). Ethnic group thought of as lake-dwelling fishers and gatherers.

uta anqa (Ay.). "House outdoors," patio.

uywa (Ay.). Domesticated animal.

uywa ispira (Ay.). Part of a llama sacrifice, "animal vespers."

uywiri (Ay.). Type of chthonic power, "those who own/raise the herds"; a household's caretaker hill.

vara (Sp.). Staff of office (see *tata rey*).

vecino (Sp.). Townsman with fully vested rights (colonial); nonindian townsman (modern).

visita (Sp.). Ritualized administrative tour; census, formal census record.

wak'a (Ay.). Sacred place or place spirit.

wasu wariri (Ay.). Drink server; lit: "cup bearer."

wila (Ay.). Blood; red.

Wila Qullu (Ay.). Lit., "blood mountain," mountain of Potosí; fig., "money."

wilara (Ay.). Sacrificial rite.

wilats kasta (Ay.). "Bloodline"; lineage figured through matrilineal or matrilateral links, or ascending kindred on mother's side.

yanani (Ay.). A duality, symmetry, pair; or one that completes a pair.

Yanaqi (Ay.). K'ulta ayllu, formerly of the upper moiety.

yatiri (Ay.). Healer, diviner; lit. "one who knows"; shaman.

References

MANUSCRIPT SOURCES

Archivo de Derechos Reales, Corte Superior de Oruro (ADRO)

Provincia Abaroa, Libro de Propiedades, 1923–24, partida no. 35. "Títulos de la comunidad de Aullagas y Arouma en Abaroa." 18 fols.

Provincia Abaroa, Libro de Propiedades, 1923–24, partida no. 136. "Títulos de orígen de la comunidad o ayllo Quillacas de la provincia Abaroa."

Provincia Abaroa, Libro de Propiedades, 1934–36, partida no. 79. "Títulos de origen protocolizados a solicitúd de Demetrio Gómez, Hernán Copacallo, etc." (1895 document citing composición titles, seeking exemption from visita and exvinculación). 15 fols.

Provincia Abaroa, Libro de Propiedades, 1931–33, partida no. 27. "Títulos de propiedad de los indigenas de la comunidad de Condo. (1619 composición in favor of Juan António Martínez Taquimallcu, gob. de Condocondo y Azanaques)." 40 fols.

Archivo General de Indias (AGI)

Charcas 32, item 12. Charcas, September 5, 1565. "Ynformaciones de la Villa Imperial del Asiento de Potosí sobre que se le hagan las mercedes contenidas . . ." 190 fols.

Charcas 49. La Plata, 1610. "Marcos Goncález de Quebedo en nombre de don Felipe Soto y don Felipe Conde caçíques prençipales del pueblo de Neustra Señora de Belén . . . sobre . . . la posesión a las tierras de Pinapina." 20 fols.

Charcas 53, item 1. Charcas, 1622. "Memorial de don Diego Copatete cacique principal de los indios Quillacas y Asanaques."

Charcas 79, no. 19. La Plata, 1606. "Ynformaçión fecha de ofiçio en la rreal audiençia de los charcas de las buenas partes del bachiller Hernán Gonçález de la Casa cura de la cathedral de la Plata. Va ante su magestad en el rreal consejo de las yndias cerrada y sellada [un visto por Fray Diego de la Barreva de Ayala]." 74 fols.

Charcas 96, no. 11. La Plata, 1658. "Probanza de servicios y méritos del bachiller don Sebastián de Aguilar, cura propietario de San Miguel de Aullagas y San Francisco de Coroma." Ca. 45 fols.

Escribanía de Camara (EC) 497-B:

Pieza 4. Madrid, 1565. "Autos del secuestro de los bienes de Hernán Vela."

Piezas 5–6. "Herederos de Hernán Vela sobre el valor de Siete Yglesias." 1,566 fols.

Pieza 16. "Autos presentados por parte de los yndios aullagas . . . contra Hernán Vela ." 68 fols.

EC 497-C. Pieza 23. 1560. "Memorial del pleito entre doña Ana Gutiérrez muger que fue de Hernán Vela difunto . . . y los indios del pueblo y repartimiento de los Aullagas . . ." 211 fols.

Lima, July 20, 1563. "Autos seguidos entre don Diego de Carbajal . . . contra el fiscal de S. M. sobre la encomienda de yndios de Guadachiri . . ."

EC 844-A. La Plata, 1583. "Lucas de Murga Menchaca, Cathalina Gutiérrez, etc., con los Indios Ullagas."

Indiferente General 422 [L. 16]. Fols. 206v–207 [RC, Madrid, 05-31-1535].

Indiferente General 532. Fols. 27v–28r. Real Cédula directed to the Audiencia del Nuevo Reino de Granada, 1549. "Juntas de indios en pueblos formados; Alcaldes hordinarios e regidores cadañeros."

Indiferente General 1624. "Expedientes y respuestas a la pertetuidad de las encomiendas de Indias vistas en la junta de la perpetuidad." Fols. 1–904 (1542–86).

Justicia 434, Pieza 1. Lima, 1563. "El fiscal de S.M. con Antón Ruiz Mestizo sobre la contradicción de la perpetuidad."

Justicia 434, Pieza 2. Lima, 1563. "Preceso hecho por el Doctor Cuenca oydor de la audiencia de los reyes contra Antonio Ruiz, mestizo, y lengua, o interprete y vezino del Cuzco. Sobre la contradicción de la perpetuidad, y lo que dió a entender a los yndios."

Justicia 651. La Plata, 1571. 3 piezas. "Los yndios de . . . Chayanta con doña Juana de los Rios sobre los demasiados tributos que les pide." 500 fols.

Justicia 653. La Plata. 1579. "Los yndios de . . . Sacaca con los herederos de don Alonso de Montemayor sobre lo que el dicho don Alonso cobró demasiado de los dichos yndios." (Entire legajo).

Justicia 667. La Plata, January 8, 1550. "Cumplimiento e diligençias que la justicia de la Villa de Plata hizo cerca de la libertad que los yndios que estan en las minas de Potosí tienen de yrse a sus tierras sin que nadie se lo impida."

Justicia 667. Potosi, May 8, 1550. "Suplicación e ynformación fecha por parte de los vezinos de la Villa de Plata y los vezinos de las ciudades del Cuzco y de La Paz açerca de mandar salir los yndios de las minas lo qual se hizo ante la justicia mayor de la Villa de Plata."

Justicia 1134. April 18, 1551. "Ynformación hecha por el señor don Lorenzo de Estopiñan y Figueroa sobre quan probechoso les es a los caciques e indios estar en Potosí." 13 fols.

Patronato 126, section 6. 1582. "Informaciones de los buenos servicios de Diego Pantoja de Chaves."

Quito 45. Memorial de don Juan Colque Guarache. (Also contains "Segunda información . . . ," 1576–77.)

9.5.1.2. Intendencia de La Plata o Charcas 1751–52. (Unnumbered letters).

1751. "Carta de don Pablo de la Vega y traslado de escritos sobre la rebelión de Cagchas en Puna y Potosí, hecho por orden de don Domingo de Xauregui, presidente de la audiencia de La Plata."

"Carta y expediente de Geronimo Gomes Trigoso, Asoguero, al superintendente de Potosí, sobre los Cagchas de Potosí."

9.5.2.1. Intendencia de La Plata 1780–81, Copiador de cartas.

November 15, 1780. "Carta de don Manuel Alvaréz Villaroél . . . coronel del Batallón de Milicias en el asiento de Minas de Aullagas . . . Escrito en 24 de Sept., 1780."

9.6.2.5. Potosí 1607–1750. (Unnumbered letters).

1750. "Carta del General don Pedro Flores de Cáseres, corregidor de la provincia de Porco, a los justicias de La Plata y Potosí, sobre la rebelión de Cacchas en Puna y Potosí."

9.10.3.7. Representaciones y Quexas de Provincias 1689–91. (Unordered cuadernos).

"Quexas del Cura de Pilaia y Paspaia," 1689.

9.14.8.7. "Potosí mita, 1795–97."

9.14.8.8. "Potosí mita, 1795–97."

9.17.1.4. Alto Perú Padrones 1645–86. (Unordered cuadernos).

"Padrón del pueblo de Condocondo," 1645.

"Padrón de los yndios de Challapata," 1645.

"Padrón del pueblo de San Lucas de Payacollo," 1646.

"Padrón de San Miguel de Aullagas," 1645.

"Padrón de los yndios Quillacas," 1645.

9.17.2.5. "Retasa de Francisco de Toledo," 1575. Anonymous copy of 1785.

9.20.4.4. Padrones de Indios 1623–46. (Unordered cuadernos).

"Padrón del pueblo de Talavera de la Puna," 1645.

9.30.2.3. Interior, Legajo 9.

Expediente 16, "Autos formados . . . sobre el tumulto de Condocondo," 1780.

9.36.6.1. Tribunales, Legajo 85.

Expediente 17. "Testimonio de los documentos calificativos de los servicios y méritos del governador del pueblo de Chaianta, don Diego Colque Guarache—y comprovantes de su Noblesa," 1796.

13.18.4.3. Padrones La Plata 1616–1725, Legajo 57. (Unordered cuadernos).

"Padrón . . . indios del pueblo de Condocondo residentes en Potosi."

"Padrón . . . indios del pueblo de Challapata residentes en Potosi."

"Padrón de Aullagas," 1684.

"Padrón de Toledo," 1684.

"Padrones de diferentes pueblos de la provincia de Paria hechos por el corregidor e la de los Amparaes por haver hallado los yndios de ellos en su distrito," 1684.

"Informes y Sumarios de Retasas de Paria," 1726.

13.18.5.1. Padrones La Plata, 1725–54 [unordered notebooks].

"Padrones . . . de la provincia de Paria," 1683–84.

"Padrón del pueblo de Atun Quillacas," 1683.

"Padrón del pueblo de Aullagas," 1683.

"Padrón y revisita—originarios y forasteros del pueblo de San Lucas de Paiacollo—y parcialidades de Quillacas, y Azanaques de la provincia de Paria," 1752.

13.18.5.3. Padrones La Plata 1770–79, Legajo 62. Libro 3, "Retasa de Ullagas," 1779.

13.18.6.1. Padrones La Plata 1793–95, Legajo 65. Libro 3, "Revisita de la provincia de Paria," 1795.

13.18.7.2. Padrones Potosí 1612–19. "Rebisita del pueblo de Macha de la Corona Real por el governador Antonio Salgado," 1619. (Probanza de don Juan de Castro y Paria, 1612).

Archivo General de Simancas, Spain (AGS)

Diversos de Castilla. Leg. 40, fol. 13, "Relaçion de los lugares que se an bendido con sus alcavalas y terçias desde el año de 1557 a esta parte . . ."

Mercedes y Privilegios 335. Venta de la villa de Siete Iglesias a Hernán Vela, vecino de Alaejos, por el importe de 3,400,000 mrs.

Archivo Histórico Nacional, Spain (AHN)

Sección Osuna. Pleitos y alcabalas de Siete Iglesias, s. XVI–XVII.

Sección de Diversos:

Docs. de Indias, no. 58. "Noticias sobre la batalla entre el Virrey B. Núñez Vela y Gonzalo Pizarro."

Docs. de Indias, no. 145. September 5, 1556. Gante. "Provisión de Felipe II en que mando que sin más dilación se proceda a dar a perpetuidad los repartimientos de indios a los conquistadores y pobladores del Perú." 2 fols.

Docs. de Indias, no. 152. Principios de 1558. Memorial que el obispo fray Bartolomé de las Casas y fray Domingo de Santo Tomás, provincial de la Orden de Santo Domingo en el Perú, dirigen al emperador, en nombre de los caciques e indios de aquel virreinato, contra la perpetuidad de las encomiendas, ofreciéndole a cambio cierta cantidad de ducados de oro y plata. Copia simple siglo xix, 4 hojas cuarto.

Docs. de Indias, no. 171. February 7, 1561. Toledo. Provisión de Felipe II al virrey del Perú, conde de Nieva, pidiéndole informe sobre la conveniencia de los repartimientos de indios, a perpetuidad, solicitados por los españoles en las provincias de su gobierno, en vista del memorial que le han presentado fray Domingo de Santo Tomás, provincial que fué de los dominicos, y el obispo fray Bartolomé de las Casas, en nombre de los caciques y naturales, en contra de esta concesión. 2 fols.

Docs. de Indias, no. 181. March 14, 1562. Lima. Carta de fray Domingo de Santo Tomás, dominico, a Felipe II manifestando que las encomiendas de indios a perpetuidad eran contra el servicio de Dios y contra la conciencia, hacienda, y señorío del rey. 2 fols.

Archivo de Hacienda y Tesoro, Prefectura de Oruro

Expediente de Amparo Administrativo, 1968. "Comunarios del ayllu Collana vs. Pablo Choquecallata et al., ayllu Cahualli, por destrucción, incendio, y saqueo de casas y escuela." 12 pp. (truncated).

Expediente de Proceso Administrativo, September 23, 1966. "Creación del Cantón Cahuayo, Provincia Abaroa. Demandante: Comunidad Sullcayana." 26 fols. (with map).

Expediente de Proceso Administrativo, August 20, 1987. "Creación del Cantón Cruce Culta." 40 fols. (with maps).

Protocolización de documento sobre deslinde de la estancia Uncallita y Jachuipiña, del ayllo Cahualli-abajo, Cantón Culta. December 16, 1970.

Archivo Histórico de Potosí (AHP)

Cajas Reales 18. Tasa de la visita general de Francisco de Toledo.

Visitas y Padrones, Cuaderno de la visita del duque de la Palata (1683), Repartimiento de Puna.

Archivo Judicial de Oruro (AJO)

Legajo 1680–82. "Cabesa de proceso de jilsa, contra don Martín Nina, Oruro, 1680."

Legajo 1779–82 (misfiled). "Cabesa de proceso contra Domingo Ramírez, Oruro, 1680."

Archivo Nacional de Bolivia, Sucre, Bolivia (ANB)

ALP Minas, tomo 45, no. 5. "Don Juan Francisco Choquetijlla, governador y casique principal de Jatun Quillacas . . ." 1693.

ALP Minas, tomo 125, no. 17. "Don Luis Enrríquez de Guzman Conde de Alva de Aliste y de Villa Flor gentil hombre de la cámara de Su Magestad. . . ." 1667.

Expedientes Coloniales (EC) 1588, no. 5. "Reclamación de don Miguel García Colque sobre el casicazgo del repartimiento de Quillacas."

EC 1611, no. 8. "Los yndios de Tacobamba contra los quillacas, Asanaques sobre que sean hechados de las tierras de Guache y Sarotala."

EC 1613, no. 19. "Probanza de Fernando de Mesa."

EC 1618, no. 5. "Los yndios de Santiago de Aymaya con Gaspar de la Rúa Hinojosa."

EC 1666, no. 37. "Don Felipe Choqueticlla contra. . . ."

EC 1738, no. 62. "Juicio contra don Pedro Norverto Chungara por atroces, por don Pascual, Estevan, Asencio y Gregorio Mamani y demas yndios . . . de Challapata."

EC 1743, no. 9. "Don Matheo Alexandro de la Cruz Condori [cacique principal] contra don Pedro Norberto Chungara [governador]. . . ."

EC 1744, no. 63. "Demanda por Francisco Caro Campo, casique de Condo Condo, contra los comunarios de Tinquipaya, Macha, Chayanta, por despojo de Tierras."

EC 1744, no. 72. "Provisión Real de deslinde y amojonamiento de varias tierras situadas en la doctrina de Sapse (partido de Yamparaez) propias de los originarios de Jatun Quillacas, Guari, Pocpo, y Aullagas."

EC 1747, no. 12. "Reclamo de don Gregorio Feliz Llanquipacha, para la posición de casique principal y governador de Condo Condo. El decreto se le despache título en forma."

EC 1755, no. 20. "Autos seguidos por don Francisco Choqueticlla, contra doña Paula Choqueticlla sobre el arrendamiento de la hacienda y molinos de Tacovilque en la doctrina de San Pedro de Micani, provincia Chayanta."

EC 1756, no. 41. "Petición de José Guarcaya, indio principal a nombre del común de indios de Condocondo, para que se les disminuyen los gastos que tienen . . . en las fiestas. . . ."

EC 1759, no. 139. "Challapata, para ver a cual de estos por derecho de sangre le corresponde desempeñar el cacicazgo del mencionado pueblo."

EC 1771, no. 143. "Testimonio de los títulos de propiedad de Quillacas y Carangas del valle de Cochabamba, dados por Luis López Obispo de Quito [in 1593]."

EC 1775, no. 165. "Autos seguidos por Luis Guarcaya, Santos Gonzáles, y otros . . . sobre el Casicasgo de Condocondo [urinsaya]."

EC 1776, no. 24. "Autos seguidos . . . sobre capítulos puestos contra el Cacique y Comunidad de indios de Challapata."

EC 1777, no. 139. "Expediente de la demanda puesto por los yndios de Condo Condo contra el cobrador de repartos del corregidor de al provincia de Paria don Narciso de San Juan y Mansilla."

EC 1778, no. 127. "Testimonio de cuentas del reparto hecho en la provincia de Paria por el corregidor de ella don Manuel de la Bodega y Llano, año de 1777."

EC 1781, no. 83. "Autos formados sobre el tumulto que acaheció en el pueblo de Condo Condo; y muertes que executaron en los Llanquipachas."

EC 1787, no. 39. "Auxilio que piden las comunidades de indios de los pueblos de Guari y Aullagas de la caja de censos."

EC 1787, no. 101. "Informe del subdelegado de Paria sobre la necesidad que hay de visitar las tierras de su partido."

EC 1792, no. 42. "Expediente promovido por doña Narsisa Choqueticlla casica de Quillacas y pueblo de Pocpo, sobre que don Manuel Mostajo le debuelva los papeles y documentos condusentes a las tierras de su comunidad."

EC 1792, no. 108. "Demanda puesta por don Ambrosio Miguel de la Cruz Condori, gobernador de los ayllus Sullca, Andamarca, y Changara . . . en nombre de la comunidad de Challapata, contra destrozos y invasiones de tierras hecho por los indios de Condocondo."

EC 1797, no. 25. "Queja entablada por los indios de Culta contra el casique cobrador de tributos."

EC 1804, no. 193. "Expediente seguido en la villa de Potosí por el testamento hecho de don Juan Choqueticlla Colqueguarachi en el año 1707 por la india Antonia Copatiti Colqueguarachi, indígena principal de los Quillacas." (Includes sixteenth-century material).

Fotocopias, 1603. García de Llanos, "Descripción de Potosí."

SG 1781, no. 42. "Expediente sobre los alborotos de los yndios de Yocalla, Yura y Puna." 8 fols. (Carta del cura de Culta Joseph Balzeda al Gob. de Potosí Jorge Escobedo, February 18, 1781).

Archivo Obisbal de Oruro (AOO)

Libro I de Bautismos, San Pedro de Condo, 1571.
Libro I de Bautismos, San Juan del Pedroso de Challapata, 1575.

Archivo de la Real Académia de Historia Española (ARAH)

9.29.5.5927. Relación de la villa de Medina y lugares de su jurisdicción que remitió a la camara en el año 1571 el corregidor.

Archivo de la Real Chancillería de Valladolid (ARChV)

Hijosdalgo, 119–7. "Proceso de Hernando Vela vezino de la villa de halahejos sobre su hidalguía." 1535.

Archivo del Tribunal de Poopó, Dept. of Oruro, Bolivia (ATP)

Expediente 11 (without title and incomplete). 1574–75. Probanza de Juan Colque Guarache.

Expediente 12 (without title, incomplete, and disordered). 1678. Autos sobre las tierras del repartimiento de Quillacas y Asanaques en el Cerro de Turqui y valle de Tarapaya.

Archivo y Biblioteca Arquidiocesanos de Sucre (ABAS)

Causas contra ecclesiásticos, no. 5020. "Condo. Licencia para capilla, 1626." 10 fols.

OTHER SOURCES

Abercrombie, Thomas A. 1986. The Politics of Sacrifice: An Aymara Cosmology in Action. Ph.D. dissertation, University of Chicago.

Abercrombie, Thomas A. 1991. To Be Indian, to Be Bolivian: "Ethnic" and "National" Discourses of Identity. In Greg Urban and Joel Sherzer, eds., *Nation–States and Indians in Latin America*, 95–130. Austin: University of Texas Press.

Abercrombie, Thomas A. 1992. La fiesta del carnaval postcolonial en Oruro: Clase, etnicidad y nacionalismo en la danza folklórica. *Revista andina* 10(2):279–352.

Abercrombie, Thomas A. 1993. Caminos de la memoria en un cosmos colonizado: Poética de la bebida y la consciencia histórica en K'ulta. In Thierry Saignes, ed., *Borrachera y memoria: La experiencia de lo sagrado en los Andes*, 139–170. La Paz: HISBOL/IFEA.

Abercrombie, Thomas A. 1996. Q'aqchas and the Plebe in "Rebellion": Carnival vs. Lent in 18th-century Potosí. *Journal of Latin American Anthropology* 2(1): 62–111.

Acosta, Antonio. 1987. La extirpación de las idolatrías en el Perú: Origen y desarrollo de las campañas: A propósito de *Cultura andina y represión,* de Pierre Duviols. *Revista andina* 9: 171–195.

Acosta, José de. 1977. *Historia natural y moral de las indias.* (1590). Facs. ed. with introduction by Barbara G. Beddall. Valencia: Albatros Ediciones (Valencia Cultural, S.A.).

Adelaar, William F. H. 1990. The Role of Quotations in Andean Discourse. In Harm Pinkster and Inge Genee, eds., *Unity in Diversity: Papers Presented to Simon C. Dik on His 50th Birthday.* Dordrecht: Foris Publications.

Adorno, Rolena. 1986. *Guaman Poma: Writing and Resistance in Colonial Perú.* Austin: University of Texas Press.

Adorno, Rolena. 1992. The Discursive Encounter of Spain and America: The Authority of Eyewitness Testimony in the Writing of History. *William and Mary Quarterly* 49(2): 210–228.

Adorno, Rolena, ed. 1982. *From Oral to Written Expression: Native Andean Chronicles of the Early Colonial Period,* Syracuse, N.Y.: Maxwell School of Citizenship and Public Affairs.

Albó, Xavier. 1975. La paradoja aymara: Solidaridad y faccionalismo. *Estudios andinos* 11: 67–109

Albó, Xavier. 1976. ¿Khitipxtansa? ¿Quiénes somos? Identidad localista, étnica y clasista en los Aymaras de hoy. *América indígena* 39(3): 477–528.

Albó, Xavier. 1979. The Future of Oppressed Languages in the Andes. In W. McCormack and S. A. Wurm, eds., *Language and Society,* 309–331. The Hague: Mouton.

Albó, Xavier. 1980. *Lengua y sociedad en Bolivia, 1976.* La Paz: Instituto Nacional de Estadística.

Albó, Xavier. 1987. From MNRistas to Kataristas to Katari. In Steve J. Stern, ed., *Resistance, Rebellion, and Consciousness in the Andean Peasant World, 18th to 20th Centuries,* 379–419. Madison: University of Wisconsin Press.

Albó, Xavier. 1991. El retorno del indio. *Revista andina* 9(2): 299–366.

Albó, Xavier. 1992. El Thakhi o "camino" en Jesús de Machaqa. In Raquel Thiercelin, ed., *Cultures et sociétes Andes et Méso-Amérique: Mélanges en hommage à Pierre Duviols,* vol. 1, 51–65. Aix-en-Provence: Publications de l'Université de Provence.

Albó, Xavier, and CIPCA team. 1972. Dinámica en la estructura inter-comunitaria de Jesús de Machaca. *América indígena* 32(3): 773–816.

Albó, Xavier, Tomás Greaves, and Godofredo Sandoval. 1983. *Chukiyawu, la cara aymara de La Paz,* vol. 3: *Cabalgando entre dos mundos.* La Paz: CIPCA.

Albornóz, Cristóbal de. 1989. Instrucción para descubrir todas las huacas del Piru y sus camayos y haziendas. (1581/1585) In C. de Molina and C. de Albornóz, *Fábulas y mitos de los incas,* ed. Henrique Urbano y Pierre Duviols, 135–198. Cronicas de America, vol. 48. Madrid: Historia 16

Albornóz, Cristóbal de. 1990. Las informaciones de Cristobal de Albornoz. (1569–84). In Luis Millones, ed., *El retorno de las huacas: Estudios y documentos sobre el Taki Onqoy: Siglo XVI,* 255–296. Lima: Instituto de Estudios Peruanos.

Allen, Catherine J. 1988. *The Hold Life Has.* Washington, D.C.: Smithsonian Institution Press.

Anonymous Jesuit. 1879. Relación de las custumbres antiguas de los naturales del Pirú. (c. 1590). In *Tres relaciones de antigüedades peruanas,* 137–227. Madrid: Imprenta y Fundición de M. Tello.

Anonymous Jesuit. 1968. *Relación de las costumbres antiguas . . .* (1620?). Biblioteca de Autores Españoles, vol. 209. Madrid.

Ares Queija, Berta. 1984. La danza de los indios: Un camino para la evangeli-zación del virreinato del Perú. *Revista de Indias* 44(174): 445–463.

Arnold, Denise. 1988. Matrilineal Practice in a Patrilineal Setting: Ritual and Metaphors of Kinship in an Andean Ayllu. Ph.D. thesis, University of London.

Arnold, Denise. 1992. The House of Earth-Bricks and Inka Stones: Gender, Memory and Cosmos in Qaqachaka. *Journal of Latin American Lore* 17(1): 3–69.

Arnold, Denise. 1993. Adam and Eve and the Red-Trousered Ant: History in the Southern Andes. *Travesia* (King's College, London) 2(1): 49–83.

Aronld, Denise, and Juan de Dios Yapita. 1992a. Fox Talk: Addressing the Wild Beasts in the Southern Andes. *Latin America Indian Literatures Journal* 8(1): 9–37.

Arnold, Denise, and Juan de Dios Yapita. 1992b. Sallqa: Dirigirse a las Bestias Silvestres en los Andes Meridionales. In Denise Arnold, Domingo Jiménez, and Juan de Dios Yapita, eds., *Hacia un orden andino de las cosas,* 175–212. La Paz: HISBOL/ILCA.

Arnold, Denise, Domingo Jiménez, and Juan de Dios Yapita. 1992. *Hacia un orden andino de las cosas*. La Paz: HISBOL/ILCA.

Arriaga, Father Pablo José de. 1968. *The Extirpation of Idolatry in Peru*. Trans. L. Clark Keating. Lexington, Ky.: University of Kentucky Press.

Arzáns de Orzua y Vela, Bartolomé. 1965. *Historia de la Villa Imperial de Potosí*. (1735). 3 vols. Ed. Lewis Hanke and Gunnar Mendoza. Providence, R.I.: Brown University Press.

Arze, Silvia. 1991. La rebelión en los ayllus de la provincia colonial de Chayanta, 1777–1781. *Estado y sociedad: Revista boliviana de ciencias sociales* (La Paz) 7(8): 89–110.

Asad, Talal. 1987. Are There Histories of Peoples without Europe? *Comparative Studies in Society and History* 29: 594–607.

Aylmer, G. E., ed. 1975. *The Levellers in the English Revolution*. Ithaca: Cornell University Press.

Bakewell, Peter J. 1984. *Miners of the Red Mountain*. Alburquerque, N.M.: University of New Mexico Press.

Bakhtin, M. M. 1981. Forms of Time and of the Chronotope in the Novel. In Michael Holquist, ed., *The Dialogic Imagination*, 84–258. Austin: University of Texas Press.

Bakhtin, M. M. 1984. *Rabelais and His World*. Trans. Hélène Iswolsky. Bloomington: Indiana University Press.

Bandelier, Adoph F. A. 1910. *The Islands of Titicaca and Koati*. New York: Hispanic Society of America.

Barker, Francis, Peter Hulme, and Margaret Iversen, eds. 1994. *Colonial Discourse/Postcolonial Theory*. New York: St. Martin's Press.

Barnadas, Josép M. 1973. *Charcas, 1535–1565: Orígenes históricos de una sociedad colonial*. La Paz, Bolivia: CIPCA.

Barragán, Rossana. 1990. *Espacio urbano y dinámica étnica: La Paz en el siglo XIX*. La Paz: HISBOL.

Barragán, Rossana. 1992. Entre polleras, lliqllas y ñañacas: Los mestizos y la emergencia de la tercera republica. In S. Arze, R. Barragán, et al., eds. *Etnicidad, economia, y simbolismo en Los Andes*, 85–127. La Paz: HISBOL/IFEA.

Barragán, Rossana. 1994. *¿Indios de arco y flecha? Entre la historia y la arqueología de las poblaciones del Norte de Chuquisaca (siglos XV–XVI)*. Sucre, Bolivia: Ediciones ASUR 3.

Barstow, Jean. 1979. An Aymara Class Structure: Town and Community in Carabuco. Ph.D. dissertation, University of Chicago.

Barstow, Jean. 1981. Marriage between Human Beings and Animals: A Structuralist Discussion of Two Aymara Myths. *Anthropology* 5(1): 71–88.

Bastien, Joseph. 1978. *Mountain of the Condor: Metaphor and Ritual in an Andean Ayllu*. St. Paul: West Publishing Co.

Baudin, Louis. 1928. *L'empire socialiste des Inkas*. Paris: Institut d'Ethnologie.

Befu, Harumi. 1974. An Ethnography of Dinner Entertainment in Japan. *Arctic Anthropology* II (suppl.): 196–203.

Behar, Ruth. 1994. *Translated Woman.* Boston: Beacon Press.

Bennassar, Bartolome. 1979. *The Spanish Character.* Berkeley: University of California Press.

Bernaldo de Quirós, Constancio. 1975. *La picota: Crímenes y castigos en el país castellano en los tiempos medievales.* (1907). Madrid: Turner.

Bernand, Carmen, and Serge Gruzinski. 1988. *De l'Idolatrie: Une archéologie des sciences religieuses.* Paris: Seuil.

Bertonio, Ludovico. 1984. *Vocabulario de la lengua aymara.* (1612). Facs. ed. Cochabamba, Bolivia: CERES, Museo Nacional de Etnografía y Folklore, and the Instituto Frances de Estudios Andinos.

Bertonio, Ludovico. 1879. *Arte y grammatica muy copiosa de la lengua aymara.* (1603). Rome: Luis Zannetti, facs. ed., Leipzig: Teubner.

Betanzos, Juan de. 1987. *Suma y narracion de los Incas.* (1551). Ed. María del Carmen Martín Rubio. Madrid: Ediciones Atlas.

Biersack, Aletta. 1989. Local Knowledge, Local History: Geertz and Beyond. In Lynn Hunt, ed., *The New Cultural History,* 72–96. Berkeley: University of California Press.

Bilinkoff, Jodi. 1989. *The Avila of Saint Teresa: Religious Reform in a Sixteenth-Century City.* Ithaca: Cornell University Press.

Boas, Franz. 1940. *Race, Language and Culture.* New York: Macmillan

Bolton, Ralph, and Enrique Mayer, eds. 1977. *Andean Kinship and Marriage.* Washington, D.C.: American Anthropological Association.

Boone, Elizabeth Hill, and Walter D. Mignolo, eds. 1994. *Writing Without Words: Alternative Literacies in Mesoamerica and the Andes.* Durham, N.C.: Duke University Press.

Bourdieu, Pierre. 1977. *Outline of a Theory of Practice.* Chicago: University of Chicago Press.

Bourdieu, Pierre. 1979. The Kabyle House or the World Reversed. In *Algeria 1960,* 133–153. Cambridge: Cambridge University Press.

Bourguet, Marie Noelle, Lucette Valensï, and Nathan Wachtel, eds. 1986. *Between Memory and History.* (Special issue of *History and Anthropology* 2[2]). New York: G&B Harwood.

Bouysse-Cassagne, Thérèse. 1975. Pertinencia etnica, status económico y lenguas en Charcas a fines del siglo XVI. In N. D. Cook, ed., *Tasa de la visita general de Francisco de Toledo,* 312–328. Lima: Universidad Nacional Mayor de San Marcos.

Bouysse-Cassagne, Thérèse. 1978. L'espace aymara: Urco et uma. *Annales E. S. C.* 33(5–6): 1057–1080.

Bouysse-Cassagne, Thérèse. 1987. *La identidad aymara: Aproximación histórica.* La Paz: HISBOL/IFEA.

Bouysse-Cassagne, Thérèse. 1988. *Lluvias y cenizas: Dos Pachacuti en la historia.* La Paz: HISBOL.

Bouysse-Cassagne, Thérèse. In Press. De Empedocles a Tunupa: Evangeliz ación, hagiografia y mitos. In Thérèse Bouysse-Cassagne, ed., *Saberes y Memorias en los Andes: Homenaje a Thierry Saignes,* 151–206. Lima: Institute Frances de E Studios Andinos.

Briggs, Lucy Therina. 1991. El k″arik″ari en dos textos de lengua aymara: Análisis morfosintáctico y del discurso. Paper read at the 47th Congreso Internacional de Americanistas, Tulane University, July 7–11.

Briggs, Lucy Therina. 1993. *El idioma Aymara: Variantes sociales y regionales.* La Paz: ILCA.

Brown, Jonathan, and John H. Elliott. 1980. *A Palace for a King.* New Haven: Yale University Press.

Buechler, Hans. 1980. *The Masked Media: Aymara Fiestas and Social Interaction in the Bolivian Highlands.* New York: Mouton.

Buechler, Hans, and Judith Marie Buechler. 1971. *The Bolivian Aymara.* New York: Holt, Rinehart and Winston.

Burga, Manuel. 1988. *Nacimiento de una utopía.* Lima: Insituto de Apoyo Agrario.

Burga, Manuel. 1992. El Corpus Christi y la nobleza Inca colonial: Memoria e identidad. In Heraclio Bonilla, ed., *Los conquistados: 1492 y la población indígena de las Américas,* 317–330. Quito: Tercer Mundo Editores/FLACSO/Libri Mundi.

Burke, Peter, ed. 1991. *New Perspectives in Historical Writing.* University Park: Pennsylvania State University Press.

Burkhart, Louise M. 1989. *The Slippery Earth: Nahua-Christian Moral Dialoque in Sixteenth-Century Mexico.* Tucson: University of Arizona Press.

Cajías de la Vega, Fernando. 1978. La población indígena de Paria en 1785. In Martha U. de Aguirre et al., eds., *Estudios bolivianos en homenaje a Gunnar Mendoza L.,* 41–100. La Paz, Bolivia.

Cajías de la Vega, Fernando. 1987. La sublevación tupacamarista de 1780 en Oruro y las provincias aledañas: Sublevación de indios y revuelta criolla. Ph.D. thesis, Universidad de Sevilla.

Callapiña, Supno, y otros Khipukamayuqs. 1974. *Relación de la descendencia, gobierno y conquista de los Incas.* (1542–1608). Prologue by Juan José Vega. Lima: Ediciones de la Biblioteca Universitaria.

Cangiano, María Cecilia. 1988. Curas, caciques, y comunidades en el Alto Perú: Chayanta a fines del siglo xvii. Unpublished manuscript. Jujuy.

Capoche, Luis. 1959. *Relación general de la Villa Imperial de Potosí.* (1585). Biblioteca de Autores Españoles, vol. 12. Madrid.

Carmagnani, Marcello. 1988. *El regreso de los dioses: El proceso de reconstitución de la identidad étnica en Oaxaca, siglos XVII y XVII.* México: Fondo de Cultura Económica.

Caro Baroja, Julio. 1965. *The World of the Witches.* Trans. from the Spanish by O. N. V. Glendinning. Chicago: University of Chicago Press.

Carter, Willaim E. 1964. *Aymara Communities and Bolivian Agrarian Reform.* Social Science Monograph No. 24. Gainesville: University of Florida.

Carter, William E. 1968. Secular Reinforcement in Aymara Death Ritual. *American Anthropologist* 70: 238–263.

Carter, William E. 1977. Trial Marriage in the Andes? In Ralph Bolton and Enrique Mayer, eds., *Andean Kinship and Marriage*, 177–216. Washington, D.C.: American Anthropological Association.

Carter, William E., and Mauricio Mamani P. 1982. *Irpa Chico: Individuo y comunidad en la cultura aymara*. La Paz: Librería-Editorial Juventúd.

Celestino, Olinda, and Albert Meyers. 1981. *Las Cofradías en el Perú: Región central*. Editionen der Iberoamericana: Reihe 3, Monographien u. Aufsätze; 6. Frankfurt/Main: Verlag Klaus Dieter Vervuert.

Cereceda, Verónica. 1986. The Semiology of Andean Textiles: The Talegas of Isluga. In John V. Murra, Nathan Wachtel, and Jacques Revel, eds., *Anthropological History of Andean Polities*, 149–173. New York: Cambridge University Press.

Cereceda, Verónica. 1987. Aproximaciones a una estética andina: De la belleza al tinku. In Thérèse Bouysse-Cassagne, Olivia Harris, Tristan Platt, and Verónica Cereceda, eds., *Tres reflexiones sobre el pensamiento andino*, 133–231. La Paz: HISBOL.

Certeau, Michel de. 1984. *The Practice of Everyday Life*. Trans. Steven F. Rendall. Berkeley: University of California Press.

Chance, John K., and William B. Taylor. 1985. Cofradías and Cargos: An Historical Perspective on the Mesoamerican Civil Religious Hierarchy. *American Ethnologist* 12(1): 1–26.

Choque Canqui, Roberto. 1979. Las haciendas de los caciques "Guarachi" en el Alto Perú. *América indígena* 4:733–748.

Choque Canqui, Roberto. 1986. *Las masacres de Jesús de Machaca*. La Paz: Ediciones Chitakolla.

Choque Canqui, Roberto. 1992. Los Aymaras y la cuestión colonial. In Heraclio Bonilla, ed., *Los conquistados: 1492 y la problación indígena de las Américas*, 127–146. Quito: Tercer Mundo Editores/FLACSO/Libri Mundi.

Christian, William A. 1981. *Local Religion in Sixteenth Century Spain*. Princeton: Princeton University Press.

Cieza de León, Pedro. 1984. *Crónica del Perú, Primera Parte*. (1553). Lima: Pontificia Universidad Católica del Perú.

Cieza de León, Pedro. 1986. *Crónica del Perú, Segunda Parte (El señorío de los Incas)*. (1553). Lima: Pontifica Universidad Católica del Perú.

Clifford, James. 1988. *The Predicament of Culture: Twentieth-Century Ethnography, Literature, and Art*. Cambridge, Mass.: Harvard University Press.

Clifford, James, and George E. Marcus, eds. 1982. *Writing Culture: The Poetics and Politics of Ethnography*. Berkeley: University of California Press.

Cobo, Father Bernabé. 1979. *History of the Inca Empire*. (1653). Trans. Roland Hamilton. Austin: University of Texas Press.

Cobo, Father Bernabé. 1990. *Inca Religion and Customs*. Trans. Roland Hamilton. Austin: University of Texas Press.

Cock C., Guillermo, and Mary E. Doyle. 1979. Del culto solar a la clandestinidad de Inti e Punchao. *Historia y cultura* (Lima) 12: 51–73.

Cohn, Bernard. 1980. History and Anthropology: The State of Play. *Comparative Studies in Society and History* 22: 198–221.

Cohn, Bernard. 1987. *An Anthropologist among the Historians and Other Essays.* Delhi: Oxford University Press.

Cole, Jeffrey A. 1985. *The Potosí Mita, 1573–1700: Compulsory Indian Labor in the Andes.* Stanford: Stanford University Press.

Collins, Jane L. 1988. *Unseasonal Migrations: The Effect of Rural Labor Scarcity in Peru.* Princeton: Princeton University Press.

Comaroff, Jean. 1985. *Body of Power, Spirit of Resistance: The Culture and History of a South African People.* Chicago: University of Chicago Press.

Comaroff, John L. 1987. Of Totemism and Ethnicity: Consciousness, Practice and the Signs of Inequality. *Ethnos* 52(3–4): 301–323.

Comaroff, Jean, and John L. Comaroff. 1991. *Of Revelation and Revolution: Christianity, Colonialism and Consciousness in South Africa,* vol 1. Chicago: University of Chicago Press.

Comaroff, John L., and Jean Comaroff. 1992. *Ethnography and the Historical Imagination.* Boulder: Westview Press.

Condarco Morales, Ramiro. 1966. *Zárate el "Temible" Wilka: Historia de la rebelión indígena de 1899.* La Paz.

Condori Chura, Leandro, and Esteban Ticona Alejo. 1992. *El escribano de los caciques apoderados/Kasikinakan purirarunakan qillqiripa.* La Paz: HISBOL/THOA.

Connerton, Paul. 1989. *How Societies Remember.* Cambridge: Cambridge University Press.

Conrad, Geoffry W., and Arthur A. Demarest. 1984. *Religion and Empire: The Dynamics of Aztec and Inca Expansionism.* Cambridge: Cambridge University Press.

Cook, Noble David. 1981. *Demographic Collapse: Indian Peru, 1520–1620.* Cambridge: Cambridge University Press.

Cook, Noble David, ed. 1975. *Tasa de la visita general de Francisco de Toledo.* Lima: Universidad Nacional Mayor de San Marcos.

Cook, Noble David, and Alexandra Parma Cook. 1993. *Good Faith and Truthful Ignorance: A Case of Transatlantic Bigamy.* Durham, N.C.: Duke University Press.

Crandon-Malamud, Libbet. 1993. *From the Fat of Our Souls: Social Change, Political Process, and Medical Pluralism in Bolivia.* Berkeley: University of California Press.

Cummins, Tom. 1994. Representation in the Sixteenth Century and the Colonial Image of the Inca. In Elizabeth Hill Boone and Walter D. Mignolo, eds., *Writing Without Words,* 188–219. Durham, N.C.: Duke University Press.

Davis, Natalie Zemon. 1987. *Fiction in the Archives: Pardon Tales and Their Tellers in Sixteenth-Century France.* Stanford: Stanford University Press.

Davis, Natalie, and Randolph Starn, eds. 1989. *Memory and Counter-Memory.* Special issue of *Representations* (26).

del Río, Mercedes. 1989. Estructuración étnica Qharaqhara y su desarticulación colonial. *Historia y cultura* (La Paz) 15: 35–73.

del Río, Mercedes. 1990. La tributación indígena en el repartimiento de Paria, siglo xvi. *Revista de Indias* 50(189): 397–429.

del Río, Mercedes, and José M. Gordillo. 1993. *La Visita de Tiquipaya (1573): Análisis étno-demográfico de un padrón toledano.* Cochabamba, Bolivia: UMSS–CERES–ODEC/FRE.

Demarest, Arthur A. 1981. *Viracocha: The Nature and Antiquity of the Andean High God.* Cambridge, Mass.: Harvard University Press.

Desan, Susan. 1989. Crowds, Community, and Ritual in the Work of E. P. Thompson and Natalie Davis. In Lynn Hunt, ed., *The New Cultural History,* 47–71. Berkeley: University of California Press.

Díaz de Castillo, Bernal. 1964. *Verdadera y notable relación del descubrimiento y conquista de la Nueva España y Guatemala.* Vol. 1. Guatemala City: Centro Editorial "José de Pineda Ibarra."

Diez de Medina, Francisco Tadeo. 1981. *Diario de alzamiento de indios conjurados contra la ciudad de Nuestra Señora de La Paz, 1781.* Transcription, introduction, notes by María Eugenia del Valle de Siles. La Paz: Don Bosco/Banco Boliviano Americano.

Diez de San Miguel, Garcí. 1964. *Visita hecha a la provincia de Chucuito por . . . en el año 1567.* Ed. John V. Murra. Lima: Casa de la Cultura.

Dillon, Mary F., and Thomas Abercrombie. 1988. The Destroying Christ: An Aymara Myth of Conquest. In Jonathan D. Hill, ed., *Rethinking History and Myth,* 50–77. Urbana: University of Illinois Press.

Duviols, Pierre. 1973. Huari y llacuaz, agricultores y pastores: Un dualismo prehispánico de oposición y complementaridad. *Revista del Museo Nacional* (Lima) 39: 153–192.

Duviols, Pierre. 1976. La capacucha: Mecanismo y función del sacrificio humano, su proyección, su papel en la política integracionista, y en la economía redistributiva del Tawantinsuyu. *Allpanchis* 9: 11–57.

Duviols, Pierre. 1977. *La destrucción de las religiones andinas (durante la conquista y la colonia).* Trans. Alber Maruenda. Instituo de Investigaciones Históricas: Serie de Historia General, No. 9. México: Universidad Nacional Autónoma de México.

Duviols, Pierre. 1986. *Cultural andina y represión: Procesos y visitas de idolatrías y hechicerías: Cajatambo, siglo XVII.* Cusco: Centro Bartolomé de Las Casas.

Duviols, Pierre. 1993. Estudio y comentario etnohistórico. In Joan de Santa Cruz Pachacuti Salcamaygua, *Relación de antigüedades deste reyno del Perú,* 11–26. (Estudio ethnohistórico y lingüístico de Pierre Duviols y César Itier). Cusco: Institut Français d'Etudes Andines, Centro Bartolomé de Las Casas.

Earls, John. 1969. The Organization of Power in Quechua Mythology. *Journal of the Steward Anthropological Society* 1(1): 63–82.

Earls, John, 1971. The Structure of Modern Andean Social Categories. *Journal of the Steward Authropoligical Society* 3(1):69–106.

Elliott, John H. 1970. *The Old World and the New,* Cambridge: Cambridge University Press.

Espejo Ayka, Elvira. 1994. *Jiccha nä parlt' ä: Ahora les voy a narrar.* Ed. Denise Y. Arnold and Juan de Dios Yapita. La Paz: UNICEF/Casa de las Américas.

Espinoza Soriano, Waldemar. 1969. El "Memorial" de Charcas: "Crónica" inédita de 1582. *Cantuta: Revista de la Universidad Nacional de Educación* (Chosica, Perú), 117–152.

Espinoza Soriano, Waldemar. 1981. El reino Aymara de Quillaca-Asanaque, siglos XV y XVI. *Revista del Museo Nacional* (Lima) 45: 175–274.

Estenssoro Fuchs, Juan Carlos. 1992. Los bailes de los indios y el proyecto colonial. *Revista andina* 20(2): 353–404.

Estete, Miguel de. 1924. *Noticia del Perú.* (1535?). Colección de libros y documentos referentes a las historia del Perú, series 2, vol. 8. Lima.

Estete, Miguel de. 1987. Noticia del Perú. (1535?). In F. Carrillo, comp., *Cartas y cronistas del descubrimiento y la conquista.* Lima: Editorial Horizonte.

Evans-Pritchard, E. E. 1962. Anthropology and History. In his *Essays in Social Anthropology,* 45–65. London: Faber and Faber.

Fabian, Johannes. 1983. *Time and the Other: How Anthropology Makes Its Object.* New York: Columbia University Press.

Fabian, Johannes. 1990. Religious and Secular Colonization: Common Ground. *History and Anthropology* 4: 339–355.

Farriss, Nancy M. 1968. *Crown and Clergy in Colonial Mexico, 1759–1821: The Crisis of Ecclesiastical Privilege.* London: Athlone Press.

Farriss, Nancy M. 1984. *Maya Society under Colonial Rule: The Collective Enterprise of Survival.* Princton, N.J.: Princton University Press.

Farriss, Nancy M. 1987. Remembering the Future, Anticipating the Past: History, Time and Cosmology among the Maya of Yucatan. *Comparative Studies in Society and History* 29: 566–593.

Faubion, James D. 1993. History in Anthropology. In B. Siegel, A. Beals, and S. Tyler, eds., *Annual Review of Anthropology,* vol. 22, 35–54. Palo Alto, Calif.: Annual Reviews.

Fiedler, Carol Ann. 1985. Corpus Christi in Cuzco: Festival and Ethnic Identity in the Peruvian Andes. Ph.D. dissertation, Tulane University.

Field, Les W. 1994. Who Are the Indians? Reconceptualizing Indigenous Identity, Resistance, and the Role of Social Science in Latin America. *Latin American Research Review* 29(3): 237–248.

Florescano, Enrique. 1992. La conquista y la tranformación de la memoria indígena. In Heraclio Bonilla, ed., *Los conquistados: 1492 y la población indígena de las Américas,* 67–102. Quito: Tercer Mundo Editores/FLACSO/ Libri Mundi.

Flores Galindo, Alberto. 1987a. Comunidades y doctrinas: La disputa por las almas: Sierra Central (1608–1666). In H. Bonilla et al., eds., *Comunidades campesinas,* 137–150. Chiclayo, Perú: Centro de Estudios Sociales Solidaridad.

Flores Galindo, Alberto. 1987b. *Buscando un Inca: Identidad y utopía en los Andes*. Lima: Instituto de Apoyo Agrario.

Flores Ochoa, Jorge A., ed. 1977. *Uywamicheq punarunakuna: Pastores de Puna*. Lima: Instituto de Estudios Peruanos.

Flynn, Maureen. 1989. *Sacred Charity: Confraternities and Social Welfare in Spain, 1400–1700*. Ithaca: Cornell University Press.

Fogelson, Raymond. 1989. The Ethnohistory of Events and Non-events. *Ethnohistory* 36: 133–47.

Font Ríus, José María. 1954. Les villes dans l'Espagne du moyen age: Histoire de leurs institutions administratives et judiciares. *Recueils de la Société Jean Bodin pour l'Histoire Comparative des Institutions*, vol. 6: *La ville*, part 1, 263–295. Brussels: Universite Libre de Bruxelles.

Franquemont, Edward M., Christine Franquemont, and Billie Jean Isbell. 1992. Awaq Ñawi: El ojo del tejedor: La práctica de la cultura en el tejido. *Revista andina* 10(1): 47–80.

Fraser, Valerie. 1990. *The Architecture of Conquest: Building in the Viceroyalty of Peru, 1535–1635*. New York: Cambridge University Press.

Friedlander, Judith. 1975. *Being Indian in Hueyapan: A Study of Forced Identity in Contemporary Mexico*. New York: St. Martin's Press.

García-Canclini, Nestor. 1992. *Culturas híbridas: Estrategias para entrar y salir de la modernidad*. Buenos Aires: Editorial Sudamericana.

Geertz, Clifford. 1980. *Negara: The Theatre State in Nineteenth-Century Bali*. Princton: Princton University Press.

Gell, Alfred. 1992. *The Anthropology of Time*. London: Berg.

Gibson, Charles. 1964. *The Aztecs under Spanish Rule: A History of the Indians of the Valley of Mexico, 1519–1810*. Stanford: Stanford University Press.

Giddens, Anthony. 1984. *The Consitution of Society: Outline of the Theory of Structuration*. Berkeley: University of California Press.

Gill, Lesley. 1994. *Precarious Dependencies: Gender, Class, and Domestic Service in Bolivia*. New York: Columbia University Press.

Gillis, J. R., ed. 1994. *Commemorations: The Politics of National Identity*. Princton: Princeton University Press.

Ginzburg, Carlo. 1982. *The Cheese and the Worms: The Cosmos of a Sixteenth Century Miller*. New York: Penguin.

Girault, Louis. 1987. *Kallawaya: Curanderos itinerantes de los Andes*. La Paz: UNICEF/OPS/OMS.

Gisbert, Teresa. 1980. *Iconografía y mitos indígenas en el arte*. La Paz: Gisbert y Cia.

Gisbert, Teresa, and José de Mesa. 1985. *Arquitectura andina. 1530–1830: Historia y análisis*. Colección Arzans y Vela. La Paz: Embajada de España en Bolivia.

Gisbert, Teresa, Silvia Arze, and Martha Cajías. 1987. *Arte textil y mundo andino*. La Paz: Editorial Gisbert.

Gisbert, Teresa, Juan Carlos Jemio, Roberto Montero, Elvira Salinas, and María Soledad Quiroga. 1996. Los chullpares del Río Lauca y el Parque Sajama. *Revista de la Academia Nacional de Ciencias de Bolivia*, no. 70. La Paz.

Glave, Luis Miguel. 1989. *Trajinantes: Caminos indígenas en la sociedad colonial, siglos XVI/XVII*. Lima: Instituto de Apoyo Agrario.

Godoy, Ricardo A. 1990. *Mining and Agriculture in Highland Bolivia: Ecology, History, and Commerce among the Jukumanis*. Tucson: University of Arizona Press.

Góngora, Mario. 1975. *Studies in the Colonial History of Spanish America*. Cambridge: Cambridge University Press.

González Echevarría, Roberto. 1990. *Myth and Archive: A Theory of Latin American Narrative*. New York: Cambridge University Press.

González Holguín, Diego. 1952. *Vocabulario de la lengua general de todo el Peru, llamada lengua qquichua o del Inca, compuesto por el padre . . . , de la compañia de Jesús, natural de Caçeres*. (1608). Ed. Raúl Porras Barrenechea. Lima: Imprenta Santa María.

Goody, Jack. 1986. *The Logic of Writing and the Organization of the State*. Cambridge: Cambridge University Press.

Goody, Jack, ed. 1968. *Literacy in Traditional Societies*. Cambridge: Cambridge University Press.

Gose, Peter. 1986. Sacrifice and the Commodity Form in the Andes. *Man* 21: 296–310.

Gose, Peter. 1991. House Rethatching in an Andean Annual Cycle: Practice, Meaning, and Contradiction. *American Ethnologist* 18(1): 39–66.

Gruzinski, Serge. 1989. Individualization and Acculturation: Confession among the Nahuas of Mexico from the Sixteenth to the Eighteenth Century. In Asunción Lavrin, ed., *Sexuality and Marriage in Colonial Latin America*, 96–117. Lincoln: University of Nebraska Press.

Gruzinski, Serge. 1993. *The Conquest of Mexico: The Incorporation of Indian Societies into the Western World, 16th–18th Centuries*. Trans. from the French by Eileen Corrigan. Cambridge, England: Polity Press. (Originally published as *La colonisation de l'imaginaire*, [Paris: Editions Gallimard, 1988]).

Guaman Poma de Ayala [Waman Puma], Felipe. 1980. *El primer nueva corónica y buen gobierno*. (1613). 3 vols. Ed. John V. Murra and Rolena Adorno; translations and textual analysis of the Quechua by Jorge L. Urioste. México: Siglo XXI Editores.

Guevara-Gil, Armando, and Frank Salomon. 1994. A Personal Visit: Colonial Political Ritual and the Making of Indians in the Andes. *Colonial Latin American Review* 3(1–2): 3–36.

Guilarte, Alfonso María. 1987. *El régimen señorial en el siglo XVI*. 2d ed. Madrid: Universidad de Valladolid—Caja de M. P. de Salamanca.

Gurevich, A. 1976. Time as a Problem of Cultural History. In L. Gardet, A. Gurevich, A. Kagame, C. Laree, A. Naher, et al., *Cultures and Time*, 229–243. Paris: UNESCO Press.

Gutiérrez de Santa Clara. 1963. *Historia de las guerras civiles del Perú.* Biblioteca de Autores Españoles, vol. 165. Madrid.

Halbwachs, Maurice. 1925. *Les cadres sociaux de la mémoire.* Paris: Presses Universitaires de France.

Halbwachs, Maurice. 1941. *La topographie légendaire des Evangiles en Terre Sainte.* Paris: Presses Universitaires de France.

Halbwachs, Maurice. 1994. *On Collective Memory.* Chicago: University of Chicago Press.

Haliczer, Stephen. 1981. *The Comuneros of Castile: The Forging of a Revolution, 1475–1521.* Madison: University of Wisconsin Press.

Hanke, Lewis. 1949. *The Spanish Struggle for Justice in the Conquest of America.* Philadelphia: University of Pennsylvania Press.

Hanke, Lewis. 1956–57. The 1608 Fiestas in Potosi. *Boletín del Instituto Riva-Agüero* (Lima) 3: 107–128.

Hanks, William. 1990. *Referential Practice: Language and Lived Space among the Maya.* Chicago: University of Chicago Press.

Hardman, M. J. 1981. *The Aymara Language in Its Social and Cultural Context.* Gainesville: University Presses of Florida.

Hardman, M. J. 1986. Data-Source Marking in the Jaqi Languages. In Wallace Chafe, ed., *Evidentiality in North and South America,* 113–136. Norwood, N.J.: Ablex.

Hardman, M. J., Juana Vásquez, and Juan de Dios Yapita, eds. 1975. *Aymara ar yatiqañataki* [To learn Aymara]. 2d ed., 3 vols. Ann Arbor, Mich.: University Microfilms.

Hardman, M. J., Juana Vásquez and Juan de Dios Yapita, eds. 1988. *Aymara: Compendio de estructura fonológica y gramatical.* La Paz: Gramma Impresión and ILCA.

Hardoy, J., and R. P. Schaedel, eds. 1969. *El proceso de la urbanización en América desde sus orígenes hasta nuestros días.* Buenos Aires.

Harmann, Inge Maria. 1988. Collective Labor and Ritual of Reciprocity in the Southern Bolivian Andes. Ph.D. disseration, Cornell University.

Harris, Olivia. 1978a. El parentesco y la economía vertical en el ayllu Laymi (norte de Potosí). *Avances* (La Paz) 1: 51–64.

Harris, Olivia. 1978b. Kinship and the Vertical Economy of the Laymi Ayllu, Norte de Potosí. *Actes du XLII Congrés International des Americanistes (Paris 1976),* vol. 4, 165–178. Paris.

Harris, Olivia. 1978c. Complementarity and Conflict: An Andean View of Women and Men. In J. LaFontaine, ed., *Sex and Age as Principles of Social Differentiation,* 21–40. ASA Monograph 17. London: Academic Press.

Harris, Olivia. 1978d. Del l'asymétrie au triangle: Transformations symboliques au nord de Potosí. *Annales E.S.C.* 33(5–6): 1108–1126.

Harris, Olivia. 1980. The Power of Signs: Gender, Culture, and the Wild in the Bolivian Andes. In C. MacCormack and M. Strathern, eds. *Nature, Culture and Gender,* 70–94. Cambridge: Cambridge University Press.

Harris, Olivia. 1982. The Dead and Devils among the Bolivian Laymi. In Maurice Bloch and Jonathan Parry, eds., *Death and the Regeneration of Life,* 45–73. Cambridge: Cambridge University Press.

Harris, Olivia. 1986. La pachamama: Significados de la madre en el discurso boliviano. In Verena Stolcke, ed., *Mujeres latinoamericanas: Diez ensayos y una historia colectiva,* 57–80. Lima: Flora Tristán (Centro de la Mujer Peruana).

Harris, Olivia. 1987. Phaxsima y qullqi: Los poderes y significados del dinero en el norte de Potosí. In O. Harris, B. Larson, and E. Tandeter, eds., *La participación indígena en los mercados surandinos: Estrategias y reproducción social, siglos XVI a XX,* 235–280. La Paz: CERES.

Harrison, Regina. 1989. *Signs, Songs, and Memory in the Andes.* Austin: University of Texas Press.

Hemming, John. 1970. *The Conquest of the Incas.* New York: Macmillan.

Hernández Príncipe, Rodrigo. 1923. Mitología andina. (1624). *Inca* 1: 24–68.

Herzfeld, Michael. 1991. *A Place in History: Social and Monumental Time in a Cretan Town.* Princeton: Princeton University Press.

Hidalgo Lehuede, Jorge. 1983. Amarus y Cataris: Aspectos mesiánicos de la rebelión indígena de 1781 en Cuzco, Chayanta, La Paz y Arica. *Chungara* 10: 117–138.

Hinojosa, Eduardo. 1903. *Origen del régimen municipal en León y Castilla.* Madrid.

Hobsbawm, Eric, and Terence Ranger, eds. 1983. *The Invention of Tradition.* New York: Cambridge University Press.

Hopkins, Diane, and Albert Meyers, eds. 1988. *Manipulating the Saints: Religious Sodalities and Social Integration in Post-Conquest Latin America.* Hamburg: Wayasbah.

Howard-Malverde, Rosaleen. 1990. *The Speaking of History: "Willapaakushayki," or Ways of Telling the Past.* Institute of Latin American Studies, Research Papers, no. 21. London: University of London.

Huanca, Tomás. 1989. *El yatiri en la comunidad aymara.* La Paz: Ediciones CADA.

Hunt, Lynn. 1989. Introduction: History, Culture, and Text. In Lynn Hunt, ed., *The New Cultural History,* 1–24. Berkeley: University of California Press.

Hunt, Lynn, ed. 1989. *The New Cultural History.* Berkeley: University of California Press.

Hutton, Patrick H. 1993. *History as an Art of Memory.* Hanover, N.H.: University Press of New England.

Hyslop, John. 1979. El área Lupaqa bajo el dominio incaico: Un reconocimiento arqueológico. *Historica* 3(1): 53–78.

Hyslop, John. 1984. *The Inca Road System.* New York: Academic Press.

Isbell, Billie Jean. 1977. "Those Who Love Me": An Analysis of Andean Kinship and Reciprocity within a Ritual Context. In Ralph Bolton and Enrique Mayer, eds., *Andean Kinship and Marriage,* 81–105. Washington, D.C.: American Anthropological Association.

Isbell, Billie Jean. [1978] 1985. *To Defend Ourselves: Ecology and Ritual in an Andean Village*. 2d rev. ed. Prospect Heights, Ill.: Waveland Press.

Iwasaki, Fernando. 1994. Mujeres al borde de la perfección: Rosa de Santa María y las alumbradas de Lima. *Hispanic American Historical Review* 73(4): 581–613.

Izco Gastón, Javier. 1992. *La doble frontera: Ecología, política y ritual en el Altiplano central*. La Paz: HISBOL.

Izco Gastón, Javier, Ramiro Molina Rivero, and René Pereira Morató, eds. 1986. *Tiempo de vida y muerte*. La Paz: Consejo Nacional de Población–IDRC.

Jiménez de la Espada, Marcos, ed. 1965. *Relaciones geográficas de Indias*. (1881–97). 3 vols. Madrid: Biblioteca de Autores Españoles.

Julien, Catherine J. 1982. Inca Decimal Administration in the Lake Titicaca Region. In G. A. Collier, R. I. Rosaldo, and J. D. Wirth, eds., *The Inca and Aztec States, 1400–1800*, 119–151. New York: Academic Press.

Julien, Catherine J. 1983. *Hatunqolla: A View of Inca Rule from the Lake Titicaca Region*. Publications in Anthropology, vol. 15. Berkeley: University of California Press.

Julien, Catherine J. 1995. Oroncota entre dos mundos. In Ana María Presta, ed., *Espacio, etnías, frontera: Atenuaciones políticas en el sur del Tawantinsuyu, siglos XV–XVII*, 97–160. Sucre: Ediciones ASUR.

Kagan, Richard L. 1981. *Lawsuits and Litigants in Castile, 1500–1700*. Chapel Hill: University of North Carolina Press.

Kagan, Richard L. 1986. Philip II and the Art of the Cityscape. *Journal of Interdisciplinary History* 17(1): 115–135.

Kellogg, Susan. 1994. Histories for Anthropology: Ten Years of Historical Research and Writing by Anthropologists, 1980–1990. In Eric H. Monkkonen, ed., *Engaging the Past: The Uses of History across the Social Sciences*, 9–47. Durham: Duke University Press.

Kelly, John D., and Martha Kaplan. 1990. History, Structure, and Ritual. In B. Siegel, A. Beals, and S. Tyler, eds., *Annual Review of Anthropology*, vol. 19, 119–150. Palo Alto, Calif.: Annual Reviews.

Klein, Herbert S. 1992. *Bolivia: The Evolution of a Multi-Ethnic Society*. 2d ed. New York: Oxford University Press.

Kolata, Alan. 1994. *The Tiwanaku*. New York: Blackwell.

Kretch, Shepard, III. 1991. The State of Ethnohistory. In B. Siegel, A. Beals, and S. Tyler, eds. *Annual Review of Anthropology*, vol. 20, 345–375. Palo Alto, Calif.: Annual Reviews.

La Barre, Weston. 1948. *The Aymara Indians of the Lake Titicaca Plateau, Bolivia*. Washington, D.C.: American Anthropological Association.

Ladurie, Emmanuel Le Roy. 1979. *Montaillou: The Promised Land of Error*. New York: Vintage Books.

Langer, Eric D. 1990. Andean Rituals of Revolt: The Chayanta Rebellion of 1927. *Ethnohistory* 37(3): 227–253.

Larson, Brooke. 1988. *Colonialism and Agrarian Transformation in Bolivia: Cochabamba, 1550–1900*. Princeton: Princeton University Press.

Las Casas, Bartolomé de. 1958. *Apologética histórica,* vol. 3. Biblioteca de Autores Españoles, vol. 105. Madrid.

Lechner, J. 1981. El concepto de "policía" y su presencia en la obra de los primeros historiadores de Indias. *Revista de Indias* 41:395–409.

Le Goff, Jacques. 1992. *History and Memory.* Trans. Steven Rendall and Elizabeth Claman. New York: Columbia University Press.

Leonard, Irving. [1949] 1992. *Books of the Brave: Being an Account of Books and of Men in the Spanish Conquest and Settlement of the Sixteenth-Century New World.* Berkeley: University of California Press.

Leveau, Philippe. 1983. La ville antique et l'organisation de l'espace rural: *Villa, ville, village. Annales E.S.C.* 38: 920–942.

Levillier, Roberto D., ed. 1918. *La audencia de Charcas: Correspondencia de presidentes y oidores, documentos del Archivo de Indios,* vol. 1: *1561–1579.* Madrid: Colección de publicaciones históricos de la Biblioteca del Congreso Argentino.

Levillier, Roberto D., ed. 1929. *Ordenanzas de don Francisco de Toledo, virrey del Perú, 1569–1581.* Madrid: Imprenta de Juan Pueyo.

Lewin, Boleslao. 1957. *La rebelión de Túpac Amaru.* Buenos Aires: Hachette.

Liebscher, Verena. 1986. *La iconografía de los queros.* Lima: Herrera Editores.

Liffman, Paul. 1977. Vampires of the Andes. *Michigan Discussions in Anthropology* 2: 205–226.

Llanque Chana, Domingo. 1990. *La cultura Aymara: Desestructuración o afirmación de identidad.* Lima: Instituto de Estudios Aymaras.

Lockhart, James. 1968. *Spanish Peru, 1532–1560: A Colonial Society.* Madison: University of Wisconsin Press.

Lockhart, James. 1972. *The Men of Cajamarca: A Social and Biographical Study of the First Conquerors of Peru.* Austin: University of Texas Press.

Lockhart, James. 1992. *The Nahuas after the Conquest: A Social and Cultural History of the Indians of Central Mexico, Sixteenth through Eighteenth Centuries.* Stanford: Stanford University Press.

Lohmann Villena, Guillermo. 1966. La restitución por corregidores y encomenderos: Un aspecto de la incidencia Lascasiana en el Perú. *Anuario de estudios americanos* (Seville) 23:21–89.

MacCormack, Sabine. 1984. From the Sun of the Incas to the Virgin of Copacabana. *Representations* 8: 30–60.

MacCormack, Sabine. 1985. "The Heart Has Its Reasons." Predicaments of Missionary Christianity in Early Colonial Peru. *Hispanic American Historical Review* 65(3): 443–466.

MacCormack, Sabine. 1988a. Atahualpa y el libro. *Revista de Indias* 48: 693–714.

MacCormack, Sabine. 1988b. Pachacuti, Miracles, Punishment, and Last Judgment: Visionary Past and Prophetic Future in Early Colonial Peru. *American Historical Review* 93(4): 960–1006.

MacCormack, Sabine. 1991. *Religion in the Andes*. Princeton: Princeton University Press.

Málaga Medina, Alejandro. 1974. Las reducciones en el Perú durante el gobierno del virrey Francisco de Toledo. *Anuario de estudios americanos* 31: 819–842.

Málaga Medina, Alejandro. 1975. Las reducciones en el Virreinato del Perú, 1532–1580. *Revista de historia de América* (México) 80: 9–42.

Mallon, Florencia E. 1992a. Entre la Utopía y la marginalidad: Comunidades indígenas y culturas políticas en México y los Andes, 1780–1990. *Historia mexicana* 42(2): 473–504.

Mallon, Florencia E. 1992b. Indian Communities, Political Cultures, and the State in Latin-America, 1780–1990. *Journal of Latin American Studies* 24: 35–53.

Mallon, Florencia E. 1994. The Promise and Dilemma of Subaltern Studies: Perspectives from Latin American History. *American Historical Review* 99(5): 1491–1525.

Mannheim, Bruce. 1986. Popular Song and Popular Grammar, Poetry and Metalanguage. *Word* 37(1–2): 45–75.

Mannheim, Bruce. 1991. *The Language of the Inka since the European Invasion*. Austin: University of Texas Press.

Maravall, José Antonio. 1963. *Las comunidades de Castilla: Una primera revolución moderna*. Madrid: Revista de Occidente.

Maravall, José Antonio. 1972. *Estado moderno y mentalidad social (siglos XV a XVII)*. Madrid: Revista de Occidente.

Maravall, José Antonio. 1979. *Poder, honor y élites en el siglo VXII*. Madrid: Siglo XXI.

Maravall, José Antonio. 1984. Trabajo y exclusión: El trabajador manual en el sistema social de la primera modernidad. In J. A. Maravall, ed., *Estudios de historia del pensamiento español*, 363–392. Madrid: Ediciones Cultura Hispánica.

Maravall, José Antonio. 1987. *Culture of the Baroque*. Minneapolis: University of Minnesota Press.

Martínez, Gabriel. 1976. El sistema de los uywiris en Isluga. In *Homenaje al Dr. Gustavo Le Paige*, 255–327. Antofagasta, Chile: Universidad del Norte.

Martínez, Gabriel. 1983. Los dioses de los cerros en los Andes. *Journal de la Société des Américanistes* 69:85–115.

Martínez, Gabriel, 1987. *Una mesa ritual en Sucre: Aproximaciones semióticas al ritual andino*. La Paz: HISBOL/ASUR.

Martínez, Gabriel. 1989. *Espacio y pensamiento: Andes meridionales*. La Paz: HISBOL.

Martínez, Gabriel. 1992. La dimensión espiritual y conceptual de un proyecto de desarrollo: El proyecto textil Jalq'a Tarabuco. In Johnny Dávalos, Verónica Cereceda, and Gabriel Martínez, *Textiles Tarabuco*. Sucre, Bolivia: Ediciones ASUR.

Martínez Cereceda, José L. 1991. Acerca de las etnicidades en la puna árida en el siglo XVI. In S. Arze, R. Barragan, L. Escobari, and X. Medinaceli, eds., *Etnicidad, economía y simbolismo en los Andes*. 2d Congreso Internacional de Ethnohistoria, Coroico. La Paz: HISBOL-IFEA-SBH-ASUR.

Martínez Cereceda, José L. 1995. *Autoridades en los Andes, los atributos del señor*. Lima: Pontificia Universidad Católica del Perú, Fondo Editorial.

Marx, Karl. 1963. *The Eighteenth Brumaire of Louis Bonaparte*. (1852). New York: International Publishers.

Matienzo, Juan de. 1967. *Gobierno del Perú*. (1567). Travaux de l'Institut français d'etudes andines, vol 11. Lima and Paris.

Mayer, Enrique. 1977. Beyond the Nuclear Family. In Ralph Bolton and Enrique Mayer, eds., *Andean Kinship and Marriage*, 60–80. Washington, D.C.: American Anthropological Association.

Mayer, Enrique. 1982. *A Tribute to the Household: Domestic Economy and the Encomienda in Colonial Peru*. Institute of Latin-American Studies. Austin: University of Texas.

Medlin, Mary Ann. 1984. Awayqa Sumaj Calchapi: Weaving, Social Organization, and Identity in Calcha, Bolivia. Ph.D. dissertation, University of North Carolina, Chapel Hill.

Mercado de Peñalosa, J. 1965. Relación del la provincia de Pacajes. (1583). In *Relaciones geográficas de Indias—Perú*, vol. 1, 334–341. Biblioteca de Autores Españoles, vols. 183–185. Madrid.

Meyerson, Julia. 1990. *Tambo*. Austin: University of Texas Press.

Mignolo, Walter D. 1993. Misunderstanding and Colonization: The Reconfiguration of Memory and Space. *South Atlantic Quarterly* 92(2): 209–260.

Mignolo, Walter D. 1994. Signs and Their Transmission: The Question of the Book in the New World. In Elizabeth Hill Boone and Walter D. Mignolo, eds., *Writing Without Words*, 220–270. Durham: Duke University Press.

Millones, Luis. 1990. *El retorno de las huacas: Estudios y documentos del siglo XVI*. Lima: IEP-Sidea.

Miranda, Lucas, and Daniel Moricio. 1992. *Testimonios de vida Ura-Moratos*. La Paz: ASUR-HISBOL.

Mitchell, Timothy. 1991. *Colonising Egypt*. Berkeley: University of California Press.

Molina, Cristóbal de (El Cuzqueño). 1916. *Relación de las fábulas y ritos de los Incas*. (c. 1575). Ed. Horacio Urteaga and Carlos A. Romero. Colección de libros y documentos referentes a la historia del Perú, series 1, vol 1. Lima.

Molina, Cristóbal de (El Cuzqueño). 1989. Relación de las fábulas i ritos de los ingas . . . In Cristóbal de Molina and Cristóbal de Albornóz, *Fábulas y mitos de los Incas*, 47–134. Ed. Henrique Urbano and Pierre Duviols. Crónicas de América, 48. Madrid: Historia 16.

Molina Rivero, Ramiro. 1986a. Estrategias socio económicas y reproductivas en la comunidad de Pampa-Aullagas, Oruro. In Javier Izko Gastón, Ramiro Molina Rivero, and René Pereira Morató, eds., *Tiempo de vida y muerte*. La Paz: Consejo Nacional de Población–IDRC.

Molina Rivero, Ramiro. 1986b. *Etnicidad y marginalidad: Los Aymaras y Urus del lago Poopó*. La Paz: UNICEF.

Molinié-Fioravanti, Antoinette. 1987. El regreso de Viracocha. *Bulletin de l'Institute français d'études andines* 16(3–4): 71–83.

Molinié-Fioravanti, Antoinette. 1991. Sebo bueno, indio muerto: La estructura de una creencia andina. *Bulletin de l'Institut français d'études andines* 20 (1): 79–92.

Momigliano, Arnaldo. 1977. *Essays in Ancient and Modern Historiography*. Oxford: Basil Blackwell.

Monast, Jacques E. 1972. *Los indios Aimaraes: ¿Evangelizados o sólamente bautizados?* Buenos Aires.

Morales, Adolfo de, ed. 1977. *Repartimiento de tierras por el Inca Huayna Cápac (Testimonio de un documento de 1556)*. Cochabamba: Museo Arqueológico, Universidad Mayor de San Simón.

Morote Best, Efraín. 1951–52. El degollador (ñaqaq). *Tradición* (Cusco) 11: 67–91.

Morris, Craig. 1979. Maize Beer in the Economics, Politics, and Religion of the Inca Empire. In C. F. Gastineau, W. J. Darby and F. B. Turner, eds., *Fermented Food Beverages in Nuturition*. New York: Academic Press.

Morris, Craig, and Donald E. Thompson. 1985. *Huánuco Pampa: An Inca City and Its Hinterland*. London: Thames and Hudson.

Moseley, Michael E. 1992. *The Incas and Their Ancestors: The Archaeology of Peru*. New York: Thames and Hudson.

Moxó, Salvador de. 1964. Los señoríos: En torno a una problemática para el estudio del régimen señorial. *Hispania* 24: 185–236, 399–430.

Munn, Nancy D. 1992. The Cultural Anthropology of Time: A Critical Essay. *Annual Review of Anthropology* 21: 93–123.

Murra, John V. 1962. Cloth and Its Functions in the Inka State. *American Anthropologist* 65: 710–728.

Murra, John V. 1964. Una apreciación etnológica de la visita. In Garcí Diez de San Miguel, *Visita hecha a la provincia de Chucuito por Garcí Diez de San Miguel en el año 1567*, 421–444. Ed. John V. Murra. Lima: Casa de la Cultura del Perú.

Murra, John V. 1964. Rebaños y pastores en la economía del Tawantinsuyu. *Revista peruana de cultura* 2: 76–101. (Republished in Murra 1975a, 117–144).

Murra, John V. 1967. La visita de los chupachu como fuente etnológica. In Iñigo Ortiz de Zúñiga, *Visita de la provincia de León del Huánico (1562) por Iñigo Ortiz de Zúñiga*, vol. 1, 381–406. Ed. John V. Murra. Huánuco, Peru: Universidad Hermilio Valdizán.

Murra, John V. 1968. An Aymara Kingdom in 1567. *Ethnohistory* 15(2): 115–151. (Republished in revised Spanish translation in Murra 1975a, 193–223).

Murra, John V. 1970. Current Research and Prospects in Andean Ethnohistory. *Latin American Research Review* 61: 3–36. (Republished in Spanish translation in Murra 1975a, 275–312).

Murra, John V. 1972. El control vertical de un máximo de pisos ecológicos en las sociedades andinas. In Iñigo Ortiz de Zúñiga, *Visita de la provincia de León de Huánuco* (1562) *por Iñigo Ortiz de Zúñiga,* vol. 2, 430–476. Ed. John V. Murra. Huánuco, Peru: Universidad Hermilio Valdizán. (Republished in Murra 1975a, 59–115).

Murra, John V. 1975a. *Formaciones económicas y políticas del mundo andino.* Lima: Instituto de Estudios Peruanos.

Murra, John V. 1975b. Las etno-categorías de un khipu estatal. In Murra, *Formaciones económicas y políticas del mundo andino,* 243–254. Lima: Instituto de Estudios Peruanos.

Murra, John V. 1977. La correspondencia entre un "capitán de la mita" y su apoderado en Potosí. *Historia y cultura* (La Paz) 3: 45–58.

Murra, John V. 1978. La guerre et les rebellions dans L'expansion de l'etat Inka. *Annales E.S.C.* 33(5–6): 926–935.

Murra, John V. 1984. Andean Societies before 1532. In Leslie Bethell, ed., *The Cambridge History of Latin America,* vol. 1. Cambridge: Cambridge University Press.

Murra, John V. 1989. Cloth and Its Functions in the Inka State. In Annette B. Weiner and Jane Schneider, eds., *Cloth and Human Experience.* Washington, D.C.: Smithsonian Institution Press.

Murua, Martin de. 1952–54. *Historia general del Perú.* Introduction and notes by M. Ballesteros. Madrid.

Nader, Helen, 1990. *Liberty in Absolutist Spain.* Baltimore: Johns Hopkins University Press.

Nash, June. 1979. *We Eat the Mines and the Mines Eat Us: Dependency and Exploitation in Bolivian Tin Mines.* New York: Columbia University Press.

Nora, Pierre. 1984. *Les lieux de la mémoire.* 3 vols. Paris: Gallimard.

Nuñez, Lautaro, and Thomas D. Dillehay. 1979. *Movilidad giratoria, armonia social y desarollo en los Andes Meridionales: Patrones de tráfico e interacción económica.* Antofagasta: Universidad del Norte.

O'Brien, J., and W. Roseberry, eds. 1991. *Golden Ages, Dark Ages: Imagining the Past in Anthropology and History.* Berkeley: University of California Press.

Ong, Walter J. 1988. *Orality and Literacy: The Technologising of the Word.* New York: Methuen and Co.

O'Phelan Godoy, Scarlett. 1985. *Rebellions and Revolts in 18th Century Peru and Upper Peru.* Cologne: Böhlau Verlag.

Orlove, Benjamin. 1994. Sticks and Stones: Ritual Battles and Play in the Southern Peruvian Andes. In D. Poole, ed., *Unruly Order: Violence, Power, and Cultural Identity in the High Provinces of Southern Peru.* Boulder: Westview Press.

Pachacuti Yamqui, Joan de Santa Cruz. 1968. *Relación de antigüedades deste reyno del Perú.* In Crónicas peruanas de interés indígena, Biblioteca de Autores Española, vol. 209. Madrid.

Pachacuti Yamqui, Joan de Santa Cruz. 1993. *Relación de antigüedades deste reyno del Perú.* Estudio ethnohistórico y lingüístico de Pierre Duviols y César Itier. Cusco: Institut Français d'Etudes Andines, Centro de Estudios Regionales Andinos Bartolomé de las Casas.

Pagden, Anthony. 1983. *The Fall of Natural Man.* Cambridge: Cambridge University Press.

Parmentier, Richard. 1987. *The Sacred Remains: Myth, History and Polity in Belau.* Chicago: University of Chicago Press.

Pärssinen, Martti. 1992. *Tawantinsuyu: The Inca State and Its Political Organization.* Studia Historica 43. Helsinki: Societas Historica Finlandiae.

Paulson, Susan. 1990. Double-talk in the Andes: Ambiguous Discourse as Means of Surviving Contact. *Journal of Folklore Research* 27(1–2): 51–65.

Pease, Franklin. 1973. *El dios creador andino.* Lima: Mosca Azul Editores.

Pease, Franklin. 1978. Los visitas como testimonio andino. In Félix Miró-Quesada, Franklin Pease, and David Sobrevilla, eds., *Historia: Problema y promesa,* vol. 1, 437–453. Lima: Pontificia Universidad Católica del Perú.

Pease, Franklin. 1992. *Curacas, reciprocidad y riqueza.* Lima: Pontificia Universidad Católica del Perú.

Pease, Franklin, ed. 1977. *Collaguas I.* Lima: Pontificia Universidad Católica del Perú.

Penry, S. Elizabeth. 1993. The Moral Economy of the Andean World. *South Eastern Latin Americanist* 37(2): 22–36.

Penry, S. Elizabeth. 1996. Transformations in Indigenous Authority and Identity in Resettlement Towns of Colonial Charcas (Alto Perú). Ph.D. dissertation, University of Miami.

Pérez Bocanegra, Juan. 1631. *Ritual formulario e institución de Cura, para administrar a los naturales de este Reyno . . .* Lima.

Platt, Tristan. 1978a. Symétries en miroir: Le concept de yanantin chez les Macha de Bolivie. *Annales E.S.C.* 33(5–6): 1081–1107.

Platt, Tristan. 1978b. Acerca del sistema tributario pre-toledano en el Alto Peru. *Avances* (La Paz) 1: 33–46.

Platt, Tristan. 1982a. *Estado boliviano y ayllu andino: Tierra y tributo en el norte de Potosí.* Lima: Instituto de Estudios Peruanos.

Platt, Tristan. 1982b. The Role of the Andean Ayllu in the Reproduction of the Petty Commodity Regime in Northern Potosí (Bolivia). In David Lehmann, ed., *Ecology and Exchange in the Andes,* 27–69. Cambridge: Cambridge University Press.

Platt, Tristan. 1983. Identidad andina y conciencia proletaria: Qhuyaruna y ayllu en el norte de Potosí. *HISLA revista latinoamericana de historia económica y social* 2: 47–73.

Platt, Tristan. 1984. Liberalism and Ethnocide in the Southern Andes. *History Workshop Journal* 17: 3–18.

Platt, Tristan. 1987a. The Andean Experience of Bolivian Liberalism. In Steve J. Stern, ed., *Resistance, Rebellion, and Consciousness in the Andean Peasant World, 18th to 20th Centuries,* 280–323. Madison: University of Wisconsin Press.

Platt, Tristan. 1987b. Entre ch'awxa y muxsa: Para una historia del pensamiento politico Aymara. In Thérèse Bouysse-Cassagne, Olivia Harris, Tristan Platt, and Verónica Cereceda, eds., *Tres reflexiones sobre el pensamiento andino,* 61–132. La Paz: HISBOL.

Platt, Tristan. 1987c. The Andean Soldiers of Christ: Confraternity Organization, the Mass of the Sun and Regenerative Warfare in Rural Potosí (18th–20th Centuries). *Journal de la Société des Américanistes* 73: 157–175.

Platt, Tristan. 1992. The Sound of Light: Speech, Script and Metaphor in the Southern Andes. In S. Arze, R. Barragan, L. Escobari, and X. Medinacelli, eds., *Ethnicidad, economía, y simbolismo en los Andes,* 439–466. La Paz: HISBOL/IFEA/SBH-ASUR.

Platt, Tristan, Thérèse Bouysse-Cassagne, Olivia Harris, and Thierry Saignes, eds. In press. *Qaraqara/Charka: Fuentes para el estudio de una confederación Aymara (siglos XV-XVII).* La Paz: CDA-IFEA-HISBOL.

Pocock, D. 1967. The Anthropology of Time Reckoning. In J. Middleton, ed., *Myth and Cosmos,* 303–314. New York: Natural History Press.

Polo Ondegardo, Juan. 1916a. *Los errores y supersticiones de los indios, sacadas del tratado y averiguación que hizo el licenciado Polo.* (1554). Ed. Horacio Urteaga and Carlos A. Romero. Colección de libros y documentos referentes a la historia del Perú, series 1, vol. 3, 3–44. Lima: Sanmarti y Cía.

Polo Ondegardo, Juan. 1916b. *Relación de los fundamentos acerca del notable daño que resulta de no guardar a los indios sus fueros.* (1571). Ed. Horacio Urteaga and Carlos A. Romero. Colección de libros y documentos referentes a las historia del Perú, series 1, vol. 3, 45–186. Lima: Sanmarti y Cía.

Polo Ondegardo, Juan. [1584] 1916c. *Instrucción contra las ceremonias ritos que usan los indios, conforme al tiempo de su infidelidad.* Ed. Horacio Urteaga and Carlos A. Romero. Colección de libros y documentos referentes a la historia del Perú, series 1, vol. 3, 189–208. Lima: Sanmarti y Cía.

Polo Ondegardo, Juan. 1940. Informe del . . . al Lic. Briviesca de Muñatones sobre la perpetuidad de las encomiendas en el Perú. (1561). *Revista histórica* 13: 125–196.

Polo Ondegardo, Juan. 1990. *El mundo de los Incas:* "Relación de los fundamentos acerca del notable daño que resulta de no guardar a los indios sus fueros, 1571. ed. Laura González and Alicia Alonso. Crónicas de América, 58. Madrid: Historia 16.

Ponce Sanjines, Carlos. 1969. *Tunupa y ekako: Estudios arqueoiógicos acerca de las efigies precolombinas de dorso adunco.* La Paz.

Poole, Deborah. 1984. Ritual-Economic Calendars in Paruro: The Structure of Representation in Andean Ethnography. Ph.D. dissertation, University of Illinois, Urbana-Champaign.

Poole, Deborah. 1992. Antropología e historia andinas en los EE.UU: Buscando un reencuentro. *Revista andina* 10(1): 209–245.

Powers, Karen V. 1991. Resilient Lords and Indian Vagabonds: Wealth, Migration, and the Reproductive Transformation of Quito's Chiefdoms, 1500–1700. *Ethnohistory* 38(3): 225–249.

Pratt, Mary Louise. 1992. *Imperial Eyes: Travel Writing and Transculturation.* New York: Routledge.

Presta, Ana María, ed. 1995. *Espacio, etnías, frontera: Atenuaciones políticas en el sur del Tawantinsuyu, siglos VX–XVII.* Sucre: Ediciones ASUR.

Price, Richard. 1990. *Alabi's World.* Baltimore: Johns Hopkins University Press.

Rama, Angel. 1982. *Transculturación narrativa y novela latinoamericana.* Mexico City: Siglo XXI.

Ramírez, Susan E. 1987. The "Dueño de Indios": Thoughts on the Consequences of the Shifting Bases of Power of the "Curaca de los Viejos Antiguos" under the Spanish in Sixteenth-Century Peru. *Hispanic American Historical Review* 67(4): 575–610.

Ramírez, Susan E., ed. 1989. *Indian-Religious Relations in Colonial Spanish America.* Syracuse: Maxwell School of Citizenship and Public Affairs, Syracuse University.

Ramírez del Aguila, Licenciado Pedro. 1978. *Noticias políticas de Indias.* (1639). Transcription by Jaime Urioste. Sucre: Imprenta Universitaria.

Ramos Gavilán, Fray Alonso. 1976. *Historia de Nuestra Señora de Copacabana.* (1621). La Paz: Academia Boliviana de Historia.

Randall, Robert. 1993. Los dos vasos: Cosmovisión y política de la embriaguez desde el inkananto hasta la colonia. In Thierry Saignes, ed., *Borrachera y memoria: La experiencia de lo sagrado en los Andes,* 73–112. La Paz: Hisbol/IFEA.

Rappaport, Joanne. 1990. *The Politics of Memory: Native Historical Interpretation in the Colombian Andes.* Cambridge: Cambridge University Press.

Rappaport, Joanne. 1994. *Cumbe Reborn.* Chicago: University of Chicago Press.

Rasnake, Roger N. 1986. Carnaval in Yura: Ritual Reflections on Ayllu and State Relations. *American Ethnologist* 13(4): 662–680.

Rasnake, Roger N. 1988a. *Domination and Cultural Resistance.* Durham, N.C.: Duke University Press.

Rasnake, Roger N. 1988b. Images of Resistance to Colonial Domination. In Jonathan D. Hill, ed., *Rethinking History and Myth: Indigenous South American Perspectives on the Past,* 136–156. Urbana: University of Illinois Press.

Rivera Cusicanqui, Silvia. 1978a. El mallku y la sociedad colonial en el siglo vxii: El caso de Jesús de Machaca. *Avances* (La Paz) 1: 7–27.

Rivera Cusicanqui, Silvia, and Tristan Platt. 1978b. El impacto colonial sobre un pueblo Pakaxa: La crisis del cacicazgo en Caquingora (urinsaya), durante el siglo VXI. *Avances* (La Paz) 1: 7–27.

Rivera Cusicanqui, Silvia. 1986. *Oprimidos pero no vencidos: Luchas del campesinado aymara y qhechwa, 1900–1980.* La Paz: HISBOL.

Riviére, Gilles. 1982. *Sabaya: Structures socio-économiques et représentacions symboliques dans le Carangas (Bolivie).* École des Hautes Études en Sciences Sociales, thèse de 3ᵉ cycle, Paris.

Riviére, Gilles, 1983. Quadripartition et idéologie dans les communautés aymaras de Carangas (Bolivie). *Bulletin de l' Institut français d' études andines* 12 (3–4): 41–62.

Riviére, Gilles. 1991. Lik'ichiri y kharisiri: A propósito de las representaciones del "Otro" en la sociedad aymara. *Bulletin de l'Institut français d' études andines* 20 (1): 23–40.

Rockefeller, Stuart Alexander. 1995. The Gaze Sucks: On Looking, Stealing Fat, and the Play of Difference in Quirpini—Bolivia and Elsewhere. Unpublished paper presented to the Latin American History Workshop, University of Chicago.

Rosaldo, Renato. 1980. *Ilongot Headhunting 1883–1974: A Study in Society and History.* Stanford: Stanford University Press.

Rosaldo, Renato. 1982. From the Door of His Tent: The Fieldworker and the Inquisitor. In James Clifford and George Marcus, eds., *Writing Culture: The Poetics and Politics of Ethnography,* 77–97. Berkeley: University of California Press.

Roseberry, William. 1989. *Anthropologies and Histories: Essays in Culture, History, and Political Economy.* New Brunswick, N.J.: Rutgers University Press.

Rösing, Ina. 1990. *Introducción al mundo Callawaya.* Cochabamba–La Paz: Los Amigos del Libro.

Rostworowski de Diez Canseco, María. 1981. La voz parcialidad en su contexto de los siglos XVI y XVII. In Marcia Koth de Paredes and Amalia Costelli, eds., *Ethnohistoria y anthropología andina, segunda jornada del Museo Nacional de Historia,* 35–45. Lima: Centro de Proyección Cristiana.

Rostworowski de Diez Canseco, María. 1988a. Prólogo. In María Rostworowski and Joyce Marcus, eds., *Conflicts over Coca Fields in XVIth-century Perú,* 69–81. Ann Arbor: Museum of Anthropology, University of Michigan.

Rostworowski de Diez Canseco, María. 1988b. *Historia del Tawantinsuyu.* Lima: Instituto de Estudios Peruanos.

Rowe, John H. 1945. Absolute Chronology in the Andean Area. *American Antiquity* 10(3): 265–284.

Rowe, John H. 1954. El movimiento nacional Inca del siglo vxiii. *Revista Universitaria* (Cusco) 107: 7–47.

Rowe, John H. 1980. An Account of the Shrines of Ancient Cuzco. *Ñawpa Pacha* 17: 1–80.

Rowe, William, and Vivian Schelling. 1991. *Memory and Modernity: Popular Culture in Latin America.* London: Verso.

Rubin, Miri. 1991. *Corpus Christi: The Eucharist in Late Medieval Culture.* Cambridge: Cambridge University Press.

Rumeu de Armas, Antonio. 1974. *Itinerario de los Reyes Católicos (1474–1516).* Madrid: Consejo Superior de Investigaciones Científicas.

Sahlins, Marshall D. 1983. Distinguished Lecture: Other Times, Other Customs: The Anthropology of History. *American Anthropologist* 85(3): 517–544.

Sahlins, Marshall D. 1985. *Islands of History.* Chicago: University of Chicago Press.

Saignes, Thierry. 1978a. Niveles de segmentación y de interdigitación en el poblamiento de los valles de Larecaja. In Marcia Koth de Paredes and Amalia Castelli, eds., *Etnohistoria y antropología andina,* 141–144. Lima: Museo Nacional de Historia.

Saignes, Thierry. 1978b. De la filiation a la résidence: Les ethnies dans les vallées de Larecaja. *Annales E.S.C.* 33(5–6): 1160–1181.

Saignes, Thierry. 1984. Nota sobre la contribución regional a la mita de Potosí a comienzos del siglo XVII. *Historiografía y bibliografíía americanistas* (Seville) 24: 3–21.

Saignes, Thierry. 1985a. *Caciques, Tribute, and Migration in the Southern Andes: Indian Society and the 17th Century Colonial Order (Audiencia de Charcas).* Institute of Latin American Studies Occasional Papers, no. 15. London.

Saignes, Thierry. 1985b. Algún día todo se andará: Los moviemientos étnicos en Charcas (siglo XVII). *Revista andina* 3(1): 425–450.

Saignes, Thierry. 1987. De la borrachera al retrato: Los caciques andinos entre dos legitimidades (Charcas). *Revista andina* 5(1) 139–170.

Saignes, Thierry. 1993. Borracheras andinas. ¿Por que los indios ebrios hablan en español? In Thierry Saignes, ed., *Borrachera y memoria: La experiencia de lo sagrado en los Andes,* 43–72. La Paz: HISBOL/IFEA.

Salazar-Soler, Carmen. 1993. Embriaguez y visiones en los Andes: Los Jesuitas y las "borracheras" indígenas en el Perú (siglos XVI–XVII). In Thierry Saignes, ed., *Borrachera y memoria: La experiencia de lo sagrado en los Andes,* 23–42. La Paz: HISBOL/IFEA.

Sallnow, Michael J. 1987. *Pilgrims of the Andes: Regional Cults in Cusco.* Washington, D.C.: Smithsonian Institution Press.

Salomon, Frank. 1981. Killing the Yumbo. In Normal E. Whitten, Jr., ed., *Cultural Transformations and Ethnicity in Modern Ecuador,* 162–209. Urbana: University of Illinois Press.

Salomon, Frank. 1982. Chronicles of the Impossible: Notes on Three Peruvian Indigenous Historians. In Rolena Adorno, ed., *From Oral to Written Expression: Native Andean Chronicles of the Early Colonial Period,* 9–39. Latin American Series, Foreign and Comparative Studies Program, no. 4, Maxwell School of Citizenship and Public Affairs, Syracuse University, Syracuse, N.Y.

Salomon, Frank. 1986. *Native Lords of Quito in the Age of the Incas: The Political Economy of North Andean Chiefdoms.* Cambridge: Cambridge University Press.

Salomon, Frank. 1987. Ancestor Cults and Resistance to the State in Arequipa, ca. 1748–1754. In Steve J. Stern, ed., *Resistance, Rebellion, and Consciousness in the Andean Peasant World, 18th to 20th Centuries,* 148–165. Madison: University of Wisconsin Press.

Salomon, Frank, and George Urioste, trans. 1991. *The Huarochirí Manuscript.: A Testament of Ancient and Colonial Andean Religion,* by anonymous author (n.d.). Austin: University of Texas Press.

Salomon, Noël. 1973. *La vida rural castellana en tiempos de Phelipe II.* Barcelona: Planeta.

Sánchez, Ana. 1991. *Amancebados, hechiceros y rebeldes (Chancay, siglo XVII).* Archivos de historia andina, 11. Cusco: Centro Bartolomé de las Casas.

Sarabia Viejo, Maria Justina. 1986, 1989. *Francisco de Toledo: Disposiciones gubernativas para el virreinato del Perú, 1569–1574.* 2 vols. Seville: Escuela de Estudios Hispano-Americanos.

Sarmiento de Gamboa, Pedro. 1942. *Historia de los Incas.* (1572). Buenos Aires: Emecé Editores.

Scott, James C. 1985. *Weapons of the Weak: Everyday Forms of Peasant Resistance.* New Haven: Yale University Press.

Schwartz, Barry. 1982. The Social Context of Commemoration: A Study in Collective Memory. *Social Forces* 61(2): 374–401.

Seed, Patricia. 1991. Colonial and Postcolonial Discourse. *Latin American Research Review* 26(3): 181–200.

Seed, Patricia. 1992. Taking Possession and Reading Texts: Establishing the Authority of Overseas Empires. *William and Mary Quarterly* 49(2): 183–209.

Serulnikov, Sergio. 1988. *Tomás Catari.* Buenos Aires: CERES.

Serulnikov, Sergio. 1989. *Reivindicaciones indígenas.* Buenos Aires: CERES.

Sharp, Jim. 1991. History from Below. In Peter Burke, ed., *New Perspectives in Historical Writing.* University Park: Pennsylvania State University Press.

Sikkink, Lynn Louise. 1994. House, Community, and Marketplace: Women as Managers of Exchange Relations and Resources on the Southern Altiplano of Bolivia. Ph.D. dissertation, University of Minnesota.

Silverblatt, Irene M. 1987. *Moon, Sun, and Witches: Gender Ideologies and Class in Inca and Colonial Peru.* Princeton: Princeton University Press.

Silverblatt, Irene M. 1988a. Political Memories and Colonizing Symbols: Santiago and the Mountain Gods of Colonial Peru. In Jonathan D. Hill, ed., *Rethinking History and Myth: Indigenous South American Perspectives on the Past,* 174–194. Urbana: University of Illinois Press.

Silverblatt, Irene M. 1988b. Imperial Dilemmas, the Politics of Kinship, and Inca Reconstructions of History. *Comparative Studies in Society and History* 30: 83–102.

Silverstein, Michael. 1976. Shifters, Linguistic Categories and Cultural Description. In K. Basso and H. Selby, eds., *Meaning in Anthropology*, 11–55. Albuquerque: University of New Mexico Press.

Silverstein, Michael n.d. Metaforces of Power in Traditional Oratory. Unpublished manuscript.

Solano, Francisco de. 1975. Urbanización y municipalización de la población indígena. In Solano, *Estudios sobre la ciudad iberoamericana*. Madrid.

Solórzano y Pereyra, Juan de. 1972. *Política indiana*. (1647). 5 vols. Madrid: Companía Iberoamericana de Publicaciones.

Sommer, Doris. 1991. *Foundational Fictions: The National Romances of Latin America*. Berkeley: University of California Press.

Spalding, Karen. 1974. *De indio a campesino: Cambios en la estructura social del Perú colonial*. Lima: Instituto de Estudios Peruanos.

Spalding, Karen. 1984. *Huarochiri: An Andean Society under Inca and Spanish Rule*: Stanford: Stanford University Press.

Stein, William W. 1961. *Hualcan: Life in the Highlands of Peru*. Ithaca, N.Y.: Cornell University Press.

Stern, Steve J. 1982. *Peru's Indian Peoples and the Challenge of the Spanish Conquest: Huamanga to 1640*. Madison: University of Wisconsin Press.

Stern, Steve J. 1993. Prologue. In *Peru's Indian Peoples and the Challenge of the Spanish Conquest: Huamanga to 1640*, xxi–iii. 2d rev. ed. Madison: University of Wisconsin Press.

Stern, Steve J., ed. 1987. *Resistance, Rebellion, and Consciousness in the Andean Peasant World, 18th to 20th Centuries*. Madison: University of Wisconsin Press.

Stocking, George W., ed. 1991. *Colonial Situations: Essays on the Contextualization of Ethnographic Knowledge*. History of Anthropology, vol. 7. Madison: University of Wisconsin Press.

Sturtevant, William 1966. Anthropology, History, and Ethnohistory. *Ethnohistory* 13: 1–51.

Szeminski, Jan. 1987. Why Kill the Spaniard? New Perspectives on Andean Insurrectionary Ideology in the 18th Century. In Steve J. Stern, ed., *Resistance, Rebellion, and Consciousness in the Andean Peasant World, 18th to 20th Centuries*. Madison: University of Wisconsin Press.

Tandeter, Enrique. 1981. La producción como actividad popular: "Ladrones de minas" en Potosí. *Nova Americana* (Turin) 4: 43–65.

Tandeter, Enrique. 1993. *Coercion and Market: Silver Mining in Colonial Potosí, 1692–1826*. Albuquerque: University of New Mexico Press.

Taussig, Michael T. 1980. *The Devil and Commodity Fetishism in South America*. Chapel Hill: University of North Carolina Press.

Taussig, Michael T. 1987. *Shamanism, Colonialism, and the Wild Man: A Study in Terror and Healing*. Chicago: University of Chicago Press.

Taussig, Michael T. 1989. History as Commodity in Some Recent American (Anthropological) Literature. *Critique of Anthropology* 9: 7–23.

Taylor, Gerald. 1980. Supay. *Amerindia* (Paris) 4: 47–63.

Taylor, Gerald. 1987. *Ritos y tradiciones de Huarochiri: Manuscrito Quechua de comienzos del siglo XVII.* Lima: IEP/IFEA.

Tedlock, Barbara, and Dennis Tedlock. 1985. Text and Textile: Language and Technology in the Arts of the Quiché Maya. *Journal of Anthropological Research* 41(2) :121–146.

Thomas, Nicholas. 1989. *Out of Time: History and Evolution in Anthropological Discourse.* Cambridge: Cambridge University Press.

Thompson, I. A. A. 1979. The Purchase of Nobility in Castile, 1552–1700. *Journal of European Economic History* 8(2): 313–360.

Thomson, Sinclair S. 1996. Colonial Crisis, Community, and Andean Self-Rule: Aymara Politics in the Age of Insurgency (Eighteenth-Century La Paz). Ph.D. dissertation, University of Wisconsin–Madison.

Titu Cusi Yupanqui, don Diego de Castro. 1985. *Ynstruçion del Ynga don Diego de Castro Titu Cussi Yupangui para el muy illustre señor el liçençiado Lope Garçía de Castro, governador que fue destos Reynos del Piru, tocante a los negoçios que con Su Magestad, en Su Nonbre, por Su Poder a de trator; la qual es esta que se sigue . . .* (1570). Ed. Luis Millones. Lima.

Toledo, Francisco de. 1975. *Tasa de la visita general.* (1583). Introduction and paleography by Noble David Cook. Lima: Universidad Nacional Mayor de San Marcos.

Tomoeda, Hiroyasu. 1985. The Llama Is My Chacra: Metaphor of Andean Pastoralists. In S. Masuda, I Shimada, and C. Morris, eds., *Andean Ecology and Civilization,* 277–300. Tokyo: University of Tokyo Press.

Torero, Alfredo. 1987. Lenguas y pueblos altiplánicos en torno al siglo xvi. *Revista andina* 5(2): 329–405.

Torero, Alfredo. 1990. Procesos lingüísticos e identificación de dioses en los Andes centrales. *Revista andina* 8(1): 253–256.

Torero, Alfredo. 1992. Acerca de la familia lingüística uruquilla (Uru-Chipaya). *Revista andina* 10(1): 171–191.

Torrico, Cassandra. n.d. Living Weavings: The Symbolism of Bolivian Herders' Sacks. Mimeo. Museo Nacional de Etnografía y Folklore, La Paz.

Troll, Carl. 1968. The Cordilleras of the Tropical Americas: Aspects of Climate, Phytogeographical and Agrarian Ecology. In C. Troll, ed., *Geoecology of the Mountainous Regions of the Tropical Americas,* 15–65. Bonn. Geographisches Institut der Universitat.

Tschopik, Harry. 1951. The Aymara of Chucuito, Peru. *Anthropological Papers of the American Museum of Natural History* 44(2).

Turino, Thomas. 1993. *Moving Away from Silence: Music of the Peruvian Altiplano and the Experience of Urban Migration.* Chicago: University of Chicago Press.

Turner, Terence S. 1980. The Social Skin. In Jeremy Cherfas and Roger Lewin, eds., *Not Work Alone,* 112–140. London: Temple Smith.

Turner, Terence S. 1984. Dual Opposition, Hierarchy, and Value. In J.-Cl. Galey, ed., *Différences, valeurs, hiérarchie,* 335–370. Paris: École des Hautes Études en Sciences Sociales.

Turner, Terence S. 1988. Ethno-ethnohistory: Myth and History in Native South American Representations of Contact with Western Society. In Jonathan D. Hill, ed., *Rethinking History and Myth: Indigenous South American Perspectives on the Past,* 235–281. Urbana. University of Illinois Press.

Urban, Greg, and Joel Sherzer, eds. 1991. *Nation-States and Indians in Latin America.* Austin: University of Texas Press.

Urbano, Henrique. 1981. *Wiracocha y Ayar: Héroes y funciones en las sociedades andinas.* Cusco: Centro Bartolomé de las Casas.

Urbano, Henrique. 1988. Thunupa, Taguapaca, Cachi: Lógica y sociedad en los Andes. *Revista andina* 11: 201–224.

Urbano, Henrique. 1989. Introducción. In Cristóbal de Molina and Cristóbal de Albornóz, *Fábulas y mitos de los incas,* ed. Henrique Urbano and Pierre Duviols, 9–41. Crónicas de América, 48. Madrid: Historia 16.

Urbano, Henrique. 1990. Mythic Andean Discourse and Pilgrimages. In A. Morinis and N. Ross Crumrine, eds., *Pilgrimage in Latin America.* New York: Greenwood Press.

Urioste de Aquirre, Martha. 1978. Los caciques Guarache. In Martha U. de Aguirre et al., eds., *Estudios bolivianos en homenaje a Gunnar Mendoza L.,* 131–140. La Paz.

Urton, Gary. 1981. *At the Crossroads of the Earth and the Sky: An Andean Cosmology.* Austin: University of Texas Press.

Urton, Gary. 1984. *Chuta:* El espacio de la práctica social en Pacariqtambo, Perú. *Revista andina* 2(1): 7–56.

Urton, Gary. 1988. La arquitectura pública como texto social: La historia de un muro de adobe en Pacariqtambo, Perú (1915–1985). *Revista andina* 6(1): 225–263.

Urton, Gary. 1990. *The History of a Myth: Pacariqtambo and the Origin of the Inkas.* Austin: University of Texas Press.

Urton, Gary. 1994. A New Twist in an Old Yarn: Variation in Knot Directionality in the Inka Khipus. *Baessler-Archiv Beiträge Zur Völkerkunde,* n.s., 42: 271–305.

Vaca de Castro. Antonio. 1929. Discurso sobre la descendencia y gobierno de los Incas [Información de los quipucamayocs (1541–44?)]. In Horacio Urteaga, ed., *Colección de libros y documentos referentes a la historia del Perú,* series 2, vol. 3, 1–53. Lima.

Vaca de Castro, Cristóbal. 1980. Ordenanzas de tambos. (1543). *Revista histórica* (Lima) 3(4): 427–492.

Valeri, Valerio. 1985. *Kingship and Sacrifice: Ritual and Society in Ancient Hawaii.* Trans. P. Wissing. Chicago: University of Chicago Press.

Van Kessel, Juan. 1992. *Cuando arde el tiempo sagrado.* La Paz: HISBOL.

Vansina, Jan. 1985. *Oral Tradition as History.* Madison: University of Wisconsin Press.

Varón Gabai, Rafael. 1982. Cofradías de indios y poder local en el Perú colonial: Huaraz, siglo XVII. *Allpanchis* 17(20): 127–166.

Varón Gabai, Rafael. 1990. El taki onqoy: Las raíces andinas de un fenómeno colonial. In L. Millones, ed., *El Retorno de las Huacas,* 331–406. Lima: Instituto de Estudios Peruanos.

Varón Gabai, Rafael, and Auke Pieter Jacobs. 1987. Peruvian Wealth and Spanish Investments: The Pizarro Family during the Sixteenth Century. *Hispanic American Historical Review* 67(4): 657–695.

Vega, Garcilaso de la. 1966. *Royal Commentaries of the Incas and General History of Peru,* trans. with an introduction by Harold V. Livermore, forwarded by Arnold J. Toynbee, 2 vols. Austin: University of Texas Press.

Wachtel, Nathan. 1973. *Sociedad e ideología.* Lima: Instituto de Estudios Peruanos.

Wachtel, Nathan. 1977. *The Vision of the Vanquished.* New York: Barnes and Noble Imports.

Wachtel, Nathan. 1978. Hommes d'eau: Le problème Uru (XVIe–XVIIe siècle). *Annales E.S.C.* 33(5–6): 1127–1159.

Wachtel, Nathan. 1981. Los mitimas del valle de Cochabamba: La política de colonización de Wayna Capac. *Historia Boliviana* (Cochabamba) 1(1): 21–57.

Wachtel, Nathan. 1982. The Mitimas of the Cochabamba Valley: The Colonization Policy of Huayna Capac. In George A. Collier et al., eds., *The Inca and Aztec States, 1400–1800,* 199–235. New York: Academic Press. (English translation of Wachtel 1981).

Wachtel, Nathan. 1990. *Le retour des ancétres: Les indiens urus de Bolivie, XXe–XVIe siècle: Essai d'histoire regressive.* Paris.

Wachtel, Nathan. 1992. Note sur le probléme des identités collectives dans les Andes méridionales. *L'Homme* 122–124, 32(1-3-4): 39–52.

Wachtel, Nathan. 1994. *Gods and Vampires: Return to Chipaya.* Chicago: University of Chicago Press.

Weiner, Annette B., and Jane Schneider. 1989. *Cloth and Human Experience.* Washington, D.C.: Smithsonian Institution Press.

Weismentel, M. J. 1991. Maize Beer and Andean Social Transformations: Drunken Indians, Bread Babies, and Chosen Women. *MLN* 106(4): 861–880.

West, Terry L. 1981a. Llama Caravans of the Andes. *Natural History* 90(12): 62ff.

West, Terry L. 1981b. *Sufriendo nos vamos: From a Subsistence to a Market Economy in an Aymara Community of Bolivia.* Ph.D. dissertation, New School for Social Research. Ann Arbor, Mich.: University Microfilms.

White, Haydon. 1978. The Forms of Wildness: Archaeology of an Idea. In White, *Tropics of Discourse: Essays in Cultural Criticism,* 150–182. Baltimore: Johns Hopkins University Press.

White, Haydon. 1989. New Historicism: A Comment. In H. Aram Veeser, ed., *The New Historicism,* 293–302. New York: Routledge.

Wildman, John, Sir. 1647. *Putney Projects. Or the Old Serpent in a New Forme. Presenting to the View of All the Well Affected in England, the Serpentine*

Deceit of Their Pretended Friends in the Armie . . . Composed by . . . John Lawmind. London.

Wolf, Eric. 1982. *Europe and the Peoples without History.* Berkeley: University of California Press.

Yapita M., Juan de Dios. 1968. *Alfabeto fonémico del idioma aymara.* La Paz, Bolivia: INEL.

Yapita M., Juan de Dios. 1992. Kunturinti liq'uchinti: Análisis lingüistico de un sallqa de Oruro. *Latin American Indian Literatures Journal* 8(1): 38–68.

Yates, Francis. 1966. *The Art of Memory.* London: Routledge and Kegan Paul.

Zárate, Agustín de. 1862. *Historia del descubrimiento y conquista de la provincia del Peru, y de las guerras, y cosas señaladas en ella, acaecidas hasta el vencimiento de Gonzalo Pizarro, y de sus sequaces, que en ella se rebelaron, contra su Magestad.* (1555). Biblioteca de Autores Españoles, vol. 26, 459–574. Madrid: Ediciones Atlas.

Zavala, Silvio A. 1971. *Las instituciones jurídicas en la conquista de América.* 2d ed. Mexico: Porrúa.

Zavala, Silvio A. 1973. *La encomienda indiana.* 2d ed. Mexico: Editorial Porrúa.

Zorn, Elayne. 1996. Marketing Diversity: Global Transformations in Cloth and Identity in Highland Peru and Bolivia. Ph.D dissertation, Cornell University.

Zuidema, R. T. 1977. The Inca Kinship System: A New Theoretical View. In R. Bolton and E. Mayer, eds., *Andean Kinship and Marriage,* 240–281. Washington, D.C.: American Anthropological Association.

Zuidema, R. T. 1964. *The Ceque System of Cuzco: The Social Organization of the Capital of the Inca.* Leiden: E. S. Brill.

Zuidema, R. T. 1989a. The Moieties of Cuzco. In D. Maybury-Lewis and U. Almagor, eds., *The Attraction of Opposites: Thought and Society in the Dualistic Mode,* 255–276. Ann Arbor: University of Michigan Press.

Zuidema, R. T. 1989b. A Quipu Calendar from Ica, Peru, with a Comparison to the Ceque Calendar from Cuzco. In A. F. Aveni, ed., *World Archeoastronomy,* 341–351. Cambridge: Cambridge University Press.

Zuidema, R. T. 1990. *Inca Civilization in Cuzco.* Trans. Jean-Jacques Decoster. Austin: University of Texas Press.

Zulawski, Ann. 1995. *They Eat from Their Labor: Work and Social Change in Colonial Bolivia.* Pittsburgh: University of Pittsburgh Press.

Index

559

Bull's horn: and documents in boundary markers, 286; on ritual altar, 347; as pututu in land wars, 490*n57*

Burial, 69, 76, 241, 452*n4*. *See also* Cemetery; Funerary ritual; Chullpa tombs

Cabildo. *See* Town council

Cacachaca (people). *See* Qaqachaka

Cacachaca (town): pilgrimage to Condo by authorities of, 122; ayllus of, 254; from annex to town, 284; power of attorney to Corcino Pérez, 306

Cacha (town): destroyed by Tunupa-apostle, 206, 208

Cacique, term used for kuraqa and mallku, 462*n20*

Cacique cobrador: non-hereditary post from 1790s, 303; in contemporary Culta. *See also* Jilaqatas

Caciques, colonial: resistance and accommodation by, 151, 216; probanzas of, 154–61, 159–61; under Inca rule, 161–62; and social memory, 162–63, 227; opposition to perpetuity of encomienda, 217–18, 477*n3*, 478*n4*; undercut by Toledan reforms, 224–25, 226, 252; as collaborators, 225; noble pretensions of, 226; as captains of mita in Potosí, 231, 234–35; and drinking in Potosí, 234; and town councils after reducción, 246; Toledo's speech to, 250–51; recruitment of forasteros by, 278; reducción caciques litigate boundaries, 284, 286, 302–3, 493*n80*; Taquimalco purchases in composición, 285, 302, 493*n80*; as targets of rebellion, 294–96, 302–3, 492*nn69, 70*; "hispanization" and pacts with corregidores of, 296, 302–3; collateral lineages of, 303; naming practices of, 466*n34*. *See also* Cacique cobrador; Colque Guarache, don Juan; Choqueticlla (lineage); Chungara, Lope; Condori, Ambrocio de la Cruz; Guarache, Juan; Llanquipacha, don Gregorio Feliz; Llanquipacha, Lucas Feliz; Taquimalco

Cahuayo (town): pilgrimage to Condo from, 122; ayllu of, 254; from hamlet

to annex to town, 284; power of attorney to Corcino Pérez, 306; cantonization of, 313; switch in department affiliation of, 313

Caisa (town): extirpation in, 267

Cajamarca (Inca town). *See* Atahuallpa, capture of

Calcha (town and people): ethnography of, 449*n1*

Calendar, contemporary K'ulta, 330. *See also* Jesus Christ *vs.* Supay-Chullpas myth; Space-time, social

Calendar, pre-Columbian and colonial: eschatology of Christian, 17; of Cusco, 175; and constellations, 184; colonization by Christian in reducción towns, 252, 256. *See also* Buena policía; Space-time, social

Camino, don José, interviews of, 453*n7*

Campesino: use of term, xviii, 451*n12*; in reference and address, 45; as euphemism, 309; *vs.* vecino, and positional identity, 451*n13*. *See also* Social categories

Cañari (people): as Spanish allies, 138

Canas. *See* Qana

Canchis. *See* Kanchi

Cantares, Spanish, 167

Cantón, unit of Bolivian administrative structure, 310, 454*n2*. *See also* Cantonization

Cantonal authorities. *See* Authorities of Santa Bárbara de Culta; Corregidor; Town council, republican

Cantonization: process of, 310–14, 446*n8*; petition of Ayllu Qullana, 311; petition of Alax-Kawalli, 311–12; of Ayllu Yanaqi, 312; of Cahuayo, 313; as latter-day reducción process, 313–14; and implementation of plan, 332; and fiesta-cargo career alternations, 370; in Provincia de Abaroa, 454*n2*

Capac hucha: compared to visita, 17–18; as Inca succession ritual, 140; sacrifices of, 171; as sacrificed person, 173; and cumbi cloth, 173, 187, 472*n49*; Guarache in, 445*n2*; Molina on, 468*n44*

Colque Guarache, don Juan: slurred by Charka caciques, 156; quipus of, used by Anonymous Jesuit, 184, 234, 258; genealogy of depicted as path, 227, 228; and mita duties in Potosí, 230, 231–33; reassertion of rule in Potosí mita, 233; and libations in Potosí, 234–35; cumbi kamayuqs of, 234–35; and creation of interculture in Potosí, 235; special influence on Toledan ordinances, 251; acquires street in Tacobamba for ayllu Ilawi, 255, 482*n38*; Cochabamba fields assigned by Toledo, 464*n25*; as leader of purported Lutheran revolt, 486*n48*

Colque Guarache, don Juan, probanzas of: described, 5, 159–61, 445*n3*; service of father Guarache to Incas in, 130, 159–60; as collaboration, 152; service to Spaniards in, 159; as event chronology, 159, 227; as ethnohistorical source, 160; genealogy in, 160–61, 227, 465*nn31, 32*, 466*nn33, 34*; as approximation of Spanish relación narrative, 226; as response to Toledan reforms, 226; use of by descendants, 227; services in Potosí mita in, 232; Espinoza version *vs.* mss, 464*n27*; on diarchies of Killaka and Incas, 464*nn27, 29*, 465*n30*

Colque, don Juan, "el Mozo": trained by Jesuits, 261; Capoche on, 484*n42*

Colque, doña María: as Oruro vendor, 7; portrait of, 94, 95

Colque Guarache lineage: "family path" of, 228; mnemonic techniques of distinct generations, 261

Commemoration: of land possession act, 9; Halbwachs on, 11; in 16th-century Spain, 17; of War of the Pacific, 91; of Eucharist, 167; of life of Jesus Christ, 252, 262

Compadrazgo, and patron-client ties, 47

Composición de tierras: in Choquecallata document, 284–89, 446*n8*; process of, 284–291; of 1590s by Fray Luis López, 285; Taquimalco purchase of Asanaqi lands, 285, 302; of 1640s by José de la

Vega Alvarado, 287; documents of interpreted in 1790s Condo *vs.* Challapata land war, 302–3; and Corcino Viscarra in 1868, 305; titles of and privatization, 305–9; and Corcino Pérez petition, 306, 439; and tribute exemption, 307–8, 439

Comsa, don Pedro, contra perpetuity, 217, 477*n4*

Concatenation, or braiding: of libation dedications, 365; of fiesta-cargo careers, 370, 371, 376, 396; of pillu visits, 372–73; of hamlet and town centered sacrifices in fiesta, 375; of rites of incoming and outgoing fiesta sponsors, 376; of dancing and fighting units, 384, 393. *See also* Recursion, formal

Condenados (ghosts), 64, 69, 76

Condo (people). *See* Quntu

Condo, San Pedro de (town): pilgrimage to by K'ulta authorities, 120, 458*n24*; social memory in, 154; refounded in visita general, 238, 482*n31*; ayllus of, 253; parish registers of, 256–58, 483*n39*; hamlets and chapels of, 273–75; hamlets become annexes, annexes seek autonomy, 284; litigation and land war with Challapata, 289, 302–3, 446*n8*; colonial fiesta sponsorship in, 292, 491*n64*; 1774 rebellion against caciques in, 294–95; represented to state by Corcino Pérez in 1894, 306; mayordomos of, 483*n40*

Condocondo. *See* Condo, San Pedro de (town)

Condor: addressed as mallku, 120; in oral narrative, 322; house as "nest" of, 334; wifetakers as in marriage rites, 343, 498*n19*; as familiar in ch'iyar yatiri shamanism, 417; as analog of Nina Willka's dove, 420. *See also* Mallku

Condori, Ambrocio de la Cruz (cacique of Challapata): litigation with Llanquipacha of Condo, 302–3

Confession: as relación, 170; quipus used in, 178, 260; pre-Columbian and colonial, 268–269

335, 337; and performance of uywa
ispira memory path, 347–49, 351–60;
quwa performed by, 360–61; llama
sacrifices of, 361–62; as part-time
Jallqa, 506*n8*
Mamani hamlet. *See* Vila Sirka.
Manco Inca: crowned by Pizarro, 139;
mistreatment by Spaniards, 141;
submission to Spaniards, 459*n7*
Manxa-Kawalli (ayllu of K'ulta): and
fiesta participation, 97; tinku with
Alax-Kawalli, 100; land war against
Qullana, 311; libations to mountain
deities of, 355. *See also* K'ulta (people)
Manxa-pacha (underworld or inner
space-time): "Christian" *vs.* "native"
content, 110; libations to gods of, 122;
chullpas as portals to, 181; creation of
with alax-pacha, 330–31; western path
to, 337; libations to in alcohol,
351–62. *See also* Alax-pacha
Maravall, José Antonio, 447*n11*
Markets: of Oruro, 39; of La Paz, 39,
450*n8*
Marriage: and patriline exogamy, 73; and
house construction, 333; genealogical
reckoning for, 340; libations of, 340;
prohibitions, 340; rites of, 340; herding
and predation metaphors in, 342–43;
and alliance, 343; groom as condor in,
343; and sister exchange, 343; rituals
of, 343, 498*n19*; as first step in ritual
career, 369; sacrifice in, 498*n18*; laritas
and ipalas in interpatriline relations,
498*n19*; mock, in mita ritual, 508*n20*
Marta, doña. *See* Cariri, doña Marta
Marx, Karl, 3
Mass: payment for, 106; indian
performance of, 270–271; colonial
priests' refusal to celebrate in Culta,
273
Materialism: in Andean ethnography, xviii
Matienzo, Juan de: against public
drinking, 216; plan for reducción town,
240
Matriliny: Arnold on, 341; in ayllu as
circulating connubium, 341; *vs.*
patriliny, 342
Matronyms. *See* Surnames

Mayordomo: type of fiesta sponsor, 81;
term of office of, 90; activities during
fiesta of Guadalupe, 98; duties of, 104;
and libations for church construction,
104; Culta church, parish registers of,
122; established in reducciones, 244; of
confraternity to Santa Bárbara, 273; of
colonial Condo, 292; of Culta in 18th
century, 298; of Condo, 483*n40*;
libations and collection of money in
limusna waku, 509*n25*. *See also* Fiesta
sponsorship; Fiesta, saint's, structure of
Mayruwiri. *See* Ancestors
Meaning: cultural, deployment of, 19;
sacrificial, entombed in letters, 170;
intersubjectivity of, and habitual
practice, 448*n13*
Memorial de Charcas, 154–57, 159. *See
also* Probanzas
Memory: archival *vs.* landscape, 9–10;
collective, and writing, 11–12; and rote
memorization, 13; LeGoff on collective,
17; arts of, 17, 189; and
countermemory, 23, 182; local in
Cantón Culta, 45; and landscape, 116;
ordering of, 117; Andean techniques of,
178; Toledo on caciques', 251;
genealogical, 340; and drink, 499*n22*;
and ethnography, 499*n22*. *See also*
Amnesia; Genealogy; Landscape;
Memory paths; Social memory; Writing
Memory paths (amt'añ t'akis): vignette of,
6; general description of, 113, 346; and
colonialism, 114; described as amnesia
techniques, 140, 216; and boundary
pilgrimages, 291; and Pablo
Choquecallata, 319; and other forms of
t'aki, 321, 346; single libation in,
346–47, 349–50; Mamani performance
of during uywa ispira, 347–49,
351–60; gender parallel performance
of, 349, 351, 354, 500*n27*, 502*n33*;
kinds of, 350; types and tokens of deity
forms in, 350–51, 352; modular
segments and formal recursion in, 351,
359; concentric spacio-temporal
hierarchy in, 359; gendered landscapes
in, 359, 500*n27*; formal parallelism and
metaphor in, 359–60; manxa-pacha

Qullasuyu (*continued*)
administration of, 153; macro-moiety division of, 153; preconquest social structure in, 154–57; division of suyus in Colchacollo chacara, 157; chullpa construction in, 182; lack of narrative sources from, 197; microcosm of in Potosí mita, 231; pilgrimage to Porco wak'a and reintegration of, 267; Almagro looting in, 461*n12. See also* Inca (people and empire)

Qullqa (storehouses), of heavens, 184

Quntu (people): ethnography of, 121, 449*n1. See also* Condo, San Pedro de (town)

Qurikancha of Cusco, compared to Pantheon, 470*n45*

Q'uwa: decoration and burning of untu llantiru figurines in, 360–61, 377, 388. *See also* Incense offering; Sacrifice, structure of

Race, *vs.* class and ethnicity, 463*n23. See also* Social categories

Ramírez del Águila, Licenciado Pedro: on indian Christ of Tacobamba, 486*n47;* on Colque Guarache Lutheran revolt, 486*n48*

Ramos Gavilán, Fray Alonso: on Tunupa as apostle, 205–6; on Copacabana miracles, 206

Ranger Battalion of Challapata, and Ché, 454*n9*

Rappaport, Joanne, xviii, 119

Rasnake, Roger N., xviii

Rebellion, indigenous: caciques killed and priests spared in 18th century, 294, 301; led by town councilmen in 18th century, 294; of 1774 in Condo, 294; tinkus as platform for, 294, 295, 300–301; in Culta, 295, 297–98, 437–38, 492*n74, n75;* in Challapata, 296–298, 492*n70;* in Chayanta, 298–300, 492*n69;* in Aullagas (of Chayanta), 300; Spaniards called apostates in, 300; Christian devotion in, 300–301; in La Paz, 300–301; of Tupac Catari, 300–301, 449*n1;* of Zárate Willka in 1899, 308,

449*n4;* of 1920s, 308–9, 449*n4;* and 1950s revolution, 309; of 1750 in Lima, 492*n68;* of Macha, 492*n73. See also* Catari, Tomás; Tupac Amaru I; Tupac Amaru II; Tupac Catari

Recipocity: asymmetrical, 162; and gifts of drink, 349; and revenge, 512*n34. See also* Ayni; Gifts; Paq"ara; Paq"arayaña

Reconquest, Spanish, as crusade, 132

Recursion, formal: in weaving process and design, 180; in libations, 351, 359; in fiesta ritual, 505*n4*

Reducción: as transformation in lived space and time, 237; Real Cédula of 1549 on, 237, 428–29; process of, 238; as doctrina, 239; jurisdictions of, 239; similarity to Castilian villas, 239; layout of, 239; Matienzo proposal for, 239; civilizational project in, 240; as amnesia technique, 240, 250, 252; town councils of, 241–46; imperial mapping, visiting, and archiving of, 247; surveillance and discipline in, 247–49, 252; Toledan intructions for creation of, 248; of Tinquipaya, 248, 429–35; Sanabria on buena policía in, 248, 434–35; Toledan explanation to caciques of, 250–51; effects within Asanaqi diarchy, 252–58; Zárate of Tacobamba, 255; depopulation of and conversion to ritual center, 283–84; 18th-century multiplication of, 284; hamlets modeled on, 284; diarchy fissioning through border squabbles among, 288; role in 18th-century rebellions, 294; Málaga Medina on, 482*n33;* Fraser on, 482*n34. See also* Buena policía; Calendar, pre-Columbian and colonial; Discipline, work; Ordinances of Toledo; Surveillance; Town councils, colonial; Visita general of Toledo

Regidores (aldermen), established in reducciones, 244

Registro civil of Culta, 60, 68, 340

Relaciones: interests in, 136; as curriculum vitae, 169; and the novel, 415. *See also* Archival culture; Chronicles; Fiction; Probanzas

104; apparition of, 117, 272, 458*n20;*
apparition of, 272; foundation of
cofradía of, 272–73; purchase of by
Chiris of Ayllu Kawalli, 273
Santa Cruz, Mariscál Andrés de, 91
Santa Rosa de Lima, questioned by
Inquisition, 266; penitential practices of,
279
Santa Teresa de Avila, questioned by
Inquisition, 266
Santo Tomás (apostle), and Tunupa, 205,
208. *See also* San Bartolomé; Tunupa;
Taguapaca
Santo Tomás, Fray Domingo de: shown
ceque system of Pocona by Polo, 187;
and perpetuity, 217
Sap"i. *See* Roots
Sapsi paxsi, ritual of Potosí mitayos, 222
Sarmiento de Gamboa, Pedro: inquisitorial
techniques and Andean narrative,
193–194, 474*n59;* on Inca origins,
200–203; on Viracocha as creator,
200–203; on Babel, 201; on creation at
Paqariqtambo *vs.* Tiwanaku, 201; on
universal flood, 201; on Viracocha and
Taguapaca, 201; on destruction of
Cacha by fire, 203; reads Andean
narrative into universal history, 203; on
tyranny of Incas, 474*n60*
School teacher, in Santa Bárbara de Culta,
61
Schools: of Cruce, 44, 45; in Santa
Bárbara de Culta, 61; of province and
cantón capitals, 310
Schwartz, Barry, 129
Scott, James C., 24
Scribes. *See* Notaries
Scripture. *See* Bible
Secret practices. *See* Clandestine practices
Seed line. *See* Mujuts kasta
Semiotics, and cultural closure, 111,
447n13. *See also* Functionalism;
Structuralism
Señorío: granting of, 132; Andean
diarchies and federations interpreted as,
134. *See also* Encomienda
Serenas (Sirens), and musical inspiration
at waterfalls, 330. *See also* Musical
instruments; Samiris

Sermon, of priest of Santa Bárbara de
Culta, 106
Shamanic practices: intercultural, 115,
417–18, 420; abogado as saint
intercessor in, 104; Nina Willka chapel
practices, 278–81, 420; Tios of mines,
and saints, 402, 505*n6;* surti wala
shaman whistles, 417; 503*n44;* and
Bolivian politics, 418; mentioned, 83,
84, 414. *See also* Ch'iyar yatiri;
Kallawaya; Sorcery; Yatiris
Sheep: sacrifice of, 105; libations to, 356
Shops of vecinos, 98
Sikkink, Lynn, 458*n24*
Sikus. *See* Musical instruments
Silences: documentary, 15; ethnographic,
15; structure of, 15
Siles Suazo, Hernán: votes for in national
elections, 452*n6*
Silu (saint peak), rites at altar of, 344, 345
Silverblatt, Irene, xviii
Simonides of Ceos, 16
Sindicatos (peasant unions): formation of
in agrarian reform, 309; in Ayllu
Qullana, 311
Sister's husband. *See* Tullqa
Siwaruyu-Arakapi (diarchy): granted in
encomienda to Francisco Pizarro, 149;
disaggregated from Killaka federation,
149, 232; map of, 158; under Colque
Guarache rule in Potosí mita, 232. *See
also* Coroma; Puna, Nuestra Señora de
la Talavera de; Tomahavi, Todos Santos
de
Skulls: in money increase rites, 124;
chicha drunk from, 295
Smith, Raymond T., xxi
Social agency: and history, 16, 400;
construction of, 114; colonial narratives
about, 205; and Jesus Christ *vs.*
Supay-Chullpa myth, 328–32; and
social process, 328–30; and social
memory, 400–401
Social categories: and euphemism,
450*n12;* hypostatization of, 450*n12.*
See also Blanco; Campesino; Cholita;
Cholo; Criollo; Ethnicity; Español;
Indian; Indio; Mestizo; Mulato; Negro;
Race; Social class; Spaniard